THE
unofficial GUIDE®
ᵀᴼ Mexico's Best Beach Resorts

4TH EDITION

THE *unofficial* GUIDE®

TO Mexico's Best Beach Resorts

4TH EDITION

MARIBETH MELLIN
with JANE ONSTOTT

WILEY

Please note that prices fluctuate in the course of time, and travel information changes under the impact of many factors that influence the travel industry. We therefore suggest that you write or call ahead for confirmation when making your travel plans. Every effort has been made to ensure the accuracy of information throughout this book, and the contents of this publication are believed correct at the time of printing. Nevertheless, the publishers cannot accept responsibility for errors or omissions or for changes in details given in this guide or for the consequences of any reliance on the information provided by the same. Assessments of attractions and so forth are based on the authors' own experiences; therefore, descriptions given in this guide necessarily contain an element of subjective opinion that may not reflect the publisher's opinion or dictate a reader's own experience on another occasion. Readers are invited to write the publisher with ideas, comments, and suggestions for future editions.

Published by:
John Wiley & Sons, Inc.
111 River Street
Hoboken, NJ 07030-5774

Produced by Menasha Ridge Press

Cover design by Michael J. Freeland

Interior design by Vertigo Design

For information on our other products and services or to obtain technical support, please contact our Customer Care Department within the United States at 800-762-2974, outside the United States at 317-572-3993, or by fax at 317-572-4002.

Wiley also publishes its books in a variety of electronic formats. Some content that appears in print may not be available in electronic formats.

ISBN: 978-0-470-37997-4

Manufactured in the United States of America

5 4 3 2 1

CONTENTS

LIST *of* MAPS

ACKNOWLEDGMENTS

WE ARE SINCERELY GRATEFUL for the assistance we received while working on this book. Our families are familiar with the rigors of writing a travel guide, and always come up with ingenious solutions to our dilemmas. And our research and office team is our family—both literally and figuratively! Susan Humphrey is an excellent investigator with great organizational and writing skills. Gary Grimaud never ceases to amaze with his knowledge of geography and the sea.

Mexico is a subject dear to our hearts, and we're always eager to learn more about our adopted country. Fortunately, the people of Mexico are generous with their knowledge and insights. This book benefits from input and advice from friends and associates, including Ignacio Acosta, Conchita Aguirre, Javier Aranda, Lourdes Arellano, Pegge Bastress, Alvaro Campos Langarica, Jeanette Chin, Isauro Cruz, Gina Machorro Espinosa, Arely Figueroa, Lydia Gregory, Bill Horn, Ana Mari Irabien, Fernando Lizarraga, Ron Mader, Patricia Lopez Mancera, Raul Marrufo, Georgina Rodriguez Martinez, Walter DeMirci, Andria Mitsakos, Carlos Mora, Carolina Delgadillo Novelo, Pia M. Oberholzer Herger, Martha Paredes, Laura Perez, Nathalie Pilovetzky, Javier Rosenberg, Luisa Sanchez, Roger Sauri, Nathalie Thenoux, Israel Urbina, Clarita Wisner, and Olga Zmork. Countless tourism officials, tour guides, concierges, and cab drivers have given us the lowdown on their favorite places . . . and then helped us get there!

We thank Bob Sehlinger of Menasha Ridge Press for creating the *Unofficial Guides* and president Molly Merkle for her faith in our work. Editor Ritchey Halphen demonstrated admirable patience and encouragement as the project came together. They are a pleasure to work with, and have helped make this guide a valuable resource for anyone interested in the pleasures of Mexico.

—*Maribeth Mellin and Jane Onstott*

ABOUT *the* AUTHORS

Maribeth Mellin is an award-winning journalist who has covered various aspects of Mexico for more than two decades. Her experiences there began with a long backpacking journey in the 1970s that took her from Baja to the tip of the Yucatán Peninsula. She covered the U.S.–Mexico border as a senior editor with *San Diego Magazine* and as a contributor for the *Los Angeles Times,* then left full-time employment when a publisher asked her to write a book on the coastal resorts of Mexico. Since then, Maribeth has authored or contributed to more than 20 travel books about Mexico and has received the prestigious Pluma de Plata award for her writing about the country. She also has authored books on Costa Rica, Peru, Argentina, Hawaii, and San Diego, where she lives just a few blocks from the beach with her husband, Gary. Her writings on social, legal, and medical issues, along with her travel articles, have garnered more than two dozen awards from journalism organizations.

Jane Onstott earned a bachelor's degree in Spanish language and Hispanic literature from San Diego State University, with a year's study in Madrid. Since then she has lived and traveled extensively in Mexico and Latin America. She worked as head of the Communication and Information office of the Charles Darwin Research Station in the Galápagos Islands, and has worked as a Spanish-language interpreter and translator in Mexico and the United States.

Jane has collaborated with colleague and friend Maribeth Mellin on several books, including *San Diego Best Places* (Sasquatch Books, 2002) and *The Insiders' Guide to San Diego* (Globe Pequot Press, 2004). A San Diego resident, Jane travels to Mexico often to work for a variety of travel publications. Her book *National Geographic Traveler Mexico* describes the country's culture and history and gives information about its most fascinating cities, towns, beaches, and archaeological sites. For more about Jane, visit **www.janewrites.com**.

INTRODUCTION

■ WHY WE LOVE MEXICO

VIBRANT, VIVID, PASSIONATE, MAGNIFICENT—such words barely begin to describe the allures of Mexico. Six thousand miles of coastline frame a majestic tapestry of mountains, deserts, and forests within the Estados Unidos Mexicanos (the country's official name). To the west, the Pacific Ocean pounds the slinky Baja California Peninsula. The Sea of Cortez separates the peninsula and mainland Mexico, which curves between the Sea of Cortez and the Gulf of Mexico. The Caribbean Sea washes over the east coast of the Yucatán Peninsula, itself bordered by the jungles and rainforests of Guatemala and Belize. And to the north, the United States of America shares coastline, deserts, rivers, mountain ranges, and a border with Mexico.

A lineup of top-notch coastal resorts contributes to Mexico's immense popularity as a vacation destination. Mexico received more than 22.6 million international visitors in 2008, representing a 5.9 percent increase over 2007. That number continues to increase as visitors return time and again, designing vacations to suit their moods. Some devote considerable downtime to lounging on golden sands and soaking up sun and fun. Others use the coastal resorts as bases for exploring archaeological sites and colonial cities. At times, these eager visitors devour popular resorts and attractions like swarms of busy army ants; this guide shows you how to avoid such scenes.

Travelers tend to get hooked on Mexico once they feel comfortable with its quirks. As a rule, the people of Mexico are kind, friendly, generous, and extremely polite. Mexican cuisine, with its delicious tropical fruits, shellfish, chiles, and homemade tortillas, is celebrated throughout the world, but you'll rarely find authentic Mexican cooking outside the country. The sound of Mexico is musical and rhythmic, and there's a song for every occasion. Though tranquil fishing villages may become internationally famous beach resorts, travelers still swing in hammocks under coconut palms at semisecret hideaways, and the flavor of Mexico remains palpable even at the most modern destinations.

Some visitors are disconcerted by Mexico's foreignness, poverty, and vitality. Even the most modern resort areas, such as Los Cabos and Cancún, aren't like South Beach, Maui, or the Virgin Islands. Everything is different in Mexico—and we like it that way.

This is the land of *mañana,* and the efficiency some travelers expect is the exception rather than the norm. It helps if you get into vacation mode immediately, throwing off the chains of life in the fast lane. Forget about scheduling your time, and go with the flow. Accidents and illnesses are all possible, just as they are in most travel situations. But you'll be able to find English-speaking doctors and pharmacists who can help with any medical situation. Crime occurs at about the same rate as at tourist areas all over the world. Petty theft, graft, and rip-off schemes are far more prevalent than violent crimes. Some visitors may encounter subtle scams and briberies. We'll help you see them coming and steer clear of unpleasantness.

That said, the pleasures of traveling in Mexico far outweigh the inconveniences. Visitors return to Mexico because they love the music, color, flavor, and sensibilities that are at the heart of Mexican culture. Where else can you climb Maya pyramids looming from steamy jungles in the morning and, in the afternoon, swim with angelfish in crystalline coves? Or dance barefoot on the sand to the sounds of mariachis and marimbas? Few places can match Mexico's mystique. With this guide, we'll help you have the most pleasurable vacation possible. Very soon, you'll no doubt love Mexico as much as we do.

ABOUT *This* GUIDE

WHY *UNOFFICIAL?*

MOST MEXICO TRAVEL GUIDES FOLLOW the tracks of the typical tourist, sending everyone to the well-known sights without offering any information about how to do this painlessly. They reflexively recommend mainstream and chain restaurants and accommodations, and they fail to recognize the limits of human endurance in sightseeing. This guide is different. We understand that a traveler's first foray into Mexico can be intimidating, and perhaps even overwhelming. We've been traveling there for nearly three decades and have found solutions to most complications and concerns.

We'll tell you what we think of certain tourist traps and famous restaurants and accommodations, how to stay off the beaten track, and ways to spend less money on one thing so you can spend more on another. We'll complain about rip-offs, advise you on bargains, and steer you out of the crowds for a break now and then. We also hope to give you the kind of information that will make you love Mexico all the more—some of the endearing eccentricities that make you realize you're definitely not in Kansas anymore.

The majority of U.S. visitors to Mexican resorts stay seven days. How much can you squeeze into that time? How much do you want to see? What are your priorities, and how can they best be served? Like any worthwhile undertaking, a trip to Mexico requires some preparation and strategy to make the place reveal its charms.

We have done the footwork. We've checked out the accommodations to find the best deals and the most interesting amenities, and tested the restaurants' cuisine, service, and ambience. We've got the lowdown on the nightlife from those who regularly crawl through their fair share of clubs. If a museum is dull or an attraction ridiculously overpriced, we'll tell you so. We hope in the process to make your visit more fun, efficient, and economical.

We've tried to anticipate the special needs of older people, families with young children, families with teenagers, solo travelers, people with physical challenges, and those who have a particular passion for adventure, archaeology, sports, shopping, or spas. We hope to keep the quality of your visit high and the irritation quotient low.

Please remember that prices and admission hours change constantly. We've listed the most up-to-date information we can get, but it never hurts to double-check times and prices.

ABOUT UNOFFICIAL GUIDES

READERS CARE ABOUT AUTHORS' OPINIONS. The authors, after all, are supposed to know what they are talking about. This, coupled with the fact that the traveler wants quick answers (as opposed to endless alternatives), dictates that travel authors should be explicit, prescriptive, and—above all—direct. The authors of the *Unofficial Guide* try to do just that. We spell out alternatives and recommend specific courses of action. We simplify complicated destinations and attractions to allow the traveler to feel in control in unfamiliar environments. Our objective is not to give the most information or all the information, but the most accessible, useful information.

An *Unofficial Guide* is a critical reference work; we focus on a travel destination that appears to be especially complex. Our authors and researchers are completely independent from the attractions, restaurants, and accommodations we describe. *The Unofficial Guide to Mexico's Best Beach Resorts* is designed for individuals and families traveling for fun as well as for business, and it will be especially helpful to those visiting Mexico for the first time. The guide is directed at value-conscious, consumer-oriented adults who seek a cost-effective but not spartan travel style.

SPECIAL FEATURES

- Vital information about traveling to and within Mexico
- Friendly introductions to Mexico's beach resorts
- Listings keyed to your interests, so you can pick and choose
- Advice to sightseers on how to avoid the worst crowds; advice to business travelers on how to avoid excessive costs
- Recommendations for sights off the beaten tourist path but no less worthwhile
- Maps to make it easy to find the places you want to visit
- Accommodation and restaurant listings that help you narrow your choices quickly, according to your budget and preferences
- A table of contents and detailed index to help you find things fast

WHAT YOU *WON'T* GET

- Long, useless lists where everything looks the same
- Information that gets you to your destination at the worst possible time
- Information without advice on how to use it

HOW THIS GUIDE WAS RESEARCHED AND WRITTEN

IN PREPARING THIS BOOK, we took nothing for granted. We thought back to our first visits to Mexico and remembered our earliest dilemmas. We talked with travelers visiting Mexico for the first time and with those few who say they'll never cross the border again. We listened to their questions, concerns, and misconceptions. Our goal is to help you enjoy Mexico to its fullest and learn to love this exciting country.

We visited each accommodation, restaurant, shop, and attraction, conducted detailed evaluations, and rated each according to formal criteria. While working as independent and impartial observers, we asked fellow travelers what they thought of the destinations and businesses. We paid particular attention to those who visit Mexico regularly and those who work in the tourism sector. We listened to their praise and complaints, and we took their comments into account when rating each entry.

In compiling this guide, we recognize that a tourist's age, background, and interests strongly influence his or her reactions to Mexico's array of beach resorts and attractions. Some may be delighted with a destination that offers endless rounds of golf. Others want culture and art. Our objective is to provide readers with sufficient description, critical evaluation, and pertinent data such that knowledgeable decisions can be made according to individual tastes.

LETTERS, COMMENTS, AND QUESTIONS FROM READERS

MANY OF THOSE WHO USE THE *Unofficial Guides* write to us asking questions, making comments, or sharing their own discoveries and lessons learned in Mexico. Readers' comments and observations are frequently incorporated in revised editions and contribute immeasurably to its improvement. We appreciate all correspondence, both positive and critical, and encourage our readers to continue writing.

How to Write the Authors

Maribeth Mellin and Jane Onstott
The Unofficial Guide to Mexico's Best Beach Resorts
P.O. Box 43673
Birmingham, AL 35243
mbmellin@aol.com (Maribeth), mexicoguru@yahoo.com (Jane)

When you write, be sure to put your return address on your letter as well as on the envelope—sometimes envelopes and letters get separated. Remember, our work takes us out of the office for long periods of time, so forgive us if our response is delayed.

Reader Survey

At the back of this guide, you will find a short questionnaire that you can use to express opinions concerning your Mexico visit. Clip out the questionnaire along the dotted line and mail it to the address above.

The Unofficial Guide Web Site

The Web site of the *Unofficial Guide* Travel and Lifestyle Series, providing in-depth information on all *Unofficial Guides* in print, is at **www.theunofficialguides.com**.

ALPHABETIZING IN SPANISH

This book contains dozens of accommodation and restaurant profiles listed alphabetically in each regional chapter. Note that articles in Spanish grammar—*el, la, las,* and *los*—are disregarded when alphabetizing, just as *the* is disregarded when alphabetizing in English. So, for example, if you're trying to find the profile for a restaurant called La Cabaña de Caleta, you'd look under C for "Cabaña" instead of L for "La." The indexes in the back of this book work the same way.

HOW INFORMATION IS ORGANIZED: BY SUBJECT AND BY GEOGRAPHIC DESTINATION

TO GIVE YOU FAST ACCESS to information about the best of Mexico's beach resorts, we've organized the information into the following chapters:

Part One, Planning Your Visit to Mexico

This chapter holds the answers to many of your most important questions. We cover health and safety issues, give you tips on getting to Mexico easily and efficiently, and discuss when and why to visit each destination.

Part Two, Accommodations and Restaurants

Many hotel chains familiar to travelers around the world have properties at Mexico's beach resorts; some have rooms and facilities exactly like those you would find in Chicago or New York City. Some travelers find great comfort in this familiarity. But we love finding the perfect Mexican room—one that has character, comfort, and a few eccentricities. And we love staying in hotels, both simple and luxurious. Mexico is blessed with wonderful one-of-a-kind small inns, from opulently restored haciendas to mom-and-pop hostels that feel like home. A few resort areas have spectacular pleasure palaces that command some of the highest room rates in the world. In our overview of the accommodation scene, we discuss why we chose the accommodations included in each regional chapter and explain our detailed rating system.

We've taken the same approach with restaurants. Countless readers and friends have asked us if they can drink the water, eat the lettuce, or find fine dining in Mexico. The answer to all three questions is yes—if you know what you're doing. Rest assured that nearly every major city in Mexico has a Subway, Domino's Pizza, or Burger King. But why eat as you would at home? In this chapter, you'll learn how to stock your hotel room with reliable food staples and sample the local cuisine wisely and safely. Once you've eaten at a few of our recommended restaurants, you'll start craving homemade tamales, lobster with made-in-the-moment tortillas, and seafood tacos. We've rated our chosen restaurants to give you a complete overview of what to expect. After all, dining may well be your largest vacation expense (after you've paid to get there and set up housekeeping). We'll help you find whatever you desire, be it comfort food or something unique and exciting.

Part Three, Arriving and Getting Oriented

Are you afraid you'll stick out like a gullible tourist when you arrive in Mexico? Do you think people will try to take advantage of your inexperience? Relax, and read our tips in this chapter. We'll tell you if you should drive at your destination or take a cab, and we'll give you information on getting around safely and inexpensively. We'll teach you how to bargain at markets and shop for fine art in galleries. We'll reveal the secrets the locals already know and the tips that will make you feel like a savvy traveler.

Parts Four to Fourteen, the Destinations

As our world evolves into a global marketplace, certain businesses have become omnipresent. But familiarity doesn't ensure success. All hip, popular tourist destinations change constantly. We've seen restaurants backed by celebrities come and go in Cancún, and we've watched entrenched clubs such as Hard Rock Cafe sell thousands of T-shirts in Los Cabos.

The competition for your vacation cash is fierce, and resort areas compete with historical, natural, and man-made attractions. Golf courses, spas, and flashy shopping malls have become de rigueur in large-scale tourist destinations. Adventure tours are popping up everywhere, and travelers can watch whales from kayaks in the Sea of Cortez or dive with giant mantas and tiny seahorses off the shores of Zihuatanejo.

In each regional chapter, we provide an overview of the attractions and experiences that makes each destination different. Some places have fascinating museums and archaeological sites. Most have sunset cruises and other boat trips and seemingly endless shopping options. We'll show you how to get the most out of your vacation dollars by suggesting only the best touring options.

WHERE SHOULD I GO?

IT'S HARD TO CHOOSE AMONG MEXICO'S BEACH DESTINATIONS. A dozen places immediately come to mind, each with a distinctive character and attributes. This book includes the most popular resort areas on the Caribbean and Pacific coasts, along with Los Cabos on the Sea of Cortez. We've chosen to cover areas that have modern airports and high-quality accommodations, restaurants, and attractions. We list the highlights below by region, in the order in which they appear in this book, and provide in-depth coverage in the regional chapters.

CANCÚN

GATEWAY TO THE MEXICAN CARIBBEAN and the Yucatán Peninsula. Comfortable for the uninitiated, too gringo-ized for die-hard Mexicophiles. English and dollars as common as Spanish and pesos. Lots of familiar accommodation, restaurant, and shop names. Varied nightlife scene. Easy access to famous Maya ruins. Best for those seeking familiarity, pampering, and moderate prices.

ISLA MUJERES

A LAID-BACK HAMMOCK-LOVER'S island in the Caribbean that's become a cult destination for budget and high-end travelers alike. Plenty of inexpensive to moderate accommodations and restaurants. A few exquisite boutique inns. Great snorkeling, fair diving, good shopping, no golf. Perfect for low-energy, easygoing relaxation.

COZUMEL

SCUBA DIVING IS THE MAIN ATTRACTION HERE. A couple of modest archaeological sites, lots of empty, windswept beaches, a traditional town with main plaza. Several good restaurants, fun sidewalk cafes, interesting shopping, a wide range of accommodations with

Comparison of Mexico's Beach Resort Destinations

	CANCÚN	ISLA MUJERES	COZUMEL	CARIBBEAN COAST	MAZATLÁN
Accommodations	★★★★½	★★★	★★★½	★★★★★	★★★½
Amenities	★★★★★	★½	★★★★	★★★	★★★½
Beaches	★★★★	★★★★	★★★★½	★★★★★	★★★½
Dining	★★★★	★	★★★★	★★★½	★★★½
Recreation	★★★★★	★★★★	★★★★	★★★★	★★★
Diving	★★	★★★½	★★★★★	★★★★★	★
Fishing	★★	★★	★★★	★★★	★★★★½
Golf	★★★	–	★★	★★	★★
Nightlife	★★★★	★★	★★½	★	★★★½
Shopping	★★★	★★★	★★★	★★½	★½
Family-friendliness	★★★★★	★★★½	★★★★	★★★★	★★★★
Peace and Quiet	★	★★★★	★★½	★★★★★	★★½
Culture	★½	★★	★★★½	★★★★	★★★★

a few chain properties. One golf course, with others in the works. Mexico's number-one cruise-ship destination (which can make the downtown area and the most popular dive sites terribly crowded). A diver's paradise and a favorite for romantic escapes.

THE CARIBBEAN COAST

THE FASTEST-GROWING RESORT AREA in Mexico includes the **Riviera Maya,** from Cancún to the Maya ruins at Tulum, and the **Costa Maya** on the southern stretch of the coast to Xcalak, near Belize. A lineup of large, all-inclusive resorts interspersed with small boutique accommodations and budget hostelries. Several marinas, two cruise-ship piers, golf course developments, and **Playa del Carmen,** a backpacker village turned trendy, hip city with excellent restaurants, high-quality folk art shops, and a long, sugary beach. Several archaeological sites, excellent diving, bird-watching, adventure tours. A high-energy choice for explorers. Offers plenty of luxurious hideaways.

MAZATLÁN

A REAL MEXICAN CITY with a large port and cruise-ship dock, an established tourist zone (called the **Zona Dorado**), and a traditional downtown with old mansions decorated with elaborate wrought-iron gates and balconies. Two busy central plazas and a traditional

PUERTO VALLARTA	IXTAPA AND ZIHUATANEJO	ACAPULCO	PUERTO ESCONDIDO	HUATULCO	LOS CABOS
★★★★★	★★★	★★	★	★★½	★★★★★
★★★★½	★★	★★	★	★★	★★★★★
★★★★	★★★½	★	★★★	★★★★½	★★
★★★★★	★★½	★★★½	★★	★	★★★★★
★★★★	★★	★★★	★½	★½	★★★★½
★★★	★★★★	★★½	★½	★★½	★★★
★★★½	★★★★	★★★★	★★	★★	★★★★★
★★★★★	★½	★	–	★	★★★★★
★★★★★	★★★½	★★	½	★★½	★★★½
★★★★	★★★	★★★	★★½	★★½	★★★★
★★★½	★★½	★½	★★★★	★★★★★	★★★★
★★★★★	★½	★★★	★½	★	★½

Mexican market. Great sportfishing and excellent seafood restaurants. Marinas, golf courses, and new resort developments. Easy access to mountain towns and seaside villages. Relatively inexpensive and traditional.

PUERTO VALLARTA

A PICTURESQUE CITY WITH COBBLESTONE STREETS, whitewashed buildings with red-tile roofs, and a backdrop of jungle-clad mountains. Long stretches of beach north and south of town lined with first-class high-rise hotels. Excellent Italian, Mediterranean, and nouvelle-Mexican restaurants. High-quality galleries displaying fine art and folk art from around the country. Several marinas, a half-dozen golf courses, and upscale resort developments. Ideal for culture vultures. The coastline south of Puerto Vallarta, called the **Costalegre,** is dotted with exclusive resorts.

IXTAPA AND ZIHUATANEJO

IXTAPA IS A MASTER-PLANNED destination with golf courses, a hotel zone along the beach, and several shopping and dining centers. Zihuatanejo is an overgrown fishing village. Budget accommodations are located in town by the plaza and moderate to expensive hotels are found on beaches and on the cliffs above them. A few

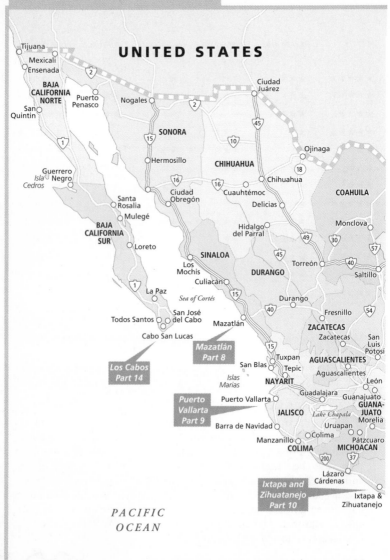

Mexico's Beach Resorts

UNITED STATES

Tijuana
Mexicali
Ensenada
BAJA CALIFORNIA NORTE
Puerto Penasco
San Quintin

Nogales

Ciudad Juárez

SONORA

Hermosillo

CHIHUAHUA

Ojinaga

Chihuahua

COAHUILA

Guerrero Negro
Isla Cedros

Santa Rosalia
Mulegé

Ciudad Obregón

Cuauhtémoc

Delicias

Monclova

BAJA CALIFORNIA SUR

Loreto

Hidalgo del Parral

Torreón

Saltillo

Los Mochis

SINALOA

Culiacán

DURANGO

La Paz
Sea of Cortés

Durango

Fresnillo

San José del Cabo

ZACATECAS

Todos Santos

Mazatlán

Zacatecas
San Luis Potosi

Cabo San Lucas

Mazatlán Part 8

San Blas

Tuxpan

AGUASCALIENTES

Tepic

Aguascalientes

León

Los Cabos Part 14

Islas Marias

NAYARIT

Guadalajara

Guanajuato

GUANA-JUATO

Puerto Vallarta Part 9

Puerto Vallarta

JALISCO

Lake Chapala

Morelia

Barra de Navidad

Uruapan

Pátzcuaro

Manzanillo

Colima

MICHOACAN

COLIMA

Lázaro Cárdenas

Ixtapa and Zihuatanejo Part 10

Ixtapa & Zihuatanejo

PACIFIC OCEAN

0   150 mi
0   150 km

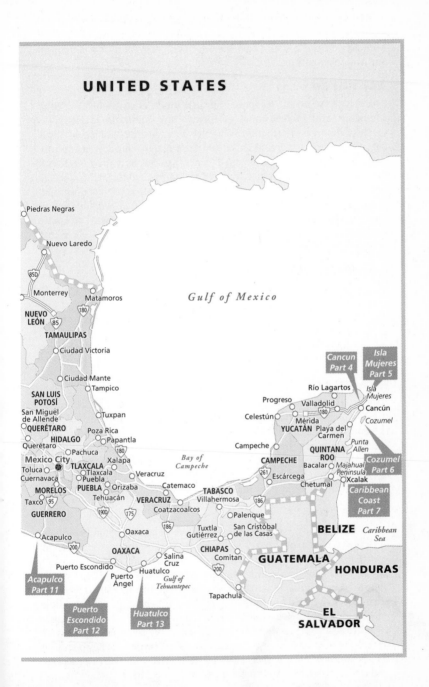

of the country's best boutique hotels are located here. The combo makes it ideal both for those who enjoy experiencing traditional Mexico and those who want a modern resort with all the amenities and total relaxation.

ACAPULCO

ONCE GLAMOROUS, Acapulco has lost much of its cachet. Wealthy Mexicans and international celebrities still maintain lavish villas on the cliffs over spectacular Acapulco Bay, but they see a side of the city most regular travelers miss. **Old Acapulco** has modest accommodations, a working waterfront, a central plaza, and the famed cliff divers. The long, unsightly, noisy **Costera,** the boulevard following the bay's contour, has the largest concentration of accommodations and restaurants. Las Brisas is the classy area with luxurious hotels and gourmet restaurants. The newest development, **Acapulco Diamante,** has golf courses, large resorts, and boutique hotels. Exciting nightlife is one of Acapulco's main attractions.

PUERTO ESCONDIDO

SURFERS MAKE PILGRIMAGES to the waves at **Playa Zicatela,** which is consistently ranked among the top surf spots in the world. Travelers hang out at small, moderately priced accommodations, eat seafood and fresh pasta at restaurants by the sand, shop for batik sarongs from Bali, or bird-watch in nearby lagoons. Great for budget travelers and those eschewing tourist resorts.

HUATULCO

NINE GORGEOUS BAYS at the foot of the Sierra Madre del Sur on the Oaxacan Coast. Upscale accommodations, all-inclusives, and the golf course are clustered around one bay; the marina and seaside cafes around another. Inland is **La Crucecita,** a pseudo-traditional Mexican village with a plaza, market, and budget to moderately priced hotels. The best activities are boat trips, kayaking, and snorkeling within the bays. Wonderful for total relaxation.

LOS CABOS

LOCATED AT THE SOUTHERN TIP of the Baja California Peninsula, between the Sea of Cortez and the Pacific. Famous for excellent sportfishing, it has become Mexico's number-one golf destination. **San José del Cabo** is a semitraditional town gentrified by expatriates. **Cabo San Lucas** is party central, with raucous clubs that attract a young, partying crowd and busy marinas sheltering handsome yachts. High-end developments and exclusive hotels and spas are located along the 18-mile, beach-front corridor that separates the two. Few options for budget travelers. Great for wealthy escapists, those willing to splurge on spectacular rooms, interesting restaurants, and overpriced taxis, and the families who fill huge time-share properties.

A **BRIEF HISTORY** *of* **MEXICO**

MODERN MEXICO

MEXICO ENTERED A NEW POLITICAL ERA at the turn of the 21st century. In the country's most transparent election ever (which isn't saying a lot), Vicente Fox Quesada, of PAN (Partido de Acción Nacional), won the presidency over PRI (Partido Revolucionario Institucional) opponent Francisco Labastida, ending more than seven decades of one-party politics. Mexicans were more shocked than anyone about this unexpected turn of events, and since that time many governorships and mayoral elections have gone to PAN and other political parties.

The change in the power structure had been building for decades. Issues long buried by politicians and the press began surfacing after the 1985 Mexico City earthquake. Thousands died in the quake, and the city's infrastructure took a major beating. And it seems the tremors shook more than the ground. Political consciousness and protest, already on the rise because of a drastic peso devaluation in 1982, grew. Carlos Salinas de Gortari was elected president in 1988. Though he ran under the PRI banner, he proved far different from his predecessors. The Harvard-educated Salinas had a global outlook on economics. Under the banner of Solidarity, he encouraged his fellow countrymen to unite and move forward into the world. Statues to solidarity still stand beside roads and bridges as a testimony to progress.

The North American Free Trade Agreement (NAFTA) was signed by Salinas and President Bill Clinton in 1993. In 1994, Subcomandante Marcos and the rifle-toting Zapatistas took over the plaza in San Cristóbal de las Casas, one of the most indigenous cities in Mexico. Demanding equal rights and justice for disenfranchised peoples of Chiapas and throughout country, the Zapatistas became a visible force in the global media. Later that year, PRI presidential candidate Luis Donaldo Colosio was assassinated in Tijuana. Ernesto Zedillo, a longtime PRI bureaucrat, was elected president. In December 1994 the peso was once again devalued and a serious recession soon followed. Salinas gradually emerged as one of the most corrupt politicians in a blatantly corrupt system. His brother, Raúl Salinas, was accused of earning millions of dollars through drug trafficking and political corruption and was imprisoned for murdering a PRI official. Ex-President Carlos Salinas left Mexico and eventually settled in Ireland. T-shirts bearing a picture of the ex-president as a convict, rat, and bandito appeared in souvenir stands.

The PRI weakened during Zedillo's presidency. Scandals about past injustices took center stage. The people were ready for change. Charismatic Vicente Fox Quesada—a tall, dignified rancher and one-time Guanajuato state governor and Coca-Cola de Mexico executive wearing cowboy boots and a big belt buckle—stood out among the presidential hopefuls in 2000. He vowed to get down to business and lead the country into the new millennium with honesty and businesslike acumen. And he won.

But the PRI was not dead. Fox's administration was plagued with the usual difficulties encountered by presidents with oppositional legislative houses. Made up of executives rather than politicians, Fox's cabinet wasn't prepared to deal with the gridlock and stubborn determination of the PRI's operatives. PRI regained popularity in the countryside, and PRI candidates won several local elections. Fox's six-year term ended in 2006, when he was replaced by PAN bureaucrat Felipe Calderón. The PRI candidate trailed a distant third throughout the contest, but the race between liberal candidate Andrés Manuel López Obrador and Calderón was as close as could be. Calderón was declared the winner, but by just 0.6% of the votes. López Obrador contested the election, citing irregularities in nearly 30% of precincts. A recount of 9% of the vote—mandated by the Federal Election Institute—showed irregularities but upheld Calderón as the winner.

With such a lackluster mandate to govern, Calderón faced challenges and contention on all sides. López Obrador continued to lead protests against the election results for many months following Calderón's inauguration. Meanwhile, the teacher's union in Oaxaca had strengthened its annual summer protests seeking higher wages.

But far more daunting challenges were building along the northern border. As Calderón was taking office, the leaders of Mexico's narcotics cartels began fighting for control of major drug routes through Mexico. The new president immediately declared war on the cartels, sending military troops to small mountain towns where opium poppies and marijuana were grown and harvested. More troops joined police forces in the border areas to stop the flow of drugs into the United States. Though the resulting conflicts have been extremely violent, more than 22 million tourists visited Mexico in 2008, making tourism the country's third-largest moneymaker.

Calderón faces myriad battles as he nears the middle of his six-year term. The value of the peso dropped about 30% in the first quarter of 2009, which increased foreign investment in Mexico but burdened the country's citizens. Tourists, on the other hand, found a wealth of bargains and the opportunity for inexpensive vacations close to home. Calderón announced that the government would win the war on drugs by the end of his term in 2012. The issue will surely dominate during the next election, as Mexico's political parties claim the power to solve the country's problems.

ANCIENT MEXICO

LIKE THAT OF MOST COMPLEX CIVILIZATIONS, the history of Mexico is a rich cultural tapestry of intricate variation in texture and hue. Over the millennia, cultures have coexisted and clashed, alternately sharing ideas and sacrificing each other to the gods of rain, fertility, and war. New evidence of early cultures is constantly being unearthed as farmers till the earth and city workers install underground cables.

MIGRATION AND EARLY CIVILIZATIONS

HUMAN BEINGS FROM ASIA FIRST BEGAN infiltrating the wide-open spaces of the New World between 30,000 and 40,000 years ago. Crossing the narrow, ice-covered Bering Strait, small bands of nomadic hunter-gatherers migrated across North and South America.

By about 4000 BC, people were cultivating plants—including squash, beans, chiles, and corn—and thus reducing the need to wander and forage. Larger communities developed, more sophisticated tools were made, and, eventually, woven vessels and ceramic containers and utensils were added to the more rustic stock of stone implements. Specialization of tasks led to the stratification of working, ruling, and artisan classes.

The Olmecs are the first culture known to have diversified in such a way. At sites such as Tres Zapotes and San Lorenzo, in the modern state of Veracruz, artisans carved giant heads of basalt stone that modern scholars think portrayed important leaders or citizens. The immense stones, some weighing 40 and 50 tons, were mined hundreds of miles away in the Tuxtla Mountains, proving that the Olmecs of 1000 BC excelled not only in craftsmanship but in engineering as well.

Other objects carved by Olmec artisans were apparently made to be more easily transported, and archaeologists have found small jade figurines of Olmec origin as far north as Tula (north of Mexico City) and south into modern Central America. In trading, divergent cultures shared not only material objects but also political, cultural, and artistic ideas—everything from local deities to architectural innovations.

Another of Mexico's oldest civilizations arose in south-central Mexico, in modern-day Oaxaca. The Zapotecs created elaborate, extensive cities, such as hilltop Monte Albán, and developed one of the continent's earliest systems of hieroglyphic writing. Zapotec artifacts have been found as far away as Teotihuacán, a contemporary kingdom north of present-day Mexico City. Thought to have been built by relatives of the Totonacs (with whose aid the Spanish conquered the Aztecs 1,000 years later), Teotihuacán was larger, richer, and more powerful than any European civilization of its time. Built facing a promenade lined with brilliant palaces and temples, the great pyramids of the sun and the moon still stand as a reminder of that ancient city, which, like many others, was abandoned at the peak of its power.

The Maya were another advanced civilization that periodically abandoned sophisticated cities for reasons unknown. By the dawn of the Christian era, the Maya already excelled in mathematics, astronomy, and architecture. From dazzling cities in the lowlands of the Yucatán Peninsula to highland Chiapas and into modern Central America, they developed several highly accurate calendars. Both the ritual, moon-based calendar of 260 days and the 365-day solar calendar were used to determine auspicious and unlucky days and to predict events. Other cultures, such as the Zapotecs, used these types of calendars as well, but only the Maya developed the Long Count, used to record historic events. Royal marriages, deaths, coronations, and births were carved in limestone stelae (inscribed stone slabs) and molded stucco lintels for all the community to see.

The Maya and most other prehispanic Mesoamerican cultures practiced both human sacrifice and ritual cannibalism. (Commoners were never permitted to eat human flesh, a rite and a delicacy reserved for nobles.) Contrary to popular mythology, virgins were not the traditional sacrificial victims. Seasoned warriors were commonly killed, bearing messages of the triumph of their enemies for the gods. Often leaders captured in battle were pitted against their conquerors in ritual ball games: The winner lived, and the loser died. Starvation, mutilation, and other tactics made certain the odds were irreversibly stacked in favor of the host team's captain.

CONQUEST AND COLONIZATION

ARRIVING IN THE NEW WORLD in the early 16th century, the Spanish conquistadors found evidence of human sacrifice wherever they turned. Their repugnance at this practice led them to attempt both the conquest and the conversion of the Mesoamerican people. Against enormous odds, they succeeded in both endeavors.

Conquistador Hernán Cortés set sail from Cuba in February 1519. An adventurous man who had traveled to the New World to escape romantic entanglements in the Old, Cortés possessed a strong will and daring character that made possible one of the most fascinating and implausible conquests in history. Factors such as good luck, great timing, and an enormous pool of wrathful enemies helped the Spanish defeat the well-organized and mighty Aztec army.

From the moment the Spanish set foot in Mesoamerica, they heard tales of the fearsome Aztecs who, from their island city surrounded by mountains, held a huge number of subjects in a merciless grip. Compared to the Zapotecs, Totonacs, and other kingdoms that paid tribute to their overlords, the Aztecs were cultural upstarts. Their mighty kingdom at Tenochtitlán—which dazzled Cortés and his men with its complexity and beauty—had not even been founded two centuries before.

This great and powerful civilization was descended from one of the barbaric Chichimec tribes that migrated from the harsher regions to the north. A few centuries of intermarriage with more cultured plateau peoples and a series of fearless and sage leaders led the

Aztecs to dominate most of the tribes in central and southern Meso-america by the time the Spanish arrived in the early 16th century.

By epic coincidence, Cortés's fleet arrived in a year that held great significance for the indigenous people. The benign god-king Quet-zalcoatl (Kukulkán to the Maya) had, according to legend, sailed away to the east centuries before, promising to return in the year 1 Reed, which corresponded to 1519. By the time Moctezuma II, the Aztec emperor, had decided that Cortés was not the god returning to reclaim his throne, the tiny Spanish force had been reinforced by large groups of Aztec enemies. Even with these allies, the conquest in retrospect seems no less than miraculous.

Spanish forces numbered some 400, while among the Aztec Empire of more than 10 million were hundreds of thousands of well-trained, well-armed warriors. Yet only two years after their incursion into Mesoamerica, the Spanish had reduced Tenochtitlán to ruins and set about rebuilding the city, and others like it, in the image of Spain.

The acquisition of native allies was facilitated by another stroke of luck for the Spanish. Among a group of slaves given them by their early hosts and most formidable allies, the Tlaxcalans, was a young woman called Malinalli, or Malinche. A willing ambassador for Cortés, she won the Spanish many allies with her translations and diplomacy and provided them with insight into the indigenous mind.

Malinche, renamed Doña Marina by the Spanish, bore Cortés a son and lived to relative old age. Many natives were not so fortunate, as imported diseases such as measles and smallpox killed them in vast numbers. Those who survived were swiftly incorporated into the viceregal system of government. Under the powerful Audiencias, answerable only to the King of Spain, the vast majority of natives and mestizos (those of mixed Spanish and indigenous descent) became virtual slaves for their European masters. Indigenous chiefs and lords who converted readily to Christianity were rewarded with positions of some importance and power, while those who persisted in wor-shipping the old gods were brutally tortured and ultimately killed.

Colonial rule lasted just shy of three centuries, from 1521 to 1810. During that period, Spain recouped many thousands of times over its tiny initial investment. The twin mountain ranges, the Sierra Madre Oriental and Sierra Madre Occidental, were seamed with the pre-cious gold that had first attracted Cortés and his men to the Aztec capital. And tons of ingots of silver filled the holds of ships bound for Manila and ultimately Spain. The Old World diet was enriched by wonderful foods from the new continent, including chocolate, squash, chiles, tomatoes, and turkey.

MEN OF THE CLOTH

CULTURE IS NEVER STATIC, and its dissemination is rarely, if ever, one-way. Although the majority of the population was too poor to enjoy these innovations, the Spaniards introduced the New World to wheat, chicken and eggs, goats, cows, and cheese. Along with new foods and infectious disease, the newcomers also introduced the Catholic faith.

Franciscan friars got the jump on converting the natives, carving a niche for themselves early on in Mexico's highly populated central plateau. The Dominicans soon followed, building sumptuous monasteries and churches in Oaxaca; while the more restrained and thrifty Jesuits led forays in the harsher, more sparsely populated northern deserts and the barren Baja California Peninsula. Many converts died of disease or overwork. Some of the most reluctant tribes retreated to the least hospitable parts of the land to avoid contact with the new taskmasters.

Given the treatment of their comrades, avoiding the Europeans was not unwise. Untold numbers spent their lives as chattel slaves, working in the fields, or deep within dangerous mines. Life expectancy was short, and despite advocates such as Chiapas's Bishop Bartolomé de las Casas, the subjugated natives were treated abominably by their white masters.

INDEPENDENCE AND THE *PORFIRIATO*

DESPITE THE ILL TREATMENT OF NATIVES and mestizos and their place at the bottom of the social pyramid, Mexican independence was not a class struggle. It was instigated by wealthy landowners, principally *criollos* inspired by the French and American revolutions and dissatisfied with the status quo. But although upper-crust liberals provided the brains, the masses—peasants who could be mobilized with promises of land and freedom—provided the cannon fodder. Not long into the war, which broke out in 1810, the primary leaders were captured and executed. The severed heads of Padre Miguel Hidalgo and Ignacio Allende, along with two compatriots, hung for the duration of the war from La Alhóndiga, a royalist stronghold in Guanajuato, to discourage would-be rebels.

Even considering the many obstacles to winning such a war and the rebels' lack of organization, Spanish resistance was lackluster and the Treaty of Cordoba ended hostilities in 1821. Little changed for the average person, with the Catholic church and the wealthy still firmly in control of the country, the economy, and the welfare of the masses.

The new order called for a constitutional monarch; "Emperor" Agustin de Iturbide reigned only briefly before his regime was replaced by a republic. When Iturbide attempted a comeback several years later, he was promptly executed.

The chaotic post-independence years made the new nation a convenient target for foreign invasions. During one of his many short stints as president, General Antonio López de Santa Anna lost Texas to the United States, prompting Mexico's northern neighbor to initiate further aggressions. Few battles were fought, and relatively few lives lost, in the Mexican-American War from 1846 to 1848. However, the end result was disastrous for Mexico, which lost nearly half of its land—including the present-day states of Utah, Colorado, Nevada, Arizona, and California—to the United States.

Frustrated with the chaos and disorder of the early 19th century, intellectual reformists attempted to wrestle control from both bureaucrats and the church. Liberal lawyer Benito Juárez, from Oaxaca state, ushered in the Reform Laws in the mid-19th century, which reduced the wealth and power of both the military and the church. Naturally, these reforms ignited immediate hostilities. After a three-year war, the liberals under Juárez had the dubious good fortune to rule, acquiring a government that was weak, corrupt, and inept, as well as bankrupt.

Stability was still a pipe dream. A French invasion soon replaced Juárez with Austrian Archduke Maximilian of Hapsburg. After just a few short years (1864–67) in his delightful palaces in Mexico City and Cuernavaca, the emperor was executed by liberals who reinstated Juárez to the presidency. Separation of church and state and other liberal reform laws were affected, although the conservative general Porfirio Díaz did little to implement any tenets of agrarian reform during his 34-year "presidency."

The period of time during which Porfirio Díaz ruled, 1876–1909, is known as the *porfiriato*. The country in general prospered as foreign investments rose, railroads were constructed, and lovely Art Nouveau buildings were commissioned in downtown Mexico City. The turn of the 19th century in Mexico was good for the moneyed few, but bad for the dispossessed masses. Díaz ruled with an iron hand. His handpicked rural police strongly "discouraged" resistance to his policies in the countryside, while adversaries in the city simply disappeared. During his rule, hundreds of thousands of peons were sold into slavery in mines, factories, and plantations—all of which naturally prospered.

THE TURN OF THE 20TH CENTURY AND THE MEXICAN REVOLUTION

THE HACIENDAS OF THE YUCATÁN benefited enormously from the *porfiriato*. The thin, poor soil of the peninsula, all but ruined by previous plantings of sugarcane and tobacco, put out banner yields of *henequen*, or sisal, used to make rope and twine. The natural fibers made from this agave plant were in demand around the world, and the hacienda owners reaped huge profits with which they built grand palaces. They furnished these with European marble, carpets, and furnishings purchased during visits of months or even years abroad at the cost of hundreds of thousands of native lives.

Despite their financial fortune, not all of Mexico's wealthy elite were content to prosper at the expense of their less fortunate countrymen. Rich, conservative northerner Francisco I. Madero brought about the Mexican Revolution (1911–1920) by campaigning against Porfirio Díaz in a rare election, for which Madero fought in 1910. Joining the conflict, Emiliano Zapata fought for agrarian reforms for landless peasants in his native Morelos. Others, such as Pancho Villa and Venustiano Carranza, added to the color as well as the chaos. With no consensus among leaders and more than one major political agenda, the Mexican Revolution was drawn out and costly. More than a million lives were lost, mostly civilians, and the country's economy was ruined.

Mexico's current constitution was ratified in 1917, but the war raged on until 1920. Although it was one of the new constitution's major tenets, agrarian reform was not implemented until 1934 and the election of president Lázaro Cárdenas. The popular president from Michoacán redistributed millions of acres of land, allowing Mexico's marginalized poor to form community-owned *ejidos,* or farms. Perhaps even more radical was his decision to nationalize all railroads and the petroleum industry, thereby ridding the country of foreign economic control.

The rule of Lázaro Cárdenas ushered in more changes, in the form of a new political party, the precursor of the well-known PRI, or Partido Revolucionario Institucional. This political party ruled with virtual impunity for the greater part of the 20th century, controlling the countryside in local elections and the nation with consecutive presidencies until the year 2000.

Much has changed since the PRI lost control of the country with the inauguration of Vicente Fox Quesada of the PAN party in 2001. The subsequent inauguration of PAN candidate Felipe Calderón in 2006 continued the move away from institutionalized politics tightly controlled by wealthy and powerful families. But this political leap into the 21st century has brought with it enormous changes and difficulties. The government is waging war with drug cartels while attempting to provide a better quality of life for its citizens. More and more foreigners are investing in residential communities as large investors create entire new resorts along the coastlines, providing jobs that keep Mexicans close to home. The next few years should be very interesting as political parties, social advocates, foreign investors, and more than 100 million Mexican citizens attempt to work together to help Mexico reach First World status.

PART ONE

PLANNING *your* VISIT *to* MEXICO

■ AIR TRAVEL

MEXICO'S COASTAL RESORTS receive numerous flights from U.S. cities, especially from each airline's airport hub. Flights with connections at major hub cities in the United States are available to all the destinations in this book. See each regional chapter for more information on airlines.

The airlines listed in the table on the next page provide flights to resort areas. Schedules and destinations change seasonally and continue to adjust as all airline companies reduce and consolidate their flights due to rising operational costs. As a rule, more flights are available during the winter high season than in the summer. We've listed the destinations each airline normally serves, but the situation could certainly change before you travel.

Many foreign airlines have agreements with Mexican carriers. For instance, you can book a flight on American Airlines from London to Acapulco, transferring in Dallas to an Aeroméxico flight to Acapulco operated by Delta. Aeroméxico also has direct flights between several European and North American cities and Mexico City and is part of the SkyTeam code-sharing alliance with Delta and Continental. If you're coming from Australia, American Airlines connects with Mexicana flights through Los Angeles. Mexicana also has alliances with Air Japan and Air New Zealand. **British Airways** (☎ 800-AIRWAY; **www.britishairways .com**) makes Mexico connections from London via Miami or Dallas–Fort Worth.

Travelers will most likely have flights connecting in Mexico City when traveling to Acapulco and Ixtapa-Zihuatanejo, Puerto Escondido, and Huatulco. You may find less-expensive flights available to other Mexican destinations as well if you're willing to change planes in Mexico City.

RESORT AIR SERVICE

AIRLINE | PHONE | WEB SITE

Alaska Airlines | ☎ 800-252-7522 | www.alaskaair.com
Cancún, Los Cabos, Mazatlán, Puerto Vallarta, and Ixtapa-Zihuatanejo

American Airlines | ☎ 800-433-7300 | www.aa.com
Puerto Vallarta, Los Cabos, Acapulco, Ixtapa-Zihuatanejo, Cozumel, and Cancún

America West/US Airways | ☎ 800- 428-4322 | www.usairways.com
Acapulco, Cancún, Los Cabos, Cozumel, Puerto Vallarta, Mazatlán, and
Ixtapa-Zihuatanejo

Continental Airlines | ☎ 800-231-0856 | www.continental.com
Los Cabos, Puerto Vallarta, Ixtapa-Zihuatanejo, Acapulco, Huatulco, Cozumel,
and Cancún

Delta | ☎ 800-241-4141 | www.delta.com
Acapulco, Cancún, Puerto Vallarta, Los Cabos, Mazatlán, and Ixtapa-Zihuatanejo

Northwest Airlines | ☎ 800-225-2525 | www.nwa.com
Note: *Except for Cancún, all are seasonal—Acapulco, Cancún, Cozumel, Puerto Vallarta,
Los Cabos, Mazatlán, and Ixtapa-Zihuatanejo.*

United Airlines | ☎ 800-538-2929 | www.united.com
Mexico City, Cancún, Cozumel, Los Cabos, Ixtapa-Zihuatanejo, and Puerto Vallarta

*Often, the best flights to the resort areas, and the best airfares, are available on the Mexican airlines.
Both airlines listed below have direct flights from the United States to the coast, and flights that connect
through Mexico City to the following resorts.*

Aeroméxico | ☎ 800-237-6639 | www.aeromexico.com
Acapulco, Puerto Vallarta, Cancún, Cozumel, Los Cabos, Mazatlán, Huatulco, and
Ixtapa-Zihuatanejo

Mexicana | ☎ 800-531-7921 | www.mexicana.com
Mexicana has flights to all the resort cities listed in our book, with most routed through Mexico City.

MEXICO CITY INTERNATIONAL AIRPORT

unofficial **TIP**
If you have fewer than
three hours between
flights, it's best to remain
inside the security-
cleared area.

First-time Mexico travelers may find the idea of
changing flights at Mexico City's Aeropuerto
Internacional Benito Juárez intimidating. But
the capital city's airport has improved dramat-
ically and layovers aren't terribly daunting.
Both the international and national terminals
have restaurants, shops, Internet cafes, and
airline club rooms inside security. Smoking is
allowed in designated clusters of tables and chairs and in some restaurants and bars in the layover areas.

With more time, you can exit through baggage claim and wander the airport's vast public areas. Bookstores and newsstands stocked with the latest books and magazines on Mexican art, architecture, culture, archaeology, and travel are great places to while away the hours. Check out the pharmacies selling the latest must-have supplies, from retinol wrinkle-reducing creams to nicotine patches, and the liquor stores with in-vogue tequilas. Art exhibits fill the vast spaces between the two terminals. The international terminal has the fanciest facilities, including the second-floor food court serving everything from sushi to cookies.

Two hotels are close to the Mexico City airport in case of overnight delays. Both are expensive but accommodating. **The Camino Real Aeropuerto** (☎ 800-722-6466 U.S., 55-3003-0033 Mexico; **www .caminoreal.com**) faces the airport and is accessed via a pedestrian sky-walk from Terminal B. The hotel has changed names several times and has long been our favorite place to hang out between flights. The 24-hour restaurant serves good Mexican and international comfort food in a calm setting; the buffet breakfast is a good deal and the management doesn't mind if you linger over your meal for hours. The gym is open to nonhotel guests for a fee. You can spend many hours walking the treadmill, swimming laps, and showering in this health club—it's a great way to break up a long journey. Massages and beauty services also are available. Be forewarned: There aren't any lounge chairs by the pool or other places to sleep. The airport **Hilton** (☎ 800-HILTONS or 800-445-8667 U.S.; 55-5133-0505 Mexico; **mexico city.hilton.com**), on the third floor of the international terminal, is a bit more formal. Hanging out is frowned upon, and the gym isn't open to the public. The restaurant is open to nonguests, however, and is blissfully quiet. If you need a nap and a shower between flights, a day-use room, to be used a maximum of six hours between 9 a.m. and 8 p.m., rents for $142, and junior suites rent for $149.

> *unofficial* **TIP**
> To call Mexico from the United States, dial ☎ **011** (international access code), then ☎ 52 (Mexico's country code), then the area code and local phone number. In Mexico, area codes have three digits and local numbers have seven digits—except in Mexico City, Guadalajara, and Monterrey. Phone numbers in those places have two-digit area codes and eight-digit local numbers.

AIRFARE CONSOLIDATORS

Flight consolidators are a good way to shop for the best deal. Consolidators buy up blocks of unsold seats from airlines and resell them to you. These companies deal with a fluid product and a rapidly changing marketplace, and many operate under several different names geared to particular customer interests (domestic versus international travel, group versus solo travel, and the like).

Among the myriad airfare consolidators, some of the most popular, stable, and relatively trustworthy include **JustFares** (☎ 800-766-3601; **www.justfares.com**), **Flight Coordinators** (☎ 800-544-3644; **www.flightcoordinators.com**), **Fly4Less** (no phone; **www.fly4less.com**), and **FlyCheap.com** (no phone; **www.flycheap.com**). The travel section of most Sunday newspapers also is a good source for flight-consolidator ads. Some consolidators deal primarily with domestic tickets, and while they may get you a ticket to Mexico, it might be the same price as the published fare from an airline with more restrictions. The Internet has made it easy to shop around for fares, but keep in mind that *caveat emptor*—buyer beware—remains the rule, especially in the more shady corners of the Web. Before you go searching the Internet or use a consolidator, check prices with the big airlines to get a ballpark figure of how much your desired ticket may cost. You may actually get a better deal working directly with an airline or a good travel agent. No matter how you book your ticket, pay with a credit card so you can contest a suspicious deal. Make sure you're booked on a scheduled flight and not a charter flight (unless you've agreed to fly on a charter), and call the airline to confirm the reservation and the seat assignment.

Package Vacations

Deals including airfare, accommodation, and some meals and tours are common and can help you save money and planning time. It's often easier to go with a package rather than searching for bargain airfares, car rentals, rooms, and tours. But there are caveats. Make sure the package includes the type of room and tours you really want. Having airport transfers included is a great idea—it helps you avoid the taxi hustle at the airport. If car rental is included, make sure it's the type of car you want. Get absolutely every detail in writing.

   Travelocity (☎ 888-709-5983; **www.travelocity.com**) and other Web sites offer package vacation deals for the major beach resorts of Mexico. Most can arrange the entire trip including air travel, shuttle service from the airport, hotel reservations, and meals. **Mexicana Airlines' Vacation Travel Plus** (☎ 800-531-7921; **www.mexicana.com**) and **Aeroméxico Vacations** (☎ 800-245-8585; **www.aeromexicovacations.com**) incorporate reduced airfare with accommodations. Packages are available for all budgets and can greatly ease the work involved in planning a trip. When you book a trip through **American Express Vacations** (☎ 888-297-0403), you can use any agent to book standard reservations or ask for a concierge-level travel agent who will create a customized package including everything from private guides to dinner reservations and spa treatments. The company offers a Travel Protection Plan with insurance covering almost every conceivable glitch. Contact American Express to find an agent in your area. **Classic Vacations** (☎ 800-635-1333; **www.classicvacations.com**) creates customized vacations that can include first-class air and luxury hotels along with all other details; they offer trip insurance as well. More mainstream companies book packages including either charter flights or scheduled airline flights. **Apple Vacations** (☎ 800-727-3400; **www.applevacations.com**) is one of the largest package operators in Mexico, along with **Funjet** (☎ 888-558-6654; **www.funjet.com**), SunTrips (☎ 800-514-5194; **www.suntrips.com**), and **Pleasant Holidays** (☎ 800-742-9244; **www.pleasantholidays.com**). These companies work with groups and individuals and offer some amazingly inexpensive deals.

THINGS *to* KNOW *before* YOU GO

TRAVEL INSURANCE

YOUR OWN INSURANCE COMPANY may offer some form of travel insurance, so check first with them before buying any additional coverage. You can purchase insurance for travel canceled due to any number of factors, such as emergencies related to your own or your family's health, death in the family, business emergencies, and so on. You also can purchase insurance to cover lost luggage, medical emergencies, or other unfortunate eventualities. Trusted sellers include **Travel Guard International** (☎ 800-826-4919; **www.travelguard.com**); **Travel Insured International** (☎ 800-243-3174; **www.travelinsured.com**); or **Access America** (☎ 800-729-6021; **www.accessamerica.com**). **Sanborn's Mexico Insurance** (☎ 800-222-0158; **www.sanbornsinsurance.com**) specializes in auto insurance for travel in Mexico but also provides individual and group medical insurance, as well as medical evacuation insurance.

LUGGAGE

EVERY AIRLINE HAS DIFFERENT RULES, so find out before you get to the airport how many bags can be checked, their maximum weight, and the size and weight of carry-ons, as well as any baggage fees that are charged in addition to the price of the ticket. With more stringent security enforcement, be careful not to bring forbidden items in your carry-on bags or on your person. The U.S. Transportation Security Administration at **www.tsa.gov** lists what you can and cannot take with you on the plane. Be prepared to have your checked and carry-on luggage opened and examined frequently—hasty packers may be embarrassed by the public display of their disarray. Cameras and laptops often undergo intense scrutiny. Make sure your batteries are in good shape so you can turn electronic items off and on frequently when so requested by security agents.

VALUABLES

BE SURE TO BRING VALUABLES, such as cameras, laptops, jewelry, money, and anything particularly fragile or precious, on the plane with you. Only certain types and small amounts of medications such as insulin may be brought on board with you (check with the airline or the TSA; see above). In general, it makes little sense to flash around expensive watches, gold chains, and other baubles in any tourist resort, unless you're staying at a high-end resort and have access to a good security system. Our advice is to leave such items at home.

MEDICATIONS

BRING AN EXTRA SUPPLY OF ANY MEDICINE you are taking, along with a copy of the prescription. If you lose your medication, it will help to know its generic name in order to get a new prescription.

unofficial **TIP**
Contrary to a popular misconception, Mexican pharmacists are forbidden from selling some medications, particularly narcotics, without a prescription.

Pharmacies in Mexico are far more accessible than those in the United States, and pharmacists can usually supply an appropriate medication if you are feeling ill. Few prescription sleep aids or medications newly approved in the States are available for purchase with or without a 'script. Some travelers try to buy drugs in Mexico without a doctor's prescription, sometimes successfully. We caution against attempting this transaction, as penalties can be stiff. If there is a chance that you may run out of your medication, ask your doctor for a back-up prescription. Also bring along a spare pair of eyeglasses or contact lenses, or carry the prescription with you.

PERSONAL ELECTRONICS

ELECTRICAL CURRENT IN MEXICO IS 110-volt, 60-cycle AC. Brookstone, Radio Shack, and most travel-gear stores and catalogs sell converters that adapt voltages to any appliance, which will be helpful for travelers coming from the United Kingdom. The outlets in some Mexican hotels have space for two flat prongs; bring a three-prong adapter if needed.

Laptops

The electrical current is reasonably consistent in most resort areas. We're most comfortable using battery power when working on our laptops, using the hotel's electricity to recharge the battery. Hooking up your modem can be a major hassle. Many hotels have digital phone systems or switchboards that won't recognize your telephone modem's way of dialing. Ask to use a direct outside line. Wireless Internet access is becoming more common in the public areas of hotels throughout Mexico, as are in-room high-speed connections for an additional fee. (Many Internet cafes will allow you to hook up your laptop for considerably less expense than at a hotel, though there's an added hassle involved in lugging your computer around.)

unofficial **TIP**
Don't despair if you can't get a Wi-Fi connection immediately. If you're told such a connection exists, roam about with your computer and try several areas (hotel lobbies are normally best). Often, claims regarding Wi-Fi service in all rooms are wildly exaggerated.

Cell Phones

Cellular coverage is good in most Mexican resort areas, but there's little reliable coverage outside of heavily populated areas. The signals are not particularly strong, so hills, mountains, or large buildings can weaken service or block it entirely.

Some American cellular phone companies have "roaming" agreements in Mexico, but others do not. Sometimes, even the representatives of the cellular companies don't really understand what kind of coverage they provide. One *Unofficial Guide* researcher was told by a Verizon operator that his phone would not work anywhere in Mexico—and yet, even while in a remote part of Baja, the phone automatically connected to a Mexican cellular network with no problems. If you want to use your cellular phone in Mexico, call your service provider to find out what Mexican coverage they have (or think they have) and what additional rates apply (about $2 a minute is standard, or about half that if you purchase a monthly international plan).

If you'd rather pick up a phone once you arrive, cell phones are available for rent at the Mexico City airport but not at most regional airports. Hotels are the best source of information about rentals; some concierges can arrange to have a phone available when you arrive. You can pay a per-minute charge by credit card or pre-pay for a certain number of minutes. Phone kits are available, consisting of a phone, charger, and calling card.

Another option is to rent a Mexico-friendly cell phone before you go. The phone is mailed to your home, you get the number in advance, use the phone on your trip, and mail it back when you return. Just like the rentals described above, you can pay as you go or prepay for a certain number of minutes. If you really want to be sure of a connection, you can shell out big bucks for a satellite cell phone which should function even in remote areas. Companies that rent all kinds of cell phones for use in Mexico (and many other countries around the world) include **RoadPost** (☎ 888-290-1616; **www.roadpost.com**), **Cellular Abroad** (☎ 800-287-5072; **www.cellular abroad.com**), **World Cellular Rentals** (☎ 877-626-0216; **www.world cr.com**), **Ace Telecom** (☎ 877-223-8353; **www.acetelecom.com**) and **Roberts Rent-A-Phone** (☎ 800-964-2468; **www.roberts-rent-a -phone.com**).

INTERNET AND E-MAIL

INTERNET CAFES ARE COMMON in Mexico, and we've listed several in the regional chapters. Some hotels offer Internet access for their guests; some now have wireless access in their lobbies. Most Internet service providers (such as AOL and Earthlink) allow you to check e-mail remotely via their Web sites; consult your service provider. You can sign up for free e-mail accounts with services such as **Gmail** (**www.gmail.com**), **Hotmail** (**www.hotmail.com**) and **Yahoo!** (**www .yahoo.com**), all of which can be checked from anywhere that has a connection to the Web.

unofficial **TIP**
Arrange your car rental online while in Mexico for considerable savings over U.S. rates. Reserve the car through the rental Web site (or other travel site), then take your confirmation code to the office and pay the lower rate. When comparing prices, it's imperative to determine which taxes, fees, and types of insurance are included in the price being quoted, as these will add considerably to the price.

CAR RENTAL

THE MINIMUM AGE REQUIREMENT to rent a car in Mexico varies anywhere from 21 to 25 years depending on the company. Companies willing to rent to a person younger than 25 may include a surcharge in their rental fee. The rates at many of the resort areas are high. If you are traveling from the United States, you may get a better deal from an international agency if you book before you go. The major agencies have counters at the larger resorts. Locally owned and operated rental companies are a bit more risky, as their fleet may not be well maintained. Be sure to check the condition of the car before you leave the lot and make note of any dents, as you will be charged for any "new" wear and tear when you return the car.

MONEY

DOLLARS ARE NEARLY AS COMMON AS PESOS in many major resort areas. Travelers on short trips to Cancún and Los Cabos don't even bother changing their money. But if you're staying longer, planning to shop a lot, or intend to travel around to remote areas, you're best off carrying pesos. You can change money at some banks before you travel or at the airport when you arrive. *Casas de cambio,* or currency exchanges, are found in most of the larger cities

> *unofficial* **TIP**
> Travelers coming from Europe or Australia should bring U.S. dollars or travelers checks; you will get a much better exchange rate for your money in Mexico.

and will give you a favorable exchange rate, as will the banks. Large hotels will usually change traveler's checks and foreign dollars, but don't expect as many pesos for your dollar.

There are ATMs in major cities and resort areas. ATMs can also be found in many small towns, but in case there isn't one or it's not working or out of money, make sure to carry some cash if you leave the big city. Don't forget to memorize your PIN before you leave home. Many travelers are finding they get the best exchange rate at ATMs; check to see what your bank charges for such transactions before leaving home, but the fee also depends on what the Mexican bank you use charges. Banks charge a flat fee for transactions, while creditcard companies charge interest from the day of withdrawal. Either of these charges may negate the favorable exchange rate. Find out before you leave what the maxi-

> *unofficial* **TIP**
> Carry small bills in pesos and dollars for tips and small purchases.

mum amount is that you can withdraw from your account via ATMs. Also, notify your credit-card companies about your travel plans. When those companies see your cards being used in a foreign country, they will sometimes flag your cards as possibly stolen—which can result in their ceasing to honor purchases until you call and verify your identity. You can do so by calling the company's office in the U.S. collect.

THE WEATHER

MEXICO MEASURES ITS WEATHER IN DEGREES CELSIUS (Centigrade) rather than Fahrenheit, so you might want to memorize a few conversions (see chart). You can check out the weather before you go from any number of Web sites. **Weather Underground** (**www .wunderground.com**) lists dozens of cities in Mexico with current temperature (in degrees Celsius and Fahrenheit), heat index, relative humidity, and other conditions. **The Weather Channel** (**www.weather .com**) and **CNN** (**www.cnn.com**) also have comprehensive, up-to-the-minute information on weather conditions in Mexico.

In a country as large as Mexico, weather is determined by many factors, including altitude, proximity to the coast, longitude, and latitude. June through October are generally the wettest months,

CONVERTING CELSIUS TO FAHRENHEIT

Convert temperatures (approximately) from Celsius to Fahrenheit by doubling the Celsius temperature and adding 30 degrees. Here are some more exact numbers:

CELSIUS	FAHRENHEIT	CELSIUS	FAHRENHEIT
–3°	26.7°	10°	50°
–1°	30.2°	15°	49°
0°	32°	20°	68°
1°	33.8°	25°	77°
5°	41°	30°	86°
10°	50°	37°	98.6°

with late September and October bringing the occasional hurricane to the Gulf and southern-Pacific coasts. Baja is dry and hot, with the sun shining approximately 350 days a year in Cabo San Lucas. *Chubascos* (hurricanes) do blow through Los Cabos every few years, bringing high winds and heavy rains. They sometimes cause considerable short-term damage to hotels, golf courses, and roads. But businesses usually get back up and running quickly.

The best time to see those bright, sunny beaches depicted in travel posters is between December and June. Rain showers and fierce storms are possible from July through November, and you can actually spend a week without seeing the sun. We were in Acapulco during a tropical storm recently. It rained fiercely for four days, and we waded through two feet of water when sightseeing. On the upside, Acapulco was washed clean and looked like the jungle it once was. We had lots of time for reading, spa treatments, and doing nothing—a lovely concept at times. We'll go into more detail about what to expect weather-wise in the regional chapters.

WHAT TO BRING

WHAT TO BRING DEPENDS on where you are going, but these general items will come in handy everywhere:

- This book
- Small English–Spanish dictionary or phrase book
- Good map of the city or cities you will be visiting
- $50 in single dollars or the equivalent in pesos for tips, tax rides, and small purchases
- Money belt
- Good day pack or shoulder bag
- Small, collapsible umbrella and/or folding rain poncho (wet season)

- Currency converter or small calculator
- Portable electrical transformer (if you're from the United Kingdom) and plug adapters
- Digital camera with extra memory cards; if you carry a film camera, bring extra film
- Battery charger
- Favorite snacks
- Good walking shoes
- Broad-spectrum sunscreen and a hat
- Insect repellent
- Earplugs (for planes and noisy hotels)

CLOTHING

THE BEACH RESORTS ARE INFORMAL, and you can spend much of your time in your bathing suit and cover-up. Shorts and T-shirts are acceptable nearly everywhere, except in dinner restaurants. Even there, jackets are rarely required for men. You'll do fine with a lightweight pair of slacks and a few button-down, polo, or Hawaiian-style shirts. Women dress up in sundresses and high-heeled sandals for fancy dinners. Some discos prohibit guests from wearing sneakers, beach sandals, shorts, or T-shirts. As a rule, customers at Mexican discos are stylishly dressed.

Given the tropical climate at most beach resorts, you'll want to bring plenty of extra shirts and an extra bathing suit. Shoes that will remain comfortable when your feet are swollen and sweaty are a must. If you're visiting during the winter, bring a jacket or sweatshirt—the winds can get very chilly, even during the day. A windbreaker or sweatshirt comes in handy for boat trips year-round.

unofficial **TIP**
If you'll be staying at upscale resorts, check their dress codes for fancy restaurants. We once were unable to sample any of the gourmet restaurants at a high-end all-inclusive resort because men were required to wear closed-toe leather shoes (an absurd rule in the tropics).

WHEN TO GO

WINTER IS THE TRADITIONAL TRAVELER SEASON, with hotel rates reaching their peak in December and early January, around the holidays. Reservations for this time of year need to be made well in advance. November (before Thanksgiving) can be a perfect time of year in many parts of Mexico, just after the rainy season but before high season begins. The weeks between Easter and Memorial Day, before the rain begins and the humidity rises, are also relatively uncrowded and pleasant. Prices tend to drop in May and June, but the same cannot be said for the humidity. If you can stand the hot temperatures, look for bargains between June and October. This trend is changing, however, as more and more families are taking their summer vacations in Mexico. July and August are often very busy. Mexican families tend to vacation at the beach during that time, packing the hotels. European travelers also flock to the coast (particularly the Caribbean) during July and August. Some accommodations will raise their rates for these months and then drop them again in September.

GATHERING INFORMATION

YOUR BEST SOURCES OF INFORMATION are the central toll-free number for information in the United States at ☎ 800-44-MEXICO and the Web site **www.visitmexico.com.** Operators at the 800 number will take your address and will snail-mail you brochures. Some operators will answer questions about airlines and destinations. *Note*: There are no offices in Australia or New Zealand.

Web Sites

Web sites come and go, but the ones listed on page 34 have been around awhile and should provide you with useful information and links to other sites. We also list relevant sites in the regional chapters.

SPECIAL CONSIDERATIONS *for* TRAVELING *to* MEXICO

PASSPORTS, VISAS, AND CUSTOMS

IF YOU ARE A U.S. OR CANADIAN CITIZEN, you will need a tourist card in order to enter Mexico. If you are arriving by plane, you can get one at the airline counter or (usually) on the plane. Tourist cards also are available at Mexican embassies and consulates, and from some travel agents. The cards are free and will be issued to persons with proof of U.S. or Canadian citizenship in the form of a passport, certified birth certificate and photo ID, or notarized affidavit of citizenship. All U.S. and Canadian citizens returning to their countries of origin by plane need a passport; after June 1, 2009, all persons will need one, including those returning by land or sea. U.S. citizens wishing to obtain a passport should check the State Department's Bureau of Consular Affairs Web site (**travel.state.gov**). The name on your airline reservation must match the one on your passport or other ID.

British and Australian travelers need a valid passport as well as the tourist card. A minor child traveling with one parent, from any country, must have notarized authorization from the other parent giving permission for the child to go to Mexico. Children over age 10 must also have a tourist card. Tourist cards are valid for up to 180 days; many times Mexican immigration officials will issue fewer days, so ask for as many days initially as you'll need to complete your stay. It's inconvenient to get more once in Mexico, and there's a fee for the paperwork. Hold on to this card (actually a small slip of paper)—you'll be asked to return it as you pass through Mexican customs or at the airline counter when you exit Mexico.

The official literature says you should carry your tourist card at all times. We've never been asked to show ours, and we usually keep it with our passports in the hotel's safety deposit box. Instead, carry a driver's license or other photo ID and a copy of your passport.

Several years ago, the Mexican government instituted the DNI (Duties for Non-Immigrants), a fee that travelers must pay to enter the country. If you are arriving by air, this will automatically be included in the price of your ticket. If you cross the border by land, you will be required to pay the fee (around $20) when you get your tourist card.

WHAT YOU MAY AND MAY NOT BRING INTO MEXICO

THOSE ARRIVING IN MEXICO BY SHIP or by air may bring in $800 worth of goods per person, provided that they have been outside the United States a minimum of 48 hours. (See **www.cbp.gov/xp/cgov/travel/vacation/kbyg** for specifics on what you may bring into the US and other rules.) You also may carry with you personal items, such as a laptop computer, camera, video camera, 12 rolls of film (not closely monitored), 20 packs of cigarettes or 20 cigars, and 1 liter of wine, beer, or liquor. You must be 18 years of age to import tobacco and 21 to import liquor. Do not bring firearms or ammunition into the country unless you have written authority from the Mexican consulate or risk severe penalties and serious jail time. Obviously, street drugs such as marijuana and cocaine should not be brought across the border. Prescription drugs are best carried in their original containers, showing your name as the prescription holder.

DOLLARS AND TRAVELER'S CHECKS

THE UNIT OF CURRENCY IN MEXICO is the *peso*. The bills come in 10-, 20-, 50-, 100-, and 500-peso notes; coins of 1, 2, 5, 10, and 20 pesos look quite similar. The bills are different colors but are similar enough to be confusing. At press time, the exchange rate hovered around 13 pesos to $1. You can use U.S dollars at some resort areas, but you'll get a poor exchange rate for your money in restaurants and shops. You'll find money-exchange desks, where you can cash enough money for taxis and tips, in baggage-claim areas at most airports. An easier method is to bring along at least $20 in single bills and several $5 bills for initial expenses and tips. Traveler's checks are easily cashed at most hotels. Most money changers will only give you pesos when you cash traveler's checks. Remember, you're in a foreign country with its own currency.

unofficial **TIP**
ATMs coughing up dollars are popping up at some destinations, especially near cruise-ship piers.

MEXICO TRAVEL WEB SITES

www.amtave.org Mexican Association of Adventure Tourism and Ecotourism

www.go2mexico.com Online guide with monthly features

www.mexconnect.com Free, monthly electronic magazine

www.mexicanwave.com Excellent articles and reports on Mexican travel from the U.K. perspective

www.mexicoguru.com Offers satellite maps, up-to-date travel articles and destination pieces, as well as a fun Spanish "word of the day" and vacation quizzes.

www.mexonline.com Independent guide to Mexico

www.planeta.com Specializes in ecotourism in Mexico and other Latin American countries

www.visitmexico.com Mexico Tourism Board

EMBASSIES AND CONSULATES

THE FOREIGN EMBASSIES ARE LOCATED in Mexico City. Consulates or honorary consulates are in many resort areas (see regional chapters).

United States

The U.S. Embassy is located at Paseo de la Reforma 305; Colonia Cuauhtémoc, 06500; ☎ 55-5080-2000. The embassy's office hours are Monday through Friday, 9 a.m. to 2 p.m. and 3 p.m. to 5 p.m. Its Web site is **www.usembassy-mexico.gov.** Cost for a replacement passport is $85.

Canada

The Canadian Embassy is at Schiller 529; Colonia Polanco (Rincón del Bosque), 11580; ☎ 55-5724-7900; **mexico.gc.ca.** It's open Monday through Friday, 8:45 a.m. to 5:15 p.m.

Australia

The Australian Embassy is housed at Rubén Dario 55; Colonia Polanco, 11560; ☎ 55-1101-2200; **www.mexico.embassy.gov.au.** The embassy is open Monday through Thursday, 8:30 a.m. to 2 p.m., 3 p.m. to 5:15 p.m.; and Friday, 8:30 a.m. to 2 p.m.

United Kingdom

This embassy is located at Rio Lerma 71; Colonia Cuauhtémoc, 06500; ☎ 55-5242-8500; **ukinmexico.fco.gov.uk.** Hours are Monday through Friday, 9 a.m. to 4 p.m.

TRAVELING WITH CHILDREN

MOST MEXICANS LOVE CHILDREN and are immensely helpful and accommodating when kids are concerned. In fact, some of our best times in Mexico have involved traveling with kids. Most hotels

Mexico Tourism Board Offices

LOS ANGELES
1880 Century Park East, Suite 511
Los Angeles, CA 90067
☎ 310-282-9112

MIAMI
5975 Sunset Drive, Suite 305
South Miami Beach, FL 33143
☎ 786-621-2909

NEW YORK
400 Madison Avenue, Suite 11C
New York, NY 10017
☎ 212-308-2110

MONTRÉAL
1 Place Ville Marie, Suite 1931
Montreal, Quebec, Canada H3B 2C3
☎ 514-871-1052

TORONTO
2 Bloor Street West, Suite 1502
Toronto, Canada M4W 3E2
☎ 416-925-0704

VANCOUVER
999 West Hastings Street,
Suite 1110
Vancouver, Canada V6C 2W2
☎ 604-669-2845

UNITED KINGDOM
41 Trinity Square
Wakefield House
London, England
EC3N 4DJ
☎ 44-207-488-9392

and resorts will provide cribs, cots, and other supplies. Many of the larger resorts have kids' programs and babysitting services. See page 55 for information on hotel chains that have programs and special packages for families.

You needn't load your luggage with diapers and baby food. You can find the necessary supplies at grocery stores and markets in all resort destinations. Granted, you'll pay more for imported American brands. But you can buy Mexican brands of everything from disposable diapers to processed cheese and Bimbo bread—the whitest, blandest bread in the world—for those cheese sandwiches young kids seem to love. Most kids are content with the simplest Mexican dishes, including cheese quesadillas, chicken tacos, and bean burritos. And the resorts all have familiar burger and pizza joints.

You should bring a car seat (if you plan on having a car) and sturdy stroller for the little ones, and a few familiar toys and blankets. Ask your pediatrician for prescriptions for antidiarrheal medicines and antibiotics for kids, just in case an upset stomach occurs. You'll want to keep a close eye on your kids while they're swimming. Hotel pools and beaches normally don't have lifeguards. Bring plenty of children's waterproof sunscreen, as it's quite expensive at the resorts.

DISABLED ACCESS IN MEXICO

MEXICO IS WOEFULLY BEHIND when it comes to assisting travelers with disabilities. Many of the most enchanting hotels have narrow, uneven stairways to the rooms; many of the sidewalks are crumbling;

curb cuts are virtually nonexistent; and wheelchair-accessible restrooms are hard to find. That said, Mexicans do everything they can to assist travelers with disabilities. The newer resort areas—Cancún and Los Cabos, in particular—are more accessible. Older cities, such as Puerto Vallarta, are known for their cobblestone streets and steep hills into the jungle, which may look attractive but are difficult for anyone with a wheelchair. A few hotel chains, including Westin, Fiesta Americana, Hyatt Regency, and Marriott, have disabled-accessible rooms.

A few organizations have some helpful tips on traveling in Mexico. **Access-Able** (no phone; **www.access-able.com**) provides a limited number of links to accommodations and attractions with disabled access, along with links to publications and organizations that may be helpful.

HEALTH

"WILL I GET SICK?" This is the most common question we've heard from first-time travelers to Mexico. It's an important issue when you travel in any foreign country. Visitors to the United States have the same concerns. Often, unfamiliar water and food can wreak havoc with your digestion, especially if you tend to have a delicate stomach.

Using a large dose of common sense while traveling in Mexico will help prevent you from becoming ill during your trip. The most common ailments suffered by foreigners traveling in Mexico are upset stomach and diarrhea—usually nonfatal but unpleasant maladies. Ingesting contaminated food or water is the leading cause of this uncomfortable ailment. So is the temptation to gorge on the wonderful tropical fruits available at most resorts. Drinking too much cheap tequila (a common pitfall) will make you wish the Angel of Death would pay a merciful visit. Many a case of so-called Montezuma's revenge is caused by overindulgence in alcohol, sun, and unfamiliar foods. Stay up all night drinking tequila shooters, and you're bound to feel less than perky the next day.

Conventional wisdom advises that you drink only bottled water and other drinks, eat only fruit that can be peeled, be careful when ordering salads, avoid ice, and don't buy food from street vendors. Wash your hands often. Naturally, exceptions exist to all of these rules. Drinking bottled water is a good idea, though many modern resorts have water purification systems. Be forewarned—many hotels have bottled water in the bathrooms, and unwitting guests commonly think the water is free. Not true. There's often a hefty charge for those little bottles, but they are convenient and may satisfy your needs. We go through about one gallon of water a day—which could cost $20 or more at hotel prices. When on a budget, we usually carry one or two bottles of water to get us through the first night, then go to the nearest market and buy a few large bottles of water for the room. When you're sightseeing or hanging out on the beach, carry around bottled water to keep from getting dehydrated.

The fruit, salad, and ice issues are less clear-cut. Most traveler-oriented restaurants use purified water to clean produce and make ice, and it's usually safe to order anything on the menu. Start out slowly for the first couple of days as your body adjusts, and stick with cooked foods. If you're feeling OK, you can be more adventuresome. Some folks say it helps to take a spoonful of Pepto-Bismol before eating. Others swear that acidophilus capsules or yogurt help fight bacteria.

The rule against eating street food is wise, at least for beginners who haven't absorbed some of the local intestinal flora in their digestive tracts. Whether you follow this rule is a personal decision based on experience. Street vendors typically sell great, cheap tacos, which are safe if you stick with clean vendor stands and cooked food. Other vendors carve papayas into fanciful, edible flowers or fill paper cups with chopped pineapple sprinkled with powdered chile; ask to have yours specially made with freshly peeled fruit and you'll probably be fine. *Licuados,* fruit drinks made with water or milk, are marvelous thirst-quenchers that are sold at juice stands around the plazas. Look for bottles of purified water at the stand and watch as your drink is prepared, or order pure, freshly squeezed orange juice.

If you are stricken with diarrhea, don't allow yourself to become dehydrated. Drink plenty of bottled water, soft drinks without caffeine, or Gatorade. Chamomile and papaya tea are soothing. Don't overmedicate yourself with antidiarrheal drugs such as Lomitil or Imodium A-D. Your body is trying to get rid of unfamiliar bugs the best way it knows. Let nature follow its own course for a few days and stick with mild medications such as Pepto-Bismol. If the diarrhea or nausea persists, go to a pharmacy and ask for a stronger medication. The pharmacists at beach resorts are quite familiar with traveler illnesses, and they can typically prescribe something to get you back in shape.

A more serious health concern for travelers in Mexico is hepatitis A, a viral infection that can be caused by direct person-to-person contact, through exposure to contaminated water, ice, or shellfish harvested from sewage-contaminated water, or from fruits, vegetables, or other foods that are eaten uncooked and became contaminated during handling by infected persons. To avoid this illness, take the same precautions as listed above for diarrhea. Also, the U.S. Centers for Disease Control and Prevention (CDC) advises getting a vaccination against hepatitis A four to six weeks before your trip. It's safe to say that most travelers don't take this precaution, and few end up with hepatitis. But if you travel frequently, it's a good idea to go ahead and get the vaccination. Make sure your tetanus vaccination is up to date while you're at it. You are less likely to encounter the hepatitis B virus; it is a blood-borne disease, usually contracted by sexual contact or the sharing of needles with an infected person.

CDC recommends taking antimalaria medication if you plan on venturing into the most rural areas of tropical Mexico during your visit. Malaria, a disease characterized by flulike symptoms of fever and chills, headache, muscle aches, and general fatigue, is caused by the bite of an infected mosquito. Symptoms occur seven to nine days after being bitten. The risk of contracting malaria in the resort areas of Mexico is slim; we've never taken any antimalaria medications in Mexico and have traveled to the most remote regions without incident. It is always a good idea to take measures against mosquito bites by applying an insect repellent (preferably with DEET as the active ingredient), wearing long-sleeved shirts and long pants around sunset (the bugs are hungriest then), and making sure screens are on your windows.

Another disease caused by the mosquito bites is dengue. Symptoms of dengue include high fever, severe headache, joint pain, nausea, and vomiting. There is no vaccination and no cure except rest, pain management *not* aspirin), and hydration. A few outbreaks of dengue have occurred in southern Mexico, but they are usually confined to outlying areas. The chance that you will get dengue is remote unless there is an epidemic at the time of your visit.

Cholera is an acute intestinal infection caused by contaminated food or water that has come into contact with an infected person. The risk to travelers in Mexico is low. Common-sense sanitary precautions usually preclude getting this disease, which is characterized by diarrhea and vomiting.

Typhoid fever is a significant problem in many developing countries of the world. It is usually found in only the most rural areas of Mexico, but there are outbreaks of this food- and water-borne disease, so if you plan to travel far off the beaten path, you may want to talk to your doctor or consult the CDC Web site (see below). Check this site before your trip to make sure that no outbreaks of these diseases are in the areas you will be visiting.

If you do become seriously ill while traveling in Mexico, check with your hotel. Many have a doctor on call that can come to your room to treat you. Health care in the larger cities is good, but not always so easy to come by in the smaller towns.

MEDICAL RESOURCES

CENTERS FOR DISEASE CONTROL AND PREVENTION: Up-to-date information on vaccinations and disease outbreaks. ☎ 800-232-4636; **www.cdc.gov**.

INTERNATIONAL ASSOCIATION FOR MEDICAL ASSISTANCE TO TRAVELERS: A nonprofit organization aimed at providing advice to travelers regarding diseases found worldwide. ☎ 716-754-4883 in the U.S., ☎ 519-836-0102 in Canada; **www.iamat.org**.

MEXICO HEALTH AND SAFETY TRAVEL GUIDE: An excellent comprehensive health guide profiling 180 physicians and medical centers throughout Mexico, published by Page & Page. ☎ 866-MEDTOGO (866-633-8646); **www.medtogo.com**.

POLLUTION PROBLEMS

WATER POLLUTION IS A PROBLEM at beach resorts all over the world. Mexico has been slow to recognize and deal with this issue, though locals and frequent visitors know to stay away from certain bodies of water.

Enclosed bays tend to have the worst problems, especially in times of heavy rains when sewage may rush into the water. But even during the calmest seasons, the bays suffer from serious overuse. Motorized water toys buzz beside areas designated for swimmers in most resort bays. The health risks of swimming or playing in polluted waters (and accidentally swallowing the water) include gastrointestinal problems and possible exposure to hepatitis or infection.

Travelers would be wise to use discretion when choosing where to swim. Going into the water is safest at beaches that face the open sea, as in Cancún, the Caribbean Coast, Cozumel (away from cruise-ship piers), Isla Mujeres, Mazatlán, and the coast north and south of the Bay of Banderas in Puerto Vallarta. Areas more prone to pollution are those close to major construction, urban locales, or river mouths, such as beaches at the south side of the main towns of Puerto Vallarta and Zihuatanejo. If you're a dedicated swimmer, surfer, or water-sports buff, make sure your hepatitis and tetanus inoculations are up-to-date.

Don't let pollution concerns keep you from visiting Mexico's beach resorts. You can still listen to the water slap against the shore or fall asleep to the sound of crashing waves. Most hotels have elaborate pool areas with perfectly clean, chlorinated water. Long walks on solitary beaches are still a joy, and you can enjoy plenty of places to snorkel, dive, swim, and ride the waves. Just use common sense. If the water trapped in a busy, enclosed bay looks grimy, or if trash collects on the beach, stay on the sand. In times of heavy rains stay out of bays backed by towns. Take day trips to uncrowded beaches facing the open sea when you want to swim in saltwater. Look for tips on the best clean beaches throughout this book.

SELF-HELP

CHAPTERS OF **Alcoholics Anonymous** are active in Mexico; signs announce English-language meetings at some hotels. Check at the front desk of your hotel or look in any available English-language newspaper. You can access the Mexican Alcoholics Anonymous Web site at **www.alcoholicos-anonimos.org.mx.** In Mexico City, the phone number for general services is ☎ 55-5264-2588.

NATIONAL HOLIDAYS

GOVERNMENT OFFICES AND BANKS are closed for national holidays. Businesses close during national and local elections, and liquor sales in bars and shops are prohibited when polls are open.

Expect less than stellar service around holidays. Mexicans some-times attach a few extra days to a holiday (especially if the holiday falls on a Thursday or Tuesday), creating what's called *puente,* or bridge.

Major businesses and some museums, restaurants, and shops are closed on the following days. In addition, they may close during Holy Week (Semana Santa) and the week between Christmas and New Year's Day, although those geared toward tourism generally are not, as sales volume is high.

A Calendar of Festivals and Events

Every day is a holiday somewhere in Mexico. Births, deaths, anniversaries, and the simplest good fortune are all cause for celebra-tion. Religious holidays are honored with special fervor in various areas, as are natural and political events. The following days are especially important on the coast.

February or March

CARNAVAL (MARDI GRAS) This movable fiesta is celebrated for five days before Lent with parades, floats, all-night dances, fireworks, and cultural events. The festivities are particularly exciting in Mazatlán and Cozumel.

March and September

EQUINOX (SPRING AND FALL) March 19 to 21, September 20 to 23. A celebration is held at Chichén Itzá, an archaeological site near Cancún, to usher in the spring and fall. During the equinox, and a few days before and after, the alignment makes the shadow of a serpent appear to crawl down a corner of the Temple of Kukulkán, finally uniting with a carved snake head at the pyramid's base. Celebrants wear white and climb atop the pyramid to say prayers and receive spiritual blessings. Because rain clouds in fall tend to block the sun's shadow, the spring event is better publicized and attended.

March or April

SEMANA SANTA (EASTER WEEK) Mexican families flock to coastal resorts during the week before Easter to witness religious celebra-tions and reunite with their loved ones, and to beat the heat of interior cities. Special foods are prepared, and religious processions are common. The most interesting Semana Santa rituals take place inland in the indigenous areas of the Copper Canyon and Chiapas, and in some colonial cities such as Taxco and Oaxaca. At the beach, the celebrations are geared more toward recharging party batteries than spiritual ones, but churches are packed on Good Friday and Easter Sunday.

MEXICAN NATIONAL HOLIDAYS
January 1 New Year's Day
February 5 Constitution Day
March 21 Benito Juárez's Birthday
May 1 Labor Day
September 16 Independence Day (begins eve of September 15)
November 20 Revolution Day
December 25 Christmas Day

SPRING BREAK Cancún has become notorious for its bawdy parties and free-for-all attitude during American spring break. City leaders are trying to erase the nastier aspects of spring break and promote the destination as a family springtime escape. Some hotels actively ban underage guests and offer special packages for family vacations. Others seek out the party crowd. Mazatlán attracts a large spring-break contingent along with families. Los Cabos is gaining considerable fame with the MTV crowd. No matter where you plan to vacation, ask about the hotel's spring-break policies before booking your room.

October and November

DÍA DE LOS MUERTOS, DÍA DE TODOS SANTOS (ALL SAINTS' AND ALL SOULS' DAYS) October 31 through November 2. Celebrations in honor of a family's deceased relatives are held throughout the country in varying degrees. The customs practiced in more traditional indigenous areas have been adopted or expanded at towns on the Yucatán Peninsula and at the Pacific Coast resorts, primarily to satisfy the tourist trade. Altars with flowers, candles, skull and skeleton candies, breads, toys, and photos of the deceased are arranged in homes and at museums and shops. Día de los Muertos has become nearly as commercialized as Halloween in some areas, and altars and folk art displays are used to attract shoppers.

HALLOWEEN What better reason to dress like a clown and behave like a fool? Discos and bars hold outrageous Halloween parties for weeks before the main event. Pack your costumes and hangover remedies.

December

FIESTA DE LA VIRGEN DE GUADALUPE December 12 and preceding days. Celebration of Mexico's patron saint, the Virgin of Guadalupe, with religious parades, some on the water. Puerto Vallarta and Puerto Escondido have significant processions, the former lasting for a month preceding the holiday.

PART TWO

ACCOMMODATIONS *and* RESTAURANTS

WHERE *to* SLEEP *and* EAT

THE ACCOMMODATIONS YOU CHOOSE FOR A VACATION or business trip can make or break your experience and your impression of Mexico. Familiar international chains have accommodations at most beach resorts, and all-inclusive and time-share properties abound. Boutique and spa hotels are all the rage; some claim the same room rates you find in Hawaii. The choices can be baffling. We're here to help you make the right decision based on your budget and expectations.

unofficial **TIP**
We tend to shy away from brand-new businesses and feature those that have been around awhile and appear to have staying power.

We've included only the best accommodations in each resort, choosing about a dozen in places such as Cancún and the Riviera Maya. Our choices are subjective, based on the criteria listed on the following pages. Accommodations not reviewed aren't necessarily horrid or mediocre; to the contrary, we wish there were space to review all of our choices.

Dining being equally important, we've reviewed restaurants that offer interesting cuisine and a pleasurable gustatory experience. Again, you can use our criteria as a guideline when you're checking out hot new restaurants or recommendations from fellow travelers. For both accommodations and restaurants, we provide general advice in this chapter and specific recommendations and profiles in each of the regional chapters.

ACCOMMODATIONS *in* MEXICO

EVEN UBIQUITOUS CHAINS such as Hilton, Hyatt, and Marriott have certain quirks in Mexico. First of all, most of the staff members who work directly with guests are Mexican. Spanish is their first language, though they must speak enough English to help guests. At most accommodations, there's someone at the front desk who does speak excellent English. Second, many American travelers—especially in Cancún and Los Cabos—seem to expect the same level and style of service they'd get in the States. Pricey resorts do provide impeccable service with excellent concierges and staff, but service suffers whenever the staff is poorly paid. Mexico is a foreign country and a developing nation with its own priorities and procedures. Politeness should be more important than expediency even if you are a tourist, and patience is a virtue best learned early and practiced routinely.

WHAT TO EXPECT

At the Front Desk

Check-in goes smoothly if you have your name, confirmation number, and other vital information written down. It's also smart to find out what the accommodation's check-in time is when reserving your room. If you're arriving early, let the staff know—they can probably arrange to get you in your room early. You'll likely be tired, jet-lagged, and eager to slip into a pool or warm bath, but it's best to take care of all room requirements up front. Take it slow and easy. Ask about safe-deposit boxes. You may need to get a lock for your in-room box at the front desk.

Standard Amenities

Mexico's resort accommodations are on par with those found in other countries—in some ways. Nearly all have air-conditioning units (we've mentioned those that don't). Accommodations that cater to families, budget travelers, and time-share clients may have refrigerators and kitchenettes. More upscale properties tend to have

---

STANDARD AMENITIES CHECKLIST

We've gone through a checklist with each accommodation review, asking about amenities and services. Look for the following details in each review, and add your preferences to the list.

Bars	Massage
Beach	Organized children's activities
Business center	Restaurants
Full-service spa	Room service (limited or
Gym	around the clock)
Hot tub	Shops
Internet	Tour desk
Marina	Water-sports center

ROOM AMENITIES

We've also looked for the amenities that make a guest room comfortable and efficient, and have listed the following amenities that are available in some or all rooms.

Air-conditioning	Kitchenette
Balcony or terrace	Minibar
Bathtub (*in addition to shower*)	Ocean view
Coffeemaker (*check the minibar list* *to see if you're charged for packets of coffee*)	Refrigerator
	Safe
Fan	Whirlpool tub
Hair dryer	Windows that open (*including sliding-glass doors*)
Massage	Shops
Organized children's activities	Tour desk
Restaurants	Water-sports center
Room service (*limited or around the clock*)	

stocked minibars—beware of running up staggering bills when you've got the munchies or the kids spot the candy. Some minibars have electronic sensors that show you've moved something, so take care if you relocate hotel-stocked items in there.

Televisions are standard, but the quality of service varies. Standard TV hookups get local and national channels in Spanish. Most accommodations, however, offer cable with CNN, some form of national U.S. network station, and movie channels. Satellite TVs usually have the most options, though standards such as CNN are sometimes blocked.

Laundry service is always available; same-day service and dry cleaning are higher-end amenities. More upscale accommodations (and service-oriented chains) are putting irons and ironing boards in the rooms, and most have them available from housekeeping. Some places let you keep these throughout your stay; others expect you to use them and promptly return them, especially in high season when demand is greater.

Phones, TVs, and laundry service are givens unless otherwise mentioned. Hair dryers, safety deposit boxes, coffeemakers, and other useful amenities are often available, too. Upscale accommodations may treat their guests to turndown service, robes and slippers, and other niceties. Concierges serve as all-around assistants, arranging tours, car rentals, computer access, and almost anything a guest requests. If such perks are important to you, be sure to ask about them. Many resort accommodations have tour and car-rental desks, shops, and water sports and activity centers; others have elaborate spas, private hot tubs, multiple swimming pools, and separate pools for children. In the accommodation profiles in our regional chapters, we've listed the amenities and services at each accommodation so you can easily choose one that suits you.

Telephones

Accommodation telephone rip-off practices are alive and well in Mexico, as in the rest of the world. Expect to pay 40¢ to $1 for local calls (some accommodations charge by the minute, others by the call), and at least $2 a minute for national long-distance calls. The sky's the limit for international calls and calls to cellular phones.

unofficial **TIP**
Most hotels don't allow these phones on the premises, but you may see them close to hotels, shops, and other tourist areas. Beware.

If you plan to do much telephoning from your room, it is worthwhile to ask about the charges up front. There's usually a cost to connect with your phone-card company. Accommodations that advertise direct-dial phones and Internet connections may not have the level of service that you are expecting. Find out all the details before dialing. Should you follow the English-language instructions on cards placed beside phones entreating you to "call home," you could easily end up with a $50 charge for a five-minute call.

Computer Connections

Trying to connect to the Internet with a laptop can be absolutely infuriating, though the situation is improving thanks to wireless hookups. In some accommodations, the phone systems are digital, meaning they run off one or two outside lines that connect to a switchboard. Automatic dialing from a computer modem is difficult in such situations. If you need to use your own computer (as opposed to one in a business center or Internet cafe), ask about high-speed Internet connection in the rooms and wireless access in the room or the hotel lobby or restaurant. If connecting to the Internet is essential to you, ask if the accommodation has a business or computer center with high-speed Internet.

Purified Water

Many accommodations have water-purification systems and claim their tap water is safe for drinking. It's a questionable claim, however. The water is probably safe in the newer resort areas, including the Mexican Caribbean and Huatulco, but you can never be 100% sure. We tend to use bottled water for drinking because the infrastructure of most resort areas is overburdened. The most expensive accommodations often have the priciest water—as much as $12 for a quart of designer-label water—whereas many budget accommodations have jugs of purified water in hallway dispensers. If you drink a lot of water, you'll save considerably if you purchase it outside your hotel.

Children's Programs

Mexico is extremely family-friendly, and most resort accommodations have some form of children's activities. The major chains have kids' clubs with supervised playrooms and activities; such programs are often available only during times of high occupancy. Make sure you ask about these activities, their hours of operation, and any fees when you make your reservation. We mention children's programs in our accommodation profiles when they're readily available.

Disabled Access

Bless the wheelchair-bound who attempt forays into Mexico. For the most part, accommodations not only do not have accessible rooms, they're actually disability-challenged: Many of the most charming accommodations in Acapulco and Puerto Vallarta are built atop or below cliffs and have endless stairways for guests to maneuver. Curb cuts and elevators with Braille pads or beepers are virtually nonexistent. Fortunately, most new hotels include at least one room outfitted for wheelchair use. In the accommodation profiles, we mention rooms with at least some accommodations for persons with disabilities. For more general information and resources, see "Disabled Access in Mexico," page 35.

Taxes

The value-added tax in coastal Mexico is 15%, with an additional hotel tax of 2% (3% in Mazatlán). Always ask if the tax is included in the room rate as it often is in budget and moderately priced accommodations. Bear this in mind when comparing the cost of different properties.

Service Charges

It's becoming more common for accommodations to add a 10%-to-20% service charge to your bill; the charge is supposed to cover all tips. Ask about such charges when you check in, as there's no need to tip bellhops and waiters when there's a service charge. You may want to tip extra for special service. The practice is most common at secluded resorts in all price ranges, all-inclusives, and at the most expensive luxury resorts.

unofficial **TIP**
During holiday periods, you can be penalized for changes made months before your arrival date.

Deposits and Cancellation Charges

You can usually guarantee your room with a credit card. Sometimes the charge is actually billed—anywhere from one night's lodging to the full price of your accommodation—when you reserve; other times not until you arrive, or a few days before. Hefty cancellation fees often apply. The policies vary with the type of property, season, and level of occupancy. The familiar chain accommodations such as Marriott, Hyatt, and Best Western seem to have the most generous cancellation policies. Most require between 24 and 72 hours notice and charge no fee if advised within the prescribed time period. Other accommodations, however, may charge one or more nights' room rate as a fee for cancellations made weeks prior to the arrival date, and some will charge you to change your dates as well. Policies vary widely, so always ask before making your reservation.

GETTING A GOOD DEAL ON A ROOM

HOTEL ROOMS ARE LIKE AIRPLANE SEATS—the price you pay depends on when you book, with whom you talk, and availability. When we ask for rate sheets, we're often given complicated tables with at least four different rates depending on the season and location of the room. You're almost certain to get different rates by checking an accommodation's Web site, calling the toll-free number, and asking at the front desk. Here are some tips on how to get the best room for your money.

BOOK EARLY Many accommodations have a block of rooms that go for the lowest rates. Once they're sold out, the rates rise. If you're traveling during a holiday, book up to a year in advance. (But bear in mind the policies just mentioned in "Deposits and Cancellations Charges.")

TRAVEL IN THE OFF-SEASON Rates are generally lowest in June (and sometimes May) and from September to mid-November. Rates are highest from January through Easter, around Mexican holidays (see "National Holidays" on page 41 and "A Calendar of Festivals and Events" on pages 40–41), and in July and August, when it seems everyone in the world is on vacation.

REVIEW ROOM RATES All accommodations have what are known as rack rates, which are established six months to a year in advance. Almost no one pays this rate, except when the hotel is nearly full. Ask if you're being quoted the rack rate and if discounts or special promotions are available. Room upgrades, free nights, golf or spa treatments, and other perks are available to those willing to do a little research. Look for packages on the hotel's Web site. Then call the hotel directly (see below). Often the international toll-free operators are not familiar with local rates and occupancy.

CALL THE HOTEL DIRECTLY Many Mexican hotels have toll-free numbers that ring directly from the United States or Canada to the hotel. Don't be rattled if someone answers the phone in Spanish. Just request a clerk who speaks English. Ask as many questions you want—you might not get all the answers you need, but you'll get a feel for the place.

CHOOSE YOUR VIEWS Rates often depend on the location of your room, with top dollar going to prime ocean views. You may find, however, that you can get a larger room with a big terrace if you choose garden or pool view (beware of noise by the pool). In Cancún, rooms with lagoon views at Le Méridien, for example, overlook a vast expanse of green water, the lights of downtown, and spectacular sunsets (the sun doesn't set over the sea on the Caribbean side of Mexico). Naturally, rates go down if you stay a few blocks away from the water.

CONSIDER A PACKAGE Deals including airfare, accommodation, and some meals and tours are common and can help you save money and planning time. It's often easier to go with a package rather than searching for bargain airfares, car rentals, rooms, and tours. But there are caveats. Make sure the package includes the type of room and tours you really want. Having airport transfers included is a great idea—it helps you avoid the taxi hustle at the airport. If car rental is included, make sure it's the type of car you want. See page 28 for some recommended companies that offer packages.

TALK WITH THE PROFESSIONALS Travel agencies specialize in certain destinations and activities and can provide convenient shortcuts and aid in decision-making. We've included companies with certain specialties in Part One, Planning Your Visit to Mexico, and in the regional chapters.

CHECK THE WEB Most hotels have their own Web sites or are at least linked to a travel or property management Web site. We've found that few hotels monitor their e-mail as closely as they should, and we urge you to make final arrangements by phone. You can book hotel rooms through many of the travel Web sites listed in Part One (see page 34), but there are potential pitfalls when making your reservations on the Web. You may not get the type of room you've requested, and you may get bumped if the hotel is overbooked.

INTERNATIONAL AND NATIONAL HOTEL CHAINS

THE FOLLOWING CHAINS HAVE HOTELS in Mexico. Most are identical or nearly so to their counterparts in the United States and elsewhere. We have not included the individual properties in the hotel profiles found in the regional chapters unless they are exceptional. If you belong to a hotel points program or feel more comfortable in familiar surroundings, check out the following chains.

Best Western has moderately priced lodgings in Acapulco, Los Cabos, Cancún, Huatulco, Ixtapa, Mazatlán, and Puerto Escondido. The quality varies tremendously. Some properties are older, independent hotels with loads of character; some are bland. Ask lots of questions when you call. ☎ 800-780-7234; **www.bestwestern.com.**

Fiesta Americana is part of Grupos Posadas, a Mexican chain that also operates Fiesta Inn (similar to Holiday Inn Express or Comfort Inn) and Explorean adventure tourism lodges. They have properties in nearly every coastal resort. Fiesta Americana hotels typically have soaring palapa (palm fronds or zacate grass) roofs covering the lobbies and lots of arches, niches, and Mexican folk art as part of the decor. The Cancún and Cozumel properties are especially attractive. ☎ 800-343-7821; **www.fiestaamericana.com.**

The **InterContinental Hotels Group** (which includes the Holiday Inn, Crowne, Indigo, and Presidente hotels) has accommodations in Acapulco, Cancún, Cozumel, Los Cabos, Mazatlán, and Puerto Vallarta. The Ixtapa Presidente is an all-inclusive, and some of the other Presidentes have the option of being so. ☎ 800-327-0200; **www.ichotelsgroup.com.**

Hyatt has two properties in Cancún, both of which are older hotels that are close to convention centers. The Hyatt Cancún Caribe has a few spacious villas on the beach. ☎ 800-633-7313; **www.hyatt.com.**

Marriott has two hotels in Cancún. The **JW Marriott** has an impressive spa, while the **CasaMagna** is more mainstream. There's anpther CasaMagna in Puerto Vallarta. ☎ 888-236-2427; **www .marriott.com.**

Sol Meliá, a Spanish chain, has hotels and all-inclusive properties in Cancún, Cozumel, the Caribbean Coast, Ixtapa, Puerto Vallarta, and Los Cabos. One of the Los Cabos hotels is on the most popular beach in Cabo San Lucas; another is an all-inclusive in the more remote Corridor. Most Meliá hotels have stunning architecture. The chain is adding a new line of hotels, called ME, and is updating the decor at some existing hotels to fit this new, hip collection. ☎ 888-95-MELIA; **www.solmelia.com.**

Starwood Hotels represents Westin, Sheraton, Le Méridien, and the Luxury Collection of hotels with properties at most resort areas. The hip Nikki Beach cocktail lounge and restaurant at the Westin Puerto Vallarta draws locals to the marina neighborhood. The Cancún Westin sits between a lagoon and the beach in a less-developed area of the hotel zone. Both the Sheraton and Westin Los Cabos are in the beach-front corridor. ☎ 800-325-3589 (Luxury Collection) or 800-WESTIN 1 (Sheraton or Westin); **www.starwood.com.**

INDEPENDENT HOTELS

PLENTY OF INDEPENDENT HOTELIERS have staked a claim on Mexico's beaches, and their properties often inspire fierce loyalty. Thus it's imperative to make your reservations early. Some are like bed-and-breakfasts (which aren't as common in Mexico as in Europe) and offer meal plans.

Mexico Boutique Hotels represents one-of-a-kind inns, restored haciendas, and unique beach hotels throughout the country. Their Web site is excellent, giving a good overview of the destinations as well as the properties. They handle beach properties in Acapulco, Los Cabos, Isla Mujeres, Puerto Vallarta, Huatulco, and Zihuatanejo. ☎ 877-278-8018; **www.mexicoboutiquehotels.com.**

Small Luxury Hotels of the World has members in Acapulco, Cancún, Playa del Carmen, Costalegre, Zihuatanejo, and Los Cabos. Some are also included with Mexico Boutique Hotels. ☎ 800-525-4800; **www.slh.com.**

unofficial **TIP**

Some accommodations may require that you purchase a meal plan during especially busy times such as Christmas and Easter, and may also require a minimum two- or three-night stay.

MEAL PLANS

HOTELS OFTEN OFFER A VARIETY of meal plans that can help reduce your costs. In most cases, your room rate will not include meals, but it's always good to ask if a meal plan is offered. The most common plan is one with either a full or a Continental breakfast included in the rate. These are especially good deals when dining out involves a costly cab ride, as in Los Cabos. Plans including lunch and dinner are most commonly offered at out-of-the-way hotels, including some on the Caribbean Coast. Meal plans include the following:

European Plan (EP): Room only, no meals included.

Breakfast Plan (BP): Room rate includes breakfast.

American Plan (AP): Room rate includes breakfast, lunch, and dinner.

Modified American Plan (MAP): Room rate includes breakfast and dinner.

ALL-INCLUSIVE PROPERTIES

THE ALL-INCLUSIVE CONCEPT TOOK hold in Cancún in the 1980s and has spread to all beach resorts. Several worldwide all-inclusive companies have invested heavily in Mexican properties. Some are so enormous they feel like sandy cities. Canadians, Americans, and Europeans arrive on charter flights, stay for a week, and rarely leave the property. Many small hotels have jumped on the all-inclusive band-wagon as well. When the property is located far from restaurants, it makes sense to purchase some form of meal plan. All-inclusives have become so pervasive in the Mexican hotel scene that we describe the exceptional ones in the regional chapters. If you're looking for an easy vacation with few decisions, check out the following companies.

CLUB MED The original all-inclusive has properties in Cancún and Ixtapa. The Cancún property was completely remodeled in 2006 and has a more family-friendly approach. ☎ 888-WEBCLUB; **www .clubmed.com.**

DREAMS This relatively new company also includes Secrets resorts and a new upscale brand awkwardly named Zoestry. The Dreams properties are located in the former Camino Real hotels, which claim gorgeous beaches in Cancún and Puerto Vallarta. ☎ 866-237-3267; **www.dreamsresorts.com.**

IBEROSTAR Distinctive, upscale properties along with family-friendly, moderately priced resorts in Riviera Maya and Cozumel. The chain has five hotels in a huge compound in Riviera Maya and is building large complexes in the Riviera Nayarit, a new resort area on the Pacific Coast. ☎ 888-923-2722; **www.iberostar.com.**

OASIS Operates hotels in Playa del Carmen and the Riviera Maya as well as in Cancún. They cater to groups from Spain and other

Europeans who are familiar with the chain. ☎ 800-44-OASIS; **www
.oasishotels.com.**

PALACE RESORTS Cancún, the Rivera Maya, Cozumel, Los Cabos,
and Puerto Vallarta are home to resorts from this company. Some
properties are reserved for adults and have spectacular spas and golf
courses; others are geared toward families. ☎ 800-346-8225; **www
.palaceresorts.com.**

TIME-SHARES

TIME-SHARE AND VACATION OWNERSHIP programs are huge
at Mexico's beach resorts; in many places, the high-pressure sales
are very annoying (see "The Time-share Hustle," page 70). If you
belong to a time-share club and hope to stay in one of these areas,
book early. The resorts fill as quickly as they can be built. Some all-
inclusive companies have vacation-ownership programs as well, and
some hotels reserve a block of rooms for time-share guests. There
are advantages to staying at a hotel that's geared toward time-share
clients. Rooms usually have some form of kitchen facilities and are
set up for weeklong stays, and activities are plentiful.

BEDS BY THE BEACH

IF BEING ABLE TO STEP FROM YOUR DOOR straight onto the
sand is a top priority, you'll want to pay special attention to your
hotel's location. Each destination has beaches safe for swimmers and
beaches that are unsafe because of rough water or pollution. Note
that beaches are seriously affected by weather. Hurricane Wilma
literally wiped most of Cancún's windward beach away in October
2005 and devastated many of Cozumel's best stretches of sand. New
sand was dredged onto or trucked to the most popular beach areas.
Severe rain and windstorms can have similar effects in all areas. Here
are a few recommendations for the best beaches in each destination;
check out the regional chapters for more details:

CANCÚN Hotels close to Punta Cancún and the open coast facing the
Caribbean are best for swimming. The ocean at the south end of the
hotel zone can be rough, while that at the north can be murky and
clogged with sea grasses. Nearly nine miles of beach between Punta
Cancún and Punta Nizúc were restored in Cancún after Hurricane
Wilma, and the sand isn't as soft or as white as it was before the
storm. The second stage of the beach-reclamation project was never
completed, and beaches on the south side of Punta Cancún tend to
lose their sand with appalling frequency.

ISLA MUJERES Stay beside Playa Norte for swimming in calm water
or close to Playa Garrafón for good snorkeling.

COZUMEL Clean, white-sand beaches are the norm at hotels along
Carretera Norte, where a few clusters of coral can satisfy snorkelers.
Beaches along Carretera Sur are smaller; some hotels sit atop lime-

stone shelves and have steps down to the water. The farther south you go, the more fish you'll see while snorkeling.

THE CARIBBEAN COAST Long, white-sand beaches are one of the coast's best features, though the incessant construction of large resorts is changing the coastline. The beach at Playa del Carmen was once the most gorgeous on the coast, but rampant construction has turned the main beach into a crowded, polluted mess. As a rule, the water is clearer the farther south you go. Diving and snorkeling are best around Puerto Morelos, Paamul, Akumal, and Tankah. Serious divers should not miss Xcalak at the far southern reaches of the coast.

unofficial **TIP**
The beaches on the northern edge of Playa del Carmen are now the best places to hang out in hip beach clubs.

MAZATLÁN The majority of hotels are located along the Zona Dorada, where Playa Gaviotas is packed with people and water toys, and the water is usually clean. For more peaceful swimming, take a short boat ride to Deer Island. Waves are higher (but not fierce) at Playa Norte and Playa Olas Altas in front of hotels popular with budget travelers and surfers alike.

PUERTO VALLARTA Most resort hotels are located on the long beach north of town facing Bahía de Banderas, at Marina Vallarta, or in Nuevo Vallarta, the latter with one long, sandy beach and a private marina. Staying in downtown or close to Playa los Muertos and the mouth of the Río Cuale puts you in the middle of the dining and social scene. Many of the hotels south of town are located on small sandy coves, giving them a feeling of privacy. The exclusive resorts along the Costalegre have gorgeous beaches and safe swimming conditions.

IXTAPA AND ZIHUATANEJO Stay in Ixtapa at Playa del Palmar if you want unobstructed beach access with water toys and seas that are fairly calm—although the beach isn't terribly wide and slopes slightly down to the water. The most charming hotels in the area are close to wildly popular Playa la Ropa in Zihuatanejo. Unfortunately, this is a closed bay, which means unseen pollution may be a problem, especially after a heavy rain.

ACAPULCO Though the views of the bay and access to dining and nightlife make the Costera an ideal base for vacationers, the water here can be polluted, especially after rainstorms. Do your swimming in hotel pools. The beaches by the hotels along Acapulco Diamante are small and sometimes rocky, and the water can be rough. The hotels closer to Puerto Marqués and Playa Revolcadero have spectacular broad beaches, but the surf is rough. In general, Acapulco isn't a great destination for serious saltwater swimmers.

PUERTO ESCONDIDO Surfers are happy in the water here because the waves off Playa Zicatela are legendary. Guests at hotels near this beach benefit from the music of crashing surf—but don't go in the water unless you are an extremely experienced swimmer or surfer.

Hotels near playas Marineros and Principal are good for walking along the sand. If swimming is your main interest, head for cozy Carrizalillo and Puerto Angelito bays.

HUATULCO Bahía Tangolunda, a gorgeous deep-blue bay, is lined with hotels and water-sports centers. Chahue Bay has calm water, water toys, and a beach club. You'll find hotels, bars, and restaurants here, but not right on the water.

LOS CABOS There are precious few places to swim in the sea at Los Cabos. Hotels in San José del Cabo benefit from the sound of crashing surf—a sure sign that you'd better stay out of the rough waves. Hotels at the new Puerto Los Cabos will be at the rough ocean, which is not recommended for swimming. People staying there, as well as those staying in San José del Cabo, most often head to the beach at Chileno or Santa María Bays to swim. Hotels facing Playa Médano in Cabo San Lucas are at the center of the social beach scene, where swimmers share the water with personal watercraft, kayaks, and small boats. The hotels on the Pacific Coast face the same conditions as those in San José.

GREAT PLACES TO STAY

MEXICO'S RESORTS OFFER so many wonderful hotels that you may want to choose your room before your beach. Destination hotels where you sleep, eat, play, indulge, and never leave the property are abundant. The best are designed by Mexican architects and artisans who use the country's Spanish, Moorish, colonial, indigenous, and contemporary styles with imaginative results. Here are our top picks; all are described further in the regional chapters.

Great for Luxury

Esencia, Caribbean Coast This small, private resort combines the most gracious aspects of Mexican hospitality with serene Mediterranean architecture and high-tech accoutrements. Scriptwriters from Los Angeles and bankers from Buenos Aires feel utterly laid-back here—even if their laptops and FedEx envelopes are close at hand. The suites feel like private villas and the service is sublimely attentive and attuned to guests' moods. The food is fabulous. and the spa is a study in minimalist serenity. ☎ 877-528-3490; **www.hotel esencia.com.**

LE MÉRIDIEN CANCÚN The combination of an excellent spa, restaurants that excite gourmands, pools heated to varying temperatures, and other thoughtful touches make the hotel an elegant retreat. ☎ 800-543-4300; **www.starwoodhotels.com.**

HOTEL PRESIDENTE INTERCONTINENTAL COZUMEL This wonderful hotel's many fans waited almost a full year for the Presidente to reopen after Hurricane Wilma trashed its buildings and lush, mature palm groves. Today's Presidente is Cozumel's first truly luxurious hotel with butler service in sea-facing suites, a fabulous free-standing spa, and restaurants well worth visiting even if you're not a guest. The rooms now have a sleek design and Internet access. Many of the waiters and housekeepers have been here for decades and were employed throughout the reconstruction phase. Even if you're a first-time guest, you'll soon feel at home. ☎ 800-327-0200; **www .intercontinentalcozumel.com.**

RITZ-CARLTON CANCÚN European furnishings and paintings seem out of place at a beach resort—except at the Ritz-Carlton. Completely reconstructed after Hurricane Wilma drenched the walls and plush furnishings, Cancún's finest hotel reopened looking almost exactly like it did before the storm. A culinary center outfitted with Viking appliances offers cooking classes and wine tastings that are great fun. ☎ 800-241-3333; **www.ritzcarlton.com.**

ROSEWOOD MAYAKOBA Sleek modernist architecture and spacious suites buried along canals and mangrove lagoons make this new Riviera Maya property an absolute standout. The service is impeccable, the amenities luxurious, and the food outstanding. ☎888-767-3966; **www.rosewoodmayakoba.com.**

LAS VENTANAS AL PARAÍSO, LOS CABOS The stonework in the pathways winding past infinity pools and restaurants is mesmerizing; each piece was laid by hand in swirling patterns. Telescopes point from the suites to whales breaching in the Sea of Cortez; still, it's hard to turn your eyes from the hand-built furniture, cushy beds, and ethnic ornaments. Bathrooms are among the best anywhere, with deep soaking tubs and glass jars filled with oils and salts. The spa's desert-clay and hot-rock treatments are pure Baja, as is the tequila-and-ceviche bar. The food is divine. ☎ 888-767-3966; **www.lasventanas.com.**

Great for Romance

CAMINO REAL ZAASHILA, HUATULCO An oasis of calm chic and non-trendy charm, the Camino Real emanates elegance and comfort. Because of its location at the rocky end of Bahía Tangolunda, the beach is private (or it feels like it is) and perfect for splashing, swimming, and snorkeling. Lounge chairs are built into the pool, which segues, amoeba-like, under a bridge; the whole effect is icy-blue cool. Beds and linens are sublimely cozy. ☎ 800-722-6466; **www.caminoreal .com/zaashila.**

HACIENDA SAN ANGEL, PUERTO VALLARTA Watch the sunset over Banderas Bay from a guest room decorated in period antiques or perhaps one with private patio, wet bar, and trickling stone fountain in this sumptuously decorated, restored *casona* in the heart of the old city. ☎ 322-222-2692; **www.haciendasanangel.com.**

LA CASA QUE CANTA, ZIHUATANEJO Adobe walls (OK, the adobe is plastered onto cement), thatched roofs covering soaring ceilings, and a saltwater pool filled by a waterfall give you an idea of the unique craftsmanship of this lovely resort overlooking picturesque Bahía de Zihuatanejo. The infinity pool starred (along with Al Pacino and Chris O'Donnell) in *Scent of a Woman*. Beautiful flower-petal arrangements appear on your bed each day to add a luxuriant touch of class. ☎ 888-523-5050; **www.lacasaquecanta.com.**

MAJAHUITAS RESORT, PUERTO VALLARTA What could be more romantic than being marooned on a white-sand beach that can be reached only by boat? No TVs, phones, computers—just candlelight, a cushy king bed, and a hammock for two. ☎ 831-336-5036; **www .majahuitas-resort.com.**

VILLA ROLANDI, ISLA MUJERES Guests arrive on the villa's yacht from Cancún and tend to stick close to the pool and their suites when in residence. You can see the green-blue Caribbean from the hot tubs on the balconies and showers in the suites—and the shower turns into a steam room when you turn a few knobs. The restaurant is exceptional and privacy is assured. ☎ 998-877-0700; **www .villarolandi.com.**

Great for Families

CASA ROSADA, PUERTO ESCONDIDO Families feel at home in this cluster of bungalows in a residential neighborhood complex close to small markets and a five-minute walk to the beach. Kids can play in an enclosed garden while parents relax by the pool. Calle 3a Sur 303; no phone; **www.casa38.com.**

CLUB MED IXTAPA Parents can have nonstop fun at the recently reinvented Club Med Ixtapa, both with the kids and on their own. Babies from age 4 months up receive super attention from friendly staff, and teens are equally pampered with age-appropriate activities. Even the evening entertainment includes tiny tots dressed in clown suits or other fun attire, while older kids and adults swing from real circus trapezes. ☎ 755-553-1000 or 800-WEBCLUB U.S. and Canada; **clubmed.com.mx.**

DREAMS CANCÚN RESORT AND SPA Kids ride water bikes in the lagoon beside the beach at the former Camino Real hotel, now an all-inclusive resort. Movies by the pool, casino nights, and volleyball games keep all ages entertained. The quieter area with a tiny, secret beach is best for honeymooners and those seeking seclusion. The Puerto Vallarta also is great fun for families. ☎ 998-848-1700, 866-2-DREAMS U.S. and Canada; **www.dreamresorts.com.**

DREAMS HUATULCO There's so much to do at this all-inclusive on Tangolunda Bay. Kids' clubs are separated by age, so even teens enjoy the water sports and classes offered at their level. The 24-hour service is a pampering touch. ☎ 958-583-0400 or 866-2-DREAMS U.S. and Canada; **www.dreamresorts.com.**

HOTEL PLAYA MAZATLÁN Kids as well as adults get a charge out of the Mexican Fiesta variety show, and whole families get onto the dance floor both before and after the performers do their thing. Programs exist to keep the kids amused year-round, and the beach is just outside your door. ☎ 800-762-5816 U.S. and Canada; **www .hotelplayamazatlán.com.**

Great for Budget Travelers

BRISAS DEL MAR, ZIHUATANEJO The junglelike setting on a hillside above Playa la Madera is unusual for a budget hotel. Once on the beach you'll want to linger rather than hike the hill back to the rooms; fortunately, the restaurant and bar are right on the sand. Rooms have big balconies with hammocks and chaise lounges. ☎ 755-554-2142; **www.brisasdelmar.net.**

FRANCIS ARLENE, ISLA MUJERES It's not on the beach, but this family-run hotel is a winner due to its cleanliness and accommodating staff. It's just a block from the open sea and a few blocks from Playa Norte, the most popular beach. ☎ 998-877-0310; **www.francisarlene.com.**

LOS MILAGROS, LOS CABOS Attentive and informative owners and rooms that feel like home are among the pluses at this small inn a few blocks from the beach in Cabo San Lucas. Good budget restaurants are located nearby. ☎ 624-143-4566 Mexico; 718-928-6647 from the U.S.; **losmilagros.com.mx.**

MISION DE LOS ARCOS, HUATULCO Across the street from the plaza in La Crucecita, this gem is well situated for those who want some action. If it were on the beach, it would easily garner far higher room rates. The architecture and decor are surprisingly elegant. ☎ 958-587-0165; **www.misiondelosarcos.com.**

EL REY DEL CARIBE, CANCÚN Travelers concerned with environmental issues are pleased with the emphasis on solar energy and recycling here. All guests enjoy the shady garden, complimentary Continental breakfast, and informative staff. ☎ 998-884-2028; **www .reycaribe.com.**

SIESTA INN, LOS CABOS In the land of $300-a-night hotel rooms, this winner manages to offer mini-apartments with kitchenettes for a mere fraction of the going rate in the area. The bulletin board is filled with tips on budget restaurants and transportation. ☎ 866-271-0952; **www.cabosiestasuites.com.**

unofficial **TIP**
Our favorite hotel in Playa del Carmen just happens to fit into the budget category—a major accomplishment in this ultrahip neighborhood.

LA TORTUGA, PLAYA DEL CARMEN, CARIBBEAN COAST People are a huge part of the attraction here—bellhops cheerfully walk you to the pharmacy, find a parking space for your car, and haul your bags up narrow stairways to immaculately clean, white, spacious rooms. Front-desk clerks hand out coupons for free breakfast and beach club passes and quickly adjust to your quirks. There's wireless Internet (and a couple of computers) by the pool and bar, and lots of places to visit with newfound friends. ☎ 984-873-1484; **www.hotellatortuga.com.**

MEXICO ACCOMMODATIONS RATED AND RANKED

WE'VE RANKED NEARLY 150 ACCOMMODATIONS in Mexico and have picked only the best in each category. Just because a hotel has only one star for its overall rating doesn't mean it's inferior. We genuinely like every hotel in this book. Our star system is based on room quality (cleanliness, spaciousness, views, amenities, visual appeal), value, service, and location. Each regional chapter features a list showing how the hotels in that region stack up against each other, followed by detailed profiles of each property. A budget hotel may have a higher overall rating than a far more luxurious one because of the warmth of its staff members or the immense value it offers. Our ratings are independent of any travel organization or club. The evaluations are also Mexico-specific and are compared with other properties in the country.

OVERALL RATING The overall rating takes into consideration all facets of a hotel. A property with a prime location, excellent restaurants, or a gorgeous lobby might rank better despite mediocre rooms. Conversely, an over-priced property with elaborate facilities and rooms and little character may rank lower overall.

ROOM-QUALITY RATING The room quality rating only considers the hotel room itself. Obviously, a room's size, quality of furnishings, and level of cleanliness are prime factors in room quality. However, *Unofficial Guide* researchers also take careful note of the things most guests notice only when something is awry: noise levels, lighting, and temperature control.

VALUE RATING The value rating is a combination of the overall and room quality ratings along with the cost of an average guest room. This indicates a general idea of value for money. If getting a good deal means the most to you, choose a property by looking at the value rating.

WHAT THE STAR RATINGS MEAN	
★★★★★	Best of the best
★★★★½	Excellent
★★★★	Great
★★★½	Very good
★★★	Good
★★½	Fine
★★	Has some things going for it
★½	Good for the cost
★	Economical

COST Hotel cost is indicated by a range of $ signs. The rates listed below are based on the one-night rack rate for a standard ocean-view room (or suitable equivalent) during the tourism high season, which runs from December through Easter. However, these ratings are most useful in terms of comparing one property to another. Don't be intimidated by the cost indicators; quite often, lower (and higher) prices are available at most hotels, depending on the room category.

$$$$$	Above $350
$$$$	$250–$350
$$$	$150–$250
$$	$100–$150
$	Below $100

Room taxes (15% to 18%) and the mandatory service charges included in the bill at some hotels may make rates higher. Always ask if these and any other additional charges (such as parking) are included in the quoted rate. If you're into exercising, ask if there is an additional charge to use the fitness facilities.

RESTAURANTS *in* MEXICO

MEXICO'S REGIONAL CUISINES ARE KNOWN for their variety, spice, and uniqueness. Outside tourist restaurants, some of the dishes served in Oaxaca aren't commonly seen on menus in Mazatlán. They've got their own prized recipes. But ask around, and you'll find favorite dishes from nearly every part of the country at the coastal resorts. The people who clean your hotel room, serve your meals, and handle your messages come from all over Mexico. They tend to live in enclaves with others from their state or region, and they set up home-style taco stands and cafes in their neighborhoods. Serious gourmands can search out the best mole or pozole. But most travelers don't have the time or inclination. Fortunately, every resort area has a few restaurants specializing in Mexico's regional cuisine.

Equally exciting for curious palates is the evolving coastal cuisine spreading from the Caribbean to the Pacific and the Sea of Cortez. Chefs from every major culinary hot spot wander through Mexico at some point in their careers. Many have fallen in love with a particular resort and started their own restaurants. They've taken Pacific Rim, Asian, French, and Italian techniques and recipes and mixed them with local ingredients. The results are often surprising and stimulating.

TRADITIONAL INGREDIENTS

THE HUMBLE TORTILLA IS THE STAFF of life in Mexico, so essential that its price is regulated by the government. Every town and city has *tortillerías* where *masa,* finely ground cornmeal, is pressed into flat disks that are synonymous with Mexican food. Tortillas made from cornmeal are the basis for tacos, enchiladas, gorditas, chalupas, and other "finger foods" served at parties or in lieu of a larger meal. Tortillas made from white or wheat flour are commonly served with specific meals, such as *queso fundido* (cheese fondue). Many foreigners prefer flour tortillas and can freely request them in most tourist-oriented restaurants.

Beans are standard fare as well, but their preparation varies with the region. On the Caribbean side of Mexico, *frijoles negros* (black beans) are served as a side dish or in a soup. Refried mashed pinto beans (*frijoles refritos*) are more common on the Pacific. *Frijoles charros* are "cowboy beans" cooked with onions and bacon and served in a soupy consistency. Rice is another common side dish; many restaurants serve white rice with vegetables rather than "Spanish rice" and beans with their entrees.

The chile pepper defines Mexican cuisine—and causes uninitiated diners to fear regional dishes. But chiles needn't be fiery hot and are often used for subtle flavoring. An exception is the chile habanero, which often appears as an accompaniment to dishes in Yucatán and the Caribbean. It's one of the hottest chiles in the country—taste it sparingly. Almost as fiery are the ubiquitous jalapeño and serrano chiles. *Guajillo* chiles add a smoky flavor to fish and meat dishes; *poblanos* ranging from mild to medium-spicy are stuffed with cheese or meat, lightly battered, and fried to make chiles rellenos. If you're wary, ask how hot (*picante*) a dish is and order accordingly.

The abundance of semitropical and tropical fruits make dining in Mexico a joy. Fresh mango, papaya, passion fruit, *pitahaya,* star fruit, and *guanábana* appear on huge fruit platters at breakfast buffets, along with watermelon, pineapple, and all sorts of bananas. Fresh fruit with yogurt and granola makes a delicious, healthful breakfast, and *licuados* (fruit blended with water, milk, or sometimes yogurt) are available everywhere. Street vendors carve papayas in floral shapes and slice mangos into cups, then sprinkle them with powdered chiles and a squeeze of lime for a healthful, refreshing snack. Because many fruits can be peeled, you can safely consume them in abundance (but be aware that a sudden diet of lots of fresh fruit can cause digestive disturbances).

The vegetable situation has improved immensely over the years. In the past, entrees were often served with an unappealing pile of boiled *chayote* (a mild, rather flavorless cousin of the zucchini) and carrots. Today, chefs use baby vegetables from organic farms and prepare stunning salads with arugula, radicchio, and a wide range of lettuces. Most establishments—but especially the traveler-oriented places—use purified water to clean their vegetables. Ask if you're unsure, and if you're not satisfied, stick with cooked vegetables.

Beef raised in the northern cattle ranches in Mexico is served throughout the country. But many restaurants at the coast are now importing U.S. steaks to please American palates. Mexican beef dishes use thin cuts rather than thick steaks, and the beef is marinated and grilled as in *carne asada*. Flavorful pork shows up as tender *carnitas*, served with hot tortillas and beans and rice. Tripe is used in *menudo,* and fried pork skin is a popular snack called *chicharrones* (known to us gringos as pork rinds). *Cabrito* (baby goat) is traditionally roasted over a spit and served in chunks with tortillas. The head, called the *cabecita,* is considered a delicacy. Chicken is abundant—and is best when roasted golden on a spit.

LIQUID GOLD AND OTHER DELIGHTFUL DRINKS

ASK TEN FANS OF MEXICO to name their favorite drink, and you might get ten different responses. You'll find Coca Light (Diet Coke) and Squirt if you must have them and bottles of purified water chilling in oversized market refrigerators. But the variety of drinks found in Mexico—both familiar and unusual—makes it worthwhile to stray from the safe realm of soft drinks into the realm of the unknown.

The flavors of drinks cold and hot are truly astonishing. Sure, you can get tomato, grapefruit, or orange juice for breakfast, but the tomato juice will undoubtedly be canned. How about fresh berry juice? Or guava, mango, papaya, or watermelon juice? Try a delicious mixture such as our favorite, fresh-pressed carrot juice mixed with orange juice. You'll fulfill all your daily fruit and veggie requirements at one sitting. *Aguas frescas,* often served during the midday meal, are watered-down versions of fresh fruit juices. A glass of watermelon water is as delicious as the better-known thirst-quencher lemonade.

Other cool drinks are unique to Mexico or to Latin America. *Agua de jamaica* is a bright-red drink found throughout Mexico. While it may have as much sugar as Kool-Aid, it is made from the flower of the jamaica plant and does have some nutritional value. *Horchata* is a refreshing, semisweet beverage of filtered rice water flavored with slivers of almond. Served on the beach, chilled coconuts get rave reviews from children and adults alike. The "milk" is watery, cool, and although fairly tasteless, still refreshing. Some adults can't resist doctoring their coconut, adding a dash of firewater and perhaps pineapple juice to turn the otherwise innocent beverage into an alcoholic *coco loco.*

There's no dearth of liquor and liqueurs made in Mexico, which is good because the imported stuff is usually twice the price. Tequila—from unaged, white tequila to golden *tequila añejo* (aged in an oak barrel for at least a year)—is ever present. Mescal, a similar distillation of the other agave plants, is produced throughout southern Mexico and, while it generally has less finesse than tequila, comes in a variety of flavors and cream versions that make it more palatable to the public.

So many delicious types of beer are brewed in Mexico that we'd be hard-pressed to name them all. There's the ever-present Corona, beneficiary of a well-orchestrated ad campaign, as well as darker and more distinctive brews such as the sweet, rich Negra Modelo and the regional Montejo, made in the Yucatán. Wineries in northern Baja California produce quite respectable wines. L.A. Cetto is the largest vintner; others such as Mogor Badam produce fewer than 10,000 bottles a year. Monte Xanic is one of our favorite labels.

If you want that warmth in your belly to come from something that's not alcoholic, there's nothing as satisfying as a cup of Mexican hot chocolate, called simply *chocolate*. Order it made with water or, for an even richer taste, with milk. Like hot chocolate, *atole* is a pre-Hispanic drink that is still vastly popular. Made of ground cornmeal or rice, and sweetened with sugar, it is served warm and often accompanies a rural evening meal. A delicious combination of hot chocolate and atole is called *champurrado*. The drink is beaten with a special wooden beater to whip it into a warm, frothy, soothing drink.

In the cities and countryside alike, the most common hot beverage is one of the world's favorites: coffee. In the tourist enclaves, you'll find espresso and cappuccino as well as *café americano,* or American-style coffee. And yes, there is a Starbucks in Cancún. If you're in a restaurant specializing in Mexican food, by all means try a traditional *café de olla,* literally, coffee from the pot. Ground coffee is boiled along with cinnamon sticks and brown sugar, then strained. The result is delicious but not too sweet, and 100% *mexicano*.

SEAFOOD PRIMER

SEAFOOD IS UNQUESTIONABLY THE MAIN INGREDIENT in coastal kitchens, and the key to ordering great fish is in knowing what's fresh. Nearly everyone wants to order lobster at least once while vacationing by the sea. You know what? The lobster is rarely fresh, and nothing is quite as disappointing as a mushy, previously frozen lobster for $30 or more. There are specific seasons when lobster can be caught; the dates vary with the location. A few chefs buy their lobster from farms where the tasty crustaceans are grown and harvested specifically for restaurants. Always ask if it's fresh or fresh frozen (frozen right when caught). If it's not, you'll be much happier with the catch of the day.

Chefs typically choose their fish daily from local anglers in early morning or late afternoon. The simplest preparation, *a la parrilla* (on the grill) is often the best, though chefs go to grand extremes to invent their own signature fish dishes. Grilled fish can be served

Guide to the Mexican Menu

Achiote Annatto seed prepared as a sauce or marinade for chicken or fish

Botana Appetizer

Carne asada A thin cut of flank steak, grilled

Carne asada a la tampiqueña A plate of *carne asada* served with beans, guacamole, cheese enchilada, and often *chile relleno* or *rajas de chile*

Cazón Shark

Chalupa Similar to a *gordita,* this fried corn-cake appetizer is usually sprinkled with meat and/or cheese.

Chaya A leafy green plant made into a refreshing, cool drink or added to *tamales* and other foods

Chile Chiles come in many dozens of varieties, from mild to searing hot. Different condiments, or *salsas,* are made from dried or fresh chiles to accompany almost every Mexican meal.

Chile relleno A *poblano* chile (mildly spicy) stuffed with cheese or ground meat and spices, egg-battered, and deep-fried

Cochinita pibil Marinated pork baked in banana leaves

Churro A dessert of deep-fried dough dusted in cinnamon and sugar

Dzotobichay A Yucatecan roll of cornmeal, pumpkin seeds, and *chaya* in tomato sauce

Enchiladas Tortillas dipped in a piquant sauce, rolled around cheese or another filling, and baked with more sauce and cheese

Fajitas Strips of beef or chicken grilled with bell pepper and onion, often served with beans, rice, guacamole, and, of course, tortillas

Flan Egg custard with a caramelized sugar topping

Flor de calabaza Squash blossom

Guacamole Mashed avocado spiced with lemon, chile, and grated onion; often served with corn tortilla chips

Helado Ice cream. Also called *nieve.*

Huachinango a la veracruzana Whole red snapper in a sauce of onions, tomatoes, peppers, and green olives

Huitlacoche Black fungus scraped from corn; an ancient delicacy

with a variety of sauces and marinades, including *mojo de ajo* (with butter or oil and lots of charred garlic) or *al ajillo* (with garlic and chiles). Breaded and fried fish is called *empanizado*. Fish tacos (*tacos de pescado*) are all the rage. The most traditional consists of a soft corn tortilla wrapped around a strip of batter-fried fish topped with chopped cabbage and cilantro, salsa, and a squeeze of lime.

Mole negro A rich sauce of chocolate, chiles, stale tortillas, and many other spices and ingredients, usually served over turkey or chicken; also called *mole poblano*

Panucho An appetizer similar to a *chalupa*

Pescado Fish

Pescado a la talla Butterflied fish, Guerrero state–style, rubbed with seasonings and grilled

Pescado tikin-xic Fish in achiote marinade; also spelled *tikin-shik*

Pipián A spicy green (*verde*) or red (*rojo*) sauce often served over chicken

Poc-chuc Marinated and grilled pork from Yucatán.

Postre Dessert

Quesadilla A flour (or sometimes corn) tortilla folded around melted cheese

Rajas de chile Mild chile pepper strips grilled with onions

Sincronizada Quesadilla with ham

Sopa de tortilla Chicken-based soup with fried tortilla strips, onion, and tomato, usually garnished with avocado and sour cream

Taco A corn tortilla with one of various fillings. Varies from region to region and may use a folded fresh or fried tortilla, or be rolled and deep-fried (usually called a *taquito*)

Tamal A rectangular cake of cornmeal steamed in banana leaves or corn husks. *Tamales* may be plain, sweet, or savory.

Torta A sandwich on a bread roll

Tortilla A pre-Hispanic food still served with most Mexican meals. Corn cooked and milled with lime is pressed by hand or machine into thin "cakes" and baked on a hot griddle. Flour tortillas, more common in northern Mexico, are made with lard or vegetable oil.

Tostada A crunchy corn tortilla topped with meat or beans, cheese, and garnishes

Totopopos Fried corn-tortilla triangles served as an appetizer or with meals

Xtabentun A sweet liqueur of anise and honey made in the Yucatán

Shrimp cocktails usually include giant *camarones* from the Gulf of Mexico or the Pacific. Ceviche—a seafood cocktail of fish marinated in lime, with chopped onions, tomatoes, and chiles—is usually wonderful, but make sure the fish is thoroughly "cooked" by the lime juice. It should look white and firm. If it smells fishy or has a rubbery texture, send it back. Ceviche *acapulqueño* (Acapulco style) contains ketchup or cocktail sauce. Octopus, or *pulpo*, is appearing on menus more frequently in both types of cocktails, as is conch.

Most coastal restaurants have red snapper (*huachinango*) on the menu, along with sea bass. *Dorado* (called mahimahi elsewhere) is found throughout Mexico, as are tuna, marlin, and wahoo. Xref is a primer with the Spanish names for the fish commonly caught and served fresh in Mexico. Other fish, such as salmon, will have been flown in from elsewhere.

Atún (tuna) Yellowfin, bluefin, and albacore tuna appear seasonally. Yellowfin is a pale, rosy color and has a high fat content that makes it perfect for grilled steaks or thinly sliced sashimi. Bluefin is darker in color and has a stronger flavor. Albacore is white and mild.

Dorado (mahimahi) Firm, light flesh cooks to delicate, sweet white meat.

Bonetero (wahoo) Delicate pink meat changes to flaky and sweet when cooked.

Huachinango (red snapper) This reliable standard has firm, pink flesh that works well with sauces and spices. It's often cooked Veracruz-style, with a sauce of tomatoes, onions, bell peppers, and olives.

Pez vela (marlin) Though the Spanish name literally means "sailfish," it's used for "marlin" as well. Fisherman catch blue, white, and striped marlin when in season, and they are encouraged to tag and release the fish to protect the species. Marlin isn't a great eating fish. Some people like grilled marlin steaks, but the flavor is strong and the meat tough. It's best smoked—or returned to the sea.

GREAT PLACES TO EAT

Best Romantic Restaurants

- **Baikal** Carretera Escénica 22, Acapulco Diamante; ☎ 744-446-6845
- **La Habichuela** Avenida Margaritas 25, Cancún; ☎ 998-884-3158
- **Mi Cocina** Boulevard Mijares 4, Los Cabos; ☎ 624-142-5200
- **Cafe des Artistes** downtown Puerto Vallarta; Avenida Guadalupe Sánchez 740; ☎ 322-222-3229
- **Tentaciones** Camino Escénico a Playa la Ropa, Zihuatanejo; ☎ 755-554-3443

Best Family Restaurants

- **Bisquets Obregón** Avenida Nader 9, Cancún; ☎ 998-887-6876
- **Chico's Paradise** Carretera a Manzanillo, Km 20, La Junta, Puerto Vallarta; ☎ 322-222-0747
- **El Jardín** Playa Zicatela; Calle del Morro s/n, Puerto Escondido; ☎ 954-582-2315
- **Emilio's** Paseo de las Garzas s/n, across from Hotel Ixtapa Palace, Ixtapa; ☎ 755-553-1583
- **Jeanie's Waffle House** Avenida Rafael Melgar between Calles 9 and 11, Cozumel; ☎ 987-872-4145

- **100% Natural** Costera Alemán 34, Old Acapulco; ☎ 744-484-8440

- **Panamá** Avenida Camarón Sábalo 400; Zona Dorada, Mazatlán; ☎ 669-913-6977

- **Pancho's** Hidalgo and Zapata, just off Boulevard Marina, Cabo San Lucas; ☎ 624-143-0973

- **Senor Frog's** Fracc. El Guitarrón; Carretera Escénica 28 at La Vista, Acapulco; ☎ 744-446-5734

Best Mexican Restaurants

- **El Arrayán** Allende 344 at Miramar, Downtown Puerto Vallarta; ☎ 322-222-7195

- **El Chilar** Juárez at Morelos, Los Cabos; ☎ 624-142-2544

- **Labná** Avenida Margaritas 29, Cancún; ☎ 998-892-3056

- **Paloma Bonita** Boulevard Kukulkán, Km 9, Cancún; ☎ 998-848-7000

- **El Sabor de Oaxaca** Avenida Guamúchil 206, Huatulco; ☎ 958-587-0060

- **Santa Fe** Playa Zicatela; Calle del Morro; Puerto Escondido; ☎ 954-582-0170

- **Yaxche** Calle 8 between Avenidas 5 and 10, Playa del Carmen; ☎ 984-873-2502

Best Gourmet Restaurants

- **Aïoli** Boulevard Kukulkán Km 14, Cancún; ☎ 998-881-2260

- **Baikal** Carretera Escénica 16, Fraccionamiento Guitarrón, Acapulco; ☎ 744-446-6845

- **Bouganvilleas** Playa Bacocho at Hotel Villa Sol; Avenida Loma Bonita 2, Fracc. Bacocho; ☎ 954-582-0350

- **Cafe des Artistes** Guadalupe Sanchez 740, downtown Puerto Vallarta; ☎ 322-222-3229

- **Casa Rolandi** Fraccionamiento Laguna Mar, Isla Mujeres; ☎ 998-877-0700

- **Club Grill** Ritz-Carlton Cancún, Retorno del Rey 36, off Boulevard Kukulkán Km 14; ☎ 998-881-0808

- **Pitahayas** Highway 1, Km 10, Los Cabos; ☎ 624-145-8010

- **Tentaciones** Camino Escénico a Playa la Ropa, Zihuatanejo; ☎ 755-554-3443

- **Trío** Guerrero 264, downtown Puerto Vallarta; ☎ 322-222-2196

Best International Cuisine

- **Daiquiri Dick's** Olas Altas 314, Puerto Vallarta; ☎322-222-0566

- **El Olvido** Costera Alemán s/n, in the Plaza Marbellas, Acapulco; ☎ 744-481-0203

- **Restaurant Frankfurt** Col. E. Zapata; Basilio Badillo 378; Puerto Vallarta; ☎ 322-222-2071

Best Seafood

- **La Cabaña de Caleta** Old Acapulco Playa Caleta s/n; ☎ 744-482-5007
- **Garrobo's** Downtown Zihuatanejo; Juan N. Alvarez 52; ☎ 755-554-6706
- **Lorenzillos** Boulevard Kukulkán, Km 10.5, Cancún; ☎ 998-883-1254
- **Nick-San** Boulevard Marina, Los Cabos; ☎ 624-143-4484

MEXICO RESTAURANTS RATED AND RANKED

RESTAURANTS OPEN AND CLOSE FREQUENTLY in resort areas, so most of those we've included have a proven track record. Our lists are highly selective. Just because a particular place is not reviewed does not necessarily indicate that the restaurant is not good, only that it was not ranked among the best in its genre. Restaurants with only one star in any category are still very good, just not as special as those with more stars.

In each regional chapter, we provide rankings that show how the restaurants in that area compare. In addition, we also provide detailed profiles for the best restaurants and for those that offer some special reason to visit, be it decor, ethnic appeal, or bargain prices. Each profile features an easily scanned heading that allows you, in just a second, to check out the restaurant's name, cuisine, overall rating, cost, quality rating, and value rating.

CUISINE In beach resorts where chefs are constantly pushing the envelope to create their own distinctive dishes, categorizing cuisine becomes a challenging endeavor. Mexican regional cuisine itself is an *olio* of recipes from all over the country twisted and shaped by a chef's preferences. A restaurant may serve chiles rellenos, for example, but the chef skips the traditional cheese and stuffs his chiles with lobster. Many chefs prefer not to be categorized at all, as they are afraid this will limit others' perception of their creativity. In most cases, we let restaurant owners or chefs name their own categories. In many cases, fusion cuisines are called simply "contemporary or international cuisine." You can get an idea of the type of food served from the heading, and then glean a better understanding by reading the detailed descriptions of specialty items and other recommendations.

OVERALL RATING The overall rating encompasses the entire dining experience, including style, service, and ambience, in addition to the taste, presentation, and quality of the food. Five stars is the highest rating possible and connotes the best of everything. Four-star restaurants are exceptional, three-star restaurants are well above average, and two-star restaurants are good. Some inexpensive restaurants are included in these higher categories because of the exceptional value and cuisine. One star indicates an average restaurant that demonstrates an unusual capability in some area of specialization—for example, an otherwise unmemorable place that has great fish tacos.

COST The expense description provides a comparative sense of how much a complete meal will cost. A complete meal for our purposes consists of an entree with a vegetable or side dish. Appetizers, desserts, drinks, and tips are excluded. Categories and related prices are as follows:

Inexpensive $10 and less per person

Moderate $10–$20

Expensive More than $20 per person

QUALITY RATING The quality rating ranks food quality on a scale of one to five stars, where five stars is the best rating attainable. It is based expressly on the taste, freshness of ingredients, preparation, presentation, and creativity of the food served. There is no consideration of price. If you want the best food available, and cost is not an issue, you need look no further than the quality ratings.

VALUE RATING If, on the other hand, you are looking for both quality and value, then you should check the value rating. Remember, the perception of value can vary from state to state and country to country. Mexico's resorts are traveler destinations, so restaurant prices probably compare favorably with prices in Miami, Los Angeles, and other major tourist destinations, but not so favorably with smaller, rural towns in Mexico. But don't think you'll eat cheaply just because you're in Mexico. Because it is a common perception that hotel restaurants are universally overpriced (where else would you pay $4 to $6 for a glass of orange juice?), we have indicated restaurants of this sort with a two-star rating rather than a discouraging single star. The two-star rating is meant to convey that yes, the restaurant charges perhaps more than you would pay for a similar entree somewhere else, but because the setting, service, and preparation are exceptional, it's still worth the splurge. We wouldn't want to rate the restaurant as a one-star, perhaps causing you to automatically forgo what could be a satisfying dining experience. The value ratings are defined as follows:

unofficial **TIP**
The older resort areas, including Mazatlán and Zihuatanejo, tend to have more inexpensive restaurants than Los Cabos or Cancún.

★★★★★	Exceptional value; a real bargain
★★★★	Good value
★★★	Fair value; you get exactly what you pay for
★★	Somewhat overpriced
★	Significantly overpriced

PAYMENT We've listed the types of credit cards accepted at each restaurant using the following codes:

AE American Express	MC MasterCard
DC Discover	V Visa

PART THREE

ARRIVING *and* GETTING ORIENTED

ARRIVING *by* AIR

THE FIRST THING MOST PEOPLE SEE at Mexico's beach resorts is an airport, which can be downright dismaying. Getting through customs and gathering your bags are fairly straightforward chores. Passing through the inevitable barrage of shouting cab drivers, time-share hustlers, rental-car agents, and other buskers is another matter completely. Blessed be the traveler whose name appears on a placard held high by a trusted guide or driver.

unofficial **TIP**
Many package tours include airport transfers that can make arrival less complicated. Look for a sign with the name of your tour company outside the airport exit. The drivers will have your name on a list and will whisk you off to the beach with ease.

IMMIGRATION

VISITORS ENTERING MEXICO MUST PRESENT a tourist card. The form, officially called the FMT (Folleto de Migración Turística), is usually handed out by airlines at check-in or during the flight. Fill out the top and bottom sections, sign on front and back, and be prepared to show your passport or certified birth certificate and picture ID (see "Passports, Visas, and Customs," page 32).

Be prepared for any number of scenarios upon landing. Some flights are routed through Mexico City's Benito Juárez Airport, necessitating a flight change. We have experienced instances when we were required to retrieve our luggage from the baggage department and submit it for inspection by the immigration officials. Other times, we have been swept along with only a cursory review of our person and carry-on luggage before being allowed to continue on to the gate to await our next flight. The walk from plane to immigration may be long, so try to keep your carry-on luggage light and easy to handle. When making your reservations, allow sufficient time for connections between flights, taking into account the possibility of an extensive search. Airline security in Mexico has been tightened and increased as it has in most countries of the world. Have your paperwork ready as you head through the lines and treat everyone with courtesy and respect.

unofficial **TIP**
Once you've shown your passport and tourist card, you'll receive the bottom half of the card. Don't lose it because you must turn it in to immigration officials at the end of your stay.

BAGGAGE CLAIM

UNLESS YOU'RE MAKING A CONNECTING FLIGHT, after receiving your tourist card you'll enter the baggage claim area. Most are fairly sophisticated setups with conveyer belts and attendants, but carts are usually nonexistent. Instead, passengers hire porters to haul luggage through customs. This is a good way to go if it's your first time in a Mexican airport. A porter will guide you to your desired mode of transportation. If your bags are missing, be sure to fill out the airline form as precisely as possible and hold on to your luggage tags. Write down as many names and phone numbers as you can while going through the process, and be sure to have the correct phone number for your hotel at hand. It may take a bit of persistence to track down lost bags, especially when you have connecting flights. Call the number the airline gives you frequently. If there's a language problem, ask someone at your hotel to help. In most cases, the airline will deliver the bags to your hotel. Before you go, pack your bathing suit, sandals, and a pair of shorts or skirt in your carry on—it makes the wait for your real clothes more tolerable.

CUSTOMS

INTERNATIONAL ARRIVALS MUST FILL OUT a customs form to enter Mexico, which uses the red-light, green-light system of selecting victims for secondary inspection. After you hand over a form listing the number of parcels you're bringing into the country, you're asked to push a button that lights either a red or green light. If you hit the red, you'll have to open your bags for inspection. Items that attract customs officials' attention include electronic equipment such as computers and cameras, food, and household items that may be subject to duty. If you're carrying new cameras and such for your trip, bring along the receipts.

GETTING TO YOUR HOTEL FROM THE AIRPORT

THE EASIEST AND MOST EXPENSIVE WAY to travel from the airport to your hotel is by private taxi. Official taxi stands are usually located within and outside the baggage claim area and post the prices to various destinations. Vans are becoming a more popular taxi option, especially at family-oriented destinations such as Cancún and Puerto Vallarta, and they are an expedient choice for groups of three or more.

The Time-share Hustle

A few years back, the shouts of time-share reps grew so loud at the Los Cabos airport that officials had to silence the din. They ruled that anyone who yelled at incoming passengers would be banned from hawking free rides and other come-ons. An amazing chorus of whispers replaced the verbal onslaught, and passengers felt as though they were passing through a hissing tunnel.

The hottest commodity for sale at the airports is transportation (see "Getting to Your Hotel from the Airport," page 69). If someone offers you a free ride to your hotel, rest assured you'll face a heavy-duty sales pitch along the way. In essence, you get a free ride, and the sales force gets a captive audience (diving out of a moving vehicle is discouraged). Enthusiastic salespersons offer all sorts of bargains during the journey; they only want a few hours of your time.

Your best bet is to ignore every come-on until you've gathered your bags and wits. Unless you want to hire a porter to haul your bags, don't let anyone grab them from your grip. Teams of men work for tips by leading passengers to various taxis and vans, and they can be rather aggressive in soliciting your business. Basically, don't get caught up in the noisy bustle that greets each arriving plane.

If you're trying to travel on a strict budget, the *colectivos* are your best bet. They are operated by the taxi drivers' union (a strong force in Mexico) and are minivans that travel along a fixed route for a fixed fare, stopping at several hotels en route. The trip may be tedious— many of the resort airports are located ten miles or more from the hotel zones and the additional stops can make the ride last an hour or more. Buy *colectivo* tickets at the official taxi counter. Package tours often include airport transportation in the mix, which simplifies everything and saves money. The larger local and international companies often have vans for their clients and whisk them off to hotels efficiently.

The most expensive resorts or those that are located far from the airport also offer airport transfers, usually for a fee. Check with your hotel when making reservations.

ARRIVING *by* CAR

MEXICO'S MOST POPULAR BEACH RESORTS lie far from the U.S. border, and travelers on short vacations usually don't arrive by car. But thousands of part-time Mexico residents, retirees, and travelers on extended journeys drive their own cars into Mexico every year and have no problems. However, there are some definite do's and don'ts.

MEXICAN AUTO INSURANCE

GETTING MEXICAN INSURANCE BEFORE your trip should be one of your top priorities. **Sanborn's Mexican Insurance** (☎ 800-222-0158; **www.sanbornsinsurance.com**) offers several types of policies and is a great source of driving info. Daily, weekly, and yearly Mexican insurance coverage is available. Most regular policies issued in the United States will cover you and your car if you drive into Mexico (AAA, for example, covers both collision and liability), but Mexico doesn't recognize them and you must purchase Mexican auto insurance as well. Some rental-car companies in the United States (but not all) will sell Mexican insurance riders along with their policies effective in the United States, but you need to request it at the time of reservation. If you forget until the last minute, there are "drive-up" windows selling insurance near many border crossings between Mexico and the United States.

REQUIRED DOCUMENTS

THE MEXICAN GOVERNMENT HAS INSTATED SEVERAL legal hoops to jump through if you plan on driving past the border zone (which includes the Baja California Peninsula and the Sonora Free Trade Zone). If you don't own the vehicle outright or if it is a rental car, a notarized letter of permission is required from the lien holder or lending institution, authorizing you to take the car into Mexico. If you purchase Mexican auto insurance from your rental car company, they'll include all the proper documentation for you.

If you drive your own car into Mexico, you'll need to bring your automobile registration. You will also need your tourist card and a valid driver's license. Once you have these documents ready, present them to the Vehicular Control Module at the border crossing customs office in order to obtain an importation permit. You will be required to post a bond, equal to the value of your car, or present an international credit card that will be charged $30. The name on the registration and the credit card must be the same, and the owner of the vehicle must be present. The permit is valid for six months and must be turned in to customs when you drive the car back out of Mexico. Heavy fines are levied for the vehicle remaining longer than six months. Keep these documents in the car at all times while driving in Mexico.

GETTING *around*
THE MEXICAN COAST

EACH RESORT AREA HAS ITS QUIRKS when it comes to transportation. In some areas, using public buses is a breeze. Cancún, for instance, has well-marked buses running the length of the hotel zone into downtown. Some of the buses are in horrid condition, mind you, but it's nice to be able to travel nearly anywhere you want for less than a dollar. Acapulco, Puerto Vallarta, and Mazatlán are easy bus-riding towns while Los Cabos is less user-friendly. Look for specific tips on riding local buses in the regional chapters.

TAXIS

TAXIS ARE THE MAIN FORM OF TRANSPORTATION for many travelers and locals. Cabs can be cheap if you look like you live in the area. Act like a tourist and you'll often pay far more. Most resorts now have official taxi fares, and drivers are supposed to carry charts explaining the fares. Many hotels list common taxi fares on boards at their front doors, and porters are happy to confirm the fare for you.

unofficial **TIP**
Using a file card or small notebook, make a crib sheet converting pesos to dollars in the most common denominations. You can check it quickly when negotiating prices in markets and taxis.

The oft-repeated key to riding taxis without getting ripped off deserves repeating. Settle the fare before the driver steps on the gas. If you're having a language problem or aren't sure what the driver is saying, confirm the fare in writing. We find the easiest way to handle the situation is to fix in your mind what you know is the proper fare, then announce that fare to the driver before you close the cab door. Check the hotel boards, inquire with resort staff, and ask other passengers what they pay for standard taxi routes.

We usually enjoy using taxis in Mexico. Many drivers are eager to practice their English and help with your Spanish, and the ensuing conversations can be informative. But recent encounters with some cab drivers have made us more wary. A few quadrupled the standard fare; others tried to give us less change when we paid (a common occurrence on buses as well).

If you're having trouble handling the taxi-driver hustle, try not to let it spoil your experience. Learn the fares and always carry small 10- and 20-peso notes and smaller change. Paying the exact fare makes everything easier.

If you meet a driver with whom you communicate well, ask about a private tour. Taxi drivers make great driver-guides, and they usually charge about $20 per hour depending on how far they'll drive. They'll take you from place to place, wait while you're touring around, and show you places you've never heard of. Hotel porters can arrange private taxi tours, but the fare might be higher.

RENTING A CAR

HAVING A CAR GREATLY EXPANDS your touring options. All the major U.S. car-rental agencies have desks at the beach resort airports, and most hotels have an agency in-house. Driving is fairly easy in most of the destinations in this book, and we usually recommend renting a vehicle at some point during your trip. The selection of rental vehicles has greatly improved in Mexico in recent years. Choices range from small sedans without air or music to new minivans with all the bells and whistles. Jeep-like vehicles without tops are popular with day-trippers; keep in mind that there's nowhere to stash your gear, and the sun gets mighty hot after a while.

The best way to ensure that you'll get the type of car you want when you want it is to make a reservation with an international company before your trip. If you're the type of person who needs all the details in place before relaxing, rent your car while at home. If you don't mind making last-minute decisions, wait till you reach your destination. Rates are sometimes (but certainly not always) lower in Mexico, and every destination has local rental companies. Local choices may range from serviceable to eccentric to dilapidated, though.

Obey all the rules you would when renting a car anywhere. Read the fine print. Examine your insurance options. Check with your car-insurance carrier and credit-card company—they *may* offer some form of insurance for rentals, but as stated on page 71, the Mexican government will not necessarily honor it in the case of an accident. Examine the car closely. We once rented a real lemon in Cozumel because it was the only car available. But we made sure the rental agent listed the missing spare tire and window crank on the form.

unofficial **TIP** Compare online car-rental rates at Internet cafes; you may be able to book the car online and save considerable money. You usually won't need to give a credit-card number to hold a car—and it's best not to give out any financial information over the Internet while traveling.

During most vacations at Mexico's coastal resorts, you need a rental car only for a few days. Use the central tourist zone as your base and figure out how many far-flung attractions you'll want to visit. Accessible and inexpensive public transportation makes it easy to get around the older cities or resorts, including Mazatlán, Acapulco, and Puerto Vallarta, and you need a car only for a day or two to explore the outlying areas. Having a car for the entire length of your stay is worth the expense in Los Cabos, where taxis charge exorbitant rates and the distances are great between good restaurants, beaches, hotels, and the airport. Wheels are a must if you're exploring any of the coastlines and changing hotels every few days. Check out the driving tips in each regional chapter for more specifics.

Driving in Mexico

Approach Mexico's roads as a kind of go-kart ride turned mad. In general, the pavement is in poor condition, and street signs are a novelty. Conditions are typically better in modern resorts,

When looking for an address you may not have a street number to guide you. Many locales don't assign street numbers; instead, you'll have an address like "Carretera Escenica s/n." The "s/n" stands for *sin número*–"without number." So all you'd know is that this address is somewhere on Carretera Escenica. Fortunately, for most addresses covered in this book, such areas are small enough that you can find your destination quickly just by driving on the correct road (the hotels will be in the hotel zone, restaurants will be near the beach, etc.). In places where this might be confusing, we'll help you out by providing extra landmarks and directions to get you where you want to go.

including Cancún, Cozumel, and Huatulco. Drivers are a mix of locals determined to prevail against their adversaries and befuddled travelers trapped in a maze.

Your driving experience is greatly affected by your destination, but there are certain commonalties. Be wary of truck and bus drivers, who rule the roads. Taxis are like ants scurrying around obstructions. Once a sign of prosperous growth, traffic lights (*semáforos*) have become all too common. Drivers usually respect red and green lights; but yellow is fair game for anybody.

Each region has its quirks, however. Cancún's street cops seem to work on commission, earning their salaries by handing out tickets (see more on the *mordida* under "Things the Locals Already Know," page 78). Potholes, sudden *vados* (dips) in the road, and construction crews are common on the Corridor highway in Los Cabos. Acapulco's Costera is a confounding series of *glorietas* (traffic circles) attached by a straightaway. Puerto Vallarta's Old Town area is best avoided by anyone in a vehicle who prefers to move at a steady pace rather than dealing with stop-and-go traffic. On the other hand, we enjoy driving Highway 307 along the Caribbean Coast but bemoan the surge of traffic and billboards. Taking a day to cruise along the single road on the windward coast of Cozumel is a joy; ditto Isla Mujeres. There are many grand drives around Mexico's coastal resorts. See each chapter for ideas.

The rules for driving in Mexico are so basic they're legendary. Keep the following concepts in mind.

DON'T DRIVE AT NIGHT. The old chestnut still holds true, though it's often ignored. If you find night driving unavoidable, know where you're going, figure out the least complicated route, and have a designated driver. If alcohol is involved, take a cab. Don't take long journeys at night—it's too easy to get lost, and streetlights are sometimes rare. If you're traveling in a rural region, you could suddenly encounter a wayward cow or a primitive roadblock of boulders or tree trunks.

OBEY THE SPEED LIMIT. That may sound like a joke, but trust us: *nobody* in Mexico drives the posted speed limit. Half the time you can't even find a sign (the usual limit on highways is 100 kmh, or 60 mph). We've been known to be rather lead-footed on rural roads and long stretches of toll freeways between destinations. But we've noticed an increasing tendency for local police to pull over travelers for bogus, as well as legitimate, reasons (see the section on the *mordida* on page 78).

FOLLOW THE FLOW. Many heavily trafficked cities and towns have one-way streets with no signs indicating the proper direction (Playa del Carmen, San José del Cabo, Crucecita). Watch which way other drivers turn and in which direction cars are parked. Closely examine the signs and traffic flow at *glorietas* (traffic circles); if in doubt, go around until you've found your proper turnoff.

GET A MAP AND DIRECTIONS. Most resort areas are developing so fast that maps are obsolete right after they're printed. Your rental agency should provide a decent map of the immediate area. Get any Mexico maps you can from an auto club or bookstore before leaving home. If you plan on driving extensively on back roads, look for Guía Roji maps in stores at home and at your destination—they're excellent, but expensive. Directions are easily obtained for standard in-town trips to restaurants or well-trodden traveler routes. Most hotel desks have printouts of directions and maps as do tour desks. If you're roaming around in a quandary, stop and ask several people for directions. As a rule of thumb, follow the route indicated by at least two sources.

WATCH OUT FOR SMALL TOWNS AND SPEED BUMPS. Many of the coastal resorts abut small villages and towns that have been forced to adapt to a steady stream of trucks and cars. The solution to slowing drivers down? *Topes,* or speed bumps. Almost anyone who's driven around Mexico has a version of the Tale of the Hidden Tope. They're driving along at a spirited clip, ignoring warning signs, when suddenly the car hits a huge bump in the road and lurches into the air. Dented axles, broken oil pans, and sore skulls are common. You may be approached by neighborhood kids and their parents selling bags of papayas and mangos, or spot a roadside stand. Don't be in such a hurry that you can't stop and wander around town for a while.

WAVE TO THE GREEN ANGELS. The Angeles Verdes (Green Angels) are heroes to any driver who's been blessed with their roadside assistance. They patrol the roads in marked green vehicles and pull off when they see anyone in trouble by the side of the road. They help change tires, usually carry enough extra gas to get you to the next station, and are great at minor auto repairs. You may have to pay for parts, and should give a tip. As a rule, Mexican drivers are eager to help out when you're stuck on the road, and mechanics can rig something together to keep you going.

KNOW YOUR RIGHTS. Accidents are inevitable if you drive a lot anywhere. Small fender benders are best handled between the drivers or with the rental company. Involve the police only if it's a major smash-up. The officials treat accidents as crime scenes and detain both parties until guilt is assigned. This could mean time in jail. Insist on speaking with your insurance company as soon as possible (make sure you get a list of phone numbers when you rent your car). We can't stress enough the importance of insurance (see "Mexican Auto Insurance," page 70). If you're driving without insurance, have an accident, and the police get involved, you will almost certainly face heavy fines and may even be arrested. Even one night in a Mexican jail is too many.

OTHER TRANSPORTATION OPTIONS

YOU HAVE PLENTY OF OPTIONS to avoid the whole driving hassle—a good idea if you're new to Mexico. Having a private driver and guide is by far the best choice. Hotels and tour companies can arrange this service, or you can wing it and hire a taxi driver.

Tour companies abound at every destination, and tours are often included in vacation packages and time-share deals. Ask for the details—length of travel time to and from the attraction and exactly what's included in the price—before signing up. Find out if you'll be herded around with a busload of strangers or transported in a van with more personalized service. Companies that specialize in specific tours are listed in the regional chapters.

THINGS *the* LOCALS *already* KNOW

COMPUTER CONNECTIONS

INTERNET CAFES CAN BE FOUND in busy resorts and small towns. While some are still using dialup connections, making surfing the Internet frustratingly slow, more and more places offer broadband. And wireless is increasingly common in hotel lobbies and restaurants. The cafes are busiest during lunchtime and just after work and school hours, when locals are Web-surfing and checking e-mail.

Some accommodations provide in-room Internet; many, including budget hotels, have a business center or computer where you can check your e-mail. Wireless access is becoming more common at hotels. But even if you're using your own computer to dial up to a local connection, you'll still be paying the hotel's phone fees. t's easiest and cheapest to go to an Internet cafe—you can type e-mails ahead of time, save to a memory stick, and take them with you to the cafe to upload.

CRIME

UNFORTUNATELY, MEXICO'S BORDER AREAS have become battle-grounds as drug cartels clash with each other and the police. In February 2009, the situation grew so serious that the U.S. State Department issued a travel alert cautioning vacationers to be aware of increasing violence in Mexico. The alert emphasized that most of the problems were taking place in the northern border states, far from the beach resorts (Cancún, for example, is 2,012 miles from Tijuana). The government did not officially warn citizens to stay away from all parts of Mexico, but it did caution tourists to be aware of their surroundings. In response to the alert and increased media coverage of the drug wars, Mexico's tourism officials have enacted measures to enhance safety for travelers.

Tourists should take the same precautions that they would any-where else in the world, using old-fashioned common sense: Leave the flashy jewelry at home. Carry your cash and passport in a money belt while traveling. At your destination, take only the money and credit cards you will need for the day, and leave the rest in the hotel safe. Hold tightly to your bag or purse, and don't leave it unattended. A man's wallet in his back pocket is an obvious target. Use licensed cabs everywhere—the cab's registration papers (with a photo of the driver) should be posted by the dashboard. Most importantly, stay away from trouble. Avoid areas where prostitution and drug use occur, and don't wander around inebriated at night.

Physical crime is less common at Mexican resorts than it is in U.S. cities. It's illegal to carry a firearm, and shootings are unusual. If you are the victim of a serious crime, contact your near-est consulate immediately. Before traveling, check the state Department's Web site (**travel.state.gov**) for alerts and current information on consular offices.

> *unofficial* **TIP**
> The emergency phone numbers in Mexico (equivalent to 911 in the United States) are ☎ 060 and ☎ 066.

GAYS AND LESBIANS

MEXICO IS A CONSERVATIVE AND PRIMARILY Catholic country, and homosexuality is tolerated but not outwardly encouraged. As you would expect, the larger cities and resorts have a more con-spicuous gay scene than the rural areas. In general, gays and lesbians who travel within Mexico are treated with respect. The **Gay Mexico Network,** a Web site (in English) devoted to gay issues and gay travel in Mexico, can be found at **www.mexgay.com.** The travel agency **Arco Iris** (☎ 800-765-4370; **www.arcoiristours.com**) specializes in gay-friendly Mexico travel.

MAGAZINES AND NEWSPAPERS

MEXICO DOES NOT HAVE A NATIONAL ENGLISH-LANGUAGE newspaper at press time. A local abbreviated edition of the

Miami Herald is available where gringos congregate, especially on the Caribbean side of the country, and some of the expensive hotels carry the *New York Times* or a shorter faxed edition of the *Times*. Many of the more popular U.S. magazines (*Time, Newsweek, People*) are available in English and Spanish editions.

MAIL

MAIL SERVICE IN MEXICO has improved in the last few years, but it's still not as efficient as we have come to expect in the United States or Great Britain. International mail sent from Mexico may take as long as three weeks to reach its destination. Make sure to write the name of the country and *por avión* (air mail) on the envelope. Sending packages by mail out of the country can be especially trying; if possible, have the shop where you make your purchases ship them for you. Post offices (*correos*) are generally open from 9 a.m. to 5 p.m. (sometimes 3 p.m.) during the week and 9 a.m. to 12:30 p.m. on Saturday, but hours vary from place to place.

MONEY AND CREDIT CARDS

CREDIT CARDS ARE READILY ACCEPTED at most hotels and restaurants in the resort towns. Carry traveler's checks if possible as well as a couple hundred dollars of cash for emergencies. Some smaller stores and restaurants accept none of the above. ATMs that accept universal credit and debit cards are located all around the tourist areas; look for them on main streets, in shopping centers, and in hotels. Most dispense pesos, but we have seen machines in Los Cabos that dispense dollars.

Lost or Stolen Credit Cards

Report missing credit cards to the police and the 24-hour (U.S.-based) lost-or-stolen-card bureaus below. Credit-card companies allow you to call their local numbers in the United States in emergencies.

American Express ☎ 800-528-4800; 01-55-5326-2660 (collect in Mexico); ☎ 336-393-1111 (call collect to U.S.)

MasterCard ☎ 800-307-7309; 001-800-307-7309 (toll-free in Mexico)

Visa ☎ 800-847-2911; 001-800-847-2911 (toll-free in Mexico)

THE *MORDIDA*

THE SYSTEM OF SLIPPING AN OFFICIAL a bit of cash to speed up inconvenient transactions has long been a part of life in Mexico, but it's one that tourists should approach with great caution. The *mordida*, as a bribe is called, is like a tip—one used to smooth over awkward situations or pesky bureaucratic red tape. The *mordida* is most commonly used during traffic stops. Some stops are justified; some are simply excuses for bald-faced extortion. Either way, it's easiest to ask how much the "fine" is and hand over the cash on the spot.

The government is trying to discourage this practice, however, and asks drivers to insist on receiving an official ticket and paying traffic fines at the police station. This simple request may discourage a police officer from further action if the charge is bogus. Even if the charge is warranted, you still may pay far less by following legal channels and dealing with the situation in an official setting. If you feel you've been extorted, contact the local tourist office and lodge a complaint. Do not attempt to use the *mordida* for any situation except the most minor traffic violations. Certainly do not try to hand over bribes at the accident scene. For anything serious, follow through on all standard channels and procedures, just as you would at home.

PUBLIC TOILETS

MEXICO'S RESTROOM SITUATION has improved considerably. Most tourist accommodations, restaurants, and attractions have modern plumbing with flushing toilets, toilet paper, and paper towels or hand dryers. Buildings that haven't been modernized have less reliable plumbing; you'll often encounter signs asking you to dispose of all paper products in a trash can by the toilet. Look for public restrooms at shopping malls and large supermarkets. If you're desperate, wander into a hotel lobby as if you're a prospective guest.

RADIO

AMERICAN ROCK 'N' ROLL IS PREVALENT at Mexican resorts. Most have a local classic-rock station playing tunes that make you feel like you've run into a long-lost friend. You're sure to hear The Beatles, Bruce Springsteen, and a heavy dose of disco. You also can find stations broadcasting the latest Latin music and Spanish oldies. It's fun to tune into call-in shows—helps keep your slang up to date.

SHOPPING

BARGAINING IS STILL ACCEPTABLE (even in the most upscale resort areas) in the artisan and public markets. It is customary to begin your bargaining at approximately half to two-thirds of the asking price and inch up from there. Asking for a reduced price at most brick-and-mortar shops will probably get you nowhere, but it never hurts to ask politely. Often, hotel shops and galleries have impressive selections of sportswear and well-made, authentic folk art at set prices.

Store Hours

Stores in Mexico are generally open between 9 a.m. and 7 or 8 p.m., with an occasional break of a couple hours in midafternoon (2 to 4 p.m.). This is especially true of the tropical climes. More and more stores in resort areas are remaining open on Sunday, too.

TELEPHONES

MAKING LONG-DISTANCE PHONE CALLS is expensive in Mexico. Many hotels add on exorbitant charges for local calls as well—make sure to get a list of the charges before picking up the phone. Ignore all come-on signs saying CALL HOME, DIAL 800, and so forth. The companies involved often tack on a hefty surcharge or use the most expensive carrier for your call.

The most practical, least expensive way to make calls is to use a phone card. **Telmex** phone-company cards come in denominations of 50 and 100 pesos. Stick the card into a phone with a slot, and a digital readout lets you know how many pesos you have left. Figure on using at least a 50-peso card if you're making a long-distance call. Calls to the United States cost about 50¢ per minute with a Telmex card. The cards are available at small shops, newsstands, and pharmacies. In some areas, private phone companies have installed card machines beside their public phones. These cards usually charge about $1 per minute to call the States.

We've noticed that some self-contained resorts don't have pay phones anywhere on the property—a definite rip-off as far as we're concerned. Look for phones in shopping malls—it's usually quieter than calling from the street. Coin-operated phones are nearly extinct.

For international calls from Mexico, dial ☎ **00,** then the country code, then the area code and number. The country code for the United States and Canada is ☎ **1,** for the United Kingdom ☎ **44,** for Australia ☎ **61,** and for New Zealand ☎ **64.** To reach Mexico from the United States, dial ☎ **011** (the international connection), then ☎ **52** (Mexico's country code), followed by the area code and local number.

To dial long distance within Mexico, dial ☎ **01,** then the area code and phone number. The area codes changed throughout the country in 2001, creating massive confusion. The change finally standardized phone numbers in Mexico . . . almost. All area codes now have three digits and local numbers have seven digits—except in Mexico City, Guadalajara, and Monterrey. There, the area codes have two digits and local numbers have eight digits.

Businesses have had a hard time keeping up with Mexico's constantly changing phone system. Brochures, business cards, and other materials often have older phone numbers with only five or six digits. See the regional chapters for info on local calls.

TELEVISION

THE MAJORITY OF HOTELS AND RESORTS in Mexico have either cable or satellite television available in the guest rooms, including CNN, some version of ESPN, and English-language movies. In some cases, there's also pay-per-view movies and access to U.S. networks, and you'll find yourself watching the local news from Denver or Dallas. We find it interesting to watch some local television, if only to check on the weather. Keep the local channels on in the background to become accustomed to hearing Spanish.

TIPPING

TIPPING IS EXPECTED IN the resort areas of Mexico. In some hotels, a daily gratuity charge is added to your bill—ask about the policy when you check in and tip accordingly. Gratuities are usually included in the room rate at all-inclusive accommodations. More restaurants are adding the tip to the bill, tacking on a 10%-to-15% service charge; still, nobody minds receiving a little extra cash for good service. Look closely before paying. Mexico has a service-oriented economy, and many workers depend upon the kindness of strangers for much of their income. Some say travelers (especially Americans) have raised the cost of tips, and workers have come to expect a generosity that locals can't match. We usually tip the high end of standard rates at major tourist areas and expensive businesses. Remember to tip tour guides and drivers. Though the tour may be included in some package or deal, dive masters, boat crews, and other guides are usually tipped.

Here are some guidelines on various kinds of tips:

BELLMEN AND PORTERS 10 pesos ($1) per bag.

CAB DRIVERS Normally not tipped just for the ride, but are tipped an additional $1 to $3 if they help with your bags or provide extra services.

HOUSEKEEPERS 10 pesos ($1) per day.

RESTROOM ATTENDANTS Many restaurants and discos have attendants that keep restrooms clean, hand each patron paper towels, and supervise an array of hairsprays, perfumes, and makeup implements (in the fancy discos). They expect a small tip, perhaps 3 to 10 pesos (25¢ to $1) depending on services rendered. In many cases, tips are their only income.

TOUR GUIDES About 10% of the tour's price; more for personalized service.

DRIVERS About 5% of the tour's price or $5 minimum per day.

WAITERS Start at 10% and work your way up to 15% if the service is exceptional.

PART FOUR

CANCÚN

MEXICO'S RESORT BOOMTOWN

MASTER-PLANNED CANCÚN IS THE COUNTRY'S most successful vacation destination. More than 3 million visitors stop by each year. They all leave with strong opinions. Lots of people say they hate Cancún—it's too touristy, too Americanized, too artificial. Others think it's an absolute paradise of white beaches, incredible blue water, fabulous hotels, and great restaurants, shopping, and nightlife. Reality, as always, lies somewhere in between.

 unofficial **TIP**
Hurricane Wilma nearly devastated Cancún's hotel zone in October 2005, but the area recovered quickly. The beaches were completely restored with sand pumped from the sea, though they lost their soft white-talcum consistency. The recovery didn't last long, though, and many beaches have washed away again. If sand is in your plans, ask about the beach before booking your room.

Cancún *is* beautiful, no doubt. Arriving planes fly above miles of dense green jungle before reaching a blue-on-blue panorama of sky and sea. It's the obvious place for a resort, as the government's tourism developers realized in the early 1970s. They quickly turned a narrow spit of sand into a 12-mile-long sampler of Everyman's vacation dream. Hotels of every imaginable architectural style rose on man-made beaches facing the open sea. Before long, languid sunbathers were lounging under the shade of palapas and sipping piña coladas at swim-up bars. Somebody put in a convention center; somebody else created a golf course. Everybody wanted in on the action.

Today's Cancún is an amalgamation of international hotels, restaurants, shops, and attractions. There is, quite literally, something for everyone—albeit something homogenized. When you visit Cancún, you're not really going to Mexico. Instead, you're headed into Las Vegas by the sea (sans gambling, though it's always rumored to be coming soon). The people who live in Cancún mostly came from elsewhere, though the city's been around long enough that second-generation residents are now driving cabs, cleaning hotel rooms, and running restaurants. Other workers from nearly every part of Mexico live in instant neighborhoods.

Most visitors never see this side of Cancún: the crowded rows of prefab houses and apartment buildings. They do sample a bit of downtown Cancún, often referred to as **El Centro,** shopping in public markets and dining in fine restaurants. But the majority of tourism-oriented businesses are located on the waterfront strip called the *zona hotelera* (hotel zone), which is shaped like the number 7, with the sea on one side and a series of vast lagoons on the other. At the top-east tip of the 7, downtown gives way to the hotel zone. At the foot of the 7, the zone connects to the mainland at Punta Nizúc, near the airport. Boulevard Kukulkán runs the length of the zone, and addresses are usually given in kilometers, with the lowest numbers closest to downtown.

There's so much to do in Cancún that you could hang around for a week or more. Die-hard shoppers ramble through a series of shopping malls. Water-sports enthusiasts have their choice of swimming, snorkeling, diving, sailing, fishing, Jet Skiing, kayaking, and more. Foodies can choose from dozens of restaurants. Families are well taken care of, and many hotels have children's programs and activities. Hotels capture their guests with spectacular pools, spas, and beaches; some are so grand you never want to leave the grounds.

Many of the best attractions—Maya ruins, theme parks, underwater preserves, islands—involve day trips away from your hotel. Tours are big business in Cancún. Sleek air-conditioned buses stream away to the Maya ruins at **Chichén Itzá** and **Tulum,** the water parks at **Xcaret** and **Xel-Há,** and beaches along the **Riviera Maya.** Boats float from marinas to beach parks on **Isla Mujeres,** coral reefs by **Punta Nizúc,** and sunset cruises along the shoreline. You may want to plan your tours before even reaching Cancún; making so many decisions can ruin a relaxing vacation.

There's a downside to paradise, naturally. The hotel zone becomes ever more crowded and has lost much of its early beauty. The lagoons and reefs have been drastically affected by construction and overuse. Hurricane Wilma actually helped Cancún in some ways. Workers

---

THE MANY NAMES OF KUKULKÁN

Boulevard Kukulkán, the main road through Cancún's hotel zone, is spelled several different ways depending on where you look or whom you ask. We've settled on "Kukulkán." (Note that "Plaza Kukulcán" is indeed spelled differently, however.)

quickly realized their lives depended on tourism, and a sense of genuine hospitality has returned. Movers and shakers realized that Cancún needed a serious new master plan to protect its image and reputation. They're trying to tone down the attention paid to spring break—a notoriously bawdy bash that's gotten way out of hand. One hopes they look beyond short-term payoffs and pay attention to the future of Cancún.

QUICK FACTS *about* CANCÚN

AIRPORT AND AIRLINES Nine miles southwest of downtown is **Cancún International Airport** (☎ 998-886-0028), the second-busiest international airport in Mexico. Most major Mexican, European, Canadian, and U.S. airlines fly into Cancún from the hub cities; connecting flights are available. **Alaska Airlines, American Airlines, America West–US Airways, Continental, Delta, Frontier,** and **Northwest** all fly nonstop from U.S. hubs to Cancún. **Aeroméxico** and **Mexicana** fly from Miami and Mexico City. **Varig, Iberia,** and **KLM** fly to Cancún from Europe. Many charter airlines travel nonstop to Cancún from major cities in the United States, Canada, Europe, and Australia. A new international terminal opened at the airport in 2008, greatly easing congestion at concessions (expensive water and snacks, pricey souvenirs) and in the parking lot. Tickets for a *colectivo* from the airport to your hotel can be purchased at the counter by the exit; prices vary between $8 and $15 depending upon location. Taxis from the airport to hotels cost around $45 to $55.

unofficial **TIP**
Many of Cancún's visitors are traveling on packages that include hotel transfers. Agents for hotels and tour companies await customers beyond the baggage claim area and time-share touts, and line up just outside the exit doors.

CLIMATE Cancún's high season (November to April) is mild, breezy, and temperate, with an occasional shower. Summer and fall are less predictable and are often hot and steamy. High buildings block the sea breeze, and you can work up a major sweat walking around in the hotel zone (we recommend doing your exploring in the early morning or at night). The average temperature is 80°F; night temperatures can dip to the high 60s in December and January.

DRIVING Major car-rental companies have desks at the airport and in hotels. You don't need a car if you're staying put in Cancún and taking organized tours. In fact, driving in the hotel zone can be a major hassle with slow traffic, lots of stoplights, endless buses, and local cops who enjoy passing out speeding tickets. If you want to explore the coast and archaeological sites, rent a car for a day or two rather than for your entire stay.

FERRIES Ferries to Isla Mujeres run from the Embarcadero in the hotel zone and from the town of Puerto Juárez north of Cancún. The Embarcadero ferries are the most convenient and run several

THREE STATES IN ONE

The Yucatán Peninsula is bisected into three states. **Quintana Roo,** one of Mexico's youngest states, runs in a skinny strip along the Caribbean Coast. Cancún is its most famous destination (and largest income generator), but the capital of the state is 237 miles south at Chetumal, on the border with Belize. The islands of Cozumel and Isla Mujeres are part of Quintana Roo. **Yucatán,** the largest state on the peninsula, forms a triangle from the peninsula's northern coast on the Gulf of Mexico to a narrow V at the juncture of Quintana Roo and the state of **Campeche.** Yucatán's capital city of Mérida is the seat of both the peninsula's ancient and modern worlds; it was originally built by the Spanish conquistadors with stones from the destroyed Maya city of T'Ho. Chichén Itzá, one of the most popular attractions near Cancún, is in the state of Yucatán. Campeche's eponymous capital city is the best-preserved example of Mexico's colonial-era walled cities and is a UNESCO (United Nations Educational, Scientific and Cultural Organization) World Heritage Site. Its southern jungles smother dozens of Maya archaeological sites. Campeche is also the country's largest oil producer, and the coastline along the gulf is lined with oil platforms.

times a day, depending on the season. Less expensive ferries run every half hour from 8 a.m. to 8 p.m. from Puerto Juárez; you'll need to take a cab or bus to catch the boat. To get a ferry to Cozumel, you must travel to Playa del Carmen, 42 miles south of Cancún.

GETTING AROUND Taxis are available at all hotels and malls and are easily flagged down on the street. Rates are fixed, though the zone system can be confusing. *Cancún Tips* puts a list of taxi fares at the front of each issue of the magazine; rip it out and carry it with you. Taxi rates in downtown are cheap; most trips should cost less than $8.

The bus system through the hotel zone and into downtown is one of the best in any resort area, but most buses are rundown and lack cool air. Still, for about $1 per person, you can ride the length of the hotel zone into town. The buses are not air-conditioned and are very crowded around 5 p.m. when workers are headed home. Hand your fare to the driver and wait for a ticket and change. Ruta 1 and Ruta 2 buses run between the hotel zone and downtown.

INTERNET ACCESS Lots of signs advertise Net cafes, but the reality often doesn't live up to the hype. Rates are high, and some cafes consist of a few computers in the middle of a shopping mall with rock music blaring in the background. Try **Web @ Internet** (Avenida Tulum 51; ☎ 998-887-2833), **Internet B@r** at the Forum (Boulevard Kukulcán Km 9; ☎ 998-883-1042), and **Kukulkán Plaza** (Boulevard Kukulcán Km 13; ☎ 998-193-0161).

RIP-OFFS AND SCAMS In the past we'e encountered a discouraging tendency among cab and bus drivers to rip off travelers, typically giving less change than you're due. Fortunately, the rip-offs are less

Isla Cancún

To Puerto Juárez ↑
and Punta Sam

Av. López Portillo

Av. Bonampak

Cancún City

See "Downtown Cancún" Map

Av. Tulum

307

Boulevard Mujeres

Ferry to Isla Mujeres

Bahía de Mujeres

0 — 2 mi
0 — 2 km

Km 3
Km 3.5
Km 4
Playa Linda
Km 5

❷

Playa Tortuga
❺

Punta Cancún
㉒
❽

Plaza Caracol

Km 7.5
⑩ Km 8
Km 7
㉑
⑲
Km 8.5 ❶
㉓ ㉜
㉚

Km 9
㉗ Km 9.5
㉘
㉛ Km 10
⑯
⑱
㉕ ㉖

Pok-Ta-Pok Golf Course ⛳

Canal Nichupté

Laguna Bojórquez

Playa Chacmool

⑪

Km 11.5

Laguna de Nichupté

Laguna del Amor

To Tulum
& Chetumal

Km 12

La Isla Shopping Village
⑰ ❼
㉔ ❸

Gulf of Mexico

Mérida
YUCATÁN

Isla Mujeres
● **Cancún**
○ *Cozumel*

Playa del Carmen

YUCATÁN PENINSULA

CAMPECHE
QUINTANA ROO

Caribbean Sea

㉙
⑬
⑮
㉚ ⑫

Caribbean Sea

Km 14

Beach 🏖
Golf ⛳
Ruins

Laguna Inglé

Canal Nizúc

To Airport
Paseo Kukulkán

Boulevard Kukulkán

❻ Km 16
❾
❹
Playa Delfines

⑭ Km 20
Punta Nizúc

21. Ty-Coz

● **ATTRACTIONS**
1. Cancún Convention Center
2. El Embarcadero
3. Interactive Aquarium
4. Playa Delfines
5. Playa Tortuga
6. Ruinas del Rey

■ **ACCOMMODATIONS**
7. Aqua Cancún
8. Dreams Cancún Resort and Spa
9. Gran Meliá Cancún
10. Hotel Presidente Inter-Continental Cancún
11. Hyatt Cancún Caribe Villas and Resort
12. Le Méridien Cancún Resort and Spa

13. Ritz-Carlton Cancún
14. Westin Resort and Spa Cancún

◆ **RESTAURANTS**
15. Aïoli
16. Cambalache
17. La Destilería
18. Lorenzillo's
19. 100% Natural
20. Puerto Madero

✿ **NIGHTCLUBS**
22. Azucar
23. Carlos'n Charlie's
24. Cinemark Cancún
25. The City
26. Coco Bongo
27. Dady'O
28. Dady Rock
29. The Grill
30. Le Méridien Lobby Bar
31. O Ultra Lounge
32. Señor Frog's

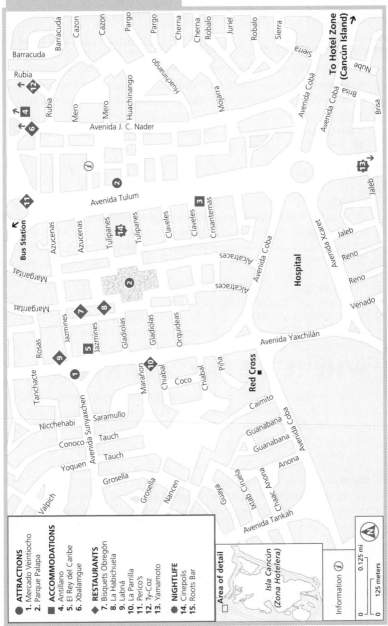

Downtown Cancún

To Hotel Zone (Cancún Island)

Avenida J. C. Nader

Avenida Tulum

Avenida Coba

Hospital

Bus Station

Avenida Yaxchilán

Red Cross

Avenida Tankah

Area of detail

Isla Cancún (Zona Hotelera)

Information ⓘ

0   0.125 mi

0   125 meters

ATTRACTIONS
1. Mercado Veintiocho
2. Parque Palapa

ACCOMMODATIONS
4. Antillano
5. El Rey del Caribe
6. Xbalamgue

RESTAURANTS
7. Bisquets Obregón
8. La Habichuela
9. Labná
10. La Parrilla
11. Perico's
12. Ty-Coz
13. Yamamoto

NIGHTLIFE
14. Cinepolis
15. Roots Bar

common since Wilma convinced most workers that happy tourists are essential to Cancún's economy. Do check the amount of change you receive from cab drivers and shop clerks. Carry lots of small bills and change, and try to give the driver the correct fare. Check fare boards in front of hotels, ask your hotel's porters about fares, and check *Cancún Tips*. Drivers who pick up passengers at the front doors of hotels typically charge more than those flagged down on the street.

TELEPHONES The area code for Cancún is ☎ **998.** All local telephone numbers have seven digits. Calls to Isla Mujeres and Playa del Carmen are long distance.

TOURIST INFORMATION The **Cancún Convention and Visitors Bureau** (☎ 998-881-2745; **www.cancun.travel**) is in the Convention Center (Boulevard Kukulcán Km 9). Open Monday through Friday, 9 a.m. to 6 p.m. (the posted hours are not always followed), the office is stocked with maps and promotional magazines but is more of a business center than a tourist-information office. Other helpful Web sites include **www.cancun.bz** and **www.travelyucatan.com.** If you lose your passport or have a complaint against some local agency or business, contact the **Consumer Protection Agency** (Avenida Cobá 10; ☎ 998-884-2369), open Monday through Friday, 8 a.m. to 2 p.m. and Saturday, 10 a.m. to 1 p.m.

Cancún Tips, an oversized glossy magazine, is invaluable for its maps, ads, and lists of taxi fares and bus routes. Pick one up as soon as you get to town. The local edition of the *Miami Herald* has a special section for the region with feature articles and news.

WHERE *to* STAY *in* CANCÚN

CANCÚN'S SKINNY HOTEL ZONE looks like a beach version of the Las Vegas Strip, with its architecturally staggering chorus line of vanity structures. Most hotels were remodeled and even rebuilt after Hurricane Wilma, improving facilities and furnishings in the process. The hurricane didn't discourage hoteliers, though. Nearly every hotel chain you can imagine has at least one property. **Sol Meliá** has two, **Fiesta Americana** has three, **Riu**'s two hotels dominate the Convention Center neighborhood, and the **Palace Resorts** has gobbled up huge chunks of land. If you're most comfortable with a familiar name, check our list of hotel chains in Part Two, Accommodations and Restaurants (see page 48), and see if your favorite a Cancún property. We've been very selective with our hotel profiles in Cancún, choosing one-of-a-kind places that stand out among the competition.

The vast majority of visitors arrive on some sort of package deal involving charter flights, transportation, tours, and other perks. Nobody pays the rack rate in Cancún—there's always some sort of deal to be had. Just make sure it includes the components you really want and not a lot of useless extras. The last time we landed

How Accommodations Compare in Cancún

ACCOMMODATION	OVERALL	QUALITY	VALUE	COST
Le Méridien Cancún Resort and Spa	★★★★★	★★★★★	★★★★	$$$$
Ritz-Carlton Cancún	★★★★★	★★★★★	★★★	$$$$$
Aqua Cancún	★★★★	★★★★½	★★★	$$$$
Gran Meliá Cancún	★★★★	★★★★	★★★½	$$$$
Westin Resort and Spa Cancún	★★★★	★★★½	★★★	$$$$
Hotel Presidente InterContinental Cancún	★★★½	★★★	★★★½	$$$
Dreams Cancún Resort and Spa	★★½	★★	★★	$$$
Hyatt Cancún Caribe Villas and Resort	★★★	★★½	★★★½	$$
El Rey del Caribe	★★½	★★★	★★★★	$
Xbalamque	★★	★★	★★	$
Antillano	★½	★★	★★½	$

at the Cancún airport, nearly everyone was whisked away in a tour company bus—airport transfers should be part of any package. There are still plenty of independent travelers in Cancún, and they run the gamut from celebrities on quick, ultraprivate escapes to backpackers headed into the Yucatán Peninsula.

Most budget hotels are located downtown, near Avenida Tulum and the bus station. Travelers with plenty of discretionary income have their pick of the hotel zone—some of the finest presidential suites you'll ever see are located in Cancún. When booking a room, pay close attention to the hotel's address. Several older properties line the beach and lagoon from Kukulkán Km 1 to Km 8, close to downtown and the Embarcadero. The beaches here weren't as damaged as others in the hotel zone and still have Cancún's famed soft white sands. Sea grass sometimes obscures the water's clarity, but it's usually fairly shallow and calm.

Rates rise as you reach the hotel zone's elbow at Punta Cancún, site of the convention center, the artisan's market, and many of the hottest discos. Cancún's fabulous beaches really start living up to their reputation at about Km 7.5 around the **Hotel Presidente InterContinental** and on to the **Dreams Cancún.** The water is calm and clear, and the beaches are clean. If you want to walk to everything you need, this is your best location. Another cluster of restaurants, malls, and hotels appears at Km 11, around Plaza Flamingo,

unofficial **TIP**
A tip for saving money: Consider choosing a room with a lagoon view rather than one overlooking the sea. If you're up high enough, the views of the sunset, green mangroves, and city lights are spectacular.

and again around La Isla and Plaza Kukulcán around Km 13. The beaches from Punta Cancún north were replenished after Wilma with sand dredged from the bottom of the sea. The sand isn't as white and soft as it was before and is eroding once again. Beaches come and go with the tide and season. Many hotels have made up for the lack of sand with elaborate pool decks. The beaches grow less crowded around the **Ritz Carlton, Le Méridien,** and other luxury hotels. Hotels from here to Km 20, at Punta Nizúc, tend to be expansive, but not necessarily expensive. They're more self-contained, and the quality of their beaches depends on how much sand has been trucked in at the moment. The water tends to be choppier here; sometimes the waves are high enough for boogie boards. Guests staying in this area rely on taxis and buses to get to the popular restaurants and malls.

ACCOMMODATION PROFILES

Antillano $

OVERALL ★½	QUALITY ★★	VALUE ★★½

Avenida Claves at Avenida Tulum, SM22; ☎ 998-884-1132; fax 998-884-1878; www.hotelantillano.com

Always clean and well maintained, the Antillano rises over Avenida Tulum, a very busy thoroughfare. The hotel is an excellent base for those traveling on a strict budget. Buses run from here to nearly everywhere, yet you can get a quiet room facing the side and back streets or the interior pool courtyard. The desk clerks and housekeepers are amenable, informative, and always willing to help budget travelers get the most from their Cancún experience. The pool's peaceful setting is a real plus for an inexpensive urban hotel.

SETTING AND FACILITIES

Location Downtown in the middle of the tourist zone, within walking distance of a bus station.

Dining Drinks and snacks at counter by front desk, Continental breakfast included in rate.

Amenities and services Pool.

ACCOMMODATIONS

Rooms 48.

All rooms AC, cable TV, telephone.

Some rooms Refrigerators.

Comfort and decor Rooms are small but with enough room for two suitcases; thin mattresses. Hallways are a bit dark, and you're at the mercy of central air-conditioning.

PAYMENT, RESERVATIONS, AND RESTRICTIONS

Deposit Negotiable.

Credit cards AE, MC, V.

Check-in/out 3 p.m./1 p.m.

Aqua Cancún $$$$

OVERALL ★★★★	QUALITY ★★★★½	VALUE ★★★

Boulevard Kukulcán, Km 12.5; ☎ 998 881 7600; 800 343 7821; fax 998 881 7601; www.feel-aqua.com

Aiming to please all the senses, the high-concept Aqua is filled with scents and unusual sights. Aromatherapy is big here, as is a New Agey ambience. Scarlet macaws fly above white-clad Tai Chi masters near the pools and the sensory gardens. Guests sip iced water while lounging on day beds in cabañas draped with white cloth, or check their e-mail with poolside Wi-Fi. Celebrity chef Michelle Berstein oversees the sleek MB dinner restaurant, and and Franco Maddalozzo does wonders with seafood at the poolside Azur. A splashy nightclub and high-tech gadgets throughout make Aqua the hippest hotel in town—for the moment.

SETTING AND FACILITIES

Location Hotel zone across the street from La Isla.

Dining 2 restaurants.

Amenities and services Beach, 8 pools, gym, spa, water-sports center, tour desk, shops, 2 bars, 24-hour room service, business center, Internet.

ACCOMMODATIONS

Rooms 371 rooms and suites.

All rooms AC, windows that open, ocean view, balcony or terrace, hair dryer, safe, minibar, coffeemaker, satellite TV, DVD/CD/MP3 player, telephone, whirlpool tubs.

Some rooms Lounge and dining areas, outdoor showers, separate bedrooms, private pool, disabled access.

Comfort and decor A soothing pale-blue-and-white color scheme is enhanced by mirrors reflecting sky and sea vistas. It's easy to linger late in the cloudlike beds. Lots of techie gadgets, including espresso machines and home-theater systems, may confound the uninitiated—make sure the porter explains everything. Rooms lack info booklets, which leaves guests wandering about until they figure out the property.

PAYMENT, RESERVATIONS, AND RESTRICTIONS

Deposit Credit-card deposit, 24-hour cancellation policy.

Credit cards AE, DC, MC, V.

Check-in/out 3 p.m./noon.

Dreams Cancún Resort and Spa $$$

OVERALL ★★½	QUALITY ★★	VALUE ★★

Punta Cancún s/n; ☎ 998-848-7000; 866-2-DREAMS U.S. and Canada; fax 998-848-7001; www.dreamsresorts.com

The all-inclusive Dreams has the advantage of an idyllic location at the tip of Punta Cancún in the middle of the hotel zone. The pyramid-shaped building and adjacent tower were built for the Camino Real, one of Cancún's first hotels, in the style of Mexican architect Ricardo Legoretta. The lobby building, with long, open-air corridors, faces a freshwater lagoon where dolphins swim within view of guests walking to the beach. The tower building sits at a place where some small Maya ruins are thought to have been an observation point. Snorkeling is best off the tiny beach on the south side of the tower. Some rooms were renovated after Wilma, but some rooms and the public spaces are rundown. Contests, movies, and games are held around the pool area and in the ballrooms, and the all-inclusive program includes an excellent seafood restaurant by the beach. A separate interactive dolphin facility has taken over the lagoons in front of the hotel. Guests in rooms facing the lagoons get a full-on view of the dolphins. Dolphin activities are not included in the all-inclusive plan.

SETTING AND FACILITIES

Location Hotel zone at Punta Cancún.

Dining 4 restaurants, all-inclusive.

Amenities and services Beach, 2 pools, gym, spa, water-sports center, tour desk, organized children's activities, shops, 5 bars, 24-hour room service, business center, Internet.

ACCOMMODATIONS

Rooms 379 rooms and suites.

All rooms AC, windows that open, ocean view, balcony or terrace, hair dryer, safe, minibar, coffeemaker, satellite TV, telephone.

Some rooms Fan, bathtub, whirlpool tub, VCR, high-speed Internet, non-smoking, disabled access.

Comfort and decor Simply decorated with white walls and drapes, bright blue and pink pillows, light wood furnishings, plenty of room to spread out your belongings, and spacious bathrooms. Though the furnishings and textiles have become worn in some rooms, the rooms are spacious and airy with marble floors, white cotton rugs by the beds, floor-to-ceiling windows, and large closets. Rooms on the first floor have hammocks on balconies.

PAYMENT, RESERVATIONS, AND RESTRICTIONS

Deposit 2 nights charged if cancellation occurs less than 72 hours before arrival.

Credit cards AE, DC, MC, V.

Check-in/out 3 p.m./noon.

Gran Meliá Cancún $$$$

OVERALL ★★★★	QUALITY ★★★★	VALUE ★★★½

Boulevard Kukulkán Km 16.5; ☎ **998-881-1100 or 800-336-3542; fax 998-881-1740; www.solmelia.com**

You can't miss this series of glass pyramids between the beach and the boulevard—the place looks like a modern Maya city. The Meliá is a good choice for those seeking a long, relatively quiet stretch of beach and five-star service and facilities. A post-Wilma makeover added a spiffy sushi lounge, fitness center, and spa and modernized the overall look, giving the rooms and public areas a sophisticated, sleek appearance. Vines hanging from interior balconies flourish in the light that streams through the trapezoidal glass roof, making the atrium lobby feel like a greenhouse. The restaurants are remarkably good.

SETTING AND FACILITIES

Location Hotel zone close to La Isla shopping center and AquaWorld marina.

Dining 6 restaurants.

Amenities and services Beach, 2 pools, hot tub, gym, spa, tour desk, organized children's activities, shops, 5 bars, 24-hour room service, business center, Internet, 9-hole golf course.

ACCOMMODATIONS

Rooms 676 rooms and suites.

All rooms AC, windows that open, bathtub, hair dryer, safe, minibar, coffee-maker, plasma screen TV, telephone.

Some rooms Ocean view, balcony or terrace, nonsmoking, disabled access, butler service.

Comfort and decor The adults-only Royal Service wing of the hotel is worth the splurge for its private lounge, swimming pool, and beach palapas shading Bali beds (think white mattresses) rather than lounge chairs. The nonexclusive area is pretty special as well. The rooms have a cool, minimalist beige-and-white decor with touches of orange to perk things up.

PAYMENT, RESERVATIONS, AND RESTRICTIONS

Deposit Credit card guarantee; 3-day cancellation policy.

Credit cards AE, MC, V.

Check-in/out 3 p.m./noon.

Hotel Presidente InterContinental Cancún $$$

OVERALL ★★★½	QUALITY ★★★	VALUE ★★★½

Boulevard Kukulkán Km 7.5; ☎ 998-848-8700 or 888-424-6835; fax 998-883-2515; cancun.interconti.com

We love greeting the porters and housekeepers at the Presidente, one of Cancún's first hotels. Many of the staff members have been here for more than a decade and greet guests like old friends. The architecture is sleek and clean and has benefited from a complete remodel post-Wilma. The lobby is now airy and open with views of the sea, and a new beach bar is the best sunset watching spot in the hotel zone. Residential complexes on both sides of the hotel keep the beach uncrowded, and the clear, calm water is perfect for swimming and snorkeling. The lack of balconies for the rooms is a disappointment, but many of Cancún's older hotels suffer from the same problem yet remain popular with longtime fans.

Location Hotel zone near Plaza Caracol.

Dining 2 restaurants.

Amenities and services Beach, 2 pools, 3 hot tubs, gym, massage, water-sports center, tour desk, organized children's activities, shops, 2 bars, 24-hour room service.

ACCOMMODATIONS

Rooms 299 rooms and suites.

All rooms AC, bathtub, hair dryer, safe, minibar, coffeemaker, cable TV, telephone.

Some rooms Windows that open, ocean view, balcony or terrace, whirlpool tub, nonsmoking, disabled access.

Comfort and decor We love the cool marble floors, light pine furnishings, and clean white decor broken up with splashes of coral-colored fabrics. But the rooms are outdated compared with the competition, and bathrooms and TVs need upgrading. Rooms without balconies are disappointing—don't stay there unless you're on a strict budget. Those with balconies on the club floors are best.

PAYMENT, RESERVATIONS, AND RESTRICTIONS

Deposit Credit card; 3-day cancellation policy; penalties vary with season.

Credit cards AE, DC, MC, V.

Check-in/out 3 p.m./noon.

Hyatt Cancún Caribe Villas and Resort $$

OVERALL ★★★	QUALITY ★★½	VALUE ★★★½

Boulevard Kukulkán Km 10.5; ☎ 998-848-7800 or 800-633-7313 U.S. and Canada; fax 998-883-1514; www.hyatt.com

The main hotel building sits behind a series of tile-roofed beachfront villas bordered by generous lawns, gardens, and a curving beach. The hotel's lush trees and gardens were stripped bare by Wilma, but green leaves are sprouting everywhere and the tropical feeling is almost back. During the ten months it was closed, the Hyatt upgraded the rooms and facilities with marble flooring, a new infinity pool and whirlpool, and a sea-view fitness center. The Blue Bayou restaurant is back and often packed with regulars who enjoy the outstanding food and fine jazz groups who perform in the lounge.

SETTING AND FACILITIES

Location Hotel zone.

Dining 3 restaurants.

Amenities and services Beach, 2 pools, 1 hot tubs, gym, massage, tour desk, organized children's activities (in summer only), shops, 2 bars, 24-hour room service, business center.

ACCOMMODATIONS

Rooms 239 rooms and suites.

All rooms AC, windows that open, balcony or terrace, bathtub, hair dryer, coffeemaker, minibar, flat-screen TV, safe, telephone, high-speed Internet.

Some rooms Ocean view, hot tub, disabled access.

Comfort and decor Some rooms are decorated in white and Mediterranean blue, others in beige on white with marble floors and large bathrooms with bathtubs and rain showers. Regency Club rooms and suites have private concierge, Continental breakfast, afternoon cocktails, and a private beach area and pool.

PAYMENT, RESERVATIONS, AND RESTRICTIONS

Deposit Credit card; 3-day cancellation policy.

Credit cards AE, MC, V.

Check-in/out 3 p.m./noon.

Le Méridien Cancún Resort and Spa $$$$

OVERALL ★★★★★	QUALITY ★★★★★	VALUE ★★★★

Retorno del Rey 37-1 at Boulevard Kukulkán Km 14; ☎ 998-881-2200 or 800-543-4300; fax 998-881-2201; www.starwoodhotels.com

A small street cuts between Kukulkán and the beach to reach this exclusive housing and hotel area. Limos and sports cars pull up to Le Méridien's pillared porte cochere, and guests enter a sunlit atrium lobby in the stunning Art Deco–style building. Once settled into their subtly elegant rooms, guests have little reason to leave the property. The freestanding Spa del Mar is one of our favorites in Cancún (it's open to the public by appointment). Though the setting is chic and elite, the courteous, friendly staff members make everyone feel at home. The resort is an excellent choice for families because the well-equipped children's center is open daily year-round. The three pools are set at different temperatures and are staggered down a slight hill to the slender beach—similar thoughtful touches make guests feel special. Consider a breakfast (the buffet at Aïoli restaurant is superb), dinner, or spa treatment here as your special splurge if you're staying elsewhere. The restaurant le St. Trop opened on the beach in 2006, giving diners a chance to sample the chef's masterpieces under the stars. There's a lot to be said for professional pampering.

SETTING AND FACILITIES

Location Hotel zone in a private area off a side road called Retorno del Rey.

Dining 2 restaurants.

Amenities and services Beach, 3 pools, hot tubs, gym, spa, water-sports center, tour desk, organized children's activities, shops, 2 bars, 24-hour room service, business center, Internet.

ACCOMMODATIONS

Rooms 213 rooms and suites.

All rooms AC, windows that open, ocean view, bathtub, hair dryer, minibar, coffeemaker, satellite TV, DVD, telephone, Internet.

Some rooms Balcony or terrace, whirlpool tub, refrigerator, kitchenette, nonsmoking, disabled access.

Comfort and decor The soft beige, gray, coral, and green color scheme adds an elegance that's not overwhelming. Bathrooms have separate shower and tub. Least-expensive rooms do not have balconies; some more expensive rooms have extra-large balconies with lounge chairs.

PAYMENT, RESERVATIONS, AND RESTRICTIONS

Deposit Credit card; 3-day cancellation policy.

Credit cards AE, DC, MC, V.

Check-in/out 3 p.m./noon.

El Rey del Caribe $

OVERALL ★★½	QUALITY ★★★	VALUE ★★★★

Avenida Uxmal 24 (at Nader); ☎ 998-884-2028; fax 998-884-9857; www.reycaribe.com

This is one of our favorite budget hotels in Mexico. A veritable jungle of trees and bushes surrounds the low-lying buildings and small pool where guests gather for snacks and drinks. The owner is extremely conscious about environmental impact, recycling and using solar power for heaters and clothes dryers. There's no restaurant, but you can get juices and purified water at the lobby, where signs are posted announcing Tai Chi classes and other activities.

SETTING AND FACILITIES

Location Downtown, in a quiet neighborhood within easy walking distance of bus stops.

Dining No restaurant, but there are several in the immediate area; Continental breakfast is included in the rate, which lowers if you skip breakfast.

Amenities and services Pool, hot tub, massage.

ACCOMMODATIONS

Rooms 25.

All rooms AC, ceiling fan, kitchenette, cable TV, telephone, nonsmoking.

Some rooms Pool-front.

Comfort and decor Rooms are compact and have beds on cement platforms. Though simple, they're well maintained, and the ambience and camaraderie among guests make up for basic accommodations.

PAYMENT, RESERVATIONS, AND RESTRICTIONS

Deposit Credit card deposit; 8-day cancellation policy; penalties negotiable.

Credit cards MC, V.

Check-in/out 2 p.m./noon.

Ritz-Carlton Cancún $$$$$

OVERALL ★★★★★	QUALITY ★★★★★	VALUE ★★★

Retorno del Rey 36, off Boulevard Kukulkán Km 14; ☎ 998-881-0808 or 800-241-3333; fax 998-885-0815; www.ritzcarlton.com

The Ritz-Carlton underwent a massive renovation after Wilma and was closed for nearly a year before reopening as the most elegant hotel in Cancún. Despite the opportunity to become more casual, the hotel remains an anomaly on the white sands of Cancún, with European antiques, silk wallpaper, thick carpets, and glittering chandeliers. Guests who will follow the Ritz anywhere are pleased with the attention to detail, impeccable service, and luxurious amenities, which have been updated to include espresso machines and LCD TVs in the rooms. The food is exceptional, and guests can learn to cook like a Ritz chef at the Culinary Center. Local musicians, foodies, and like-minded guests choose the hotel's Club Grill for special occasions. The Ritz also offers dining in private cabañas on the beach. The Kayanta Spa specializes in treatments using regional ingredients and techniques.

SETTING AND FACILITIES

Location Off the hotel zone on a private road.

Dining 3 restaurants.

Amenities and services Beach, 2 pools, hot tub, gym, spa, tour desk, organized children's activities, shops, 4 bars, 24-hour room service, business center, Internet.

ACCOMMODATIONS

Rooms 365 rooms and suites.

All rooms AC, windows that open, ocean view, bathtub, hair dryer, safe, minibar, satellite TV, VCR/DVD/CD, high-speed Internet.

Some rooms Balcony or terrace, whirlpool tub, nonsmoking, disabled access

Comfort and decor. The subdued rosy-beige color scheme, soft lighting, upholstered furnishings, and plush carpeting reflect the traditional Ritz style. Marble bathrooms glow with flattering lighting and have makeup mirrors; in a bow to the times, the showers have rainshower heads. Some suites have a private dressing area; others can be set up with a baby's nursery.

PAYMENT, RESERVATIONS, AND RESTRICTIONS

Deposit Flexible.

Credit cards AE, DC, MC, V.

Check-in/out Flexible.

Westin Resort and Spa Cancún $$$$

OVERALL ★★★★	QUALITY ★★★½	VALUE ★★★

Boulevard Kukulkán Km 20; ☎ 998-848-7400 or 800-228-3000 U.S. and Canada; fax 998-885-0666; www.westincancun.com

If you're looking for seclusion and privacy, the Westin is an excellent choice. It sits between a lagoon and the ocean, with beaches on both sides (watching the sunset is best from the lagoon beach) and expanses of undeveloped shoreline. Long, stark hallways lead from the lobby to the hallways; windows recessed in ultramarine blue niches frame stunning views of the sea. The Westin is the last property in the hotel zone and shops and restaurants are not within easy walking distance. But the bus stops by the entrance, cabs are plentiful, and you're removed from the zone's noise and bustle. Now a Starwood property, the hotel has all the brand's special touches, including Heavenly Beds and a Heavenly Spa with *temazcal*, a steam bath based on Maya healing practices. Pets are welcome, and the kid's club is a separate building on the lagoon side between the two towers.

SETTING AND FACILITIES

Location Southern hotel zone near Punta Nizúc.

Dining 3 restaurants.

Amenities and services 2 beaches, 4 pools, 5 hot tubs, gym, spa, water-sports center, tour desk, organized children's activities, shops, 3 bars, 24-hour room service, business center, Internet.

ACCOMMODATIONS

Rooms 379.

All rooms AC, bathtub, hair dryer, safe, minibar, coffeemaker, cable TV, telephone, high-speed Internet.

Some rooms Windows that open, ocean view, balcony or terrace, whirlpool tub, nonsmoking, disabled access.

Comfort and decor Rooms are delightfully comfortable with the trademark Westin Heavenly Bed as the main attraction. The stark white on white decor, broken by touches of blue in the furnishings, gives a sense of space, and sleeping with the sliding doors open is pure bliss. Bathrooms are large, with separate showers and tubs.

PAYMENT, RESERVATIONS, AND RESTRICTIONS

Deposit Credit card guarantee; 24-hour cancellation policy.

Credit cards AE, DC, MC, V.

Check-in/out 3 p.m./noon.

Xbalamque $

OVERALL ★★	QUALITY ★★	VALUE ★★

Avenida Yaxchilán 31; ☎ 998-884-9690; fax 998-8887-3055; www.xbalamque.com

The combination of a good restaurant and cantina, a bookshop and coffeehouse, and artistic decor makes this a standout in the budget category. Quality is slipping, however, and the staff could use a good pep talk concerning courteous service. The facilities and rooms need attention and updating as well. Most times, Xbalamque is filled with travelers who want to be in the heart of the city, near the bus station and locals' neighborhoods and businesses.

SETTING AND FACILITIES

Location Downtown near Parque Palapa, the bus station, and restaurants.

Dining 2 restaurants, 1 coffeehouse.

Amenities and services Pool, spa, gym, shop, bar.

ACCOMMODATIONS

Rooms 80 rooms, 12 suites.

All rooms AC, cable TV, telephone.

Some rooms Nonsmoking.

Comfort and decor Though somewhat run-down, the rooms are comfy with thoughtful touches such as good bedside lighting, ample tiled bathroom counters, and small desks.

PAYMENT, RESERVATIONS, AND RESTRICTIONS

Deposit 2-night deposit to reserve; penalties for cancellation during high season and holidays; 48-hour cancellation policy in low season; 5-day policy in high season.

Credit cards No credit cards.

Check-in/out Negotiable.

 # WHERE *to* EAT *in* CANCÚN

IN CANCÚN, THERE'S A RESTAURANT for every sort of appetite. If you're most comfortable eating familiar foods, you won't be disappointed. And if you've heard about chain restaurants that aren't in your neck of the woods, you'll probably find them in Cancún. We've left out most of the chains, but there are some standouts. The **Rainforest Cafe** in the Forum Plaza has a misty, jungle decor that's cool and refreshing, and their juice bar is a great place to recoup your energy. The **Hard Rock Cafe** has enough distractions for families with teens, as do **El Shrimp Bucket, Señor Frog's,** and **Carlos'n Charlie's.** Prices are similar to those in California or Florida, and dress is casual. Reservations are a must in the high season at many places, and they are a good idea anytime if you're traveling with kids and don't want to wait around. Some places that don't normally accept reservations will make them for parties of six or more. There are several free publications listing restaurant menus and tips; look for *Restaurante Menu Mapa* and *Cancún Menus*.

RESTAURANT PROFILES

Aïoli ★★★★★

MEXICAN/MEDITERRANEAN	EXPENSIVE	QUALITY ★★★★★	VALUE ★★★

Hotel zone just past Plaza Kukulkán, in Le Méridien Hotel; Boulevard Kukulkán Km 14; ☎ 998-881-2260

Reservations Essential in high season.

Entree range $17–$36.

Payment AE, MC, V.

How Restaurants Compare in Cancún

RESTAURANT | CUISINE | COST	OVERALL	QUALITY	VALUE
Aïoli | Mexican/ Mediterranean | Exp	★★★★★	★★★★★	★★★
Puerto Madero | Argentine Steak House | Exp	★★★★½	★★★★½	★★★
Cambalache | Steak House | Exp	★★★★	★★★★	★★★★
La Habichuela | Caribbean | Exp	★★★★	★★★★	★★★★
La Parrilla | Traditional Mexican | Mod	★★★★	★★★★	★★★★
Labná | Yucatecan | Mod	★★★★	★★★★	★★★★
La Destilería | Regional Mexican | Exp	★★★½	★★★	★★★
Yamamoto | Japanese | Mod	★★★	★★★	★★★★
Lorenzillo's | Seafood | Exp	★★★	★★★	★★★
Ty-Coz | Sandwiches | Inexp	★★★	★★★	★★
100% Natural | Health Food | Inexp	★★½	★★½	★★★★
Bisquets Obregón | Mexican | Inexp	★★	★★	★★★
Perico's | Mexican | Mod	★★	★½	★

Service rating ★★★★.

Parking Valet.

Bar Extensive imported liquor and wine list.

Dress Bring out the best dress, jewels, and linen slacks.

Disabled access Yes.

Customers Discerning diners with discretionary income.

Hours Daily, 6:30 a.m.–11 p.m.

SETTING AND ATMOSPHERE Views of the ocean or pool, covered terrace seating available, fine crystal and courtly service.

HOUSE SPECIALTIES Breakfast buffet; duck breast with honey-and-lavender sauce; lobster tail with a fricassee of vegetables, bouillabaisse sauce, and polenta gnocchis. Specialties change with the season.

SUMMARY AND COMMENTS Champagne or mimosas served in delicate flutes make a great accompaniment for the sublime breakfast buffet, and dinner is a glorious affair with perfect service, excellent wines, and outstanding cuisine with a Provençal flair. The Caesar salad is topped with shrimp and kalamata olives, the shrimp cream soup with lobster ravioli is divine, and the tuna carpaccio is so fresh it tastes of the sea. And that's just the starters (we've been known to choose appetizers and soups or salads for our meal, since we must leave room for dessert). The Angus filet with foie gras and chaterelle mushrooms is a standout, as is the marinated boquinete baked in a salt crust. The coffee drinks topped with fresh whipped cream could stand in for dessert, but they're even better when accompanied with a hot-chocolate fondant with pistachio ice cream.

Bisquets Obregón ★★

MEXICAN	INEXPENSIVE	QUALITY ★★	VALUE ★★★

**Downtown (other locations opening in hotel zone); Avenida Nader 9;
☎ 998-887-6876**

Reservations Not accepted.

Entree range $2–$6.

Payment MC, V.

Service rating ★★★.

Parking Limited street parking.

Bar Full service.

Dress Casual.

Disabled access Yes.

Customers Locals and travelers, families (kid's menu).

Hours Daily, 7 a.m.–1 a.m.

SETTING AND ATMOSPHERE Bustling coffee shop packed almost constantly; noise level is high. Separate nonsmoking area.

HOUSE SPECIALTIES *Café con leche,* biscuits, pastries, omelets.

SUMMARY AND COMMENTS Waiters pour the *café con leche* Veracruz style, using big separate pots filled with strong dark coffee and steaming milk. Other waiters carry around trays of fresh biscuits and pastries—the choices are irresistible. Breakfast is the main event, served all day, along with sandwiches and full meals.

Cambalache ★★★★

STEAK HOUSE	EXPENSIVE	QUALITY ★★★★	VALUE ★★★★

**Hotel zone in Forum Plaza, Boulevard Kukulkán Km 9;
☎ 998-883-0902; www.grupocambalache.com**

Reservations Recommended.

Entree range $12–$27.

Payment AE, MC, V.

Service rating ★★★★½.

Parking In Forum Plaza lot.

Bar Full service, imported wines.

Dress Smart casual.

Disabled access Yes.

Customers Travelers and locals on big night out.

Hours Daily, 1 p.m.–1 a.m.

SETTING AND ATMOSPHERE Tango music plays in the background and waiters in white shirts and ties bustle about wood tables crowded in several dining rooms. The raised seating areas to the sides of the main dining room are more romantic.

HOUSE SPECIALTIES Beef, suckling pig on a spit, souffléd fried potatoes.

SUMMARY AND COMMENTS Argentina meets Mexico at this wildly popular restaurant where diners sate cravings for prime meat. The beef is displayed on a tray; waiters are adept at describing the various cuts and the sweetbread and sausage appetizers. Salads are big enough for two and the meat is best served Argentine style, grilled and served on platters with a salad of tomatoes and onion, and baskets of fried potatoes. Cambalache is more casual than Cancún's other steak houses, and the prices here are lower for meats of similar quality.

La Destilería ★★★½

REGIONAL MEXICAN   EXPENSIVE   QUALITY ★★★   VALUE ★★★

Hotel zone, across from Plaza Kukulcán; Boulevard Kukulkán Km 12.65; ☎ 998-885-1087

Reservations Accepted; recommended for groups.

Entree range $11–$25.

Payment AE, MC, V.

Service rating ★★★★.

Parking Small lot.

Bar Full service, 150 brands of tequila.

Dress Casual.

Disabled access Restrooms are upstairs.

Customers Mexicans familiar with the chain, travelers looking for good Mexican food.

Hours Daily, 1 p.m.–midnight.

SETTING AND ATMOSPHERE Designed to resemble a tequila distillery and museum with room-size vats, large pipes, and other accoutrements around the dining room and bar. Check out the old black-and-white photos of tequila distillery workers. Comfortable and casual, yet you could dress up for a special night out.

HOUSE SPECIALTIES Pork ribs with spicy tamarind sauce and smoked jalapeño chile peppers, seafood and mango salad, chicken *pipián* (sauce with nuts, chiles, and spices).

SUMMARY AND COMMENTS It's not just a restaurant—it's an experience. The menu is unusual for the area, with lots of regional meat dishes from Jalisco and Sonora (and a chile rating for spiciness). The company is from Guadalajara, and the city's renowned mariachis are ever-present. Sample rare tequilas and *panuchos, chalupas,* and *sopes* in the bar.

La Habichuela ★★★★

CARIBBEAN	EXPENSIVE	QUALITY ★★★★	VALUE ★★★★

Downtown; Avenida Margaritas 25; ☎ 998-884-3158

Reservations Recommended.

Entree range $13–$21.

Payment AE, MC, V.

Service rating ★★★★.

Parking Street parking.

Bar Full service.

Dress Dressy casual.

Disabled access Possible.

Customers Couples, some families, professionals at lunch.

Hours Daily, 1 p.m.–midnight.

SETTING AND ATMOSPHERE The back garden, with Maya carvings and statues, is one of the most romantic places in Cancún, filled with twinkling candlelight. The back of the menu includes a guide to the replicas of Maya altars, masks, and carved columns that decorate the garden area.

HOUSE SPECIALTIES *Cocobichuela* (lobster and shrimp in curry sauce, served in a coconut shell and garnished with tropical fruit), seafood parade platter.

SUMMARY AND COMMENTS The Pezotti family, owners of several Cancún restaurants, created this special, romantic retreat in 1977, and it remains a delight. Try the famed cream of *habichuela* (string bean) soup, ginger shrimp, or *filete á la tampiqueña,* a traditional Mexican sampler platter. Finish with a snifter of *xtabentun,* a sweet liqueur said to be a Maya aphrodisiac.

Labná ★★★★

YUCATECAN	MODERATE	QUALITY ★★★★	VALUE ★★★★

Downtown; Avenida Margaritas 29; ☎ 998-892-3056

Reservations Recommended.

Entree range $7–$30.

Payment AE, MC, V.

Service rating ★★★★.

Parking Street.

Bar Full service.

Dress Dressy casual.

Disabled access Yes.

Customers Travelers.

Hours Daily, noon–midnight.

SETTING AND ATMOSPHERE Soaring arches filled with Maya carvings loom over the long dining room and linen tablecloths; casual but classy.

HOUSE SPECIALTIES *Cochinita pibil* (marinated pork baked in banana leaves), lobster a *xtabentun* (lobster with xtabentun liqueur), *pescado tikin-xic* (fish in achiote marinade—also spelled *tikin-shik*).

SUMMARY AND COMMENTS The Pezotti family has filled a long-vacant niche by providing a stunning restaurant serving traditional Yucatecan cuisine. Dishes you won't see anywhere else are on the menu, including *queso relleno* (Edam cheese stuffed with ground pork, raisins, capers, and olives); *pavo en pipián* (turkey in pumpkin-seed sauce); and *poc chuc* (grilled pork tenderloin). It's a culinary adventure worth experiencing.

La Parrilla ★★★★

TRADITIONAL MEXICAN	MODERATE	QUALITY ★★★★	VALUE ★★★★

Downtown; Avenida Yaxchilán; ☎ 998-287-8119

Reservations Not accepted.

Entree range $8–$20.

Payment AE, MC, V.

Service rating ★★★★.

Parking Limited street parking.

Bar Full service.

Dress Casual.

Disabled access None.

Customers Locals and return visitors.

Hours Daily, noon–10 p.m.

SETTING AND ATMOSPHERE The rambling interior is designed to resemble a Mexican hacienda with murals of gardens and flowers on the walls and a central courtyard where a weekend buffet is served.

HOUSE SPECIALTIES Carne asada, mole, margaritas.

SUMMARY AND COMMENTS One of the few big Mexican restaurants that attracts a largely local crowd, La Parrilla is the place to go when you're craving tacos, burritos, enchiladas, and refried beans that haven't been tamed for tourists' tastes. The Saturday and Sunday lunch buffet is fabulous. Cooks stand behind flaming grills in the courtyard dishing up seasoned pork, chicken, and strips of beef in piping-hot tortillas; side dishes cover most Mexican favorites. Plan on lingering at least two hours.

Lorenzillo's ★★★

SEAFOOD	EXPENSIVE	QUALITY ★★★	VALUE ★★★

Hotel zone on the lagoon; Boulevard Kukulkán Km 10.5; ☎ 998-883-1254

Reservations Recommended.

Entree range $14–$30.

Payment AE, MC, V.

Service rating ★★★.

Parking Valet and self parking.

Bar Full service.

Dress Casual.

Disabled access Possible, but not officially set up for wheelchairs.

Customers Lots of regulars who wouldn't leave Cancún without eating lobster here.

Hours Daily, noon–midnight.

SETTING AND ATMOSPHERE Watch the sun set over the lagoon from a large, palapa-covered deck or inside the main dining room full of nautical touches.

HOUSE SPECIALTIES Lobster fresh from the restaurant's farm.

SUMMARY AND COMMENTS There's no guarantee the lobster served elsewhere is fresh. Here, the live spiny lobsters are displayed for your selection, then prepared, steamed, and served with drawn butter, in coconut milk, or with a poblano-chile sauce. Coconut shrimp, garlicky shrimp and scallops, and prime rib and steaks are available for those who can't bear to see their lobster snatched from the tank. Families fill the place in early evening; romantic types should wait until about 8 p.m. Light meals and snacks are served at the pier bar.

 100% Natural ★★½

HEALTH FOOD	INEXPENSIVE	QUALITY ★★½	VALUE ★★★★

Middle of the hotel zone, near Hotel Presidente InterContinental; Boulevard Kukulkán Km 8.5; ☎ 998-883-1184

Reservations Not accepted.

Entree range $3.50–$12.

Payment AE, MC, V.

Service rating ★★.

Parking Small shopping-center parking lot.

Bar Full service.

Dress Casual.

Disabled access Yes.

Customers Athletes, vegetarians, locals, and travelers.

Hours Daily, 24 hours.

SETTING AND ATMOSPHERE Green-and-white walls and furnishings, lots of plants.

HOUSE SPECIALTIES Salads, pastas, steamed veggies.

SUMMARY AND COMMENTS You'll find several branches of this Mexican chain in the hotel zone and downtown; we like the proximity to hotels and the calm pace at this location. Healthy plants and healthful food are the hallmarks. Their salads are lifesavers, full of fresh veggies washed in purified water. End your long nights here, with a dose of vitamins before bed.

 **Perico's** ★★

MEXICAN	MODERATE	QUALITY ★ ½	VALUE ★

Downtown; Avenida Yaxchilán 61; ☎ 998-884-3152

Reservations Accepted for large groups only.

Entree range $14–$40.

Payment AE, MC, V.

Service rating ★★★.

Parking Street parking.

Bar Full service.

Dress Casual.

Disabled access None.

Customers Travelers.

Hours Daily, 1 p.m.–1 a.m.

SETTING AND ATMOSPHERE Wild and crazy decor with wall-sized murals, papier-mâché figurines and skeletons, and Mexican folk art hanging all about. Families might choose to dine early, as it gets quite boisterous after 9 p.m.

HOUSE SPECIALTIES Fajitas, *Plato Pancho Villa* (beef medallions served with a tamale, quesadilla, and refried beans).

SUMMARY AND COMMENTS Excess is the hallmark of this family-owned party restaurant. It's much like Señor Frog's, but more Mexican in decor and ambience. The requisite shooters, dancing among tables, and drinking games prevail at night—beware of consuming too much cheap tequila. The food is not stellar, but the portions are large enough for two people to share an entree. You'll likely spend some time at the bar waiting for a table. See how many personalities you can recognize in the mural behind the bar—look for Albert Einstein, Che Guevara, Fidel Castro, and the Mexican comic Cantinflas. Kids are delighted by the decor and comical waiters—just be sure to dine early so they miss the tequila-fueled excesses.

Puerto Madero ★★★★½

ARGENTINE STEAK HOUSE	EXPENSIVE	QUALITY ★★★★½	VALUE ★★★

Hotel zone; Boulevard Kukulkán Km 9; ☎ 998-885-2829

Reservations Recommended.

Entree range $20–$40.

Payment AE, MC, V.

Service rating ★★★★.

Parking Valet.

Bar Full service.

Dress Dressy casual.

Disabled access Yes.

Customers Local professionals.

Hours Daily, 1 p.m.–1 a.m.

SETTING AND ATMOSPHERE Stylish wood and brick decor reminiscent of beef houses in Buenos Aires. Gets crowded and noisy after 9 p.m.

HOUSE SPECIALTIES Grilled rib-eye steak, New York steak, sashimi, fried souffléd potatoes.

SUMMARY AND COMMENTS Cancún's hipsters stop here for huge beef dinners before heading out for a night of club hopping. Models, celebrities, and musicians air kiss as they mingle with the crowd in the main dining room; the outdoor deck overlooking the lagoon is a bit more sedate. Groups dining on expense accounts take up large tables. Count on sharing side dishes and desserts, as the portions are huge and everything's excellent. Though other high-end hip restaurants have opened nearby, this remains a local favorite, with the best food and social scene.

Ty-Coz ★★★

SANDWICHES	INEXPENSIVE	QUALITY ★★★	VALUE ★★

Downtown beside Commercial Mexicana supermarket, Avenida Tulum, SM 2, ☎ 998-884-6060; Boulevard Kukulkán Km 8, across from Hotel Presidente InterContinental, ☎ 998-883-3564

Reservations Not accepted.

Entree range $4–$8.

Payment Cash only.

Service rating Counter service.

Parking Large lot downtown; small strip-mall lot in hotel zone.

Bar No alcohol.

Dress Casual.

Disabled access None.

Customers Locals primarily, some travelers.

Hours Monday–Friday, 9:30 a.m.–11 p.m.; take-out available.

SETTING AND ATMOSPHERE Large counter at front where diners place orders; tables and counters with bar stools in fairly quiet dining area decorated with original art.

HOUSE SPECIALTIES Baguette and croissant sandwiches; the specialty includes smoked turkey, ham, chicken breast, salami, and three cheeses.

SUMMARY AND COMMENTS Locals rave about the sandwiches made to order at this little cafe. Stop by for a Parisian breakfast of hard-boiled eggs and croissants, or choose the German plate of cold meats and cheese with Dijon mustard for lunch or dinner. Pick up take-out before heading out on a day trip, or relax over English tea or *café con leche* (coffee with milk) any time of day. The hotel-zone location is strictly takeout, with a few tiny tables by the street.

Yamamoto ★★★

JAPANESE	MODERATE	QUALITY ★★★	VALUE ★★★★

Downtown on a quiet residential street; Avenida Uxmal 31 SM3; ☎ 998-887-3366

Reservations Accepted.

Entree range $8–$20.

Payment AE, MC, V.

Service rating ★★★.

Parking Street parking.

Bar Full service.

Dress Casual.

Disabled access Possible; there are a few tables by the sushi counter and steps to the dining room.

Customers Locals, neighborhood residents.

Hours Monday–Saturday, 1:30–11 p.m.; Sunday, 1:30–10 p.m.; take-out and delivery available.

SETTING AND ATMOSPHERE Minimalist decor with a sushi counter by the front door and a large white dining room with light wood tables.

HOUSE SPECIALTIES Sushi, sashimi, pork with ginger sauce.

SUMMARY AND COMMENTS This out-of-the-way Japanese restaurant serves the best sushi, sashimi, and teppanyaki dishes in town and has long been a local favorite. They'll arrange transportation for you, and they treat customers like special guests. The tempura is perfectly fried, and the fried-noodle and teriyaki dishes are in the inexpensive range. It's a pleasant change for a peaceful lunch or dinner and a blessing for vegetarians, as there are many veggie and tofu dishes on the menu.

SIGHTSEEING *in* CANCÚN

THE *ZONA HOTELERA*, OR HOTEL ZONE, sometimes called **Isla Cancún** (though it's not actually an island), is a city unto itself containing enough shopping malls and restaurants to keep many visitors content. Outside the water activities, the shopping malls are the main attraction and contain play zones for kids along with abundant shops and restaurants. Downtown Cancún, also called **El Centro,** is a sprawling warren of neighborhoods called *supermanzanas,* or by the abbreviation "SM." Addresses may include a street name and an SM code, which helps cab drivers find obscure locations. Most of the sights of interest to travelers are within walking distance of Avenida Tulum, which offers several stops for the hotel-zone buses.

ATTRACTIONS

THE HOTEL ZONE'S ATTRACTIONS LINE Boulevard Kukulkán from El Centro to **Punta Nizúc** We've listed them in that order, starting with the marina where some ferries depart for **Isla Mujeres.** The ferry terminal (still sometimes called Playa Linda) is part of **El Embarcadero** (Boulevard Kukulkán Km 4; ☎ 998-849-4848).

The big complex at the water's edge includes shops and snack bars, and the water's edge is lined with tour boats, yachts, and ferries. Though there was once a fabulous folk art museum here, it's closed now, and the Embarcadero is mostly populated by tour and ferry passengers.

The **Cancún Convention Center** (Boulevard Kukulkán Km 9; ☎ 998-883-0199) sits in the center of the widest part of Boulevard Kukulkán at the juncture of the two branches of the hotel zone's 7 shape.

At the **Interactive Aquarium** (Boulevard Kukulkán Km 25; ☎ 998-883-0411), a scuba diver with a microphone answers questions about the fish darting about within an enormous aquarium. Outdoor pools hold rays and dolphins for petting, and you can arrange to dive in a shark cage or interact with dolphins for an additional fee. There is a restaurant and bar, plus lockers and showers for cleaning up after a dive. Open daily from 9 a.m. to 7 p.m.; admission is $14 for adults, $10 for children.

Ruinas del Rey (Boulevard Kukulkán Km 18.5; ☎ 998-883-2080) is the largest archaeological zone in Cancún; archaeologists think it may have been a royal burial site. The ruins themselves aren't nearly as impressive as those found elsewhere on the peninsula, but the site feels totally removed from the surrounding hotels, thanks to its location near the lagoon. The site is open daily from 9 a.m. to 4:30 p.m.; admission is $3.

BEACHES

ALL THE BEACHES IN THE HOTEL ZONE are public, though nonguests may be discouraged from lingering on the sands in front of specific hotels, and new condo towers block access to formerly popular beaches. Security guards keep nonguests from using beach chairs and other facilities, and generally make them feel uncomfortable. Sand erosion has destroyed many beaches facing the open sea; those facing Isla Mujeres are in better shape. **Playa Tortuga** (Km 7) is the best for calm water and rental centers with water toys, and **Playa Delfines** (Km 18) at the far southern end of the hotel zone is wonderful for sunsets and rough waves. There's fairly good body surfing at Playa Delfines if you know what you're doing; novices shouldn't try swimming in the rough waters. This is one of the most popular beaches with locals.

EL CENTRO

DOWNTOWN IS UNDERGOING a bit of a renaissance, though it will never resemble a traditional Mexican city. After all, it's only been around since 1974. **El Centro,** the area most often frequented by travelers, lies along Avenida Tulum's west side. The city planners didn't pay much attention to the central plaza and church; their 1970s look is boring. The central square, called **Parque Palapa** (between *avenidas* Tulum and Yaxchilán), has been updated with a stage and amphitheater area, and locals gather at taco stands edging the plaza. There's a pedestrian walkway called Andador Tulipanes between the two main avenues that run past the plaza, where Friday-night concerts draw a lively crowd.

Mercado Veintiocho, west of Avenida Yaxchilán at Avenida Sunyaxchén, has become the center of downtown's shopping action for travelers. The market covers several city blocks and offers stalls selling papayas, chiles, plastic buckets, and handicrafts. Look for hammocks, hats, sandals, and pottery here, and stop at one of the market cafes for lunch. The adjacent Plaza Bonita has some good folk art shops and a great hammock store, El Aguacate. Avenida Tulum is lined with budget accommodations and department stores. East of Tulum street you'll find some interesting small restaurants and accommodations in residential neighborhoods.

TOURS *and* SIDE TRIPS *from* CANCÚN

CHICHÉN ITZÁ

LOCATED 179 KILOMETERS (112 miles) west of Cancún, **Chichén Itzá** is the most famous Maya site on the Yucatán Peninsula. Tour companies offer day trips to the ruins from Cancún, but we're hesitant to recommend them. There simply isn't enough time to absorb the beauty and magic of the 10-square-kilometer site. The drive takes about two-and-a-half or three hours each way; more if you're on a tour bus that stops at several hotels to pick up clients. That gives you two or three hours at the site, at the hottest and most crowded time of the day. Archaeology buffs are much happier spending at least one night at the **Hotel Mayaland** (☎ 998-887-0870 or 800-235-4079 from the United States) near the back entrance to the site. Admission to the site includes the eerie nightly sound and light show, so you might as well have the whole experience.

Whether you're staying the night or visiting for a day, consider renting a car. The drive along the toll road (*autopista*) between Cancún and Chichén Itzá is a breeze. In fact, the road is so straight it's almost boring. Try to leave as early as possible—the site opens at 8 a.m. and tour buses don't begin to clog the parking lot until 10:30 or so. When the crowds and heat become overwhelming, retreat to one of the hotels near the site for lunch, then return for more explorations in the afternoon. You may want to take the local highway back to Cancún, passing through small villages and stopping to see the restored 17th-century monastery in the bustling town of **Valladolid.**

No matter how you get there, you need at least five hours to give Chichén Itzá its due. The city is believed to have been inhabited from AD 432 to AD 1224, with long periods of intermittent abandonment. The architecture of its 30 to 40 explored structures combines techniques from several Maya groups and the Toltecs; the result is an impressive complex of pyramids, temples, plazas, and tombs.

The 98-foot-high **El Castillo** rises above the site's vast lawns and reconstructed buildings in Chichén Nuevo, where most of the major structures are located. The four-sided pyramid is topped by a temple dedi-cated to Kukulkán. Called a priest, king, or god, Kukulkán is the Maya version of Quetzalcoatl, a mysterious plumed serpent. The Aztecs who encountered Hernán Cortés in the 16th century thought he was Quetzalcoatl returning to his people; the results were disastrous for Mexico's indigenous tribes. The Maya had virtually abandoned Chichén when the conquistadors arrived, which helped preserve the structures. Spanish warriors and missionaries were interested in conquering and converting the populace, not preserving history.

Pathways through low, dry grass lead to the ball court, with its bas-relief depictions of warriors and the ritual decapitation (believed to be the winner's reward). If you and a companion stand at opposite ends of the court and whisper, you'll be able to hear each other. Near the court is a stone platform carved with a series of human skulls; a pathway north leads to the Cenote Sagrado, where divers have discovered skeletons and precious artifacts from the sinkhole's depths.

Southwest of El Castillo, a dirt road leads to **Chichén Viejo** (Old Chichén). This area is usually less crowded than the other, especially if you walk all the way south to the **Casa de las Monjas** (Nunnery), one of the site's more ornate structures, with latticework and animal carvings. A narrow, nearly hidden path southeast of the Nunnery leads to piles of barely excavated edifices buried in vines. The most famous building in Chichén Viejo is the snail-shaped **Caracol,** used as an observatory. The unusual round building has eight windows that correspond with the cardinal directions in a low tower. Visitors are prohibited from climbing most of the structures at the site.

Chichén Itzá is open 8 a.m. to 5 p.m. daily. Admission is $9, and there is an additional $12 fee to bring in a video camera. The entryway includes a good museum and relief map of the site, along with a few shops, a restaurant, and large restroom areas. Guides are available, and handicraft stands line the parking lot.

ISLA HOLBOX

DOCILE WHITE-SPOTTED WHALE SHARKS—the biggest fish in the sea—migrate to the Gulf of Mexico north of the Yucatán Peninsula from May to September. Intrepid travelers quickly follow, setting up camp on Isla Holbox (pronounced **HOLE**-bosh). The island, part of the Yuum Balam Reserve, sits eight miles off the northeast tip of the Yucatán Peninsula where the Caribbean Sea meets the Gulf of Mexico. The leeward side is lined with mangroves where white pelicans, pink flamingos, and black cormorants nest. A white-sand beach popular with pregnant sea turtles fringes the windward shores. About 1,200 islanders live here year-round, fishing and tending to travelers who've discovered the Mexican Caribbean's last fantasy island.

Cell phones don't work on Isla Holbox. The sole Internet cafe isn't as popular as one might think. After a couple of barefoot-in-the-sand days on the island, e-mail becomes an unwelcome intrusion. Hammocks are the most popular amenities at the two-dozen or so small hotels; air-conditioning is still a luxury. Fish is the dietary staple, naturally. The lobster pizza and pasta, octopus and conch ceviche, and grilled catch-of-the-day at restaurants around the main plaza and on the beach are superb.

Isla Holbox isn't for everyone. It's one of the buggiest places we've ever been. Showers must always be followed by a liberal cloud of bug spray—the mosquitoes and sand fleas are legendary. Getting here involves a three-hour drive (or a three- to five-hour bus ride) from Cancún to Punta Chiquila on the peninsula's north coast, followed by a 45-minute ferry ride. Yet some travelers are content to visit Holbox on day trips from Cancún.

The whale sharks are the main lure. Swimming with these 60-foot-long creatures is an awesome experience. Local captains pilot small skiffs about two hours offshore to reach the sharks, who approach the boat fearlessly. After the whales have checked out the boats, two passengers are allowed to enter the water with a guide. Humans must swim madly to keep up with the sharks (who appear from the boat to move imperceptibly as they glide away). Lucky swimmers end up floating beside the shark's head, looking into its marblelike eyes. As the shark moves, the swimmer feels a rush of water from the gills as the shark ingests sea water and filters the plankton that serve as its sustenance. Far too soon the dorsal fin sways through the water and the shark is gone. During July and August, when the sharks are most plentiful, repeat performances are usually the norm.

Isla Holbox is worth visiting even without the marine display. A plaza with a palm thatch to covered playground sits three sandy blocks from the beach and the pueblo consists of a small grid of unnamed streets with the requisite church, telegraph office, *panadería* (bakery), and produce market. Most of the accommodations front the leeward coast, where the shallow, calm water is an incomparable shade of green. Local fisherman offer tours to Isla Pasión (Passion

Island), Isla Pájaros (Bird Island), and a cool freshwater spring in the mangrove lagoon. Rental golf carts are available for exploring the 26-mile-long island, and it's easy to pass several days just walking along the beach looking for shells, lingering at cafes in town, and hanging out in a hammock.

Our favorite hotel on Holbox is **Xaloc,** with 18 bungalows along palm-lined pathways by the beach and two pools. Mosquito nets cover king-size beds set in the middle of circular rooms; hammocks hang on the porches. Bathrooms have two sinks in a long vanity counter, powerful hot-water showers, and enough shelves and hangers for bathing suits and shorts. Thus far, the Spanish owners have resisted the lure of air-conditioning (which helps keep rates low), and ceiling fans stir the steamy air. Phone ☎ 984-875-2160; 800-728-9098 U.S.; **www.mexicoboutiquehotels.com.** The inexpensive **Hotelito Casa las Tortugas** is a bit closer to town and loaded with Italian whims and the character of its owners. Bungalows painted green, pink, and yellow surround gardens right by the beach; hammocks hang every-where. The restaurant serves superb espresso and breakfasts. ☎ 984-875-2129; **www.holboxcasalastortugas.com.**

Eco Colors (see below) offers weekly trips from Cancún to Holbox. Trips include the whale sharks when they're around, and concentrate more on the aquatic-bird nesting on Bird Island the rest of the year.

ECOTOURISM

DESPITE HAVING ENVELOPED OR CONSUMED most every-thing natural in its immediate vicinity, Cancún is surrounded by nature preserves, tiny villages, and islands filled with birds. Tours go to **Sian Ka'an,** the UNESCO biosphere reserve south of Tulum (see the following page) for bird-watching and boat trips through mangrove lagoons.

Eco Colors (Calle Camarón 32, SM 27; ☎ 998-884-3667; **www .ecotravelmexico.com**) covers the area with day and overnight trips that include camping, tromping through remote archaeological sites, biking the coast, and other adventures. Their auto tour incorporates your desires (ruins, snorkeling, and so on) in customized car trips with built-in hotel reservations and a list of suggested restaurants.

It takes about three hours to drive from Cancún to Sian Ka'an, which doesn't give you much time to explore the region on a day trip. We prefer spending at least one night in the park's Visitor Center, managed by Eco Colors. During the summer months, sea turtles come onto the park's beaches to lay their eggs late at night, and crocodiles can be seen during nighttime kayak trips year-round. Sea birds greet the dawn, and kayaking through the park's mangrove lagoons is best in early morning when the birds are active. Eco Colors is the oldest ecotourism company in the region, and one of

THE MAYA WORLD

Cancún is the gateway to Mexico's Maya world, where pyramids, homes, and temples rise above the jungle throughout the Yucatán peninsula in the states of Quintana Roo (home of Cancún), Yucatán, and Campeche. Three large archaeological sites—Chichén Itzá, Cobá, and Tulum—lie within a few hours' drive from Cancún and the Caribbean Coast, and the landscape throughout the area is dotted with structures built by the Maya. At Xcaret, granddaddy of the Caribbean Coast's theme parks, dozens of ancient Maya structures have been restored and a reproduction of a Maya village accurately displays the lifestyle of the modern Maya. Canals constructed by the Maya in mangrove lagoons lead to the sea at the Sian Ka'an Biosphere Reserve, a UNESCO World Heritage Site. (See page 110 for a more thorough description of Chichén Itzá; the other sites are covered in the Caribbean Coast chapter.) Trying to decide which sites to visit during a Cancún vacation can be frustrating. The following chart gives an opinionated overview of the highlights of each site and information on the logistics of getting there. Several companies in Cancún (listed in Tours, page 116) offer guided tours to the sites.

Chichén Itzá

WHY GO A dramatic introduction to the Maya, with restored pyramids, temples, an observatory, a ball court, and all the important edifices of a major ceremonial center.

DISTANCE 179 kilometers (112 miles) west of Cancún. TRAVEL TIME 2½–3 hours each way by car or tour bus. TOURING TIME At least 5 hours to see the main structures; overnight is best.

HIGHLIGHTS The spiral Observatory and lacy latticework on the Casa de las Monjas (climb to the top for the best view of the site); visions of sunken treasure and skeletons in the Cenote Sagrado; echoed whispers across the ball court.

Cobá

WHY GO The site still feels wild and undiscovered; it's possible to get lost (and found) on jungle paths here.

DISTANCE 170 kilometers (105 miles) southwest of Cancún. TRAVEL TIME 2 hours each way. TOURING TIME 5 hours by foot, 3 by bike.

HIGHLIGHTS Climbing Nohuch-Mul while wild parrots fly overhead; riding mountain bikes over ruts and vines on side pathways to clusters of half-excavated structures.

Sian Ka'an Biosphere Reserve

WHY GO Total immersion in nature; it's the only place in Mexico where you can cruise in a kayak or small boat through canals built by the Maya while watching for crocodiles, sea turtles, and flamingos.

DISTANCE 145 kilometers (90 miles) southwest of Cancún. TRAVEL TIME 3–3½ hours each way. TOURING TIME 8–9 hours on an organized or self-driving tour. Spending the night at the Visitor Center lets you search for turtles and crocodiles at night and aquatic birds at dawn.

HIGHLIGHTS Summer night tours to watch sea turtles build their nests on the reserve's beaches; spotting tiny temples amid the mangroves; snorkeling off secluded beaches.

Tulum

WHY GO For the sheer beauty of the 1,000-year-old walled fortress above the Caribbean Sea. The site is easily covered in a couple of hours, leaving time to visit other interesting attractions in the area.

DISTANCE 130 kilometers (81 miles) south of Cancún. **TRAVEL TIME** 2–2½ hours each way. **TOURING TIME** 2–3 hours.

HIGHLIGHTS The Castillo above a white-sand beach (a good place to swim after your tour) and the relief of the "bee god" at the Temple of the Descending God.

Xcaret

WHY GO For the most comprehensive overview of the Yucatán Peninsula's flora, fauna, culture, and history.

DISTANCE 80 kilometers (50 miles) west of Cancún. **TRAVEL TIME** 1½–2 hours each way. **TOURING TIME** 5 hours minimum.

HIGHLIGHTS The butterfly pavilion, aviary, and coral aquarium for nature; Maya village and cemetery for culture. *Xcaret at Night,* a song-and-dance spectacle with more than 200 performers, would show well on PBS. The authenticity and choreography are fantastic. Skip buying dinner tickets—the food's not that great, and the service detracts from the show.

GETTING THERE We're accustomed to renting a car for Cancún side trips and find driving far more pleasurable than riding in a tour bus. By leaving Cancún early in the morning, you'll miss rush-hour traffic and arrive at your destination long before group tours. Workers are far more prevalent than travelers when the sites open, and it's actually possible to imagine the preconquest scenery from atop tall pyramids. With a car at hand, you can break for lunch when the tour buses arrive or move on to other attractions. It costs about $80 a day to rent a car with automatic transmission and air-conditioning in Cancún.

Reaching the sites on a tour bus does have its advantages, especially if you're uncomfortable driving in unfamiliar places. If you decide to take a tour, try for one that leaves Cancún by 7 a.m. If you're going to Xcaret, you'll most likely be at the park all day and half the night and don't need to rush for an early start.

TOURING TIPS As at Disneyland, head for the most popular structures first. Photos at most structures are best taken before the glare is too bright.

The clichés about drinking water, sunscreen, and hats apply. Bug repellent is a must at Cobá. You'll be glad you remembered to stash an extra T-shirt in your bag, along with more film (or space on your digital camera's memory chip) than you imagined needing.

unofficial **TIP**
At Tulum, you can no longer climb atop the gray *castillo* rising alone beside the turquoise sea, but you can get some good photos if you climb the slight hill just south of the structure.

the best in the country. Their tours are always enjoyable and highly informative.

Alltournative (Avenida 38N, between Avenidas 1 and 5; ☎ 984-873-2036; **www.alltournative.com**) in Playa del Carmen (see Part Seven, page 200) will pick up passengers staying in Cancún who wish to join their day-long tours to Maya villages and ruins; tours include kayaking, rappelling, mountain biking, and lunch at a Maya village. The company, which works with local Maya communities to help provide tourism revenue, also has overnight camping tours.

Kolumbus Tours (Puerto Juárez; ☎ 998-884-5333; **www.kolumbus tours.com** uses replicas of historic sailing ships for bird-watching tours to Isla Contoy, a nature preserve near Isla Mujeres. The boats sail from Puerto Juárez, north of Cancún, but the company offers free transportation from hotels.

TOURS

TOURS AND ACTIVITIES ARE OFTEN INCLUDED in vacation packages; the savings on entry fees and transportation can be significant. Every hotel has some kind of tour desk for making independent reservations; consider your options before making a decision, and don't necessarily go for the lowest price. Creature comforts such as air-conditioned buses and meals make tours more pleasant experiences. **Mayaland Tours** (Robalo 30, SM 3; ☎ 998-884-4512 or 800-235-4079 from the United States; **www.mayaland.com** is one of the largest and oldest companies in Cancún. They offer bus tours to Chichén Itzá from Cancún, including admission, guided tour, and buffet lunch, as well as self-driving tours and overnight stays at the Mayaland Hotel by the ruins. Mayaland can arrange transportation to the city of Mérida and the surrounding attractions, and has day tours to Tulum and the aquatic theme parks of Xel-Há and Xcaret. **Intermar Caribe** (Avenida Tulum 225 at Avenida Jabalí, MS 20; ☎ 998-881-0000; **www.travel2mexico.com**) is another established company with knowledgeable agents; they have the tours mentioned above and can book most Cancún activities. **Best Day Tours** (Boulevard Kukulkán Km 5.5, in the lobby of the Gran Caribe Real Hotel; ☎ 998-881-1329, **www.bestday.com** offers everything from bullfight tours to lobster-dinner lagoon cruises and bar-hopping tours that take in several Cancún nightspots with one fee covering transportation and all drinks.

BOAT TOURS

YOU SHOULD GET OUT ON THE WATER at some point during your vacation, and there are plenty of ways to do so. Daytime boat cruises usually involve a bit of snorkeling and time for sunbathing on the ship or a beach. **Bluewater Tours** (Boulevard Kukulkán Km 6.5; ☎ 998-849-4444) has trimarans and fast catamarans departing from the Embarcadero for daily snorkeling and sunning trips. **SubSea**

Explorer departs from the AquaWorld marina (Boulevard Kukulkán Km 15.2; ☎ 998-848-8327; **aquaworld.com.mx**) daily and travels submerged along a small section of sponges and coral by the lagoons. Turtles, parrotfish, and tiny blue neons are easily visible. The ship is small and stuffy, however, and anyone with a tendency toward claustrophobia may be uncomfortable.

One of the most popular day trips from Cancún is a boat ride to **Isla Mujeres,** a small island eight miles offshore (for extensive details, see Part Five, Isla Mujeres). **El Garrafón** is an underwater reserve where the snorkeling is much better than anywhere in Cancún. The beaches on the leeward side of the island have been taken over by tour companies hosting theme dinners after sunset cruises. Some island tours include time for shopping in the brightly colored Caribbean-style homes along the town's main streets. Several companies offer tours to the island.

100% Vela Cancún (Boulevard Kukulkán Km 3.5; ☎ 998-849-4900) sails catamarans toward Isla Mujeres for snorkeling, then a Mexican lunch buffet on the beach and cocktails on the way back to Cancún.

Dolphin Discovery (Boulevard Kukulkán Km 5.5, at Playa Langosta next to Casa Maya Hotel; ☎ 998-849-4758) takes passengers to Isla Mujeres to swim with dolphins—a pricey and memorable experience.

Dinner and dancing boat cruises are popular nightlife options. Night tours have a theme—sunset, dinner, pirates, parties—and cruise along the Cancún skyline in early evening. **Caribbean Carnaval** (El Embarcadero, Boulevard Kukulkán Km 4; ☎ 998-884-3860) sails to Isla Mujeres for an all-inclusive dinner and dance fest on a private beach.

kids The two replicas of 17th-century galleons in the fleet for **Captain Hook Pirate Ship** (El Embarcadero, Boulevard Kukulkán Km 4; ☎ 998-849-4451) cruise along the hotel zone's coastline as pirates shoot cannons and serve lobster dinners.

The **Columbus Lobster Dinner Cruise** (Royal Mayan Marina, Boulevard Kukulkán Km 16.5; ☎ 998-849-4748) travels through Laguna Nichupté while a lobster-and-steak dinner is served on deck. **AquaWorld's Cancún Queen** (Boulevard Kukulkán Km 15.2; ☎ 998-848-8327; **aquaworld.com.mx**) is a more rowdy affair with a three-course dinner, open bar, live band, and drinking games.

kids XCARET

YOU CAN'T MISS THE SIGNS FOR **Xcaret,** a combination water park, nature and culture center, and entertainment venue 72 kilometers south of Cancún (for more details, see page 115 of this chapter and page 203 of Part Seven). Packages, including transportation from Cancún, are available. Get information at the Xcaret Information Center (Boulevard Kukulkán Km 9.5; ☎ 998-883-0470). The park is at Highway 307, 72 kilometers south of Cancún, between Playa del Carmen and Tulum (☎ 984-871-5200; **www.xcaret.com**).

EXERCISE *and* RECREATION *in* CANCÚN

CANCÚN'S 12-MILE-LONG HOTEL ZONE is a perfect course for marathons (one is held annually around the beginning of November) and triathlons alike. Kayaking in the lagoons is popular with bird-watchers and nature lovers. But most travelers seem to prefer getting a rush from water sports. Personal watercraft are extremely popular and are available for rent at hotel beaches and marinas. Kids, in particular, get a kick out of banana boats, which look like inflated versions of their namesake surging through the water. Parasailing is popular and available on beaches and at the lagoon. Keep safety in mind, and don't use any equipment that seems fishy or poorly maintained—you will usually have to sign forms releasing equipment owners from all liability for accidents.

BULLFIGHTS

BULLFIGHTS ARE HELD ON WEDNESDAYS at 3:30 p.m. at the **Cancún Bullring** (Boulevard Kukulkán at Avenida Bonampak, SM 4; ☎ 998-884-8248). It's easiest to purchase tickets through a travel agency or your hotel concierge, although you can also purchase them at the ticket window. Prices start at around $25 per person.

GOLF

THE OLDEST AND MOST WELL-KNOWN COURSE in Cancún is the **Club de Golf Cancún** (Boulevard Kukulkán Km 7.5; ☎ 998-883-1230, **www.cancungolfclub.com**); formerly known as Pok-Ta-Pok. Designed by Robert Trent Jones Sr., the 18-hole course offers wonderful views of the ocean and lagoon against a backdrop of small Maya ruins. The club facilities include a putting green, driving range, tennis courts, and a pro shop.

The par-72, 18-hole professional course at the **Hilton Cancún Club de Golf** (Boulevard Kukulkán Km 17; ☎ 998-881-8016) was completely rebuilt after Hurricane Wilma; turf was replaced and many holes redesigned. Improved facilities include a driving range, clubhouse with restaurant, and pro shop with equipment rental. Transportation to the course is available from the hotel lobby.

The **Moon Palace Spa & Golf Club** (Highway 307 Km 340; ☎ 998-881-6000) is the only Nicklaus Signature Course in the Cancún region. Totaling 10,798 yards of play, the three, nine-hole, par 36 courses surrounded by natural mangroves are located on the grounds of the enormous Moon Palace Resort. Transportation from Cancún is available for those who purchase a golf package.

The **Meliá Cancún Beach and Spa Resort** (Boulevard Kukulkán Km 16.5; ☎ 998-881-1100) has a 53-par, nine-hole course with dazzling ocean views.

WATER SPORTS

SEVERAL MARINAS ARE LOCATED ON THE LAGOONS and coastline and offer everything from diving to parasailing. **AquaWorld** (Boulevard Kukulkán Km 15.3; ☎ 998-848-8300; **aquaworld.com.mx**) is a huge complex with a cornucopia of water activities, including snorkeling tours to the reefs at Punta Nizúc, dinner cruises on the *Cancún Queen,* jungle tours through Nichupté Lagoon on personal watercraft, scuba diving on reefs and in *cenotes* (subterranean freshwater pools with underwater caves), and the aforementioned parasails towed by boats.

Scuba Diving and Snorkeling

Cancún has few coral reefs, and those that exist have been "loved" to death. Still, dive companies manage to find a few sites worth exploring. **Punta Nizúc** is the most popular diving and snorkeling area, but the last time we were there the reefs were practically barren. Diving off **Punta Cancún** is more rewarding, though you need to be wary of currents. Serious divers should skip the marina tours and contact dive companies that offer small-boat trips to out-of-the-way sites along the coast and cenote diving. **Scuba Cancún** (Boulevard Kukulkán Km 5; ☎ 998-849-5255) and **Solo Buceo** (Boulevard Kukulkán Km 9; ☎ 998-883-3979) are two reputable companies that offer dive trips and instruction.

▮ SHOPPING *in* CANCÚN

AT LEAST A HALF-DOZEN SHOPPING MALLS are in the hotel zone, each with a distinctive character. Most have ATMs and/or money-exchange offices, some kind of Internet cafe, and several restaurants. They also serve as good reference points when looking for addresses while dotting the hotel zone with convenient parking and bus stops. **Plaza Caracol** (Boulevard Kukulkán Km 8.5; ☎ 998-883-1038) is good for basic beach clothes and gear. Several popular restaurants have sidewalk views on the ground floor, and shops carrying everything from sportswear to serapes fill the two air-conditioned levels. **Forum by the Sea** (Boulevard Kukulkán Km 9; ☎ 998-883-4425) is at the center of a busy nightlife area and has several restaurants including a Rainforest Cafe and Hard Rock Cafe. Farther along the hotel zone, **Plaza Flamingo** (Boulevard Kukulkán Km 11; ☎ 998-883-2945) sits beside the lagoon and is more refined despite one's initial impression (its most visible businesses are **Pat O'Brien's, Outback Steakhouse,** and **Jimmy Buffet's Margaritaville.**) You can find some decent Mexican crafts in small shops here.

   La Isla (Boulevard Kukulkán Km 12.5; ☎ 998-883-5025) is the most fun to walk around these days. It's meant to resemble Venice, perhaps, and was expanded along the edge of the lagoon in 2006. Bridges and landscaped walkways lead over canals and around

unofficial **TIP**
The Kukulkids play zone at Kukulcán Plaza is a great distraction for children. The climbing equipment, small rides, and enclosed trampolines help work off energy.

several groupings of shops, restaurants, and attractions. The **Interactive Aquarium** is here, along with movie theaters, high-end shops, and a Liverpool, U.K., department store. **Kukulcán Plaza** (Boulevard Kukulkán Km 13; ☎ 998-885-2200) underwent a complete makeover in 2006 and is the most upscale mall. One end is devoted to Luxury Avenue, a duty-free shop displaying everything from Baccarat to Swatch. The marble-and-glass design, with wall-length waterfalls and bubbling fountains, is unlike anything else around and is an excellent landmark defining the beginning of the more exclusive section of the hotel zone.

Downtown, the **Plaza las Américas** (Avenida Tulum 260; ☎ 998-887-4839) is a godsend for everyone on the coast. Residents love the plush movie theaters, department stores, restaurants, and convenient parking, and they stock up on clothing, housewares, and other supplies, too. The **Comercial Mexicana** (Avenida Tulum at Avenida Uxmal; ☎ 998-880-9164) is a longtime favorite for everything from beer to aspirin to walking shoes, and it's located near a stop for the bus to the hotel zone.

The main sources for Mexican arts and crafts are the designated artisan's markets. **Coral Negro** (Boulevard Kukulkán Km 9, next to the convention center) is justifiably called the Flea Market. Its stalls are packed with goods suiting every trend of the moment—it's the place to get temporary or permanent tattoos along with tacky souvenirs. **Ki Huic** (Avenida Tulum 17, SM 3; ☎ 998-884-3347) has been around almost since Cancún began attracting travelers, and this tired complex of vendors' stands looks its age. The prices are ridiculously high here, but competent hagglers may find some treasures amid the junk. **Mercado Veintiocho** (Avs. Yaxchilán and Sunyaxchén) has become *the* place to shop for better-quality items, including guayabera shirts, hammocks, purses from Guatemala, and woven belts and shawls from Chiapas and Oaxaca. Check out the shops in the adjacent Plaza Bonita as well.

NIGHTLIFE *in* CANCÚN

CANCÚN THROBS WITH AN IRREPRESSIBLE BEAT after dark, as if everyone has absorbed solar energy by the pool. Parents and kids head for restaurants that include plenty of distractions after taking in a game of minigolf or some video-arcade craze. Lots of folks board boats for dinner and booze cruises; others dress up and dine after 9 p.m.—the appropriate hour to begin nighttime activities in Mexico. Restaurants become nightclubs as the night wears on, and diners gather at the bar to listen to jazz or the latest DJs spinning house mixes. Discos and dance and music clubs don't really hit their stride until midnight when locals join travelers on the dance floor.

The long lines in front of **Coco Bongo** (Boulevard Kukulkán Km 9.5; ☎ 998-883-5061; **cocobongo.com.mx**) are proof this 1,800-person capacity club is one of the hottest nightspots in town. The musical mix of rave, hip-hop, and disco is a crowd pleaser, as are the Vegas-style shows with dancers mimicking Michael Jackson, Madonna, and other pop stars as lights flash and trapeze artists swing above the dance floor. Next door **The City** (Boulevard Kukulkán Km 9.5; ☎ 998-883-4187; **www.thecitycancun.com**) is an entertainment mega-plex with a beach club, restaurant, cocktail lounge, and nightclub. DJ Paul Van Dyck headlined the club's reopening in March 2005, when crowds far exceeded the club's 7,000-guest capacity. A marquee lists upcoming events.

Dinner segues into wild dancing at **Carlos'n Charlie's** (Boulevard Kukulkán Km 8.5; ☎ 998-883-4467) and **Señor Frog's** (Boulevard Kukulkán Km 9.5; ☎ 998-883-1092), where waiters and customers dance to music on the tables, in the aisles, and anywhere they can find. Señor Frog's post-hurricane revamp included an indoor swimming pool—a good place to cool down after a dance marathon. **Perico's** (see "Where to Eat in Cancún," page 106) has a similar scene downtown (minus the pool).

Anyone who loves to dance has ample opportunity to strut his or her stuff in Cancún. Serious discos with laser and light shows, huge dance floors, and a stylish crowd include **Dady'O** (Boulevard Kukulkán Km 9.5; ☎ 998-883-3333), the spawn of a famed Acapulco disco that attracts a stylish, younger set. The crowd isn't allowed to relax at **Dady Rock** (Boulevard Kukulkán Km 9.5; ☎ 998-883-3333), where DJs and waiters entice dancers into competitions.

The best salsa club in Cancún is **Azucar** (next to the **Dreams Cancún Resort and Spa,** Boulevard Kukulkán Km 9; ☎ 998-883-7000). The live bands are always incredible—we were once captivated by an all-female Cuban group that kept the dance floor packed until dawn. The clientele is sophisticated and chic, and watching the experts do the salsa and merengue is a treat.

Electronic music and sophisticated decor make **O Ultra Lounge** (Boulevard Kukulkán Km 9.5; ☎ 998-883-3333) a favorite among local office workers and travelers seeking a more sophisticated scene. Stylish couples and singles sip bellinis in the lounge, and dance wherever they wish.

The Grill at the Ritz-Carlton (Retorno del Rey 36; ☎ 998-881-0808) hosts live jazz bands in a classy ambience perfect for sipping after-dinner brandies. **Le Méridien's** lobby bar (Boulevard Kukulkán Km 14; ☎ 998-881-0808) has pianists and other musicians playing some nights—but if there's a big soccer game happening the TV might be on. The mood varies with the guests, who make themselves at home everywhere. Downtown, **Roots Bar** (Avenida Tulipanes 26, near Parque Palapa; ☎ 998-884-2437) is a live-tunes haven for musicians playing everything from fusion to flamenco.

For movie buffs, **Cinepolis** (Plaza las Américas, Avenida Tulum, SM 4 and 9; ☎ 998-884-4056) is the largest cinema complex in Cancún, with 12 screens showing current films, some in English. **Cinemark Cancún** (Boulevard Kukulkán Km 12; ☎ 998-883-0576) in Las Isla has five screens showing first-run movies.

PART FIVE

ISLA MUJERES

An ISLAND RETREAT

MORE CARIBBEAN, CASUAL, and noncommercial than Cancún and Cozumel, Isla Mujeres is the perfect place for a do-nothing vacation. You can tour the five-mile-long island in a day—if you really take your time—which makes it a popular day trip from Cancún. But you can easily avoid the crowds during your sojourn and thoroughly enjoy the island's laid-back nightlife.

Most of the island's visitors spend considerable time on **Playa Norte,** which extends from the ferry pier to the northern tip of the island and has every sort of amusement you might desire. Early mornings are best for snorkeling around **El Garrafón,** a marine park turned major tourist attraction, or tooling around the island in a golf cart. A few other sights provide diversion, and you won't want to miss the cemetery, pirate's hacienda, and turtle farm. But that's about it for serious sightseeing.

unofficial **TIP**
Isla Mujeres fared far better than Cancún during Hurricane Wilma's onslaught in October 2005. Parts of the island were flooded but most of the low-rise buildings were quickly repaired. Playa Norte actually gained more sand, or, as the locals like to say, Isla gained the sand Cancún lost.

Isla Mujeres—"The Isle of Women," or Isla for short—was purportedly dedicated to the goddess Ixchel by the Maya. A small shrine sits at the island's southern tip, near the lighthouse. The island was given its current name by Francisco Hernández de Córdoba, who arrived with the Spanish conquistadors and explorers in 1517. The skinny limestone strip was of little use to the Spaniards until the pirate era in the 1800s, when swashbucklers stored their booty in caves and wooed local maidens (in their own inimitable style). It was hardly on the map until Cancún emerged with its chain of lights just eight miles west across the Caribbean.

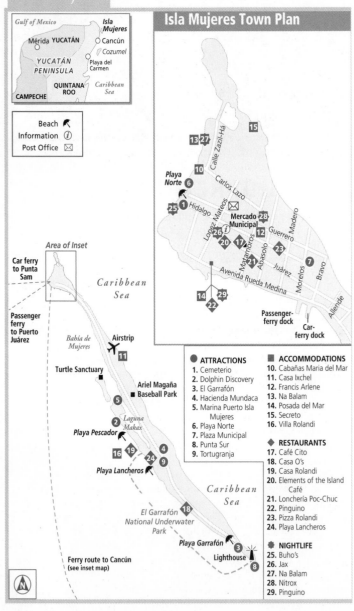

Isla Mujeres

Isla Mujeres Town Plan

Gulf of Mexico

Mérida YUCATÁN

Isla Mujeres

○ Cancún

⬭ Cozumel

YUCATÁN PENINSULA

Playa del Carmen

QUINTANA ROO

Caribbean Sea

CAMPECHE

Beach 🢄
Information ⓘ
Post Office ✉

Calle Zazil-Há

Carlos Lazo

Playa Norte

Hidalgo

López Mateos

Mercado Municipal

Matamoros

Guerrero

Madero

Abasolo

Juárez

Morelos

Bravo

Allende

Avenida Rueda Medina

Passenger-ferry dock

Car-ferry dock

Area of Inset

Car ferry to Punta Sam

Caribbean Sea

Passenger ferry to Puerto Juárez

Bahía de Mujeres

Airstrip ✈

Turtle Sanctuary

Ariel Magaña ■ Baseball Park

Laguna Makax

Playa Pescador 🢄

Playa Lancheros 🢄

Caribbean Sea

El Garrafón National Underwater Park

Playa Garrafón 🢄

Lighthouse

Ferry route to Cancún
(see inset map)

● **ATTRACTIONS**
1. Cemeterio
2. Dolphin Discovery
3. El Garrafón
4. Hacienda Mundaca
5. Marina Puerto Isla Mujeres
6. Playa Norte
7. Plaza Municipal
8. Punta Sur
9. Tortugranja

■ **ACCOMMODATIONS**
10. Cabañas Maria del Mar
11. Casa Ixchel
12. Francis Arlene
13. Na Balam
14. Posada del Mar
15. Secreto
16. Villa Rolandi

◆ **RESTAURANTS**
17. Café Cito
18. Casa O's
19. Casa Rolandi
20. Elements of the Island Café
21. Lonchería Poc-Chuc
22. Pinguino
23. Pizza Rolandi
24. Playa Lancheros

✹ **NIGHTLIFE**
25. Buho's
26. Jax
27. Na Balam
28. Nitrox
29. Pinguino

From the 1960s to the mid-1980s, Isla was favored by backpacking travelers who wanted nothing more than a hammock under the palms and a freshwater shower. Campgrounds outnumbered hotels, and happy campers wandered barefoot on sandy streets. A few cafes served tacos and pizza, and a dozen hotels catered to those who preferred beds, bathrooms, and clean towels. Serious tourism was just beginning to develop when Hurricane Gilbert blew through in 1988, leaving massive destruction in its wake. It took a long time for Isla to recover—the government's attention was focused on Cancún's nearly instant makeover. The government acted far more efficiently after Hurricane Wilma in 2005, clearing rubble from the streets and handing out paint to business owners on the waterfront.

Today, Isla is prettier than it's been in decades, with fresh coats of yellow, blue, and red paint on wooden houses and shops. The long white beaches are raked daily, the palms are flourishing, and business owners are seriously courting travelers. The only thing missing is the hammock campgrounds.

Instead, Isla has several really good accommodations in the budget and moderate price ranges and a new wave of small boutique hotels. Tourists here are a blend of beach lovers who've been coming here for decades and newcomers seeking small-town life rather than the flash and glitz of a major beach resort.

QUICK FACTS *about* ISLA MUJERES

AIRPORT Isla has an airstrip, but it's primarily used by the military—there are no commercial flights. Visitors typically arrive and depart at the Cancún airport and take a ferry to the island (see below). You shouldn't have to overnight in Cancún unless your flights arrive late at night or leave early in the morning. In those cases, it's best to book a room in Cancún to avoid stressful situations.

CLIMATE Isla benefits from sea breezes that keep temperatures down, but it still has a tropical climate. Hurricanes are especially dangerous here. If you hear of a hurricane warning, go to the mainland. The average monthly temperature dips gently between 90°F and 80°F.

FERRIES Most visitors and locals arrive via the ferries from the Puerto Juárez or the Cancún hotel zone. If you're arriving in Cancún by air, you can get to Puerto Juárez, about 10 kilometers north of Cancún, by taxi, bus, or private transport. Tour companies can arrange transfers between the airport and the ferry terminal. The ride takes about 20 minutes and costs about $10 each way in a shared vehicle or $43 each way in a private vehicle. Arrange this type of private transfer before you travel by contacting **Best Day** (☎ 998-881-7206; **www .bestday.com**). Tell them you want direct service to Puerto Juárez and not a shared vehicle with passengers going to other locations. **Cancún Valet** (☎ 998-892-4014; **www.cancunvalet.com**) charges $40 one-way or $75 roundtrip for a van holding ten persons. Alternately, you can hire a taxi for about $15 each way. The least expensive way to reach the ferry is to take the public bus to the Cancún bus station (make sure it's not headed to Playa del Carmen) and a bus to Puerto Juárez; The cost is about $5 and the trip will take about 90 minutes.

The Puerto Juárez terminal has lockers, restaurants, and a porter to help with your bags. Ferries run every half hour, 6 a.m. to 11 p.m., and cost $3.50. The trip takes about 20 minutes. Schedules change frequently, so check the schedule board by the ticket window for your return time as well as your trip over to the island.

> *unofficial* **TIP**
> Some hotels on Isla offer transfer service from the Cancún airport or a private boat from one of the piers. Ask when making reservations.

More-expensive shuttles travel between the Embarcadero in Cancún's hotel zone and Isla Mujeres. The boats run five times a day from 9 a.m. to 9 p.m. and cost $15. Ferries arrive at Isla Mujeres's main dock at Avenida Medina and Calle Morelos. Count on the whole journey from the airport to Isla taking at least 90 minutes (longer if you're traveling by bus) if everything runs efficiently. There is also a car ferry from Punta Sam, north of Puerto Juárez, but there's no reason to bring a car to this tiny island unless you intend to move in.

> *unofficial* **TIP**
> Be sure to allow plenty of time for the ride back to town, no matter how you choose to tour around. Even tiny Isla has a bit of a rush hour in early evening.

GETTING AROUND Cars are unnecessary on Isla. Most people get around on scooters or in golf carts. Both can be rented at hotels and businesses in town; typical costs are $40 for 24-hours' worth of golf cart, and $25 to $35 a day or $11 per hour for a moped. Traffic putters along at about 20 mph. Even taxi drivers tend to drive at a leisurely pace. You often see caravans of golf carts headed to Garrafón; many Cancún tour companies include these merry little parades in their Isla tours. The leaders guide their troops to the side of the road occasionally, allowing other drivers to pass. Bicycles are available for rent, and they are great for short trips but the heat can get you down on long rides.

INTERNET ACCESS Air-conditioning and speedy DSL connection make **Isla Mujeres Internet Café** (Avenida Madero 17) popular. The charge is about $1 for 30 minutes. They'll let you hook up your laptop here. **Digitcenter** (Plaza Isla Mujeres) offers both broadband and Wi-Fi connections for your laptop as well as computers where you can check your mail.

TELEPHONES The area code is ☎ 998; all local phone numbers have seven digits. The old numbers were six digits only (and locals still

unofficial **TIP**
Several social-service agencies accept donations of clothing, school materials, toys, and medical supplies, and many frequent Isla travelers bring a suitcase full of gifts. For a list of agencies, see www.isla-mujeres.net.

refer to them this way). Add a 7 to the front of six-digit local numbers.

TOURIST INFORMATION The **Tourist Information Office** (Avenida Medina 130; ☎ 998-877-0307) is open Monday to Friday, 8 a.m. to 8 p.m. The clerks distribute brochures and information and can be of help with reservations and questions. **La Isleña** (Avenida Morelos between Avenida Medina and Avenida Juárez; ☎ 998-877-0578) has long been a great source of information. They run snorkeling and boat trips and are generous with info and assistance. **Isla Mujeres Net** (**www.isla-mujeres.net**) and **isla-mujeres.com.mx** are good sources for basic information.

WHERE *to* STAY *in* ISLA MUJERES

MANY OF ISLA'S ACCOMMODATIONS are clustered around Playa Norte and the town and are moderately priced. But a new wave of small boutique hotels has raised the island's profile. These private, serene inns are perfect for those who want total peace and relaxation. There are no major chain hotels on the island and only one all-inclusive (so far).

unofficial **TIP**
To save time, bring sufficient cash to cover meals, shopping, and incidentals while on the island. There's only one bank and a couple of money-exchange stands.

Rates increase significantly around holidays, so book your hotel room early. Depending on your flight times, you may have to overnight in Cancún; most hotels

How Accommodations Compare in Isla Mujeres

ACCOMMODATION	OVERALL	QUALITY	VALUE	COST
Villa Rolandi	★★★★	★★★★	★★★½	$$$$
Na Balam	★★★½	★★★★	★★★	$$$$
Casa Ixchel	★★★½	★★★	★★	$$
Secreto	★★★½	★★★½	★★½	$$$
Posada del Mar	★★★	★★★	★★★★	$
Cabañas Maria del Mar	★★	★★	★★★	$–$$
Francis Arlene	★½	★★	★★★★	$

will suggest the best place to stay in your price range. **Mornings in Mexico** (no phone; **www.morningsinmexico.com**) reserves rooms in several hotels and manages condo rentals. It's often easier to go through this local site than to try to call hotels yourself—especially if you don't speak Spanish.

Four Seasons Travel (☎ 800-555-8842; **www.yucatanres.com**) has specialized in Isla for years and can guide you to the right property.

ACCOMMODATION PROFILES

 Cabañas Maria del Mar $–$$

OVERALL ★★	QUALITY ★★	VALUE ★★★

Avenida Arq. Carlos Lazo No. 1; ☎ 998-877-0179 or 800-223-5695 U.S. and Canada; fax 998-877-0213; www.cabanasdelmar.com

This is one of Isla's oldest hotels, with plenty of modifications through the years. The least-expensive bungalow rooms face the gardens and pool in a two-story palapa-roofed building; rooms connect for families and groups. The Tower section is a two-story Mexican-style building with red-tile roofs holding 24 large rooms with refrigerators and wood furnishings; second-story rooms have a beach view from the balcony. The Castle section is across the street and has large rooms with refrigerators and large terraces overlooking the beach.

SETTING AND FACILITIES

Location On Playa Norte.

Dining 1 restaurant, complimentary Continental breakfast.

Amenities and services Beach, 2 pools, tour desk.

ACCOMMODATIONS

Rooms 73.

All rooms AC, fan, refrigerator.

Some rooms Ocean view, windows that open, balcony or terrace, satellite TV.

Comfort and decor Management is casually efficient and can help with every-thing from sending your piles of clothes to the laundry to arranging group functions. Guests wander barefoot between rooms, pool, and beach. The gardens provide shade and add to the hotel's character; they also harbor mosquitoes. You may need to use repellant in the evening. The restaurant's Buho's bar on Playa Norte is *the* gathering spot for tourists and locals at sunset.

PAYMENT, RESERVATIONS, AND RESTRICTIONS

Deposit 2-night deposit required; 15-day cancellation in low season, 30 days in high season for full refund.

Credit cards MC, V.

Check-in/out Noon/noon.

Casa Ixchel $$

OVERALL ★★★½	QUALITY ★★★	VALUE ★★

Avenida Martinez; ☎ 998-888-0107; www.casaixchelisla.com

A spiritual, holistic vibe resonates through this serene sanctuary on the island's windward side facing the open sea. The buildings are stark white, with slatted wood shading over sundecks and balconies. Internationally recognized shaman Heliodoro Benavides visits several times a year to conduct energy-balancing sessions and preside over weddings. Spa treatments are offered on an ocean-view terrace, and there is space for yoga sessions. The beach is rocky and the sea can be rough. But on calm days the snorkeling is great, and you might see dolphins swimming just offshore. Children are welcome at Christmas and Easter, but this isn't a great place for families.

SETTING AND FACILITIES

Location On the road paralleling the windward side.

Dining 1 restaurant.

Amenities and services Beach, spa, Internet.

ACCOMMODATIONS

Rooms 10.

All rooms Fan, windows that open, small kitchen, nonsmoking.

Some rooms AC, ocean view, balcony or terrace, large bathtub, separate bedroom, terrace.

Comfort and decor Rooms are named Love, Bliss, Contemplation, and such and are meant to inspire tranquility. Most have large tubs stocked with herbs and salts for leisurely soaking, and all have cushy beds with white linens. Those with full kitchens are stocked with French-press coffeemakers, refrigerators, and stovetop burners. Rates vary greatly, as all rooms are different.

PAYMENT, RESERVATIONS, AND RESTRICTIONS

Deposit Credit card, $25 nonrefundable service charge for cancellations more than 45 days before reserved date; more expensive penalties closer to date, and no refunds 14 days before arrival date.

Credit cards AE, MC, V.

Check-in/out 3 p.m./noon.

Francis Arlene $

OVERALL ★½	QUALITY ★★	VALUE ★★★★

Avenida Guerrero No. 7; ☎ 998-877-0310 or 998-877-0861;
www.francisarlene.com

We're fond of this family-run budget hotel on a back street in town. The Magañas keep their coral-colored buildings immaculately clean, and guests tend to return year after year. Though it's not on the beach, the hotel is a short walk from the open sea and about a 10-minute walk from Playa Norte. A small courtyard separates the buildings. Room rates are quoted in pesos and are very reasonable. If you ask for them in dollars, they get higher. E-mail responses are sometimes tardy—it's best to book through Mornings in Mexico (see page 128).

SETTING AND FACILITIES

Location On a back street in downtown between the bay and sea.

Dining No restaurant.

Amenities and services No extra services, no luggage storage.

ACCOMMODATIONS

Rooms 24.

All rooms Fans, refrigerators, no phones, no TV.

Some rooms AC, kitchenette, balcony.

Comfort and decor The rooms, simply decorated with tiled floors and floral bedspreads, are immaculately clean. There's always someone from the family on hand to help with any questions.

PAYMENT, RESERVATIONS, AND RESTRICTIONS

Deposit Credit-card deposit, fully refundable if canceled within 30 days of scheduled stay.

Credit cards Cash only, no credit cards.

Check-in/out Flexible.

Na Balam $$$$

OVERALL ★★★½	QUALITY ★★★★	VALUE ★★★

Calle Zazil-Há 118, Playa Norte; ☎ 998-877-0279; fax 998-877-0446; www.nabalam.com

An emphasis on health and serenity prevails at this extremely popular beachfront hotel. The beachside section has lush gardens around rooms facing the sea. The section on the other side of the road has a pool. The owner has filled the place with folk art, mostly from Chiapas and Guatemala. *Na balam* means "tiger" in Maya, and the cat's image appears in statues and on the hotel's stationery. Check the Web site for packages. The hotel sometimes hosts yoga workshops and weddings, and offers yoga classes. Breakfast and light meals are served in the casual snack bar by the beach, which is open until sunset. Dinner in the more formal (read: shoes and shirts required) Zazil Ha is a candlelit delight, and the chef is a pro at creating delicious vegetarian meals. Rates are significantly lower from May to December.

SETTING AND FACILITIES

Location Playa Norte.

Dining 1 restaurant, 1 snack bar.

Amenities and services Beach, pool, massage.

ACCOMMODATIONS

Rooms 33.

All rooms AC, fan, safe deposit box, terrace or balcony.

Some rooms Ocean view, windows that open, whirlpool tubs on the terrace, kitchen.

Comfort and decor The large rooms have white textiles, white walls, graceful wood furnishings with ornate carvings, peaked palapa ceilings, separate seating and dining areas, and folk-art decorations. Three suites are much larger and have king-size beds and whirlpool tubs. The rooms don't have TVs or other electronic gear; Internet access is available in the lobby.

PAYMENT, RESERVATIONS, AND RESTRICTIONS

Deposit 1-night deposit.

Credit cards MC, V.

Check-in/out 3 p.m./noon.

Posada del Mar $

OVERALL ★★★	QUALITY ★★★	VALUE ★★★★

Avenida Rueda Medina 15-A; ☎ 998-877-0044; fax 998-877-0266; www.posadadelmar.com

Some island regulars wouldn't consider staying anywhere but this rambling oldie that attracts a mixed bag of travelers. Families are happy with the large, simple rooms impervious to the wear of sand and wet clothes. Travelers counting their pesos find the hotel comfortable and accessible to town and the beach. The pool is buried in trees, lawn, and rock arches, and sits beside the palapa bar with its swing chairs and affable bartender. Hammocks swing under palm trees in a quiet, shady area near the pool. The pace is slow and congenial, especially if you speak a bit of Spanish. The restaurant serves breakfast, lunch, and dinner, and the palapa bar by the pool is a great place to hang out—literally—in swings at the bar.

SETTING AND FACILITIES

Location Across the street from Playa Norte near ferry pier.

Dining 1 restaurant.

Amenities and services Pool, tour desk.

ACCOMMODATIONS

Rooms 61.

All rooms AC, fan, windows that open, cable TV.

Some rooms Ocean view, balcony or terrace, bathtub, refrigerator, disabled access.

Comfort and decor The newest section's rooms are more refined, with niches, reading lamps over the beds, and sliding glass doors to the gardens. Mini-suites are the largest rooms and have refrigerators and microwaves. There's no elevator.

PAYMENT, RESERVATIONS, AND RESTRICTIONS

Deposit 1- to 2-night deposit before arrival, 3-day cancellation policy.

Credit cards AE, MC, V.

Check-in/out 3 p.m/1 p.m.

Secreto $$$

OVERALL ★★★½	QUALITY ★★★½	VALUE ★★½

Sección Rocas, Lote 11, Punta Norte; ☎ 998-877-1039, 998-877-1048, or 800-728-9098 U.S. and Canada; www.hotelsecreto.com; www.mexicoboutiquehotels.com

A white-on-white, ultraprivate retreat on a small beach near Playa Norte, Secreto looks very LA or South Beach. White gauze curtains flow from canopies over the beds; white walls angle around a lobby/lounge and pool. One expects to hear some sort of ethereal music in the background; thankfully, the guests determine the ambience. There's a two-night minimum stay; five nights minimum between December 20 and January 8.

SETTING AND FACILITIES

Location Near Na Balam on Half Moon Beach.

Dining No restaurant; complimentary Continental breakfast; room service from local restaurants.

Amenities and services Beach, pool, tour desk, room service, Internet.

ACCOMMODATIONS

Rooms 9.

All rooms AC, windows that open, ocean view, balcony or terrace, safe, refrigerator, satellite TV, CD, nonsmoking, Wi-Fi.

Some rooms King bed.

Comfort and decor Minimalists love the rooms' clean, fresh look; hermits and romantics enjoy the private terraces overlooking Half Moon Beach. The beach and water are visible from some beds when the sliding glass doors are open, and couches face the candlelit terraces. Towels are fluffy and soft, sheets crisp and cool, and iPods come pre-loaded with your style of music.

PAYMENT, RESERVATIONS, AND RESTRICTIONS

Deposit 2-night, nonrefundable deposit charged to credit card to reserve; 25% of balance if cancelled within 90 days, 50% if cancelled within 60 days, 100% charges for less than 30 days.

Credit cards AE, MC, V.

Check-in/out 3 p.m./noon.

Villa Rolandi $$$$

OVERALL ★★★★	QUALITY ★★★★	VALUE ★★★½

Fraccionamiento Laguna Mar; ☎ 998-877-0700 or 998-877-0100; www.villarolandi.com

This romantic boutique hotel gives Isla a certain cachet as a glamorous hideaway. Other island hotels have updated their rooms and amenities to meet this competition, but Rolandi still holds a special charm. Its restaurant is a standout. Privacy is protected; only guests are allowed by the horizon pool and small beach. The hotel is ideal for honeymooners and couples on romantic getaways—or celebrities who book the whole place. Complimentary Continental breakfast is slipped through a little niche in each suite each morning. A new thalassotherapy spa adds another level to the experience, with water therapies along with massages, wraps, and other spa treatments. Guests can book transfers from Cancún on the hotel's yacht. *Note:* Guests must be at least 13 years old.

SETTING AND FACILITIES

Location Between Laguna Makax and the sea facing Cancún.

Dining 1 restaurant.

Amenities and services Beach, pool, spa, gym, Internet.

ACCOMMODATIONS

Rooms 35 suites.

All rooms AC, ocean view, balcony or terrace, safe, minibar, satellite TV, CD.

Some rooms Nonsmoking, outdoor hot tub.

Comfort and decor The attention to detail is exceptional, with comfortable seating areas by the balconies and terraces (those away from the pool are designed for privacy), cushy beds with fine linens, and cozy robes in the spacious closets. The bathrooms have fabulous showers with dueling showerheads, jets, a small seat, and stereo speakers; they can be used as steam rooms. Green-marble counters have plenty of room for your toiletries, and there's a separate vanity area. All that's missing are hammocks on the terraces.

PAYMENT, RESERVATIONS, AND RESTRICTIONS

Deposit Credit card required to make reservation.

Credit cards AE, MC, V.

Check-in/out 3 p.m./noon.

WHERE *to* EAT *in* ISLA MUJERES

ISLA HAS A SURPRISING NUMBER and variety of restaurants. Many are clustered around the pedestrian zone on Avenida Hidalgo; those on the north end by the nightclubs tend to change names and management but are fun places to eat tacos and pizza while watching the crowd. Many of the hotels have good or even excellent restaurants; along with those listed in this section are **Zazil Ha** in the Na Balam and **La Cazuela** at the Roca Mar by the seafront *malecón* (promenade). You'll find several small palapa-covered beach bars and neighborhood

How Restaurants Compare in Isla Mujeres

RESTAURANT | CUISINE | COST	OVERALL	QUALITY	VALUE
Casa Rolandi | Gourmet Italian | Exp	★★★★	★★★½	★★★
Casa O's | Seafood/steak | Mod	★★★½	★★★	★★½
Pinguino | Mexican/seafood | Mod	★★★	★★★	★★★★
Pizza Rolandi | Italian | Mod	★★★	★★★	★★★
Playa Lancheros | Seafood | Inexp	★★½	★★★	★★★
Elements of the Island Café | Swiss/Breakfast | Inexp	★★½	★★½	★★½
Café Cito | Crêpes/international | Inexp	★½	★½	★★
Lonchería Poc-Chuc | Mexican/Yucatecan | Inexp	★	★	★★★

restaurants along the road to El Garrafón. Stop by for a cold drink and snack, and you're sure to get a feel for the Mexican residents of the island. All restaurants are casual; some do not accept credit cards.

RESTAURANT PROFILES

Café Cito   ★½

CRÊPES/INTERNATIONAL	INEXPENSIVE	QUALITY ★½	VALUE ★★

Downtown; Matamoros 42; ☎ 998-877-1470

Reservations Not accepted.

Entree range $3–$8.

Payment Cash only.

Service rating ★★.

Parking Street.

Bar No.

Dress Casual.

Disabled access Limited.

Customers Regular locals, travelers.

Hours Daily, 8 a.m.–2 p.m., year-round; open for dinner in high season.

SETTING AND ATMOSPHERE Glass tops cover arrangements of shells on sand on tables painted Mediterranean blue.

HOUSE SPECIALTIES Crêpes, waffles.

SUMMARY AND COMMENTS Visitors linger over newspapers and postcards as they sip espresso with their croissants. Crêpes filled with fruit, ice cream, or other treats, and baguettes stuffed with cream cheese and avocado or melted cheese with tomatoes are served for breakfast and lunch. This is a great, quiet place to take a breather when shopping downtown.

Casa O's ★★★½

SEAFOOD/STEAK	MODERATE	QUALITY ★★★	VALUE ★★½

Close to El Garrafón on south side of island; Carretera Garrafón s/n;
☎ **998-888-0170**

Reservations Recommended.

Entree range $8–$18.

Payment MC, V.

Service rating ★★★★.

Parking Street.

Bar Full service; good selection of wines from California, Mexico, France, and Chile.

Dress Casual.

Disabled access Not good.

Customers Locals on special nights out, travelers.

Hours Daily, 1–9 p.m.; closed October.

SETTING AND ATMOSPHERE A wooden walkway winds over a stream to a large palapa by the sand, where tables are covered in linens and candlelight sparkles on crystal.

HOUSE SPECIALTIES Lobster bisque, spiny lobster, Black Angus beef, shrimp kabobs.

SUMMARY AND COMMENTS Book a table for just before sunset, order a bottle of imported wine, and settle back for a romantic, enjoyable evening. Prices are high for the island, but the setting and delicious food are worth the splurge. If you can't spring for the lobster, try the fresh fish *veracruzano* style, with onions and tomatoes. Don't miss the Key lime pie. It seems your name must end in an O to work as a waiter here (hence Casa O's); it also helps to speak English and/or French and be sincerely accommodating.

Casa Rolandi ★★★★

GOURMET ITALIAN	EXPENSIVE	QUALITY ★★★½	VALUE ★★

Hotel Villa Rolandi by Laguna Makax; Fraccionamiento Laguna Mar;
☎ **998-877-0700**

Reservations Recommended.

Entree range $13–$30.

Payment AE, V, MC.

Service rating ★★★.

Parking Street.

Bar Full service.

Dress Casual chic.

Disabled access Yes.

Customers Hotel guests, island visitors, day-trippers from Cancún.

Hours Daily, 8 a.m.–10:30 p.m.

SETTING AND ATMOSPHERE Casually elegant open-air restaurant over the water fronting the main dining room; tables are set with linen cloths and crystal.

HOUSE SPECIALTIES Seafood carpaccio, black ravioli filled with shrimp, shrimp with saffron and sambuca, lamb chops.

SUMMARY AND COMMENTS Isla's leading gourmet restaurant is run by the Swiss-Italian family whose restaurants are renowned in the area for their wood-burning ovens and fabulous pizza. But the cuisine here is far more refined. White truffle oil is drizzled on carpaccio, arugula and radicchio cover salad plates, and homemade ravioli is filled with venison. Linger over a long lunch or dinner, and don't skip any courses. Finish with the silky passion fruit mousse or panna cotta with berries.

Elements of the Island Café ★★½

SWISS/BREAKFAST	INEXPENSIVE	QUALITY ★★½	VALUE ★★½

Downtown; Avenida Juárez 64 between Lopez Mateos and Matamoros; ☎ 998-877-0736

Reservations Not accepted.

Entree range $3–$7.

Payment Cash only.

Service rating ★★★.

Parking Some street parking.

Bar No.

Dress Casual.

Disabled access Possible at outdoor tables.

Customers Travelers and locals seeking healthful meals.

Hours Thursday–Tuesday, 7:30 a.m.–1 p.m.

SETTING AND ATMOSPHERE Wood tables, chairs and benches on sidewalk and inside a bright airy dining room with bulletin boards and lots of windows.

HOUSE SPECIALTIES Apple strudel, muesli, quiche.

SUMMARY AND COMMENTS Breakfast is a delight at this small cafe in an apartment building (vacation rentals available). If you crave natural yogurt, granola, and fresh fruit, look no further—and the muesli is great as well. Eggs are scrambled with *chaya* (similar to spinach) or fried and served with tasty potatoes. A few sandwiches are available as well, along with individual quiches. You could easily make a sinful meal of apple strudel topped with vanilla ice cream.

Lonchería Poc-Chuc ★

MEXICAN/YUCATECAN	INEXPENSIVE	QUALITY ★	VALUE ★★★

Downtown; Avenida Juárez at Abasolo; no phone

Reservations Not accepted.

Entree range $2–$7.

Payment Cash only.

Service rating ★★.

Parking Street.

Bar No.

Dress Casual.

Disabled access None.

Customers Locals, budget travelers.

Hours Monday–Saturday, 8 a.m.–10 p.m.

SETTING AND ATMOSPHERE Tiny, bare-bones restaurant a few steps above the street, with seven wobbly wooden tables.

HOUSE SPECIALTIES *Poc-chuc, panuchos,* tacos.

SUMMARY AND COMMENTS Few places in Isla's traveler areas serve authentic Yucatecan dishes. Most of the standards (see our "Guide to the Mexican Menu," pages 62–63) are on the menu at this little neighborhood restaurant, where meals are served on plastic plates and diners tend to be taking a break from jobs at nearby businesses. The *poc-chuc* (marinated, grilled pork chop) is a good choice, as is *cochinita pibil* (marinated pork baked in banana leaves). The cooking is simple, and portions are small.

 Playa Lancheros ★★½

SEAFOOD	INEXPENSIVE	QUALITY ★★★	VALUE ★★★

Middle of the west coast of the island, just past the hacienda Mundaca on the way to Garrafón; no phone

Reservations Not accepted.

Entree range $8–$15.

Payment No credit cards.

Service rating ★½.

Parking Street.

Bar Beer, tequila, rum.

Dress Beach casual.

Disabled access Difficult.

Customers Locals on weekend afternoons, travelers during the week.

Hours Daily, 11 a.m.–sunset.

SETTING AND ATMOSPHERE Beach basic, with palapas for shade over picnic tables, children playing in the sand nearby.

HOUSE SPECIALTIES Ceviche, *pescado tikin-xic.*

SUMMARY AND COMMENTS A classic Mexican Sunday afternoon includes a long, leisurely lunch with the whole family. On Isla, the generations gather on the beach at this casual cafe. They visit over platters of mixed seafood ceviche, and Yucatecan *pescado tikin-xic,* the freshest fish of the day seasoned with *achiote* (reddish annatto seed), baked in banana leaves and served with fresh tortillas, shredded cabbage, and limes. The beer bottles accumulate, someone pulls out a guitar, and everyone sings melancholic ballads. Only the setting sun forces the sated diners to disperse. This is the perfect place to experience this family tradition and enjoy a superb meal. The menu includes barbecued chicken, guacamole, and nachos.

Pinguino ★★★

MEXICAN/SEAFOOD	MODERATE	QUALITY ★★★	VALUE ★★★★

Downtown across from the main beach; Avenida Rueda Medina 15-A; ☎ 998-877-0044

Reservations Accepted.

Entree range $7–$12.

Payment MC, V.

Service rating ★★★.

Parking Street.

Bar Full service.

Dress Casual.

Disabled access Yes.

Customers Hotel guests, island visitors, locals.

Hours Daily, 7 a.m.–10 p.m.

SETTING AND ATMOSPHERE Large dining room set just above the sidewalk, across from the beach. Tables on the balcony at the rail have excellent sunset view. New furnishings and post-Wilma renovations have updated this old favorite.

HOUSE SPECIALTIES Seafood soup, seafood platter for two, lobster.

SUMMARY AND COMMENTS Everything the cooks prepare is fresh and yummy, from the fruit and yogurt at breakfast to the fabulous lobster tail at dinner. The cuisine isn't gourmet, but it's very good—and the setting is more peaceful than at restaurants in the middle of town. Try the enormous platter of grilled fish and shellfish for two.

Pizza Rolandi ★★★

ITALIAN	MODERATE	QUALITY ★★★	VALUE ★★★

Downtown; Avenida Hidalgo 110; ☎ 998-877-0429

Reservations Not accepted.

Entree range $6–$13.

Payment AE, V, MC.

Service rating ★★★.

Parking Limited street parking.

Bar Full service.

Dress Casual.

Disabled access Limited.

Customers Everybody on the island.

Hours Daily, 11 a.m.–11:30 p.m.

SETTING AND ATMOSPHERE Front tables face the pedestrian sidewalk; in the back, a huge dining room sits in a courtyard beneath the Hotel Belmar. Try for a table away from the wood-burning oven.

HOUSE SPECIALTIES Lobster pizza, baked chicken, coconut ice cream with Kahlúa.

SUMMARY AND COMMENTS It seems every visitor has at least one meal at this island institution (sister to the more gourmet Casa Rolandi). The pizzas are crisp and loaded with toppings of your choice; salads are fresh and bountiful; and there are plenty of other pasta, seafood, and beef selections. The crowd is convivial—you might run into fellow travelers you've met during your ramblings or locals who've helped you at shops and hotels.

SIGHTSEEING *in* ISLA MUJERES

ISLA SEEMS TO FLOAT LIKE A REEF ATOP THE WATER. It's so skinny—half a mile at its widest point—and so flat you can easily imagine the sea washing right over it. Most of the residences and businesses sit atop the northern section on a fairly substantial hunk of ground between the **Bahía de Isla Mujeres** and the open sea. The town extends from the ferry pier on the bay at Avenida Medina four blocks northeast to a *malecón* (waterfront promenade) facing the sea.

Shops, budget hotels, and restaurants line the ten cross-streets running east to west. It's pretty hard to get lost, but the streets sometimes seem like a maze. The **Plaza Municipal** is little more than a cement slab in front of the undistinguished city hall at Juárez and Bravo; a pedestrian walkway leads to the *malecón*, a great place to stroll any time of day.

ATTRACTIONS

Playa Norte, WHICH RUNS FROM AVENIDA MEDINA to land's end, is the center of the action for most of Isla's visitors. The beach faces shallow, crystalline, calm water and is dotted with palapa-roofed bars and a few hotels. Umbrellas, lounge chairs, and some beach toys are available for rent. Fortunately, there aren't a lot of powered watercrafts buzzing about. A sandy road runs parallel to the beach past the **Cemeterio** (Cemetery) on Calle Zazil-Há. The pirate Fermín Mundaca had his tomb with skull and crossbones put here, though he was buried elsewhere. The monument is here, but it's unmarked and hard to find. The seaside cemetery is packed with floral bouquets (many plastic) and plaster angels.

Avenida Medina runs southwest nearly the whole length of the island; the name of the street eventually changes to Carretera Garrafón. Another unnamed road branches off Medina at the south edge of **Laguna Makax,** a large lagoon that shelters the busy **Marina Puerto Isla Mujeres.** The marina has 70 slips, gas, and a large boat-yard where all the vessels from Cancún are maintained.

Dolphin Discovery (☎ 998-193-3360; **www.dolphindiscovery.com**) is on the bay side of the road. It is recommended that you make reservations in advance if you want to swim, dive, or simply have an encounter with the dolphins. The facility is open from 9 a.m. to 5 p.m. Prices start at $69 for adults and $59 for children for a simple dolphin encounter.

kids Another road juts west to **Playa Lancheros,** where the water is calm and there are plenty of palms for shade. This is a good spot to stop for a swim and lunch. Nearby **Tortugranja** (☎ 998-877-0595) is a science center focused on protecting the sea turtles that lay their eggs on Isla's beaches. A few turtles are being raised in the center's outdoor tanks; inside the buildings are aquariums and exhibits on sea turtles, plus a shop selling books, videos, and turtle-oriented souvenirs. The center is fascinating (kids love the baby turtles), and its proceeds help protect the turtles and their eggs and babies. To get there, take Avenida Rueda Medina south of town; about a block southeast of Hacienda Mundaca, take the right fork (the smaller road that loops back north); the entrance is about a half kilometer (quarter mile) farther, on the left. Admission is $3, and the center is open daily, 9 a.m. to 5 p.m.

A crumbling rock archway marks the entrance to **Hacienda Mundaca** (no phone), built by the pirate Fermín Mundaca for an island girl he loved. As the legend goes, the maiden didn't return his affection, and Mundaca lived a lonely life amid his tropical gardens and rambling estate. He deserted the hacienda and died in Mérida. Some guides say the Mundaca story is bunk, and that a slave-trader impersonated the pirate. Whoever built the hacienda left it to crumble into ruins that travelers and locals enjoy exploring. The municipality has taken over the grounds and turned it into a park and zoo. Spider monkeys, white-tailed deer, a boa constrictor, and a jaguar are kept in roomy cages with plaques bearing the names of the animals in Maya; crocodiles sun at the edge of ponds. The remains of a chapel, cannons, and a few buildings are buried in thick bushes and vines. It's a pleasant, shady place to wander about for an hour. Bring bug repellent and go early, before the sun makes the jungle setting hot and steamy. The hacienda is located east off Avenida Rueda Medina. Take the main road southeast from town to an S-curve at the end of Laguna Makax, and then turn left onto a dirt road. Open daily, 9 a.m. to 5 p.m.; admission is $1.

The biggest attraction on Isla is **El Garrafón** (Carretera El Garrafón, 2.5 km (1.5 miles) southeast of Playa Lancheros; ☎ 998-193-3360 (park), 866-393-5158 in the U.S.; **www.garrafon.com**), an underwater preserve and marine park. The same people who created Xcaret (see Part Four, Cancún, page 115) took over the neglected park a few years ago and turned it into a commercial complex that is now run by Dolphin Discovery. Snorkeling here can be an adventure, depending on the currents, because the water swirls around rocky inlets. But you'll see large schools of parrotfish, angelfish, and other sea creatures. Hammocks hang under palms along a grassy slope above the water; some visitors set up housekeeping in this area for the day. Beach chairs and palapas are set on various sand areas, and there are large shower, locker, and scuba and snorkel rental facilities. Admission rates vary. All-inclusive rate, including meals and domestic alcohol, costs about $50 for adults and children if you're staying on the island, or $89 adults, $65 kids under age 12 including transportation from Cancún. More expensive packages include international-liquor, zip-line, and bicycle tours. Tours from Cancún arrive throughout the day. If you're staying on the island, get here early to avoid the crowds. The park is open daily, 9 a.m. to 5 p.m.

Garrafón's management has taken over the southern tip of the island, site of the lighthouse and small Maya temples believed to have been pilgrimage sites for women. You now have to pay an admission fee of $5 to enter the area called **Punta Sur.** A pathway lined with enormous metal sculptures leads to the ruins atop a ragged cliff. Admission to this area is included in the Garrafón admission package.

unofficial **TIP**
The snorkeling is just as good, if not better, in the waters near the park. Garrafón de Castilla next door charges just $2 for use of showers, bathrooms, and a small beach.

TOURS *and* SIDE TRIPS *from* ISLA MUJERES

BOAT TOURS

BOAT CAPTAINS WHO RUN SNORKELING, diving, and sightseeing trips congregate at the **Sociedad Cooperativa Turística** (Avenida Medina just north of the pier; ☎ 998-877-0714 or 998-877-1304). Most of the boats are small skiffs (called *pangas*) that comfortably carry four to six people. You can hire one to cruise along the bay side of the island to Garrafón and the waters below the lighthouse. Captains arrange various types of tours that last four hours and can include food and drink.

unofficial **TIP**
Hire a boat for a couple of hours around sunset and have the captain putter around the coast for a gorgeous view of Cancún with the sky streaked pink and gold.

The system is very informal; you just shop around until you get a captain and price you like. Typically, four hours of fishing close to shore costs $100, while eight hours farther out costs $240. Consider getting a boat with an awning or some form of shade—it may cost more, but it will save your skin from burning. The captains also run sportfishing trips; some will take you to Puerto Juárez for less money than the ferry. The journey can get rough, however.

ISLA CONTOY

BIRDERS IN PARTICULAR ARE FASCINATED with **Isla Contoy,** 19 miles north of Isla Mujeres. The four-mile-long island is a haven for herons, flamingos, spoonbills, petrels, and dozens of other migratory species. The island has been a wildlife sanctuary since 1981 and has gone through several migrations of its own. At times, visitors have been allowed to go onshore and visit a small museum; at other times, they were restricted to a small landing area. There have even been times when the island was completely off limits. The whims of various marine, military, and environmental agencies are unpredictable. These days the island has hiking trails, a museum, a small souvenir shop, picnic areas, and bird-watching areas. **Amigos de Isla Contoy** (☎ 998-884-7483 in Cancún; **www.islacontoy.org**) monitors the environmental issues on the island and is a great source of info. Tours to Contoy usually include lunch, which often consists of grilled fish caught along the 45-minute trip to the island. Shop around the **Sociedad Cooperativa Turística** (Avenida Medina just north of the pier; ☎ 998-877-0714 or 998-877-1304) for a tour, which usually lasts about four hours and costs $38 to $50. Ask if the boat actually stops at the island; if so, you must pay a $5 authorization fee. Stop by the co-op's offices and inspect the boats, talk with the captains and set up your trip a few days before you want to go, if possible.

Serious bird-watchers and nature lovers may want to set up their trip in advance, which can be difficult through the Cooperativa. **Captain Tony** (☎ 998-877-0229; **www.isla-mujeres.net/capttony/home.htm**) gets rave reviews for his Contoy trips. **La Isleña** (Avenida Morelos between Avenida Medina and Avenida Juárez; ☎ 998-877-0578) runs tours to Isla Contoy and has a stand in front of the shop staffed by friendly clerks who are loaded with local tips. Tours leave from the dock at 8:30 a.m. daily and include a light breakfast, snorkel dive, tour of the lee side of Isla Contoy, and a fresh-cooked lunch, all for $40. **Captain Ricardo Gaitan** (Fraccionamiento I Madero; ☎ 998-877-1363; **www.isla-mujeres.net/contoy/home.htm**) runs trips to the island either by motorboat or sailboat. The trip includes lunch, drinks, fishing along the way, and snorkeling opportunities. Both companies offer fishing and snorkeling tours.

EXERCISE *and* RECREATION *in* ISLA MUJERES

SCUBA DIVING AND SNORKELING

El Garrafón is the obvious place to snorkel, but the admission is steep. However, the fish don't stick to the park's boundaries, and you can snorkel other places without paying a huge fee. At **Garrafón de Castillo** (☎ 998-877-0107), just north of the park, the proprietors charge a paltry $2 for visitors to snorkel off the shores and coves adjacent to the park. Showers and restrooms are available. Snorkeling is sometimes good off Playa Norte between Na Balam and the tip of the island by the Avalon resort if the tide is high.

The scuba diving off Isla doesn't compare to Cozumel's and the mainland reefs. But a certain kind of diver can't resist **Las Cuevas de los Tiburones Dormidos** (Caves of the Sleeping Sharks). The caves, about three miles northeast of the island, were discovered by a fisherman diving for lobster. He noticed that the sharks in this certain area seemed lethargic; Jacques Cousteau, *National Geographic,* and Ramón Bravo (Mexico's leading shark expert) came by and made the caves famous. Blacktip and bull sharks hover in the caves as if sleeping, and divers can swim about the area without attacks. The dive is for only the most experienced divers, however, as the sharks stick between 80 and 150 feet below the surface. More-accessible dive sites include **Los Manchones,** a two-kilometer set of reefs about ten minutes from Isla by boat. Isla's dive shops have also started running whale shark tours in summer. The docile giant sharks migrate to the waters north of Isla, near Isla Holbox. The trip is a full-day adventure and there's no guarantee you'll see the sharks. But when you do, it's an awesome experience. The whale sharks sometimes come closer to Isla Mujeres, and the trip isn't as arduous (see "Isla Holbox," page 112). **Delfin Sea Hawk Divers** (Avenida Lazo; ☎ 998-877-0296; **www.isla-mujeres.net/seahawkdivers**) run trips to several local sites including the Caves of the Sleeping Sharks.

SHOPPING *in* ISLA MUJERES

ISLA'S SHOPS ARE MORE INTERESTING than those in Cancún if you're looking for folk art and ethnic souvenirs. Juan Carlos Peña has assembled an exceptional collection of masks at **Aztlán** (Calle Madero; ☎ 998-877-0419). Unlike the manufactured pieces you see at most shops, Peña's masks are the real thing, handmade in Guerrero, Michoacán, and other folk-art centers. **Emilio Sosa Medin** (no phone) creates extraordinary papier-mâché *alebrijes* (dragons) and masks at his shop on López Mateos between Guerrero and Hidalgo.

His most spectacular pieces take many months to create and cost hundreds or thousands of dollars. The arcades along Avenida Hidalgo and Matamoros sell batik sarongs from Bali, manufactured Mexican pottery and jewelry, and some original crafts. **Artesanías Arco Iris** (Avenida Juárez at Hidalgo; no phone) accepts credit cards and is packed with hammocks, embroidered dresses, Oaxacan rugs, and other good-quality arts and crafts. The **Mercado de Artesanías** (Avenidas Matamoros and Lazo) has several stands displaying a wide range of goods from Guatemalan textiles to Oaxacan pottery. **De Corazón** (Avenida Abasalo between Avenidas Hidalgo and Guerrero; ☎ 998-100-1211) displays handcrafted soaps and herbal teas made on the island along with paintings, clothing, and jewelry created by local artists.

The aromas from **Panadería la Reina** (Avenida Madero at Juárez; ☎ 998-877-0419) are irresistible—stop by for *bolillos* (soft rolls), *empanadas,* ham-and-cheese rolls, cookies, and other treats. You can put together a picnic lunch here or buy a few snacks for your room (note that they're closed on Sunday). Isla's **Mercado Municipal** is a small affair on the north end of Guerrero. It's a good place to buy fresh tropical fruit (mangoes are best in May and June), tortillas, and veggies.

unofficial **TIP**
Isla Mujeres is a conservative and family-oriented community, and rowdy behavior is frowned upon. This isn't the best destination for party lovers.

NIGHTLIFE *in* ISLA MUJERES

THE NIGHTLIFE SCENE ON ISLA GETS MORE active every year. Lately, the action takes place on the north end of avenidas Guerrero and Hidalgo. The street is closed to vehicles, and the walkway is crammed with sidewalk tables spilling out from bars and cafes. The names of the businesses change, and popularity is based on the type of visitors on the island. In August, it has a very European flair, while Mexicans prevail around Easter and Semana Santa. **Jax** (Avenida Mateos 42; ☎ 998-877-1218) has a sports bar with satellite TV and good burgers on the first floor and an open-air restaurant and bar with a sea view on the second. On Playa Norte, the beach bars at **Buho's** (Cabañas Maria del Mar, Avenida Arq. Carlos Lazo 1; ☎ 998-877-0179) and **Na Balam** (Calle Zazil-Há No. 118, Playa Norte; ☎ 998-877-0279), stay crowded under the moonlight. **Pinguino** (Avenida Rueda Medina 15, at Hotel Posada del Mar; ☎ 998-877-0044) was one of Isla's first late-night hangouts, and it remains a good place to mingle with locals. Move from here to the hotel bar seemingly buried in jungle beside the pool, and grab a swing seat at the bar. Dancers delight in the salsa nights and rock nights at **Nitrox** (Avenida Matamoros 87; ☎ 998-887-0568).

PART SIX

COZUMEL

CRUISING *to* A QUIET ISLAND

YOU HAVE TO STAY A FEW NIGHTS, far from the cruise-ship piers and tourist attractions, to appreciate the languid lifestyle, awesome snorkeling and diving, and multiethnic character of this Caribbean island. Sadly, most of the tourists who visit Cozumel arrive on cruise ships—the island is the busiest cruise port in Mexico. There are at least three ships in port most days, and few times when there isn't a white behemoth on the horizon. It's a shame the passengers get such a limited view of Cozumel, one of Mexico's most charming and loveable destinations. Once the site of religious pilgrimages by Maya women, Cozumel became a mecca for scuba divers after Jacques Cousteau stopped by in the 1960s. Word of the chain of reefs, underwater canyons, and walls off the island's shores soon spread. Cozumel has been on lists of the world's top-ten dive sites for decades, and it marks the beginning of the **Palancar Reef** (also called the Maya Reef), the second-longest barrier reef system in the world. That it has become a major cruise port alarms environmentalists. The ships arrive north of the **Cozumel Underwater Marine Park,** but accidents do happen. If you're a scuba diver and you haven't been to Cozumel, you'd better get here soon.

Cozumel is calmer than Cancún, more compact than the Caribbean Coast, and more sophisticated than Isla Mujeres. The selection of hotels, restaurants, and activities is varied—and even those seeking extravagant luxury find suitable

unofficial **TIP**
Hurricane Wilma hovered here for more than 36 hours in October 2005, ravaging the coastline, tearing apart cruise-ship piers, and flooding streets and homes. But Cozumel's recovery has been amazing: infrastructure was quickly repaired, and cruise ships (critical to the local economy) soon returned. The waterfront *malecón* in downtown San Miguel was rebuilt and looks better than ever. Most hotels underwent complete renovations, modernizing their facilities and room amenities.

lodgings. Cozumel benefits from being a long-standing community confined within 189 square miles of scrubby jungle, white-sand beaches, and city streets. The only town is **San Miguel,** which begins at the leeward waterfront and spreads out along the west side of the island. The central plaza is a classic with its ornate gazebo, blossoming flamboyant trees, and plentiful park benches. It's just a block from the ferry dock and is at its finest on Sunday evenings when bands playing everything from military marches to mambo attract local crowds. Even when there isn't live music, somebody brings large speakers and sets the tune for dancing. The sound of prayers and singing resounds from the **Iglesia de San Miguel,** which sits in the midst of the tourist-oriented pedestrian zone. Try to include a Sunday in your stay.

Cozumel is only 33 miles long and 9 miles wide, and it has few main roads. The Carretera runs along the waterfront nearly the length of the leeward side of the island, changing names along the way. In the south, it's called Carretera Sur, and sometimes Carretera a Chankanaab (the road to **Chankanaab**). In town it becomes Avenida Rafael Melgar, then Carretera Norte. At the southern tip of the island, Carretera Sur cuts inland to the windward side of the island and runs along the coast. Pretty simple, all in all.

Calle 11, near the giant **Chedraui** supermarket and **Cineopolis** movie theater, is the main road into the commercial and residential areas of town. The Boulevard Aeropuerto Internacional runs inland at the north end of town by the Navy base and becomes the Carretera Transversal, crossing through residential neighborhoods and low jungle to the windward side. Most of the northern part of the island is undeveloped. A dirt road leads to private residences and the **Punta Molas** lighthouse at the northern tip.

QUICK FACTS *about* COZUMEL

AIRPORT AND AIRLINES **Cozumel Airport** (☎ 987-872-0928) is just a few miles north of San Miguel. *Colectivos* (shared vans) carry travelers from the airport to their hotels for about $7 to $20 per person; you'll pay about double that for individual service. Private taxis can be hired from the hotel zone ($9 to $25 from the all-inclusives at the south tip) and downtown (about $5) to the airport. Airline service varies with the season.

American Airlines operates a daily flight from Dallas. **Continental Airlines** operates a daily flight from Houston and **US Airways** flies daily from Charlotte **Mexicana** has nonstop service from Mexico City. **US Airways** has flights from Charlotte, North Carolina, and Delta flies three days a week from Atlanta, Georgia. Frontier has a Saturday flight from Denver, Colorado. **Mayair** operates several shuttle flights between Cozumel and Cancún. Airline service comes and goes with the season and there are usually more options in the inter season.

You can also fly in and out of Cancún and take a bus to Playa del Carmen for the ferry to Cozumel. The **Riviera** bus line has frequent bus service from the Cancún airport to Playa del Carmen.

unofficial **TIP**
Beware of baggage restrictions on the small planes from the mainland. Some allow only one bag and charge for more—a considerable expense for travelers with dive gear. Choose a flight on a larger plane, and ask about restrictions when you buy your ticket.

DRIVING Car rentals abound, and the vehicles are often in rough shape. The least-expensive cars rent for about $50 a day, including taxes and insurance. Most insurance policies don't allow you to take the vehicle off paved roads— a prohibition that's often ignored. Major agencies, including **Avis** and **Executive,** have desks at the airport, and there are several independent local agencies.

Mopeds and scooters are extremely popular with locals and travelers. They're also terribly dangerous, especially for first-timers. Helmets are required and provided with rentals. Use them. People are forever falling off these bikes, scraping their sunburns miserably, and more-serious accidents are common. Try to stick to the shoulder of the road. Taxi drivers tend to get frustrated when stuck behind a puttering scooter. Mopeds rent for about $25 per day; insurance is included.

FERRIES Passenger ferries connect Playa del Carmen (☎ 987-873-0067) and Cozumel's main pier (☎ 987-869-2775), running most every hour on the hour between 5 a.m. and 11 p.m. (check current schedule, as hours vary with the season and there may be reduced service). The trip takes 45 minutes and may be canceled in inclement weather. The fare is around $14 for adults and $8 for children. A vehicle ferry departs from the Calica terminal pier (☎ 987-872-7688), south of Playa del Carmen. The fare starts at about $55 for small cars (more for larger vehicles) and $5 per passenger.

GETTING AROUND Taxis here are far from cheap, but they do have set rates. Expect to pay between $9 and $12 from downtown to Parque Chankanaab, and between $18 and $40 from downtown to the southern all-inclusive resorts. The set rates are posted at the ferry pier, cruise-ship piers, and hotels, and many drivers carry complicated rate and zone charts. For half-day trips around the island, consider renting a cab by the hour or day. Drivers charge upwards of $15 an hour. You can hire a radio cab or make a complaint at **Sitio de Taxis** (Taxi Syndicate; ☎ 987-872-0041). Local public bus service runs through San Miguel and the urban neighborhoods, but not along the hotel zones.

INTERNET ACCESS More hotels on Cozumel are offering computer hookups and Wi-Fi in the rooms or public spaces. If you need Internet

Cozumel Island

Gulf of Mexico

Isla Mujeres

Mérida

YUCATÁN

Cancún

Cozumel

YUCATÁN
PENINSULA

Playa del
Carmen

QUINTANA
ROO

*Caribbean
Sea*

CAMPECHE

*Caribbean
Sea*

Punta Molas Lighthouse
Punta Molas

Laguna Xlapak

Punta Norte
Isla de la
Pasión

13

Castillo
Real

14

Downtown Pier
7 **15**

Punta Langosta
Cruise-ship Pier

← To Playa
del Carmen
(45 mins.)

✈ Airport

17 San Miguel
de Cozumel

5

*Cozumel
Channel*

8 **10**

6

Santa Rosa

Playa Bonita

N. Paraíso Reef

Car Ferry

S. Paraíso Reef

4 **1** *Laguna
Chankanaab*

*Chankanaab
Reef*

Santa Cecilia

*Tormentos
Reef*

11

Punta Morena

*Yucab
Reef*

*Santa
Rosa
Reef*

9 Playa San
Francisco

2

Playa Chen Río

*San
Francisco
Reef*

12

16

Punta Chiqueros

*Palancar
Reef*

Playa
Palancar

El Mirador

Palancar Reef

Tumba de
Caracol

*Laguna
Colombia*

*Caribbean
Sea*

3

Punta Sur
Punta Celarain

Punta Celarain Lighthouse

Airport ✈
Beach ⚓
Ferry Route
Ruins

| 0 | 5 mi |
| 0 | 5 km |

● **ATTRACTIONS**
1. Discover Mexico
2. El Cedral
3. Faro de Celarain Eco Park
4. Parque Chankanaab
5. San Gervasio

■ **ACCOMMODATIONS**
6. Hotel Cozumel
and Resort

7. Coral Princess
8. Cozumel Palace
9. Fiesta Americana Cozumel
Dive Resort
10. Hotel Cozumel and Resort
11. Hotel Presidente
InterContinental Cozumel
12. Iberostar Cozumel
13. Meliá Cozumel All-Inclusive
Beach and Golf Resort

14. Playa Azul

◆ **RESTAURANTS**
15. La Cabaña del Pescador
Lobster House
16. Coconuts
17. Jeanie's Beach Club

San Miguel de Cozumel

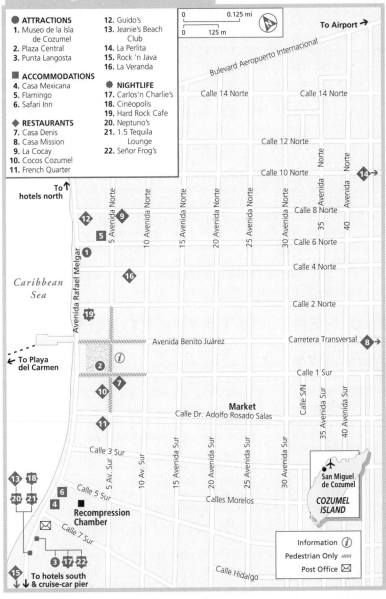

● **ATTRACTIONS**
1. Museo de la Isla de Cozumel
2. Plaza Central
3. Punta Langosta

■ **ACCOMMODATIONS**
4. Casa Mexicana
5. Flamingo
6. Safari Inn

◆ **RESTAURANTS**
7. Casa Denis
8. Casa Mission
9. La Cocay
10. Cocos Cozumel
11. French Quarter
12. Guido's
13. Jeanie's Beach Club
14. La Perlita
15. Rock 'n Java
16. La Veranda

♣ **NIGHTLIFE**
17. Carlos'n Charlie's
18. Cinéopolis
19. Hard Rock Cafe
20. Neptuno's
21. 1.5 Tequila Lounge
22. Señor Frog's

0   0.125 mi
0   125 m

To Airport →

Bulevard Aeropuerto Internacional

Calle 14 Norte   Calle 14 Norte

Calle 12 Norte

Calle 10 Norte

Calle 8 Norte

Calle 6 Norte

Calle 4 Norte

Calle 2 Norte

Avenida Rafael Melgar

5 Avenida Norte
10 Avenida Norte
15 Avenida Norte
20 Avenida Norte
25 Avenida Norte
30 Avenida Norte
35 Avenida Norte
40 Norte

To ↑ hotels north

Caribbean Sea

← To Playa del Carmen

Avenida Benito Juárez

Carretera Transversal **→**

Calle 1 Sur

Market
Calle Dr. Adolfo Rosado Salas

Calle 3 Sur

5 Av. Sur
10 Av. Sur
15 Avenida Sur
20 Avenida Sur
25 Avenida Sur
30 Avenida Sur
35 Avenida Sur
40 Avenida Sur
Calle S/N

Calle 5 Sur

Calles Morelos

Recompression Chamber

Calle 7 Sur

To hotels south & cruise-car pier

Calle Hidalgo

San Miguel de Cozumel

COZUMEL ISLAND

Information ⓘ
Pedestrian Only ////
Post Office ✉

access frequently, be sure to ask about access before booking a room. Many hotels have a computer you can use to check your e-mail; charges range from free to $8 an hour. The **Crew Office** (Avenida 5, No. 201, between Calle 3 Sur and Avenida Rosada Salas; ☎ 987-869-1485) is a friendly spot with lots of computers, high-speed Internet, laptop stations, long-distance phone booths, and a book exchange.

Coffee Net (Avenida Rafael Melgar near Calle 25; ☎ 987-872-6394) is easily located and has reasonable prices.

TELEPHONES The area code is ☎ **987.** All phone numbers should have seven digits, with a three-digit area code. If you run across an older, six-digit local number, add an 8 at the beginning.

TOURIST INFORMATION The **Cozumel Island Hotel Association** (Calle 2 Norte at Avenida 15; ☎ 987-872-3132; fax 987-872-2809) offers information about tours and other things as well as the scoop on island accommodations. The **Cozumel Tourism Promotion Board** is located in the same building with different phone number (☎ 987-872-7585). The Web site at **islacozumel.com.mx** is very informative.

Cozumel My Cozumel (**www.cozumelmycozumel.com**) has great chat boards with lots of tips and recommendations. Vacation-home rental agencies and real-estate agencies have informative Cozumel Web sites. The sites **www.islacozumel.org** and **www.gocozumel.com** are particularly up to date.

WHERE *to* STAY *in* COZUMEL

unofficial **TIP**
As the coral heads start growing again, the fish are slowly returning close to shore, and the snorkeling is getting better at beach clubs. But it's best to head out farther on a boat tour to see corals, sponges, and swarms of tropical fish.

COZUMEL'S LEEWARD SHORE is lined with hotels. Few have more than 200 rooms, and there are dozens of small, one-of-a-kind properties. The southwest side of the island, along Carretera Sur, is ideal for serious divers who want quick access to prime reefs and walls. At the far south end of the island, all-inclusive hotels claim miles of beach and scrubby jungle. The water isn't always clear in this area. If snorkeling from shore is important, you're better off farther north. On the other hand, prime dive sites are a short boat ride away.

These all-inclusives still have the *cozumeleño* pace and ambience—it's not like they could be dropped on to Cancún's shores. Cabs to town are costly from these places; ask if there's a shuttle or try to share a van with a group. Some all-inclusives have deals with bars and restaurants in town that give discounts if you're wearing the hotel's annoying plastic bracelet. Be sure to get out at least for a day and explore the archaeological sites, parks, and town.

How Accommodations Compare in Cozumel

ACCOMMODATION	OVERALL	QUALITY	VALUE	COST
Hotel Presidente InterContinental Cozumel	★★★★★	★★★★★	★★★★	$$$–$$$$$
Cozumel Palace	★★★★	★★★★	★★★	$$$$
Playa Azul	★★★★	★★★½	★★★★	$$$
Iberostar Cozumel	★★★½	★★★½	★★★★	$$$$
El Cid La Ceiba	★★★½	★★★½	★★★	$$-$$$
Hotel Cozumel and Resort	★★★	★★½	★★★½	$$
Meliá Cozumel All-Inclusive Beach and Golf Resort	★★★	★★	★★★★	$$$$
Casa Mexicana	★★★	★★★	★★	$$
Coral Princess	★★½	★★½	★★	$$$
Safari Inn	★★	★★½	★★★★½	$
Flamingo	★★	★★	★★★	$
Fiesta Americana Cozumel Dive Resort	★★	★★	★★	$$

Chankanaab separates the all-inclusives from the next group of hotels to the north, which have access to great offshore dive sites and rocky beaches. The **Puerto Maya Pier** marks the beginning of Cozumel's more crowded region. Accommodations between here and town cater to divers and face views of gorgeous water and cruise ships that dwarf the island's hostelries. Budget hotels line the streets of downtown, which isn't a bad place to stay. Decent beaches lie within walking distance and countless places to dine and drink.

Older hotels, private residences, and condos are sprinkled along Cozumel's best beaches on the north side of town, beyond the Navy base. Plenty of divers stay on this end of the island; they may have a longer boat ride to the reefs, but the water here is perfect for swimming and kiteboarding. Room rates tend to be lower on the north side of town, and the cruise ships float far off on the horizon.

Most accommodations offer dive or golf packages. Rates are highest around Christmas and stay high until after Semana Santa (Easter week). They're lowest from post-Easter to June and again from September to November (hurricane season).

ACCOMMODATION PROFILES

Casa Mexicana $$

OVERALL ★★★	QUALITY ★★★	VALUE ★★

Avenida Rafael Melgar between Calles 5 and 7; ☎ 987-872-9090 or 877-228-6747 U.S. and Canada; fax 987-872-9073; www.casamexicanacozumel.com

It took daring to build this chic hotel right on the main drag along the downtown waterfront, but the gamble worked. A sweeping escalator leads from the sidewalk to a lobby that's part waterfront lounge and part reception area. The architect cleverly stacked rooms, terraces, and balconies so that inside rooms face trees, bright yellow walls, and water fountains—though some face each other or unsightly roofs. The company also has the budget Hotel Bahía and Suites Colonial in town; make reservations through the same toll-free number.

SETTING AND FACILITIES

Location Avenida Rafael Melgar between Calles 5 and 7, near Punta Langosta.

Dining No restaurant; complimentary breakfast buffet in lobby.

Amenities and services Room service, Internet.

ACCOMMODATIONS

Rooms 90.

All rooms AC, balcony, bathtub, hair dryer, satellite TV, telephone, high-speed Internet.

Some rooms Ocean view.

Comfort and decor The rooms are more stylish than in most downtown hotels; bathrooms are especially posh with marble vanities, bathtubs, and thick, soft towels.

PAYMENT, RESERVATIONS, AND RESTRICTIONS

Deposit Credit-card deposit; 3-day cancellation policy in high season and 1-day policy in low season.

Credit cards AE, MC, V.

Check-in/out 2 p.m./noon.

 ### El Cid La Ceiba $$–$$$

OVERALL ★★★½	QUALITY ★★★½	VALUE ★★★

Carretera a Chankanaab Km 4.5; ☎ 987-872-0844 or 866-306-6113 U.S.; fax 987-872-0065; www.elcid.com

A longtime favorite on Cozumel, La Ceiba was in desperate need of a makeover when the El Cid company from Mazatlán stepped in. They totally remodeled the rooms and facilities (and had to redo some of their work after Wilma) and the hotel is once again an excellent choice for those seeking lots of activities, good Mexican food at the restaurant, and a beach stocked with lounge chairs and palapas. Cruise ships docked at the nearby pier detract from the scenery, however. The main pool is small (and popular with cruise activities staff who keep the tone very upbeat). A second tide pool area in a quieter part of the property has a waterfall cascading into a rocky pool filled with fish—you can slip from here into the water and snorkel with sergeant majors and parrotfish. Both European and all-inclusive plans are available. The food is decent and sometimes excellent—stick with Mexican dishes.

SETTING AND FACILITIES

Location North of San Miguel by Puerto Maya.

Dining 1 restaurant, all-inclusive plan available.

Amenities and services Beach, 2 pools, hot tub, gym, spa, water-sports center, dive shop, tour desk, children's activities, room service, dock.

ACCOMMODATIONS

Rooms 60.

All rooms AC, windows that open, balcony or terrace, hair dryer, safe, coffee maker, kitchenette, cable TV.

Some rooms Ocean view, living room, 2 bathrooms, kitchenette or full kitchen, nonsmoking, disabled access.

Comfort and decor The rooms are eminently practical for divers, families, and travelers who enjoy having lots of space to set up housekeeping. The balconies have straight-on views of the sea and massive cruise ships at the dock. Separate tubs and showers and lots of hooks for wet clothing make the bathrooms a pleasure. Some rooms have a Murphy bed or pullout couch.

PAYMENT, RESERVATIONS, AND RESTRICTIONS

Deposit Credit-card guarantee; nonrefundable cancellation fee of at least 72 hours (higher at holidays).

Credit cards AE, MC, V.

Check-in/out 2 p.m./noon.

Coral Princess $$$

OVERALL ★★½	QUALITY ★★½	VALUE ★★

Carretera Norte Km 2.5; ☎ 987-872-3200 or 800-253-2702 U.S. and Canada; fax 987-872-2800; www.coralprincess.com

This old favorite has been remodeled with a pleasing tropical flair and fresh paint and furnishings. The pool and beach areas are ideal for the location, with plenty of sand and a casual beach bar. Limestone shelves leading into the water and a reef right off shore make for good snorkeling. The suites are popular with time-share guests, but there's no time-share pressure.

SETTING AND FACILITIES

Location North of town near the marina.

Dining 1 restaurant.

Amenities and services Beach, 2 pools, hot tub, gym, massage, water-sports center, dive shop, tour desk, shops, room service, Wi-Fi.

ACCOMMODATIONS

Rooms 136 rooms and suites.

All rooms AC, balcony or terrace, hair dryer, safe, refrigerator, coffeemaker, cable TV.

Some rooms Ocean view, bathtub, refrigerator, kitchenette, nonsmoking.

Comfort and decor The rooms vary considerably in size and decor, from small, standard rooms to fresh, clean, tropical-looking studios and villas. The studios with separate bedrooms and kitchenettes are delightfully spacious and comfortable, but not luxurious. They're great for longer stays when you want to set up temporary housekeeping.

PAYMENT, RESERVATIONS, AND RESTRICTIONS

Deposit Credit-card guarantee; 3-day cancellation policy; penalties differ with season and package.

Credit cards AE, DC, MC, V.

Check in/out 4 p.m./noon.

Cozumel Palace $$$$

OVERALL ★★★★	QUALITY ★★★★	VALUE ★★★

Avenida Rafael E. Melgar, Km 1.5; ☎ 987- 9430 or 800-635-1836 U.S. and Canada; fax 987-872-9431; www.palaceresorts.com

This older hotel was gutted (on purpose, with additional help from Hurricane Wilma) and room space has expanded to generous proportions. The pool area and beach areas are a bit cramped but you can always slip into the sea for some good snorkeling right off shore. Many guests are familiar with Palace Resorts, which has at least a dozen properties in Mexico. The Palace Passport Program (an added expense) allows guests to use facilities at other Palace resorts (a great benefit when ferrying over to their Playa del Carmen hotel). The hotel is strictly all-inclusive, which makes it more expensive than other hotels in this neighborhood.

SETTING AND FACILITIES

Location 10-minute walk south of town.

Dining 3 restaurants.

Amenities and services Beach, 2 pools, gym, spa, water-sports center, dive shop, tour desk, shops, room service, Internet.

ACCOMMODATIONS

Rooms 176 rooms and suites.

All rooms AC, balcony or terrace, bathtub, coffeemaker, fan, hair dryer, safe, minibar, ocean view, satellite TV.

Some rooms Nonsmoking.

Comfort and decor The rooms are attractive, with hammocks on the balconies, double Jacuzzis in the seating area, and a calm beige and white color scheme.

PAYMENT, RESERVATIONS, AND RESTRICTIONS

Deposit Credit-card guarantee; penalties differ with season and package.

Credit cards AE, DC, MC, V.

Check-in/out 4 p.m./1 p.m.

Fiesta Americana Cozumel Dive Resort $$

OVERALL ★★	QUALITY ★★	VALUE ★★

Carretera Sur Km 7.5; ☎ 987-872-9600 or 800-343-7821 U.S. and Canada; fax 987-872-2666; www.fiestaamericana.com

Completely refurbished after Wilma, this well-designed property is located across the street from the beach; a beach club, dive shop, restaurant, and pool are accessible via a bridge over the road. Soaring palapa roofs, archways, and amiable staff members all increase the comfortable feeling. The hotel is in an isolated area, however, and is best suited to dedicated divers more interested in the reefs than diversions on land.

SETTING AND FACILITIES

Location South coast near Chankanaab.

Dining 3 restaurants.

Amenities and services Beach, pool, gym, water-sports center, tour desk, organized children's activities, shops, room service.

ACCOMMODATIONS

Rooms 224 rooms, including 56 casitas.

All rooms AC, windows that open, satellite TV, coffeemaker.

Some rooms Fans, ocean view, balcony or terrace, minibar, disabled access, nonsmoking.

Comfort and decor Casitas along garden pathways behind the hotel are more spacious and have outdoor sinks and space for gear. Rooms on the highest floors overlooking the water are great as well. All rooms have light-wood furnishings with tropical floral fabrics and large bathrooms.

PAYMENT, RESERVATIONS, AND RESTRICTIONS

Deposit Credit-card guarantee; make changes 24 hours before arrival or forfeit 1 night's fee.

Credit cards AE, MC, V.

Check-in/out 3 p.m./1 p.m.

Flamingo $

OVERALL ★★	QUALITY ★★	VALUE ★★★

Calle 6N 81; ☎ 987-872-1264 or 800-806-1601 U.S. and Canada; fax 954-351-9740 in the U.S; www.hotelflamingo.com

Book far in advance if you want to stay at downtown's legendary budget haven. The Flamingo is a classic, meeting all needs for low rates while remaining classy. Soothing yellow walls, lots of plants in the courtyard, and a spacious lobby cafe make it so comfortable guests like to hang out with each other and share tips and info. The rooftop Villa Flamingo has a separate living room, full kitchen, and terrace overlooking town and water. The Aqua restaurant and bar is a great place to hang out if you want to trade tips with other travelers.

SETTING AND FACILITIES

Location North side of downtown near the Cozumel Museum.

Dining 1 restaurant.

Amenities and services Room service, Internet.

ACCOMMODATIONS

Rooms 16 rooms, 1 penthouse.

All rooms AC, cable TV.

Some rooms Windows that open, kitchen.

Comfort and decor Casual, with white stucco walls and simple metal-frame furniture.

PAYMENT, RESERVATIONS, AND RESTRICTIONS

Deposit Credit-card deposit; 30-day cancellation policy, 2-night penalty (longer at holidays).

Credit cards MC, V.

Check-in/out 2 p.m./noon.

Hotel Cozumel and Resort $$

OVERALL ★★★	QUALITY ★★½	VALUE ★★★½

Carretera Sur Km 1.7; ☎ 987-872-9020 or 877-454-4355 U.S. and Canada; fax 987-872-2154; hotelcozumel.com.mx

As an all-inclusive, this rather standard hotel is one of the best values on the island. It's located across a busy street from the beach, but a tunnel leads under the road to a large beach club with a small patch of sand, a saltwater pool, plenty of sunbathing space, a dive center, and a restaurant. Back at the hotel, the pool is enormous, supposedly the largest on the island. The food in the restaurant is very good, especially if you stick with the Mexican choices on the menu. Snack bar food is less satisfying. Rooms have irons and ironing boards—still not a standard amenity in Cozumel hotels. Both all-inclusive and European meal plans are available. A small convention center was added to the property in 2006.

SETTING AND FACILITIES

Location About a 15-minute walk south of downtown.

Dining 3 Restaurants, all-inclusive.

Amenities and services Beach, 2 pools, 2 hot tubs, gym, water-sports center, tour desk, organized children's activities, shops, Wi-Fi in lobby, Internet, room service.

ACCOMMODATIONS

Rooms 181.

All rooms AC, windows that open, balcony or terrace, bathtub, hair dryer, safe, cable TV.

Some rooms Ocean view, nonsmoking.

Comfort and decor The 3-story buildings (with elevators) frame lawns, gardens, and the pool, and the grounds are expansive enough that you can find a quiet corner. Most rooms are large and have a table with chairs beside sliding-glass doors, and plenty of closet and dresser space. Rooms have irons and ironing boards—still not a standard amenity in Cozumel hotels—and would be perfect for business travelers if they had Internet hookups.

PAYMENT, RESERVATIONS, AND RESTRICTIONS

Deposit Credit-card deposit; 1–3-day cancellation policy according to seasons.

Credit cards AE, MC, V.

Check-in/out 3 p.m./noon.

Hotel Presidente InterContinental Cozumel $$$–$$$$$

OVERALL ★★★★★	QUALITY ★★★★★	VALUE ★★★★

Carretera a Chankanaab Km 6.5; ☎ 987-872-9500 or 800-327-0200 U.S. and Canada; fax 987-872-9501; www.intercontinentalcozumel.com

One of our favorite hotels in the whole country, the Presidente has maintained a Mexican sense of gracious comfort for more than two decades. It was absolutely devastated by Wilma, with landscaping that's grown over decades totally wiped out. Fortunately, the owners decided to revamp the entire property while rebuilding it. The makeover took more than a year, but was well worth the wait. Returning guests see plenty of familiar faces among the waiters and porters, but the rooms have been upgraded to "hip hotel" standards, with gourmet coffeemakers, rain showers in outdoor gardens, and MP3 docks bedside. The lavish, full-service Mandara Spa is reason alone to stay here—but then there's the second pool, the freshly raked white-sand beach, and the prime snorkeling waters. Fine Italian cuisine is served in the gourmet Antonio di Roma restaurant, while the palapa-shaded El Caribeno serves tangy ceviches, fresh guacamole, and other treats. You'll pay dearly to enjoy all the luxuries here, but it's worth it.

SETTING AND FACILITIES

Location South end of the island, in a private setting near Chankanaab.

Dining 2 restaurants.

Amenities and services Beach, 2 pools, hot tub, gym, spa, organized children's activities, shops, 24-hour room service, business center, Internet.

Rooms 220.

All rooms AC, balcony or terrace, hair dryer, minibar, CD/DVD, Wi-Fi.

Some rooms Ocean view, bathtub, safe, coffeemaker, disabled access, outdoor shower, plasma-screen TV, butler service.

Comfort and decor The hotel has fewer rooms than it did before the storm, to allow the new ocean suites to grow to more than 700 square feet each. Butlers, ocean-view bathtubs, cushy towels, and silken linens are among the many improvements.

PAYMENT, RESERVATIONS, AND RESTRICTIONS

Deposit Credit-card deposit; 3-day cancellation policy; penalties vary with the season.

Credit cards AE, DC, MC, V.

Check-in/out 3 p.m./noon.

Iberostar Cozumel $$$$

| OVERALL | ★★★½ | QUALITY | ★★★½ | VALUE | ★★★★ |

**Carretera Sur Km 17; ☎ 987-872-9900 or 888-923-2722 U.S.;
fax 987-872-9909; www.iberostar.com**

Casual and comfortable, the Iberostar stands out among the all-inclusives covering the southeast end of Cozumel. The lobby is actually a nice gathering spot with plenty of comfy couches, tour desks, and a full bar. Pathways meander through gardens to the rooms, pool, and beach; it's the kind of place where you can wander around barefoot (sandals are required in most restaurants) in a bathing suit and sarong for days on end. Several parts of the hotel were reconstructed after Wilma, but the casual vibe remains.

SETTING AND FACILITIES

Location Far south end of island.

Dining 4 restaurants.

Amenities and services Beach, 3 pools, hot tub, gym, spa, water-sports center, tour desk, organized children's activities, shops, Internet.

ACCOMMODATIONS

Rooms 306.

All rooms AC, fan, balcony or terrace, hair dryer, safe, minibar, satellite TV.

Some rooms Ocean view, bathtub, coffeemaker, kitchenette.

Comfort and decor The architecture is reminiscent of the older resorts on the Caribbean Coast, with several 8-unit buildings with palapa roofs, wood balconies with hammocks, and wrought iron and wood furnishings. Most of the rooms are surrounded by trees and gardens; it's a long walk to the beach from those set by the restaurant and lobby. Only a few are on the beach; try to get units 1103 or 1104.

PAYMENT, RESERVATIONS, AND RESTRICTIONS

Deposit Credit-card deposit; 1-night penalty if cancelled less than 24 hours in advance, does not apply for holiday season.

Credit cards AE, DC, MC, V.

Check-in/out 3 p.m./noon.

 ## Meliá Cozumel All-Inclusive Beach and Golf Resort $$$$

OVERALL ★★★	QUALITY ★★	VALUE ★★★★

Carretera Costera Norte Km 5.8; ☎ 987-872-0411 or 888-95MELIA U.S. and Canada; fax 987-872-1599; www.solmelia.com

Golf privileges at the Cozumel Country Club, a soft, white-sand beach, plenty of space to roam, and unlimited free food and drink make this Meliá all-inclusive an excellent choice for families The hotel, which once was headquarters for honchos attending regional summits, attracts a mixed crowd. The kids cluster around their Flintstones-themed designated pool and activity center. Honeymooners and more-solitary types take rooms on the south side of the property around a larger pool. Each group stakes out its turf on the long beach. Two children age 12 and under (per family) stay and eat free with their parents.

SETTING AND FACILITIES

Location Across street from the golf course on far north end of hotel zone.

Dining 3 restaurants.

Amenities and services Beach, 2 pools, gym, massage, water-sports center, tour desk, organized children's activities, shops.

ACCOMMODATIONS

Rooms 147 rooms and suites.

All rooms AC, windows that open, balcony or terrace, bathtub, hair dryer, safe, satellite TV.

Some rooms Ocean view, minibar, nonsmoking, disabled access.

Comfort and decor This older, well-maintained hotel was one of the first all-inclusives on the island and now benefits from proximity to the golf course. It has a pleasant, relaxing ambience. The beach and calm, clear water seem to go forever.

PAYMENT, RESERVATIONS, AND RESTRICTIONS

Deposit Credit-card deposit; 72-hour cancellation policy.

Credit cards AE, MC, V.

Check-in/out 3 p.m./noon.

Playa Azul $$$

OVERALL ★★★★	QUALITY ★★★½	VALUE ★★★★

Carretera Costera Norte Km 4; ☎ 987-869-5160; fax 987-869-5173; www.playa-azul.com

The owners have taken one of Cozumel's first beach hotels and turned it into a classy boutique inn with something for families, singles, and couples. They are big supporters of the Cozumel Country Club and offer free tee times with the room rate—some guests golf daily. Small, tasteful touches such as hand-painted ceramic wall sconces and artful mirrors enhance the decor. Most of the suites are enormous, with large showers, plenty of bathroom counter space, and pale green, blue, and yellow textiles. The standard rooms are small. It's fun to wander between the hotel beaches here. Several rocky outcroppings cup small coves perfect for snorkeling.

SETTING AND FACILITIES

Location North of town across from the La Cabaña del Pescador restaurant.

Dining 1 restaurant; full breakfast included in rate.

Amenities and services Beach, pool, massage, water-sports center, tour desk, shops, room service, Internet.

ACCOMMODATIONS

Rooms 50.

All rooms AC, windows that open, balcony or terrace, hair dryer, safe, minibar, coffeemaker, satellite TV.

Some rooms Ocean view, nonsmoking, living room, hot tub, kitchen.

Comfort and decor Light, tropical decor with thoughtful design touches such as small vanity niches with mirrors. The ambience is romantic, yet the beach and hotel are popular with families who favor this area. Service is personable, and info on activities is readily available. Master suites have oceanfront balcony, living room, and private hot tub; the garden house has full kitchen, separate bedrooms and living room, but no ocean view.

PAYMENT, RESERVATIONS, AND RESTRICTIONS

Deposit Guarantee with credit card; 3-day cancellation policy; stiffer policies at holidays.

Credit cards AE, MC, V.

Check-in/out 3 p.m./noon.

Safari Inn $

OVERALL ★★	QUALITY ★★½	VALUE ★★★★½

Avenida Rafael Melgar at Calle 5; ☎ 987-872-0101; fax 987-872-0661; www.aquasafari.com

One of our favorite bare-bones budget hotels sits atop our favorite dive shop on the downtown waterfront. It's basic and perfect for dive buddies who don't care about frills. The owner also rents delightful, moderately priced condos at Condumel on the north coast. With hammocks in the living rooms, full kitchens, deep bathtubs, and terraces or balconies right over the water, these condos are idyllic for a few nights (or months). The hotel is better for short stays, and perfect if you want to walk out the front door and jump into a dive boat.

SETTING AND FACILITIES

Location Across from the downtown waterfront between the passenger ferry pier and Punta Langosta.

Dining No facilities, but lots of restaurants nearby.

Amenities and services Water-sports center, shop.

ACCOMMODATIONS

Rooms 12.

All rooms AC, cable TV.

Some rooms Beds for up to 5 persons.

Comfort and decor Clean white walls, enough space to spread out your bags, powerful hot-water showers. Street noise inevitable.

PAYMENT, RESERVATIONS, AND RESTRICTIONS

Deposit Negotiable.

Credit cards MC, V (no credit cards at Condumel).

Check-in/out Flexible.

WHERE *to* EAT *in* COZUMEL

COZUMEL SLIPPED INTO FAST-FOOD-FRANCHISE hell when it became a cruise-ship haven. Until then, the golden arches and other universal signs were absent. But now the island has brand-name burgers (local kids adore the second-story McDonald's on the waterfront), pizza, a Hard Rock Cafe, and Baskin-Robbins ice cream. But plenty of small restaurants serve everything from lobster to jambalaya. Many are owned by foreign residents who couldn't bear to leave the island.

unofficial **TIP**
Stick bug repellent in your bag if you're dining in a courtyard. Mosquitoes love damp places with plenty of human victims.

The tourist area of downtown has dozens of restaurants, and you'll find some pleasant surprises in the back neighborhoods. Yucatecan cuisine is less prevalent than you would expect. Look for *cochinita pibil* (marinated pork baked in banana leaves) and *pescado tikin-xic* (fish with achiote). Prices are lower here than in Cancún (but they're creeping up), and the quality is pleasantly high. Dress is always casual, and it's become more important to make reservations at the popular spots.

RESTAURANT PROFILES

La Cabaña del Pescador Lobster House ★★

LOBSTER	EXPENSIVE	QUALITY ★★	VALUE ★½

North hotel zone across from Playa Azul Hotel;
Carretera Costera Norte Km 4; ☎ 987-872-0795

How Restaurants Compare in Cozumel

RESTAURANT | CUISINE | COST	OVERALL	QUALITY	VALUE
Guido's | Italian | Mod	★★★★	★★★★	★★★½
La Cocay | Mediterranean | Exp	★★★★	★★★½	★★★
French Quarter | Cajun | Exp	★★★½	★★★	★★★
Rock 'n Java | Breakfast/pastries | Inexp	★★★	★★★	★★½
La Veranda | Caribbean | Exp	★★★	★★★	★★½
Casa Denis | Mexican/ Yucatecan | Inexp	★★½	★★½	★★★
Casa Mission | Mexican | Mod	★★½	★★½	★★
Coconuts | Mexican | Mod	★★½	★★	★★
Cocos Cozumel | Breakfast | Mod	★★	★★★	★★
Jeanie's Beach Club | Breakfast/Mexican | Inexp	★★	★★★	★★
La Cabaña del Pescador Lobster House | Lobster | Exp	★★	★★	★½
La Perlita | Mexican Seafood | Mod	★½	★★	★★★

Reservations Not accepted.

Entree range $12–$25.

Payment Cash only.

Service rating ★★.

Parking Street parking.

Bar Full service.

Dress Casual.

Disabled access Manageable, no stairs.

Customers Travelers.

Hours Daily, 6–10 p.m.

SETTING AND ATMOSPHERE A bridge leads through tropical gardens to a large rustic restaurant with a long front counter where you place your order. Choose a lobster by weight, then wait for the meal at your table.

HOUSE SPECIALTIES Lobster and fixings.

SUMMARY AND COMMENTS Craving lobster? That's good, because it's the main attraction, though the menu also includes shrimp, chicken, and steak. Entrees are served with white rice and bland vegetables; one wishes they'd include refried beans and tortillas.

Casa Denis   ★★½

MEXICAN/YUCATECAN	INEXPENSIVE	QUALITY ★★½	VALUE ★★★

Calle 1 Sur 132 between Avenidas 5 and 10; ☎ 987-872-0067

Reservations Not accepted.

Entree range $3.50–$10.

Payment No credit cards.

Service rating ★.

Parking Limited street parking.

Bar Beer, tequila, some other liquors.

Dress Casual.

Disabled access Possible, at sidewalk tables.

Customers The full gamut from first-time tourists to local families who've lived here for generations.

Hours Daily, 8 a.m.–8 p.m.

SETTING AND ATMOSPHERE One of the oldest restaurants on the island in a yellow wooden house in the middle of the shopping and dining area near the plaza. Some wobbly tables on the sidewalk, others in a small, dark dining room and more in a back courtyard.

HOUSE SPECIALTIES *Cochinita pibil* (marinated pork baked in banana leaves), tacos.

SUMMARY AND COMMENTS A stop at Casa Denis for a least a beer and excellent guacamole is a must for any visitor. The waiters look like they've been here since the place opened in 1945, so don't expect speedy service. Seats at sidewalk tables are best since it gets pretty warm inside. The food is *puro mexicano*—real Mexican—and served on scratched plastic dishes. This is a good place to sample Yucatecan homestyle cooking.

Casa Mission   ★★½

MEXICAN	MODERATE	QUALITY ★★½	VALUE ★★

Back street in downtown, about 20 blocks from the waterfront; Avenida Juárez at Calle 55A; ☎ 987-872-1641

Reservations Recommended for groups.

Entree range $3.50–$30.

Payment AE, MC, V.

Service rating ★★★.

Parking Plenty of street parking.

Bar Full service.

Dress Evening casual wear.

Disabled access Possible, but there are a couple of steps to restrooms.

Customers Travelers fond of the Mission restaurants in town who have found this out-of-the-way location.

Hours Daily, 4–11 p.m.

SETTING AND ATMOSPHERE An old hacienda-style home with the restaurant confined to the covered veranda. Expansive gardens with fountains and tropical birds.

HOUSE SPECIALTIES Seafood platter, fajitas.

SUMMARY AND COMMENTS Yes, there is a lion in residence here; he's part of the family. The operators of the Mission restaurant in the tourist zone of San Miguel took over this square block of gardens and a long-neglected old house and turned it into a lovely home similar to what you'd find in colonial Mexico. The setting outshines the food. Arrive early so you can see the gardens, mango and *guanábana* (soursop) trees, and the decorative items from Dolores Hidalgo and other folk-art centers on the mainland. The food is typical tourist Mexican, bountiful and rather bland.

La Cocay ★★★★

MEDITERRANEAN	EXPENSIVE	QUALITY ★★★½	VALUE ★★★

Downtown; Calle 8 Norte 208; ☎ 987-872-4407 or 987-872-5533

Reservations Accepted.

Entree range $8–$22.

Payment MC, V.

Service rating ★★.

Parking Limited street parking.

Bar Full service.

Dress Resort casual.

Disabled access Yes.

Customers Local business professionals, tourists seeking a refined cuisine in a sophisticated setting.

Hours Monday–Saturday, 6–11 p.m.

SETTING AND ATMOSPHERE Artsy dining room with evocative black-and-white photographs of Mexico City and Cuba on the walls and subdued lighting, courtyard framed by trees.

HOUSE SPECIALTIES Sautéed chicken livers, seared tuna with wasabi, chocolate torte.

SUMMARY AND COMMENTS Chef Margarita Estrella prepares duck with blueberry cassis sauce, filet mignon with garlic mashed potatoes, and other dishes you won't see at other island restaurants. Prices are high and the quality a tad inconsistent, but that doesn't discourage diners seeking a classy evening. Soft jazz plays in the background and the wine list showcases some fine Mexican Merlots. If you can't manage a big splurge, come by for the cheese plate or canapés with hummus, goat cheese, or duck pâté.

Cocos Cozumel ★★

BREAKFAST	MODERATE	QUALITY ★★★	VALUE ★★

Downtown pedestrian area; Avenida 5 Sur 180; ☎ 987-872-0241

Reservations Not accepted.

Entree range $4–$10.

Payment Cash only.

Service rating ★★★★.

Parking Limited street parking.

Bar None.

Dress Casual.

Disabled access Plenty of room for wheelchairs in dining area, fairly easy bathroom access.

Customers Local gringos and travelers.

Hours Tuesday–Sunday, 6 a.m.–noon; closed September and October.

SETTING AND ATMOSPHERE U.S.-style coffee shop with several tables in a dining room cooled by a fan and a few tables on the sidewalk. Waiters carry coffeepots about and are quick to take and serve orders. Friendly and casual.

HOUSE SPECIALTIES Eggs with green chilies and melted cheese, home-fried potatoes and bacon with eggs cooked exactly as you please, homemade muffins.

SUMMARY AND COMMENTS We can't be on Cozumel without stopping by to sit at the counter and chat with the owners about new happenings and old friends. Cocos is a family-run operation with a generous, friendly ambience.

Coconuts ★★½

MEXICAN	MODERATE	QUALITY ★★	VALUE ★★

Windward Coast Road

Reservations Not accepted.

Entree range $6–$15.

Payment Cash only.

Service rating ★.

Parking Sandy parking lot.

Bar Full service.

Dress Casual, bathing suits are fine.

Disabled access None.

Customers Locals and travelers touring the windward coast. The scene can get rowdy as beachgoers stop by for cold beers and loud music.

Hours Daily, 11 a.m.–sunset.

SETTING AND ATMOSPHERE Open air, palapa-covered beach cafe with a circular central bar, wood tables, and chairs inside and outside on small patches of level dirt.

HOUSE SPECIALTIES Octopus ceviche, shrimp with garlic.

SUMMARY AND COMMENTS This funky and fun bar sits atop a small hill overlooking the gorgeous sea on the windward coast. The proprietor keeps scrapbooks filled with photos of happy tourists showing off their tanned chests and bikinis. The food is excellent, from the fresh chips and homemade salsa to the whole grilled fish.

French Quarter ★★★½

CAJUN	EXPENSIVE	QUALITY ★★★	VALUE ★★★

Downtown tourist zone; Avenida 5 Sur between Avenida Salas and Calle 3; ☎ 987-872-6321

Reservations Advisable in high season.

Entree range $9–$25.

Payment AE, MC, V.

Service rating ★★★.

Parking Plenty of back-street spaces.

Bar Full service, large selection of imported beers and liquors.

Dress Sundresses, tropical shirts, nice shorts.

Disabled access Steep stairway leads to dining room, but there's a bar with dining tables and restrooms at street level.

Customers Travelers, locals seeking quiet camaraderie.

Hours Daily, 4–11 p.m.

SETTING AND ATMOSPHERE Cool rooftop terrace on a side street located downtown.

HOUSE SPECIALTIES Étouffée, crawfish, blackened catch of the day.

SUMMARY AND COMMENTS You won't find Louisiana-style cuisine anywhere else on the island, or a more congenial bar favored by local business owners. Owner Mike Slaughter thought he would just stay a few days on the island—he's lasted for several years and runs a friendly, relaxing restaurant with great food. Try the crab cakes, spinach salad, catfish, or imported steaks.

Guido's ★★★★

| ITALIAN | MODERATE | QUALITY ★★★★ | VALUE ★★★½ |

North side of downtown waterfront; Avenida Rafael Melgar 23 between Calles 6 and 8 Norte; ☎ 987-872-0946

Reservations Not accepted.

Entree range $5–$15.

Payment MC, V.

Service rating ★★★.

Parking Limited street parking.

Bar Full service.

Dress Casual.

Disabled access Manageable.

Customers Travelers who have a meal here whenever they're on the island; cruise-ship captains and crew; locals.

Hours Monday–Saturday, 11 a.m.–11 p.m.

SETTING AND ATMOSPHERE Pizza parlor with wood-burning oven and tables under posters of Italy; back courtyard with large trees and vines climbing down from the second-story balcony.

HOUSE SPECIALTIES Pizza, calzone, seafood specials, coconut ice cream with Kahlúa.

SUMMARY AND COMMENTS Formerly (and forever in locals' minds) called Rolandi's, this upscale pizza parlor is known for its wonderful puffy garlic bread, crisp pizza crusts with generous toppings, innovative seafood dishes (try the sea bass wrapped in spinach or tuna with manchego cheese), and comfortable, peaceful courtyard. Stop by when you want something familiar and soothing or an unusual twist on the catch of the day.

Jeanie's Beach Club ★★

| BREAKFAST/MEXICAN | INEXPENSIVE | QUALITY ★★★ | VALUE ★★ |

Avenida Rafael Melgar at Calle 11; ☎ 987-878-4647

Reservations Accepted.

Entree range $8–$15.

Payment Cash only.

Service rating ★★★.

Parking Street parking.

Bar Full service.

Dress Casual.

Disabled access Yes.

Customers Locals who work for the dive shops and hotels, travelers familiar with the name, tour groups.

Hours Daily, 6 a.m–10 p.m.

SETTING AND ATMOSPHERE Streetside cafe with a few sidewalk tables and a larger, palapa-covered dining room in back. Festive decor and attentive, friendly service.

HOUSE SPECIALTIES Waffles with bacon and eggs or *huevos rancheros,* chocolate-chip waffles.

SUMMARY AND COMMENTS This popular waffle shop has morphed into a downtown beach club with free Wi-Fi and a snorkeling and Snuba concession. Longtime local fans still stop by for their waffle fix, but the majority of daytime diners come from the cruise ships. The place is most crowded in early morning as divers and dive masters fuel up on carbs.

La Perlita ★½

| MEXICAN/SEAFOOD | MODERATE | QUALITY ★★ | VALUE ★★★ |

Deep in downtown on a hard-to-find street; Avenida 65 Norte 499 between Calles 8 and 10 Norte; ☎ 987-872-3452

Reservations Not accepted.

Entree range $8–$15.

Payment MC, V.

Service rating ★★★.

Parking Street parking.

Bar Full service.

Dress Very casual.

Disabled access No special accommodations, but at sidewalk level.

Customers Locals.

Hours Daily, 10 a.m.–7 p.m.

SETTING AND ATMOSPHERE Fishnets and buoys hang above a few tables in the small dining room, where a TV plays in one corner and neighbors wander by for coffee or lunch.

HOUSE SPECIALTIES The freshest fish possible, *filete relleno perlita* (fish fillet with shellfish, ham, and bacon), whole fried fish.

SUMMARY AND COMMENTS Visit this neighborhood fish market–turned–restaurant for the absolute freshest catch of the day. Fishermen bring their catch to the restaurant in early evening; it's displayed in the market the next morning and served in the restaurant. The menu is filled with crab and shrimp cocktails, spicy seafood soup, whole fried fish (usually snapper), crab tacos, and the chef's concoctions of the catch of the day.

Not for queasy eaters who prefer familiar surroundings, but a great find for off-the-beaten-path explorers.

Rock 'n Java ★★★

BREAKFAST/PASTRIES	INEXPENSIVE	QUALITY ★★★	VALUE ★★½

On the waterfront just north of downtown; Avenida Rafael Melgar 602; ☎ 987-872-5440

Reservations Not accepted.

Entree range $4–$10.

Payment MC, V.

Service rating ★★.

Parking Street parking.

Bar None.

Dress Casual.

Disabled access Possible.

Customers Locals and tourists.

Hours Sunday–Friday, 7 a.m.–10 p.m.; Saturday, 7 a.m.–2 p.m.

SETTING AND ATMOSPHERE Long display case with cakes and pies, tables scattered about large room with ocean view, bookshelves piled with used books for sale.

HOUSE SPECIALTIES Apple pie, steamed veggies, natural yogurt with granola and fruit.

SUMMARY AND COMMENTS The menu is tempting any time of day, whether you're hankering for a mango milkshake or grilled cheese with tomato and avocado. Vegetarians are in luck here and can make a full dinner out of a baked potato stuffed with cheese. The coffee's strong (brewed decaf is available), as is the AC, and the Beatles, Elton John, and Billy Joel play in the background. You'll see locals reading their newspapers, tourists browsing through used books, and regulars who can't make it through the day without stopping by for some java and local news. The owners recently opened a Thai noodle house nearby.

La Veranda ★★★

CARIBBEAN	EXPENSIVE	QUALITY ★★★	VALUE ★★½

North side of downtown tourist zone; Calle 4 Norte 140, between Avenidas 5 and 10 Norte; ☎ 987-872-4132

Reservations Accepted.

Entree range $12–$22.

Payment MC, V.

Service rating ★★.

Parking Street.

Bar Full service with imported wines and liquors, martinis.

Dress Dressy casual.

Disabled access Yes.

Customers Travelers, some locals.

Hours Daily, 4 p.m.–midnight.

SETTING AND ATMOSPHERE The wooden house could be in Bermuda or the Caymans; the decor is nautical Caribbean. Best seats are in the back garden amid candlelight.

HOUSE SPECIALTIES Poblano chili stuffed with seafood, coconut shrimp with pineapple salsa.

SUMMARY AND COMMENTS A satisfying change of pace, this romantic restaurant serves seafood and meats with a tropical flair. Mango and pineapple show up frequently in sauces, as do roasted peppers and garlic. The menu is ambitious and usually successful. Try the bananas flambé for desert.

SIGHTSEEING *in* COZUMEL

IF YOU HAVE A FEW DAYS OR MORE on the island, take your time exploring its many attractions. You can take a cab to the beach parks and spend the day, rent a car or hire a cab to explore the windward side of the island, and concentrate your downtown sightseeing into a couple of mornings and evenings.

ATTRACTIONS

 COZUMEL HAS PLENTY OF ATTRACTIONS, and many of them are mobbed when cruise ships are in port. The water is the main draw, and **Parque Chankanaab** (Carretera Sur Km 9; ☎ 987-872-2940 park) is the best place for sampling Cozumel's underwater delights. It's been a national park since 1980, so the fish and lobsters that hang out here feel pretty safe. Snorkelers see tropical fish in the lagoon's shallow waters; the offshore diving is less spectacular. Wilma wreaked havoc with the park's botanical gardens, but the trees are coming back to life and the gardens now have an oval Maya house, called a *na,* and replicas of Maya statues. A separate concessionaire runs a swimming-with-dolphins program. The dolphin program is well run, overall, but its location close to the reefs is unfortunate, as algae from the dolphin enclosures harms fragile coral. Facilities at Chankanaab include lockers, showers, dive companies, equipment rental, and a very good restaurant—try the grilled fish or ceviche. Admission is $16 for adults and $8 for children ages 3–11.

Faro Celarain Eco Park, southernmost point of Carretera Sur (☎ 987-872-2940 or 987-872-0914), is a 247-acre nature preserve with protected lagoons, small Maya ruins, and a nautical museum in the **Faro de Celarain** (Celarain Lighthouse). Visitors must leave their cars at the entrance and ride on bicycles or trucklike passenger vehicles through the park to the various attractions. Certain areas along the beach are designated swimming, snorkeling, and kayaking areas. The park is open daily, 9 a.m. to 4 p.m.; admission is about $10; free for children under age 8. What you're paying for here is access to a pristine beach, and your contribution helps maintain the area and keep developers at bay. If you go, be sure to bring your swimsuit, fins, snorkel gear, or any other sports equipment you have, and plan to spend a lovely day at the beach.

The tourist-oriented area of **San Miguel** is bisected by Avenida Benito Juárez and Avenida 5. The passenger-ferry pier sits at the foot of Juárez, which runs inland to the **Plaza Central.** We've noticed that few day-trippers venture into or past the plaza—a misfortune for local businesses, but a delight for those in the know. A section of Avenida 5 and surrounding streets is closed to vehicular traffic, making it a pleasant place to stroll past shops and cafes. The same cannot be said for Avenida Rafael Melgar along the *malecón*, or waterfront, where salespeople stand outside jewelry and souvenir shops offering deals on gems and serapes.

A cruise-ship dock marks the southern end of downtown at **Punta Langosta** (Avenida Rafael Melgar 599; ☎ 987-872-7860; **www.punta langosta.com**), a two-story shopping mall. The soaring, shiplike architecture defines the area and somewhat confines the customers who just want to eat, drink, and shop for jewelry and clothing with familiar labels. An enclosed walkway over the street leads from the ship terminal to the shopping center. The parking lot in back is a great place to stash your car while you're exploring town, and the center has money-exchange windows, a good deli, clean restrooms, and a game arcade.

To get an overview of the island's topography, history, and culture, be sure to visit the **Museo de la Isla de Cozumel** (Avenida Rafael Melgar between Calles 4 and 6 Norte; ☎ 987-872-1475) near the north end of the waterfront. One of the best community museums in Mexico, this two-story building was one of the island's first hotels and now holds fascinating exhibits on coral, shells, the Maya, conquistadors, pirates, and more current history. The second-story cafe at the front of the building is perfect for sipping coffee while watching the waterfront. It's open daily, 9 a.m. to 5 p.m.; admission is $3 and free for children under age 8.

An overview of Mexico's many cultures is presented in a multiscreen film at **Discover Mexico** (Carretera Sur Km 5.5; ☎ 987-857-2820; **www.discovermexico.org**). The indoor museum contains collector-quality folk art from throughout Mexico, while the outdoor park displays replica of Mexico's most famous archaeological and architectural sights. There's a Disney-like Mexican food

unofficial **TIP**
Discover Mexico offers a combination package including bilingual guided tours of both Discover Mexico and Chankanaab Park. Tickets cost $34 for adults and $24 for children.

stand outside, and a fabulous museum store at the exit. Guides are available at the entrance. The place is open Monday through Saturday, 8 a.m. to 6 p.m.; admission is $10.

Cozumel's archaeological sites are small and far less impressive than those on the mainland. Tours to Chichén Itzá and Tulum are readily arranged through tour operators. On the island, don't miss **San Gervasio** (4.5 miles down the San Gervasio access road off the Carretera Transversal; no phone). Dedicated to the goddess Ixchel who ruled the moon and fertility, the classic- and post-classic-style temples and the surrounding area were occupied from AD 300 to 1500. Maya women from the mainland brought tributes to Ixchel to ensure their fertility. There is evidence of limestone roads called *sacbes* running from these shrines in the jungle to the coast. You can see the site in an hour or two, tops. Guides are available at the entry gate, and it's open daily, 7 a.m. to 4 p.m.; admission is $5, free for children under age 11.

A side road leads off the Carretera Sur to **El Cedral,** a small agricultural settlement that's been in existence since before the Spaniards arrived in 1518. The Maya temple and structures that were once a thriving community are gone, but the town is still very traditional. The annual fiesta held here in May is a major event, drawing people from all over the island. The weeklong fair includes cockfights, music, and real, down-home Maya cooking. To get there, turn inland at Carretera Sur Km 17.5. The church and a few homes are located about two miles inland.

You get a whole different perspective of Cozumel by driving along the windward coast, where beaches are carved from the limestone shelf and waves crash against the shore. Stop by one of the rustic beach cafes along the road. **Chen Río** and **Mezcalitos** both serve great grilled fish and are filled with families on weekends.

TOURS *and* SIDE TRIPS *from* COZUMEL

TOUR COMPANIES TEND TO CONCENTRATE on the cruise ships and take large groups on shore excursions. Ask for a more personalized tour with a private guide—it might be a bit more expensive, but it's worth it. **Fiesta Cozumel** Cozumel (Calle 11 Sur 598, between Avenidas 25 and 30; ☎ 987-872-4311, fax 987-872-0433, **www.fiesta holidays.com**) is one of the island's largest agencies and offers everything from car rental to flights to excursions to Chichén Itzá.

BOAT TOURS

 Atlantis Submarine (Carretera a Chankanaab Km 4; ☎ 987-872-5671; **www.goatlantis.com**) offers one-and-a-half-hour submarine rides. If you're lucky, you might spot a sea turtle floating by. Tours depart daily on the hour, 9 a.m. to 2 p.m.; price is $79 adults, $45 children.

HORSEBACK TOURS

Aventuras Naturales (Avenida 35, No. 1081; ☎ 987-872-1628 or 858-366-4632 in the U.S.; **www.aventurasnaturalascozumel.com**) offers guided horseback tours of Maya ruins and the beach. Prices start at $30 for a two-hour tour. They also have jungle Jeep and bicycle tours. **Rancho Buenavista** (Avenida Rafael Melgar and Calle 11 Sur; ☎ 987-872-1537) takes visitors on four-hour trips through the jungle from the ranch at the south end of the island; prices begin at $65.

JEEP TOURS

Wild Tours (☎ 987-872-5876; **www.wild-tours.com**) offers several caravan ATV rides in the northeast side of island, some combined with snorkeling and lunch. Rates start at $75 for a two-hour tour of the jungle.They also offer horseback riding.

EXERCISE *and* RECREATION *in* COZUMEL

MOST OF THE ACTION TAKES PLACE IN THE WATER. Even joggers on the sides of the Carretera have favorite spots where they jump in the water at the end of their runs. The **Cozumel Mini Golf** (Avenida 15 at Calle 1 Sur; ☎ 987-872-6570), known locally as Golfito, is a challenge for everyone with its streams and ponds. It's open daily, 9 a.m. to 9 p.m., and costs $7, $5 for children. Otherwise, a few hotels have a tennis court or two.

GOLF

THE COURSE AT THE **Cozumel Country Club** (Carretera Norte Km 5.8; ☎ 987-872-9570, fax 987-872-9590; **cozumelcountryclub.com.mx**) is much lauded by players and golf publications. The 18-hole, 6,743-yard, par-72 course was laid out by the Nicklaus Design Group on the north end of the island's windward side. Its development was closely monitored by environmentalists, and it has become a haven for birds and iguanas. Audubon International certified the course as a Cooperative Sanctuary in 2006. Greens and fairways meander through scrub jungle and past lagoons, and sand traps are actually made of crushed coral. Some hotels include a complimentary round of golf in room rates or golf packages. Greens fees ($149) include a shared golf cart, and rental clubs and shoes are available.

SCUBA DIVING AND SNORKELING

EVEN CLAUSTROPHOBES AND NONSWIMMERS can't resist peeking into the clear water off Cozumel's white-sand beaches. Striped sergeant majors swarm around dock pilings, rocky coves, and the outdoor decks on seaside restaurants—they've learned where to find easy dining. Before Hurricane Wilma, parrotfish, angelfish, tiny blue neons, and yellow tangs hung close to shore, but they disappeared when the raging surf tore up the coral. Life is gradually returning to Cozumel's shallow waters, but it's now best to head away from shore on a boat tour to see the most creatures.

unofficial **TIP**
Many dive shops offer snorkeling tours to the best reefs, and some will take snorkelers along with divers on their boats. Snorkeling with a dive master is a great way to spot creatures you could easily miss on your own.

Divers have long been enamored with Cozumel's reefs, swim-through canyons, coral pinnacles, and deep walls. The underwater landscape was transformed by the storm, which tore apart coral and sponges in some areas. But there are still plenty of great dive spots, and those who've been here before are curious to see how their favorite reefs have been transformed. New coral and sponges are growing and baby fish swarm around as if in a watery nursery.

Cozumel is a particularly good dive destination because there's something for every level of expertise, from beginning snorkelers to advanced divers. The water rarely dips below 75°F, and the clarity is astonishing. You can be swimming 20 feet beneath the surface and still see clouds floating by in the sky. Much of the time in the water is spent drift-diving—floating along with the current past brain coral, sponges, and schools of neon-colored fish.

More than 50 dive shops and operations offer a wide range of services. The **Aquatic Sports Operators Association** (ANOAAT) (☎ 987-872-5955; **www.anoaat.com**) has listings of affiliated dive operations. Many shops offer resort courses with classes in swimming pools and shallow water. The certification allows you to go on shallow dives with a dive master, and it's a good way to get hooked on scuba. Various levels of certification classes are available. Some clients do all their class and pool work at home, then finish their open-water training with a Cozumel dive shop.

Make sure you dive with a certified dive master, and try to stay away from the cattle boats carrying 20 or more divers to one site. Ask if the boat has drinking water and refreshments. Divemasters should instruct you to keep your hands and feet off delicate corals and sea fans—don't touch the critters either. Most of the standard dive sites are part of the marine sanctuary, and the inhabitants are off-limits. You can easily rent all the gear you need at a shop, though dedicated divers bring all the latest equipment in their giant dive bags. Snorkeling equipment is also readily available. The **Cozumel Recompression Center** (Calle 5 Sur 21; ☎ 987-872-1430) has a hyperbaric chamber and doctors who know how to deal with everything from jellyfish stings to the bends.

We have found several dive shops to be reliable, courteous, and safe. **Aqua Safari** (Avenida Rafael E. Melgar 429, between Calles 5 and 7 Sur; ☎ 987-872-0101; **www.aquasafari.com**) offers just about every kind of diving, along with accommodations. Reputable and responsible, the company has been around for decades. They have a second location at the Cozumel Palace hotel. Along with dive and snorkel trips, **Blue Angel Dive Shop** (☎ 987-872-1631 or 866-779-9986 toll-free in the U.S.; **www.cozumel-diving.net/blueangel**) runs combo snorkel and dive trips so families and friends with different levels of experience can get out in the water together.

Scuba Du (Presidente InterContinental; ☎ 987-872-9505; **www.scubadu.com**) also has been around a long time. They offer dives and classes, and they arrange snorkeling and sportfishing trips. **Aldora Divers** (Calle 5 Sur 37; ☎ 987-872-3397 or 649-723-0667 from the United States; **www.aldora.com**) provides computers for all their divers and specializes in dive sites off the south tip of the island—advanced divers get a chance to check out reefs, tunnels, and walls away from the crowds. They also offer dives off the windward coast.

Del Mar Aquatics (Costera Sur Km 4; ☎ 987-872-5949; **www.delmaraquatics.com**) is based at the Casa del Mar hotel across the street from the water and pier, and offers boat dives and instruction. **Dive Paradise** (Calle 3 Sur between Avenida Rafael Melgar and Avenida 5); ☎ 987-869-0503; **www.diveparadise.com**) also offers snorkeling trips and dive instruction and has shops at several hotels and downtown. Though they're becoming a larger company with four locations (including the Hotel Cozumel Resort and Hotel Villablanca), they still offer personalized service. Experienced divers can check out the island's caverns and caves with **Yucatch Expeditions** (Calle 3 Sur at Avenida 5; ☎ 987-113-7044; **www.yucatech.net**).

SPORTFISHING

ANGLERS ARE ALLOWED TO FISH OUTSIDE the marine park, and many find fertile fishing grounds there. Marlin, dorado, snapper, and tuna abound in various seasons, and the island holds several fishing tournaments, including the **International Rodeo of Sport Fishing** in May. Some companies also offer bonefishing on the northern side of the island. For information or to charter a your own boat, contact **3 Hermanos** (☎ 987-872-6417; **www.cozumelfishing.com**) or **Albatros Deep Sea Fishing** (☎ 987-872-7904 or 888-333-4643; **www.cozumel-fishing.com**).

SHOPPING *in* COZUMEL

COZUMEL USED TO HAVE A FEW GALLERIES selling high-quality folk art, but the focus has turned to items favored by cruise-ship passengers. Jewelry shops abound. One outfit, called **Diamonds International,** has at least three large shops on Avenida Rafael Melgar (such as the one at Avenida Melgar 131; ☎ 987-872-5333). **Los Castillo** in Punta Langosta (☎ 987-869-2978) is a high-end national chain known for its silver from Taxco. This shop displays fine Mexican silver jewelry and objets d'art, and also has a large selection of inexpensive earrings, charms, and necklaces. Punta Langosta was supposed to have an extraordinary selection of high-end designer boutiques and galleries. But the businesses in the center tend toward fast food (Baskin-Robbins, Burger King, coffee, mediocre sushi), standard jewelry, perfume, souvenir shops, and Versace and Swatch outlets. However, **Super Deli** in Punta Langosta (☎ 987-869-1757) carries an amazing selection of U.S. snacks and drinks—even Fritos, an abomination in the land of *totopos* (fried corn tortillas). The wine selection includes imports, and several wines are available in splits. Prices are high.

Los Cinco Soles (Avenida Rafael Melgar at Calle 8; ☎ 987-872-2040) has the best overall selection of souvenirs from throughout Mexico. The shop used to carry exceptional handcrafted folk art as well as manufactured pottery and clothing, but the selection has become more mainstream. Still, it's a fascinating place, with room after room of everything from placemats to pricey Talavera pottery. Fine tequilas are sold in one room—tasting is encouraged. **Pancho's Backyard** restaurant (behind the shop; ☎ 987-872-2141) serves excellent margaritas and gourmet Mexican cuisine. Avenida Melgar is lined with huge souvenir shops all selling the same onyx bookends, slogan T-shirts, and woven blankets. Wander a few blocks behind Melgar to find a more varied selection. **Bugambilias** (Avenida 10 Sur by Calle 1 Sur; ☎ 987-872-6282) sells good hammocks. Arts and crafts vendors are largely confined in the **Mercado de Artesanías** on Calle 1 behind the plaza and to smaller markets by the cruise-ship piers.

NIGHTLIFE *in* COZUMEL

COZUMEL ISN'T MUCH OF A LATE-NIGHT PARTY TOWN. Locals and residents wander around Punta Langosta and along the waterfront around sunset, diners fill restaurants about 7 p.m., and most doors are shut by 11 p.m. **Carlos'n Charlie's** (Punta Langosta; ☎ 987-869-1646) takes up the north side of the shopping center at sidewalk level; **Señor Frog's** (also at Punta Langosta; ☎ 987-869-1646) commands the upper section. Part of a Mexican chain familiar to many travelers, the two restaurant-bars dominate the dancing and partying scene. The food is dependably good, the music deafening, and the dancing gets wilder and more fun as the night wears on. **Hard Rock Cafe** (Avenida Rafael Melgar 2-A by the ferry pier; ☎ 987-872-5273) has an excellent live rock band that gets everyone dancing. The scene is a bit more sophisticated at **1.5 Tequila Lounge** (Avenida Rafael Melgar at Calle 11 Sur; ☎ 987 872 4421). Martinis beat out margaritas as the drink of choice, and sushi supplants tacos.

There are several bars along Avenida Rafael Melgar near the piers. None charge a cover, so you can wander in and out until you find a place to land. Many restaurants have live mariachi, marimba, or guitar music at dinner. **Neptuno** (Calle 11 at Avenida Rafael Melgar; ☎ 987-872-1537) has been the main disco for at least a decade. It moved around the corner in 2008 to make way for a mega–grocery store and now has two levels with dance floors and upgraded sound systems. It opens around 10 p.m. The seven-screen **Cineópolis** (Avenida Rafael Melgar by Calle 11; ☎ 987-869-0799) shows some English-language movies and movies with English subtitles.

PART SEVEN

The **CARIBBEAN COAST**

The **RIVIERA MAYA** and **MORE**

FLY ABOVE THE CARIBBEAN COAST south of Cancún, and you see endless shades of blue water and long, sparkling-white beaches backed by dense green cushions of vines and trees. Then you spot a bunch of buildings squished together as if a giant cookie cutter slashed through the jungle to make way for a city. The same scene appears frequently all along the coastline between the vibrant cityscape of Cancún and the border between Mexico and Belize. The Caribbean Coast, once a tranquil hangout for backpackers stretching every peso to the max, is Mexico's fastest-growing resort area.

In the past two decades, this strip of idyllic blue coves and talcum-soft beaches has undergone a startling transformation. Highway 307 south of Cancún was once a two-lane country road where modern Maya pedaled three-wheeled bicycles called *triciclos*. Today, tour buses and rental cars roar past a few brave cyclists commuting to work on the modern four-lane highway (which is being widened once again in places). Signs for huge all-inclusive resorts, small hideaways, and residential developments dot Highway 307. Theme parks, archaeological sites, and nature reserves pull in huge crowds of day-trippers from Cancún. Many inevitably want to return.

The coastline begins near Cancún's international airport; several large, all-inclusive resorts line the road to the town of **Puerto Morelos,** 22 miles south. The **Riviera Maya**—a now-famous name coined by tourism developers—begins a few miles south at Punta Bete and extends 75 miles down the coast to the UNESCO Biosphere Reserve at **Sian Ka'an.** It encompasses dozens of resort developments, small communities, and towns, and has become a well-known and desirable destination.

*un*official **TIP**
Trucks pull in and out of construction sites all along Highway 307. Slow down if you see one starting to enter the road—they're not going to get out of your way.

The Yucatán's Upper Caribbean Coast

0   25 mi
0   25 km

Airport ✈
Ferry route – – –
Reef ⦀⦀⦀⦀
Ruins ≣

Isla Holbox

Isla Contoy

El Cuyo

Holbox

Chiquilá

RÍO LAGARTOS NATURE RESERVE

Isla Mujeres

Punta Sam
Cancún
Puerto Juárez

Isla Cancún

○Buenaventura

QUINTANA ROO

YUCATÁN

180

180D

Caribbean Sea

3 **11**

toll road

180D

free road

Nuevo Xcan

Puerto Morelos
10
Punta Maroma

7

307

Chemax

To Valladolid & Chichén-Itzá

180

Playa Xcalacoco **9**   *Punta Bete*

Mayakoba
Xcaret
Puerto Calica Cruise Port
Paamul **8**

6

Playa del Carmen

ISLA DE COZUMEL

Cobá

Puerto Aventuras
Xpu-ha
13   **5**
Akumal
4   Aktun Chen
Hidden Worlds Cenotes
Tankah   **Xel-Há**
Tulum

San Miguel de Cozumel

Ferry
Ferry

Tulum **14**

Chunyaxché
15 **12**   *Caribbean Sea*
2 **1**

Muyil

Boca Paila

307

SIAN KA'AN BIOSPHERE RESERVE   Punta Allen

Chumpón

Vigia Chico

Bahía de la Ascensión

Felipe Carrillo Puerto
↓ To Majahual and Xcalak

Peninsula Vigia Grande

UNITED STATES

Gulf of Mexico

MEXICO

Area of detail

Mexico City ★

BELIZE

PACIFIC OCEAN

GUATEMALA
EL SALVADOR   **HONDURAS**

■ **ACCOMMODATIONS**
1. Ana y José Hotel & Spa
2. Azulik Resort
3. Ceiba del Mar Beach & Spa Resort
4. Club Akumal Caribe and Villas Maya
5. Esencia
6. Fairmont Mayakoba and Rosewood Mayakuba
7. Hotel Marina El Cid

8. Hotel Paamul
9. The Tides Riviera Maya
10. Maroma Resort & Spa
11. Zoestry Paraiso de la Bonita
12. Las Ranitas
13. Vista del Mar

◆ **RESTAURANTS**
14. Don Cafeto's
15. Mezzanine

Playa del Carmen is the hub of the Caribbean Coast, and the fastest-growing city in Mexico. Its Avenida Quinta (Fifth Avenue) is the hippest shopping and dining area on the Yucatán Peninsula. Twenty years ago, Playa was the commercial hub of the coast, with the largest bus terminal, the ferry to Cozumel, and a scattering of small hotels and campgrounds. Phones were nearly nonexistent, and most streets consisted of rutted dirt. Today, Playa has traffic lights, paved boulevards, and more than 200,000 residents.

Xcaret is the most famous attraction on the coast, a man-made museum of all that is precious in Yucatán. A few miles south, tour buses pack parking lots near the ancient Maya site of **Tulum,** with its splendid limestone temples standing sentry above the Caribbean Sea.

Sian Ka'an protects lagoons, shore, and sea south of Tulum and the highway cuts a bit inland to traditional towns and villages sans global fast-food franchises and fancy hotels. The southern stretch of the coast, long the purview of escapists, has now been dubbed the **Costa Maya.** Slated for extensive tourism development, this region now receives cruise ships at **Majahual.** Travelers and cruise-ship passengers explore recently restored Maya archaeological sites and dive and snorkel at untrammeled coral reefs. The Mexican Caribbean ends at **Chetumal,** capital of the state of Quintana Roo.

INTRODUCTION *to* *the* CARIBBEAN COAST *of* MEXICO

THIS CHAPTER INCLUDES MORE THAN A dozen destinations and recommendations on where to stay, eat, and play. As the Caribbean Coast continues to develop, several of these areas will become independent beach destinations and the region will resemble Mexico's Pacific Coast, aka the Mexican Riviera. An international airport is in the works for Tulum, and Chetumal's runways are receiving more flights. For now, we've placed dozens of disparate destinations under one the Caribbean Coast heading and recommended our favorite places to explore.

THE ACCOMMODATIONS SCENE

MORE THAN 200 ACCOMMODATIONS line the shores and streets of the Caribbean Coast. Historically, this region has been a natural

How Accommodations Compare on the Caribbean Coast

ACCOMMODATION	OVERALL	QUALITY	VALUE	COST
AKUMAL				
Club Akumal Caribe and Villas Maya	★★★	★★★	★★★	$$–$$$
Vista Del Mar	★★★	★★★	★★★	$
MAJAHUAL-XCALAK				
Costa de Cocos	★★★	★★★	★½	$$$
MAYAKOBA				
Rosewood Mayakoba	★★★★★	★★★★★	★★★★	$$$$$
Fairmont Mayakoba	★★★★½	★★★★½	★★★★	$$$$$
PAAMUL				
Hotel Paamul	★★★	★★	★★★★	$
PLAYA DEL CARMEN				
Deseo Hotel and Lounge	★★★	★★★	★★½	$$$$
La Tortuga Hotel and Spa	★★½	★★½	★★★	$$
Hacienda del Caribe	★½	★★	★★★★	$
PLAYA XCALACOCO				
The Tides Riviera Maya	★★★★★	★★★★★	★★★★	$$$$$
PUERTO MORELOS				
Zoetry Paraiso de la Bonita	★★★★★	★★★★★	★★★★	$$$$$
Ceiba del Mar Beach & Spa Resort	★★★★	★★★	★★	$$$
Hotel Marina El Cid	★★★	★★★	★★★	$$$
PUNTA MAROMA				
Maroma Resort & Spa	★★★★	★★★★½	★★★	$$$$$
TULUM				
Ana y José Hotel & Spa	★★★½	★★★½	★★★	$$$
Las Ranitas	★★½	★★★	★★	$$
Azulik	★★	★★½	★★	$$$
XPU-HA				
Esencia	★★★★★	★★★★★	★★★★	$$$$$

canvas where independent investors and hoteliers expressed their creativity. That's still the case, though the dreams tend to be more elaborate and expensive. Nearly every hotel conglomerate in the world seems to want in on the action. Several luxury travel companies have properties in the works, especially around Mayakoba, an emerging golf, hotel, and residential resort just north of Playa. The most exclusive properties tend to be self-contained and removed from outside restaurants and attractions. Most offer meal plans and gourmet dining. All-inclusive resorts designed to keep their guests captive for at least a week are immensely popular here. Palace Resorts has gobbled up enormous chunks of jungle and coast for self-contained, all-inclusive resorts, as have Barcelo and Iberostar. Hundreds of travelers arrive each week on charter flights from Canada, Italy, Spain, and the U.S. They're immediately bused with their fellow passengers to resorts designed to please each nationality. These guests get a subdued taste of the Mexican character of the region and all the necessary accoutrements for a week's R&R. We've reviewed only a few exceptional all-inclusives here, preferring to concentrate on smaller one-of-a-kind properties. Campgrounds and budget accommodations have nearly disappeared, though some remain on the outskirts of the main towns. If you're seeking that old-time tradition, check out the hotels along the highway around Playa del Carmen and Tulum.

Sensations Travel, a booking company specializing in small hotels, represents several small inns and private villas around Playa del Carmen and Tulum. Check them out at **www.sensationstravel.com.** Two U.S. expatriates who've settled on the coast have one of the best Web sites about the area and also represent several rental villas and condos at **www.locogringo.com.**

THE RESTAURANT SCENE

unofficial **TIP**
The most accessible large grocery store in the area is the Chedraui supermarket on Highway 307 just south of Playa del Carmen (across the traffic light at the intersection with Avenida Juárez). If you're staying awhile and watching your expenses, you can stock up on everything from bottled water to imported wines there.

THE CARIBBEAN COAST DOESN'T HAVE as many independent restaurants as one might expect. Because so many of the hotels are all-inclusive or so exclusive they're far removed from towns, guests tend to eat most of their meals at their hotels. Playa del Carmen has become a culinary hotbed with restaurants run by well-traveled European and Mexican chefs. The variety of cuisine is astounding, covering everything from authentic Yucatecan specialties to caviar and foie gras. It's common for hotel rooms in this area to have small refrigerators, and many resorts have at least some rooms with kitchenettes.

TOURING THE COAST

YOU'LL LIKELY RAMBLE all around the coast if you're staying any length of time.

Hotels have tour desks that can arrange nearly any adventure you'd like to experience, but independent explorers will want a rental car for at least a day or two. The easiest way to handle transportation is to arrange transportation to your hotel when you make your reservations (usually for an extra fee), relax for a few days, and restrict your drive-around sightseeing to a few days. Tour companies located in Cancún and Playa del Carmen will pick up passengers at most coast hotels. Scuba diving, snorkeling, and other water-sports are the main activities along the coast, and most hotels have beach activity-centers.

QUICK FACTS *about the* CARIBBEAN COAST

AIRPORT AND AIRLINES The international airport for the area is in Cancún (see Part Four, Cancún [page 84] for details). Arrange transportation to your hotel in advance, if possible. There's usually a fee for airport transfers; it can be as high as $100 each way. Transports are often included in vacation packages. Taxis and *colectivos* run from the airport to coastal towns. Public buses run from the airport to Playa del Carmen.

CLIMATE The coast is blessed with sea breezes that usually aren't blocked by large buildings. You'll be thrilled to have air-conditioning during the summer months, however, when the heat and humidity are sweltering. Tropical storms and hurricanes can produce high winds and rain from June through October, and you could get stuck in your room for days on end. That's a rare occurrence, however. Usually the rains fall for a few hours in the afternoon, right around siesta time.

DRIVING Highway 307 runs south from Cancún to Chetumal and has four lanes between Cancún and Tulum. The traffic can be horrendous, especially around Playa del Carmen where everything comes to a standstill at times. Tour buses barrel down the road. If you're not sure of your turn-off, stay in the right-hand lane.

FERRIES Passenger ferries to Cozumel depart from Playa del Carmen almost hourly from 5 a.m. to 11 p.m. There's often a two-hour gap between trips in midday. Schedules are not consistent, however. Check with your hotel for a current schedule. On the speediest boats, you can reach the island in 45 minutes. There are ticket booths at the foot of the ferry pier; call ☎ 984-879-3113 or visit **crucerosmaritimos.com.mx**

unofficial **TIP**
When booking your room, ask how long it takes to travel from the Cancún airport to the hotel. The drive to Tulum, for example, can last 90 long minutes. The distance may determine your decision, especially if you have a late arrival or early departure. Consider spending your first and last nights in Cancún or Puerto Morelos.

How Restaurants Compare on the Caribbean Coast

RESTAURANT | CUISINE | COST	OVERALL	QUALITY	VALUE
PLAYA DEL CARMEN			
La Casa del Agua | International | Exp	★★★★	★★★★★	★★★
Yaxche | Nouvelle Yucatecan | Mod	★★★★	★★★★★	★★★
Sur | Argentine/Beef | Exp	★★★	★★★	★★★
Babe's Noodles and Bar | Thai | Inexp	★★★	★★★	★★★★
Palapa Hemingway Restaurant | Mexican/American | Mod	★★	★★★	★
El Tacolote | Mexican | Inexp	★★	★★	★★★
TULUM			
Mezzanine | Thai | Mod	★★★★	★★★★	★★★½
Don Cafeto's | Mexican | Inexp/Mod	★★	★★½	★★

for schedule updates. The fare is $12. Vehicle ferries depart several times a week from Calica, south of Playa; for schedules and fares call ☎ 984-871-5100. The trip takes two hours; passenger fare is $6, and vehicle fare is $67.

GETTING AROUND Many of the resort hotels in this area are designed to hold guests captive, keeping them entertained for days on end. But there's much to explore, and it's a shame not to join a tour or two or wander about on your own in a rental car. There are desks for every major car-rental company at the Cancún airport; some have offices in Playa del Carmen. Hotels also can arrange car rentals. Your choice of vehicles is vast—Corvettes, Suburbans, even Minis are available for rent. You don't need four-wheel drive unless you expect to do some major off-roading in the rainy season.

INTERNET ACCESS Some hotels have Internet access from on-site computers or Wi-Fi in public areas. A few now have Internet connections in the rooms, though it isn't common.If frequent and efficient connection is important, ask in advance. **Cybernet Caseta Telefónica** (Avenida 5; ☎ 984-872-1246) in Playa del Carmen is an efficient one-stop shop for making long-distance calls, exchanging faxes, or checking e-mail and the Internet. **Au Cacao Chocolate Café** (Avenida 5 at Calle Constituyentes; ☎ 984-803-5748) in Playa del Carmen has Wi-Fi hotspots for customers.

TELEPHONES There are three area codes for this region. Puerto Morelos uses the same code as Cancún, ☎ **998.** Playa del Carmen, Tulum, and the areas in between have a ☎ **984** area code. Majahual and the Costa Maya are in the ☎ **983** area code. You'll see all sorts of numbers on business cards and brochures. The local number should have seven digits. Calls between the three area codes are long distance.

TOURIST INFORMATION The Riviera Maya has an excellent tourism bureau that assists travelers in finding their way around the coast. The main office is on Carretera 307 at Calle 28, ☎ 984-859-2170, or visit **www.rivieramaya.com.** Other Web sites with travel info abound; check out **www.locogringo.com, www.cancunsouth.com,** and **www.playa.info.**

PUERTO MORELOS

BLESSEDLY RESISTANT TO CHANGE, the small coastal town of Puerto Morelos is 22 miles south of Cancún. The town center is modest, with a central plaza, church, and small markets and cafes. Fishermen bring their daily catch to the pier, where anglers and divers can arrange trips with boat captains.

Expats and Cancún workers who don't mind the commute live in small houses and handsome villas on the outskirts of town, while the fishermen's families stick close to the plaza and pier. Until recently, hotel choices were modest and few, and Puerto Morelos was favored by backpackers and reclusive types. But growth has arrived in the form of exclusive resorts that have replaced the jungles north and south of town, where the El Cid Marina opened in 2006. There's just enough to see and do in Puerto Morelos to make it a perfect base for trips into Cancún and all around the coast. The town's artisan collective sells hammocks, pottery, and souvenirs from a row of stands a block south of the plaza. Scuba-diving operators are located by the town pier, and a few small shops and cafes sit around the main plaza. While the white-sand beaches are beautiful in this area, the sea is shallow and sea grass often makes swimming difficult. Most hotels have piers extending to deeper water and boat trips to nearby reefs. For information check **www.visitpuertomorelos.com.**

WHERE TO STAY IN PUERTO MORELOS

Ceiba del Mar Beach and Spa Resort $$$

OVERALL ★★★★	QUALITY ★★★	VALUE ★★

Avenida Niños Héroes s/n, Puerto Morelos; ☎ 998-872-8060 or 877-545-6221 U.S.; fax 998-872-8061; www.ceibadelmar.com

After Hurricane Wilma trashed this lovely spa hotel, the owners spent nearly a year rebuilding and redesigning the property to make it even more exclusive, secluded, and sublimely comfortable. Palm palapas top three-story buildings with whirlpool tubs and sundeck on the roof, and each building has a dedicated concierge, called a "host." The suites are comfortable, with hammocks hanging on the balconies. The pool winds along a white beach, and the main restaurant sits beside a stream. Another restaurant, Arrecife, has a raw bar serving carpaccios, ceviches, sushi and sashimi. A *temazcal* cave opens on the sand—this ancient steam-and-mud treatment is de rigueur at Mexican spas. The spa itself is located in a separate building and offers all the latest treatments performed by excellent therapists. A well-stocked library has DVDs available free of charge, and guests can use the hotel's bicycles without charge. The resort only accepts children ages 15 and older. Small pets are welcome.

SETTING AND FACILITIES

Location On the beach just north of Puerto Morelos.

Dining Restaurant, meal plans available.

Amenities and services Beach, 2 pools, hot tub, gym, spa, water-sports center, tennis, bicycles, tour desk, shop, 24-hour room service, wireless Internet.

ACCOMMODATIONS

Rooms 88 suites.

All rooms AC, fan, windows that open, ocean view, balcony or terrace, bathtub, hair dryer, safe, minibar, satellite TV, VCR/DVD, Internet.

Some rooms Nonsmoking, disabled access, plasma screen TV, sitting room, plunge pool, hot tub.

Comfort and decor Wood shutters open from above the large soaking tub to the balcony and ocean view. The furnishings and linens were upgraded in the remodel, and all rooms have Egyptian cotton sheets, pillow menus, and soft cotton robes. Hammocks hang on the balconies and terraces. Ask for a second-floor room for more privacy. Rooms vary widely in amenities; the penthouse suites have spot-on views of the sea, private elevator access, and hot tubs. Plan includes Continental breakfast slipped through a niche in the closet each morning.

PAYMENT, RESERVATIONS, AND RESTRICTIONS

Deposit Credit-card deposit for 1-night rate; cancellation policy varies starting with forfeiting 1-night rate with a 14-day cancellation policy. Three-night minimum stay in August; 7-night minimum stay from December 23 to January 1.

Credit cards AE, MC, V.

Check-in/out 3 p.m./noon.

 Hotel Marina El Cid $$$

OVERALL ★★★	QUALITY ★★★	VALUE ★★★

Highway 307, Km 298; ☎ 998 872-8999 or 800-525-1925 U.S.; fax 998-872-8998; www.elcid.com

Residents of Puerto Morelos were concerned when construction began on this private marina and resort hotel just south of town. Both have opened, and though they're certainly not low-key, they're not as large as they could be. The company has enough land to build 1,000 hotel rooms, but is planning to build only 350 in the near future. The 200 suites now available are located in low-rise buildings set on curving pathways past lawns and a spectacular pool with a rocky island, waterfalls, and waterslide. The scene is quieter on the north side of the property by the adults-only pool, actually a large, shallow whirlpool big enough for a dozen or more. Spa treatments are performed at a raised treatment area draped in white gauze close to the adult pool; a spa is in the works. The food is good for an all-inclusive; the best dishes are prepared at the poolside Hacienda El Arrecife and the casual La Marina beside boats bobbing at their slips.

SETTING AND FACILITIES

Location Just south of the town of Puerto Morelos.

Dining 4 restaurants, all-inclusive.

Amenities and services Beach, 1 pool, hot tub, spa services, water-sports center, room service, wireless Internet access in lobby, marina.

ACCOMMODATIONS

Rooms 200.

All rooms AC, windows that open, balcony or terrace, hair dryer, safe, complimentary minibar, coffeemaker, satellite TV.

Some rooms Ocean view, living room, two bathrooms, kitchenette, hot tub, nonsmoking, disabled access.

Comfort and decor The good-sized suites have wet-bar areas with coffeemakers and all-inclusive stocked minibars (beer, soda, water). Small balconies overlook pools or the long white beach; beds are comfy and there are enough tables and chairs to spread out your stuff. Those who enjoy a good soak might be disappointed—none of the bathrooms have tubs. The Platinum Club Level Service, which is a $40-per-night upgrade, includes better linens, a pillow menu, butler service, and goodies such as a bottle of sparkling wine.

PAYMENT, RESERVATIONS, AND RESTRICTIONS

Deposit Credit-card guarantee with 2-night deposit; nonrefundable cancellation fee of at least 14 days (higher at holidays).

Credit cards AE, MC, V.

Check-in/out 2 p.m./noon.

Zoetry Paraiso de la Bonita $$$$$

OVERALL ★★★★★	QUALITY ★★★★★	VALUE ★★★★

Highway 307 Km 328; ☎ 998-872-8300 or 888-496-3879 U.S. and Canada; fax 998-872-8301; www.zoetryresorts.com

This extravagant resort is a destination hideaway for upscale guests seeking curative spa treatments. The Thalasso Center was designed under the strict supervision of experts in this system that uses fresh, heated seawater to encourage an exchange of minerals and toxins between the blood and the water. It is a serious spa where therapists create weight-reduction, healing, and beautification programs for their clients. But you needn't sign on for an intense spa experience. Individual treatments are available, and the stunning hotel has excellent restaurants, a long private beach, and suites with dramatic decor. Guests are offered all sorts of complimentary treats during their stay, including tequila in the rooms, Continental breakfast, afternoon tea with finger sandwiches, and a never-ending supply of flavored iced teas. Now managed by the creators of the Dreams and Secrets all-inclusive resorts, Paraiso de la Bonita is the first property in the company's luxury brand.

SETTING AND FACILITIES

Location Bahía Petenpich, just north of Puerto Morelos.

Dining 3 restaurants.

Amenities and services Beach, pool, hot tub, gym, spa, water-sports center, tour desk, shop, 24-hour room service, Internet.

ACCOMMODATIONS

Rooms 90 suites.

All rooms AC, fan, windows that open, ocean view, balcony or terrace, bathtub, whirlpool tub, hair dryer, safe, minibar, satellite TV/DVD, Internet.

Some rooms Nonsmoking, disabled access, plunge pools.

Comfort and decor Suites are designed with Balinese, African, Asian, and other themes and are almost overwhelmingly ostentatious. The beds, however, are fabulous, covered with Frette linens and piles of pillows. Bathrooms have Bulgari toiletries and sunken-marble tubs that take forever to fill with water. Suites on first floor have plunge pools outside; those on upper stories have balconies with hammocks.

PAYMENT, RESERVATIONS, AND RESTRICTIONS

Deposit Credit-card guarantee with 1-night deposit, 24-hour cancellation policy, 60-day cancellation policy for holidays.

Credit cards AE, MC, V.

Check-in/out 3 p.m./noon.

WHERE TO EAT IN PUERTO MORELOS

YOU'LL FIND SEVERAL SMALL CAFES ON THE STREETS around the central plaza. Seafood is the specialty at **Restaurante Los Pelicanos** (Avenida Melgar at Avenida Tulum; ☎ 998-871-0014). A large palapa covers the simple seaside cafe, where you can spend hours watching boats pass. **John Gray's Kitchen** (Avenida Niños Héroes; ☎ 998-871-0665) is open for dinner only and closed on Mondays, but that doesn't keep diners from Cancún and the Riviera Maya away. The chef has a loyal following and prepares excellent steaks, seafood, and continental cuisine. **Hola Asia** Avenida Tulum across from the plaza; ☎ 998-871-0679) is a hit for its Chinese, Japanese, and Thai dishes—and takeout is available.

PUNTA MAROMA

LONG A SECLUDED ESCAPE FOR THE RICH and famous, Maroma is undergoing massive development. Ultra high-end Capella is building a resort by Maroma's gorgeous beach, and the Secrets Maroma all-inclusive opened nearby in 2008. All the hotels here are private and exclusive—at least when it comes to road access. But there's nothing to keep lookie-loos from wandering by on the beach, if they can find beach access.

Maroma Resort & Spa $$$$$

OVERALL ★★★★	QUALITY ★★★★½	VALUE ★★★

Highway 307 Km 51; ☎ 998-872-8200 or 800-237-1236 U.S.;
fax 998-872-8220; www.maromahotel.com

Ultraexclusive and private, Maroma sits at the end of a long road amid 500 acres of beach and a coconut plantation. Founder and architect Jose Luis Moreno teamed up with Orient Express Hotels in 2002 and expanded this much-celebrated hideaway to a include oceanfront suites and the Kinan Spa. The cluster of curving white structures buried in palms and gardens faces the beach, where nearly everyone, it seems, is perfectly tanned and toned. The buildings were designed by Moreno in alignment with the stars and energy channels; Maroma exudes a tranquility that soon calms even the most stressed-out high-powered guests. Evenings are especially lovely, with nearly 1,000 candles burning along the pathways and staircases. Morning coffee on your private veranda and trips to the nearby reefs are included in the room rate. Check out the extensive collection of books and magazines in the library, where the concierge awaits to arrange anything you need. The food is exceptional, with Yucatán-inspired cuisine and freshly baked pastries and breads that send guests off to the gym. Maroma's beach was named "Top Beach of the World's 10 Best Beaches" by the Travel Channel.

SETTING AND FACILITIES

Location 20 miles south of Cancún International Airport.

Dining 3 restaurants.

Amenities and services Beach, pool, hot tub, gym, spa, water-sports center, tour desk, shop, 24-hour room service, Internet.

ACCOMMODATIONS

Rooms 65.

All rooms AC, fan, windows that open, balcony or terrace, bathtub, hair dryer, safe, minibar, CD, high-speed Internet, no TV.

Some rooms Ocean view, nonsmoking, disabled access, separate bedrooms, plunge pool, fitness equipment.

Comfort and decor A soothing sense of style prevails, with white-gauze netting over the beds, hand-loomed rugs, bamboo shutters, and enormous bathtubs with hand-painted Mexican tiles. Cotton caftans are supplied in each room, and guests tend to wear them to the spa and pool.

PAYMENT, RESERVATIONS, AND RESTRICTIONS

Deposit Credit card; 14-day cancellation policy (requires notice in writing).

Credit cards AE, DC, MC, V.

Check-in/out Noon/3 p.m.

PLAYA XCALACOCO

THE CAMPGROUNDS AND RUSTIC *cabañas* that once claimed this perfect beach are gone. The more luxurious Tides (formerly Ikal del Mar) is located on a quiet section of the beach, and vacation homes and condo developments are under construction nearby.

The Tides Riviera Maya $$$$

OVERALL ★★★★★   QUALITY ★★★★★   VALUE ★★★★

Highway 307 40 miles south of Cancún airport; ☎ 984-877-3000 or 800-578-0281 U.S.; fax 984-877-3008; www.tidesrivieramaya.com

Unlike some of the new upscale properties on the coast, The Tides blends with the natural terrain. It started as Ikal del Mar ("poetry of the sea" in Maya), and the latest owners have pretty much left perfection alone, while adding luxurious amenities like mayordomos in charge of each guest's needs. Motorized vehicles are left outside the gates, and night lighting consists of torches that don't compete with the starlit sky. The villas are surrounded by lush tropical gardens and have private pools; there's also a pool by the seven-mile–long beach. The separate spa facilities include a *temazcal* (Maya-style sauna), steam room, Jacuzzi, Swiss shower, Tai Chi and yoga classes, and beauty salon. Treatments use local herbs and flowers and include massages, wraps, and facials. Children under age 16 are not permitted, but pets under six pounds are allowed.

SETTING AND FACILITIES

Location 3 miles north of Playa del Carmen.

Dining 2 restaurants.

Amenities and services Pool, hot tub, spa, water-sports center, tour desk, shop, 24-hour room service, Internet.

ACCOMMODATIONS

Rooms 30 villas.

All rooms AC, balcony or terrace, bathtub, hair dryer, safe, satellite TV, DVD, CD, complimentary minibar.

Comfort and decor Simple yet utterly enchanting, the white-on-white decor enhances the beauty of native hardwoods and soaring palapa roofs. The beds, draped in white gauze, sit in the middle of the rooms, with headboards and night-stands with reading lamps. Egyptian-cotton sheets, fluffy duvets, and down pillows make them irresistible. The bathrooms have twin sinks. All villas have private plunge pools on the terraces. Wander the grounds in daylight to pinpoint your villa's surroundings, as it can be hard to find your way home in the dark night.

PAYMENT, RESERVATIONS, AND RESTRICTIONS

Deposit Credit-card guarantee with 50% of stay total required at booking; 14–21-day cancellation policy; all cancellations forfeit $100.

Credit cards AE, DC, MC, V.

Check-in/out 2 p.m./noon.

■ MAYAKOBA

THIS HIGH-END RESORT DEVELOPMENT just north of Playa del Carmen takes the Riviera Maya to a whole new level. The name translates from Mayan as "City on the Water," and a city it is—though one totally devoted to vacationing. An 18-hole Greg Norman–designed golf course called El Camaleón winds from a long beach though mangrove lagoons and jungle. When completed, Mayakoba will hold several high-end hotels and residential communities. First in the lineup are the Fairmont, which opened in 2006, then the Rosewood, a 2008 addition. Now a Banyan Tree, scheduled to open in 2009, is under construction.

WHERE TO STAY IN MAYAKOBA

 Fairmont Mayakoba $$$$$

OVERALL ★★★★½	QUALITY ★★★★½	VALUE ★★★★

Highway 307, Km 298; ☎ 984-206-3000, 800-257-7544, or 800-544-6088 U.S.; fax 984-206-3030; www.fairmont.com/mayakoba

This sprawling property has an unusual design for a beach resort—most of the rooms sit beside lagoons rather than sand. Motorized lunches transport guests through canals from the soaring lobby, past an island that holds most of the swimming pool and recreation facilities, The canals continue along under bridges linking the golf course, rooms, and beach. Golf carts cover the area more rapidly, and are posted near all rooms (as are bikes you can borrow to peddle around). The two-story Willow Spa is a great place to hang out—its rooftop lap pool is the best place for a serious swim, and the gym has every gizmo your muscles demand. A second pool, gourmet restaurant, and water-view suites line the long, white beach.

SETTING AND FACILITIES

Location Mayakoba, just north of Playa del Carmen.

Dining 3 restaurants, deli.

Amenities and services Beach, 2 pools, spa, room service, wireless Internet.

ACCOMMODATIONS

Rooms 401 rooms and suites.

All rooms AC, fan, windows that open, balcony or terrace, bathtub, hair dryer, safe, minibar, TV/DVD/CD, Internet.

Some rooms Nonsmoking, disabled access, ocean view.

Comfort and decor Sitting on your deck in the morning watching egrets and herons is sublimely relaxing, as is padding around your studio-sized suite with its earth-toned furnishings, large dressing area with double closets, and bathroom that looks like its buried in jungle. Wooden slatted doors close off the bathing and sleeping areas and open to the jungle or ocean views.

PAYMENT, RESERVATIONS, AND RESTRICTIONS

Deposit Credit-card guarantee; 7-day cancellation policy.

Credit cards AE, DC, MC, V.

Check-in/out 2 p.m./noon.

 Rosewood Mayakoba **$$$$$**

OVERALL ★★★★★	QUALITY ★★★★★	VALUE ★★★★

Highway 307, Km 298; ☎ **984-875-8000 or 888-767-3966 U.S.;**
fax 984-875-8001; www.rosewoodmayakoba.com

Gracious, amiable service is the hallmark of this gorgeous all-suite resort buried within a protected reserve. The great outdoors—a template of green tropical forest, mangrove lagoons, white sand, and blue sea—is never far from view even inside the suites, thanks to outdoor showers and huge glass doors opening to the scenery. The restaurants and bars (including a seductive tequila library lounge) offer enough delicious options to keep guests from roaming away from the property. The main pool flows beneath the lobby and gourmet restaurant beside a jade-green lagoon, and a smaller pool sits just above the talcum-white beach.

SETTING AND FACILITIES

Location Mayakoba, just north of Playa del Carmen.

Dining 2 restaurants.

Amenities and services Beach, 2 pools, hot tub, gym, spa, water-sports center, tour desk, shops, 24-hour room service, Wi-Fi and high-speed Internet.

ACCOMMODATIONS

Rooms 128 suites.

All rooms AC, fans, windows that open, sundecks or patios, bathtub, garden showers, plunge pool, hair dryer, safe, minibar, TV/DVD/CD, Internet.

Some rooms Nonsmoking, disabled access, ocean view, separate bedrooms, butlers.

Comfort and decor The designers thought of every detail to encourage luxurious comfort, from the sublime beds with ocean- or jungle-views to the dual sinks with plenty of counter space and the generous closets. Pleasurable amenities include a bottle of primo tequila, fresh fruit, large tubs, plush towels, deluxe toiletries, and iPod docks.

PAYMENT, RESERVATIONS, AND RESTRICTIONS

Deposit 2-night deposit; 14-day cancellation policy.

Credit cards AE, DC, MC, V.

Check-in/out 3 p.m./3 p.m.; both are flexible.

PLAYA DEL CARMEN

TWO DECADES AGO, Playa del Carmen (often just called "Playa") was a small town with dirt streets and a few casual hotels and campgrounds. Now it's one of the fastest-growing cities in Mexico, with a 20% annual growth rate and about 200,000 residents. Although the infrastructure has undergone improvements, it can't keep up with the growth, and the streets are jam-packed with cars, buses, and tour vans. Playa's acclaimed long, white beach was destroyed when a developer was allowed to build a large hotel and jetty just a few blocks from the main part of town. The hotels and restaurants packed together on the sand haven't helped. The best beach area is now north of town in the rapidly growing neighborhood around Avenida Constituyentes and Calle 38.

Playa's eclectic, sophisticated selection of restaurants, shops, and hotels just keeps getting better as the town grows. Playa easily rivals Cancún as a vacation destination, especially if you enjoy a vibrant, youthful scene. While Cancún is jam-packed with franchise hotels and restaurants, Playa has a more individualistic feel. Travelers enjoy hanging out in the cafes and on the beach, making friends with fellow explorers, and exchanging tips. By staying in Playa you're close to Tulum, Xcaret, the Cozumel ferry, and many of the coast's good diving and snorkeling areas. Prices are a bit lower than in Cancún (though that's changing rapidly) and there are more options for budget travelers.

Playa is the commercial center for the coast and has banks, a post office, auto-repair and rental shops, gas stations, supermarkets, warehouse stores (Office Depot, Sam's Club), and vigilant cops who love handing out tickets. Avenida Juárez is the main road into town from the highway, and it's always congested. Several of the streets leading off Juárez are one-way, though there aren't always signs telling you so. If you're driving, find a place to park (there's a pay lot on Avenida 10 on the north side of Juárez) and sightsee on foot.

WHERE TO STAY IN PLAYA DEL CARMEN

IT SEEMS NEARLY EVERY OTHER BUILDING in Playa is a hotel. Styles and prices vary greatly, though the general trend is toward pricey, boutique-style inns. Some of the oldest and least-expensive properties have joined together to form the Association of Small Hotels; you can check them out on the Web at **www.hotelesplayadelcarmen.com. Villas Playa del Carmen** (☎ 984-803 1543; **www.villasplayadelcarmen.com**) also handles villa and condo rentals in the area.

Accommodation Profiles

Deseo Hotel and Lounge $$$$

OVERALL ★★★	QUALITY ★★★	VALUE ★★½

Avenida 5N and Calle 12; ☎ 984-879-3620 or 800-186-6978 U.S.; fax 984-879-3621; www.hoteldeseo.com

The first in Playa's growing number of utterly hip hotels, Deseo is an adults-only, white-on-white spectacle where every element is designed to create a chic, minimalist scene. Stairs lead up from the busy street to the

playa del carmen

■ **ACCOMMODATIONS**
1. Deseo Hotel and Lounge
2. Hacienda del Caribe
3. La Tortuga Hotel and Spa

◆ **RESTAURANTS**
4. Babe's Noodles and Bar
5. La Casa del Agua
6. Palapa Hemingway
    Restaurant
7. Sur
8. El Tacolote
9. Yaxche

● **NIGHTLIFE**
10. Alux
11. Básico
12. La Bodeguita del Medio
13. Blue Parrot
14. Capitan Tutix
15. Deseo
16. Diablito Cha-Cha Cha
17. Frida Bar
18. La Santanera
19. Pure Night

Post Office

Calle 14
New Bus Station
Calle 12
Calle 10
Calle 8
Calle 6
Calle 4
Calle 2
Avenida Juárez

1st N.

Caribbean Sea

Pedestrians Only

Av. 5

← To Highway 307

Av. 35
Av. 30
Av. 25
Av. 20
Av. 15
Av. 10

Calle 1

Pedestrians Only

Calle 1

Ferry pier
to Cozumel
(Muelle)

0   164 feet
0   50 meters

dark-wood sun terrace, pool, and rooms; there's no elevator. The staff and clients sometimes have a rather elitist attitude, depending on the current guests. Continental breakfast is included in the room rate. The bar and pool are the center of the action, with drinks and snacks served to guests lounging on padded sun beds shaded by white-gauze canopies. The hotel is on a busy street but guests have access to a beach club.

SETTING AND FACILITIES

Location In the midst of Avenida 5.

Dining Bar with snacks.

Amenities and services Pool, hot tub, massage, room service, Internet.

ACCOMMODATIONS

Rooms 18 rooms.

All rooms AC, safe, minibar.

Some rooms Balcony, bathtub, satellite TV.

Comfort and decor Beds covered in pristine white linens are centered away from the walls and look out to balconies strung with hammocks. Claw-foot bathtubs sit outside the bathrooms; hooks for hats and beach towels hang behind a gauze drape. Suites have a tub in the middle of the room, and curtains instead of bathroom doors; several have large balconies. Rooms are stocked with condoms, incense, and earplugs to block the noise from the bar. Most have sliding doors that open to the pool area.

PAYMENT, RESERVATIONS, AND RESTRICTIONS

Deposit Credit-card deposit, 7-day cancellation policy.

Credit cards AE, MC, V.

Check-in/out 3 p.m./1 p.m.

Hacienda del Caribe $

OVERALL	★½	QUALITY	★★	VALUE	★★★★

Calle 2N 130; ☎ 984-873-3132; fax 984-873-1149; www.haciendadelcaribe.com

This three-story hotel (no elevator) has the feel of a Yucatecan hacienda in the middle of the city. The rooms are surprisingly quiet given the proximity to Avenida 5, and the large, guarded parking lot behind the hotel is a major plus. The small courtyard pool is surrounded by plants and patio tables, and the building is filled with charming, artistic touches including reproductions of Diego Rivera paintings.

SETTING AND FACILITIES

Location Just off Avenida 5.

Dining Restaurant; Continental breakfast included in room rate.

Amenities and services Pool.

ACCOMMODATIONS

Rooms 34 rooms.

All rooms AC, fan, safe, minibar, cable TV.

Some rooms Windows that open.

Comfort and decor Rooms have red-tile floors, tables and chairs made with leather and woven strips of wood, carved and painted wooden headboards, brightly colored curtains and bedspreads, and stenciling on white walls. Some have king-size beds, domed-brick ceilings, and sliding-glass doors that open to views of the street and a bit of beach. Rooms are looking a bit worn down these days and have considerable competition. But the hotel is just two blocks from the beach and close to the bus station.

PAYMENT, RESERVATIONS, AND RESTRICTIONS

Deposit Credit-card deposit to confirm reservation; cancellation policy flexible.

Credit cards MC, V.

Check-in/out 3 p.m./noon.

La Tortuga Hotel and Spa $$

OVERALL	★★½	QUALITY	★★½	VALUE	★★★

Avenida 10, between Calles 12 and 14; ☎ 984-873-1484; fax 984-873-0798; www.hotellatortuga.com

Peaceful, yet in the midst of the action, La Tortuga is one of our favorite hotels for its homey, comfortable feeling. We always find it a traveler's dream come true, and often check in without reservations, only to get an upgraded room for whatever rate we're paying. The staff couldn't be any more accommodating, and the whole place feels like a jungle hideaway. The buildings frame a freeform pool in a small garden beside a lounge area with couches, tables, and wireless Internet access. Stairways lead to rooms with all sorts of configurations and views, and a quietness prevails despite the nearby nightlife action. A breakfast buffet (included) is served in the restaurant between the pool and the street. Guests have free passes to Mamita's beach club. All sorts of soothing and nourishing treatments are available at the adjacent Izta Spa. Guests receive a discount on parking at a nearby indoor lot. *Note:* This is not a hotel for kids—all guests must be age 17 or older.

SETTING AND FACILITIES

Location On a side street 1 block from Avenida 5 in Playa.

Dining 1 restaurant.

Amenities and services Beach club, 1 pool, hot tub, spa services, wireless Internet access in lobby.

ACCOMMODATIONS

Rooms 51.

All rooms AC, fan, windows that open, hair dryer, coffeemaker, safe, TV.

Some rooms Whirlpool tub, balcony or terrace, pool access from terrace.

Comfort and decor The design is practical yet pleasing, with lots of built-in counter space and niches where you can stash your stuff. Bedside lamps offer good lighting and the beds are comfy, though not plush. Decorations are minimal—just stencils of turtles and fish on the walls, small TVs and *saltillo* (terra-cotta) tiled floors—but the overall look is clean and fresh.

PAYMENT, RESERVATIONS, AND RESTRICTIONS

Deposit Credit card; 14-day cancellation policy.

Credit cards MC, V.

Check-in/out Flexible.

WHERE TO EAT IN PLAYA DEL CARMEN

THERE'S NO SHORTAGE OF DINING OPTIONS in Playa. Italian restaurants have long prevailed—there's a large community of Italian expatriates here, along with Germans and North Americans. They've opened restaurants that rival those in Cancún, offering a wide range of cuisines. Coffeehouses abound, as do casual beach bars. The sidewalk on Avenida 5 is like a giant meeting place where locals and frequent visitors hang out at their favorite cafes and greet friends as they pass by. Some restaurants segue into bars and lounges after dinner and have live music on weekends. Dining isn't cheap along Avenida 5, but there are alternatives on Avenida Juárez and the back streets of town.

Restaurant Profiles

Babe's Noodles and Bar ★★★

| THAI/EUROPEAN | INEXPENSIVE | QUALITY ★★★ | VALUE ★★★★ |

**Calle 10, between Avenidas 5 and 10; ☎ 984-804-1998,
www.babesnoodlesandbar.com**

Reservations Not accepted.

Entree range $6–$15.

Payment MC, V.

Service rating ★★½.

Bar Full service.

Parking Limited street parking.

Dress Casual.

Disabled access None.

Customers Locals getting together for a drink and inexpensive meal.

Hours Daily, 5–11 p.m.

SETTING AND ATMOSPHERE Tables are packed on the sidewalk and in the bar/restaurant at this popular gathering point. It gets noisy, but it's a fun spot for dining inexpensively.

HOUSE SPECIALTIES Pad Thai, red curry with shrimp, Swedish meatballs.

SUMMARY AND COMMENTS A Swedish couple opened Babe's after traveling around Mexico and deciding to settle in Playa. It's been a favorite spot with locals ever since. The vibe is upbeat and friendly, and the food's great, especially if you want a filling meal of noodles, cheese, and veggies for just a few pesos. Another location opened in 2006 on Avenida 5 between Calles 28 and 30 in a neighborhood that's become the latest hip hangout.

La Casa del Agua ★★★★

| INTERNATIONAL | EXPENSIVE | QUALITY ★★★★★ | VALUE ★★★ |

Avenida 5 at Calle 2 Norte; ☎ 984-803-0323

Reservations Recommended in high season.

Entree range $16–$29.

Payment MC, V.

Service rating ★★★★.

Bar Full service, imported wines.

Parking Limited street parking.

Dress Dressy casual.

Disabled access None.

Customers Locals and travelers enjoying a special night out.

Hours Daily, 11:30–midnight.

SETTING AND ATMOSPHERE A winding stairway leads up from the street to the second-story dining room and patio. Tables are spread far enough apart for quiet conversation; the best seats are on the patio. A street-level bistro gives a full-on view of the crowds of shoppers—the upstairs outdoor patio is more private.

HOUSE SPECIALTIES Chicken with spaetzle, steak Roquefort, steak served with *huitlacoche* (a dark, pungent, mushroomlike fungus that grows on corn).

SUMMARY AND COMMENTS The Spath family, who've long been involved in tourism in the Riviera Maya, have created a delightful restaurant with an unusual menu that includes several European favorites. You might want to eat here several times, sampling seafood risotto, thick steaks, and fabulous ice-cream creations.

Palapa Hemingway Restaurant ★★

MEXICAN/AMERICAN	MODERATE	QUALITY ★★★	VALUE ★

Northern Fifth Avenue; Avenida 5 between Calle 12 and Calle Corazón; ☎ 984-803-0003

Reservations Accepted for groups.

Entree range $7–$14.

Payment MC, V.

Service rating ★★.

Bar Full service.

Parking Limited street parking.

Dress Casual.

Disabled access Limited.

Customers Locals and travelers.

Hours Daily, 8 a.m.–midnight.

SETTING AND ATMOSPHERE Open to the sidewalk, the dining room walls are covered with boldly colored, abstract murals and historical photos of Cuba. The palapa is supported by twisted tree trunks and a large, living tree.

HOUSE SPECIALTIES Grilled steaks and seafood with a Caribbean flair salmon in three-cheese sauce.

SUMMARY AND COMMENTS The decor is as stimulating as the food, which blends Caribbean and Mexican flavors.

Sur ★★★

ARGENTINE/BEEF	EXPENSIVE	QUALITY ★★★	VALUE ★★★

Avenida 5 at Calles Corazón and 14; ☎ 984-873-2995

Reservations Accepted.

Entree range $15–$30.

Payment AE, MC, V.

Service rating ★★★.

Bar Full service.

Parking Limited street parking.

Dress Casual.

Disabled access Limited.

Customers Locals and travelers.

Hours Daily, noon–11:30 p.m.

SETTING AND ATMOSPHERE 2-story building nearly buried in trees and vines, hardwood floors, blue-and-white linens.

HOUSE SPECIALTIES Empanadas, steaks, sausage.

SUMMARY AND COMMENTS Carnivores look no further. This palace of meat serves beef the Argentine way, with plenty of fat for extra flavor. The marinated *arrachera* steak is thin and tender, but if you're really craving beef go for the half-pound *churrasco* steak. The *chimichurri* sauce of oil and spices is excellent—go ahead and spoon it onto the fresh bread as well as the beef. The menu has seafood, pasta, and chicken offerings as well.

El Tacolote ★★

MEXICAN	INEXPENSIVE	QUALITY ★★	VALUE ★★★

Avenida Juárez near Avenida 5; Avenida Juárez 105; ☎ 984-873-1363

Reservations Not accepted.

Entree range $6–$15.

Payment AE, MC, V.

Service rating ★★★.

Bar Full service, tropical cocktails.

Parking Limited street parking.

Dress Casual.

Disabled access Limited.

Customers Locals and travelers.

Hours Daily, noon–11 p.m.; delivery available.

SETTING AND ATMOSPHERE Simple restaurant and take-out stand.

HOUSE SPECIALTIES Tacos, fajitas, marinated beef.

SUMMARY AND COMMENTS You can eat inexpensively here by sticking with beef, pork, and chicken tacos or cheese quesadillas. The full meals are more expensive, but there's enough food for two. Choose from several no-meat or fish selections, including vegetable fajitas.

Yaxche ★★★★

NOUVELLE YUCATECAN	MODERATE	QUALITY ★★★★★	VALUE ★★★

Downtown; Calle 8, between Avenidas 5 and 10; ☎ 984-873-2502; www. mayacuisine.com

Reservations Recommended for dinner.

Entree range $11–$25.

Payment AE, MC, V.

Service rating ★★★½.

Bar Full service.

Parking Limited street parking.

Dress Casual.

Disabled access Limited.

Customers Residents and travelers come from throughout area for frequent meals.

Hours Daily, noon–midnight.

SETTING AND ATMOSPHER The front dining room and back garden are filled with Maya touches, including reproductions of stone pillars and carvings of Maya deities. Tables beside the garden fountain are nicest. The expanded dining room now has air-conditioning.

HOUSE SPECIALTIES Lobster flambéed with *xtabentun* (a local liqueur), *tikin-xic* (fish baked in banana leaves), *epazote* shrimp.

SUMMARY AND COMMENTS The best regional restaurant on the coast has garnered awards and much praise for its innovative renditions of traditional Maya recipes. The chef uses chipotle chiles, *achiote*, banana leaves, *epazote*, and other regional ingredients to create extraordinary meals. Definitely a must for at least one meal—you may return for more.

SIGHTSEEING IN PLAYA DEL CARMEN

BETWEEN THE WATER, beach, **Avenida 5** (also called La Quinta), and the inner city, there's plenty to see and do in Playa, and it serves as a perfect headquarters for those traveling without cars. Buses and taxis are readily available, and Playa is the locus of many tour and sporting companies. Shops, restaurants, and businesses clustered around the pier and plaza cater to day-trippers for the most part, while those on the north end of Avenida 5 cater to a more discerning and relaxed clientele. **Calle Corazón,** a pedestrian corridor at Calle 12, between Avenida 5 and 10, is lined with several good shops and restaurants. The far northern section of La Quinta, past Avenida Constituyentes, is rapidly becoming the hippest part of town with coffeehouses, cafes, and folk-art shops. You can see almost everything on foot, unless you're staying in **Playacar**. Within Playacar, wildlife fans will want to check out **Xaman-Há,** a small aviary open daily, 9 a.m. to 5 p.m.; Paseo Xaman-Há, Playacar; ☎ 984-873-0593; admission $8.

unofficial **TIP**
Some hotels in Playacar have bike rentals, which can drastically cut the expense of visiting Playa del Carmen. Just remember that you could get overheated and sunburned if biking around in midday.

TOURS AND SIDE TRIPS FROM PLAYA DEL CARMEN

Alltournative (Avenida 38N between Avenidas 1 and 5; ☎ 984-803-9999; **www.alltournative.com**)

has tours to Maya villages near Cobá that include kayaking, rappelling, zip lines, mountain biking, tours of the archaeological site, and lunch at a Maya village. Their inland Jeep safaris open up a side of the peninsula that many travelers don't see, and the Maya villages they work in seem to have benefited from the attention. The tour to the village of Pac-Chen has garnered some ecotourism awards. Tours cost about $124 adults, $105 for kids under age 12. They have stands with staff explaining the tours on Avenida 5 between Calles 12 and 14 and between Calles 26 and 28.

EXERCISE AND RECREATION IN PLAYA DEL CARMEN

PALACE RESORTS, WHICH HAS SEVERAL all-inclusive hotels in the Riviera Maya including one in Playacar, has taken over the **Playacar Club de Golf** (Paseo Xaman-Há, Playacar; ☎ 984-873-4960). The 18-hole, par-72 course designed by Robert Von Hagge is the centerpiece of the Playacar development, and it runs past hotels, villas, small Maya ruins, and white beaches. Greens fees are $180 on an all-inclusive plan including shared cart, drinks, and snacks.

Scuba diving on the reefs and at nearby *cenotes* is popular, and there are several dive shops in Playa. Some shops offer dive and hotel packages. **The Abyss Dive Shop** (Calle 1 between Calles 12 and 14, beachfront; ☎ 984-873-2164, **www.abyssdiveshop.com**) offers technical dives, reef, wreck and cave diving, and other water sports. Another long-timer, **Tank-Ha** (Avenida 5 between Calles 8 and 10; ☎ 984-873-0302, www.tankha.com) is well established.

The redoubtable **ATV Explorer** (Highway 307 between Playacar and Xcaret; ☎ 984-873-1626; **www.atvexplorer.com**) has a two-hour tour that combines riding ATVs through the jungle, swimming in a *cenote,* and exploring the area's ruins and caves. Cost is $50 for a person riding double and $59 for a person riding single. Advance reservations are recommended.

SHOPPING IN PLAYA DEL CARMEN

PLAYA IS A SHOPPER'S DELIGHT, with more variety than anywhere else in the region (including Cancún). Avenida 5 is packed with shops selling jewelry, folk art, sarongs, and swimsuits. **Paseo del Carmen,** an open-air mall near the ferry pier, has several sportswear shops, bars, and restaurants in a pleasant setting with fountains and plenty of benches for resting between shopping forays. **Plaza Pelicanos** on Avenida 10 between Calles 8 and 10 includes three movie theaters, a few boutiques, and a food court. Many shops take at least one form of credit card, but they may add an extra charge for the service. Check out the tiny shop called **The Bone House** (Calle 8 between Avenidas 5 and 10; no phone) for intricate carvings with Maya designs. **La Calaca** (Avenida 5 N between Calles 12 and 14; ☎ 984-873-0174) has one of the best selections of folk art, including Oaxacan wood carvings, lacquered trays and boxes, miniature skeleton dioramas, and papier-mâché figurines. The masks and papier-mâché figures hanging outside **Pachamama** (Calle Corazón between Calles 12 and 14; ☎ 984-803-3355) lure you into a shop stocked with miniature dioramas and skull and skeleton figurines. **El Arbol de la Vida** (Avenida 5 between Calles 28 and 30) is a collector's gallery with gorgeous weavings, pottery, and carvings.

Mundo Maya (Avenida 5N between Calles 14 and 16; ☎ 984-803-0821) sells prehispanic musical instruments, a wide array of Mexican CDs, original artworks, and souvenirs. Some of the finest amber jewelry you'll ever find is displayed at **Ambar Mexicano** (Avenida 5 between Calles 4 and 6; ☎ 984-873-2357). The excellent workmanship comes from artists in Chiapas.

NIGHTLIFE IN PLAYA DEL CARMEN

THE MAIN NIGHTLIFE CHOICES along the coast vary with your hotel. If you're staying at an all-inclusive property, options usually include a few bars and live shows or dances that change nightly. The many small properties dotting the coast usually have a bar or lounge where the action depends upon the guests' sense of camaraderie. The nightly Maya show at **Xcaret** (see right) is a major attraction for travelers staying anywhere between Cancún and Tulum. If you have a car, your choices for evening entertainment are more diverse. Make reservations in advance for dinner at various hotels and restaurants along the coast, and linger around the grounds.

Playa del Carmen has the most active nightlife scene. Avenida 5 (also known as Fifth Avenue) pulsates at night, especially when tour groups from cruise ships descend. Most restaurants stay open until the crowd wears down, and many have sidewalk tables where friends gather late into the night. Some restaurants have live music after dinner, especially when tourism is high. The bars at the ultrahip hotels **Deseo** (Avenida 5 at Calle 12; ☎ 984-879-3620) and **Básico** (Calle 10 at Avenida 5; ☎ 984-879-4448) throb with house music at night, when guests and locals lounge about on plush mattresses or practice their moves at salsa lessons.

The **Blue Parrot** (Calle 12 at Avenida 1; ☎ 984-873-0083) hosts live bands nightly until midnight. DJs spin techno, lounge, and house music at **Diablito Cha-Cha Cha** (Calle 12 at Avenida 1; ☎ 984-803-3695) from Thursday to Saturday nights. The restaurant serves great sushi, clams, pulpo, and other small plates. Diehards usually move on from here to the two-story **La Santanera** (Calle 12 between Avenidas 5 and 10; ☎ 984-803-4771) where dancing and general revelry hits its peak on the second-story dance floor. The ambience is a tad more subdued in the first-floor lounge area.

Live groups play smooth jazz at **Frida Bar** (Avenida 5 at Calle 12; ☎ 984-973-2222) amid—you guessed it—reproductions of Frida Kahlo paintings. Discos aren't usually Playa's thing, but locals are thoroughly enjoying the dance floors and 70s and 80s music at **Pure Night** (Calle 6 between Avenidas 5 and 10; ☎ 987-803-2656).

There is also a dance scene at **Alux** (Avenida Juárez at Calle 55 Sur; ☎ 984-803-0713). Mojitos and cigars are de rigueur at **La Bodeguita del Medio** (Paseo del Carmen, no phone), a branch of the famed Havana bar and restaurant. Live jazz plays nightly. Dancers and drinkers frolic barefoot in the sand at **Capitan Tutix** (Calle 4 at the beach; ☎ 984-873-1748), which now has a second location in Tulum (Avenida Tulum at Cobá crossroad; no phone).

XCARET

kids THE MAYA USED THE NATURAL COVE at **Xcaret** as a port and settlement in the postclassic period. It was a secret, sacred spot for hundreds of years, until a modern developer spotted it as the ideal location for a large-scale experiment. Miguel Quintana has transformed a 250-acre plot of jungle and beach into an ecologically oriented theme park that attracts thousands of visitors each month. Most are shuttled down from Cancún and spend the day and evening immersed in a replica of all that's special about the region. Attractions include an underwater river ride, swim-with-dolphins program, horseback riding, butterfly pavilion, aviary, aquarium, botanical garden, and on and on. Several postclassic Maya structures (AD 1200–1500) have been reconstructed. The largest cluster is lit with torches during the park's nightly show called *Noche Espectacular*. It is truly spectacular, with dancers recreating the history of Mexico (the battle between the Aztecs and conquistadors is quite impressive). The last half of the show includes the famous regional folkloric dances from throughout Mexico, with elaborate costumes and choreography. The show is surely the most comprehensive in Mexico, and gives a thorough overview of the country's many cultures.

Future plans include making Xcaret a home port for a large cruise line. The 769-room, all-inclusive Grand Xcaret by Occidental Hotel opened in 2004, ready for cruise passengers beginning or ending their journeys here. Both the port and the hotel have stirred up considerable controversy as locals protest further development. The coastline is definitely being impacted by all the construction in the area, and some fear that more cruise ships will increase the chances of serious damage to the reefs.

You'll pay nearly as much as it costs to take the family to Disneyland; all-inclusive packages covering activities and transportation are the best deal. Count on spending the day and evening to get the most for your money. If you can't last that long, go in mid-afternoon and stay for the show. Admission is $69 adults, $34.50 kids ages 5 to 12; round-trip transportation from Playa del Carmen and Riviera Maya hotels is $10. Meals and swimming with dolphins cost extra. Highway 307, 50 miles south of Cancún, between Playa del Carmen and Tulum; ☎ 984-873-2643, 998-881-2451 in Cancún; ☎ 984-803-1298 in Playa del Carmen; **www.xcaret.net**.

PAAMUL

CAMPERS, ESCAPISTS, AND BUDGET TRAVELERS are delighted to find this isolated beach, where solitude and simplicity are the main attractions. There's just one hotel (see below) with a campground, restaurant, and dive shop—all you need for a relaxing vacation.

Hotel Paamul　$

OVERALL ★★★	QUALITY ★★	VALUE ★★★★

Highway 307 Km 85; phone and fax ☎ 984-875-1051; www.paamulcabanas.com

A two-story hotel has replaced the longtime cabañas on Paamul's white-sand beach, with nothing to block the view of the sea. Behind the buildings is a large campground with spaces for tents, RVs, and basic campers who just want to string a hammock between trees. The campground is packed during the winter—it's one of the few places on the coast that accepts RVs and offers reduced weekly and monthly rates. The palapa-roofed restaurant and bar serve decent, reasonably priced meals; bring snacks if you're staying awhile. The dive shop offers snorkel and dive trips to the nearby reef, plus dive certification; a small market at entrance sells cold drinks and supplies.

SETTING AND FACILITIES

Location　Paamul, 10 miles south of Playa del Carmen.

Dining　1 restaurant.

Amenities and services　Beach, pool, water-sports center.

ACCOMMODATIONS

Rooms　13 rooms; 200 campsites.

All rooms　AC, windows that open, ocean view, balcony or terrace, refrigerator, microwave.

Some rooms　The master suite has a full kitchen and bedroom.

Comfort and decor　A room with air-conditioning on the beach in the Riviera Maya for less than $100 is almost impossible to find. These are perfectly service-able with two double beds, sand-proof tiled floors, and hot showers. Call ahead to reserve, as they fill quickly.

PAYMENT, RESERVATIONS, AND RESTRICTIONS

Deposit　50% deposit required to hold reservation, paid by check or wire trans-fer to hotel's account; 1-week cancellation policy.

Credit cards　Cash only.

Check-in/out　Noon/noon.

PUERTO AVENTURAS

A MASTER-PLANNED DEVELOPMENT, Puerto Aventuras has the largest full-service marina on the coast, and it's favored by yachties and part-time villa and condo owners. The complex includes a nine-hole golf course, a small shopping area with a few restaurants and cafes, and the **Museo CEDAM** (Mexican Underwater Expeditions Club; no phone) covering the history of shipwrecks on the reefs and Mexican scuba diving. The museum is generally open daily with a break in midday, but hours are erratic; a voluntary donation is requested for admission. Because of the marina, Puerto Aventuras lacks good beaches. For more information on the Puerto Aventuras area, contact the Puerto Aventuras resort at ☎ 984-873-5000 (for golf-course info, call ☎ 984-873-5111), or visit **www.puertoaventuras.com.**

XPU-HA

Esencia $$$$$

OVERALL ★★★★★	QUALITY ★★★★★	VALUE ★★★★

Highway 307 at Xpu-ha; ☎ 984 873 4830 or 877-528-3490 U.S.; fax 984 873 4836; www.hotelesencia.com

Want to feel like you're staying in a private villa on the beach? You belong at Esencia. Once a private compound built for an Italian duchess, this small hotel now has a series of gorgeous rooms in the original villa and several newer Mediterranean-style buildings on the secluded property. Privacy is insured—there'sonly a small sign for the hotel at the side of Highway 307, and the turnoff leads to a wooden stick and palm frond traditional Maya *na* (house) on a dirt road. Guests are led down a jungle path to the main building, which looks as though it belongs the Italian Riviera—except for the Mexican Caribbean's sparkling white sand and nearly translucent aquamarine sea. Though the setting is classic, the amenities are high-tech—iPod hookups, speakers everywhere, plasma-screen TVs, shades that open and shut by remote control. Though simple in design, the spa is excellent and soothing. Meals at the poolside restaurant and the more formal dinner restaurant are also sublime—you need to stay at least a week to sample everything.

SETTING AND FACILITIES

Location Xpu-Ha, between Playa del Carmen and Tulum.

Dining 2 restaurants.

Amenities and services Beach, 2 pools, spa, room service, wireless Internet access.

ACCOMMODATIONS

Rooms 29 suites.

All rooms AC, fan, windows that open, balcony or terrace, bathtub, hair dryer, safe, minibar, TV/DVD/CD, Internet.

Some rooms Nonsmoking, disabled access, plunge pools, ocean view, several bedrooms, full kitchen.

Comfort and decor The rooms in both the villa section and newer two-story are simply elegant, with white walls, mahogany-wood accents, 600-thread count sheets, and classy Moulton Brown amenities. Bathrooms have rainshower shower heads and separate bathtubs; closets are enormous. Two cottages are outfitted for families accustomed to traveling with their nannies and have multiple bedrooms, private pools, and kitchens.

PAYMENT, RESERVATIONS, AND RESTRICTIONS

Deposit Credit-card guarantee with 50% deposit; nonrefundable cancellation fee of 21 days; $100 penalty for changes.

Credit cards AE, MC, V.

Check-in/out 2 p.m./noon.

AKUMAL

CONDOS, PRIVATE VILLAS, AND SMALL HOTELS line the shores of **Akumal Bay** and **Half Moon Bay,** two of the loveliest bodies of water on the coast. Pablo Bush Romero, the Jacques Cousteau of Mexico, founded the Mexican Underwater Expeditions Club (CEDAM) here in 1958, leading divers in rudimentary gear to shipwrecks and pristine coral reefs. The original bungalows used by the divers are part of Akumal's main hotel, the **Club Akumal Caribe and Villas Maya** (see below), the informal hub for the many gringos who have vacation homes here. The coast's attractions are within easy driving distance, and services including a laundry and market are located just outside the gates of the hotel. There's a small commercial center called **Plaza Ukana** inside the front gate with an Internet and phone office, real estate agency, a cafe, shops, and a gym. There are several entrances to Akumal from the highway. The northern entrance, signed CLUB AKUMAL CARIBE, leads to the attractions listed under "Sightseeing in Akumal," page 208. Other entrances south of this turnoff lead to hotels and residential areas in **South Akumal** and **Aventuras Akumal.** To reach the hotels and sights profiled on the following pages, enter the gates at Club Akumal Caribe and turn left on the dirt road running along the edge of Half Moon Bay.

WHERE TO STAY IN AKUMAL

Club Akumal Caribe and Villas Maya $$–$$$

OVERALL ★★★	QUALITY ★★★	VALUE ★★★

Highway 307 Km 104; ☎ 984-875-9012 or 800-351-1622 U.S.; 800-343-1440 Canada; fax in U.S. 915-581-6709; www.hotelakumalcaribe.com

Pablo Bush Romero started this hotel for his diving buddies in the 1960s. The complex now includes bungalows, a small hotel, and rental villas spread along the edges of Akumal Bay. The setting is idyllic though not serene—Club Akumal is far too popular for that. Families gather on the long beach, while snorkelers float facedown in the bay and scuba students practice breathing underwater. Everyone is friendly and casual, given to chatting with strangers over ice-cream cones or beers. The Lol-Ha restaurant is a local institution serving Mexican and American dishes; it's open for breakfast and dinner. The adjacent snack bar serves lunch (try the tacos with *cochinita pibil*) and the pizza parlor, bar, and ice-cream stand take care of any cravings.

SETTING AND FACILITIES

Location 50 miles south of Cancún.

Dining 1 restaurant, 1 beach bar.

Amenities and services Beach, pool, water-sports center, kids' activities, shop.

ACCOMMODATIONS

Rooms 21 rooms, 40 bungalows, several villas and condos.

All rooms AC, fan, safe, refrigerator.

Some rooms Ocean view, terrace or balcony, coffeemaker, kitchenette, VCR/DVD/CD, telephone, disabled access.

Comfort and decor The plain hotel rooms are located beside the pool; some have an ocean view. The bungalows are scattered at the back of the property without ocean views, but they have more of a beachy feel. Parking is available outside the units.

PAYMENT, RESERVATIONS, AND RESTRICTIONS

Deposit By check only; strict cancellation policy charging 50% of total with less than 2 days' notice.

Credit cards AE, MC, V.

Check-in/out 3 p.m./noon.

Vista Del Mar $

OVERALL ★★★	QUALITY ★★★	VALUE ★★★

**Highway 307 Km 104; ☎ 984-875-9060 or 888-425-8625 U.S;
☎/fax in U.S. 505-992-3333; www.akumalinfo.com**

Located on a gorgeous bay in a strip of modest condos, restaurants, and vacation homes, this small, economical hotel is perfect for divers, swimmers, and escapees who want perfect calm water at their footsteps. The company also handles bookings for an adjacent complex of condos with separate bedrooms and kitchens. Rates for a one or two-bedroom condo are less than $200 except during holidays, and hotel rooms start at less than $100. Most of the neighbors are North Americans staying for months in vacation homes. Nearby small restaurants and markets make it easy for you to walk around barefoot during your entire stay, and **Akumal Dive Adventures** (**www.akum aldiveadventures.com**) can take care of your diving and snorkeling needs.

SETTING AND FACILITIES

Location Half Moon Bay, off the highway and a bit north of Club Akumal on a sandy road.

Dining 1 restaurant serving breakfast, another restaurant a few steps away is open for all 3 meals.

Amenities and services Beach, pool, water-sports center, dive shop.

ACCOMMODATIONS

Rooms 15.

All rooms AC, fan, windows that open, balcony or terrace, coffeemaker, minifridge, TV.

Some rooms Most rooms have 1 queen bed, some have 2 doubles.

Comfort and decor Bright blue, yellow, and green walls brighten the simple rooms, which are used more for storing your stuff and sleeping than leisurely TV watching. The beach is what it's all about—rooms are designed to withstand sandy feet and wet towels. None of the rooms have bathtubs.

PAYMENT, RESERVATIONS, AND RESTRICTIONS

Deposit 50 percent deposit required within 7 days of booking; final balance due 60 days before arrival. Cancellation fee; no refunds less than 30 days before arrival; $75 penalty for changes.

Credit cards AE, MC, V.

Check-in/out 3 p.m./11 a.m.

SIGHTSEEING IN AKUMAL

AKUMAL MEANS "PLACE OF THE TURTLES," and loggerhead and green turtles return to the shores of **Half Moon Bay** from May to October to dig their nests and lay their eggs. The residents of the area do their best to encourage the turtles to come ashore by limiting lighting and activities on the beach at night. The small **Centro Ecológico Akumal** (☎ 984-875-9095) at the beginning of the road around the bay offers turtle-watching tours and educates residents and guests on tips for protecting the marine environment. A donation is requested for admission.

Near the end of the bay road is **Yal Kú,** a hidden lagoon filled with tropical fish. The residents of Akumal rigorously protect the lagoon from development. Guards collect a small fee as visitors enter the parklike area around the lagoon. Lockers, restrooms, and snorkel gear rentals are available. Unlike Xel-Há and Xcaret, Yal Kú remains a natural setting with incredibly clear water; schools of bright blue and green parrotfish hang out here. Admission is $7 adults, $4 children.

unofficial **TIP**
Akumal is a major destination for sea turtles nesting on the sand in summer. The hotels refrain from using bright lights on the beach when the turtles are around and caution guests to leave the turtles and their nests alone. Akumal's ecological center has info about the turtles and their babies.

Scuba diving remains one of the area's main attractions. The **Akumal Dive Center** (at Club Akumal Caribe [see profile, page 206]; ☎ 984-875-9025; www.akumaldivecenter.com) is the area's original dive shop and a headquarters for CEDAM. The divemasters and instructors have years of dive experience in the area, and they lead professionally operated dive trips to the reefs and *cenotes*. Several levels of certification courses are offered, including a resort course that gives nondivers a feel for the underwater world. The shop rents scuba and snorkel gear, kayaks, and sailboards, and runs fishing trips.

Another established dive operation, **Akumal Dive Adventures** (at Vista del Mar Hotel;

☎ 984-875-9157 or 888-425-8625 U.S.; **www.akumaldiveadventures .com**) offers PADI instruction and different levels of certification, along with reef and *cenote* diving trips, gear rentals, and fishing excursions.

kids Located midway between Akumal and Xel-Há, **Aktun Chen** (Highway 307 Km 107; ☎ 998-892-0662; **www.aktunchen .com**) is an astonishing series of caves, caverns, and tunnels said to be five million years old. Visitors are guided through the grounds (watch out for the aggressive spider monkeys that hang about trying to steal anything they can) and into the caves, where golden-brown stalactites and stalagmites grow toward each other in eerie shapes. The pathway leads to a startlingly bright green cenote, then back out to sunlight. The park has several trails through the forest, a small zoo of local animals, and a cafe. Aktun Chen is open daily, 9 a.m. to 5p.m.; admission is $24 for adults, $13 for children.

XEL-HÁ

kids THE PEOPLE WHO BROUGHT YOU Xcaret have transformed this underwater preserve into yet another water park, with a river ride, several snorkeling areas, five restaurants, a swim-with-dolphins program, and enough distractions to perhaps justify the steep entry fee. Packages including food, drink, equipment rentals, and some activities are available and are a good deal if you plan to stay the day. The snorkeling here isn't as spectacular as it once was—perhaps the 500,000 annual visitors floating over the coral have driven the fish away. But the botanical gardens are excellent, and there are plenty of diversions for the whole family. Get here early and claim one of the shaded areas along the edges of the coves. Xel-Há is open daily, 8:30 a.m. to 6 p.m. An all-inclusive fee of $67.50 adults, $33.75 children includes meals, snorkel gear rentals, use of hammocks, and locker. The park is located on Carretera Chetumal-Cancún Km 240; ☎ 984-875-6000; **www.xelha.com**.

The **Xel-Há Archaeological Site** is located just south of the water park on the highway and has a small complex of ruins beside a shaded *cenote*. The ruins are open daily, 8 a.m. to 5 p.m., and admission is $3.50.

XEL-HÁ *to* TULUM

HIDDEN WORLDS CENOTES

IF YOU SPEND ANY TIME ON THE COAST, you'll eventually hear stories of the deep, mysterious *cenotes* buried in the jungle. Scuba divers visit this area strictly to submerge themselves in deep, dark, underground rivers and caves. At **Hidden Worlds Cenotes,** both first-time snorkelers and experienced divers find adventures that meet their excitement quotient. This well-established scuba-diving company offers snorkel and dive trips in the **Dos Ojos** and **Dreamgate** *cenotes* and bat caves. The experience is outstanding (if you don't mind dark caves). Divemasters lead you through a series of underground rivers, where you swim in cool, clear water beneath fragile stalactites illuminated by occasional rays of sunlight. The company also offers reef-diving trips and cavern- and cave-diving courses. If you prefer staying on land, there's also a zip line above the jungle canopy and a SkyCycle canopy adventure.

Hidden Worlds is open daily; tours are held at scheduled times and reservations are recommended. It's on the inland side of Highway 307 between Xel-Há and Tulum; ☎ 984-115-4514; **hiddenworlds .com.mx.**

TANKAH

SIX MILES SOUTH OF XEL-HÁ on Highway 307, another small sign marks a dirt road leading to Tankah. The best-known business in the area, **Casa Cenote** (open daily, 8:30 a.m. to 9 p.m.; ☎ 984-115-6996; **www.casacenote.com**) began as a simple restaurant between the sea and a large *cenote*. Its Sunday buffets still attract crowds of expatriates, and the business has expanded to include rental condos and casitas. Other small hotels and condo complexes have arisen in the area. There are supposed to be manatees in the *cenote,* though the shy creatures rarely make an appearance for snorkelers and divers.

TULUM

 THE LAST MAJOR STOP IN THE RIVIERA MAYA is the booming town of **Tulum,** home to the only major Maya archaeological site overlooking the sea. A road south of the ruins (accessible from Highway 307 just past the entrance to the archaeological site) has been the purview of budget travelers pleased with simple campgrounds on white sand. But air-conditioning and swimming pools have arrived, along with a more demanding clientele. Several companies known for their chic hotels have laid claim to prime beachfront land south of the ruins, and a building boom is coming. A few all-inclusives have risen, but the area still contains a few treasured hideaways interspersed with solitary beaches and coves. Recently, the government has closed some of the hotels because of land disputes. Those listed on the following pages have clear ownership papers and are not subject to sudden closures. The road gets rougher as you reach the entryway to the **Sian Ka'an** reserve, and it runs along the **Boca Paila** peninsula past long stretches of beaches and lagoons, to the small fishing village at **Punta Allen.**

Tulum is 81 miles south of Cancún on Highway 307. The highway parallels the coast through the town and is lined with auto-repair shops, markets, restaurants, and other businesses. Drivers headed south along the more solitary stretches of the highway should stock up on gas and supplies here.

WHERE TO STAY IN TULUM

Ana y José Hotel & Spa $$$

OVERALL ★★★½	QUALITY ★★★½	VALUE ★★★

Carretera Tulum-Boca Paila Km 7; ☎ 998-880-5629; fax 998-880-6021; www.anayjose.com

One of our all-time favorites on the coast is this updated cabaña-on-the-sand hotel, no longer considered rustic. Air-conditioning and fans have been added, along with phones. The modern Ana y José (named for the original owners, Ana and José Soto) has a full spa, suites, and a large pool flowing from a rock grotto.

SETTING AND FACILITIES

Location On the road south of the ruins.

Dining Restaurant.

Amenities and services Beach, pool, hot tub, spa, tour desk, shop.

ACCOMMODATIONS

Rooms 22 rooms and suites.

All rooms AC, fan, windows that open, balcony or terrace, safe.

Some rooms Ocean view, nonsmoking.

Comfort and decor Ana y José has become downright boutiquelike with the addition of five suites with gauze netting draped around king beds, tall palapa roofs, and sofabeds. One second-floor suite has a separate living room with hammock, fan, and ocean-view terrace. Even the least-expensive rooms are special, with cotton drapes and bedspreads in light peach and aqua, niches with shelves and drawers, and tiled bathrooms.

PAYMENT, RESERVATIONS, AND RESTRICTIONS

Deposit 50% deposit on credit card; 2-night penalty in case of cancellation or no-show.

Credit cards MC, V.

Check-in/out 3 p.m./noon.

Azulik $$$

OVERALL ★★	QUALITY ★★½	VALUE ★★

Highway 307 Km 4.5; ☎ 888-898-9922 U.S. and Canada; www.azulik.com; reservations, reservations@eco-tulum.com

South Beach meets Big Sur at this "eco-chic" hideaway. Spiritually inclined honeymooners and sensualists are attracted to the rustic villas sans AC (heat and humidity are intense in summer). The property is decidedly adults only (and clothing optional), with romance and health paramount. The spa offers massages and such along with a flotation chamber, lucid dreaming classes, and the attendance of a "real Maya shaman." Azulik is affiliated with the adjacent, less-expensive Cabañas Copal and Zahra.

SETTING AND FACILITIES

Location On the road south of the ruins.

Dining 1 restaurant.

Amenities and services Beach, pool, spa, tour desk, shops, room service, Wi-Fi.

ACCOMMODATIONS

Rooms 15.

All rooms Fans, windows that open, balcony or terrace, bathtub, hot tub on terrace of each villa, safe, no phone.

Some rooms Ocean view.

Comfort and decor Beds draped with mosquito netting are the focal point of rooms designed with tropical hardwoods—even the individual outdoor hot tubs and indoor bathtubs are carved from tree trunks. Though breezes usually keep the temperature comfortable, sleep can be sweaty in summer.

PAYMENT, RESERVATIONS, AND RESTRICTIONS

Deposit Payment in advance with credit card, full refund if notified 15 days in advance.

Credit cards MC, V.

Check-in/out 3 p.m./noon.

Las Ranitas $$

OVERALL ★★½	QUALITY ★★★	VALUE ★★

Carretera Tulum-Boca Paila Km 9, Tulum; ☎/fax 984-877-8554; www.lasranitas.com

A French couple turned their beachfront home into a small boutique hotel emphasizing ecological responsibility with wind generators, solar panels, and recycled water. The gardens are lush, nearly burying the tiny pool, and the hotel's golden-stucco buildings peek through the palms. The ambience is subdued, tasteful, and serene. A French chef adds a certain élan; the food is superb. Note that the hotel is closed mid-September to early November.

SETTING AND FACILITIES

Location On the road south of the ruins.

Dining Restaurant.

Amenities and services Beach, pool, massage, tour desk, Internet.

ACCOMMODATIONS

Rooms 17.

All rooms Fan, windows that open, safe, telephone, high-speed Internet.

Some rooms Ocean view, separate bedrooms, private pool, balcony or terrace.

Comfort and decor Environmental correctness reigns with the lack of AC and TV, but Ranitas isn't rustic. Rooms are subtly sophisticated, with lots of tile accents, blue and green walls with murals, painted floors, and a vast collection of frog statues and paintings (the name of the hotel means "the little frogs").

PAYMENT, RESERVATIONS, AND RESTRICTIONS

Deposit Flexible.

Credit cards Cash only.

Check-in/out 4 p.m./noon.

WHERE TO EAT IN TULUM

MOST TRAVELERS STAYING IN THE AREA eat at their hotels because few options exist in the neighborhood. If you're just spending the day, try the restaurants at the beachfront hotels or on Highway 307.

Don Cafeto's ★★

MEXICAN	INEXPENSIVE/MODERATE	QUALITY ★★½	VALUE ★★

Highway 307 in the center of Tulum's commercial district

Reservations Not accepted.

Entree range $4.50–$12.50.

Payment MC, V.

Service rating ★★★★.

Bar Full service.

Parking Street.

Dress Casual.

Disabled access Possible.

Customers Travelers staying in area and passing through; locals from nearby businesses.

Hours Daily, 7 a.m.–11 p.m.

SETTING AND ATMOSPHERE Casual sidewalk cafe that extends back from the street to a large dining room with open kitchens and bustling waiters. Check out the photos of local dignitaries on the wall behind the long back table.

HOUSE SPECIALTIES Mexican plate with bit of everything; ceviche, *huevos motuleños, chaya,* and cheese omelet.

SUMMARY AND COMMENTS The best coffee around is served at this busy cafe, where everybody staying in the neighborhood eventually stops by for an espresso or a meal. The tables are often packed at early lunchtime when tour groups stop between visiting Tulum and Xel-Há. But the food and camaraderie are worth the wait.

Mezzanine ★★★★

THAI	MODERATE	QUALITY ★★★★	VALUE ★★★½

Carretera Tulum-Boca Paila Km 1.5, Tulum; ☎ 984-131-1516; mezzanine.com.mx

Reservations No reservations.

Entree range $8–$15.

Payment MC, V.

Service rating ★★.

Bar Full service.

Parking Limited sandy street parking.

Dress Beach cover-ups.

Disabled access None.

Customers Hip, young locals enjoying a day at the beach.

Hours Daily, 8 a.m.–10 p.m.

SETTING AND ATMOSPHERE The restaurant sits above a pure white beach and has sail-like white awnings to shade outdoor tables. Lounge music plays in background. Diners wander to the beach and back with sandy feet and skimpy swimsuits.

HOUSE SPECIALTIES Spicy beef salad with mint, duck breast with mandarin and chile sauce, mango lassies.

SUMMARY AND COMMENTS Young beautiful people come from Playa and Cancún to enjoy the Ibiza-like scene at this chic boutique hotel and restaurant. The hotel's nine overpriced rooms are set away from the restaurant beside a small pool, and the whole property sits above a fabulous beach. Long lunches are the meal of choice—on weekends you could wait quite a while for a table. The food is excellent and the vibe laid-back. Disc jockeys sometimes appear in the bar at night and the place becomes a huge party house, with some revelers spending the night.

SIGHTSEEING IN TULUM

Attractions

The ruins at Tulum are the Caribbean Coast's greatest historical attraction. Thousands of day-trippers visit them almost every day. The ruins were nearly loved to death by the time the government finally stepped in and built an official entryway to the archaeological site in the early 1990s. Tour buses and cars, which once parked right beside the simple structures from the postclassic era, are now relegated to a parking lot far from the ruins. Visitors must walk or take shuttles from the entrance (complete with restrooms, shops, fast-food stands and money-exchange offices) along a quarter-mile path to reach the limestone temples and walls by the sea. Many of the most impressive buildings are roped off so that eager visitors don't climb on fragile steps.

The most majestic ruin is the **Castillo,** a short, pyramid-shaped structure atop a 40-foot cliff. Used as a watchtower by the Maya during the postclassic period (AD 900–1541), the Castillo has slotted windows facing the sea, where candle-light guided ships through coral reefs. The other structures at Tulum are largely unimpressive; the city was used as a commercial rather than cer-emonial center, and temples tend to be small. A few faded paintings at the **Temple of the Frescoes** depict Maya deities and offerings. The **Temple of the Descending God** has an interesting relief of an upside-down figure said to have been the "bee king." The setting is dramatic, with alabaster structures dotting a grassy plain. You can swim at the small cove below the ruins, but there are no facilities. A nightly sound-and-light show was added in 2008. Admission is $9 (plus $3 more if you bring a video camera).

Sian Ka'an Biosphere Reserve

Hotels and tour companies all along the coast offer tours to the **Sian Ka'an Biosphere Reserve** (Carretera Tulum-Boca Paila, 15 miles south of Tulum). The reserve, a UNESCO World Heritage Site, covers about 200,000 acres of beaches, lagoons, *cenotes,* and a series of canals and small temples built by the Maya. Tours include boating or kayaking through the canals; the bird-watching is excellent. Tours (including transportation from Cancún and the Riviera Maya) are available from the Ana y José Hotel (see profile, page 211) and start at $72. **Eco Colors** (Calle Camarón 32, SM 27, Cancún; ☎ 998-884-3667; **www.ecotravelmexico.com**) includes the reserve in its day and overnight trips ($109 per person for a full day of kayak-ing, hiking, and snorkeling at the reserve). The company operates an overnight visitors center in the park with six rustic rooms. **Muyil,** which is located within the reserve, is accessible from Highway 307 and includes several interesting Maya structures. The sea is visible from the top of the site's *castillo,* which rises almost 70 feet above a lagoon. Muyil is open daily 8 a.m. to 5 p.m., and admission is $3 (free Sunday).

Cobá

The steep pyramids of **Cobá** lie buried in dense jungle 42 kilo-meters west of Tulum. Few structures have been uncovered in the

50-square-kilometer site, which originated in AD 600 and sits amid more than 50 *sacbe* (roads) crisscrossing the peninsula. The steepest structure, **Nohoch Mul,** pokes 42 meters above the jungle. Climb to the top and be rewarded with a view of an endless sea of green treetops pierced by gray-white temples. Several lakes lie in the site, including **Lake Cobá** beside the entrance. Admission is $4, plus $6 if you bring in a video camera.

The excavated structures at Cobá are spread far apart; the easiest way to get around is to rent a mountain bike ($2.50) at the stand by the first group of structures. Men pedaling *triciclos* (three-wheeled bikes with passenger benches) also offer rides around the site for $7.50. Cobá is often muggy and buggy; bring insect repellent and plenty of water. The site is open daily, 8 a.m. to 5 p.m. Services are sparse. A few stands by the entrance sell cold drinks, snacks, and souvenirs. There is a small fee to use the fairly clean restrooms at the shops. The best place to pass a night here is the **Villa Arqueológico** (☎ 985-858-1527), one of a chain of small hotels found nearby to Mexico's archaeological sites. The hotel has a gardenlike pool area, a surprisingly good and expensive restaurant, and adequate rooms. Rates are typically about $80 per person per night, including breakfast.

Majahual

Much of the southern coastal region of the Yucatán Peninsula has been dubbed the Costa Maya and is slated for tourism development. A four-lane highway leads east of Highway 307 to the coastal village of **Majahual.** The small, humble settlement of locals and expatriates is the hub of Mexico's next Caribbean resort area; plans include marinas, golf courses, and all the modern tourism trappings. More than a dozen cruise lines use **Puerto Costa Maya** (☎ 998-267-7700; **www.costamaya-mexico.com**) as a port of call and offer tours to isolated archaeological sites and pristine (for now) coral reefs. The port reopened in 2008 after considerable repair from hurricane damage. **Playa Uvero,** 15 miles north of Majahual, has been developed as a beach playground for shore excursions; not much happens there unless a ship is in port. In Majahual, basic waterfront restaurants fill up when the ships are around. The rest of the time they serve fresh fish and beer to wandering travelers. Majahual has a few modest hotels, but most travelers who visit this area stay at one-of-a-kind inns farther south.

Majahual is the largest community on the Xcalak Peninsula, which runs south from the **Sian Ka'an Biosphere** reserve to the tiny village of **Xcalak.** Along the paved road south from Majahual, sandy side roads lead to a few small hotels catering to scuba divers and isolationists. The main attraction here is the coast's proximity to the **Chinchorro Reef Underwater National Park,** a pristine coral ring littered with shipwrecks 20 miles offshore. Chinchorro is a diver's delight. Its 24-mile-long reef is one of the healthiest in Mexican waters; the tiny islands formed on the reef's surface are home to just a few fishermen. The Navy regularly patrols the area to prevent poachers from stealing artifacts from the wrecks, but the reef is certainly in danger. There is talk of development on the reef, including recreation areas for cruise-ship passengers. Parts of the barrier reef extending from Cozumel to Belize lie close to the coastline, and snorkeling and diving are excellent even if you don't make it to Chinchorro. **www.xcalak-info.com.**

WHERE TO STAY IN MAJAHUAL AND XCALAK

Costa de Cocos $$$

OVERALL ★★★	QUALITY ★★★	VALUE ★ ½

Carretera Majahual-Xcalak Km 52; ☎ 984-831-0110; www.costadecocos.com

Divers and fly-fishing fanatics seeking uncrowded reefs head for this end-of-the-road hideaway at the edge of Xcalak. The resort has a dive shop on-site and offers trips to the nearby reefs and Chinchorro and fly-fishing trips. Kayaks are on hand for group tours or solo trips. The restaurant has become a neighborhood hangout and serves great Caribbean dishes with a spicy flair. Owners David and Ilana Randall, pioneer hoteliers in the region, are amiable, knowledgeable hosts, and staying here is a delight for those who want peaceful seclusion with exciting diversions.

SETTING AND FACILITIES

Location Southern tip of Xcalak peninsula by village of Xcalak.

Dining 1 restaurant and bar.

Amenities and services Beach, pool, water-sports center, tour desk, Internet.

ACCOMMODATIONS

Rooms 16.

All rooms Fan, windows that open, safe.

Some rooms Ocean view, coffeemaker.

Comfort and decor The 16 cabañas are built from tropical woods and have hammocks hanging in the middle (along with beds). Two rooms have 2 bedrooms and 2 bathrooms; all have stocked bookshelves and screened windows.

PAYMENT, RESERVATIONS, AND RESTRICTIONS

Deposit 2-night deposit required, payable through PayPal (**www.paypal.com** or **www.paybycheck.com**); 20-day cancellation policy.

Credit cards Cash only.

Check-in/out Flexible.

PART EIGHT

MAZATLÁN

PACIFIC PLAYAS

AFTER LOS CABOS, **Mazatlán** is Mexico's closest major resort area with international flights from the western United States and Canada. And while Acapulco has more fame and Puerto Vallarta more art galleries and fine restaurants, travelers have been blissing out in Sinaloa state's second-largest city for decades. The city is experiencing a resurgence in popularity, and the downtown area is undergoing a rennaissance.

Many visitors find everything they need in the **Zona Dorada,** a "Golden Zone" of shops, hotels, and restaurants facing **Playa Gaviotas** ("Gull Beach"), itself a long stretch of coarse, but generally clean, beige sand. Rental services on the beach offer personal water-craft, catamarans, windsurfers, and other beach toys for rent by the hour or the day; visitors need only emerge from their hotel rooms to begin the party. Lying just offshore, **Deer, Bird,** and **Sea Lion islands** pacify the Pacific, making the water at **Playa Gaviotas** acceptable for floating and swimming (although small waves tend to crash on the beach), as well as the more ambitious water sports.

If you wander beyond Playa Gaviotas and the Zona Dorada, there's plenty more to explore. The wide, long beach continues north to **Playa Sábalo** and **Punta Cerritos,** where surfers take advantage of the point break uninterrupted by barrier islands. Around this point, **Emerald Bay** is a brand-new hotel zone slated for development. Its main tenant thus far is the innovative **Pueblo Bonito Emerald Bay** and a few private condos. A second major resort development, **Estrella del Mar,** covers more than 800 acres and includes a golf course, condos and private homes (some available as vacation rentals), a boutique hotel, and a sea-turtle sanctuary.

The original tourist zone, south of the Zona Dorada, is more original and pulsing with life. In the 1950s and 1960s, hotels located along Avenida del Mar ("Sea Street") were the most posh and desirable in the city, boasting such innovations as elevators and discos. Today these hotels play second-string to the Zona Dorada properties, representing a budget option and a good choice for those seeking a more Mexican, less resortlike experience.

The beachfront *malecón,* or promenade, connecting the Golden Zone with downtown has been completely refurbished with new walkways, sculptures, landscaping, and lighting. Among the many statues and monuments along the 18-km boardwalk is an enormous copper vat honoring the local brewery. Now more than ever, this is a great place for an early morning or sunset stroll or jog. The beach fronting Avenida del Mar is called **Playa Norte.** Fishermen land their skiffs on the south end of this beach, called **Playa de los Pinos** despite a distinct lack of pine trees.

Marking the entrance to the old downtown section of Mazatlán is the **Fisherman's Monument,** where a tall pink-and-aqua obelisk towers over a statue of a fisherman and his naked woman. Continuing south you'll come to **Playa Olas Altas,** where surfers ride the waves.

Los clavadistas (the divers) are men young and old who dive into the sea for the entertainment of spectators and passersby. The distance is deceptively small, but due to the shallow water, their feat is at least as dangerous as that performed by their more famous colleagues in Acapulco. Look for these intrepid souls year-round, especially at noon and sunset, at the base of the giant Mexican flag waving next to the **Continuity of Life** statue, where a bronze couple cavorts with a team of dolphins.

Above this scene towers **Cerro de la Nevería,** which served as a lookout point during French and U.S. invasions. It got its name, "Icebox Hill," because early pioneers stashed ice from faraway ports in a small cave at its base. Next is **Cerro de la Vigía,** which overlooks downtown, the islands, the port, and the Pacific Ocean beyond. Next to a restaurant overlooking the water on all sides is a cannon that was used to repel foreign invaders, including the Americans, who occupied the port city briefly after the Mexican-American War. The last in this series of three peaks, **El Cerro del Crestón** is the long-time home of a lighthouse that townspeople and tourism pundits claim is world's highest still in operation. (According to the Mazatlán tourism board, it was second to the one on the Rock of Gibraltar, which is no longer operational.) Accessing the lighthouse, perched a smidgen more than 500 feet above the water, requires a hike of about 40 minutes up a steep path. The other two summits are accessible by car.

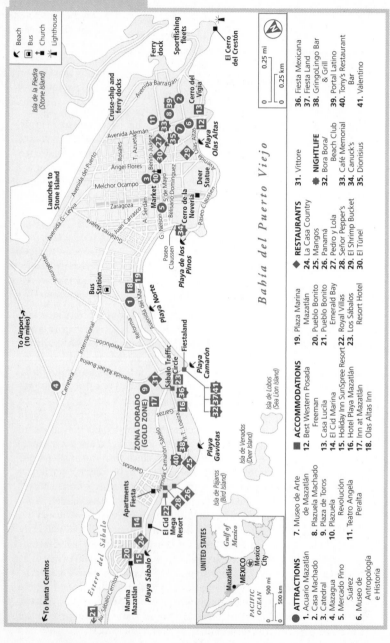

Mazatlán Area

ATTRACTIONS
1. Acuario Mazatlán
2. Casa Machado
3. Catedral
4. Mazagua
5. Mercado Pino Suárez
6. Museo de Antropología e Historia
7. Museo de Arte de Mazatlán
8. Plazuela Machado
9. Plaza de Toros
10. Plazuela Revolución
11. Teatro Angela Peralta

ACCOMMODATIONS
12. Best Western Posada Freeman
13. Casa Lucila
14. El Cid Marina
15. Holiday Inn SunSpree Resort
16. Hotel Playa Mazatlán
17. Inn at Mazatlán
18. Olas Altas Inn
19. Plaza Marina Mazatlán
20. Pueblo Bonito
21. Pueblo Bonito Emerald Bay
22. Royal Villas
23. Los Sábalos Resort Hotel

◆ RESTAURANTS
24. La Casa Country
25. Mangos
26. Panamá
27. Pedro y Lola
28. Señor Pepper's
29. El Shrimp Bucket
30. El Túnel
31. Vittore

✳ NIGHTLIFE
32. Bora Bora/Beach Club
33. Café Memorial
34. Canuck's
35. Dionisius
36. Fiesta Mexicana
37. Fiesta Land
38. GringoLingo Bar & Grill
39. Portal Latino
40. Tony's Restaurant Bar
41. Valentino

On the inlet side of this long peninsula, the **Pacífico Brewery** belches white, hops-scented smoke. This brewery pertains to Mexico's largest brewery, Grupo Modelo, which produces Pacífico along with the better-known Corona, Modelo Especial, and the dark Negra Modelo—the latter so tasty it could pass for dessert. The brewery allows group tours only. Nearby, cruise ships and ferryboats dock and depart at Avenida de la Puerta.

unofficial **TIP**
Operators and taxi drivers try to convince cruise-ship passengers that the cruise-ship pier is far from attractions, but it takes only 10–15 minutes to walk from the pier to downtown Mazatlán and the waterfront.

kids Water taxis chug across the narrow inlet, ferrying visitors to **Isla de la Piedra** ("Stone Island"). Actually a ten-mile peninsula, this is an ideal spot for cantering on horseback down the beach, taking long walks, or lingering over a picnic lunch. Although usually quite deserted, it can be crowded on Sundays when local families install themselves near the water. Vendors sell grilled shrimp, smoked fish, hamburgers, chilled coconuts, beer, and soft drinks. You can also get there by car (a rather long route—about 40 minutes—on the way to the airport) or on an organized tour (see "Sightseeing in Mazatlán," page 239).

unofficial **TIP**
Weekends are great fun on Isla de Piedra, but the water taxis back and forth can be crowded. The crowds are lightest early in the morning and in mid-afternoon.

Once you've toured Mazatlán's considerable oceanfront and gotten the lay of the land, it's time to leave your car or cab and take a walking tour of the charming historical district in **Old Mazatlán,** an 180-block district containing 479 buildings designated as historical landmarks. Many of the homes here were built in the late-19th or early-20th century, and their two- and three-story "tropical neoclassic" facades are painted in an array of pastel colors, generally with white trim around windows and doors. Wrought iron molded in extravagant designs creates balconies and covers extra-large windows that allow welcome breezes on sultry summer days. Walls up to three feet thick further insulate the well-designed structures. This neighborhood is under consideration to become a UNESCO World Heritage Site, and a number of buildings have been restored.

One of the best times to visit the city is in November and December, during the **Festival Cultural de Mazatlán,** also called Mazfest. Summer rains have clothed trees and shrubs in a mantle of green leaves, the weather is warm but not too sticky-hot, and the fishing is superb. If you don't mind afternoon rain showers (and the *occasional* hurricane), come for the **Festival Sinaloa de las Artes,** held each October. Both festivals celebrate the arts with inexpensive theater, dance, and music performances, including guitar, violin, or piano recitals, rock concerts, and opera and symphony orchestra performances, at the **Angela Peralta Theater.** Free events are presented in pretty **Plaza Machado.**

QUICK FACTS *about* MAZATLÁN

AIRPORT AND AIRLINES Serving the city of Mazatlán is **Rafael Buelna International Airport** (☎ 669-982-2177), some 18 miles south of the hotel zone. **Alaska Airlines** has service from major West Coast cities; **Continental** flies through Houston, and **America West** flies from Las Vegas and Los Angeles via its hub, Phoenix. **Northwest** offers service once weekly from Detroit, **Frontier** flies daily from Phoenix, and **Delta** has daily flights from Salt Lake City.

   Aeroméxico and **Mexicana** fly from major U.S. and Mexican cities. **Transportaciones Aeropuerto** shuttle vans deliver visitors to their hotels. To get to the airport, take a private taxi, which typically costs about $20.

DRIVING It isn't necessary to drive in Mazatlán because public transportation is abundant and inexpensive. When we drive to downtown Mazatlán, we usually parallel park near the waterfront and walk around the congested market and plaza areas. A car does come in handy if you want to check out the outlying areas, and the highways are in good shape. Mazatlán is 750 miles south of the border at Nogales; the drive normally takes two full days.

FERRIES Car and passenger ferries connect Mazatlán with La Paz, the capital of Baja California Sur; the crossing takes about 18 hours. Check the schedule at ☎ 800-122-1414 (toll-free within Mexico) and purchase tickets in advance at the ferry terminal (Prolongación Carnaval s/n, Fraccionamiento Playa Sur).

Getting Around Taxis and *pulmonías* (small open-air taxis) cruise the main tourist drag in the Zona Dorada and down-town. International car-rental agencies have counters at the international airport and major hotels. Bright green buses—newer and air-conditioned—charge less than $1 to go from downtown to the Zona Dorada and Playa Sábalo.

unofficial **TIP**
If you see the old area code, ☎ 69, add a 6 at the beginning before dialing.

TELEPHONES The area code is ☎ **669.** All phone numbers are now seven digits.

TOURIST INFORMATION Visit the helpful, bilingual, brochure-rich **State Tourism Office** (Calle Carnaval 1317; ☎ 669-981-8883), open Monday through Friday, 9 a.m. to 4 p.m. For some local dish, check out the *Pacific Pearl* (www.pacificpearl.com), a monthly, ad-driven English-language newspaper with some interesting articles. The Mazatlán Hotel Association has a helpful Web site, **www.gomazatlan .com;** the commercial Web site **mazatlan.com.mx** is also packed with good information.

WHERE *to* STAY *in* MAZATLÁN

MAZATLÁN HAS ONLY A FEW TRULY RITZY resort hotels, including the **Pueblo Bonito Emerald Bay,** far from the action in what is now being touted as "New Mazatlán." Otherwise, the classiest hotels line Avenida Camarón Sábalo and Avenida Playa Gaviotas (formerly Avenida Rodolfo T. Loaiza) in the Zona Dorada. Avenida Gaviotas zigs off Camarón Sábalo at the southern end of the zone and runs even closer to the beach in a short loop. Although not terribly glamorous, the hotel zone is packed with shops, bars, and restaurants. The beach there, **Playa Gaviotas,** is one of the nicest for swimming and is lined with vendors renting water-sports equipment. Accommodations near downtown, along Avenida del Mar and Paseo Claussen, are sold out during **Carnaval,** which normally falls in February. The rest of the time, they are preferred by those opting for less expensive or more "Mexican" accommodations. New boutique hotels are popping up in Old Mazatlán, giving tourists pleasurable downtown digs. If you're staying in this part of town strictly to save money, however, check around; some of the Zona Dorada properties offer very competitive prices, especially during low season.

ACCOMMODATION PROFILES

Best Western Posada Freeman $

OVERALL ★★	QUALITY ★½	VALUE ★★★

Avenida Olas Altas 79 Sur, ☎ 669-985-6060; 800-780-7234 U.S. and Canada; fax 669-985-6064; www.bestwestern.com

In the 1960s this was the area's fanciest hotel, boasting the city's first elevator and a popular rooftop disco. Closed for many years, it was renovated and reopened in the early 2000s. Although it's not posh or sophisticated by today's standards, the Freeman is in a great location across the street from Olas Altas beach and a short walk from downtown. We like the Freeman for its proximity to Mazatlán's cultural centers, busy traditional market, beautiful cathedral, and plazas full of people, day and night. Locals stroll along the beachfront boardwalk, admiring the views and the town's many statues. Although the rooms are new, they are small, and many are dwarfed by a king-size bed. There's an exceptional view from the rooftop pool area and a bar one floor down from which cold drinks can be delivered to the pool.

SETTING AND FACILITIES

Location Across the street from Olas Altas beach, downtown Mazatlán.

Dining Plentiful breakfast buffet included in room rate; no other meals served.

Amenities and services Pool, shop, bar, Internet, free Wi-Fi in rooms and public areas.

ACCOMMODATIONS

Rooms 64 rooms, 8 suites.

All rooms AC, fan, windows that open, hair dryer, safe, coffeemaker, cable/satellite TV, high-speed Internet, refrigerator.

Some rooms Ocean view, balcony or terrace, kitchenette, nonsmoking, disabled access.

How Accommodations Compare in Mazatlán

ACCOMMODATION	OVERALL	QUALITY	VALUE	COST
Pueblo Bonito	★★★★½	★★★★	★★★★	$$
Pueblo Bonito Emerald Bay	★★★½	★★★★	★★★	$$$
Casa Lucila	★★★★	★★★★	★★★	$$$
Hotel Playa Mazatlán	★★★½	★★½	★★★★	$$
Los Sábalos Resort Hotel	★★★	★★★	★★★★	$$
Holiday Inn SunSpree Resort	★★★	★★½	★★★★	$$–$$$
El Cid Marina	★★★	★★★	★★★	$$$
Royal Villas	★★½	★★	★★	$$
Inn at Mazatlán	★★	★★★	★★★	$$
Best Western Posada Freeman	★★	★½	★★★	$
Olas Altas Inn	★½	★★	★★	$
Plaza Marina Mazatlán	★	★	★★	$–$$

Comfort and decor Cheery drapes and upholstery, nondescript, dark-brown furnishings, cramped rooms.

PAYMENT, RESERVATIONS, AND RESTRICTIONS

Deposit Credit card; 4-day cancellation policy.

Credit cards AE, MC, V.

Check-in/out 1 p.m./12 p.m.

Casa Lucila $$$

OVERALL ★★★★	QUALITY ★★★★	VALUE ★★★

Paseo Olas Altas 16, ☎ and fax 669-982-1150; www.casalucila.com

Overlooking Playa Olas Altas, this historic home–turned–boutique hotel is the most charming hotel in downtown—and in all Mazatlán. The building's golden facade glows in the sunlight, and the interior is outfitted with sleek wooden furnishing, custom-made Italian windows and doors, and an elegant restaurant. Owner Conchita Valades Valdez named the hotel for her mother and the Fernando jazz bar for her father, famed musician Fernando Valades. She's present much of the time and makes sure her guests are comfortable. Young adults 15 and older are welcome but must have their own rooms.

SETTING AND FACILITIES

Location Eastern edge of Old Mazatlán by Olas Altas.

Dining 1 restaurant with a jazz bar.

Amenities and services Small rooftop pool, massage, room service, Internet.

ACCOMMODATIONS

Rooms 8 suites.

All rooms AC, hair dryer, safe, satellite TV, coffeemaker, nonsmoking.

Some rooms Ocean view, balcony, whirlpool tub, disabled access.

Comfort and decor Each of the eight suites has a distinct design. Those on the second and third floor have broad balconies facing the sea, and all have a sleek, minimalist style. Luxuries include king-sized beds wrapped in fine linens, large showers with Italian fixtures, and Bulgari toiletries.

PAYMENT, RESERVATIONS, AND RESTRICTIONS

Deposit Credit card; 2-day cancellation policy.

Credit cards AE, MC, V.

Check-in/out 3 p.m./noon.

El Cid Marina $$$

OVERALL ★★★	QUALITY ★★★	VALUE ★★★

**Avenida Camarón Sábalo s/n, ☎ 669-913-3333 or 888-733-7308
U.S. and Canada; fax 669-914-1311; www.elcid.com**

Catering to yachties and those with a taste for classy accommodations, the Marina El Cid is one of Mazatlán's more fashionable properties. Its full-service marina has 90 slips. The hotel, located on the edge of town, offers free shuttle service to the 27-hole golf course, restaurants, and facilities at its three other properties and a water taxi to the beach. All-inclusive packages, along with golf and fishing packages, are available.

SETTING AND FACILITIES

Location North end of Zona Dorada, Playa Sábalo.

Dining Restaurant with marina view serving international cuisine; bar.

Amenities and services Beach, 2 pools, hot tub, gym, spa, massage, marina, water-sports center, tour desk, organized children's activities, shops, bar, room service, business center, Internet.

ACCOMMODATIONS

Rooms 200 rooms and suites.

All rooms AC, ceiling fans, windows that open, hair dryer, safe, refrigerator, kitchenette, cable/satellite TV.

Some rooms Ocean view, balcony, nonsmoking, disabled access.

Comfort and decor Classy and comfortable in Mediterranean style; white walls and furnishings with blue trim, pillows, and other accent pieces.

PAYMENT, RESERVATIONS, AND RESTRICTIONS

Deposit Credit card; 3-day cancellation policy.

Credit cards AE, MC, V.

Check-in/out 3 p.m./1 p.m.

Holiday Inn SunSpree Resort $$–$$$

OVERALL ★★★	QUALITY ★★½	VALUE ★★★★

Avenida Camarón Sábalo 696; ☎ 669-913-2222 or 800-465-4329 U.S.; fax 669-914-1287; www.ichotelsgroup.com

The six-story property offers plain decor but many services and amenities. The gym boasts an ocean view and is open between 5 a.m. and 11:30 p.m. The shallow infinity pool (framed by artificial rocks) has a swim-up bar, but there's precious little shade for the plastic lounge chairs that surround it. Rooms are plain but well-maintained, and boast good mattresses, linens, and bedspreads, as well as microwaves, iron and ironing board, and desk with a lamp that's nice for writing and working.

unofficial **TIP**
The generous cancellation policy allows you to change plans right up to the evening of your reservation.

SETTING AND FACILITIES

Location Zona Dorada, Playa Sábalos.

Dining 2 restaurants; across street from popular steak house, Casa Country.

Amenities and services Beach, pool, hot tub, gym, organized children's activities, tour desk, shop, bar, room service, business center, Internet.

ACCOMMODATIONS

Rooms 186 rooms and 23 suites.

All rooms AC, windows that open, hair dryer, safe, refrigerator, coffeemaker, cable/satellite TV.

Some rooms Ocean view, balcony or terrace, kitchen, kitchenette, nonsmoking rooms, disabled access.

Comfort and decor Not stylish, but comfortable, with an emphasis on the practical, a soothing pink-and-sand color scheme.

PAYMENT, RESERVATIONS, AND RESTRICTIONS

Deposit Credit-card guarantees later arrival; 6 p.m. day of arrival without using credit card; no-shows pay 1 night.

Credit cards AE, DC, MC, V.

Check-in/out 3 p.m./noon.

 ## Hotel Playa Mazatlán $$

OVERALL ★★★½	QUALITY ★★½	VALUE ★★★★

Avenida Playa Gaviotas 202; ☎ 669-989-0555 or 800-762-5816 U.S. and Canada; fax 669-914-0366; www.hotelplayamazatlan.com

When American entrepreneur U. S. George first opened this beachfront hotel in 1955, far from the action downtown and at Olas Altas, local people must have thought him antisocial. A half-century later, the hotel is one of the most desirable properties of the happenin' hotel zone, while downtown hotels are mainly popular during Carnaval. This hotel has a reputation for looking after its clients, offering romantic music nightly in the open-air restaurant even during the low season, when many others scale down to bare-bones services. This commitment to quality also means that room maintenance is ongoing and facilities are always being upgraded. Recommended and patronized by locals as well as travelers is the Fiesta Mexicana variety show, offered two or three times a week, starting at 7 p.m.

SETTING AND FACILITIES

Location Avenida Playa Gaviotas loop, south end of Zona Dorada.

Dining 2 restaurants, 2 bars, snack bar.

Amenities and services Beach, 3 pools, 2 hot tubs, gym, massage, tour desk, organized children's activities, shops, 2 bars, room service, business center.

ACCOMMODATIONS

Rooms 418 rooms and suites.

All rooms AC, windows that open, balcony or terrace, hair dryer, cable/satellite TV.

Some rooms Ocean view, kitchenette, refrigerator, nonsmoking, disabled access.

Comfort and decor Clean, spare rooms featuring lots of white and decorative tile. Some rooms were completely renovated in 2008 with pillow-top mattresses, marble bathroom counters, and all-new furnishings.

PAYMENT, RESERVATIONS, AND RESTRICTIONS

Deposit Credit card; 3-day cancellation policy (7 days during holidays).

Credit cards AE, MC, V.

Check-in/out 3 p.m./1 p.m.

Inn at Mazatlán $$

OVERALL ★★	QUALITY ★★★	VALUE ★★★

Avenida Camarón Sábalo 6291; ☎ 669-913-5500 or 800-262-0526 U.S. and Canada; fax 669-913-4782; innatmazatlan.com.mx

This property, which started as a private residence for personal friends and segued to a time-share, now has a tower dedicated to hotel guests. The feeling, however, is still that of a time-share. All-suite rooms are ample but lack the perks of hotel chains—including bathroom toiletries and turndown service. Rooms are large and airy, and the location in the heart of the Zona Dorada is convenient for beach, restaurant, and bar-hopping. Choose from studios; one-bedroom, two-bath suites for up to four people; two-bedroom, three-bath units (both with sleeper sofa in living room); or the junior suite, with sleeping for four but no separate bedroom. A spa was added in 2007.

SETTING AND FACILITIES

Location South end of Zona Dorada.

Dining Papagayo restaurant, serving international food and a varied breakfast buffet.

Amenities and services Beach, bar, 2 pools, 2 hot tubs, gym, spa, room service, shop, tour desk, Internet.

ACCOMMODATIONS

Rooms 220 suites.

All rooms Air-conditioning, coffeemaker, microwave, ceiling fans, ocean view, balcony or terrace, cable TV.

Some rooms Internet, Wi-Fi.

Comfort and decor Standard rooms have small refrigerator and coffeemaker; all types of suites have full kitchen, at least two bathrooms, and separate AC unit in the bedroom. All have smallish balcony; plain bathrooms have shower only, with no toiletries or hair dryer. It's worth requesting a room in the spiffier tower.

PAYMENT, RESERVATIONS, AND RESTRICTIONS

Deposit Credit card; 30-day cancellation policy.

Credit cards MC, V.

Check-in/out 4 p.m./10 a.m.

Olas Altas Inn $

OVERALL ★½	QUALITY ★★	VALUE ★★

Avenida del Mar 719; ☎ 669-981-3192, 888-305-2201 U.S., or 877-836-0360 Canada; fax 669-985-3720; olasaltasinn.com.mx

About halfway between the Zona Dorada and the historical center, Olas Altas Inn sits across the street from long North Beach, where the anglers sell the catch of the day and families walk and picnic on weekends. Furnishings are budget-class, with decent mattresses and large TVs. The fifth floor houses the junior suites and the executive floor, where rooms have desks and the business center offers fax as well as secretarial and other services. These two floors also have the best ocean views.

unofficial **TIP**
Exuberant sports groups sometime take over most of the rooms, and the hotel is popular with families—not a good choice for a quiet getaway.

SETTING AND FACILITIES

Location Playa Norte.

Dining Restaurant serving Mexican and American food, poolside snack bar (high season only).

Amenities and services Pool, tour desk, shop, bar, room service, business center, Internet.

ACCOMMODATIONS

Rooms 80 rooms and suites.

All rooms AC, fan, windows that open, wireless Internet, cable/satellite TV.

Some rooms Ocean view, bathtubs, whirlpool tubs, balcony or terrace, hair dryer, minibar, kitchenette, coffeemaker.

Comfort and decor Simple decor with few surprises, pleasant or unpleasant. Rooms vary in size and have plain, white baths with sliding-door showers.

PAYMENT, RESERVATIONS, AND RESTRICTIONS

Deposit Credit card; 2-day cancellation policy.

Credit cards MC, V.

Check-in/out 3 p.m./1 p.m.

Plaza Marina Mazatlán $–$$

OVERALL ★	QUALITY ★	VALUE ★★

Avenida del Mar 73; ☎ 669-982-3622 or 866-357-5714 in the U.S.; fax 669-982-3499; www.hotelplazamarina.com

This ten-story hotel was built at the turn of the 21st century across the street from Playa Norte. Rooms and suites are more pleasant than the sometimes smoky public areas, including the bar with two pool tables and the small restaurant. The pool with waterfall is pleasant, although the bar in the middle opens only during peak occupancy, including Carnaval (usually in February), July and August school holidays, Christmas, and Easter weekends. Junior suites are ample, and with a view of the ocean from the separate bedroom and a comfortable and well-stocked kitchenette, they are a good bargain. It's geared mainly to Mexican families on vacation and Mexican business people.

SETTING AND FACILITIES

Location Playa Norte.

Dining Restaurant.

Amenities and services Pool, bar, shop, room service.

ACCOMMODATIONS

Rooms 46 rooms and 43 suites.

All rooms AC, cable TV, coffeemaker, minifridge.

Some rooms Ocean view, balcony or terrace, bathtub, hair dryer, kitchenette, high-speed Internet, disabled access.

Comfort and decor New but uninspired decor in muted shades of peach and green.

PAYMENT, RESERVATIONS, AND RESTRICTIONS

Deposit Credit card; 1-day cancellation policy.

Credit cards AE, MC, V.

Check-in/out 3 p.m./noon.

Pueblo Bonito $$

OVERALL ★★★★½	QUALITY ★★★★	VALUE ★★★★

Avenida Camarón Sábalo 2121; ☎ 669-914-3700 or 800-990-8250 U.S.; fax 669-914-1723; www.pueblobonito.com

A pretty property right in the Zona Dorada, Pueblo Bonito offers junior suites sleeping up to four persons and luxury suites that sleep up to six. Ceilings are domed, floors are cool, white tile, and the plush living room furniture centers around a wood-and-glass table. Pillowtop mattresses make beds super snuggly; ample balconies have towel racks as well as comfy chaise lounges for stretching out and admiring the sea. Time-share owners settle in for a week or more and often claim prime rooms months in advance. Right on the beach, and offering organized kids' activities and kitchenettes in all suites, this is a good choice for families with children.

SETTING AND FACILITIES

Location Zona Dorada, Playa Gaviota.

Dining 3 restaurants.

Amenities and services Beach, 2 pools, hot tub, gym, massage, water-sports center, tour desk, organized children's activities, shops, 4 bars, tennis courts, spa, room service, Internet.

ACCOMMODATIONS

Rooms 247 suites.

All rooms AC, fan, windows that open, ocean view, balcony or terrace, bathtub, hair dryer, refrigerator, coffeemaker, kitchenette, cable/satellite TV, high-speed Internet.

Some rooms Disabled access.

Comfort and decor Tasteful, muted, and pleasant decor, each suite with comfortable sitting area or living room. Kitchenettes have microwaves, toasters, and pretty blue-and-white, Talavera-style place settings.

PAYMENT, RESERVATIONS, AND RESTRICTIONS

Deposit Credit card; 3-day cancellation policy (1 night charged); 2 nights charged for no-shows.

Credit cards AE, MC, V.

Check-in/out 10 a.m./4 p.m.

Pueblo Bonito Emerald Bay $$$

OVERALL ★★★½	QUALITY ★★★★	VALUE ★★★

Avenida Ernesto Coppel Compaña s/n, ☎ 669-989-0525 or 800-990-8250 U.S. and Canada; fax 669-988-0718; www.pueblobonito.com

Nonconformist hotelier Ernesto Coppel has expanded his hotel empire with this sister to six other properties, one in Mazatlán's Zona Dorada, four in Los Cabos, and one in Puerto Vallarta. The hotel sits almost alone in "New Mazatlán," an exclusive zone under development near Punta Cerritos. A PETA-unfriendly safari theme dominates Kelly's Bar, decorated in tiger heads and black-and-white photos of successful hunts. Everything else about the new property, however, is tastefully done and carefully executed. Pretty grounds with flower-filled planters and fountains surround the pool and the oceanfront restaurant. Rooms are beautifully decorated with pastel walls and vibrant but tasteful bedspreads and drapes in tropical colors. Marble floors in the junior suites lead out onto ocean-view balconies with plush chaise lounges; because of this, we prefer them to master suites, which have a separate bedroom but no balcony. There are activities for all ages here, such as Spanish, bartending, and cooking classes, aquaerobics, and bingo. The resort opened a freestanding spa featuring chromotherapy, aromatherapy, and water-reflexology paths in 2009, giving guests yet another reason to never leave the property.

unofficial **TIP**
Although it's far from the action of the Zona Dorada, there's a free shuttle to Pueblo Bonito Mazatlán.

SETTING AND FACILITIES

Location Beach north of Punta Cerritos; off connecting road to Highway 15, about 6 miles north of downtown.

Dining Indoor and outdoor dining, 2 restaurants.

Amenities and services Beach, 2 pools, 2 hot tubs, gym, spa, tour desk, organized children's activities, shops, 4 bars, 24-hour room service, Internet.

ACCOMMODATIONS

Rooms 258 suites.

All rooms AC, fan, windows that open, ocean view, bathtub, hair dryer, safe, refrigerator, coffeemaker, kitchenette, cable/satellite TV, high-speed Internet.

Some rooms Balcony or terrace, nonsmoking, disabled access.

Comfort and decor Sophisticated tropical-style furnishings and tasteful, light pastel walls with white crown molding. Very comfortable feather-top beds, choice of pillow style; sink area separates toilet from deep tub.

PAYMENT, RESERVATIONS, AND RESTRICTIONS

Deposit Credit card; 3-day cancellation policy (1 night charged); 2 nights charged for no-shows.

Credit cards AE, MC, V.

Check-in/out 10 a.m./4 p.m.

Royal Villas $$

OVERALL ★★½	QUALITY ★★	VALUE ★★

Avenida Camarón Sábalo 500; ☎ 669-916-6161 or 800-898-3564 U.S.; fax 669-914-0777; royalvillas.com.mx

The sound of water falling on rocks permeates a high-ceilinged lobby, decorated in sky blue and mauve. It is not elegant but has a comfortable, accessible feeling. The lobby leads directly to the small poolside bar, fronted by the beach at Playa Gaviotas. The restaurant is set back behind the pool and doesn't have much of an ocean view. One- to three-bedroom suites, with one to three bathrooms and multiple balconies, are available. Kids and teens enjoy the foosball and Ping-Pong tables in the recreational room; adults also enjoy billiards; and separate men's and women's saunas are available for further R&R.

SETTING AND FACILITIES

Location Zona Dorada, Playa Gaviotas.

Dining 2 restaurants.

Amenities and services Beach, pool, hot tub, gym, massage, tour desk, organized children's activities, shops, bar, room service, business center, Internet.

ACCOMMODATIONS

Rooms 125 suites.

All rooms AC, balcony, hair dryer, safe, refrigerator, coffeemaker, kitchenette, cable/satellite TV, high-speed Internet, Wi-Fi in guest rooms and public areas.

Some rooms Ocean view, tub, nonsmoking, disabled access.

Comfort and decor Rooms are spare and modern, with Italian-style floor tiles and minimal art. The larger suites have multiple balconies and round glass-top dining tables dividing the living area from the kitchenette.

PAYMENT, RESERVATIONS, AND RESTRICTIONS

Deposit Full amount on credit card; 1-day cancellation policy (2 days in high season).

Credit cards MC, V.

Check-in/out 3 p.m./noon.

Los Sábalos Resort Hotel $$

OVERALL ★★★	QUALITY ★★★	VALUE ★★★★

Avenida Playa Gaviotas 100; ☎ 669-983-5333, 800-528-8760 U.S., or 877-756-7532 Canada; fax 669-983-8156; www.lossabalos.com

One of Mazatlán's best values, this classy hotel has plenty of services and amenities. Its stylish rooms feature simple but modern decor. The spa offers manicures, facials, and skin and body treatments, and the U-shaped pool meanders from shallow to deep. Polished limestone floors and dark-brown wicker chairs with comfortable cushions lend elegance to the large, open lobby. On the grounds, immaculate green lawns are bordered by banana trees and flowering shrubs. Joe's Oyster Bar is a favorite hangout for young *mazatlecos,* and marimba musicians entertain daily, noon to 4 p.m., at Bar Gaviotas.

SETTING AND FACILITIES

Location Playa Sábalos, south end of Zona Dorada.

Dining 5 restaurants, including Joe's Oyster Bar, Taco Show for DJ-spun hip-hop and live performance; and Vittore, across the street, for tasty Italian fare in this upbeat bar-restaurant.

Amenities and services Beach, pool, hot tub, gym, spa, massage, water-sports center, tour desk, shops, 2 bars, room service, business center, Internet.

ACCOMMODATIONS

Rooms 200 rooms and suites.

All rooms AC, windows that open, balcony or terrace, hair dryer, safe, coffeemaker, cable/satellite TV.

Some rooms Ocean view, balcony or terrace, nonsmoking.

Comfort and decor Firm mattresses, closets, marble headboards, and simple-yet-pleasing decor. The third-story rooms with balconies facing the beach are the best choice.

PAYMENT, RESERVATIONS, AND RESTRICTIONS

Deposit Credit card; 3-day cancellation policy.

Credit cards AE, MC, V.

Check-in/out 3 p.m./noon.

WHERE *to* EAT *in* MAZATLÁN

MAZATLÁN'S RESTAURANTS TEND TO SERVE great food centered around beef and shrimp, which are among the state's most important exports. There's no dearth of fresh fish either. Fillets are served many ways, but the masterpiece of the sea is the *sarandeado*, a whole, butterflied fish with the skin rubbed with salt and garlic and grilled over a charcoal fire. Also typical to the region is *molcajete*, a bubbling pot of grilled meat or chicken in a flavorful smoky chile sauce called *adobo*, served with grilled onions, tomatoes, fresh cheese, and tortillas. Most of Mazatlán's restaurants are informal, and many are a great value.

RESTAURANT PROFILES

La Casa Country ★★★

STEAK	INEXPENSIVE/MODERATE	QUALITY ★★★	VALUE ★★★

**Zona Dorada; Avenida Camarón Sábalo s/n, opposite Holiday Inn;
☎ 669-916-5300**

Reservations Accepted but rarely necessary.

Entree range $7–$18.

Payment AE, MC, V.

Service rating ★★★★.

Parking Lot.

Bar Full service specializing in margaritas made with seasonal fruits.

Dress Casual; cowboy gear a plus.

Disabled access None.

Customers Locals and travelers in search of grilled American cuts and *carne asada*.

Hours Daily, noon–2 a.m.

SETTING AND ATMOSPHERE Western decor with lots of wood, stuffed soaring eagles, loud music, and muted TVs bolted on rafters.

HOUSE SPECIALTIES Steak.

How Restaurants Compare in Mazatlán

RESTAURANT	CUISINE	COST	OVERALL	QUALITY	VALUE
Señor Pepper's	Steak	Mod	★★★★½	★★★★½	★★★
Mangos	Mexican/International	Inexp/Mod	★★★★	★★★★	★★★½
Pedro y Lola	Mexican	Mod	★★★½	★★★½	★★★½
La Casa Country	Steak	Inexp/Mod	★★★	★★★	★★★
Vittore	Italian	Mod/inexp	★★★	★★★	★★★
Panamá	Mexican/Dessert	Inexp	★★½	★★★	★★★★★
El Túnel	Mexican	Inexp	★★	★★	★★★★
El Shrimp Bucket	Seafood/Steak	Mod	★★	★★	★★★

SUMMARY AND COMMENTS Waiters in crisp white shirts, tight blue jeans, and cowboy boots join together for some not-so-spontaneous line dancing in this country-and-western–themed restaurant bar run by three brothers. This is not the place for a serious conversation: music plays loudly, and the sound bounces around the high-ceilinged space. Flags of the world hang from the rafters, and antler chandeliers light the two connecting dining rooms. Consistently good food draws locals as well as one-timers on vacation. We suggest the beef-based tortilla soup for starters, or the inexpensive mixed green salad. The *molcajete* is really wonderful—it's a sizzling pot of beef or chicken served with grilled green onions and tomato.

Mangos ★★★★

MEXICAN/INTERNATIONAL   INEXPENSIVE/MODERATE   QUALITY ★★★★   VALUE ★★★½

Zona Dorada; Avenida Playa Gaviotas 404; ☎ 669-916-0044

Reservations Accepted but rarely necessary.

Entree range $8–$16.

Payment AE, MC, V.

Service rating ★★★★.

Parking Crowded parking lot.

Bar Full service, with promotional prices and happy hour 2-for-1 drink specials, especially during off-season.

Dress Businessmen in suits, tourists in sweatsuits, teens in tight T-shirts.

Disabled access None.

Customers Travelers and young *mazatlecos* looking for action; Mexican couples and families.

Hours Sunday–Thursday, 11 a.m.–1 a.m.; Friday and Saturday, 11 a.m.–3 a.m.

SETTING AND ATMOSPHERE The bar feeling predominates; decor is secondary to food and drink.

HOUSE SPECIALTIES Appetizers, such as shrimp chimichangas; banana pie cooked in a wood-fire oven.

SUMMARY AND COMMENTS Grab a table overlooking the water, which laps the shore of Playa Gaviotas just beyond the large glass windows. Although the scene here is that of a bar (on weekends especially), you can also get yummy food. A full menu offers fish, fajitas, and steak as well as burgers and fries. Check out the varied appetizers, which come in portions that can be shared among several friends. The shrimp *chimichangas* are served as five diminutive pieces, and though eep-fried, they don't taste greasy. On the appetizer menu is the delicious *molcajete* (beef or chicken with grilled green onions and tomato). An entire squadron of waiters is on hand, mainly to chat up the female customers.

Panamá ★★½

MEXICAN/DESSERT	INEXPENSIVE	QUALITY ★★★	VALUE ★★★★★

Zona Dorada; Avenida Camarón Sábalo 400; ☎ 669-913-6977

Reservations Large groups only.

Entree range $5–$10.

Payment AE, MC, V.

Service rating ★★★.

Parking Street.

Bar No alcohol.

Dress Casual but neat.

Disabled access None.

Customers Packed with couples on dates, coworkers at lunch, families, and travelers.

Hours Daily, 7 a.m.–10 p.m.

SETTING AND ATMOSPHERE Brightly lit, clean, dinerlike atmosphere.

HOUSE SPECIALTIES Lunch specials, breakfast, and pastries and cakes, especially the *negrito de mis amores* (chocolate and vanilla cake).

SUMMARY AND COMMENTS This is a favorite with locals for big, hearty breakfasts and economical daily lunch specials, the latter prepared and set on a table at the restaurant's entrance so patrons can see what's what. It includes a fruit drink, soup, main dish, side dish, and bread or tortillas for about $8. Favorite dishes include *fajitas fiesta* (steak strips grilled with mushrooms, bacon, and bell pepper), and *asado mazatleco*, a regional dish of cubed steak and potatoes served with fresh-from-the-griddle corn tortillas and lightly refried *bayo* beans typical to the state of Sinaloa. Also worth trying are the tortilla soup and the Panamá salad of mixed

unofficial **TIP**
There are several other locations around town, including one across from the cathedral (Benito Juárez and Canizales; ☎ 669-985-1853).

greens with grilled chicken breast, onion, carrot, broccoli, and pineapple bits. Kids enjoy selecting a fresh-daily dessert from the cart, and there's lots of recognizable fare for them before they get to dessert.

 Pedro y Lola ★★★½

MEXICAN	MODERATE	QUALITY ★★★½	VALUE ★★★½

Centro; Carnaval 1303, on Plaza Machado; ☎ 669-982-2589

Reservations Yes; recommended on weekends.

Entree range $8–$14.

Payment AE, MC, V.

Service rating ★★.

Parking Limited street parking off the plaza.

Bar Full service.

Dress Casual but neat; locals dress up a bit for weekend nights.

Disabled access None.

Customers Locals and travelers wanting a night out downtown.

Hours Daily, 6 p.m.–1 a.m.

SETTING AND ATMOSPHERE Informal indoor atmosphere with brown butcher paper covering white tablecloths; outdoor tables overlook Plaza Machado. Love music indoors and outdoors most nights.

HOUSE SPECIALTIES *Pedro infante* (strips of pork in *adobada* sauce served with chorizo, vegetables, and olives).

SUMMARY AND COMMENTS Restaurants like this are what give downtown a good name. The food is reasonably priced and consistently wellprepared, and while it's popular with travelers, it isn't a touristy place. A favorite dish among seafood lovers is *camarones Pedro y Lola*—jumbo shrimp flambéed with brandy and Cointreau with an orange-brandy sauce, served with rice and roasted vegetables. For dessert, consider the homemade banana pie. The ambience is informal yet cheerful, with gargantuan, exposed redwood ceiling beams and peach-painted walls hung with oil paintings. Tables outside overlook Plaza Machado and the downtown street scene, which is closed to cars on weekend nights. Live music varies between the indoor piano bar and a guitarist singing softly outside.

Señor Pepper's ★★★★½

STEAK	MODERATE	QUALITY ★★★★½	VALUE ★★★

Zona Dorada; Avenida Camarón Sábalo s/n, across from Hotel Playa Real; ☎ 669-914-0101

Reservations Accepted.

Entree range $19–$44.

Payment AE, MC, V.

Service rating ★★★★.

Parking Lot.

Bar Full service with extensive wine and liquor list, and flaming coffees.

Dress Resort casual/dressy.

Disabled access Side-door access.

Customers Travelers and relatively affluent locals hungry for steak.

Hours Daily, 5–11 p.m.

SETTING AND ATMOSPHERE Romantic, dimly lit restaurant with fine table linens and glassware.

HOUSE SPECIALTIES Porterhouse steak and jumbo shrimp, Angus beef imported from the United States.

SUMMARY AND COMMENTS Locals save up for a special night out at this splendid restaurant near the northern end of the Zona Dorada. The ambience is elegant yet unpretentious, with potted plants, rattan furniture, and candles on every table. The refreshingly brief menu offers giant cuts of porterhouse, rib eye, and New York steaks as well as prime rib, each served with a fresh spinach garnish and fried potatoes in a creamy cheese sauce. Or order fresh lobster or jumbo shrimp accompanied by fusilli pasta in white sauce with wine, mushrooms, and Parmesan cheese. Main dishes are accompanied by an appetizer and choice of salad or soup. Some folks stop by to soak up the classy atmosphere and enjoy a drink or dessert at the small, highly polished bar in the center of the restaurant. A piano player or duo plays nostalgic or music Wednesday through Sunday after 7:30 p.m.

 ## El Shrimp Bucket ★★

SEAFOOD/STEAK	MODERATE	QUALITY ★★	VALUE ★★★

Olas Altas; Paseo Olas Altas 11; ☎ 669-981-6350

Reservations Accepted but rarely necessary.

Entree range $10–$18.

Payment AE, MC, V.

Service rating ★★★.

Parking In hotel lot.

Bar Full service, with hundreds of different tequilas; tropical drinks.

Dress Casual but neat.

Disabled access Yes.

Customers Local businessmen and politicos lingering over long breakfasts and lunches, expatriates, and first-timers encouraged by Carlos'n Charlie's connection.

Hours Daily, 6 a.m.–11 p.m.

SETTING AND ATMOSPHERE Lively, but not as nuts as others in the chain; with a colorful collection of shrimp- and beach-related icons throughout. Filled with locals in the morning for bountiful breakfasts.

HOUSE SPECIALTIES Breaded jumbo shrimp served with rice, French fries, and veggies; yummy shrimp quesadillas; huevos rancheros.

SUMMARY AND COMMENTS The first of more than 50 seafood restaurants in the Anderson's chain (including Señor Frog's and Carlos'n Charlie's), this is one of the smaller and more sedate restaurants, but still plenty lively. You'll be serenaded by live romantic music, Thursday through Saturday evenings (7 to 10 p.m.), and perhaps by mariachis during high season. If you choose to sit on the open-air, ocean-view patio, you can watch the world walk by on the busy main street. Indoors, local professionals conduct business breakfasts and power lunches in air-conditioned comfort under a canopy of colorful *piñatas*.

  El Túnel ★★

| MEXICAN | INEXPENSIVE | QUALITY ★★ | VALUE ★★★★ |

Old Acapulco; Calle Carnaval 1207; no phone

Reservations Not accepted.

Entree range $4–$6.

Payment Cash only.

Service rating ★★½.

Parking Limited street parking.

Bar No alcohol.

Dress Informal.

Disabled access None.

Customers Locals and some plucky travelers.

Hours Daily, noon–midnight.

SETTING AND ATMOSPHERE Informal, family-oriented with oil cloth on tables, brightly painted walls and unpainted cement floors.

HOUSE SPECIALTIES *Pozole;* typical Mexican "snack" foods such as tacos and tostadas in their authentic presentation.

SUMMARY AND COMMENTS Service can be annoyingly casual, but this is a fun place to eat the foods that locals love: tacos, tostadas, hamburgers, *pozole* (spicy hominy soup), and gorditas (little round maize cakes topped with shredded meat and cabbage and served with a variety of spicy salsas). Most items are ordered by the piece—that is, order one taco or a dozen. It's a great way to sample a variety of typical dishes. Here you can also get *raspados,* shaved ice with different flavorings. Located across the street from the Angela Peralta Theater, this is a good place for a late snack after a cultural event there; if you come before the event, remember the slow service and allow plenty of extra time for loitering. It's dreadfully hot in summer, so eat at the outdoor tables.

Vittore ★★★

| ITALIAN | MODERATE/INEXPENSIVE | QUALITY ★★★ | VALUE ★★★ |

Zona Dorada; Avenida Playa Gaviotas 100, across from Hotel los Sábalos; ☎ 669-986-2424

Reservations Recommended for dinner in winter.

Entree range $11–$22.

Payment AE, MC, V.

Service rating ★★★★.

Parking Large lot.

Bar Full service, with Chilean, Italian, and Mexican wines.

Dress Resort casual.

Disabled access Yes.

Customers Customers Travelers and locals out for a special Italian meal or dessert and cappuccino.

Hours Daily, noon–midnight.

SETTING AND ATMOSPHERE Warm and open, yet with modern, somewhat spare decoration and accents.

HOUSE SPECIALTIES Wood-fired pizza, rack of lamb, other Italian favorites.

SUMMARY AND COMMENTS At the front of the stylish restaurant are the bar and round bar tables with comfortable, high-backed stools. Here you can order a drink, perhaps a cappuccino laced with amaretto, and a big, yummy square of tiramisu. For dinner, head back to the adjacent dining room, where classic square tables clothed in white invite intimate tête-à-têtes under modern, dark-wood ceiling fans. Garlands of light bulbs hanging from the rafters contribute an unusual design element. Among the most popular entrees are lasagna and lamb chops, the latter served with French fries, grilled tomatoes, and eggplant stuffed with fresh goat cheese. Also recommended is a thick swordfish steak served with Italian-style rice, your choice of pasta, and vegetable. The candlelit sidewalk tables are nice in the cool of the evening.

SIGHTSEEING *in* MAZATLÁN

THERE'S A LOT TO SEE AND DO IN MAZATLÁN, quite apart from hours by the pool, at the beach, or at the resorts' boisterous bars. The city is spread out, but not too expensive to access. Use an open-air *pulmonía* to get around, which costs about the same as a taxi (minimum fare around $3). New, air-conditioned, bright-green buses run up and down the coast road between downtown, the **Zona Dorada,** and **Playa Cerritos.** And most tour operators pick up clients at their hotels for excursions in or around Mazatlán. If you have a rental car, it's fairly easy to park along the coast road or in the Zona Dorada, although parking spaces downtown are a bit harder to find.

ATTRACTIONS

IF YOUR IDEA OF A SPECTATOR SPORT includes bullfighting, check out **Plaza de Toros,** just outside the Zona Dorada on Calzada Rafael Buelna, most Sunday afternoons between December and April. Admission runs about $20 to $30.

kids 🩴 *Mazatlecos* (people from Mazatlán) are great base-ball fans, and their Pacific Coast League team, **Los Venados,** plays at Teodoro Mariscal Stadium from late October through March. These pastimes aside, many folks are happy to spend every day on the beach, and in Mazatlán, they could choose a different beach every day for a week. See the beach descriptions under "Pacific Playas," page 218.

kids For something different, take a ride on the amphibious *El Tiburón,* a World War II relic, to **Isla de Venados** (Deer Island). The ancient vessel takes about 20 minutes to reach the island from **El Centro Acuático El Cid** (see "Water Sports" under "Exercise and Recreation in Mazatlán," page 245). The 100-peso round trip leaves at approximately 10 a.m., noon, and 2 p.m., and returns at noon, 2 p.m., or 4 p.m. Although this isn't a snorkeler's paradise (despite hype to the contrary), the water is clean and calm—just right for swimming or kayaking. Rough red rocks frame the lee shore beach, and a trail leads to a panoramic view of the island. The path continues down to the rougher windward side, where a protected cove offers better snorkeling. On a calm day, it is pleasant to circumnavigate the island by kayak. To the north, **Isla de los Pájaros** is a bird sanctuary that cannot be visited, although boats may anchor offshore.

After you've parasailed, played beach volleyball, and soaked up the sun, it's time for some sightseeing in Mazatlán's historic center. After years of neglect, many of the historical buildings, mainly built between 1830 and 1913, have been restored (or at least their facades have). Wandering here for a few hours, you'll be rewarded with boutiques in renovated old homes, a few museums and galleries, and lots of photo-ops.

Start your downtown tour in the main plaza, **Plazuela Revolución,** bordered by Calles Nelson, 21 de Marzo, Flores, and Benito Juárez. The pretty square is shaded by palms and surrounded by shops and businesses. Locals take a time-out on benches in the shade, or dive into the diner below the wrought-iron bandstand in the center of the square. The north side of the square is dominated by the yellow-steepled **Catedral** at Calles Juárez and 21 de Marzo. The interior was renovated recently and boasts an ornate altarpiece of gold. Several blocks north of the cathedral lies the **Mercado Pino Suárez** (the municipal market), always a cultural eye-opener (see "Shopping in Mazatlán," page 246).

South of the main square, at Calles Carnaval and Constitución, the restored **Teatro Angela Peralta** is an ornate 19th-century building once destroyed by hurricane in the 1960s, but now reborn to host cultural events, theater, and dance. Across the street, **Café Memorial** (Calle Carnaval 1209 Sur; ☎ 669-985-4301) is a great place to stop for coffee and cake, one of their special panini sandwiches, or a full meal before or after theater events. It's open daily after 7 a.m. One block toward the ocean, **Plazuela Machado** is less formal than Plazuela Revolución. Sitting on what was once swampy, unused land, the charming, open square was an 1850s-era gift to the city by shipping magnate and successful merchant Juan Machado. Mazatlán's oldest square, it is also the most beautiful, surrounded by restaurants and cafes, and sporting a lazy, tropical feel. It's even nicer now that contiguous streets are closed to vehicular traffic Friday through Sunday after 6 p.m. People stroll around the plaza and sip refreshments at tables outside the many restaurants, bars, and cafes.

Overlooking the plaza, **Casa Machado** (Avenida Constitución 79; ☎ 669-982-1440) is a replica of 19th-century life in Mazatlán, with several rooms filled with furnishings and costumes and a film about Mazatlán's history.

In the same neighborhood, the **Museo de Arte de Mazatlán** (Venustiano Carranza at Sixto Osuna; ☎ 669-985-3502) has a permanent collection of fine art with work by Francisco Toledo, José Luis Cuevas, Rufino Tamayo, and other well-known Mexican artists. The museum is open Tuesday through Saturday, 10 a.m. to 2 p.m. and 4 to 7 p.m.; and Sunday, 10 a.m. to 2 p.m. Admission is free. Almost every Thursday evening, the museum sponsors a free or inexpensive cultural event—anything from poetry readings to jazz performances or informal theater.

Nearby, the **Museo de Antropología e Historia** (Calle Sixto Osuna off Paseo Olas Altas; ☎ 669-981-1455) is a small museum with dioramas and archaeological pieces (with labels in Spanish only) from the region. It's open Tuesday through Sunday 10 a.m. to 7 p.m.; there is no charge for admission.

kids Of more interest to children is the **Acuario Mazatlán** (Avenida de los Deportes 111; ☎ 669-981-7815), where sea-lion and bird shows are repeated several times a day. Kids get a kick out of the large playground and the tanks of more than 250 species of tropical fish. Here you'll find an aviary, gift shop, and small snack shop. It's open daily, 9:30 a.m. to 6 p.m.; admission is $6. If you prefer to get soaked yourself (instead of watching the sea lions have all the fun), take the kids to **Mazagua** (Entronque Habal-Cerritos s/n, near Playa Las Brujas; ☎ 669-988-0041), an aquatic park with wave pool, waterslides, and a snack shop. There are tables and barbecue grills where you can enjoy your own picnic lunch. Hours are Tuesday through Sunday, 10 a.m. to 6 p.m. (open some Mondays for holidays, Holy Week, July, and August). Admission is $8.

Most Mazatlán tour operators offer five- to six-hour "booze cruises" to **Isla de la Piedra.** The price varies; most cost $35 to $45 depending on the number of additional activities offered: usually horseback riding, banana boating, or snorkeling.

unofficial **TIP**
Note that the water is usually murky. Some operators offer a less expensive version, with activities optional.

TOURS *and* SIDE TRIPS *from* MAZATLÁN

CITY AND BAY TOURS, as well as tours to outlying villages, are available through several agencies. Tours to the tequila-making town of **La Noria** are available through **Marlin Tours** (Avenida Playa Gaviota 417, Zona Dorada; ☎ 669-913-5301; **www.toursinmazatlan.com.mx**). Their colonial towns tour hits Concordia and Copala with or without lunch ($40 to $50, accordingly) at rural Rancho Malpica.

Vista Tours (Camarón Sábalo 51, across from Hotel Riviera Mazatlán; ☎ 669-986-8610; **vistatours.com.mx**) offers a wide range of tours, including city tours, trips to **El Rosario, Concordia,** and **Copala** as well as a tequila tour to La Noria and an all-day birding adventure to the mangroves and islets of Bahía Santa María (10 hours, $119 per person) or Teacapán (6 hours, $90). **Olé Tours** (Avenida Camarón Sábalo 7000, Centro Comercial el Campanario; ☎ 669-916-6288; **www.ole-tours.com**) specializes in tours to **El Rosario** and to **Concordia** and **Copala** (both last 6 hours and cost $55 per person, including lunch) and can arrange private airport transfers ($100 for 4 persons).

COASTAL SINALOA

> **unofficial TIP**
> This largely undeveloped strip of coastline has been targeted for a massive development project, which will eventually contain marinas, golf courses, and resort hotels.

SINALOA IS AN AGRICULTURAL STATE, and one of the most important products along the coast south of Mazatlán is the mango, which can be purchased for a song during its season (June through September).

Foreigners, especially during winter months, set up camp along the miles of soft-sand beaches between the tiny towns of **Las Cabras** and **Teacapán,** and restaurants, simple lodgings, and RV parks are springing up to serve their needs.

In Teacapán, **Villas María Fernanda** (☎ 695-954-5393; **www.villasmaria fernanda.com**) is on the estuary near the departure point for tours. In addition to one three-bedroom apartment with complete kitchen, the five pretty villas with small kitchen, living area, bedroom, and bath are reasonably priced as are the 12 hotel rooms. There are two pools and several beaches within walking distance. The owners also offer horseback riding, bike, and lagoon trips. Next door, **Restaurant Mr. Wayne** (no phone) named for a family friend of the owners, serves breakfast and fresh seafood.

For plain lodgings on a long, wide beach, **Rancho Los Angeles** (Carretera Escuinapa-Teacapán Km 25; ☎ 695-953-1609 or 695-953-1414) has been sold and is being remodeled. There is space for some 30 RVs (full hookups). About half a mile north of Teacapán, on endless **La Tambora beach,** two seaside shanties serve beer, soft drinks, fish fillets, and other fresh seafood.

CONCORDIA AND COPALA

ABOUT 25 MILES EAST OF MAZATLÁN, **Concordia** provides a glimpse of small-town life. Don't expect oodles of excitement here, but do bring a camera loaded with film and take a stroll around town, admiring the brightly painted one- and two-story homes topped with aged brickred roof tiles. In the main square, where entrepreneurs sell trinkets and souvenirs, the 18th-century **Iglesia de San Sebastián** is said to be the state's oldest building still in use. From Concordia, tours and individual travelers generally push on through the foothills of the **Sierra Madre del Occidente** to the even smaller town of **Copala,** 15 miles beyond. Although dusty brown in the dry winter months, the brush and scrub burst into bright green leaves during and after summer rains. In Copala, wander the narrow cobblestone street past tiny houses painted in many pastel shades. Originally a mining town, Copala was founded in 1565 by the young Spanish conquistador Francisco de Ibarra. Clinging to one of the gorges that surround the town is the relatively sober, 18th-century **Iglesia de San José.** Outside, local boys tout rides on diminutive donkeys that hardly look up to the task. Although you'll see more than a few burros, this is definitely a one-horse town.

ESTUARIES AND EL ROSARIO

ABOUT 90 MILES SOUTH OF MAZATLÁN IS **El Estero de Teacapán,** the system of estuaries and mangrove swamps that dominates the southern portion of the state of Sinaloa. Lacing the coast, these mangroves are a haven for resident and migratory water species, including flamingo, heron, ibis, stork, and spoonbills. Of the eight types of mangroves found around the world, four are found in this area. Tours can be arranged through tour operators in Mazatlán, especially **Vista Tours** (Camarón Sábalo 51, across from Hotel Riviera Mazatlán; ☎ 669-986-8610 or 669-914-0187). These tours often make a short stop in **El Rosario,** a silver- and gold-mining town established in 1655. The town's main church, dedicated to Our Lady of the Rosary (for whom the town was also named), has a dazzling main altarpiece encrusted in gold. The town's foundation is laced with tunnels of now-played-out mines.

EL QUELITE

THE STATE TOURISM BOARD IS PUSHING *turismo rural,* a brand of ecotourism involving the small towns such as **El Quelite,** about 18 miles northeast of Mazatlán off Highway 15. Tours to this peaceful town of some 1,500 people include stops at the local bakery and tortilla factory, a visit to the state's largest fighting-cock breeding

unofficial **TIP**
El Quelite is home to one of the largest rooster farms, where the birds are raised for cockfighting. You can see the farm's tiny A-frame nesting huts and hundreds of birds strutting about at the edge of town.

ranch, and lunch of a typical meal of *carne asada*, beans, rice, and tortillas. Some tours may include a demonstration of Ulama, a pre-hispanic ball game. If the quiet life here in town beckons, the affable Dr. Marcos Osuna, of one of the town's most important families, has a few rooms for rent at **Mesón de los Laureanos** (Callejón Fco. Bernál 1; ☎ 669-965-4194). The cost is $68 per couple per night (breakfast and tax included), with no extra charge for a child or two; or $48 for a room in a charming adjacent house, without breakfast.

EXERCISE *and* RECREATION *in* MAZATLÁN

WITH A WEALTH OF WATER SPORTS, miles-long beaches for walking or jogging, and several impressive golf courses, there's no reason to be idle during your Mazatlán idyll. Listed below are some of the most popular recreation and exercise options.

GOLF

PART OF THE **El Cid** hotel, marina, and condo conglomerate, the **El Cid Golf and Country Club** (Camarón Sábalo s/n at the Granada Country Club; ☎ 669-913-3333, ext. 3261) is host to several national and international amateur golf tournaments each year. Greens and fairways of the 6,712-yard, 27-hole course meander around adjoining condos. There's a driving range, putting green, and clubhouse. The $58 greens fees do not include caddy ($17) or cart ($40).

Club Campestre de Mazatlán (Km 1195 Carretera Internacional Sur; ☎ 669-980-1570) is a private golf course. The main allure of this older, nine-hole course, which is in less-than-pristine condition, is its low price: less than $30 to play through twice. There's a driving range and putting green, and caddies and carts are available ($20 cart rental).

Estrella Del Mar Golf Club (Isla de la Piedra; ☎ 669-982-3300; 800-967-1889 U.S.; **www.estrelladelmar.com**) is appropriate for players of various skill levels. This 18-hole, Robert Trent Jones Jr.–designed course stretches along the sea for several miles. There's a three-story clubhouse with pro shop, restaurant-bar, and PGA pro on staff. You can rent clubs, use the driving range and practice area, and sign up for lessons or clinics. Greens fees are a bit pricey at $110 (but include cart rental); they are significantly lower in low season, May through October.

unofficial **TIP**
It's 12 miles from Mazatlán, but the greens fee includes transportation from most Zona Dorada hotels.

SPORTFISHING

MAZATLÁN IS A SUPERB DESTINATION for serious sport-fishers, who haul in thousands of game fish each year. The area's catch-and-release program is popular and helps preserve the species for future generations. The November **El Cid Billfish Classic** attracts anglers competing for more than $300,000 in prize money, including prizes for fish that are released. Sailfish are plentiful during most of the year, as are tuna and dorado. Blue and black marlin rule during summer and fall, followed by striped marlin between December and April. Other anglers vie for bottomfish: roosterfish, grouper, skipjack, pompano, Spanish mackerel, and sea bass.

Choose from more than 125 fishing boats large and small. Among the most recognized are the **Aries Fleet,** at the El Cid Marina (Camarón Sábalo s/n; ☎ 669-916-3468) and **StarFleet** (Avenida Joel Montes Camarena s/n, next to lighthouse downtown; ☎ 669-982-2665; 888-882-9614 U.S.; **starfleet.com.mx**), another full-service operator promoting catch and release. Shared boats cost around $100 per person, while boats for two to eight passengers vary in price from $260 to $485 per day. For largemouth bass, take a trip to **El Salto** reservoir northeast of Mazatlán. **Amazing Outdoors** (Camarón Sábalo 2601-4; ☎/fax 669-984-3151; **www.basselsalto.com**) offers expensive day and overnight fishing trips to the region.

SURFING

THE SURF IS BEST IN THE SUMMER MONTHS. Locals hang out at **Playa Olas Altas** downtown, where the waves crash against a shallow beach. Surfing is also good at **Isla de la Piedra,** as well as **La Escopama Beach,** and **Playa las Brujas,** both north of the Zona Dorada. **Patoles,** about one hour north of Mazatlán, is known for its right and left breaks and long waves.

TENNIS

IN ADDITION TO COURTS AT **El Cid, Hotel Playa Real** (formerly Camino Real), and **Hotel Pueblo Bonito,** you can play on one of several clay or hard courts at **Las Gaviotas Racquet Club** (Calle Ibis at Río Bravo; ☎ 669-913-5939; $14/hour hard court, $18/hour clay court). Pay by the hour for $6/hour at **Tenis Club San Juan** (across from the Hotel Costa de Oro; ☎ 669-913-5344) The three cement courts are unlit, so play ceases at dusk.

WATER SPORTS

WATER TOYS CAN BE RENTED RIGHT on the beach in the Zona Dorada, and activities include parasailing and personal watercraft and catamaran rentals. Or climb aboard a giant banana boat, where you'll be towed by motorboat for a quick trip to Deer Island (cost is about $8 per person). The **Centro Acuático El Cid** (on the beach at Avenida Camarón Sábalo s/n, between El Cid and Puesta del Sol hotels; ☎ 669-913-3333, ext. 3341) offers all of the above as well as catamaran, boogie boards, sportfishing, and excursions to Isla del Venados. Bay cruises can be booked through most any hotel, often aboard the trimaran **Kolonahe,** which berths at El Cid Marina (Camarón Sábalo s/n, ☎ 669-916-3468). Passengers have access to snorkels, fins, and kayaks, and the cost ($42 adults, $21 children ages 12 and under) includes food and drink. Or choose a four-hour sunset cruise, departing at 5:30 p.m. in summer, 4:30 p.m. in winter. There's music for dancing, and the cost ($35 for adults, less for children ages 12 and under) includes open bar.

SHOPPING *in* MAZATLÁN

MAZATLÁN'S SHOPPING SCENE has brightened in the past few years, welcoming several worthwhile folk-art shops in Old Mazatlán and the Zona Dorada. **Casa Etnika** (Calle Sixto Osuna 50, ☎ 669-136-0139) has a fun selection of ethnic folk art as well as framed photos and other works of art. It's housed in a restored mid-19th-century mansion. Near the malecón in Old Mazatlán, **Casa Antigua** (Mariano Escobedo 206 Poniente; ☎ 669-982-5236) occupies another lovely old house. Here you'll find items from throughout Mexico, including black pottery, papier-mâché, silver, pewter, and other handicrafts. Note that they're both closed on Sunday. A half block from the Angela Peralta Theater, **NidArt** (Libertad 45; ☎ 669-981-0002) occupies yet another 19th-century home, this one painted bright purple and pink. Here, an artisans' co-op offers handmade silver jewelry, sculpted leather masks, figurines and larger carved wood pieces, as well as coconut masks from Guerrero, Huichol handicrafts, and folk art from other areas of Mexico. Check out the second-floor gallery for photography and other rotating fine art exhibits. Except during the height of tourist season, it's open Monday through Saturday, 10 a.m. to 2 p.m.

unofficial **TIP**
The plaza's indoor playground area is hugely popular with families on weekends. Small rides, games, and jumping cages keep the little ones delighted while their parents visit tables and chairs throughout the area.

Mazatlán's large **Mercado Pino Suárez** (Calle Serdán and Melchor Ocampo) was built locally based on designs by Alfred Eiffel. There you'll find the usual cacophony of buyers and sellers bartering for produce, fresh fish and meat, and knock-offs of Calvin Klein jeans.

For a complete selection of moderately priced jewelry and gifts (glass objects, platters, and frames, for example) shop at **Michael Gallery** (Las Garzas 18; ☎ 669-916-5511). A second store is located across from the Balboa Club Resort (Avenida Camarón Sábalo 19; ☎ 669-916-7816). Mazatlán's biggest shopping center, **La Gran Plaza** (Avenida Reforma at Apolo; ☎ 669-986-3836) has boutiques, a movie theater with three screens, and a food court in addition to **Comercial Mexicana,** a grocery store chain, and **Fábricas de Francia,** a chain department store.

NIGHTLIFE *in* MAZATLÁN

LOCALS DECRY MAZATLÁN'S "spring-break party-on" label, but just listening to the young party animals around the pool confirms that the drink-til-you-drop scene still rages in the beachfront clubs. But for those who want more sober (or at least more stimulating) forms of entertainment, these too can be found, if you know where to look.

For a traditional Mexican show, don't miss **Fiesta Mexicana** (at Hotel Playa Mazatlán, Avenida Playa Gaviotas 202; ☎ 669-913-5320), which includes domestic cocktails, beer, and a buffet dinner along with a variety show with folk dancing, rope tricks, and a stab at comedy. Performances cost $35 and are scheduled for Tuesdays, Thursdays, and Saturdays at 6 p.m. during high season; once or twice weekly the rest of the year (often there are no shows in the lowest season, September). The live local band draws the crowd onto the dance floor before and after the variety show.

At the south end of the Zona Dorada, **Fiesta Land** (Avenida Camarón Sábalo at Avenida Rafael Buelna, Punta Camarón; ☎ 669-984-1666) is a party complex with several different venues, notably **Valentino** for romantic dining and dancing, or **Bora Bora** for dancing in abandon on the beach, as well as **Canta Bar** for karaoke, **Pepe's & Joe** for sports on TV while tipping a few, and during the day, **Bora Bora Beach Club** for combining swimming, sunning, and socializing—they also have a regulation sand volleyball court.

Of the Zona Dorada bars and nightclubs, **GringoLingo Bar & Grill** (Avenida Playa Gaviotas 313; ☎ 669-913-7737) is a popular pit stop for a drink anytime. The bar-restaurant **Mangos** (see restaurant listing, page 234) is popular with all ages and has a party-hearty reputation on weekend nights. Locals and travelers looking to steer clear of the gringo party crowd might opt instead for nearby **Tony's Restaurant Bar** (Avenida Playa Gaviotas and Avenida Camarón Sábalo; no phone) to listen to live rock or salsa from the comfort of their tables, or squeeze onto the small dance floor. The casual establishment serves beer, hard liquor, and simple snack foods like hot dogs and tacos.

Closer to downtown, a couple of personable Canadian musicians have opened **Canuck's** (Paseo Claussen; ☎ 669-981-2978), a relaxed rock and blues venue where U.S., Canadian, and Mexican flags hang from the huge, peaked, thatch roof. The food's not bad, either. A half block off Plazuela Machado, in the historic center of Mazatlán, the lounge **Dionisius** (B. Dominguez 1406; ☎ 669-985-0333), attached to Ambrosia vegetarian restaurant, is open late on weekend nights. The retro-lounge-feel bar has low, intimate booths and low lighting

unofficial **TIP**
Vendors selling jewelry, embroidered purses and blouses, used books, and paintings set up stands around Plazuela Machado on Friday and Saturday nights. The mood is festive and fun, with crowds walking about and filling tables at sidewalk cafes.

as well, perfect for an evening of conversation or schmoozing.

For a drink or coffee and a bite to eat, we like **Portal Latino** (which serves great enchiladas in *mole* sauce) at H. Frias 1305, no phone, right on Plazuela Machado, or, across from Angela Peralta Theatre, **Café Memorial** (Calle Carnaval 1209, ☎ 669-985-4301) for coffee and dessert off the cart. Locals head for a shanty on the beach at Playa La Bruja to dance to *banda* (nouveau marching band) Friday and Saturday nights, and Sunday after 5 p.m.

MAZATLÁN'S CARNAVAL

Real Navy ships engage in a firestorm of fireworks; ballerinas twirl and prance at the baseball stadium, where the conductor leads the formally dressed orchestra; oompah bands strut down oceanfront Avenida del Mar, followed by sweaty horses, flashy muscle cars, and a flatbed truck decorated like a spaceship. The five-day, pre-Lenten festival is one of the largest in Mexico, full of unexpected revelry.

Strolling vendors sell intact eggshells filled with confetti for cracking on your friend's head (or those of strangers passing by). There are all-night dances that many recover from by sipping a beer for breakfast and then sleeping all day on the beach.

For all its flamboyance and fun, Mazatlán's Carnaval is also a family affair. Poetry contests are held, and the baseball stadium ballet draws a massive crowd. Nationally and internationally recognized pop stars headline at concerts around town. A king and queen of Carnaval are named, and they preside over the festivities wearing beautiful, ornate regalia so hot and heavy that just *looking* at them in the semitropical heat can make a gringo swoon.

The celebrations have been taking place in this port city since the early 1800s, when soldiers and sailors chose the days before Lent as a time for acting up. By the early 19th century, the more dignified citizens of the booming port city decided the festivities were too ribald and boisterous. They began organizing parades, poetry competitions, and elections for the queen and the king, who was originally called *el rey feo* ("the ugly king"). He's now referred to as *el rey de la alegría*, or "the king of happiness."

Hotel rooms sell out a year in advance for the week surrounding Carnaval, and the entire town settles into some serious partying. Don't expect to receive attentive service in restaurants—nearly everyone's recovering from late-night revelries. If you're in Mazatlán for Carnaval, you'd best join in with abandon.

PART NINE

PUERTO VALLARTA

WIDE BEACHES *and* HIGH CULTURE

DIVIDE 25 MILES OF BEACHES BY A POPULATION of 350,000. Add 3.8 million visitors a year. Factor in a warm tropical climate and a thriving cultural scene. The result of this equation is Puerto Vallarta, one of Mexico's most popular and charismatic coastal resorts.

Aside from its miles of sandy beaches and rock-framed coves, Puerto Vallarta (often shortened to just "PV") also offers gourmet dining and modern art. Celebrated chefs from around the world compete for customers at restaurants serving fine Swiss, Italian, Mediterranean, and nouvelle Mexican cuisine. Others turn out more-traditional favorites (including Mexican standards and fresh grilled fish and seafood) while specializing in superb sunsets viewed from lovely venues along the beach or tucked into the hills. Set in the middle of a long, wide, blue **Bahía de Banderas** ("Bay of Flags"), Puerto Vallarta is backed by bright emerald hills that rise abruptly behind the town.

The resort area now sprawls both north and south of the original settlement, which grew up around the **Río Cuale,** the river that bisects the town and empties into the sea. **Old Vallarta**'s quaint style has considerable charm. Whitewashed stucco buildings topped with red roof tiles face narrow, uneven cobblestone streets. Sturdy fuchsia-, peach-, and rose-colored bougainvillea spill over fences and painted garden gates, their bright tropical colors commingling with cacti and succulents, slender palms, and exuberant vines.

The beauty of the setting has perhaps inspired Puerto Vallarta's large community of artists. Dozens of galleries display the works of well-known and up-and-coming creators. Most of these galleries are concentrated downtown, but the Marina Vallarta area and some of the large hotels and shopping malls also sell fine art. Shops display

The Central Pacific Coast and Costalegre

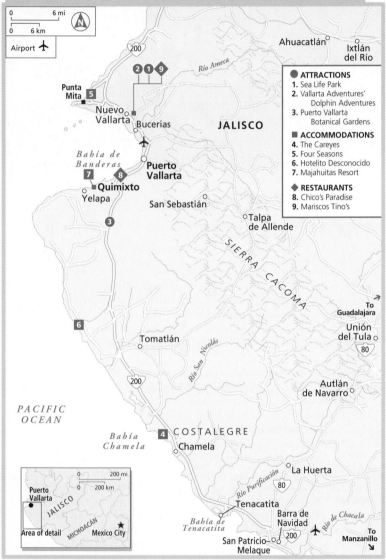

0   6 mi
0   6 km

Airport ✈

200

Río Ameca

Ahuacatlán   Ixtlán
del Río

● **ATTRACTIONS**
1. Sea Life Park
2. Vallarta Adventures'
   Dolphin Adventures
3. Puerto Vallarta
   Botanical Gardens

■ **ACCOMMODATIONS**
4. The Careyes
5. Four Seasons
6. Hotelito Desconocido
7. Majahuitas Resort

◆ **RESTAURANTS**
8. Chico's Paradise
9. Mariscos Tino's

Punta
Mita **5**

Nuevo
Vallarta   Bucerias

JALISCO

*Bahía de
Banderas*

7   **8**

**Puerto
Vallarta**

Quimixto
Yelapa

San Sebastián

3

SIERRA   CACOMA

Talpa
de Allende

To
Guadalajara

Unión
del Tula

80

6

Tomatlán

Río San Nicolás

Autlán
de Navarro

*PACIFIC
OCEAN*

200

*Bahía
Chamela*

4 COSTALEGRE

Chamela

La Huerta

Río Purificación

80

200 mi
200 km

Puerto
Vallarta

JALISCO

Area of detail *MICHOACÁN* ★ Mexico City

Tenacatita

*Bahía de
Tenacatita*

Barra de
Navidad

San Patricio–
Melaque

200

Río de Chacala

To
Manzanillo

Puerto Vallarta Hotel Zone and Beaches

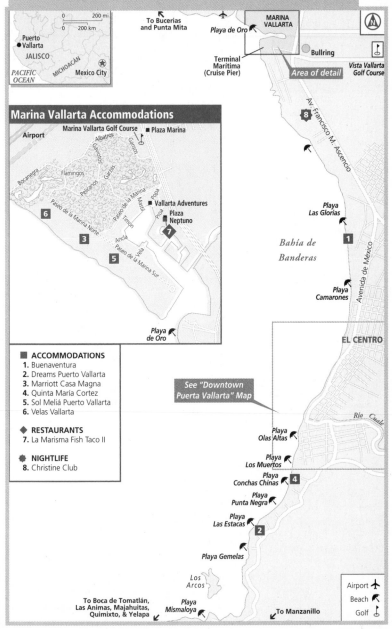

Puerto Vallarta
JALISCO
PACIFIC OCEAN
MICHOACÁN
Mexico City

0   200 mi
0   200 km

To Bucerias and Punta Mita
Playa de Oro
MARINA VALLARTA
Terminal Marítima (Cruise Pier)
Bullring
Area of detail
Vista Vallarta Golf Course

Marina Vallarta Accommodations

Airport
Marina Vallarta Golf Course
Plaza Marina
Albatros
Gaviotas
Garzas
Bocanegra
Flamingos
Pelícanos
Garzas
Popa
Paseo de la Marina
Mastil
Timon
Proa
Vallarta Adventures
Plaza Neptuno
Paseo de la Marina Norte
Ancla
Paseo de la Marina Sur
Vela
Playa de Oro

Av. Francisco M. Ascencio
Playa Las Glorias
Bahía de Banderas
Avenida de México
Playa Camarones
EL CENTRO

See "Downtown Puerta Vallarta" Map

Río Cuale
Playa Olas Altas
Playa Los Muertos
Playa Conchas Chinas
Playa Punta Negra
Playa Las Estacas
Playa Gemelas
Los Arcos

To Boca de Tomatlán, Las Animas, Majahuitas, Quimixto, & Yelapa
Playa Mismaloya
To Manzanillo

■ ACCOMMODATIONS
1. Buenaventura
2. Dreams Puerto Vallarta
3. Marriott Casa Magna
4. Quinta María Cortez
5. Sol Meliá Puerto Vallarta
6. Velas Vallarta

◆ RESTAURANTS
7. La Marisma Fish Taco II

● NIGHTLIFE
8. Christine Club

Airport ✈
Beach 🏖
Golf ⛳

Downtown Puerto Vallarta

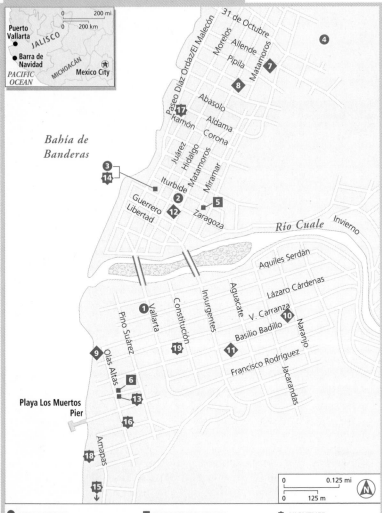

● ATTRACTIONS
1. Hotel Posada de
   Río Cuale
2. Iglesia de Nuestra
   Señora de
   Guadalupe
3. Plaza de Armas
4. Terra Noble

■ ACCOMMODATIONS
5. Hacienda San Angel
6. Los Arcos Suites

◆ RESTAURANTS
7. El Arrayán
8. Café des Artistes
9. Daiquiri Dick's
10. La Marisma Fish Taco I
11. Restaurant Frankfurt
12. Trio

❀ NIGHTLIFE
13. Apache's Bar and Café
14. Los Arcos Amphitheater
15. Blue Chairs
16. Descanso del Sol
17. Hilo
18. La Palapa
19. Señor Frog's

paintings, sculpture, multimedia art, and collector-quality folk art from around the country.

One of the things we love about Vallarta is the city's devotion to the arts. On Wednesday evenings between November and April, PV's downtown galleries participate in **Art Walk;** handing out cheap wine and peanuts to visitors who use art as an excuse to socialize. Many free cultural events are staged at the outdoor **Los Arcos** amphitheater, between the town plaza and the *malecón*, or seaside boardwalk, especially during high season (late November through Easter break). On Sunday evenings, local families and visitors might gather to see a performance of folkloric ballet or listen and dance to live salsa, Mexican ballads, or other genres of music.

At the tall pole next to Los Arcos, watch **Los Voladores de Papantla** (the Papantla Fliers) perform a ritual "dance" that involves diving head first from 100 feet up. Dressed in fantastic costumes of ribbons, velvet, tiny mirrors, and flowers, the men are anchored by an ever-unwinding rope until they lightly touch the ground. The schedule changes with the season, but between December and April it's usually on the hour between 6 and 9 p.m. Dozens of vendors who sell souvenirs as well as hot and cold drinks, crêpes, hot dogs, and ceviche have been relocated to the newer section of the *malecón*, just south of the Cuale River.

November brings events day and night, including the well-known **Festival Gourmet International in Puerto Vallarta and Nayarit (www.festivalgourmet.com)**, sailing regattas, art exhibitions, and of course, lots of live music.

A highly religious but hardly somber celebration is the annual **Fiesta de la Virgen de Guadalupe,** which honors Mexico's patron saint. The Virgin of Guadalupe is PV's patron as well, which explains the extent of her popularity. Daily processions make their way to the city's small cathedral from the end of November through her feast day, December 12. The streets are packed with spectators and participants as neighborhood associations and Vallarta churches parade to the cathedral to honor the Virgin and to seek divine favors.

The area around the **Río Cuale**—still the hub from which the town radiates—was first settled by a couple of entrepreneurial fishermen. A few years later, salt used in the smelting process was delivered to the bay here and then transported to mountain mines, so the fledgling town was called Puerto Las Peñas ("Port of Rocks"). The name was later changed to Puerto Vallarta in honor of Jalisco state governor Ignacio L. Vallarta.

The town grew slowly, with little external attention, until Mexicana Airlines brought the first travelers in the 1950s. The movie *Night of the Iguana*, based on the Tennessee Williams play, was filmed here in 1963. The actors and their entourage attracted fledgling paparazzi, and the press that was generated set PV's course straight for its current megaresort status.

For several decades the destination "Puerto Vallarta" has been understood to encompass all points along 25-mile Bahía de Banderas, as far north as Punta Mita. Today private and federally funded development of the Nayarit coast is under way, and everything and everything between San Blas and Nuevo Vallarta goes under the moniker "Riviera Nayarit." This includes the lovely northern end of Banderas Bay at **Punta Mita,** an upscale development now in its second decade. The lavish **St. Regis** joins the more established **Four Seasons** resort and two golf courses as well as private homes and condos. Currently within the 1,500-acre gated community are private villas that rent for many thousands of dollars a day, complete with staff. Beaches here are beautiful, and offshore you can spot cetaceans at the **Marieta Islands.** Humpback whales breed in these waters December through May; the nutrient-rich waters are abundant year-round with manta rays, colorful tropical fish, and other marine creatures.

Heading south from Punta Mita, you'll pass sandy and rocky beaches, surf spots, and seafood shanties on lovely beaches. Paradise is being paved, however, by upscale housing developments and hotels, including those currently being built at **Destiladeras.** The town of **La Cruz de Huanacaxtle,** a small but well-established fishing community, will maintain some of its own humble character in spite of the new Marina Riviera Nayarit, which opened in 2008. The area near the marina, however, will be transformed with new accommodations, restaurants, and shops.

A few miles south, **Bucerías** has for years been attracting expatriates and snowbirds stretching their retirement or vacation dollars—be they Canadian or U.S. Next stop is **Flamingos,** with two new condo complexes in the works. Last stop before the Jalisco state line is **Nuevo Vallarta,** a well-established all-inclusive resort destination on its own long, flat beach. Once sold as the lonely cousin to more popular Puerto Vallarta, the southern anchor of the Riviera Nayarit is slowly growing into a destination with actual character, and development of Bucerías and towns to the north makes Nuevo Vallarta guests feel less isolated. Excursion boats depart from here. Crossing into Jalisco state is the beginning of Puerto Vallarta itself. **Marina Vallarta** is a large mixed development of hotels and condominiums surrounding the cruise-ship and excursion-boat dock; 450-slip marina and yacht club; golf course; and adjacent malls, shops, and restaurants.

South of Marina Vallarta and hugging the busy coastal highway, **Zona Hotelera** (sometimes called "Zona Hotelera Norte" or simply "the hotel zone") has high-rise hotels—including the Fiesta Americana, Sheraton, and Holiday Inn—mixed in with local businesses along the busy main boulevard. Next is the Old Town, the original Puerto

Vallarta you'll see on postcards and magazine covers. Although there's beach fronting all of downtown, the spots that attract most sunbathers are **Playa Los Muertos** at the south end of downtown near the pier and, to a lesser extent, contiguous **Playa Olas Altas,** just to the north. These are lively and backed by accommodations, bars, and restaurants where sybarites repair for drinks and nourishment.

South of downtown PV are a series of beaches separated by rocky shore. The first of these, including **Conchas Chinas, Mismaloya** (where *Night of the Iguana* was filmed), and **Boca de Tomatlán** are accessible by road. Farther south, **Las Animas, Quimixto, Majahuitas, Yelapa,** and **Pisota** can be reached by boat only. Included in this chapter are the isolated, high-end resorts and rustic accommodations of **Costalegre,** a 280-mile stretch of coast between PV and Barra de Navidad to the south.

QUICK FACTS *about* PUERTO VALLARTA

AIRPORT AND AIRLINES Gustavo Díaz Ordaz International Airport (☎ 322-221-1298) is four miles out of downtown, near Marina Vallarta. Airport shuttles can be hired just outside the baggage claim (Transportes Terrestres, ☎ 322-221-1488). Rates to the different hotel zones and parts of the city are posted, but it's a confusing scene. A seat in a shared taxi van costs $6 to $10 per person, or a little more than twice that amount for a car with up to three passengers. Several airlines fly nonstop from Los Angeles (Alaska Air), Phoenix (America West/US Airways), Houston (Continental), Chicago (American), Dallas (American), and Toronto (Air Canada). **Mexicana** and **Aeroméxico** have direct flights from some U.S. cities, especially during the winter months, as well as service from Mexico City, Tijuana, Guadalajara, and many other Mexican cities.

CLIMATE Puerto Vallarta is sticky and hot in the summer. The average rainfall for July is 13 inches; the average temperature 90°F. November through June are the best months to avoid rain (temperatures dip to 80°F) although May and June can be aggressively hot. January and February are the coolest months.

DRIVING The old section of town has narrow, cobblestone streets. Parking problems have been alleviated by the construction of several controversial parking structures in the heart of the old town. Driving north and south of downtown is usually not problematic and the hotels and shops have plenty of parking. If driving from the airport, the hotel zone, or other points north of downtown, you can take the *Libramiento* (bypass road) if you want to skirt town altogether and head for points south. Still, unless you plan to do lots of exploring

unofficial TIP
It's important in PV to choose your hotel zone carefully so that you're where you want to be more often than not.

north and south of town, buses and taxis are your best options for getting around. Puerto Vallarta is 212 miles west of Guadalajara, the capital of Jalisco state, and about 280 miles north of Manzanillo, Colima.

GETTING AROUND Taxis are ubiquitous and not terribly expensive, but costs do add up depending on where you are and where you want to go. The minimum fare is about $3; the fares to downtown PV from Conchas Chinas and Mismaloya beaches, south of town, are about $7 and $9, respectively. From Marina Vallarta, most taxi drivers charge $10, but from Nuevo Vallarta, the fare jumps to around $19.

Water taxis depart from the pier next to the Hotel Rosita, at the north end downtown ($24 round-trip) and from Boca de Tomatlán ($7 each way) for Las Animas, Quimixto, Majahuitas, and Yelapa. There are usually two or three departures in the morning and the same number of return trips in the afternoon. In high season there are four departures and returns from the Los Muertos pier; half that number the rest of the year. Cost is $22 round-trip. Be sure to ask when the last water taxi returns to town, unless you plan to stay the night.

As usual in Mexico, buses are frequent, inexpensive, and travel at frightening rates of speed between traffic lights and stop signs. Buses connect the airport and downtown and en route serve the hotel zone. Marina Vallarta buses run from one end of this zone to the other. Buses running south to Conchas Chinas, Mismaloya, and Boca de Tomatlán originate downtown at the corner of Calles Basilio Badillo and Constitución).

unofficial TIP
Many properties in Nuevo Vallarta, although technically in Nayarit state, use the ☎ 322 area code. Some also adopt the PV time zone so that guests don't miss their flights: Nayarit is in mountain time and Jalisco, central time.

INTERNET ACCESS PVC@fe.com (Olas Altas 246, Col. Emiliano Zapata; ☎ 322-223-0608) is open daily from early morning until at least midnight and serves coffee, booze, snacks, sandwiches, and salads. In the hotel zone, **PV Net** (Boulevard Francisco M. Ascencio 1692, near the Hertz car rental; ☎ 322-223-1127) is open daily between 7 a.m. and 1 a.m., offers laptop connections, and charges just $1.50 per hour for regular Internet service.

TELEPHONES Puerto Vallarta's area code is ☎ 322. All local PV numbers should begin with 22 and have another five digits after that. If you come across older, five-digit numbers, just add 22 at the beginning. The area code for southern Nayarit is ☎ 329.

TIME-SHARES Booths advertising tourist information are located all over Vallarta: at the airport, hotels, and along city streets in the

How Accommodations Compare in Puerto Vallarta

ACCOMMODATION	OVERALL	QUALITY	VALUE	COST
Four Seasons	★★★★★	★★★★★	★★★	$$$$$
The Careyes	★★★★	★★★★	★★★★	$$$$$
Velas Vallarta	★★★★	★★★★	★★★★	$$$$$
Hacienda San Angel	★★★★	★★★★	★★½	$$$$$
Hotelito Desconocido	★★★★	★★★★	★½	$$$$$
Dreams Puerto Vallarta	★★★★	★★★	★★★	$$$$$
Marriott Casa Magna	★★★½	★★★½	★★★★	$$$$
Sol Meliá Puerto Vallarta	★★★	★★½	★★★★½	$$$$
Majahuitas Resort	★★½	★½	★★½	$$$$$
Buenaventura	★★	★★	★★	$$$
Los Arcos Suites	★★	★½	★★★★	$$

tourist areas. They're all connected to some commercial entity, usually a time-share property, including some attached to the larger resorts.

TOURIST INFORMATION To reach the **Puerto Vallarta Convention and Visitors Bureau,** call ☎ 888-384-6822 or log on to **www.visitpuertovallarta.com.** Or contact the national tourism board at ☎ 800-446-3942 in the United States (**www.visitmexico .com**). Once in PV, visit the **State Secretary of Tourism** at Centro Comercial Plaza Marina (☎ 322-221-2676) in Marina Vallarta or the **Municipal Tourist Board,** downtown Puerto Vallarta, on the main plaza at Independencia 123 (☎ 322-226-8080, ext. 270). For information about Nuevo Vallarta or resorts to the north, contact the **Riviera Nayarit Convention and Visitors Bureau** (Paseo de los Cocoteros, 85 Sur, at Paradise Plaza mall; ☎ 322-297-2516; **www.rivieranayarit.com**).

unofficial **TIP**
Time-share vendors can be aggressive, so don't feel compelled to answer their greetings or to make excuses about why you don't want to attend a free presentation.

WHERE *to* STAY *in* PUERTO VALLARTA

WHILE THE NUMBER OF ACCOMMODATIONS in Puerto Vallarta and vicinity has soared over the years, the area still offers a range of prices and accommodations to suit most travelers' tastes and budgets. Locations are quite varied: from the posh and pricey **Four Seasons** at Punta Mita (an hour north of PV proper, in Nayarit State) to the rustic **Lagunita Yelapa,** south of Old Puerto Vallarta and accessible only by boat, and boutique beauties of the Costalegre.

In between are the most popular options, including the original downtown digs around Playa Olas Altas and Playa Los Muertos. The latter hotels, most of them moderate in price and in amenities, are sought after for their proximity to the downtown action, with lots of shopping, bars, and restaurants.

Chain hotels and Mexican time-shares line the beach north of downtown, referred to as simply the hotel zone (*zona hotelera* or sometimes, *la zona hotelera norte*). Just to the north, Marina Vallarta's upscale hotels, condos, and 18-hole golf course surround the cruise-ship terminal, marina, and yacht club. Crossing the state line into Nayarit, you'll find another cluster of accommodations heading north from the mouth of the Ameca River, at Nuevo Vallarta. Because of their relative isolation, most of the hotels there are all-inclusives. Still more hotels are found south of downtown. These, such as the **Dreams Puerto Vallarta** and the **InterContinental,** have nice beaches but are not within easy walking distance of other hotels, shops, or restaurants. Still, it's a short cab or bus ride to Old Vallarta, and traffic here is lighter than along busy Boulevard Francisco M. Ascencio (aka "the airport road"), which connects downtown Vallarta to points north.

A few self-contained, exclusive properties dot the Costalegre, tucked into the dry-thorn forest by the sea. These are some of Mexico's most elegant hideaways, favored by reclusive celebrities and honeymooners. Most folks who stay here arrange for private transportation from PV for an extra charge of $100 or more.

As you can see, there is an enormous range of lodgings in Puerto Vallarta. It makes sense to study the options, decide what sort of vacation you want, and choose accordingly. Check Web sites and call toll-free numbers for further information and to learn of special promotions.

ACCOMMODATION PROFILES

Buenaventura $$$

OVERALL ★★	QUALITY ★★	VALUE ★★

Avenida México 1301, Col. 5 de Diciembre; ☎ 322-226-7000 or 888-859-9439 U.S.; fax 322-222-3546; hotelbuenaventura.com.mx

The location halfway between the north end of downtown and the hotel zone is a good one, but room prices have risen substantially after last year's remodeling, and several large-chain all-inclusives in the area offer an even better rate for all-inclusive. (The Buenaventura offers both plans.) Still, many people return for the more intimate setting. The open, airy, and pleasant main restaurant faces the pool and beach, where there's a friendly party feeling. Banana boats, personal watercraft, parasailing, volleyball, and more fun happen just outside on the beach during high season, and scheduled activities such as bingo, dance classes, and water polo are available.

SETTING AND FACILITIES

Location Northern edge of downtown.

Dining All-inclusive available, 2 restaurants.

Amenities and services Beach, 2 pools, hot tub, spa, massage, tour desk, business center, organized children's activities, shop, 3 bars, room service, Internet, Wi-Fi.

ACCOMMODATIONS

Rooms 215 rooms and 18 suites.

All rooms AC, windows that open, cable/satellite TV, hair dryer, safe, coffeemaker.

Some rooms Ocean view, balcony or terrace, whirlpool tub, bathtub, minibar, refrigerator, kitchenette, nonsmoking, disabled access.

Comfort and decor Comfortably furnished rooms, recently refurbished and brightened, with new wood furniture, polished limestone counters and tabletops, and comfortable new beds with white linens. When you book a "deluxe" (standard) room, request one on a higher floor with balcony looking out over the beach; these cost the same as those without, although the hotel does not guarantee availability.

PAYMENT, RESERVATIONS, AND RESTRICTIONS

Deposit Credit card; 48-hour cancellation policy.

Credit cards AE, MC, V.

Check-in/out 3 p.m./noon.

The Careyes $$$$$

OVERALL ★★★★	QUALITY ★★★★	VALUE ★★★★

Carretera Barra de Navidad a Puerto Vallarta Km 53.5; ☎ 315-351-0000 or 800-728-9098 U.S. and Canada; fax 315-351-0100; www.elcareyesresort.com

Just south of idyllic Chamula Bay, the luxurious Careyes property is bordered by a rocky cove. The ponies still run at the adjacent polo club, and the European-style spa is modern and professional. The architecture is a mix of Mediterranean and coastal Mexican called the "Careyes style," using stones, palm fronds, adobe roof tiles, and stucco detailing to create a look that seems simultaneously novel and familiar. Buildings have a wonderful palette of sunny colors and softly rounded corners. Junior suites have a large living area and plunge pool or Jacuzzi. On the lovely beach, lounges in the shade of individual palapas dot the soft sand, and yachts bob offshore. There's a wide variety of diversions, including snorkel gear, kayaks, mountain bikes, horseback riding, and fishing; there's no charge to use the spa's steam room, sauna, and hot tub. Expect a 5% surcharge on your bill at checkout.

SETTING AND FACILITIES

Location About 105 miles south of Puerto Vallarta and 60 miles north of Manzanillo airport on the Costalegre.

Dining Restaurant, delicatessen.

Amenities and services Beach, pool, hot tub, gym, spa, massage, marina, watersports center, tour desk, shops, tennis courts, 2 bars, room service, Internet.

ACCOMMODATIONS

Rooms 51 rooms and suites.

All rooms AC, fans, windows that open, hair dryer, minibar, cable TV, high-speed Internet, DVD/CD.

Some rooms Ocean view, terrace/balcony, whirlpool tub, safe, kitchenette, coffeemaker, private plunge pool.

Comfort and decor With walls painted such colors as warm ochre and sapphire blue, rooms also feature lovely, simple, Mediterranean-style furnishings that are functional and comfortable. Junior suites have large hot tubs on private balconies overlooking the beach.

PAYMENT, RESERVATIONS, AND RESTRICTIONS

Deposit Credit card; 60-day to 3-day cancellation policy, depending on season.

Credit cards AE, MC, V.

Check-in/out 3 p.m./1 p.m.

 Dreams Puerto Vallarta $$$$$ (all-inclusive)

OVERALL	★★★★	QUALITY	★★★	VALUE	★★★

Playa Las Estacas, Carretera a Barra de Navidad Km 3.5;
☎ **322-226-5000 or 866-237-3267 U.S. and Canada;**
fax 322-221-6000; www.dreamsresorts.com

This beautiful 11-story, all-inclusive property sits on its own lovely, white-sand beach south of town. Individual palapas shade comfortable lounge chairs overlooking the bay, which is calm here and great for swimming. The huge, free-form pool has a swim-up bar; activities here can make it noisy. Rooms have cool, stone floor tiles and bright accent colors, and a nice mix of contemporary furnishings and Mexican handcrafts. Some suites have a hot tub on the balcony. The spa has a second-story patio overlooking the beach with a hot tub and several massage tables. Two tennis courts are available for toning the body and destressing. The no-wristband all-inclusive policy means you can go into town without looking like a geek and also that your identity will be checked whenever you return to the resort. Tons of activities, both organized and individual, make this a great choice for active singles and families, and a variety of restaurants ensures no one gets bored with the same old buffet.

SETTING AND FACILITIES

Location South of downtown at Playa Las Estacas.

Dining 5 restaurants offering Italian, Mexican, seafood, steaks, and international food.

Amenities and services Beach, 3 pools, 3 hot tubs, gym, spa, massage, watersports center, tour desk, organized children's activities, shops, 4 bars/lounges, 24-hour room service, business center, Internet.

ACCOMMODATIONS

Rooms 337 rooms and suites.

All rooms AC, windows that open, ocean view, bathtub, hair dryer, safe, minibar, satellite TV, DVD, coffeemaker.

Some rooms Fan, balcony or terrace, whirlpool tub, nonsmoking, disabled access.

Comfort and decor All rooms have modern, comfortable furnishings and are decorated with bold accent colors in blue and aqua. The awesome view of gorgeous bay, rocks, and beach can be seen from every room and see-through balcony.

PAYMENT, RESERVATIONS, AND RESTRICTIONS

Deposit Credit card; 7-day cancellation policy with $45 per person fee.

Credit cards AE, MC, V.

Check-in/out noon/3 p.m.

Four Seasons $$$$$

OVERALL ★★★★★	QUALITY ★★★★★	VALUE ★★★

Punta Mita, Bahía de Banderas; ☎ 329-291-6000 or 800-819-5053 U.S. and Canada; fax 329-291-6060; www.fourseasons.com

Physically and financially removed from the hoi polloi, the Four Seasons invites the wealthy to relax here in peace. (Garden rooms start at around $630 per night; the 28% tax and service fees add up, too.) Whitewashed buildings with red-tile roofs dot the green, gracious grounds, and most rooms have at least a partial ocean view. Architect Diego Villaseñor designed the buildings in native, minimalist style so as not to compete with the natural setting. From the woven sisal rug in the huge, open-sided, palapa-roofed lobby, to bed tables and beds in the rooms and suites, the furnishings are highest quality, and often custom made. Jack Nicklaus designed the oceanfront golf course, one of Mexico's best. The top-drawer, Zen-inspired spa offers treatments geared to the location, including a tequila massage. An astonishing number of employees guarantees that guests' wishes will be granted quickly. Private villas with staff have been built on the grounds and these can be rented; guests have access to Four Seasons facilities.

SETTING AND FACILITIES

Location Punta Mita, 30 miles northwest of Puerto Vallarta, at Las Cuevas Beach.

Dining 3 restaurants (one at golf course).

Amenities and services Beach, 2 pools, hot tub, gym, spa, massage, watersports center, tour desk, shops, 2 bars, 24-hour room service, business center, Internet, golf, tennis, cultural center.

ACCOMMODATIONS

Rooms 114 rooms, 27 suites.

All rooms AC, fan, windows that open, balcony or terrace, bathtub, hair dryer, safe, minibar, coffeemaker, cable/satellite TV, high-speed Internet, DVD/CD.

Some rooms Ocean view, whirlpool tub, nonsmoking, disabled access.

Comfort and decor Luxurious yet simple and comfortable, with plush chaise lounges on terraces, and superb beds and linens

PAYMENT, RESERVATIONS, AND RESTRICTIONS

Deposit Credit card charge of 3 nights at time of reservation; 30-day (60 days for some suites) cancellation policy or pay full room rate for entire reservation period.

Credit cards AE, DC, MC, V.

Check-in/out 3 p.m./noon.

 ## Hacienda San Angel $$$$$

| OVERALL ★★★★ | QUALITY ★★★★ | VALUE ★★½ |

Calle Miramar 336; ☎ 322-222-2692, 877-278-8018 U.S., or 866-818-8342 Canada; fax 322-223-1941; www.mexicoboutiquehotels.com/sanangel

Although it looks like this elegant, endless mansion has existed forever, it's actually an amalgam of several contiguous homes that owner Janice Chatterton has acquired and meticulously reinvented. Everything is top-of-the-line, from building materials of stone, marble, and stucco to Talavera tiles, detailed masonry, and the antiques with which guest rooms and the soaring public spaces are decorated. Formal dining rooms segue with supreme nonchalance to covered gardens, a library, and a Talavera-lined swimming pool with fountain. There's a great city view from the third-story pool and most of the rooms.

SETTING AND FACILITIES

Location Downtown, 6 blocks uphill in from the boardwalk.

Dining Restaurant; dinner served anywhere on the property with advance notice; Continental breakfast and cocktail hour with hors d'ouevres included in room price.

Amenities and services Internet (free), 3 pools, hot tub, massage.

ACCOMMODATIONS

Rooms 16 suites.

All rooms Fan, windows that open, air-conditioning, minibar (customized), DVD.

Some rooms Ocean view, balcony or terrace, safe, bathtub.

Comfort and decor Guest rooms have comfortable mattresses and Egyptian cotton sheets and are individually decorated with ecclesiastic art. Most have at least one stunning bay view; the Celestial room has a thatch-roofed outdoor living room with wet bar, fountain, and awesome view of the cathedral and bay.

PAYMENT, RESERVATIONS, AND RESTRICTIONS

Deposit 1 night on credit card (nonrefundable); cancellation policy 45 days or forfeit entire fee.

Credit cards AE, MC, V.

Check-in/out 3 p.m./noon.

Hotelito Desconocido $$$$$

OVERALL ★★★★	QUALITY ★★★★	VALUE ★ ½

**Cruz de Loreto Tomatlán; ☎ 322-281-4010 or 800-728-9098 U.S.;
fax 322-281-4130; www.hotelito.com**

Looking for a kicked-back yet exclusive resort on a beautiful beach in the middle of nowhere? Look no further: this rustically charming hotel is far removed from the outside world. Rooms have no televisions or telephones, so you can just let go and relax. Because there are no other towns for miles around, you'll be eating in; the obligatory meal plan is $80 per person. Order coffee in the morning by raising a red flag (here we're being literal), after which you can head for the estuary-view restaurant for a big spread à la carte. The changing menu features mainly updated, wholesome Mexican standards. Go bird-watching, or grab a kayak and paddle. There's an extra charge for horseback riding, but windsurfing equipment, kayaks, and mountain bikes are provided at no extra charge. During late summer and fall, a turtle tour includes the liberation of tiny turtle hatchlings at sunset. Isolation and relaxation are key components of a Hotelito sojourn.

SETTING AND FACILITIES

Location Playón de Mismaloya near Cruz de Loreto, Costalegre.

Dining 2 restaurants, à la carte breakfast, set meals from a changing, mainly Mexican menu served in the restaurant-bar.

Amenities and services Beach, pool (salt water), cold-water Jacuzzi tub, spa, massage, water-sports center, tour desk, shop, 2 bars.

ACCOMMODATIONS

Rooms 16 rooms and 13 suites.

All rooms Fan, windows that open, nonsmoking.

Some rooms Ocean view, balcony or terrace, bathtub, whirlpool tub, disabled access.

Comfort and decor Small battery-powered fans cool bungalows that are architecturally styled after the native dwellings of the region. They have split-bamboo walls, plank floors, thatched roofs, unscreened porches, and open-air showers surounded by bamboo. The unique Mexican furniture and decorations are rustic but smart; beds have mosquito netting.

PAYMENT, RESERVATIONS, AND RESTRICTIONS

Deposit Credit card; 2-nights' deposit; 30-day cancellation policy.

Credit cards AE, MC, V.

Check-in/out 3 p.m./noon.

Majahuitas Resort $$$$$ (American Plan)

OVERALL ★★½	QUALITY ★½	VALUE ★★½

**Playa Majahuitas; ☎/fax 322-293-4506, 831-336-5036 U.S.;
www.majahuitas-resort.com**

This boutique hotel opened in 1996 to offer luxurious seclusion on a beautiful white-sand beach tucked into a small rocky cove. There's a radio for emergencies, but in general the idea here is to be incommunicado. Electric lights are also delightfully absent, and as dusk descends, candles and lanterns light the pathways, restaurant, and your own comfortable casita. (Bedtime readers don't despair, there are battery-powered reading lamps!) An open-air style lets nature invade your room, mostly in the form of sea breezes and gorgeous views. Lacy curtains provide privacy where needed. Some houses sit on stilts in the sand, others perch on the cliffs above. Each has a hammock hanging outside for maximum comfort. The price includes three meals and activities such as guided hikes and kayaks, but not drinks or transportation by boat from Puerto Vallarta.

SETTING AND FACILITIES

Location Playa Majahuitas, 13 miles southwest of Puerto Vallarta; accessible by boat only (15-minute ride) from Boca de Tomatlán.

Dining 3 meals included in price. Most people take breakfast and lunch at small tables tucked around property and sit together for a family-style dinner. Food is mostly Mexican and international, emphasizing fresh seafood and produce grown onsite.

Amenities and services Beach, pool with wading pool, massage.

ACCOMMODATIONS

Rooms 8 casitas.

All rooms Ocean view, windows that open, balcony or terrace, fan; no TV, telephone, or electrical outlets.

Comfort and decor Whitewashed walls, wood or tile floors, and exposed-beam ceilings with thatch or tile roofs. Some have an outdoor bathroom with pebble mosaic walls, others use a large rock itself as part of the structure. Mexican art and handicrafts decorate the rooms.

PAYMENT, RESERVATIONS, AND RESTRICTIONS

Deposit Credit card; 7-day cancellation policy (varies with season).

Credit cards AE, MC, V.

Check-in/out Flexible.

Marriott Casa Magna $$$$

OVERALL ★★★½	QUALITY ★★★½	VALUE ★★★★

Paseo de la Marina 5; ☎ 322-226-0000 or 800-223-6388 U.S. and Canada; fax 322-226-0060; www.casamagnapuertovallarta.com

Like the other hotels in the Marriott chain, this one has vast, elegant public spaces; the lobby gleams with marble. Rooms combine comfortable furnishings with lots of little things that add to guests' comfort level—like alarm clocks and voicemail. The enormous pool, surrounded by lacy palms, overlooks the beach where there's parasailing, volleyball, and other activities. It's walking distance (about a mile) from the marina and the shops, restaurants, and bars that surround it, and about a $10 cab ride into downtown Puerto Vallarta.

SETTING AND FACILITIES

Location Marina Vallarta on Playa Salado.

Dining 4 restaurants, including Mikado, serving good Japanese food.

Amenities and services Pool, 2 bars, hot tub, spa, gym, sauna, 3 tennis courts, 24-hour room service, beach, concierge, meeting rooms, babysitting, kids' programs, car rental, Wi-Fi.

ACCOMMODATIONS

Rooms 404 rooms, 29 suites.

All rooms Air-conditioning, windows that open, balcony, bathtub, hair dryer, safe, minibar, cable/satellite TV, coffeemaker, Wi-Fi.

Some rooms Ocean view, refrigerator, hot tub, nonsmoking rooms, several rooms for disabled guests.

Comfort and decor Comfortable furnishings and beds, sliding-glass doors that open to the ocean breeze, desks with reading lamps facilitate working vacations.

PAYMENT, RESERVATIONS, AND RESTRICTIONS

Deposit Credit card; 7-day cancellation policy.

Credit cards AE, MC, V.

Check-in/out 4 p.m./noon.

 Quinta María Cortez $$–$$$

| OVERALL ★★★ | QUALITY ★★★½ | VALUE ★★★★ |

Calle Sagitario 132; ☎ 322-221-5317 or 888-640-8100 U.S.; fax in U.S. 801-531-1633; www.quinta-maria.com

Charming and eclectic describe the seven unique apartments overlooking a rocky cove and small beach. Each is creatively decorated, and several have been used as backgrounds for fashion shoots and movies. We love the Quinta Maria because all of the suites are quirky and comfortable, and truly make you feel that you're in a beachfront home rather than in a hotel. The common sitting area has an ocean view and fireplace, but no TV (no TVs in the rooms either). To maintain the calm ambience, younger children are not generally permitted at Quinta María Cortez, although families can rent one of three villas next door at Casa Tres Vidas.

SETTING AND FACILITIES

Location Playa Conchas Chinas, south of PV.

Dining Breakfast included in room rate; otherwise, no restaurant.

Amenities and services Pool, beach, Internet, Wi-Fi (common areas only).

ACCOMMODATIONS

Rooms 7 suites, 3 villas.

All rooms Fan, windows that open, ocean view, balcony or terrace, bathtub, hair dryer, safe, coffeemaker.

Some rooms AC, kitchenette.

Comfort and decor Most suites have rooms at different levels, and each has a wonderful if slightly cluttered, homey feel.

PAYMENT, RESERVATIONS, AND RESTRICTIONS

Deposit 1 night's nonrefundable deposit; full payment due 30 days before arrival; 50% charge for cancellations 7 to 30 days prior; otherwise no refund.

Credit cards AE, MC, V.

Check-in/out 3 p.m./noon.

 Sol Meliá Puerto Vallarta **$$$$ (all-inclusive)**

OVERALL ★★★	QUALITY ★★½	VALUE ★★★★½

Paseo de la Marina Sur 7; ☎ 322-226-3000 or 800-336-3542; fax 322-226-3030; www.solmelia.com

A huge all-inclusive near the golf course in Marina Vallarta, this megaresort is spread over many acres and may require a lot of walking, despite the elevators. Rooms are ample and simply decorated in a low-key palette that doesn't distract from the beauty just beyond the sliding-glass doors. Two children age 6 or under stay free stay free with parents, and that includes meals and plentiful activities for small kids. The many conference and meeting rooms are often used for private gatherings, such as family reunions and wedding receptions, as well as business meetings. Set amid the well-crafted grounds is a humongous free-form pool with swim-up bar and two attached hot tubs. There is a wealth of activities, classes, professional entertainment, and free equipment for guests to choose from, and almost all are included in the room price. This beach was reduced by Hurricane Kenna and has rocks mixed in with grainy sand—not PV's best. Excellent all-inclusive rates make this a good choice for families looking for quality time together; the all-inclusive rate for kids ages 12 to 7 is just $44 per night.

SETTING AND FACILITIES

Location On the beach; middle of Marina Vallarta.

Dining 4 restaurants, including à la carte and buffet.

Amenities and services Beach, pool, 2 hot tubs, gym, massage, water-sports center, tour desk, organized children's activities (ages 4 months and up), shop, 3 bars, room service, Internet, Wi-Fi (lobby only).

ACCOMMODATIONS

Rooms 356 rooms, 4 suites.

All rooms AC, windows that open, balcony or terrace, bathtub, hair dryer, safe, refrigerator, cable/satellite TV.

Some rooms Ocean view, nonsmoking, disabled access.

Comfort and decor Basic, comfortable, spacious rooms with a muted color scheme.

PAYMENT, RESERVATIONS, AND RESTRICTIONS

Deposit Reserve with credit card; 72-hour cancellation policy.

Credit cards AE, MC, V.

Check-in/out 3 p.m./noon.

Los Arcos Suites $$

OVERALL ★★	QUALITY ★½	VALUE ★★★★

Manuel M. Dieguez 164, Col. E. Zapata; ☎ 322-226-7101, 800-648-2403 U.S., or 888-729-9590 Canada; fax 322-226-7104; www.playalosarcos.com

This L-shaped, four-story property is the place for independent travelers happy to trade immediate beach access and views for proximity to downtown PV's happenin' shopping and dining scene. Rates are great but tend to change month to month in the higher season. Across the street from the beach, these are comfortable—but not luxurious or arty—lodgings above the second floor that enjoy either a view of the street scene or pool area; from some you can see the ocean beyond. Many amenities such as hot tub, spa, restaurant, lively bar, and travel services are available at the busier, noisier, beach-facing sister property, Los Arcos, across the street.

unofficial **TIP**
Be aware that there's a central phone and fax number for all three, and be sure to book The Suites and make sure the cabbie delivers you there. Kitchenettes come with toaster, two-burner stove, dishes, and a small refrigerator.

SETTING AND FACILITIES

Location Olas Altas, the Heart of the Romantic Zone.

Dining No restaurant or bar, but the area is restaurant heaven.

Amenities and services Beach (at sister property across the street), restaurant, room service, pool, spa, Wi-Fi (lobby only).

ACCOMMODATIONS

Rooms 44 suites.

All rooms Air-conditioning, windows that open, kitchenette, balcony, bathtub, hair dryer, safe, refrigerator, cable TV, coffeemaker.

Some rooms Ocean view (partial).

Comfort and decor Standard hotel decor; upper-story suites get a good breeze. Regular suites have separate bedroom with door (and cost just a few dollars more); junior suites do not. Rooms overlooking the heated pool have smaller balconies but are quieter than street-facing rooms.

PAYMENT, RESERVATIONS, AND RESTRICTIONS

Deposit 1 night on credit card; 3-day cancellation policy.

Credit cards AE, MC, V.

Check-in/out 2 p.m./noon.

Velas Vallarta $$$$$ (all-inclusive)

OVERALL ★★★★	QUALITY ★★★★	VALUE ★★★★

Avenida Costera s/n, Marina Vallarta; ☎ 322-221-0091 or 866-847-4609 U.S. and Canada; fax 322-221-0755; www.velasvallarta.com

One of three beautiful PV Velas properties, this one offers the most bang for your vacation bucks. Located in the Marina district, it's a great area for biking, blading, or walking and about equidistant from downtown Vallarta

How Restaurants Compare in Puerto Vallarta

RESTAURANT	CUISINE	COST	OVERALL	QUALITY	VALUE
Trio	Mediterranean	Mod/Exp	★★★★½	★★★★★	★★★★
El Arrayán	Traditional Mexican	Mod	★★★½	★★★★	★★½
Café des Artistes	Eclectic	Exp	★★★★	★★★★	★★★
Restaurant Frankfurt	German/international	Mod	★★★★	★★★★	★★★★
Mariscos Tino's	Seafood	Mod	★★★½	★★★★	★★★★
Daiquiri Dick's	International	Exp	★★★★½	★★★★★	★★★★
Chico's Paradise	Mexican/seafood	Mod	★★	★★	★★½
La Marisma Fish Taco	Seafood	Inexp (I and II)	★★	★★★	★★★★½

and Nuevo Vallarta. Everything about the beachfront property is done on a grand scale, and textures are varied but all are natural: rough rock, smooth glass and marble, well-oiled teak. Tropical plants add color and scent. Rooms (studio-size through three-bedroom suites) are vast and airy and have fully stocked kitchenettes; the smaller ones don't have a balcony or a view. Living rooms have bright, modern, comfortable built-in couches, multiple ceiling fans, and a round glass dining table between it and the kitchenette. Flat-screen TVs finish the modern picture.

SETTING AND FACILITIES

Location Marina Vallarta.

Dining 3 restaurants; all-inclusive, buffet or à la carte. La Ribera for Mexican cuisine and Andrea for Italian (the latter must be reserved ahead).

Amenities and services Beach, spa, gym, hot tub, marina, 3 pools, 2 bars, 24-hour room service, shop, tour desk, kids' programs (ages 5–12), Internet, Wi-Fi.

ACCOMMODATIONS

Rooms 339 suites.

All rooms AC, fans, windows that open, bathtub, hair dryer, safe, minibar, coffeemaker, cable/satellite TV.

Some rooms Balcony or terrace, kitchenettes, hot tub, ocean view, nonsmoking.

Comfort and decor Rooms are casually elegant with an understated, modern Mexican theme, comfortable built-in couches, ceiling fans, and a pillow menu.

PAYMENT, RESERVATIONS, AND RESTRICTIONS

Deposit First night charge for guarantee; 14-day cancellation policy.

Credit cards AE, MC, V.

Check-in/out 3 p.m./noon.

WHERE *to* EAT *in* PUERTO VALLARTA

IF YOU LIKE TO EAT WELL, Puerto Vallarta is the destination for you. PV is known for its many fine restaurants that serve a variety of cuisines, including Italian, French, and Pan-Asian, in addition to the typical Mexican and seafood. Although the finer dining spots aren't cheap, lots of competition generally keeps prices in line. Shorts, T-shirts, and flip-flops are common attire at the less-elegant establishment, including a handful of places south of town where guests can sunbathe and swim in river-fed pools both

 unofficial **TIP**
The less-publicized, two-week May Food Festival offers three-course meals at a dozen great restaurants for $15 or $25 a pop. This is a good time to visit PV's priciest restaurants such as Cafe des Artistes.

before and after they dine. These jungle eateries include **Chico's Paradise** (Highway 200 Km 20; ☎ 322-223-6005) and **El Edén** (several miles inland on dirt road from Playa de Mismaloya; no phone).

The popular nine-day **Festival Gourmet International in Puerto Vallarta and Nayarit** has been held in mid-November since 1995. Each year, 20 or more guest chefs from different countries converge on the city to offer cooking lessons, wine tastings, and special menus for festival guests. For more information, call ☎ 322-222-2247 or visit **www.festivalgourmet.com**.

RESTAURANT PROFILES

 El Arrayán ★★★½

TRADITIONAL MEXICAN	MODERATE	QUALITY ★★★★	VALUE ★★½

Downtown Puerto Vallarta; Allende 344 at Miramar;
☎ **322-222-7195**

Reservations Recommended.

Entree range $15–$25.

Payment MC, V.

Service rating ★★★.

Parking Street.

Bar Specializing in Mexican liqueurs and tequilas.

Dress Casual.

Disabled access Yes.

Customers Repeat customers who love the homey ambience and traditional Mexican dishes with a modern twist.

Hours Wednesday–Monday, 6–11 p.m.; closed August.

SETTING AND ATMOSPHERE Casual, comfortable dining on the interior veranda of an old Puerto Vallarta home, with Huichol Indian art on the walls.

HOUSE SPECIALTIES Old-fashioned Mexican recipes such as *abuela* (grandma) used to make, not the U.S. version.

SUMMARY AND COMMENTS Very popular with foreigners, this small, inviting downtown dining room offers Mexican comfort food. Black-bean soup, *pozole* (hominy soup), beef-tip tacos, and ceviche of fish or scallops exemplify the abbreviated menu. Traditional ingredients you'll find here include the mild, green vegetable *chayote*, cactus pads, fresh white cheese, sesame seeds, and local herbs like *hoja santa* that can be found at most any marketplace in Mexico.

Café des Artistes   ★★★★

ECLECTIC	EXPENSIVE	QUALITY ★★★★	VALUE ★★★

Downtown Puerto Vallarta; Guadalupe Sánchez 740; ☎ 322-222-3228

Reservations Recommended.

Entree range $19–$40.

Payment AE, MC, V.

Service rating ★★★½.

Bar Full service bar, expanded wine list, lots of aperitifs, and various after-dinner coffee drinks.

Parking Valet.

Dress Dressy–elegant casual.

Disabled access None.

Customers Travelers, local bigwigs.

Hours Café des Artistes: nightly, 6–11:30 p.m.; Cocina de Autor: Monday–Saturday, 6–11; closed September.

SETTING AND ATMOSPHERE Romantic music; two delightful outdoor gardens; restrained elegance in Cocina de Autor.

HOUSE SPECIALTIES Cream of prawn and pumpkin soup, Kobe beef with horseradish and mild *pasilla* chile sauce.

SUMMARY AND COMMENTS Chef-owner Thierry Blouet prides himself on his original recipes combining New and Old World ingredients: think gazpacho with achiote and avocado cream. Many repeat Vallarta visitors wouldn't dream of missing the innovative dishes served on the scrumptious, multilevel garden or the cool interior space, which is mainly white on white. At the upstairs Cocina de Autor Thierry Blouet, diners choose three- to five-course bistro menus, with or without wine pairings; the decor in the 40-person upstairs dining room is exclusive and subdued. Guests from either restaurant can repair after dinner to the cigar room for smokes and after-dinner drinks. Constantini Wine Bar offers nearly 50 vintages by the glass and often has live music. There's a Thursday wine tasting at 6 p.m.

Chico's Paradise ★★

MEXICAN/SEAFOOD	MODERATE	QUALITY ★★	VALUE ★★

South of downtown, near Boca de Tomatlán; Carretera a Manzanillo Km 20, La Junta; ☎ 322-223-6005

Reservations Suggested for groups.

Entree range $11–$29.

Payment Cash only.

Service rating ★★★★.

Parking Small lot.

Bar Full service, with a fine selection of refreshing tropical drinks made with or without liquor.

Dress Casual; bathing suits acceptable.

Disabled access None.

Customers Mexican and international travelers.

Hours Daily, 10 a.m.–6 p.m.

SETTING AND ATMOSPHERE Multiple levels of tables with bright Mexican cloths overlook the Horcones River, which forms small falls and bathing pools. Hiking trails head into the hills from here, too.

HOUSE SPECIALTIES *Mariscada paraíso,* a mixed seafood grill for two people.

SUMMARY AND COMMENTS Pull up a leather chair, order a massive margarita, and prepare to spend hours here in Chico's Paradise. The food is just average; most dishes come with rice, steamed veggies, and bread, some with yummy black beans. The main reason to come is to combine dining al fresco with playing in the rocky river. Bring your swimsuit and, waiting the requisite half-hour after stuffing yourself with seafood or a massive burrito, splash about in one of a series of pools. The restaurant has expanded over the years to accommodate groups, and there are even shops selling souvenirs and sunscreen. There's an 11-line canopy tour and horseback riding, too.

 Daiquiri Dick's ★★★★½

INTERNATIONAL	EXPENSIVE	QUALITY ★★★★★	VALUE ★★★★

Los Muertos Beach; Olas Altas 314; ☎ 322-222-0566

Reservations Recommended in high season.

Entree range $15–$26.

Payment MC, V.

Service rating ★★★★.

Parking Street.

Bar Full service, wines, and daiquiris.

Dress Resort casual.

Disabled access None.

Customers Locals and travelers.

Hours Daily, 9 a.m.–10:30 p.m.; closed Tuesdays May–August and September.

SETTING AND ATMOSPHERE The beach and palm trees are the most important elements of the restaurant's decor, whether you're on the outdoor patio (closed during the wet summer season) or in the open-sided dining room.

unofficial **TIP**
Light eaters can make a meal of the shrimp-taco appetizer. Nothing could be tastier, and for small appetites, they make a perfect meal.

HOUSE SPECIALTIES Fish on a stick; shrimp tacos with hollandaise sauce. Changing daily chef's specials— at least one different appetizer, soup, and main dish each day

SUMMARY AND COMMENTS A busy outdoor patio overlooks the action on Playa de los Muertos. Inside, the setting is equally unadorned, with nothing to distract from the delicious food. There's no air-conditioning, but fresh breezes blow throw the beachfront bistro, and overhead fans swirl the air about agreeably. A variety of fresh fish filets are offered, including tuna, sea bass, and red snapper in a slightly piquant sauce. The popular shrimp tacos come in a flour tortilla with a side dish of guacamole. For dessert, you can't beat the caramelized-pear pot pie. Their signature drink is actually a handcrafted margarita with Cointreau and good tequila; among many daiquiris offered, strawberry, banana, and a blend of the two flavors are the best.

Restaurant Frankfurt ★★★★

GERMAN/INTERNATIONAL	MODERATE	QUALITY ★★★★	VALUE ★★★★

Col. E. Zapata; Basilio Badillo 378; ☎ 322-222-2071

Reservations Recommended in high season.

Entree range $12–$18.

Payment Cash only.

Service rating ★★★★.

Bar Full bar with 20 different beers, including German labels.

Parking Street.

Dress Casual.

Disabled access Yes.

Customers Locals and travelers looking for good value and tasty food.

Hours Monday–Saturday 11:30 a.m.–11:30 p.m.

SETTING AND ATMOSPHERE Inside it's a classic European farm-style restaurant with warm, faux painted gold walls, acid-washed concrete floors, and brick arches. Outdoors is a garden patio with outdoor barbecue.

HOUSE SPECIALTIES Cut-like-butter pork chops with spaetzle and warm sweet red cabbage; classic schnitzel.

SUMMARY AND COMMENTS Maybe you didn't come to Mexico to eat German food, so work into the idea slowly over a thinly sliced mahimahi carpaccio. Follow with a goat-cheese salad—Mexico has plenty of goats, no? By then you'll be hooked. Most of the moderately priced main dishes come with a choice of spatzle, French fries, country fries, or sauerkraut. Between Easter and mid-October 15, take advantage of the inexpensive dinner special where you can choose one of three starters, mains, and desserts.

La Marisma Fish Taco (I and II) ★★

SEAFOOD	INEXPENSIVE	QUALITY ★★★	VALUE ★★★★½

**Location I: corner of Naranjo and Venustiano Carranza,
Col. E. Zapata, no phone
Location II: Condominios Marina del Rey, behind Plaza Neptuno,
Marina Vallarta; ☎ 322-221-2884**

Reservations Not commonly accepted.

Entree range $5–$7; most items are à la carte.

Payment No credit cards.

Service rating ★★★.

Parking Marina–shopping center parking lot; street parking.

Bar None.

Dress Casual as can be.

Disabled access None.

Customers People looking for great seafood in a supercasual setting.

Hours *Marisma Fish Taco I:* Tuesday–Sunday, 10 a.m.–5 p.m.; *Marisma Fish Taco II:* Tuesday–Sunday, 11 a.m.–7 p.m.

SETTING AND ATMOSPHERE Marisma Fish Taco I: streetside taco stand with six wooden stools. Marisma Fish Taco II: open-sided, no air-conditioning, patio-style, no-frills dining area with white plastic tables and chairs and lazily rotating ceiling fans.

HOUSE SPECIALTIES Fish tacos, shrimp tacos, shrimp quesadillas.

SUMMARY AND COMMENTS This isn't the place to take your sweetie when you want to pop the question. But we thought you might want to know about PV's most delicious fish tacos. Order as many as you like, and doctor the battered-, deep-fried fish on a hot corn tortilla with condiments to taste: green guacamole, shredded cabbage, a squeeze of lime, and a big dollop of any salsa, from fiery to mild. Other dishes include delicious shrimp quesadillas, shrimp burgers, fruit plates, and beef burgers with fries. (The taco-stand location in Old Vallarta has a more limited menu.) The tortillas are handmade as you order, and recipes are written at the bottom of the menus. At the Plaza Neptuno location, cold beer can be made to appear, although it's not on the menu.

Mariscos Tino's ★★★½

| SEAFOOD MODERATE | QUALITY ★★★★ | VALUE ★★★★ |

Nuevo Vallarta; Boulevard Nayarit 393; ☎ 322-297-0221. The original location is in Pitillal, a Vallarta suburb (Avenida 333 at Calle Revolución; ☎ 322-224-5584; also Punta Mita's El Anclote 64; ☎ 329-291-6473)

Reservations Accepted.

Entree range $10–$20.

Payment MC, V.

Service rating ★★★★.

Bar Full service.

Parking Lot.

Dress Anything reasonable goes, although Mexican clients will dress up.

Disabled access In the restaurant, yes.

Customers Local businessmen, ladies who lunch, locals celebrating special occasions; tourists from Nuevo Vallarta and Marina Vallarta.

Hours Daily, noon–9:30 p.m.

SETTING AND ATMOSPHERE Casual yet festive alfresco dining room overlooking the Ameca River. Architects have positioned the dining room around several gnarly old trees.

HOUSE SPECIALTIES *Pescado sarandeado,* a regional presentation of butterflied red snapper rubbed with salt and herbs and cooked over charcoal.

SUMMARY AND COMMENTS Lively and unpretentious, this riverside restaurant is always abuzz at lunchtime and more mellow in the evening. A platoon of experienced waiters is on hand to greet patrons warmly and make sure plates are cleared and things running smoothly. This is the place to venture beyond ceviche and shrimp cocktail and simple fillets and try some of the restaurant's signature dishes, including *pescado sarandeado* grilled over charcoal, crab or smoked marlin tacos, shrimp empanadas, and coconut shrimp.

Trio ★★★★½

| MEDITERRANEAN MODERATE/EXPENSIVE | QUALITY ★★★★½ | VALUE ★★★ |

Guerrero 264, downtown; ☎ 322-222-2196

Reservations Recommended.

Entree range $13–$27.

Payment AE, MC, V.

Service rating ★★★½.

Parking 3-hour courtesy parking at Parque Juárez.

Bar Full service.

Dress Resort casual.

Disabled access Yes.

Customers Loyal following of local businesspeople and travelers.

Hours Daily, 6–11:30 p.m.

SETTING AND ATMOSPHERE Lovely old, two-story home often described as southern European in feel, with an intimate outdoor garden.

HOUSE SPECIALTIES Dishes are built around olive oil, fresh herbs, and locally grown produce. Locals yelp if rack of lamb with ragout disappears from the menu.

SUMMARY AND COMMENTS This is the favorite restaurant of many Puerto Vallarta residents because the setting is cozy yet elegant, and the food is consistently five-star. Organic and locally grown produce is used whenever possible, and most of the dishes reflect Mediterranean and European recipes with Mexican accents. Even standard entrees like oven-roasted rabbit and pan-roasted sea bass get a wonderful, unforgettable treatment from chef Bernhard Guth, born and raised in Germany and with culinary credentials from Italy to New York and co-chef-owner Ulf Henrickkson, of Sweden.

SIGHTSEEING *in* PUERTO VALLARTA

PUERTO VALLARTA'S MOST ARDENT ADMIRERS return year after year because the destination offers so much. At **Los Muertos Beach** downtown, multihued parasails hover high above speedboats, and the water is full of banana boats, personal watercraft, kayaks, and other toys. Restaurants and bars line the beach, vendors stroll the sand selling everything from kinda-cold Cokes to tamales, handcrafts to hair braiding.

From the Los Muertos public dock (and from Boca de Tomatlán and the pier near Hotel Rosita, at the north end of the *malecón*), water taxis depart for the more isolated hamlets and beaches to the south: **Playa Las Animas, Quimixto, Majahuitas,** and **Yelapa.** North of downtown, the hotel zone is fronted by water toys for rent, while the hotel restaurants lining the beach provide food and refreshments in the shade when the tropical sun begins to scorch. (The beach there isn't as pretty as it was since Hurricane Kenna swamped it, replacing some of the sand with fist-size rocks.) Although its beaches are less spectacular than those to the north and south, the quiet streets and sidewalks of the **Marina Vallarta** development make it a great place to walk or bike ride, and the marina itself has a good number and variety of shops and restaurants.

Entering Nayarit state, but still on **Banderas Bay** are the more self-contained, mainly all-inclusive beach hotels of **Nuevo Vallarta,** at the mouth of the **Ameca River.** En route to the end of the bay at **Punta Mita** are a series of ever-popular small towns, beaches, and coves, all rarely crowded except perhaps on weekends, when families come to spend some quality time together. This area is booming, and tourism pundits are putting on paper and breaking ground on multimillion-dollar residential and hotel projects that will significantly change this stretch of coast.

ATTRACTIONS

IN ADDITION TO ADVENTURE TREKS into the surrounding hills, bay tours, deep-sea fishing, and other aquatic sports, the place to stroll and sightsee is **Old Vallarta.** Rather than touring museums, the fun here is strolling around while admiring the architecture and the exuberant tropical flowers spilling over garden walls. Combine your stroll with shopping, snacking, and stopping for refreshments for maximum enjoyment. In the heart of downtown, the *malecón* (waterfront walkway) is a great place to pause to watch the people and sea, and to enjoy numerous whimsical statues done by some of PV's premier artists. If you tire of the bustle and hype, head four or more blocks inland to see some older homes and locals' haunts.

Adjacent to the *malecón* is the main square, the **Plaza de Armas** (Calles Zaragoza and Juárez), and the town's open-air amphitheater, **Los Arcos.** Walk to the back of the main plaza to the pretty **Iglesia de Nuestra Señora de Guadalupe,** with its distinctive, delicate crown (said to be a replica of that of the Empress Carlota, wife of Maximilian) atop the church's tall bell tower.

unofficial **TIP**
The neighborhood in the hills behind downtown is called **Gringo Gulch** for the number of wealthy North Americans who bought property here after Taylor and Burton made it the hip thing to do.

For a house and garden tour of several Vallarta villas, arrive at the **Hotel Posada del Río Cuale** (Calle Agustín Serdán 242; ☎ 322-222-1957) at 10:30 a.m. Wednesday and/or Thursday (high season only, mid-November through April). Organized by the International Friendship Club ☎ 322-222-5466, the $30 tour leaves promptly at 11 a.m.; the money benefits local charities.

Open year-round daily except Mondays, the **Puerto Vallarta Botanical Gardens** (Carretera a Barra Km 24, Las Juntas; ☎ 322-223-6182; **www.vallartabotanicalgardensac.org**) has thousands of varieties of plants and is home to brilliant butterflies and flowers. Entrance is just $3. There's an orchid house and trails leading off into the jungle; bug repellent is a must for an enjoyable day. Bring your bathing suit and spend some quality time at the river here, or have a meal in the pleasant second-story restaurant overlooking the property. It's an expensive taxi ride (about $30), but you can catch an "El Tuito" bus for less than a dollar at the corner of Calles Aguacate and Carranza, in the Romantic Zone. The bus will stop along the highway for the return trip.

Owned by artist and entrepreneur Jorge Rubio, **Terra Noble** (Tulipanes 595, Fraccionamiento Lomas de Terra Noble; ☎ 322-223-3530; **www.terranoble.com**) is a day spa (closed Sunday) offering massage, facials, manicures and pedicures, and body treatments; it's also a venue for *temazcal* sweat lodge ceremonies, weddings, and workshops. The lodge's buildings combine African and American indigenous building techniques, including the use of adobe, palm fronds, and stone—as well as recycled aluminum cans and old tires.

Vallarta Adventures' Dolphin Adventure (Boulevard de Nayarit s/n, Nuevo Vallarta Marina; ☎ 322-297-1212, ext. 3; 888-303-2653 U.S. and Canada; **www.vallarta-adventures.com**) gives cetacean-lovers the chance to pet and even smooch one or more of a dozen Pacific bottlenose dolphins. Who knows how the dolphins feel about this encounter, but most humans love it. About $80 (price for adults) gets you into waist-deep water with the dolphins; $100 lets you swim with your adorable cetaceans. Arrangements should be made at least a day ahead of time. The center is open daily.

kids **Wildlife Connection** (Francia 140, Departamento 7, Col. Versalles; ☎ 322-225-3621; **www.wildlifeconnection.com**) offers boat trips ($65 per person, about four hours) to find and interact with dolphins in the wild. Kids' price is half the adult price.

unofficial **TIP**
Most dolphin pods permit guests to get right in the water with them, but there are no guarantees.

kids **Sea Life Park** (Carretera a Tepic Km 155, across from entrance to Nuevo Vallarta; ☎ 866-393-5158 (U.S.), 866-793-1905 (Canada), 800-727-5391 (Mexico); **www.sealife parkvallarta.com**) is a water park with slides and swimming pools, a water-recreation area for small fry, and restaurant. But the park's emphasis is on the interactive dolphin experience and reservations should be made ahead of time through one of their toll-free numbers. The park is open daily between 10 a.m. and 5 p.m.; admission is $18 for adults and $14 for kids unless you're booking dolphin encounters, in which case entrance to the park is included in the price.

TOURS *and* SIDE TRIPS *from* PUERTO VALLARTA

MOST PEOPLE TAKE A BOAT TOUR, which shows them at least a slice of PV's enormous bay. Sunset cruises are popular, and most offer drinks, snacks, or dinner and dancing. In general, the more passengers the boat carries, the cheaper the fare.

Other bay tours focus on sailing, whale- and turtle-watching, and snorkel and dive trips to the **Marieta Islands** (off the northern tip of **Banderas Bay**), **Los Arcos** (for snorkeling or day or night diving), and the artificial reef at **Las Caletas. Vallarta Adventures** (see below) operates a romantic dinner cruise, "Rhythms of the Night," to **La Caleta,** where film director John Huston had his home. Passengers cruise to the rocky cove and disembark on a moonlit beach for dinner followed by a contemporary dance show in the open-air amphitheater. (Sometimes the dance comes first, making a bit of a wait for dinner.) It's touristy yes, but also an enjoyable night out on the water and the beach and the food served is surprisingly good. Their day trip is great too, offering kayaking, snorkeling, and a yummy lunch.

Sailboat cruises are available by day or night. With fewer passengers (usually between 12 and 20), this is a somewhat more luxurious way to tour, and passengers have more say about where they cruise. You can help the crew, fish, or just relax and work on your tan. Sunset sailing cruises are also available. This tour is available through several companies, including **Vallarta Adventures** (Edificio Marina Golf, Local 13-C, Calle Mástil, Marina Vallarta, and Avenida Las Palmas 39, Nuevo Vallarta; ☎ 322-297-1212 or 888-303-2653 U.S. and Canada; **www.vallarta-adventures.com**), one of Vallarta's most comprehensive tour companies.

unofficial **TIP**
Plan to get an early start, as the sea is less choppy before early afternoon, and most trips set out in the morning.

Other offerings through Vallarta Adventures include a van trip to the small mountain town of **San Sebastián del Oeste** for $80 (offered by other operators as well; see "San Sebastián del Oeste," right).

Along with other boating and fishing operators, **Ecotours** (Vallarta 243, Col. E. Zapata; ☎ 322-222-6606; **www.ecotoursvallarta.com**) offers very popular whale-sighting tours during the winter months. Humpbacks and their young are easily spotted in the bay. It's an especially dramatic moment when the gargantuan animals breach—hauling themselves partly or entirely out of the water despite their great tonnage. Dolphins can often be seen surfing the bow wake and doing some of their own acrobatics; with luck, killer whales, false killer whales, or Brydes whales can also be spotted. Ecotours also offers bird-watching tours in several different ecosystems as well as kayaking, hiking, and, depending on the time of year, turtle or other nature-oriented programs.

More than a half dozen canopy tours operate in Vallarta. The jungle scenery and abundant natural rivers makes this a magical place to zip along from platform to platform. Vallarta Adventures (see above for contact info) is recommended for those staying north of PV proper. Those staying in Old Vallarta may prefer the tour at El Edén (Calle Vallarta 228-Int.; ☎ 322-222-2516; **www.canopyeleden .com**). This jungly area was the set of the movie *Predator* with Arnold Schwarzenegger, and you can see some of the memorabilia. Zip lines cross the Mismaloya River several times; afterward you can bathe in the river or have a snack at the onsite bar-restaurant.

SAN SEBASTIÁN DEL OESTE

 San Sebastián del Oeste IS A 17TH-CENTURY MINING TOWN at about 7,000 feet above sea level. Since the mines gave out around the time of the Mexican Revolution, the population has shrunk to fewer than 1,000 people. Isolated from the modern world by a treacherous dirt road winding through the mountains, San Sebastián has maintained its charming and unique village appeal and is today accessible by a paved road. This journey provides a respite from coastal heat and a glimpse both into the state's fabulous mountain scenery and picturesque small-town life. Area tour operators make the trip by van (**Vallarta Adventures;** see below), horse (**Rancho El Charro;** see page 282), or ATV (through **Wild Vallarta,** Manuel M. Dieguez 274; ☎ 222-8928). (You can also drive up on your own for the day or overnight excursion. However this journey is not recommended during the rainy season, as mudslides are a problem.)

Once in San Sebastián, you'll walk around town, visit a family's home, and enjoy a meal of regional food at an old hacienda. **Vallarta Adventures** (Edificio Marina Golf, Local 13-C, Calle Mástil, Marina Vallarta, ☎ 322-221-0836; or in Nuevo Vallarta, Avenida Las Palmas 39, ☎ 329-297-1212; **www.vallarta-adventures.com**) offers a full-day tour for $80 per person. Similar trips are sometimes offered to slightly larger towns such as **Mascota** and **Talpa;** the latter draws some 4 million visitors a year to see the town's miracle-working Virgin of Talpa, enshrined in its Gothic-style basilica.

EXERCISE *and* RECREATION *in* PUERTO VALLARTA

THERE'S SO MUCH TO DO IN PUERTO VALLARTA, and a seemingly endless numbers of beaches on which to do it. (See the introduction to this chapter and "Sightseeing in Puerto Vallarta," page 275, for detailed descriptions of area beaches and their attractions.) Water taxis travel daily between Boca de Tomatlán, south of town (and at least once or twice from the Hotel Rosita pier and the pier at Los Muertos Beach) and the lovely beaches to the south. Less isolated than before and now offering a smattering of services and creature comforts, they are nonetheless worth exploring by off-the-beaten-trackers. Some services, such as equipment rental and parasailing, are not offered during low season or inclement weather.

Las Animas is the first beach you'll reach as you travel south from downtown. Restaurants on the sand serve fish caught fresh by local anglers. Personal watercraft can be rented, and *pangas* pull parasailers and water-skiers to and fro. **Quimixto** is a pretty place to dive—sea turtles and fish mingle with other marine life amid the coral and underwater cliffs of **Quimixto Coves.** Snorkelers hug the rocky shore. Rent horses for a ride into the foothills; the usual destination is a waterfall-fed pool that, especially in and around the wet season, is deep and perfect for a swim. Eateries on the beach sell simply prepared fish plates and Mexican snacks like enchiladas and quesadillas. Boat tours disembark here to snorkel, swim, and sun.

The home of small, exclusive Majahuitas Resort, **Majahuitas** is often visited by day cruises catering to snorkelers but there aren't any services, such as restrooms, except for hotel guests.

kids Farthest south, pretty **Yelapa** has parasailing and *pangas* for rent, as well as restaurants on the beach and its own jungle waterfall (dry in winter and spring).

unofficial **TIP**
Simple accommodations here provide an escape valve for those who can't bear to head back to civilization.

At the northern end of the palm-fringed cove, romantically rustic accommodations are available at **Lagunita Yelapa** (☎ 322-209-5056; **www.hotel-lagunita.com**). The hotel's restaurant is right on the beach. A member of Mexico Boutique Hotels, **Verana** offers pastoral elegance at a higher price, November through June. Along with an outstanding view, the eight-room, adults-only property has a stream-fed swimming pool, full-service spa, and an obligatory meal plan ($80 per person per night). There's a five-night minimum stay. For information and reservations call toll-free from the United States or Canada (☎ 800-728-9098; **www.mexicoboutiquehotels.com/verana**). Beyond Yelapa, **Pisota** is known for its clean water and white sand. It's most often visited by people spending several days in one of these seaside hamlets.

Between these beaches and downtown PV, **Mismaloya Beach** (of *Night of the Iguana* fame) has been taken over by the large La Jolla de Mismaloya Hotel, and Hurricane Kenna stole a lot of its sand. Although less inviting than before, Mismaloya offers water-sports equipment and *pangas* for rent on the beach or through waterfront restaurants. Snorkeling and diving gear can be rented from Chico's Dive Shop (in front of La Jolla de Mismaloya hotel, ☎ 322-228-0248), which also leads diving expeditions.

Not far south, the **Horcones River** runs down to meet the sea. As well as a popular restaurant, **Chico's Paradise** (Highway 200 Km 20; ☎ 322-223-6005, see "Where to Eat in Puerto Vallarta," page 271) is a great place to spend a morning or afternoon bathing in the rocky pools and small waterfalls formed by the river as it flows toward the sea.

GOLF

PRICES ARE FOR HIGH SEASON, morning hours. Expect discounts during the rainy season and for twilight golf, after 2 p.m. or so. The 18-hole, par-72 **Flamingos** course (Carretera Federal 200 Km 145, in Nuevo Vallarta; ☎ 329-296-5006; **flamingosgolf.com.mx**) was designed by Percy Clifford. Facilities include a bar, snack bar, and clubhouse, as well as a driving range and putting green. Pros can help with lessons to straighten your swing or improve your drive. The entire course was renovated in 2005. Greens fees, including cart and a bucket of balls, are $139.

Marina Vallarta Golf Course and Country Club (across from Marriott Casa Magna Resort, Paseo de la Marina s/n, Fraccionamiento Marina Vallarta; ☎ 322-221-0545; **www.marinavallartagolf.com**) is a Joe Finger–designed, 18-hole, par-71, 6,700-yard championship course. Lakes, lagoons, and other water features make the course both challenging and attractive—to golfers as well as waterfowl. Practice facilities include a putting green and driving range, and there's a small restaurant and bar and a clubhouse with showers. Greens fees are $135, including shared cart and tax.

Four Seasons Punta Mita (Punta Mita; ☎ 329-291-6000; **www.fourseasons.com/ puntamita/golf.html**) has a private Jack Nicklaus–designed course that opened in 1999. Eight of the 19 holes (yup, 19!) are on the ocean. The optional par-3 is designed for those who choose it over the 194-yard hole found on a tiny offshore islet. (Transportation to the hole is by amphibious cart, weather permitting.) *Condé Nast Traveler* readers listed the Four Seasons number one course of the world in 2006. Greens fees are $170, including shared cart. The course is open only to Four Seasons' guests, club members, and their guests.

> *unofficial* **TIP**
> Ask about promotional fees and packages for Mayan Palace. There are usually many options, and few people pay the rack rate. Currently under renovation, the new and improved course will be completed by mid-2009.

Vista Vallarta (Circuito Universidad 653, Col. San Nicolas; ☎ 322-290-0030; **www.vistavallartagolf.com**) is located 20 minutes from downtown. Two 18-hole, 72-par courses cover 550 acres. You'll enjoy great views of the bay as you play through the palm forests and natural creeks of the Jack Nicklaus–designed course. At the west end of the property, the intriguing Tom Weiskopf course offers a varied landscape of native vegetation and plenty of natural water features. Rental clubs are available, as are golf lessons, a driving range, and putting green. Greens fees are $194.

Inexperienced players and seasoned golfers alike appreciate **Mayan Palace Golf Course** (Paseo de las Moras s/n, Fraccionamiento Naútico Turístico; ☎ 322-226-4000; **www. mayanresortsgolf.com**). Half of the holes are currently under extensive renovation; to play the remaining 9 twice, green fees at this 18-hole

> *unofficial* **TIP**
> In the sticky summer months, humidity and heat are concerns for horseback riders. Things start cooling down after 2 p.m., making later-afternoon rides more appealing. However, it's also more likely to rain later in the day. Choose your poison.

course at the south end of Nuevo Vallarta are $120, including a shared golf cart. Prices will go up once the course has been renovated.

HORSEBACK RIDING

ONE OF PV'S LONG-ESTABLISHED RANCHES AND STABLES, **Rancho El Charro** (☎ 322-224-0114; **www.ranchoelcharro.com**) offers a nice variety of tours, from weeklong excursions to San Sebastián in the Sierra, to a three-hour route ($62) into the foothills. You're not riding all the time: each tour includes time for a swim and one or two meals. Guests are picked up and returned to their hotel or a location nearby.

Another long-term operator is **Rancho Ojo de Agua** (Cerrada de Cardenal 227, Fraccionamiento Aralias; ☎ 322-224-0607). Choose a three- or five-hour trip into the hills, or spend the night at their Sierra Madre camp. Cost is around $60 for a three-hour tour; five-hour tours cost about $74, including lunch. It's $420 per person for an overnight.

PARASAILING

PARASAILING IN THE BAY IS VERY POPULAR, and there are operators at major beaches during high season, including **Mismaloya, Los Muertos, the hotel zone, Marina Vallarta,** and **Nuevo Vallarta** who will happily tow you—flying high and with a colorful parasail behind you—into the sky. Rates are typically $45 for a 10-minute ride.

SCUBA DIVING AND SNORKELING

WHILE THE WATER ALONG THE PACIFIC is more turbid than in the Caribbean, the west coast offers an excellent array of marine species. Visibility is generally better in the summer than in the winter months, and the water, while warm year-round, is at least ten degrees warmer at this time. Among the most popular dive sites are **Los Arcos,** a group of picturesque rocks off the shore at **Mismaloya.** This is a good spot for night dives, as the ocean is relatively shallow, with a dramatic drop-off and plenty of different marine species. The depth around the **Marieta Islands** generally ranges from 70 to 110 feet. A varied environment of reefs, drop-offs, and caves will put you in the path of tropical fish, giant manta rays, eels, and sea turtles. During the winter, this is a good place to spot humpback whales.

Las Caletas offers shallow water and the usual tropical fish suspects, and you can loll on the picturesque beach after you dive. A bit farther away, more challenging dives await experienced divers at **Los Morros,** where you'll find more than a dozen caves and tunnels, and **Corbeteña,** known for its steep walls. Snorkeling is most popular in **Las Caletas** and the **Marietas. Chico's Dive Shop** (Díaz Ordaz 772; ☎ 322-222-1895) offers diving and snorkeling excursions to the Marieta Islands, Majahuita, El Chimo, Quimixto, and other locations.

SPORTFISHING

PUERTO VALLARTA IS AN EXCELLENT DESTINATION for sport-fishing. You'll find some sort of billfish any time of year, and sailfish year-round. There's good fishing also for amberjack, snapper, Spanish mackeral, and bonita. November, which is also dedicated to the festival of the arts, is the month for the annual **International Sailfish and Marlin Tournament** (☎ 322-222-1436; **www.fishvallarta.com**). Cash and prizes are awarded for the largest tuna, dorado, sailfish, and marlin brought in. For sportfishing boat rental, contact **Fishing with Carolina** (☎ 322-224-7250; **www.fishingwithcarolina.com**). Charter prices range from $250 for four hours (one to four passengers on a 28-foot super-panga) to $600 on a fast, 30-foot sportfisher or $850 on a 40-foot boat for up to 10 passengers. Party boats include lunch and cost $150 per person.

SHOPPING *in* PUERTO VALLARTA

PUERTO VALLARTA CAN RIGHTLY CLAIM to have some of the very best shopping (if not *the* best) of all Mexico's coastal resorts. The most concentrated selection of good shops are in Old Vallarta, but there is great shopping north of town, too. In addition to boutiques, art galleries, and outdoor markets, Puerto Vallarta has a number of shopping malls and plazas that vie for travelers' attention and discretionary income. In the hotel zone, the most popular (and pedestrian) is **Plaza Caracol,** with a grocery and department store, many small shops, and a Cinemark Theater sixplex. More upscale Paradise Plaza (in Nuevo Vallarta next to Paradise Plaza Hotel; ☎ 322-226-6700) is an air-conditioned center with more than 100 establishments, including shops, a bank, video arcade, several cafes, and a grocery store. Marina Vallarta has two fairly good shopping centers: **Plaza Marina** with Comercial Mexicana megagrocery as well as clothing and gift shops, and **Plaza Neptuno** at the northwest end of the marina. Surrounding the marina itself on three sides, a smattering of jewelers, women's clothing stores, beachwear boutiques, and liquor stores mingle with a dozen restaurants and bars.

> *unofficial* **TIP**
> Both Marina Vallarta malls have good traditional Mexican eats at casual restaurants. At Plaza Marina, tiny **8 Tostados,** in the parking lot, serves delightful seafood tostadas, and a rotisserie-chicken storefront is popular day and evening. Plaza Neptuno offers **La Marisma** (see "Where to Eat in Puerto Vallarta," page 273) for casual yet yummy seafood tacos, quesadillas, and burritos.

For fine ceramics from Mata Ortiz (the highly prized work reminiscent of Hopi and Navajo pottery), shop downtown at **Galería de Ollas**

(Corona 176; ☎ 322-223-1045). **Talavera, Etc.** (Vallarta 266; ☎ 322-222-4100) and **Majolica Antica** (Corona 191; ☎ 322-222-5118) are two small shops offering exquisite, authentic Talavera ceramics.

Open daily, the **Huichol Collection Gallery** (Morelos 490; ☎ 322-222-0182) sells lovely, if rather pricey beaded objets d'art made by the Huichol Indians of inland Jalisco and Nayarit. The artists are often on hand, demonstrating the process of making bright yarn paintings or applying tiny colorful beads to wooden forms using beeswax.

For a good variety of different types of crafts, including a large selection of woven goods and fine ceramics, visit **Querubines** (Juárez 501-A; ☎ 322-222-2988).

Many of PV's dozens of art galleries are located downtown. These include **Galería Uno** (Morelos 561; ☎ 322-222-0908), which changes exhibitions frequently (and has lots of free inaugural cocktail parties); **Arte Latinoamericana** (Josefa Ortiz Domínguez 155; ☎ 322-222-4406); and **Galería Pacífico** (Calle Aldama 174; ☎ 322-222-1982). All show contemporary paintings and sculptures by local and foreign artists. Across from the restaurant of the same name, **Gallery des Artistes** (Leona Vicario 248; ☎ 322-223-0006) sells original art and antiques, including the work of Mexican masters and contemporary Puerto Vallarta painters. **Galleria Dante** (Basilio Badillo 269; ☎ 322-222-2477) is a huge shop specializing in sculpture but selling paintings as well. These are just a few of the top spots for fine art; browsing downtown (and in the shopping centers listed on the previous page), you'll find a whole lot more.

unofficial **TIP**
Calle Basilio Badillo, formerly known as "Restaurant Row," is now even more formidable for good shopping, with lots of women's clothing, jewelry, and bathing suit boutiques.

Up and down the sliver of an island, **Isla Río Cuale,** are shops and stands selling souvenir-quality paintings as well as other inexpensive handcrafts. It's a beautiful setting, bordered by the rushing river and lined in huge old trees. Just north of the river, the **Mercado de Artesanias** (Avenidas Libertad and Miramar, near the Río Cuale) sells a large selection of silver, hand-embroidered dresses and tops, trinkets, and souvenirs, as well as food.

Two shops selling high quality, fashionable resort wear (mainly for women), accessories, and jewelry are **Maria de Guadalajara** (Morelos 550, ☎ 322-222-2387, downtown; or at Marina del Sol Condos, Plaza Marina; ☎ 322-221-2566) and **La Bohemia** (Constitución and Basilio Badillo, ☎ 322-222-3164; or in Marina Vallarta's Plaza Neptuno, ☎ 322-221-2160). For a huge selection of quality women's clothing in a variety of designer labels, visit **d'Paola,** (Agustín Rodríguez 289; ☎ 322-222-1120). The venerable shop also has a fair amount of jewelry, mainly large format, as well as its own line of pewter tableware.

NIGHTLIFE *in* PUERTO VALLARTA

LIKE ITS SHOPPING SCENE, PV's nightlife is varied and exhaustive—that is, it's as easy to come back from a PV vacation exhausted (if exhilarated) as it is return relaxed and refreshed. The dancing scene here is intense, and barhopping is an art form.

Many of the superior restaurants offer live music, with a menu that ranges from Brazilian, jazz, blues, and rock to the more traditional Mexican mariachi or marimba music. If you like traditional Mexican band music (sometimes danzón), head for the main plaza on Thursday or Sunday evenings. More concerts are held at outdoor **Los Arcos** amphitheater during holidays and major music festivals in November and May. For information about nighttime dinner, dancing, and sunset cruises, see page 277.

Between **The River Cafe** and **Le Bistro Jazz Cafe**, both on the diminutive Cuale Island in the heart of the Old Town, you're sure to find some live music you like. (Call to confirm at ☎ 322-223-0788 or 322-222-0283, respectively.) On Los Muertos Beach, **La Palapa** restaurant (Calle Pulpito 103; ☎ 322-222-5225) has live jazz or Brazilian music most evenings after 8 p.m. For a big salsa band to listen or dance to, visit the Cuban bar-restaurant **La Bodeguita del Medio** (opposite the malecón at Paseo Diaz Ordaz 858; ☎ 322-223-1586) any night except Monday. House bands (banda, mariachi) perform at **El Mariachi Loco** (Lázaro Cárdenas 254; ☎ 322-223-2205, closed Sunday) beginning at 10:30 p.m. Live tunes are a bit scarcer outside Old Vallarta; your best bet will be major hotels in the hotel zone and Marina Vallarta. Party animals will prefer such dens of earthly delights as **Bebotero** (Paseo Diaz Ordáz 522; ☎ 322-222-113-0099), which supposedly supplies live rock or reggae nightly after 10 p.m.

Some of PV's many bars and clubs offer drinking and dancing to canned music till the dawn's early light—with official or unofficial closing times between 4 and 6 a.m. Megalomania-sized **Hilo** (Paseo Diaz Ordaz 588; ☎ 322-223-5361) pumps out techno and ska for the young; equally popular is **Señor Frog's** (Morelos 518; ☎ 322-222-5171). For see-and-be-seen, the upper-crust head to **DeSantos** (Morelos 771; ☎ 322-223-3052) in downtown Vallarta, which doesn't give up until 6 in the morning on a good night.

For a full-on tropical dance venue, visit **J.B.** (Carretera al Aeropuerto Km 2.5, near Marina Vallarta; ☎ 322-224-4616). **Christine Club** (Krystal Vallarta Hotel, Avenida de los Garzas s/n; ☎ 322-224-0202) is Vallarta's best disco, known for its light show and the variety of canned music played.

There's a busy gay nightlife scene as well, centered in Old Vallarta's Romantic Zone. Open nightly after 6 p.m., **Diva's** (Madero

388; ☎ 322-222-7774) is the new kid on the block. **Apache's Bar and Café** (Olas Altas 439; ☎ 322-222-5235) attracts a gay and lesbian crowd as well as writers, poets, and fine artists of all stripes.

 The undisputed queen of Vallarta's gay scene, however, is **Blue Chairs** (Los Muertos Beach near Calle Francisca Rodriguez; ☎ 322-222-5040), which has a hotel, pool, upstairs bar, a bar on the beach (the original "blue chairs"), and weekly events: drag shows, bingo, and so on.

November celebrates a series of unrelated but similarly joyful events loosely called **Las Fiestas de Noviembre.** It seems as if every day there's at least one form of free entertainment, everything from classic guitar, rock *en español,* percussion, jazz, and dance music, to puppet shows, folkloric dance, or mariachi music, many held at downtown's outdoor Los Arcos Amphitheater. The ten-day Festival Internacional Gourmet (**www.festivalgourmet.com**), in which invited chefs collaborate with local talent to introduce new menus, draws gastronomes.

For year-round movie entertainment, check out **Multicinemas Versalles** (Avenida Francisco Villa 799, Col. Versalles; ☎ 322-225-8766); **Cineópolis** (Plaza Soriana, Avenida Francisco Villa 1642, El Pitillal; ☎ 322-225-1251), or **Cinemark** (Avenida de los Tules 178, Plaza Caracol; ☎ 322-224-8927; **cinemark.com.mx**), all of which show English-language movies with subtitles. The newest of the pack is **MMCinemas** (Boulevard Francisco M. Ascencio 2920, Plaza Galerías Vallarta; ☎ 322-221-0095), almost directly across from the cruise-ship terminal. All cost between $4 and $5 per person and give a discount on Wednesdays.

NORTH *of* PUERTO VALLARTA

NAYARIT STATE IS EXPERIENCING A BOOM. Long considered Puerto Vallarta's poor relation, Jalisco's northern neighbor is now promoting its own lovely coastline. This to the chagrin of escapists who've for years had small towns such as San Francisco and Sayulita to themselves. Now tourism pundits have dubbed the corridor from Nuevo Vallarta north to the oddly named town Lo De Marcos "Vallarta–Nayarit." A short drive from the Puerto Vallarta airport or a PV hotel, this part of the country makes a worthy destination in itself or a fun day of exploring. The following is a brief roundup of places to eat and explore.

Included in the main part of this chapter, **Nuevo Vallarta** offers mainly all-inclusive resorts on a long, wide, flat beach that extends all the way north to Bucerias. This has very much the feel of a planned vacation resort, which it is. Many guests are surprised that with traffic, it can take an hour by bus and about 40 minutes by car or taxi to downtown PV, where the action is.

On the other hand, **Bucerías,** 5 to 10 minutes north, is increasingly touristic. The beach is wide and the surf usually mild enough for casual swimming. There are few concessionaires, but plenty of good restaurants face the sand. A growing cadre of worthwhile eateries in this growing town includes Claudio's Meson Bay (Lázaro Cárdenas 17; ☎ 329-298-1634), which offers theme nights (all-you-can-eat seafood or barbecue) and good grub daily overlooking the sea, with live marimba several evenings a week.

Mark's (Lázaro Cárdenas 56; ☎ 329-298-0303; dinner only) is admired for its convivial bar and excellent international food. For martinis and fine desserts, slip up the stairs above Tapas del Mundo restaurant to **The Bar Above** (Avenidas Hidalgo and Mexico; ☎ 329-298-1194).

These and other fine restaurants are found between the main highway and the sea, along with the town square, church, handcraft market, and vacation rentals. You have to enter town north or south of the creek at one of five stoplights, depending on where you want to go. Stop at **Pie in the Sky** (Heroes de Nacozari 202; ☎ 329-298-0838), on the main highway (southernmost stoplight) for crunchy chocolate-chip cookies or blackberry-lemon pie and good strong coffee, among other delicious desserts.

A sign just north of Bucerías points the way to the fishing village of **La Cruz de Huanacaxtle,** which boasts the new private Marina Riviera Nayarit. Stop in at **Philo's** (Delfin 16; ☎ 329-295-5068, open Tuesday through Saturday, daily in high season) for eats, suds, Spanish or guitar lessons, or just to ask what's going on around town. We've had reports of great dinners, including schnitzel and veggie lasagna, at **Black Forest** (Calle Marlin 16; ☎ 329-295-5203; closed Saturday and August through early October), and the outdoor patio is simple yet chic. **Hikuri** (Calle Coral 66; ☎ 329-295-5071) has the area's best selection of Huichol crafts.

At the north end of La Cruz, families play in the mild surf of **La Manzanilla,** where *enramadas* (structures of palm) serve ceviche and sodas. Three new hotels are planned for the beach at **Destiladeras;** the high-end Capella has already broken ground.

Continue along the curve of the bay to **Punta Mita,** mostly gated now and the domain of the well-to-do. There's beach access at El Anclote, however, where a string of restaurants serve up seafood and sunsets. The most dependable is **Tino's,** and the newest and most chichi is French chef Thierry Blouet's **Cafe des Artistes del Mar** at the boutique hotel of the same name. Accommodations are found at contiguous Colonia E. Zapata and Nuevo Corral del Risco, where fishermen can be hired for boat trips to Las Marietas or offshore surfing spots.

An inland route circumvents Punta Mita en route to **Sayulita** and points beyond. Sayulita is an increasingly popular yet still unsophisticated fishing village and surf mecca. There are fewer lodgings than one might think, mainly basic digs catering to surf dogs. Restaurants worth investigating include **Si Hay Olitas** (Revolución 33; ☎ 329-291-3203), for large Mexican combo plates and seafood, and the wildly popular **Choco Banana** (Calles Revolución and Delfin; ☎ 329-291-3051) for a range of international munchies and good breakfasts. On the beach you can rent horses or snorkeling gear, take surf lessons, or book a boat excursion.

Just a few miles up the road, **San Francisco** (aka San Pancho) was a model factory town created by ex-President Echevarría. Its broad sandy streets are only slowly opening up to tourism, yet an enclave of international artists and entrepreneurs support a handful of very good restaurants and a smattering of hotels and vacation rentals. Most of the restaurants close or have reduced hours in the slow summer months. Check out **Gallo's** (Avenida Tercer Mundo 33; ☎ 311-258-4135; closed Tuesday, dinner only) for pizza and steaks; they have bands most weekends and more often in high season. **La Ola Rica** (Avenida Tercer Mundo s/n a block from the beach; ☎ 311-258-4123; closed Sunday, August through October, and when things get slow; dinner only) serves yummy international dishes and has cheerful decor; romantic, cheerful, and open **Cafe del Mar** (Avenida China 9; ☎ 311-258-4451; closed Wednesday, and August through November) is another good choice. Taco and sandwich places are found around town for cheaper, on-the-go meals; the wide beach is usually too flat for surfing, but perfect for nice long walks between the headlands.

Five minutes farther by car, **Lo De Marcos** is less sophisticated. Its bungalow-style hotels with kitchenettes cater mainly to large Mexican families from the interior; foreigners rent or own homes. This unassuming beach town represents the northernmost point of a first stage of Riviera Nayarit's development; so far, the only visible change has been a new road into town from the highway. But a metamorphosis is inevitable.

PART TEN

IXTAPA *and* ZIHUATANEJO

The TWIN PARADISES

IF EVER THERE WAS AN OVERLOOKED, underhyped beach resort in Mexico, this is it. The double destination has 16 miles of coast, and you'll find everything from long, lonely stretches of sand with only pelicans and sandpipers for company, to lovely bayside beaches where you can purchase a piña colada, a fish filet right off the grill, or a new bikini. **Ixtapa** is one of Mexico's most compact planned resorts: a miniature version of the Cancún hotel strip, but with little glitz and few gimmicks. Even the time-share scene is low-key compared with Vallarta's or Los Cabos's. **Zihuatanejo,** often short-ened to Zihua, was named by the Aztecs and conquered by the Spanish. Separated by just a few miles of—yes—more beaches, the two resorts together make one of Mexico's most laid-back vacation destinations.

Today the city of Zihua has 120,000 inhabitants, and government-sponsored housing projects clump together at the north end of town. Some 35 years ago, this was a fishing outpost with unpaved streets; electricity was a recent arrival. These civic improvements came about after Highway 200 arrived in the 1960s to connect the somnolent village to the modern world. Tourism turned from a trickle of hardy Mexico-philes to a slow-but-steady stream of beach bums, divers, and surfers enchanted by the easygoing lifestyle. The beautiful **Bay of Zihuatanejo,** surrounded by the lumpy green foothills of the **Sierra Madre Occidental,** has some of Mexico's most attractive beaches.

At the time its new neighbor Ixtapa was developed, Zihua's economy was based on fishing and agriculture. Sesame seeds, mango, guayaba, and guanábana were grown, as well as staple crops such as tomato, chiles, and corn. One of the most important export crops was *copra,* the meat of the coconut, used for soap, oil, and many other products.

Taking over an enormous coconut grove, the hotel zone named Ixtapa (which means "white place" in Nahuatl, the language of the Aztecs) opened its first hotel in 1975. In the years since, the resort has grown slowly, and even today comprises fewer than two dozen properties. Although most of Ixtapa's lodgings are not terribly glamorous or cutting edge, hotel prices here are accordingly lower than those in Mexico's better-known coastal resorts. Popular with families, Ixtapa's hotel zone is small enough to make traveling among its accommodations, restaurants, attractions, and shops both easy and inexpensive.

Ixtapa's main road, which approximates a (divided) country lane rather than a major thoroughfare, is lined with orange-flowering hedges and large ceiba trees dangling big brown pods. High-rises (but far from high) line the beach in a strip less than two miles long, while across the street, shops and restaurants cluster in a series of intermingled strip malls.

Neighboring Zihuatanejo has more mom-and-pop stores and inexpensive accommodations than Ixtapa, but it's also home to high-end boutique hotels such as **La Casa Que Canta, The Tides,** and boutique hotels whose rooms number in the single digits. In contrast to planned Ixtapa, Zihuatanejo is a real fishing town that matured quickly after Ixtapa's birth. Anglers still sell their wares beside the sea, and small homes comingle with restaurants, stores, and markets tended by easygoing merchants. On both sides of town, high cliffs frame curvaceous, seductive **Zihuatanejo Bay.**

Like Mexico's other coastal resorts, activities here center on water sports and beach-bumming. Diving and snorkeling, while not as grand as in the Caribbean, benefit from the region's varied underwater terrain, which is mainly volcanic in origin. You might take a sunset gallop along **Playa Larga,** a boat ride to **Ixtapa Island,** or a day trip to more distant beaches, each with its own appeal. Many visitors find, however, that between Ixtapa and Zihuatanejo, they really don't need to go anyplace else.

QUICK FACTS *about* IXTAPA *and* ZIHUATANEJO

AIRPORT AND AIRLINES Ixtapa-Zihuatanejo International Airport (☎ 755-554-2070) is eight miles (15 minutes) west of Zihua; Ixtapa is four miles farther. National airlines flying into Zihua include **Aeroméxico, Mexicana,** and **Magnicharter. Continental** offers nonstop service from Houston. The hub for **America West** is Phoenix. Other carriers flying into Ixtapa-Zihua include **Alaska Airlines** (from Los Angeles and San Francisco) and **American Airlines** (from Dallas). From the airport, expect to pay approximately $18 each for shared van service to Ixtapa's main hotel zone and slightly more to hotels at Playas Quieta and Larga; $15 to downtown Zihuatanejo or Playa

La Ropa. Private taxis cost about $28 and $32 between the airport and Zihua and Ixtapa, respectively. Most rental-car companies have desks at the airport.

CLIMATE Although hot and humid during the rainy season (July to October), Ixtapa-Zihua is guarded by the flanks of the Sierra Madre Occidental and receives fewer storms, and often rains of less intensity, than do resorts north and south, such as Acapulco and Puerto Vallarta. The coolest months, when temperatures dip into the low 70s or even the 60s at night, are December through February.

DRIVING Ixtapa-Zihua is about 150 miles northwest of Acapulco. The new toll road, called Carretera Siglo XXI (21st Century Highway) cuts driving time from Mexico City to six and a half hours, or three and a half hours from Morelia, Michoacán. Or, take the older, free Autopista del Sol via Acapulco, about nine hours between Ixtapa-Zihua and Mexico City.

GETTING AROUND Taxis and buses run between Ixtapa and Zihua, which are about five miles apart. Catch a bus in Zihua from the corner of Calles Morelos and Juárez. Bus stops are found up and down Paseo Ixtapa, but the bus will stop just about anywhere if it can. Cost is about $0.45 to $0.70, depending on where you get on or off. The minimum cab ride is $3; between Ixtapa and Zihuatanejo it's $5. Rates are posted in hotels, and cab drivers should produce a rate sheet upon request.

INTERNET ACCESS Zihuatanejo and Ixtapa have finally joined the 21st century and offer a number of Internet cafes in each location. Zihua's humbler and moderately priced hotels may have free Wi-Fi (lobby and/or guest rooms), while pricier places in both destinations usually charge for both Wi-Fi and high-speed cable connection: up to $40 per day for 24-hour access in your room. In downtown Zihua, **Bar-Net** (at Hotel Zihuatanejo, Calle Agustín Ramírez 2, ☎ 755-554-5330) is air-conditioned and has 16 computers at coffee-shop-style booths. It's only $2 an hour to surf the net; soft drinks, beer, chips, and Mexi finger food like tacos and quesadillas are served. In Ixtapa, stylish **Kaldhi Café** (Plaza Kiosko next to Kopados bar, ☎ 755-553-1917) opens between 8 a.m. and 11 p.m. and serves smoothies and snacks. Buy a coffee and hook up to Wi-Fi free, or use their computer for $3 per hour.

TELEPHONES The area code is ☎ **775.** All local phone numbers are seven digits.

TOURIST INFORMATION The **Convention & Visitors Bureau,** or Oficina de Convenciones y Visitantes (Paseo de las Gaviotas 12, Ixtapa; ☎ 755-553-1270; **www.ixtapa-zihuatanejo.org**), is open weekdays from 9 a.m. to 2 p.m. and 4 to 7 p.m. and offers advice about hotels, restaurants, and area activities.

unofficial **TIP**
If you run across an older, six-digit local number, add a 5 at the beginning. To a five-digit number, add 55.

Ixtapa and Zihuatanejo Area

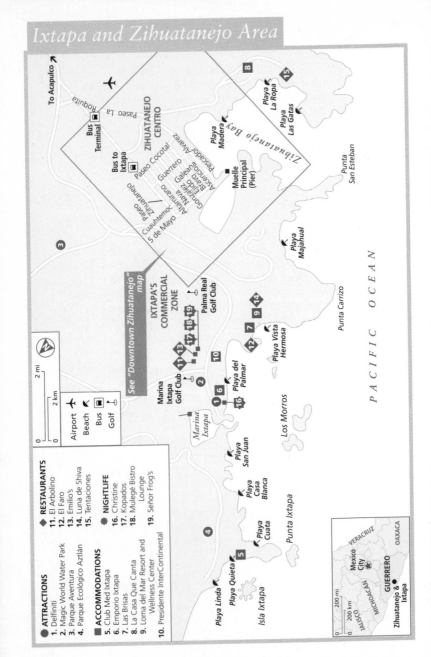

ATTRACTIONS
1. Delfiniti
2. Magic World Water Park
3. Parque Aventura
4. Parque Ecológico Aztlán

ACCOMMODATIONS
5. Club Med Ixtapa
6. Emporio Ixtapa
7. Las Brisas
8. La Casa Que Canta
9. Loma del Mar Resort and Wellness Center
10. Presidente InterContinental

♦ RESTAURANTS
11. El Arbolino
12. El Faro
13. Emilio's
14. Luna de Shiva
15. Tentaciones

✳ NIGHTLIFE
16. Christine
17. Kopados
18. Mulegé Bistro Lounge
19. Señor Frog's

N

2 mi
2 km

✈ Airport
⌿ Beach
▣ Bus
⛳ Golf

See "Downtown Zihuatanejo" map

IXTAPA'S COMMERCIAL ZONE

Marina Ixtapa Golf Club
Marina Ixtapa
Palma Real Golf Club

Playa Linda
Playa Quieta
Isla Ixtapa
Playa Cuata
Punta Ixtapa
Playa Casa Blanca
Playa San Juan
Los Morros
Playa del Palmar
Playa Vista Hermosa

ZIHUATANEJO CENTRO

To Acapulco
Paseo La Ropita
Bus Terminal
Bus to Ixtapa
Paseo Cocotal
Paseo Zihuatanejo
Cuauhtémoc
5 de Mayo
Altamirano
Nava
González
Galeana
Ejido
Guerrero
Bravo
Ascencio
Pescador
Álvarez

Playa Madera
Playa La Ropa
Playa Las Gatas
Playa Majahual

Zihuatanejo Bay

Muelle Principal (Pier)
Punta San Esteban

PACIFIC OCEAN

Punta Carrizo

VERACRUZ
Mexico City
MICHOACÁN
GUERRERO
OAXACA
JALISCO
Zihuatanejo & Ixtapa

200 mi
200 km

Downtown Zihuatanejo

ATTRACTION
1. Museo Arqueológico de la Costa Grande

ACCOMMODATIONS
2. Brisas del Mar
3. Casa de la Palma
4. La Casa Que Canta

RESTAURANTS
5. Bandidos
6. Garrobos

NIGHTLIFE
7. Bandidos

To Ixtapa

Main Bus Terminal

Tres Estrellas Bus Terminal

Avenida Morelos

Paseo Zihuatanejo

Paseo del Palmar

C. I. Altamirano

Cuauhtémoc

Avenida Nava

Benito Juárez

Municipal Market

Kioto   Plaza

C. González

Vicente Guerrero

Ejido

Juárez

Paseo de la Boquita

Calle Adelita

Camino a Playa la Ropa

5 de Mayo

Galeana

Canal

Calle Eva Zamano de Lopez Mateos

Las Salinas

Artisan's Market

N. Bravo
Pedro Ascencio

Avenida Ramírez

Álvarez

del Pescador

J.N.

Paseo

Playa Municipal

Playa Madera

Muelle Principal (Pier)

Bahía de Zihuatanejo

Playa La Ropa

Punta Godomía

Playa Las Gatas

Beach
Bus
Post Office

0   330 ft
0   100 m

WHERE *to* STAY *in* IXTAPA *and* ZIHUATANEJO

IXTAPA'S HIGH-RISE ACCOMMODATIONS march side by side up two-mile Playa El Palmar, the resort's raison d'être. A few big names, including the **Meliá Azul Ixtapa** (Boulevard Ixtapa s/n, Playa Linda; ☎ 755-555-0000) and the recently remodeled Club Med (Playa Linda;

How Accommodations Compare in Ixtapa and Zihuatanejo

ACCOMMODATION	LOCATION	OVERALL	QUALITY	VALUE	COST
Club Med Ixtapa	Ixtapa	★★★★	★★★★	★★★★	$$$$
Brisas del Mar	Zihuatanejo	★★★★	★★★★	★★★★	$$–$$$
La Casa Que Canta	Zihuatanejo	★★★★	★★★★	★★★	$$$$$
Las Brisas	Ixtapa	★★★½	★★★½	★ ½	$$$$$
Loma del Mar	Ixtapa Resort and Wellness Center	★★★	★★★★	★★½	$$$$$
Emporio Ixtapa	Ixtapa	★★★	★★★	★★★★	$$$
Presidente InterContinental	Ixtapa	★★★	★½	★★½	$$$$
Casa de la Palma	Zihuatanejo	★	★	★★★	$

☎ 755-555-1000) are found on the more solitary beaches northwest of Ixtapa, across from Ixtapa Island. Downtown Zihua offers budget lodgings, and there is a sprinkling of inexpensive and moderately priced bungalows and low-rises at La Madera and La Ropa beaches. The cliffs above the latter are home to the spectacular and expensive **La Casa Que Canta** and the new restaurant–boutique hotel **Tentaciones.**

ACCOMMODATION PROFILES

Las Brisas $$$$$

OVERALL ★★★½	QUALITY ★★★½	VALUE ★½

Playa Vista Hermosa, Ixtapa; ☎ 755-553-2121 or 888-559-4329 U.S. and Canada; fax 755-553-1038; brisas.com.mx

Designed by Ricardo Legorreta, this award-winning property (until recently part of the Westin chain) has a pyramid shape that permits a pretty ocean view from each room. In trademark Legorreta style, the terra-cotta–colored building has surprising accents of canary yellow and hot pink. Guest rooms received a $20 million renovation (finished in 2007), with new furnishings of red cedar as well as new mattresses, bedding, and hand-loomed cotton spreads. Bathrooms were redone in travertine marble. Additionally, the three-year project expanded and modernized meeting facilities, making this a good choice for conventions. All rooms have an extra-large terrace affording both sun and shade as well as hammock, chaise lounges, table and chairs. One-bedroom master suites have either a pool or a whirlpool tub on their balconies. The beach here is very private, and the hotel's restaurants first-rate. Despite the addition of warmer notes in decor and furnishings, the overall feeling of the property is modernistic.

SETTING AND FACILITIES
Location Playa Vista Hermosa, northwest of Ixtapa tourist zone.

Dining 6 restaurants, including Portofino, which won AAA's Four-Diamond Award in 2008.

Amenities and services Beach, 4 pools, gym, massage, water-sports center, tour desk, organized children's activities, shops, 2 bars, 24-hour room service, business center, Internet.

ACCOMMODATIONS

Rooms 390 rooms, 26 suites.

All rooms AC, fan, windows that open, ocean view, balcony or terrace, safe, hair dryer, minibar, coffeemaker, cable/satellite TV, Wi-Fi.

Some rooms Plunge pool, hot tub, nonsmoking, disabled access.

Comfort and decor Rooms are on the small side but have new, comfortable beds, plenty of amenities, and oh, those expansive, ocean-view balconies—with Yucatecan hammocks.

PAYMENT, RESERVATIONS, AND RESTRICTIONS

Deposit Credit card; 30-day cancellation policy or 2 nights' penalty.

Credit cards AE, MC, V.

Check-in/out 3 p.m./1 p.m.

 Brisas del Mar **$$–$$$**

OVERALL ★★★★	QUALITY ★★★★	VALUE ★★★★

Calle Eva Samano de López Mateos s/n, Playa La Madera, Zihuatanejo; ☎ 755-554-2142; fax 755-554-6710; www.hotelbrisasdelmar.com

This charmingly individualistic hotel has an ideal location, tumbling down a ton of stone steps from the road to the beach, where the restaurant and bar are located. The rambling grounds hold a kitschy kind of charm and lots of surprises: ponds of koi, caged parakeets, fountains, a riot of plants. Despite the fun and funky flair, the owner continually strives to improve facilities and services—for example, each room now has a phone and Wi-Fi access. Rooms have large balconies, tile-and-rock-mosaic floors, built-in shelves, and nice touches such as carved wood furniture and brightly glazed Talavera pottery—all of which make them seem more homey than hotel-like. The property has a game room and library, and a small spa with sauna, steam, and reasonably priced massages, facials, and other services.

unofficial **TIP**
At press time, the plan at Brisas del Mar is to put whirlpool tubs on all balconies, which may affect room price.

SETTING AND FACILITIES

Location Up many stairs from Playa La Madera.

Dining Bistro del Mar Restaurant, at the beach.

Amenities and services Beach, pool, spa, bar, Internet.

ACCOMMODATIONS

Rooms 28 rooms and suites; 1 villa on the beach.

All rooms AC, windows that open, ocean view, balcony, bathtub, hair dryer, safe, minibar, coffeemaker, cable/satellite TV.

Some rooms Whirlpool on balcony, kitchenette, refrigerator.

Comfort and decor Charming Mexican decor and furnishings, carved-wood doors, chairs, and sofas; Talavera sinks; ample balconies with padded chaise lounges and hammock.

PAYMENT, RESERVATIONS, AND RESTRICTIONS

Deposit Credit card guarantee; 1-night penalty for cancellation 48 hours after booking.

Credit cards AE, MC, V.

Check-in/out 3 p.m./noon.

Casa de la Palma $

OVERALL ★	QUALITY ★	VALUE ★★★

Calle Ciruelos s/n, across from Farmacias Similares, one block north of Boulevard Benito Juárez, behind the municipal market; ☎ 755-554-2092; www.casadelapalma.com

This small hotel without frills (and with basic English only) is a super bargain for folks who don't mind walking about ten minutes to the plaza and the town's main beach, where the fishermen pull their boats onto the sand. The three-story, family-run lodgings sits behind the municipal market. Expect tiny pink soap in the bathroom; bring your own shampoo. Older rooms downstairs have only a small window facing the hallway; ask for one of the two newer rooms upstairs with cement bathroom floor inlaid with smooth stones. Only one room—one of the two newer ones—has a narrow balcony with a hammock. Otherwise, there are a few cafe tables with chairs around the pool. The friendly owners invite guests to use the fridge or microwave off the small lobby. No elevator.

SETTING AND FACILITIES

Location Downtown Zihuatanejo.

Dining No restaurant.

Amenities and services Pool, Wi-Fi (in lobby only), free parking onsite or one block away for overflow and larger vehicles.

ACCOMMODATIONS

Rooms 17 rooms.

All rooms AC, cable TV.

Some rooms Balcony, fan, minibar (a few available for larger rooms upon request).

Comfort and decor Rooms have fresh paint and hand-loomed cotton spreads; most have carved headboards painted with cheerful suns, calla lilies, sunflowers, or swans.

PAYMENT, RESERVATIONS, AND RESTRICTIONS

Deposit Reserve only through Mexico bank deposit, or take your chances without a reservation.

Credit cards Cash only (may accept credit cards in near future).

Check-in/out 1 p.m./noon.

Club Med Ixtapa $$$$ (all-inclusive)

| OVERALL ★★★★ | QUALITY ★★★★ | VALUE ★★★★ |

Playa Quieta, Ixtapa; ☎ 755-553-1000 or 800-WEB-CLUB U.S. and Canada; clubmed.com.mx

Club Med was the first (and remains the only) resort on this lovely, palm-fringed, brown-sand beach a ten-minute drive from the main hotel zone. Rooms and public areas received a $20-million remodel in 2007, and the fresh new installations are both comfortable and—despite being geared toward families and kids—exceptionally stylish. Children from babies in cribs to age 5 are treated like royalty for a small fee, with their own napping quarters, restaurants with pint-sized tables and chairs, and age-appropriate activities. Activities for kids age 5 and older are free and abundant. The club's evening entertainment often includes guests; even tiny tots can dress up and participate. The real-life trapeze is a hit with both adults and older children, and there are no ressies needed or extra charge for kayaking, sailing, miniature golf, and much more. The main pool is open 24/7. In-room Wi-Fi is $15 per 24 hours—significantly cheaper than at some area resorts. When comparing rates with those at other all-inclusives, remember that Club Med's price includes 17% tax.

unofficial **TIP**
Club Med's Ixtapa property encompasses all of 850-meter-long Playa Quieta except a bit belonging to informal seafood restaurant Marisquería Neptuno at the north end. The government gave this land to Señor Oliverio, the current owner's father, in recognition for his services as a guide to Jacques Cousteau in the 1960s and early 1970s.

SETTING AND FACILITIES

Location On Playa Quieta, approximately 10 minutes west of Ixtapa's main hotel zone.

Dining 3 restaurants (one à la carte).

Amenities and services Beach, 3 pools, hot tub, gym, full-service spa, massage, water-sports center, tour desk, organized children's activities, shops, room service, Wi-Fi, Internet.

ACCOMMODATIONS

Rooms 283 rooms, 15 suites.

All rooms AC, fan, windows that open, hair dryer, safe, small refrigerator, coffeemaker, safe, cable TV, CD, Wi-Fi, nonsmoking.

Some rooms Ocean view, balcony or terrace, plasma TV (with cable), bathtub, disabled access.

Comfort and decor Room decor is modern Mexican, with pendant lamps, velveteen chaises, and crisp white bed linens. Suites have a bathroom connecting children's room, with twin beds, to the master bedroom.

PAYMENT, RESERVATIONS, AND RESTRICTIONS

Deposit Entire payment due at time of booking by credit card; no refunds, customers can rebook up to 1 year after cancellation.

Credit cards AE, MC, V.

Check-in/out 3 p.m./11 a.m.

La Casa Que Canta $$$$$

| OVERALL ★★★★ | QUALITY ★★★★ | VALUE ★★★ |

Camino Escenica s/n, Playa La Ropa, Zihuatanejo; ☎ 755-555-7030 or 888-523-5050 U.S.; fax 755-554-7900; www.lacasaquecanta.com

Do you have the inclination (and the money) to indulge yourself and your five senses as well? This luxurious little boutique hotel, a member of Small Luxury Hotels of the World, combines earthy elements such as thick pseudo-adobe walls, peaked thatch roofs, folk art, and superior service in a delightful marriage of style and comfort. From their perch high above the beach, hotel guests enjoy awesome views, although steps make it impractical for some folks. The beach is accessible by a stairway down the hill; about halfway down is a saltwater pool with waterfall. The spa offers facials, body wraps, and manicures as well as massage. Master suites have plunge pools and hammocks on their "living room" terraces. The eight suites of the new El Murmullo and El Ensueño villas can be rented separately or together, and each of the two villas has its own swimming pool and concierge.

unofficial **TIP**
Children under age 16 are not permitted at the hotel (except if an entire villa is booked by one group or family).

SETTING AND FACILITIES

Location Overlooking Playa la Ropa.

Dining Daily specials of Mexican seafood, in the informal pool bar; dinner in a romantic restaurant with great views.

Amenities and services Beach, 2 pools, gym, spa, tour desk, shop, 2 bars, room service, Internet (free).

ACCOMMODATIONS

Rooms 25 plus 2 villas with a total of 8 suites.

All rooms AC, fan, windows that open, ocean view, balcony or terrace, hair dryer, safe, minibar; no room TV, Internet ($10 per stay).

Some rooms Plunge pool; villa suites only have plasma TV with satellite and DVD players.

Comfort and decor Each unit has tasteful Mexican folk art and is individually decorated with impeccable taste. There's rose marble from Puebla,

Talavera pottery from Guadalajara, and copperware and carved furniture from Michoacán.

PAYMENT, RESERVATIONS, AND RESTRICTIONS

Deposit Credit card; 30-day cancellation policy (60 days during high season).

Credit cards AE, MC, V.

Check-in/out 3 p.m./1 p.m.

Emporio Ixtapa $$$

OVERALL ★★★	QUALITY ★★★	VALUE ★★★★

Boulevard Ixtapa s/n, Ixtapa; ☎ 755-553-1066 or 866-936-7674 U.S. and Canada; fax 755-553-1991; www.hotelesemporio.com

The nondescript, beige-cement exterior of this 11-story hotel belies the fresh, clean, comfortable rooms within. Suites are a good value; some have two balconies and three different ocean views. The pool is large, and there's a volleyball net for aquatic games, although shade trees and umbrellas are in short supply. The hotel, which sits smack dab in the middle of the hotel zone, has a couple of lighted tennis courts for nighttime play at no extra charge. In fact, this is the perfect hotel for folks who don't like to be "nickel and dimed." Even the Wi-Fi in guest rooms is free. FAP (Full-American Plan), including national alcoholic beverages, snacks, and three meals is also available.

unofficial **TIP**
The Emporio Ixtapa has been awarded the "Distinctivo H" award, which recommends the hotel's restaurants and other dining facilities for high standards of hygiene.

SETTING AND FACILITIES

Location Hotel zone, Playa del Palmar.

Dining 3 restaurants.

Amenities and services Beach, pool, hot tub, gym, massage, water-sports center, tour desk, organized children's activities, shops, 3 bars, room service, business center, Internet, free Wi-Fi in guest rooms (free) and lobby.

ACCOMMODATIONS

Rooms 196 rooms, 23 suites.

All rooms AC, windows that open, hair dryer, safe, minibar, cable/satellite TV.

Some rooms Ocean view, nonsmoking, disabled access.

Comfort and decor Soothing bone-color scheme with pastel spreads; modern and more traditional furnishings. Junior suites have separate bedroom (no door) with balcony, king bed, and TV; master suites have two bedrooms with doors that close and multiple ocean views.

PAYMENT, RESERVATIONS, AND RESTRICTIONS

Deposit Guarantee with credit card; 3-day cancellation policy except 1-night charge during Christmas and Easter holidays.

Credit cards AE, MC, V.

Check-in/out 4 p.m./1 p.m.

Loma del Mar Resort and Wellness Center　$$$$$

OVERALL　★★★	QUALITY　★★★★	VALUE　★★½

Calle Fragata, Lote F (neighbor to Hotel Las Brisas), Zona Hotelera II, Ixtapa; ☎ 755-555-0460; www.lomadelmar.com

If money isn't an object and you don't mind a tropical hillside view instead of an ocean vista, you can't ask for much more than this brand-new spa retreat on five acres of land. In the spacious guest rooms, organic materials blend seamlessly with stylishly modern items: look for glass, wicker, teak, or limestone tables; rattan chairs; and polished, poured-cement sinks and surrounds in fully loaded kitchens. Traditional Mexican touches include white walls, exposed ceiling beams, and red-tile floors. Most of the furniture comes from Spain, including comfortable couches in a pleasant palate of tan, ivory, and dusty red. Pendant lamps and oversized but delicate vases and candles complement the decor. The resort's claim to fame is its thalasso-wellness center and a 1,580-square-foot saltwater pool with stations for relaxing or rejuvenating different body parts. Check the hydro beds, where bubbles keep you afloat, Jacuzzi area within the pool, and volcano chambers with underwater leg massages. Outside the pool in the wellness center, masseurs give excellent Hindu, Thai, and hot-stone massages, among others. The resort borders Palma Real golf and tennis club; it's a scenic five- to ten-minute walk to the beach club.

SETTING AND FACILITIES

Location South end of Ixtapa's tourist zone.

Dining 2 restaurants (including Luna de Shiva, reviewed on page 306).

Amenities and services 3 pools (swimming, thalasso therapy, and kids' pools), spa, tour desk, some organized children's activities, bar, room service, Wi-Fi (free).

ACCOMMODATIONS

Rooms 16 suites.

All rooms AC, fan, windows that open, balcony or terrace, safe, hair dryer, full kitchen, plasma TV with satellite, DVD.

Some rooms Whirlpool tub.

Comfort and decor Modern yet comfortable and warm. Wide, fully furnished balconies overlook the thalassotherapy pool and the forested hills beyond.

PAYMENT, RESERVATIONS, AND RESTRICTIONS

Deposit Credit card; 10% penalty on cancellations less than 30 days; 1-night penalty for 15 days or less; more detailed charges online or by phone.

Credit cards AE, MC, V.

Check-in/out 4 p.m./1 p.m.

 Presidente InterContinental $$$$$ (all-inclusive)

OVERALL　★★★	QUALITY　★½	VALUE　★★½

Boulevard Ixtapa s/n, Playa del Palmar, Ixtapa; ☎ 755-553-0018 or 800-344-0548 U.S.; fax 755-553-0156; www.intercontinental.com/ixtapa

Like the food choices and amenities, the clientele of this well-situated hotel in the midst of Ixtapa's main hotel zone is varied. During the winter, it's 80 percent Canadian and American and 20 percent Mexican; those figures are reversed during school and summer holidays. You'll find tons to do here (16 hours of activities and entertainment each day), from karaoke at the bar to bingo and dance contests; cooking, bartending, and Spanish courses. Rooms vary by view, not amenities; only those in the 11-story tower (just $20 more than standard rooms) have ocean view. Only a few rooms have a balcony, but the view isn't necessarily the best from the balcony because of railing height. This is an especially good deal for families, as two kids younger than age 6 stay for no additional cost; or pay $40 per day for children ages 6 to 12. There are spinning and yoga classes as well as couples-size sauna and steam rooms. Internet access is free in the business center.

unofficial **TIP**
Wi-Fi is free in the lobby and lobby bar, but doesn't reach to guest rooms or restaurants.

SETTING AND FACILITIES

Location On the beach at Playa del Palmar, Ixtapa.

Dining 6 restaurants.

Amenities and services Beach, pools, gym, children's activities, tour desk, shops, 3 bars, business center, room service, Internet.

ACCOMMODATIONS

Rooms 408 rooms, 12 suites.

All rooms AC, windows that open, hair dryer, bathtub, 24-hour room service, cable/satellite TV, high-speed Internet.

Some rooms Ocean view, balcony or terrace, safe, minibar, coffeemaker, CD, DVD, nonsmoking rooms, disabled access.

Comfort and decor There's a pedestrian gold-and-blue color scheme with minimal wall art or decoration; Talavera ceramic soap and tissue dispensers in the bath.

PAYMENT, RESERVATIONS, AND RESTRICTIONS

Deposit Credit card; 72-hour cancellation policy (more during holidays).

Credit cards AE, MC, V.

Check-in/out 3 p.m./12 p.m.

WHERE *to* EAT *in* IXTAPA *and* ZIHUATANEJO

DINING IS A PLEASURE IN IXTAPA AND ZIHUA. Most restaurants expect only casual dress, and while cuisine centers on seafood and

How Restaurants Compare in Ixtapa and Zihuatanejo

RESTAURANT	LOCATION	CUISINE	COST	OVERALL	QUALITY	VALUE
Tentaciones | Zihua | Fusion | Exp	★★★★½	★★★★	★★★★
Luna de Shiva | Ixtapa | Nouvelle Mexican/ international | Exp	★★★½	★★★★	★★★
Garrobos | Zihua | Mexican/seafood | Mod	★★★	★★★½	★★½
Bandidos | Zihua | Mexican/seafood | Mod	★★★	★	★½
El Faro | Ixtapa | Seafood | Mod/exp	★★½	★★½	★★
Emilio's | Ixtapa | Pizza/BBQ | Mod	★★½	★★	★★★½
El Arbolito | Ixtapa | Seafood | Inexp/mod	★★	★★	★★★

regional and Mexican cuisine, there's a lot to choose from within those categories, and a sprinkling of more exotic and international dishes.

RESTAURANT PROFILES

Bandidos ★★★

MEXICAN/SEAFOOD	MODERATE	QUALITY ★	VALUE ★½

Calle 5 de Mayo No. 8, Zihuatanejo; ☎ 755-554-8072

Reservations Accepted.

Entree range $8–$17.

Payment MC, V.

Service rating ★★½.

Parking Street only.

Bar Full service.

Dress Casual.

Disabled access None.

Customers National and international travelers; locals and travelers for nightlife.

Hours Daily, 11 a.m.–2a.m. (closed Sunday, May–October).

SETTING AND ATMOSPHERE The music sets the mood: Latino, festive, and casual.

HOUSE SPECIALTIES Barbecued ribs, fish and shrimp tacos, red-snapper fillet in lobster sauce.

SUMMARY AND COMMENTS One of the few spots in town with live music, Bandidos is popular with locals and tourists alike. The casual patio is open to the street, or sit inside in the dining room or at the bar. Among the popular Mexican and seafood items on the menu are tons of different shrimp dishes, including *camarones enamoradas* ("shrimp in love"): bacon-wrapped shrimp grilled and served with tamarind sauce. Or order a hot pot of bubbling beef, chicken, fish, or shrimp served with homemade tortillas, as well as grilled onion, cactus, green onion, and bell pepper; it's called *molcajete.* The live music is gentler ballads Thursday through Saturday at around 9 p.m. and danceable Latino tunes on Friday and Saturday nights after 11 p.m.

*un*official **TIP**
Although tourist-oriented restaurants serve pozole any day of the week, this hominy soup is served traditionally—for long lunches, typically 3 to 5 or 6 p.m.–on Thursdays only. The dish originated in Chilapa, Guerrero, near the state capital of Chilpancingo.

El Arbolito   ★★

SEAFOOD	INEXPENSIVE/MODERATE	QUALITY ★★	VALUE ★★★

Centro Comercial Los Patios, Ixtapa; ☎ 755-553-3700

Reservations Rarely needed but accepted.

Entree range $8–$18.

Payment AE, MC, V.

Service rating ★★½.

Parking At the front of Los Patios outdoor mall.

Bar Full service, specializing in "black banana," with Kahlúa, coconut liqueur, pineapple juice, and banana.

Dress Casual.

Disabled access Restaurant yes, but mall bathrooms are not equipped for wheelchairs.

Customers Locals; in high season the place fills with foreigners, especially during happy hour, 5–7 p.m.

Hours Daily noon–11 p.m.

SETTING AND ATMOSPHERE Casual, open-air dining surrounded by shops. Latin pop and rock emanate from the sound system above a round bar supported by lacquered tree trunks with a palapa-thatched roof.

HOUSE SPECIALTIES Whole red snapper, shrimp soup (broth), *camaronillas* (quesadillas with shrimp).

SUMMARY AND COMMENTS In the midst of this tangle of mini-malls across from Ixtapa's main hotel zone is this low-key restaurant under multiple palm-thatched roofs. Sit at typical *equipale* (pigskin) table and chairs with bright-red tablecloths, or eat at the carved-wood bar. The food is traditional Mexican seafood: fresh fish served breaded and fried, grilled, or sautéed with garlic; sides are rice and (overcooked) vegetables. Locals favor the *campechanas,* large seafood cocktails of fish, octopus, and shrimp. The restaurant's second-floor sister restaurant in Zihua (Juan N. Alvarez 30; ☎ 755-554-6522) overlooks the basketball court–main plaza.

El Faro ★★½

SEAFOOD	MODERATE/EXPENSIVE	QUALITY ★★½	VALUE ★★

Paseo de la Colina s/n, Colonia Vista Hermosa, Ixtapa;
☎ **755-555-2525**

Reservations Recommended; ask for ocean view.

Entree range $17–$30.

Payment AE, MC, V.

Service rating ★★★½.

Parking Yes.

Bar Full service. The house specialty, the *martini oca,* is made with tangerine-flavored gin, lemon Barcadi, lemon juice, and dry Vermouth.

Dress Dress-up casual.

Disabled access None.

Customers Condo dwellers, foreign and domestic travelers, locals out for birthday or special event.

Hours Daily: 8 a.m.–noon (buffet only) and 6–10:30 p.m.

SETTING AND ATMOSPHERE The main decorations of this five-terrace (three open to the sky and two under a palapa roof), ocean-view eatery are the wide-open vistas of the waves below. Blessed by sea breezes and the sound of the surf, the architectural style is modern Mexican-Mediterranean.

HOUSE SPECIALTIES Fuente de Mariscos seafood platter with lobster, fish, octopus, shrimp, and mussels served with rice, bread, and steamed veggies; for dessert, chocolate-and-macadamia-nut crêpes.

SUMMARY AND COMMENTS What decoration can be seen is earthy and appealing; even the swirling ceiling fans evoke a *Casablanca* kind of feeling. You can splurge on lobster in season, or you can order à la carte. Don't forget to sample the homemade flan for dessert. This restaurant is on the grounds of the gated Pacífico condominium complex; just tell the guard that you're headed for El Faro.

unofficial **TIP**
If you go to El Faro for breakfast, bring a bathing suit and ride the funicular down to relatively inaccessible Vista Hermosa beach.

Emilio's ★★½

PIZZA/BARBECUE	MODERATE	QUALITY ★★	VALUE ★★★½

Paseo de las Garzas s/n, across from Hotel Ixtapa Palace, Ixtapa;
☎ **755-553-1583**

Reservations Not accepted for small parties.

Entree range $9–$21.

Payment AE, MC, V.

Service rating ★★.

Parking Lot of shopping mall.

Bar Full service.

Dress Resort casual, casual.

Disabled access None.

Customers Locals, Ixtapa hotel guests, weekend visitors from Morelia or Mexico City.

Hours Daily, 1 p.m.–midnight.

SETTING AND ATMOSPHERE A wooden deck overlooking the street, inside low lighting, basket lamps, and a polished bar.

HOUSE SPECIALTIES Barbecue pork ribs, pizza.

SUMMARY AND COMMENTS Locals come for the pizza and the convivial, unpretentious ambience. The instrumental background music is upbeat yet unobtrusive. Salads, such as the romaine with goat cheese, sun-dried tomatoes, nuts, apple chunks, and red grapes, are great to share as a first course. But the real star of the show, in addition to the very popular, slow-cooked barbecued pork ribs, are the pizzas. There's a long list of choices; most popular are the Italian, with mushrooms, serrano ham, salami, ham, and onion and the four-cheese pizza.

 Garrobos ★★★

| MEXICAN/SEAFOOD | MODERATE | QUALITY ★★★½ | VALUE ★★½ |

Downtown Zihuatanejo; Juan N. Alvarez 52; ☎ 755-554-6706

Reservations Recommended in high season for dinner.

Entree range $10–$22.

Payment AE, MC, V.

Service rating ★★★★.

Parking Street only.

Bar Full service.

Dress Casual.

Disabled access Yes.

Customers Travelers in high season; locals otherwise.

Hours Daily, 8–11 a.m., noon–11 p.m.

SETTING AND ATMOSPHERE A marine-blue color scheme prevails in this open restaurant overlooking the street. The wooden chairs, which could use cushions, discourage lingering.

HOUSE SPECIALTIES *Huachinango* Zihuatanejo: whole red snapper, butterflied, rubbed with spices and light adobo sauce, and grilled; it is absolutely fresh and deliciously straightforward. Wonderful flan made in-house with coconut milk and Kahlúa.

SUMMARY AND COMMENTS The tortillas are fresh. The salsas are hot! Waiters are friendly, so the only drawbacks are the rock-hard wooden chairs. There's a great variety of yummy items to choose from, mainly fresh fish and seafood. The appetizers make good starters to share, or as a meal in themselves. During lobster season have some delicious lobster tacos

unofficial **TIP**
At press time Garrobos
offered live trova music
from 7 to 9:30 p.m., mid-
December through April.

or lobster "steak" (pulled out of the shell) with
bacon, mushrooms, and green pepper in white
sauce. Try the "Shrimp de la Doña," six jumbo
shrimp grilled in olive oil and covered with a red
mole sauce that's spicy but not hot. This and
most entrees are served with choice of one hot
and one cold side dish: currently orange and beet
salad, apple salad, or mushrooms with lime, and baked potato or several
sautéed vegetable medleys, respectively. The food tends to be simple
and healthful, plates are well-presented, and there's an oyster bar serving
mussels, oysters, clams, and sashimi daily between noon and 5 p.m.

Luna de Shiva ★★★½

NOUVELLE MEXICAN/INTERNATIONAL   EXPENSIVE   QUALITY ★★★★   VALUE ★★★

**Loma del Mar resort, Calle Fragata, Lote F (neighbor to Hotel Las Brisas),
Zona Hotelera II, Ixtapa; ☎ 755-555-0460; www.lomadelmar.com**

Reservations Recommended for dinner.

Entree range $24–$38.

Payment AE, MC, V.

Service rating ★★½.

Parking At press time, parking around small traffic circle only (parking lot
planned for the future), with walk down steep ramp to the restaurant (or ask
receptionist for golf cart).

Bar Full service.

Dress Spiffy to casual.

Disabled access None.

Customers Wealthy spa-devotees of Loma del Mar resort, Ixtapa hotel guests.

Hours Daily 7 a.m.–10:30 p.m.

SETTING AND ATMOSPHERE Intimate, palm-thatched, open-air restaurant
overlooking the pool and Palma Real golf course

HOUSE SPECIALTIES Corn pie topped with caramel and served with coconut
ice cream and pomegranate seeds; the Cucaracha, a flaming drink prepared at your table with Kahlúa, rum, tequila, and brandy.

SUMMARY AND COMMENTS India-inspired Luna de Shiva glows romantically
in the evening when lamps, torches, and candles honoring Indian gods
are lighted. It overlooks the spa-resort's thalassotherapy pool, with
underwater lights changing from green to blue to purple. Originally
dedicated to an Asian palate, the menu has been redirected to modern Mexican and international cuisine. From Mexico City's Ambrosia
culinary school, chef Jorge Garcia creates intriguing plates. For starters
try a spreadable appetizer of white beans, chorizo, and filet of fish,
perhaps moving on to a hearts-of-palm soup or the radicchio and
bougainvillea-flower salad with light peanut dressing. Fish and meat
dishes follow, each decorated with tiny piles of spices to enhance

flavor and the twirled, cut, and deep-fried embellishments that are the norm at high-end restaurants. Under no circumstances should you decline the special corn pie drizzled with caramel and served with coconut ice cream—so save room for dessert.

Tentaciones   ★★★★½

ASIAN-MEDITERRANEAN FUSION   EXPENSIVE   QUALITY ★★★★★   VALUE ★★★★

Camino Escénico a Playa la Ropa Lote 97 (200 feet past Restaurante Kau-Kan, enter road to Casa Cuitlateca, then bear right instead of left), Zihuatanejo; ☎ 755-554-3443

Reservations Required; preferably 24 hours or more in advance but usually accepted morning of meal before noon.

Entree range $55 prix fixe menu.

Payment AE, MC, V.

Service rating ★★★½.

Parking Small lot, otherwise parking on very steep streets. It's also hard to find the first time; take a taxi!

Bar Full service, specializing in margaritas and martinis.

Dress Resort casual.

Disabled access Absolutely not; lots of steps.

Customers Upscale national and international travelers looking for a unique dining experience.

Hours Nonguests for dinner only (daily, 5–10 p.m.); hotel guests also for breakfast and lunch.

SETTING AND ATMOSPHERE Romantic, chic, and with decor that pleases but doesn't overwhelm. Enjoy amazing views of Zihua Bay from the large wooden deck, where appetizers and drinks are served. The small, classy, open-air dining room has Indonesian and Pacific Coast decor.

HOUSE SPECIALTIES Set five-course meal selected daily by the chef—no substitutions.

SUMMARY AND COMMENTS *Wow!* We love this place. The nightly menu, selected and prepared by chef Mario Ramirez Miranda, allows for deviations from his intended plan with advance notice only. It's best to just be open to what the universe has in store for you. Presentation is lovely, but it's the food's flavors that truly inspire. At one dinner we enjoyed, our carpaccio was razor-thin and—along with the mound of citrus-infused risotto—formed an integral part of the plate's decoration. The Caesar-style salad with marinated portobello mushroom was a mild interlude before an amazing cold cream-of-apple soup with curry. Equally wonderful were the main course and dessert that the 25-year-old chef from Zihuatanejo created from ingredients handpicked that morning. Along with the decor, the food blends Asian and Mediterranean flavors with great success. A grottolike, rock-lined infinity pool separates the restaurant from Tentaciones's four equally excellent suites ($370 to $420 in high season, discounted from May to mid-November).

SIGHTSEEING *in* IXTAPA *and* ZIHUATANEJO

ZIHUA IS FUN TO WANDER AROUND IN, although it has few real attractions. In the morning, check out the anglers selling their wares at the fish market, or poke your head in the tiny **Museo Arqueológico de la Costa Grande** (Paseo del Pescador s/n, by the basketball court; ☎ 755-554-7552, closed Monday); admission is only $1.

This destination is mainly about hangin' on the shore, however. The northernmost of Ixtapa's beaches, **Playa Linda** has a couple of seafood shanties, shade palapas to rent, and a long beach for brisk or leisurely walks. The surf here is gentle and the sand fine, albeit dark. Rent horses ($45 per hour through tour operators, or $20–$25 [negotiable] from the folks on the beach) and canter along the water's edge, or visit the shopping area, where the once-ambulatory vendors were herded when their growing numbers threatened to drive sunbathers to distraction. As this beach attracts local families, however, cheap bathing suits and plastic beach toys outnumber silver jewelry or other fine souvenirs.

At Playa Linda you'll find the ferry to **Ixtapa Island** ($3.50 round-trip), which is a worthwhile day trip. With four different beaches easily accessible on foot, Ixtapa Island is a great place for snorkeling, relaxing on the beach, or sitting under shade supplied by the seafood restaurants lining the shore. The most popular beach is **Playa Cuachalalate,** where you can sit in the shade, drink a cool beverage, rent kayaks or snorkel equipment, or just swim in a delicious cove where the water is clear and inviting. The ferry leaves from Playa Linda, near the Qualton Inn, about every ten minutes, 10 a.m. to 3 p.m. (less often in low season); the last boat returns to Ixtapa at 5 p.m. Double-check the ferry schedule before retiring to more secluded **Playa Carey** on the far side of the island. There are no services there, and therefore, more solitude and fewer people.

unofficial **TIP**
There are several free parking lots at Playa Linda.

Heading toward the hotel zone from Playa Linda, next is three-mile **Playa Quieta,** named for its gentle waves. This soft-sand beach is home to **Club Med,** at the south end, and a simple beachfront eatery with tables on the sand at the other end of the beach.

Fronting the hotel zone, and thus where the action is, two-mile **Playa el Palmar** faces the open sea. This is the main beach of the tourist zone, and it's great for long walks. We always spend at least one morning or afternoon parked on a chaise lounge under a cute, thatched-shade contraption that doubles as a cocktail table, people watching and ordering a soda or an appetizer to satisfy the roving resident waiters. Farther south, **Playa Vista Hermosa** is a smaller beach framed by rock formations. Although the beach is public, access is only through the Hotel Las Brisas, which perches above it, or by boat.

After Playa Vista Hermosa, the road jogs inland and continues several miles to Zihuatanejo. Fishermen sell the catch of the day at commercially oriented **Playa Principal,** which parallels downtown. Lining the beachfront road, **Paseo del Pescador,** are a multitude of shops, restaurants, and businesses.

Fishing boats leave from the municipal pier at the east end of the beach, as do water taxis to **Playa las Gatas** directly across the bay. The ten-minute boat trip from the town dock departs frequently and costs about $4.50 round-trip. Don't miss this excursion to this pretty beach at the point. It's crowded and festive on weekends, when families camp out at one of a dozen basic fish eateries just out of reach of the gentle waves. Rugged green foothills rise directly above the bay on all sides, painting a patently postcard-esque panorama—the blue ocean sparkles in the sun, and life feels sublime. There's significantly less activity mid-week.

In between Playa Principal and Playa Las Gatas is **Playa la Madera,** which at the very back of the deep bay has gentle surf, shallow water, and is popular with families. Several hotels grace this lovely beach, some on the shore and others perched on the hill above. **Playa la Ropa** also has fine white sand and offers a smattering of water sports in high season and on holidays—mainly sailboarding, parasailing, and banana boats. Hotels and restaurants offer respite from the sun in their bars and restaurants, making this stretch of sand even more inviting. A paved, lighted path connects Playa la Madera to downtown Zihua. Because pollution can be a problem in enclosed bays such as this, it's unwise to swim here right after a heavy rainstorm, when contaminants from town may enter the bay. Farther south, 1ong Playa Larga invites runs along a three-kilometer stretch of sand, and has seaside fish shanties for informal eats and refreshments. There's a formidable current along the shore and a closed-out beach break that discourages both swimming and surfing.

ATTRACTIONS

Parque Ecológico Aztlán (Camino a Playa Linda; no phone) is an ecological park that individuals or tours may access via a six-mile path for biking, blading, jogging, or walking. It originates at Marina Ixtapa and ends at Playa Linda. Here you'll see the area's two most important ecosystems, the tropical woodland and the mangrove swamp. There's no admission fee, and it's only possible to visit the park during daylight hours, as there's no electricity, either. Remember to bring insect repellant, as the bugs sometimes attack.

Parque Aventura (km 4.8 Carretera Zihuatanejo–Lázaro Cárdenas; 800 meters from Mirador Ixtapa; ☎ 755-510-0480, **parque-aventura -ixtapa.com.mx**) offers 11 zip lines totaling nearly 2,000 meters in length, ranging in height from 4 to 15 meters above the ground. Local agencies charge $50 to $60 per person for the two-hour tour, but those with their own wheels or putting two or more in a taxi ($7 to $8 each way) can save money by making their own arrangements. There's no fee to enter the park; zip-line cost is about $40 per person.

kids **Magic World Water Park** (Paseo de las Garzas s/n, part of Ixtapa Palace Hotel; ☎ 755-553-1359) has a kids' play area with pirate ship, restaurant, wave pool, giant slides, and an artificial lake. The park is open daily, 9:30 a.m. to 5:30 p.m., and admission is $6. If you owe your kids a multiday playdate, you can book a package deal (with accommodations, meals, park entrance) at the Ixtapa Palace time-share. It's most appropriate for kids ages 9 or younger, not teens.

Next to Carlos'n Charlie's, **Delfiniti** (Paseo Ixtapa s/n; ☎ 755-553-2707; **www.delfiniti.com**) offers expensive dolphin encounters. A 45-minute swim costs $119 for adults and kids age 8 and over; 20-minute encounters run $79 for adults and kids age 8 and over, $119 for kids ages 3 to 7 with an adult; a 10-minute encounter for small fry up to age 3 with an adult is $79. Try to make arrangements ahead of time online or through your hotel or tour operator.

TOURS *and* SIDE TRIPS *from* IXTAPA *and* ZIHUATANEJO

Adventours (Centro Comercial Plaza Ambiente, Ixtapa, across from Hotel Park Royal, ☎ 755-553-1069) offers the six-hour Adventure in the Island Tour ($76) combining biking, kayaking, and snorkeling. The cost includes transportation, lunch, and all equipment. They also offer a five-hour walking tour ($56) to **Parque Ecológico Aztlán,** including lunch.

Ixzi Tours (Andador Río Yextla Manzana 4, Lote 25, Colonia La Puerta del Sol, Ixtapa; ☎ 755-553-2547; **www.ixtitours.com**) arranges horseback riding on Playa Larga or from their riding stable. Time on the horse is just over an hour; including transportation from your hotel the cost is a bit steep at $50. Among many other tours, they also offer sunset cruises including open bar ($55) and several different trips to the surrounding countryside ($59 to $70).

Sunny Side (Paseo Ixtapa s/n, across from Hotel Fontan, Centro Comercial Los Patios, Local 139; ☎ 755-553-3790) arranges horseback riding as well as two-and-a-half-hour sunset cruises with open bar ($45). Also popular are day trips to **Patzcuaro** to visit coppersmiths and churches and to shop or to Acapulco to shop, see the city sights, and watch the famous cliff divers. Both trips include Continental breakfast and lunch ($148 and $130 per person, respectively).

EXERCISE *and* RECREATION *in* IXTAPA *and* ZIHUATANEJO

JUST BECAUSE YOU'RE IN A HOT, SUNNY, tropical location doesn't mean you can't rev up—it just takes a little extra effort. In Ixtapa, concessionaires rent personal watercraft, catamarans, and sailboards from the hotels along Playa el Palmar, while these toys are also found on Ixtapa Island, and in Zihua at Playa la Ropa and Playa las Gatas. Banana boats are ubiquitous, and you'll see parasailers glide over the popular tourist spots as well. There are fewer vendors during low season (May, June, September, and October) and sometimes none during inclement weather or super low season.

BIKING

A SIX-MILE BIKE PATH FOLLOWS the perimeter of the Marina Ixtapa Golf Course and then continues north through **Parque Ecológico Aztlán** (see "Sightseeing in Ixtapa and Zihuatanejo," page 309). The cement path around the golf course is smooth enough for in-line skaters. The second leg of the path is locked after 8 p.m.; security patrols cruise the area in case of accidents. A slightly shorter and hillier path connects the opposite end of Ixtapa with Zihuatanejo. It begins at the Tucan Ixtapa traffic circle, at the junction of Avenida Viveros and Boulevard Pelícanos, and ends at the Pemex station on the outskirts of Zihua.

GOLF

LOCATED AT EITHER END OF IXTAPA, the resort's 18-hole golf courses open at 7 a.m., with the last tee time at 4 p.m. Both have similar, moderate greens fees, offer a restaurant-bar, showers and lockers, and resident pro. The 18-hole **Club de Golf Marina Ixtapa** (east end of Paseo Ixtapa; ☎ 755-553-1410) was designed by Robert von Hagge in 1990. It's a par-72 with rolling greens. The abundance of water features might help you forget the heat; nonetheless, we recommend trying for an early-morning tee time, as the twilight green fee is only $5 less than the regular fee of $55, with a mandatory cart costing an additional $35. On-site are a clubhouse and pro shop, practice area, and putting green.

At the other end of Ixtapa, **Club de Golf Palma Real** (west end of Paseo Ixtapa; ☎ 755-553-1163) boasts many royal palms. Alligators roam around in their former home, but if it's any comfort, they are relocated when they surpass 12 feet in length. The clubhouse has lockers and showers, a pro shop, and a restaurant-bar. Greens fees are $85 and $65 in low season, with an additional $30 for the cart.

SCUBA DIVING AND SNORKELING

AREA SCUBA BOOSTERS (including dive-shop operators) insist that the coast here offers greater variety of terrain as well as plant and animal species than the Caribbean. This variety helps to offset poorer visibility, which generally ranges from 15 to 30 feet, although it is sometimes better in the winter months. Recommended dive spots for beginners include the coral reefs at **La Caleta de Chon.** Both beginning and advanced divers can check out the many canyons of volcanic origin, most between 30 and 100 feet deep, of **El Sacramento.** Half a dozen challenging, deeper dives await more experienced divers willing to brave the current at **Los Morros de Potosí.** One of these is **Cueva de Gertrudis** (Gertrude's Cave), where nurse sharks hang out. Several generations of PADI dive masters run **Carlo Scuba** (Las Gatas Beach; ☎ 755-554-6003; **www.carloscuba.net**) offering dive excursions, including night dives, instruction, and certification. Two-tank dives usually cost about $85 (a few dollars more for more distant Morros de Potosí), $65 for one tank.

Warm water makes snorkeling enticing most of the year, with surface temps of 85°F cooling to the low 60s February through April. The best diving months are generally November through February and July and August. The best snorkeling spots are the rocky outcroppings surrounding **Playa las Gatas,** nearby **Playa Manzanillo,** and **on Isla Ixtapa** (the latter two are accessed by boat only).

SPORTFISHING

IXTAPA-ZIHUA IS HIGHLY RATED among deep-sea fishing aficionados hunting sailfish, dorado, tuna, and blue and black marlin; a steep drop-off close to shore means you don't have to travel far to find the big game fish. Most sportfishing boats range in size from 28 to 40 feet. The **International Sailfish Tournament,** usually held the first weekend in May, is the traditional local contest. Conservationists have in recent years started the **Ixtapa-Zihuatanejo Total Tag & Release Tournament,** which includes an inshore, fly-fishing event for dorado, wahoo, roosterfish, and other denizens of the not-so-deep. See **www.ixtapasportfishing.com/tournament** for tourney details.

U.S.-based **Ixtapa Sportfishing Charters** (19 Depue Lane, Stroudsburg, PA 18360; ☎ 570-688-9466 U.S.; fax in U.S. 570-688-9554; **www.ixtapa sportfishing.com**) offers catch-and-release fishing on day charters. Their boats, 28- to 42-footers, run between $295 and $450 per day. A fleet of locally operated boats, **Coopertiva Teniente José Azueta** (☎ 755-554-2056), is found at the entrance to Zihua's main dock. Cost per boat is $180 to $250 for skiffs (locally called *pangas*) with shade and emergency bathroom, or $250 to $300 for yachts 28 to 32 feet long.

SURFING

SURFING IS POPULAR AT **Playa las Gatas** and **Playa Manzanillo,** both accessible by boat from Zihua's pier; at **Escolleras,** near Marina Vallarta; at the end of **Playa Linda, Pantla,** and **Troncones,** the latter about 30 minutes north of Ixtapa on Highway 200. The best surfing months are May through October, during the rainy season. If you want to take lessons, rent a surfboard, or join a surfing safari, contact **Catcha L'Ola** (Centro Comercial Kiosko, Local 12; ☎ 755-553-1384; **www.ixtapasurf.com**).

TENNIS

ASIDE FROM HOTEL COURTS, there are few places to play tennis. Luckily **Club de Golf Palma Real** (west end of Paseo Ixtapa, next to Hotel Barceló; ☎ 755-553-1163) offers four lighted courts available for nighttime play. The cost is $8.50 per hour for the court during daylight hours and $16 an hour when the lights are needed. The courts are open 7 a.m. to 7 p.m. daily (but arrive before 6 p.m.). In the heart of Ixtapa's main hotel zone, **Hotel Emporio Ixtapa** (Boulevard Ixtapa s/n, Ixtapa; ☎ 755-553-1066) has two lighted courts and charges non-guests $10 per hour (per court, not per person).

SHOPPING *in* IXTAPA *and* ZIHUATANEJO

FACING THE HIGH-RISE HOTELS OF IXTAPA is a series of strip malls selling everything from pharmaceuticals to fine art. They tend to segue from one mall to another, making it difficult to know exactly where you are. Because the address of each one is simply Paseo de Ixtapa s/n (or *sin numero,* which means "without street number"), locals usually identify them by the hotel that's across the street. For beachwear and women's clothing, there's the rather pricey **Aqua** (Plaza La Fuente). We recommend **La Fuente** (Centro Comercial Los Patios, across from Hotel Barceló; ☎ 755-553-0812) for a larger inventory of comfortable women's resort wear and finely embroidered *huipiles* and beaded tops from Guerrero villages as well as a small but excellent selection of folk art and handcrafts. **Tandor** (Centro Comercial La Puerta; ☎ 755-553-1628) sells quality menswear such as guayabera shirts, linen shirts and slacks, and classy shorts in a variety of colors. **Mic Mac** (Plaza La Puerta; ☎ 755-553-1733) and **Galería San Angel** (Plaza Los Patios, no phone) offer a decent selection of handcrafts, clothing, purses, masks, and Talavera lookalikes. For leather and man-made shoes and accessories, there's **Christina's Leather** (Plaza Las Fuentes; ☎ 755-553-2399). **Cielito Lindo** (Centro Comercial Los Patios, Local 26; ☎ 755-553-2714) is the place to shop for good-quality jewelry, many pieces with intriguing amber stones of red or green in addition to the more traditional gold color.

In Zihua, nine out of ten shoppers head instinctively to the **Mercado de Artesanías Turístico** (Calle 5 de Mayo between Calle Ejido and Paseo del Pescador; no phone). The specialties here are brightly painted and lacquered wooden and ceramic plates, bowls, and figures, as well as silver jewelry from Taxco. More than 250 small stalls are crowded with shell jewelry, lacquer boxes and picture frames, beach clothing, and curios and souvenirs; it's a fun place to shop and a great way to support local small businesses, although quality is just average and there's a lot of repetition. Just across the street is **Arte Mexicano Nopal** (Calle Cinco de Mayo 56, ☎ 755-554-7530). The owners shop all around Mexico for unique arts and crafts, and they sometimes find unusual things. Gifted packers, they can help your precious souvenirs arrive home in one piece. Unique and beautiful embroidered and pull-thread gifts are found at **Deshilados** (Nicolás Bravo 107; ☎ 755-554-7026) and its Ixtapa sister store (Centro Comercial Los Patios; ☎ 755-553-0221). You'll find blouses, baby clothes, table runners and tablecloths, and place mats. **Alberto's** (Cuauhtemoc 12; ☎ 755-554-2161) has been around for many years and has a good collection of gold and silver jewelry, much of it handmade at their workshop and set with semi-precious stones. **Artesanías Olinalá** (Avenida 5 de Mayo 2; ☎ 755-554-6733) has an amazing selection of lacquer trays, gourds, and other items typical of its namesake village. Quality is excellent and the workmanship must be seen to be believed. **Mercado Municipal** (Calle Benito Juárez at Antonio Nava; no phone) has some clothing and beachwear in addition to a hot-food market and alleys full of the stuff of daily living.

NIGHTLIFE *in* IXTAPA *and* ZIHUATANEJO

FOR A SUNSET COCKTAIL, the view at **El Faro** (see profile in "Where to Eat in Ixtapa and Zihuatanejo," page 304) makes this restaurant-bar a natural choice.

Bandidos (Calle 5 de Mayo at Pedro Ascencio; ☎ 755-553-8072) is a popular bar and restaurant with a dedicated clientele. Sit at the bar, a table, or on the patio overlooking the street. Juan y Sus Bandidos play an invigorating mix of salsa, merengue, and romantic music weekend nights after 11 p.m., more often during the high season or when business picks up.

For late-night dancing, **Christine** (at Hotel NH Krystal, Paseo de Ixtapa s/n; ☎ 755-553-0456) continues to be one of the area's most popular and enduring discos. The club offers ladies' night and open bar on different weekday nights, and a packed house on weekend nights. **Señor Frog's** (Centro Comercial Ixtapa; ☎ 755-553-2260) caters to all ages with food as well as lively entertainment, free-flowing libations, and loud music while **Carlos'n Charlie's** (Paseo del Mar s/n, on the beach next to the Best Western Hotel at the north end of Ixtapa's hotel row; ☎ 755-553-0085; **grupoanderson.com.mx**) caters largely to an youthful crowd, both international and national. Also in Ixtapa, **Kopados** (Centro Comercial Ixtapa, behind Señor Frog's; ☎ 755-553-2000, after 10 p.m. no cover; **www.kopadosbar .com**) is a place for dancing to salsa, Cuban music, and Latin pop under a large, second-story palapa roof. The servers and barmen are friendly, and there's live music in high season, usually December through March throughout the week and almost always on weekends the rest of the year. It's popular with younger people, and despite the music, one can actually carry on a conversation. **Mulegé Bistro Lounge** (Centro Comercial Ixtapa, next door to Señor Frog's; ☎ 755-553-3861) is a restaurant serving international food for breakfast, lunch, and dinner. After 11 p.m. they dim the lights, switch the music to house and chill out, and attract locals and travelers to their modern, white-on-white lounge for drinks and conversations with friends.

PART ELEVEN

ACAPULCO

PACIFIC PLAYGROUND

ACAPULCO IS THE MOST URBAN BEACH RESORT on Mexico's Pacific Coast. It's the largest city (population nearing 1 million) in the state of Guerrero, one of the country's least-populated states. Behind the parade of hotels along the broad **Acapulco Bay,** a major city is crammed into crowded neighborhoods that notch the mountainsides like ribbons of ore. Acapulco isn't as pretty as Puerto Vallarta, where the cobblestone streets and whitewashed homes are a beautiful cliché. Nor can its natural beauty compare with that of the planned resort areas at Los Cabos and Huatulco. Nevertheless, it's one of the most popular getaways for Mexicans from every social stratum, and it's the beach of choice for European and Canadian travelers who like a bit of down-to-earth character with their sun and fun.

Acapulco's greatest attraction is its nightlife. Vacationers and locals alike tend to come alive around sunset, when party boats cruise through the bay and villa dwellers hold chic cocktail parties. Many restaurants don't even open for dinner until 7 p.m. and don't get really busy until 9 or 10. Nightclubs open around 10 p.m. but aren't much fun until after midnight, when crowds dance to everything from 1970s disco to salsa and techno. Along the **Costera,** the scene is one of youthful exuberance as rock and roll blares from beach bars. The city literally throbs at night, and it doesn't calm down until dawn. This is one place in Mexico where you'll find restaurants open 24 hours.

Like a faded beauty queen, Acapulco keeps undergoing face-lifts. Her loyal fans overlook the flaws, but this legendary playground of the stars can appear rather unsightly to newcomers. Steep hillsides, stacked with villas and hovels alike, edge Acapulco Bay (named Bahía Santa Lucía by Spanish conquistadors). Seventies-style high-rise hotels line the central curve of the bay in the Costera, where youthful visitors screech while bungee jumping or parasailing. The streets of **Old Acapulco** are clogged with buses and cars, and the sidewalks are crumbling and crowded. In the hills on the east side of the bay, bulldozers constantly make way for more elegant neighborhoods and hotels. The place has the feel of an old resort city resting on its reputation for romance.

In its heyday, the 1940s and 1950s, Acapulco was the destination of choice for the rich-and-famous Hollywood crowd. Errol Flynn, Rita Hayworth, Cary Grant, and "The Duke" (John Wayne) took over small hotels in Old Acapulco and made them their personal playgrounds. The cliff divers of **La Quebrada** became so famous they starred in a Timex watch commercial. Mexican composer Agustín Lara played the piano as his then-wife, actress María Félix, sang and danced on the sand. The Hollywood aura settled upon Acapulco in the 1950s, and a sense of that old glamour remains intact. The Kennedys, Nixons, and Clintons all spent romantic getaways in Acapulco; Elizabeth Taylor and her third husband, producer Mike Todd, got married here. Name-dropping and star sightings are still part of the Acapulco scene—you just have to know the right places and be able to get into them.

As the legions of Mexican families who vacation here annually know, Acapulco really does have something for everyone. European budget travelers, North American snowbirds, and middle-class Mexicans gravitate to Old Acapulco, where the small hotels bear a worn patina of glamour and the large all-inclusives shelter multigenerational families. Travelers seeking moderately priced hotels and restaurants and plenty of action stay on the Costera, where the beach is packed with umbrellas and water toys. Well-heeled visitors (as well as savvy bargain-hunters) head for the villas and casitas in **Acapulco Diamante.** The most alluring discos, sumptuous restaurants, and luxurious hotels are located here, along with several golf courses and a few large resorts.

Located in Acapulco's high-end Punta Diamante district, **Mundo Imperial** was until recently the focus of what tourism folk have been calling the reinvention of Acapulco. After five years of building and an investment of some $300 million, however, construction of the luxury resort, destination spa, high-tech exposition center, and shopping promenade ground to a halt in December 2008 because of the global financial crisis. Concerts and theatrical performances do take place at The Forum—a 4,000-seat theater boasting excellent sight lines and acoustics—which opened a month before work on the rest of the project was stopped.

If the complex is completed according to the original blueprint, it will contain a state-of-the-art fitness center, five swimming pools, tennis courts, and free high-speed and wireless Internet throughout the property. There will be a pets' club, and (presumably for their human handlers) personalized butler service. Sol Imperial, a destination spa and wellness center, will offer traditional Chinese medical treatments along with a wide array of spa amenties. The centerpiece of the development is to be the 730,000-square-foot Il Duomo Convention, Exhibition, and Entertainment Center.

Given its popularity with celebrities and socialites, Acapulco is a natural setting for cultural happenings. Plácido Domingo has sung at the **Acapulco Convention Center;** sports figures show up for golf tournaments. If you believed the guides leading city and boat tours, you'd think every celebrity worth an appearance in *People* magazine has a villa overlooking the bay.

QUICK FACTS *about* ACAPULCO

AIRPORT AND AIRLINES Acapulco International Airport (☎ 744-435-2060) is 12.5 miles southeast of the Costera. **American** has a winter seasonal nonstop flight from Dallas and Chicago; **Continental** flies direct from Houston year-round and from Newark in winter; **America West** offers a nonstop flight year-round from Los Angeles and Phoenix; and **Northwest** flies from Minneapolis in winter. **Aeroméxico** and **Mexicana** have flights through Mexico City. **Transportes Aeropuerto** (☎ 744-462-1095) offers shuttle service from the airport to area hotels. Call them at least 24 hours before you need to return to the airport for your flight home. The $30 to $46 fare (depending on your hotel's location) is less than that charged by private taxis.

CLIMATE Acapulco is extraordinarily humid; it gets about 59 inches of rain annually, and temperatures hover in the high 80s—but feel hotter. Tropical storms and hurricanes pass through from June to October, when the city gets washed clean. Some roads flood in heavy rains.

DRIVING Acapulco is 229 miles south of Mexico City. A car isn't necessary when touring the area, unless you're staying at an outlying hotel in Acapulco Diamante and want to do a lot of sightseeing. Most major U.S. car rental agencies have desks at the airport and representatives at the hotels. However, because car rental prices are steep, you might spend less and avoid the hassle by simply taking taxis around town or renting one by the hour.

unofficial **TIP**
Don't get on a bus that says Caleta–Cine Rio— that route winds through the back streets of downtown and takes forever to reach the beach.

GETTING AROUND Taxis are everywhere. The blue-and-white ones are licensed and are the best option for tourists who don't speak Spanish. Whether or not the cab has a meter, confirm the fare with the driver before the cab starts rolling. Many hotels have signs listing standard fares. Rates are usually higher after 11 p.m. It's easy to take the public bus between the

Costera and Old Acapulco. To get to the former, look for buses labeled BASE (the Navy base by the former Hyatt Regency Acapulco, now the Grand Hotel); heading toward the latter, the bus should say CALETA (the beach in Old Acapulco). The fare is less than $1, and there are bus stops all along the route. Yellow buses marked Acapulco run along a route from Puerto Marqués to Caleta, along the Costera.

INTERNET ACCESS Internet "cafes" (with or without coffee, beverages, or snacks) up and down the boulevard charge about $3 per 15 minutes to $3 per hour. Many of Acapulco's moderately priced hotels offer free Wi-Fi (lobby and/or guest rooms), while pricier places usually charge for both Wi-Fi and high-speed cable connection, at a cost of $20 to $40 per day for 24-hour access in your room. Access in the lobby or lobby bar is often free.

TELEPHONES The area code for Acapulco is ☎ **744;** all local phone numbers have seven digits.

TOURIST INFORMATION The **Acapulco Convention and Visitors Bureau** (Costera Miguel Alemán 38-A, Fracc. Costa Azul, next to Kentucky Fried Chicken, on upper level of HSBC bank; ☎ 744-484-8555; **ocva@ ocvacapulco.com; visitacapulco.com.mx**) is open Monday through Friday, 9 a.m. to 6 p.m., Saturday 10 a.m. to 2 p.m. They can help with hotel reservations and information on tours and transportation. The state's **Tourist Protection Agency** or Procuraduría de la Defensa del Turista (Costera Miguel Alemán 4455; ☎ 744-484-4416) has an information booth in front of the Acapulco Convention Center where clerks assist travelers with problems such as lost passports or theft; the office is open daily, 8 a.m. to 11 p.m.

WHERE *to* STAY *in* ACAPULCO

UNLESS YOU HAVE A RENTAL CAR or endless funds for cabs, your choice of hotel greatly determines your Acapulco experience. Most of the budget accommodations are located in **Old Acapulco,** a crowded urban area packed with longstanding restaurants, cafes, public beaches, markets, and intriguing inns. You give up luxury when you stay here, but you're immersed in local character. Most boat trips depart from the main pier or yacht club in this area. The **Costera,** running along the curve of Acapulco Bay, is lined with high-rise hotels, most built in the 1970s and 1980s. It's the designated tourist zone, with lots of beach action (parasailing, banana boats, personal watercraft), plenty of places to drink and dance all night long, and several air-conditioned shopping malls. Traffic is horrendous here. When you're not facing the bay, the Costera looks rather ugly, chockablock with unattractive storefronts and choked with traffic, but it's home to the convention center and other attractions.

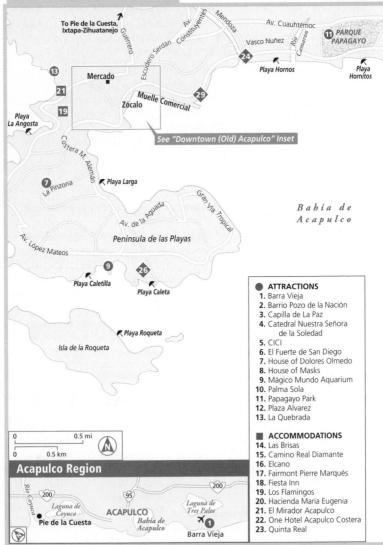

Acapulco Bay Area

To Pie de la Cuesta,
Ixtapa-Zihuatanejo

Guerrero

Av. Constituyentes
Escudero Serdán
Mendoza

Av. Cuauhtémoc

Vasco Nuñez

Río Camarón

11 PARQUE
PAPAGAYO

13

21

Mercado

24

Playa Hornos

Playa
Hornitos

19

Muelle Comercial

29

Zócalo

Playa
La Angosta

See "Downtown (Old) Acapulco" Inset

Costera M. Alemán

7

La Pinzona

Playa Larga

Av. de la Aguada

Gran Vía Tropical

*Bahía de
Acapulco*

Av. López Mateos

Peninsula de las Playas

9

26

Playa Caletilla

Playa Caleta

Playa Roqueta

Isla de la Roqueta

0   0.5 mi

0   0.5 km

N

Acapulco Region

Río Coyuca

200

95

200

Laguna de
Coyuca

ACAPULCO

Laguna de
Tres Palos

Pie de la Cuesta

Bahía de
Acapulco

Barra Vieja

1

● ATTRACTIONS
1. Barra Vieja
2. Barrio Pozo de la Nación
3. Capilla de La Paz
4. Catedral Nuestra Señora
   de la Soledad
5. CICI
6. El Fuerte de San Diego
7. House of Dolores Olmedo
8. House of Masks
9. Mágico Mundo Aquarium
10. Palma Sola
11. Papagayo Park
12. Plaza Alvarez
13. La Quebrada

■ ACCOMMODATIONS
14. Las Brisas
15. Camino Real Diamante
16. Elcano
17. Fairmont Pierre Marqués
18. Fiesta Inn
19. Los Flamingos
20. Hacienda Maria Eugenia
21. El Mirador Acapulco
22. One Hotel Acapulco Costera
23. Quinta Real

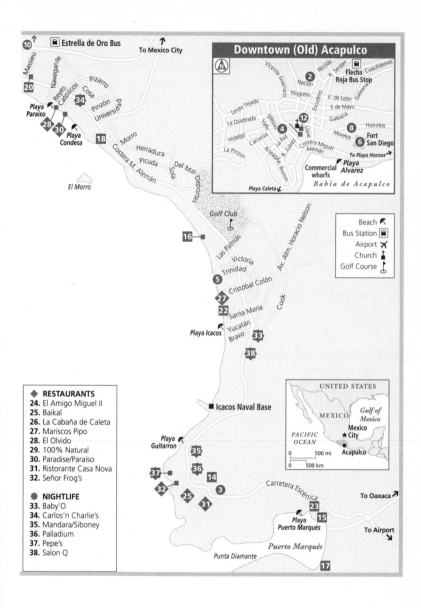

Estrella de Oro Bus

To Mexico City

10

Massieu

20

Navegante

Reyes Católicos

Pizarro

Cosa

34

Pinzón

Universidad

Playa Paraíso

28

30

Playa Condesa

18

Morro

Herradura

Picuda

Sola

Del Mar

Deportes

El Morro

Downtown (Old) Acapulco

Vicente Guerrero

Nicolás

A. Serdán

Cuauhtémoc

2

Nación

Flecha Roja Bus Stop

Progreso

Escudero

Galeana

V. de León

5 de Mayo

Lerdo Tejada

Iglesias

Galeana

La Quebrada

Valle

12

Llave

8

Hornitos

Hidalgo

Carranza

La Paz

B. Juárez

Morelos

6

Fort San Diego

La Pinzón

Anteagra

Bretón

Costera Miguel Alemán

To Playa Hornos

Commercial wharfs

Playa Alvarez

Playa Caleta

Bahía de Acapulco

Golf Club

Las Palmas

Victoria

Trinidad

Cristóbal Colón

Av. Alm. Horacio Nelson

16

5

27

22

Santa María

Cook

Playa Icacos

Yucatán

Bravo

33

38

Beach
Bus Station
Airport
Church
Golf Course

Icacos Naval Base

UNITED STATES

Gulf of Mexico

MEXICO

Mexico City

PACIFIC OCEAN

Acapulco

0 — 500 mi
0 — 500 km

Playa Guitarron

35

36

37

14

32

3

25

31

Carretera Escénica

To Oaxaca

23

15

Playa Puerto Marqués

To Airport

Puerto Marqués

Punta Diamante

17

♦ RESTAURANTS
24. El Amigo Miguel II
25. Baikal
26. La Cabaña de Caleta
27. Mariscos Pipo
28. El Olvido
29. 100% Natural
30. Paradise/Paraíso
31. Ristorante Casa Nova
32. Señor Frog's

☀ NIGHTLIFE
33. Baby'O
34. Carlos'n Charlie's
35. Mandara/Siboney
36. Palladium
37. Pepe's
38. Salon Q

The newest section of the tourist zone is located on Carretera Escénica, which climbs and dips along steep cliffs on the east side of Acapulco Bay to Puerto Marqués and the airport. Much of this area is undergoing ongoing development; in general, the region is called **Acapulco Diamante.** The newest hotels overlook Marqués Bay and are geared toward reclusive vacationers (though a few huge all-inclusive properties share the bay and Playa Revolcadero).

Choosing a hotel close to the beach in Acapulco is something of a moot point if you're hoping to swim in the bay because it's often polluted. That doesn't discourage beachgoers from zooming about on personal watercraft and banana boats. If you partake in such activities, try not to ingest a lot of water.

Acapulco's busiest seasons occur during Mexican holidays. Hotels become incredibly crowded and noisy and rooms are packed with several members of multigenerational families. Advance reservations are a must, and many hotels have severe cancellation policies.

unofficial **TIP**
The city is absolutely packed with families in August, around Christmas, and during Semana Santa (the week before Easter).

ACCOMMODATION PROFILES

Las Brisas $$$$$

OVERALL ★★★★	QUALITY ★★★½	VALUE ★★★

Carretera Escénica 5255; ☎ 744-469-6900 or 800-223-6800; fax 744-446-5332; brisas.com.mx

John F. and Jackie Kennedy honeymooned here. Need we say more? Las Brisas is relentlessly romantic and rosy pink—even the rental Jeeps look like they're blushing. Couples on their first or fifteenth honeymoons tend to get mighty cozy in serene suites with private pools and cushy, king-size beds. Confident singles are happy here as well, thanks to the tranquil surroundings and the friendly drivers who transport guests up and down the hilly, 40-acre resort compound. A shuttle runs to La Concha Beach Club, where guests play in salt- and freshwater pools or snorkel along the rocky coastline. Closer to "home," each room has its own private plunge pool. Noise from nearby discos can be a problem if you prefer leaving your shutters open to sea breezes. However, the hotel provides just the right amount of casual luxury to make guests feel pampered and refreshed. The property's beach club, restaurants, meetings rooms, and lobby were extensively revamped in 2007.

SETTING AND FACILITIES

Location In Las Brisas hills at Acapulco Diamante; rooms are staggered up steep hillsides above Carretera Escénica.

Dining 3 restaurants.

How Accommodations Compare in Acapulco

ACCOMMODATION	OVERALL	QUALITY	VALUE	COST
Quinta Real	★★★★★	★★★★★	★★★	$$$–$$$$
Fairmont Pierre Marqués	★★★★	★★★★	★★★★	$$$$
Las Brisas	★★★★	★★★½	★★★	$$$$$
Elcano	★★★½	★★★½	★★★	$$$
Camino Real Diamante	★★★	★★★	★★★	$$$$
Fiesta Inn	★★½	★★★	★★★★	$$
Los Flamingos	★★½	★★	★★★	$
Hacienda María Eugenia	★★	★★½	★★★★	$
One Hotel Acapulco Costera	★★★	★★½	★★★★	$
El Mirador Acapulco	★½	★½	★★	$$

Amenities and services Beach club, pools, spa, gym, water-sports center, children's activities (holidays only), shops, tour desk, 2 bars, 24-hour room service (extra charge), business center, Internet (Wi-Fi in the lobby, business center, and some rooms).

ACCOMMODATIONS

Rooms 214 casitas, 49 suites.

All rooms AC, fan, windows that open, balcony or terrace, hair dryer, safe, minibar, satellite TV.

Some rooms Ocean view, whirlpool tub, DVD, nonsmoking.

Comfort and decor The decor is minimalist, with low table and chairs (not comfortable for working on a laptop or writing postcards), stall showers, plush towels, and balconies or terraces with views of the bay. Coffee, fruit, and sweet breads are placed in a cubby by each room's front door every morning. A $20 million remodel in 2007 gave all rooms new bedding and flat-screen TVs and larger balconies with French-inspired furniture. In suites, luxurious and spacious marble bathrooms have rain showers in grottolike settings.

PAYMENT, RESERVATIONS, AND RESTRICTIONS

Deposit Credit-card guarantee with 1-night deposit; cancel 8 days before arrival date to avoid penalty (nonrefundable guarantees for some holidays and packages). Tipping is discouraged; instead, a $20 daily service charge is added to the bill.

Credit cards AE, MC, V.

Check-in/out 3 p.m./1 p.m.

Camino Real Diamante $$$$

OVERALL ★★★	QUALITY ★★★	VALUE ★★★

**Carretera Escénica 14; ☎ 744-435-1010 or 800-722-6466 U.S.;
fax 744-435-1020; www.caminoreal.com**

Hidden down a steep, rough road and seemingly buried in jungle, the Camino Real is perfect for reclusive vacationers. Low buildings and villas rise above a small cove in Marqués Bay, their green roofs and ivory walls blending into the rocky landscape. You'll likely ignore the outside world as you lounge about the deep, blue pools over a tiny beach. The food is great, the staff gracious and accommodating, and spa treatments are available.

SETTING AND FACILITIES

Location In Acapulco Diamante, near Las Brisas.

Dining 2 restaurants, including La Huerta, with national and international fare, inaugurated in December 2007; 2 bars.

Amenities and services Beach, 3 pools, shops, gym, spa, tour desk, organized children's activities (weekends and holidays only), room service, wireless Internet in public spaces.

ACCOMMODATIONS

Rooms 157.

All rooms AC, windows that open, balcony or terrace, fan, safe, hair dryer, minibar, satellite TV, high-speed Internet.

Some rooms Ocean view, whirlpool tub, coffeemaker, disabled access, nonsmoking.

Comfort and decor Rooms are lovely and serene, with cream-colored walls, marble floors, and large bathrooms, although some of the standard rooms are very small and others are far from the pool. Elevators connect most levels, but you may have to climb a few stairs to get around.

PAYMENT, RESERVATIONS, AND RESTRICTIONS

Deposit Credit card; 3-day cancellation policy.

Credit cards AE, DC, MC, V.

Check-in/out 3 p.m./1 p.m.

Elcano $$$

OVERALL ★★★½	QUALITY ★★★½	VALUE ★★★

**Avenida Costera Miguel Alemán 75; ☎ 744-435-1500 or
01800-090-7500; fax 744-484-2230; www.hotel-elcano.com**

You can't help but imagine what Acapulco was like in the 1950s when you enter this blue-and-white fantasy. Remodeled in the mid-1990s, the hotel has a subtle nautical design with plenty of whirring ceiling fans and wicker furnishings. Blue-tile backrests on the beds and slatted-wood lounge chairs on the balconies make the rooms feel like spacious cruise-ship cabins.

Look for murals and paintings by Cristina Rubalcava, who fancifully captures scenes of cliff divers, mermaids, and actresses dancing on the sand. If you're not staying here, have breakfast or lunch at the hotel's Bambuco Restaurant to enjoy a setting reminiscent of Casablanca. The food's great, too.

SETTING AND FACILITIES

Location Costera near Convention Center.

Dining 2 restaurants, 3 bars.

Amenities and services Beach, pool, hot tub, gym, massage, tour desk, organized children's activities (high season only), shops, room service, Wi-Fi, business center, Internet.

ACCOMMODATIONS

Rooms 180.

All rooms AC, fan, hair dryer, safe, minibar, cable TV.

Some rooms Ocean view, balcony, bathtub, Wi-Fi, disabled access.

Comfort and decor Fresh, airy feel; surprisingly quiet for the location; romantic and casual.

PAYMENT, RESERVATIONS, AND RESTRICTIONS

Deposit Guarantee with credit card; cancel 48 hours ahead with no fee.

Credit cards AE, MC, V.

Check-in/out 3 p.m./1 p.m.

Fairmont Pierre Marqués $$$$

OVERALL ★★★★	QUALITY ★★★★	VALUE ★★★★

Playa Revolcadero s/n, Col. Granjas del Marqués; ☎ 744-466-1000 or 800-441-1414 U.S., 800-257-7544; fax 744-466-1046; www.fairmont.com

Once the private vacation home of J. Paul Getty (who developed the adjacent golf course), the Pierre is a calm oasis beside the more bustling Fairmont Acapulco Princess. Guests have use of all Princess facilities—including its excellent spa—and share the long, broad beach at Playa Revolcadero. The original hotel, built in 1957, was totally remodeled and expanded in 2001. Pathways around pools and villas are lined with fountains and flowers, and the ambience is subdued.

SETTING AND FACILITIES

Location Acapulco Diamante beside the Fairmont Acapulco Princess hotel.

Dining 2 restaurants, 2 bars.

Amenities and services Beach, 3 pools, gym, spa, organized children's activities (at Fairmont Princess).

ACCOMMODATIONS

Rooms 229.

All rooms AC, safe, satellite TV.

Some rooms Ocean view, balcony or terrace, bathtub, hair dryer, high-speed Internet.

Comfort and decor The hotel was drastically remodeled in 2001 in the style of a rambling private hacienda—one with a lot of guestrooms, anyway. All rooms have sliding-glass doors opening to generously sized patios and balconies. Compared to the Fairmont Acapulco Princess, the Pierre feels like a boutique hotel. The pool areas are heavenly and peaceful, and guests tend to be more reserved and well dressed.

PAYMENT, RESERVATIONS, AND RESTRICTIONS

Deposit Guarantee reservation with credit card; cancel 3 days before arrival to avoid penalty; nonrefundable deposits required with some packages and around holidays.

Credit cards AE, MC, V.

Check-in/out 3 p.m./1 p.m.

Fiesta Inn $$

OVERALL ★★½	QUALITY ★★★	VALUE ★★★★

Costera Miguel Alemán 2311; ☎ 744-435-0500 or 800-343-7821 U.S.; fax 744-435-0509; www.fiestainn.com

A business traveler's hotel in the midst of the high-rise hotels of La Costera, the Fiesta is an efficient and quiet oasis. Amenities are few but well-suited to the clientele, who care more about practicalities than luxury. Still, families familiar with the chain and its frequent-guest program find it a good vacation escape.

SETTING AND FACILITIES

Location Costera.

Dining 1 cafe-restaurant, 1 bar.

Amenities and services Beach, pool, gym, organized children's activities, room service, business center, wireless Internet.

ACCOMMODATIONS

Rooms 220.

All rooms AC, balcony, bathtub, hair dryer, coffeemaker, cable TV, free high-speed Internet, Wi-Fi.

Some rooms Ocean view, nonsmoking, 1 room with disabled access.

Comfort and decor The hotel was very quiet when we visited, which is a major plus in the Costera. The front desk clerks are efficient and courteous. There are few frills in the rooms, which are immaculate and plain, with sinks outside the bathroom and coffeemakers, but no minibars or safe-deposit boxes. There are several meeting rooms and a good business center.

PAYMENT, RESERVATIONS, AND RESTRICTIONS

Deposit Guarantee with credit card; you forfeit cost of your entire stay if you cancel fewer than 3 days before arrival; forfeit 2 nights' deposit if you make changes or cancel fewer than 21 days before arrival during high season and holidays.

Credit cards AE, MC, V.

Check-in/out 3 p.m./1 p.m.

Los Flamingos $

OVERALL ★★½	QUALITY ★★	VALUE ★★★

Avenida López Mateos s/n; ☎ 744-482-0690; www.hotellosflamingos.com

Those who love Acapulco's Hollywood heyday have a fondness for this small, inconveniently located hotel once favored by Johnny Weissmuller, Cary Grant, John Wayne, and other celluloid heroes. If you're hoping to hang out in a hammock, sip margaritas, dine on *carne asada* and excellent guacamole, and listen to guitarists croon old boleros, this is your place. You can walk up and down the road to the center of Old Acapulco, if you must. Better to claim a room at the edge of the cliff overlooking the bay, turn on the ceiling fan, and pretend you're in a black-and-white movie (though your surroundings are largely white and pink). Most of the staff members have been around for decades, as have many of the guests.

SETTING AND FACILITIES

Location On steep street above waterfront in Old Acapulco.

Dining Restaurant, coffee shop, bar.

Amenities and services Beach club, pool, tour desk, shop, room service, Wi-Fi in lobby.

ACCOMMODATIONS

Rooms 40.

All rooms Windows that open.

Some rooms Ocean view, whirlpool, TV.

Comfort and decor White walls, large windows, and well-maintained bathrooms.

PAYMENT, RESERVATIONS, AND RESTRICTIONS

Deposit Credit card; 72 hours before arrival to avoid cancellation fees.

Credit cards MC, V.

Check-in/out 2 p.m./1 p.m.

Hacienda María Eugenia $

OVERALL ★★	QUALITY ★★½	VALUE ★★★★

Avenida Costera Miguel Alemán 176; ☎ 744-435-0660; fax 744-435-0669; haciendamariaeugenia.com.mx

By far the best budget hotel on the Costera, this little gem sits across the street from the larger hotels and beach. Its cheery arches, balconies, and pillars are meant to evoke a colonial ambience, and it works. The four-story building (sans elevator) frames a central courtyard and a long pool with a waterslide. Rooms that face the side street are best; you can actually sit on your little balcony without being deafened by traffic noise.

SETTING AND FACILITIES

Location Costera, across the street from Playa Condesa.

Dining 1 restaurant.

Amenities and services Beach club, 2 pools, Wi-Fi.

ACCOMMODATIONS

Rooms 66.

All rooms AC, bathtub, balcony, cable TV.

Some rooms Kitchenette, refrigerator, balcony, ocean view, Wi-Fi.

Comfort and decor The rooms here beat out everything else in this price range because they all have bathtubs as well as showers (uncommon in budget accommodations) and a table with four chairs. A rustic-wood theme prevails; mattresses sit on plywood platforms and are a bit thin. At times the hotel is filled with families; rooms away from the pool are quiet.

PAYMENT, RESERVATIONS, AND RESTRICTIONS

Deposit Credit-card guarantee; cancellation policy varies.

Credit cards AE, MC, V.

Check-in/out 3 p.m./1 p.m.

El Mirador Acapulco $$

OVERALL	★½	QUALITY	★½	VALUE	★★

Plazoleta La Quebrada 74; ☎ 744-483-1155, 744-483-1221, or 866-573-7197; fax 744-483-8800; hotelelmiradoracapulco.com.mx

You're almost guaranteed to come by this Acapulco institution at some point. It's one of the famed hotels favored by the 1950s Hollywood set and has a striking location atop La Quebrada, site of the cliff-diver show. Ownership has changed several times. We're fond of the simple, apartment-like suites in the 200 building overlooking the open ocean. They have kitchenettes and balconies perched over the waves. The restaurant is packed with travelers watching the show, and the staff is not always efficient. Room prices include tax, free stay for two children under age 12, and buffet breakfast for all. Cost is about half the rack rate in the off-season.

SETTING AND FACILITIES

Location La Quebrada, above Old Acapulco.

Dining 2 restaurants, 2 bars.

Amenities and services 2 pools, saltwater pool, hot tub, shops, room service.

ACCOMMODATIONS

Rooms 142, including 9 junior suites.

All rooms AC, balcony or terrace, bathtub, minibar, coffeemaker, safe, refrigerator, satellite TV, VCR.

Some rooms Ocean views, whirlpool tub, kitchenettes, nonsmoking.

Comfort and decor This old house needs a lot of work. The owners are lax with maintenance, and the hotel sits right over the open sea. But the rooms and gardens have a decidedly Mexican flair, with tiles, textiles, and fountains all evoking a sense of nostalgia. The absence of elevators makes the compound inaccessible to anyone who has trouble climbing stairs.

PAYMENT, RESERVATIONS, AND RESTRICTIONS

Deposit Guarantee reservation with credit card 24 hours before arrival.

Credit cards AE, MC, V.

Check-in/out 3 p.m./1 p.m.

One Hotel Acapulco Costera $

OVERALL ★★★	QUALITY ★★½	VALUE ★★★★

Costera Miguel Alemán 16, Colonia Costa Azul; ☎ 744-435-0470; fax 744-435-0471; www.onehotels.com

Mexico's Grupo Posadas, which has the Fiesta Americana and Fiesta Inn brands, has recently inaugurated this economy-class brand geared toward businesspeople; express check-out is designed to minimize hassle. Rooms have few amenities, but things like coffee and a safe for valuables are available in the reception area. The hotel is one block away from the beach and doesn't have the amenities that beach resorts usually have, but it's worth considering since it's brand new and very reasonably priced. The hotel has indoor parking, too.

SETTING AND FACILITIES

Location In the middle of the hotel zone.

Dining "Food corner" for Continental breakfast only.

Amenities and services Pool, business center, high-speed Internet, Wi-Fi.

ACCOMMODATIONS

Rooms 126.

All rooms AC, cable TV, Wi-Fi.

Some rooms Nonsmoking.

Comfort and decor Rooms are sleek and modern, designed for efficiency and comfort, with work desks.

PAYMENT, RESERVATIONS, AND RESTRICTIONS

Deposit Credit card; cancel before 6 p.m. same day.

Credit cards AE, MC, V.

Check-in/out 3 p.m./1 p.m.

Quinta Real $$$–$$$$

OVERALL ★★★★★	QUALITY ★★★★★	VALUE ★★★

Paseo de la Quinta 6, Acapulco Diamante Real; ☎ 744-469-1500 or 866-621-9288 U.S. and Canada; fax 744-469-1516; www.quintareal.com

There's nothing old-fashioned about this architectural masterpiece at the tip of a steep cliff over Marqués Bay. Private villas rise around the hotel as workers chip into massive, rocky hills, creating modern buttresses for exquisite homes in this upscale development. Like all hotels in this chain, the Quinta Real is quietly elegant, with 74 suites in a five-story building overlooking the pool and Punta Diamante beach. Security is tight; make reservations for a meal, or for a treatment in the excellent spa, if you want to see how celebrities relax.

SETTING AND FACILITIES

Location Acapulco Diamante near Fairmont Acapulco Princess hotel.

Dining 2 restaurants, bar.

Amenities and services Beach, 2 pools, gym, spa, marina, tour desk, organized children's activities, shops, 24-hour room service, Internet, Wi-Fi.

ACCOMMODATIONS

Rooms 74 suites.

All rooms AC, fan, windows that open, ocean view, balcony or terrace, bathtub, hair dryer, safe, satellite TV, high-speed Internet, Wi-Fi.

Some rooms Minibar, whirlpool tub, nonsmoking, disabled access.

Comfort and decor Elegant, with marble floors, cushy beds with plenty of pillows, original artwork, and attentive service.

PAYMENT, RESERVATIONS, AND RESTRICTIONS

Deposit Guarantee reservation 2 days in advance with credit card; 3-day cancellation fee.

Credit cards AE, MC, V.

Check-in/out 3 p.m./1 p.m.

WHERE *to* EAT *in* ACAPULCO

YOU CAN'T DENY THE VARIETY OF DINING OPTIONS in Acapulco, though it sometimes seems you're surrounded by fast-food joints and global chains such as Hard Rock Cafe and Planet Hollywood. There's a lot of innovative cooking taking place in the hills around Las Brisas—with a half-dozen interesting restaurants in a row along the curving road, chefs need to outwit the competition. You can find several excellent hotel restaurants as well, including **Bellavista** at Las Brisas and **Bambuco** at the Elcano.

Acapulco has a few good restaurants in the tourist areas that serve great regional food. Our local favorites include all sorts of seafood preparations with an *acapulqueño* twist. The ceviche, for example, usually includes cocktail sauce or ketchup.

The most important dish to residents of the state of Guerrero is *pozole*, a hominy stew with chicken or pork that's traditionally

How Restaurants Compare in Acapulco

RESTAURANT	CUISINE	COST	OVERALL	QUALITY	VALUE
Bailkal	International fusion	Mod/exp	★★★★★	★★★★★	★★★★½
El Olvido	International	Mod/exp	★★★★	★★★★½	★★★★
Ristorante Casa Nova	Northern Italian	Very exp	★★★½	★★★★	★★
La Cabaña de Caleta	Seafood	Inexp	★★★	★★★	★★★½
Mariscos Pipo	Seafood	Mod	★★★	★★★	★★½
El Amigo Miguel II	Seafood	Inexp	★★½	★★½	★★★
Señor Frog's	American/Mexican	Mod	★★	★★★	★★★
100% Natural	Health Food	Inexp	★★	★★½	★★★★
Paradise/Paraíso	Mexican/international	Mod/exp	★	★★	★

served on Thursdays. Look for POZOLE EL JUEVES ("Pozole on Thursdays") signs, and you're sure to find crowds lingering over big bowls of the savory broth. Trays of oregano, chopped onions, dried chiles, *chicharrones* (fried pork skins), and chunks of avocado are set beside each bowl; for some, a bottle of tequila is the requisite centerpiece.

Dinner is served exceptionally late here; some restaurants don't even open until 7 p.m., and many serve dinner until midnight. Two casual, all-night restaurants, **El Zorrito** (Costera Miguel Alemán s/n; ☎ 744-485-7914) and **El Fogón** (Costera Miguel Alemán 10; ☎ 744-484-5079), have branches along the Costera and serve standard *huevos rancheros,* tacos, enchiladas, and other stick-to-the-ribs fare.

unofficial **TIP**
Those in the know typically load up on protein and carbs before hitting the discos, then search out a 24-hour restaurant for a dawn breakfast.

RESTAURANT PROFILES

 El Amigo Miguel II ★★½

SEAFOOD	INEXPENSIVE	QUALITY ★★½	VALUE ★★★

Costera, near the fort; Costera Miguel Alemán s/n; ☎ 744-486-2868

Reservations Not accepted.
Entree range $7–$12.

Payment MC, V.

Service rating ★★.

Parking Street.

Bar Full service.

Dress Casual.

Disabled access Limited.

Customers Local families on weekend afternoons, business lunchers on weekdays.

Hours Daily, 11 a.m.–8 p.m.

SETTING AND ATMOSPHERE Enormous palapa roof over a cement-floor dining room packed with plastic tables. Crowded, noisy, fun. Try to get one of the tables at the edge of the dining room closest to the sand.

HOUSE SPECIALTIES Whole fresh lobster, *filete Miguel* (fish filet stuffed with conch, shrimp, and octopus).

SUMMARY AND COMMENTS Located on a broad beach favored by locals and anglers, Amigo Miguel is a longtime favorite for travelers seeking a break from Gringolandia. Though most of the waiters speak at least a bit of English, this is a good place to try out your Spanish while ordering grilled *huachinango* (red snapper), *tamales de pescado* (fish tamales), and whole *langosta* (lobster). The lobster is caught in the little town of Marquella south of the city, and Miguel's tends to serve it fresh when other places are using frozen lobster.

Baikal ★★★★★

INTERNATIONAL FUSION	MODERATE/ EXPENSIVE	QUALITY ★★★★★	VALUE ★★★★½

Acapulco Diamante; Carretera Escénica 22; ☎ 744-446-6845

Reservations A must.

Entree range $17 and up.

Payment AE, MC, V.

Service rating ★★★★.

Parking Adjacent lot, valet.

Bar Full service, extensive wine list.

Dress Resort Chic; dressing up advised, no shorts.

Disabled access Only in private salons; stairs to main restaurant.

Customers Residents of upscale vacation villas, travelers on a big night out.

Hours Daily, Sunday–Thursday, 7–1 p.m.; Friday and Saturday, 7 p.m.–2 a.m.; closed Monday

SETTING AND ATMOSPHERE Avant-garde elegance, with cream and white linens, and gauze drapes dividing a section of the dining room for privacy; subdued conversation; soft jazz playing in the background.

HOUSE SPECIALTIES Steamed red snapper with lobster butter; sautéed calamari with crab marmalade.

SUMMARY AND COMMENTS Chic without being pretentious, Baikal combines stunning design with exciting cuisine. A peaked palm roof covers a pond framed by blazing torches at the entryway; a curving stairway and elevator lead down to the dining room, built right into the rock with floor-to-ceiling windows facing Acapulco Bay. A mirror on the back wall reflects the scenery, and at several points during the evening underwater films display scenes of diving porpoises and spouting orcas on movie screens. The cutting-edge cuisine is invariably divine. Choose the lobster tail with goat cheese, U.S. choice steak with Roquefort, or tangy seafood salad. Portions are generous and artfully presented. Baikal is our first choice for a classic Acapulco night out.

 La Cabaña de Caleta ★★★

SEAFOOD INEXPENSIVE QUALITY ★★★ VALUE ★★★½

Old Acapulco; Playa Caleta s/n next to Hotel Acamar; ☎ 744-482-5007; www.lacabanadecaleta.com

Reservations Not normally accepted.

Entree range $8–$15.

Payment AE, MC, V.

Service rating ★★.

Parking Limited Valet parking.

Bar Full service, tasty piña coladas and margaritas.

Dress Bathing suits and cover-ups if you like, especially on the beach.

Disabled access Tables are crowded together, but staff will gladly move them to make room for a wheelchair; bathrooms are small.

Customers Beachgoers still wet and sandy.

Hours Daily, 9 a.m.–8:30 p.m.

SETTING AND ATMOSPHERE There's little difference between the beach and the restaurant, save for the tables and chairs. The thatched roof and fans do make the dining room, just above the beach, a tad cooler than it is on the sand. Families gather around long, plastic tables, while kids run around on the sand—totally casual. There are showers and lockers for those who want to shed the sandy suit, however.

HOUSE SPECIALTIES Seafood crêpes, seafood casserole, paella (on Saturday and Sunday).

SUMMARY AND COMMENTS Imelda Alvarez and her family have been running this Caleta landmark for decades, and La Cabaña is one of the most popular beach restaurants in Old Acapulco. We like it for long lunches of ceviche, *campechana* cocktails (with shrimp, octopus, and fish), shrimp crêpes, and whole snapper grilled with garlic and spices. Bring a large group, order pitchers of lemonade, and sample as many of the seafood specialties as you can.

Mariscos Pipo ★★★

SEAFOOD	MODERATE	QUALITY ★★★	VALUE ★★½

Costera, near the Convention Center; Costera Miguel Alemán 105;
☎ **744-484-0165**

Reservations Not accepted.

Entree range $9–$20.

Payment AE, MC, V.

Service rating ★★.

Parking Street.

Bar Full service.

Dress Casual.

Disabled access None.

Customers Locals on lunch and dinner breaks, large families.

Hours Daily, 1–9:30 p.m.

SETTING AND ATMOSPHERE Cavernous, hall-like dining room strewn with fishing nets, floats, and other nautical decor. Noisy and basic; plastic plates, flimsy paper napkins—and TV in the background, especially during *fútbol* (soccer) games.

HOUSE SPECIALTIES *Pulpo a la plancha* (grilled octopus), *langostinos* (crayfish), whole fried fish.

SUMMARY AND COMMENTS The best restaurant near the Convention Center, Pipo's is a local institution. Also visit branches on the beach and in downtown; all are popular and usually packed around 3 p.m. You can feast inexpensively on seafood soups, and rice with shrimp, or order a large, whole red snapper fried and served with rice and tortillas (whole fish are served by size; the largest feeds at least two hungry adults and a couple of kids). The food is all that matters; decor and comfort are secondary.

El Olvido ★★★★

INTERNATIONAL	MODERATE	QUALITY ★★★★½	VALUE ★★★★

Costera Miguel Alemán s/n, in Plaza Marbella; ☎ **744-481-0203;**
elolvido.com.mx

Reservations Suggested for dinner.

Entree range $10–$21.

Payment MC, V.

Service rating ★★★.

Parking Limited parking in Plaza Marbella lot.

Bar Full service, some imported wines.

Dress Casual but neat.

Disabled access None.

Customers Local professionals, couples, singles.

Hours Daily, 6 p.m.–1a.m.

SETTING AND ATMOSPHERE It's located at the back of a minimall and just above the beach. Tables at the edge of a railing overlook the beach scene, as it dwindles from daytime crowds to joggers and couples strolling hand-in-hand while watching the sunset. Torches and candlelight add a romantic touch, but you won't feel out of place eating alone. A small shop inside the restaurant displays handcrafted glassware and dishes.

HOUSE SPECIALTIES Chilled avocado soup, shrimp with coconut-ginger sauce.

SUMMARY AND COMMENTS Professionals working in the nearby hotels enjoy after-work drinks and dinner at this small, comfortable restaurant that they wish they could keep a secret. But word's out that "The Forgotten One" is an undeserved moniker, and reservations are a must for late weekend dinners here. The menu offers some unusual combinations such as the surprisingly tasty lamb chops with mole sauce. Take time to linger over an espresso before club-hopping.

100% Natural ★★

HEALTH FOOD	INEXPENSIVE	QUALITY ★★½	VALUE ★★★★

Old Acapulco; Costera Miguel Alemán 34; ☎ 744-484-8440; 100natural.com.mx

Reservations Not accepted.

Entree range $6–$10.

Payment AE, MC, V.

Service rating ★★.

Parking Limited street parking.

Bar Beer and wine.

Dress Casual.

Disabled access None.

Customers Office workers at lunch; vacationing vegetarians with carnivorous cronies.

Hours Daily, 7 a.m.–11 p.m.

SETTING AND ATMOSPHERE Bright white-and-green walls and linens in the dining room, tables set out on a pier over the water, casual and very clean.

HOUSE SPECIALTIES Whole-wheat waffles, *pescado enamorado* (fish stuffed with cream cheese, nuts, and spinach), *pollo goyo* (grilled chicken breast with melted cheese and mustard).

SUMMARY AND COMMENTS Several branches of this popular health-food restaurant are around town (as well as elsewhere in Mexico). We like this one for its over-the-water seating and live piano music on Saturdays and Sundays from 9 a.m. to 1 p.m. The soy burgers, platters of steamed veggies, enormous salads, and juices and smoothies (everything is cleaned with purified water) are absolute delights after too much overindulgence elsewhere. The menu isn't totally meat-free—there is a turkey-ham sandwich along with the grilled chicken and many seafood selections.

Paradise/Paraíso ★

MEXICAN/INTERNATIONAL   MODERATE/EXPENSIVE   QUALITY ★★   VALUE ★

Costera; Costera Miguel Alemán 107 by Fiesta Americana Condesa Acapulco hotel; ☎ 744-484-5988c

Reservations Accepted for large groups.

Entree range $10–$40.

Payment AE, MC, V.

Service rating ★★★.

Parking Limited street parking.

Bar Full service.

Dress Shorts and T-shirts.

Disabled access None.

Customers Young travelers looking for a wild party.

Hours Daily, noon–midnight.

SETTING AND ATMOSPHERE A wooden stairway leads down from the sidewalk to a large, open-air restaurant beside a pool and bungee-jumping apparatus. Diners have use of a saltwater swimming pool. Waiters break into song and dirty dancing every half hour; as the night goes on, diners take to the stage as well. One disconcerting point—the ladies' room door opens right onto the dining room.

HOUSE SPECIALTIES Garlic shrimp, Szechuan chicken, shrimp soup.

SUMMARY AND COMMENTS This is the best of the beach restaurant-bars lining the Costera. The waiters are relentlessly cheerful, the food is good (if overpriced), and strangers soon become friends. Screams from the adjacent bungee jumpers pierce the air, though the music gets so loud it nearly drowns them out. The menu has a good selection of Chinese rice and noodle dishes, and the drinks are enormous.

Ristorante Casa Nova ★★★½

NORTHERN ITALIAN   VERY EXPENSIVE   QUALITY ★★★★   VALUE ★★

Acapulco Diamante; Carretera Escénica 5256; ☎ 744-446-6237

Reservations Essential.

Entree range $25–$50.

Payment AE, MC, V.

Service rating ★★★.

Parking Valet.

Bar Full service, 25 brands of scotch and vodka, large list of imported wines.

Dress Dressy resort attire, collared shirts and slacks for men.

Disabled access None.

Customers Lots of repeat customers, local regulars.

Hours Daily, 7–11:30 p.m.

SETTING AND ATMOSPHERE Glass-enclosed atrium entrance, high-ceilinged dining room with chandeliers on low glow so as not to interfere with candlelight, huge floral arrangements, some tables on terraces overlooking the bay—very elegant.

HOUSE SPECIALTIES Seafood pasta, New Zealand lamb.

SUMMARY AND COMMENTS The restaurant is located right across the street from Las Brisas, which makes it popular with that hotel's guests. It's got lots of nearby competition, but regulars wouldn't splurge anywhere else. The waiters in crisp, white shirts and black vests prepare a tangy Caesar salad tableside. The entrees of choice—veal piccatta, lobster ravioli, and Norwegian salmon—are skillfully prepared and predictable. Casa Nova isn't as exciting as other restaurants in this neighborhood, but it is dependable.

Señor Frog's ★★

AMERICAN/MEXICAN	MODERATE	QUALITY ★★★	VALUE ★★★

Fracc. El Guitarrón; Carretera Escénica 28 at La Vista; ☎ 744-446-5734

Reservations Accepted but not usually necessary.

Entree range $10–$25.

Payment AE, MC, V.

Service rating ★★★.

Parking Self-parking, small parking lot.

Bar Full service.

Dress Casual.

Disabled access Yes.

Customers Travelers looking for recognizable (i.e., Americanized) Mexican food, locals for Thursday *pozole*.

Hours Daily, 10 a.m.–midnight.

SETTING AND ATMOSPHERE Casual and fun, with serapes, sombreros, piñatas, and other Mexican kitsch decorating walls and ceilings; view of the bay.

HOUSE SPECIALTIES *Pozole,* oysters, *carne asada* platters, barbecued ribs and chicken.

SUMMARY AND COMMENTS Though it's part of a chain known for its party-time theme, this Señor Frog's is more subdued and mature. The food is dependable, servings are bountiful, and the flavoring is subdued enough to soothe picky eaters. Tortilla soup, fajitas, taquitos, and caramel crêpes add a Mexican flair to a menu that aims to please. Most of the restaurants in this area are chic and expensive; this is a more moderate alternative.

SIGHTSEEING *in* ACAPULCO

ONE STREET CONNECTS NEARLY ALL of Acapulco's major sights. The main avenue running along the edge of the bay is called **Avenida Costera Miguel Alemán**—just call it the Costera and everyone will know what you mean—and connects Acapulco's three main tourism centers: **Old Acapulco,** the Costera itself, and **Acapulco Diamante.**

ATTRACTIONS

Old Acapulco contains the city's most interesting cultural sights. Located at the western curve of the bay, the area begins at **Playa Caleta,** a shallow beach jammed with umbrellas, towels, and local families. The palapa-covered restaurants along the sand serve some of the best seafood in town—if you're looking for local color, you'll find it here. The neighborhood is packed with small and medium-sized accommodations and small shops. It's a budget traveler's delight because nearly everything sold here is at least 20% cheaper than in the more modern parts of town.

 Mágico Mundo Aquarium (☎ 744-483-1215) on Playa Caleta is a water park with two seawater pools and two wildlife shows a day. On display are tropical fish, turtles, alligators, and other animals. It's a great spot for kids, who are delighted to play here all day, but adults sans kids can check out the highlights in an hour or so. Two restaurants serve burgers, hot dogs, and seafood. It's open daily, 9 a.m. to 6 p.m.; admission is $6 adults, $3 children.

Small skiffs carry passengers across the water from Caleta to **Isla de la Roqueta.** The calm waters off the island are good for swimming and snorkeling, and a few simple, beach-facing restaurants—and roving vendors—sell cold drinks and snacks. A trail leads to an old lighthouse atop the steep island. The climb takes about 20 minutes, and the view from on top is fabulous. Do this hike early in the morning, and carry plenty of water.

The center of Old Acapulco and the downtown area is the *zócalo*, also called **Plaza Alvarez.** The plaza has all the requisite elements—a central gazebo, lots of tall shade trees, shoeshine boys, flower sellers, and a few outdoor cafes—all overseen by the **Catedral Nuestra Señora de la Soledad,** a church topped with two onion-shaped domes. Party boats depart from the docks across the Costera from the plaza, and local anglers beach their *pangas* and untangle their fishing nets on the beaches east of the docks. Wander along these beaches just after dawn and you'll see shoppers examining the catch of the day as the anglers return from their nights at sea.

One of Acapulco's oldest neighborhoods, **Barrio Pozo de la Nación,** has become a stop on city tours. Small adobe buildings from the 1850s are clustered around a well that was dug to help the neighborhood avoid a cholera epidemic sweeping through the city. Young girls in frilly white dresses and boys in starched shirts and pants perform dances in front of a *capilla* (shrine) to the Virgin of Guadalupe when tour groups arrive. Barrio Pozo is buried in the back streets of downtown at Aldama between Mendoza and Ruíz de Alarcón. You might not see the dances if you're not with a group, but if you hang out around the shrine, you're sure to be approached by someone who'd love to talk about the neighborhood.

Old Acapulco is home to **La Quebrada,** where daredevil young men dive from steep, 130-foot cliffs into a rocky inlet of rushing water. The cliff divers of Acapulco are legendary, and their feats are impressive. Check it out at night, when the divers carry flaming torches into the sea. There are several platforms where viewers catch the show, watching as the divers pray at a small shrine before taking the leap. After the show, these young hunks wander through the crowd asking for donations. They deserve a tip. The divers have become such an icon that they're unionized and insured. La Quebrada is in the hills above downtown, about a five-minute cab ride from the *zócalo*. You can easily go there on your own rather than with a tour. The restaurant at the El Mirador Acapulco hotel (see profile in "Where to Stay in Acapulco") serves dinner during the shows. Though the food doesn't merit the price, it's fun to sit at the edge of the balconies and watch the divers as you sip a margarita.

The neighborhoods of Old Acapulco are filled with remembrances of past glories. Art lovers should not miss the **House of Dolores Olmedo** (Calle Inalámbrica 6, Cerro de la Pinoza; no phone). Though not an official museum, the home's exterior walls are covered with mosaic murals created by Diego Rivera during convalescence at his patron's vacation villa. The swirling red, yellow, blue, and green tiles include many of the muralist's favorite images, including serpents, the feathered spirit Quetzalcoatl, and a frog (many said Rivera looked like a giant frog).

The Costera leads west from the *zócalo* to **El Fuerte de San Diego** (Avenida Costera Miguel Alemán and Hornitos, s/n; ☎ 744-482-3828), home to an impressive historical museum. The star-shaped fort, originally constructed in 1616 and rebuilt after the 1776 earthquake, sits atop a small hill overlooking the bay. Its cannons now point at the cruise-ship terminal, amusingly enough. About a dozen rooms facing the fort's courtyard have been skillfully restored and house extensive exhibits on the region's history. It's easily one of the best museums on the coast.

Curving stone staircases lead to outdoor walkways and lookout points. The museum and fort are open Tuesday through Sunday, 9 a.m. to 6 p.m.; admission is $4, but it's free on Sundays and holidays.

Another unofficial museum, the **House of Masks** (Calle Hornitos at Morelos; ☎ 744-486-5577), down the street from the fort, contains a fascinating collection of hand-painted wood and papier-mâché masks used for dances and religious ceremonies in the state of Guerrero. The house sits on a small pedestrian walkway by the fort; ask the guards to show you the way. It's open Tuesday through Sunday, 10 a.m. to 4 p.m. There's no admission charge.

La Costera curves parallel to the bay past **Papagayo Park** (Costera Miguel Alemán and Manuel Gómez Morín No. 1; no phone) where children enjoy playing on the small amusement-park rides on Sunday afternoons (there is a small fee for each ride). It's open daily, 7 a.m. to 8 p.m.; the rides operate from 3 to 10 p.m. The beaches in this area are immensely popular with local families and are lined with a series of seafood cafes. As a gringo, you may be approached by hustlers and vendors, but you'll also enjoy conversations with *abuelas* and local kids practicing their English.

unofficial **TIP**
Take a ride in a horse-drawn *calesa* after dinner—the later you wait the less traffic will impede the pleasure of your ride. Be sure to ride on the water side of the Costera—there's nothing scenic about the other side. Rides cost about $10.

The main tourist beach is **Playa Hornos,** where vendors offer parasailing rides, personal-watercraft rentals, banana-boat rides, and all sorts of water toys for rent and sale. The beach is backed by a series of high-rise hotels where the majority of Acapulco's vacationers lounge by shimmering pools and play at beach bars. From the streets, this area is about as unsightly as a tourist zone can be. The traffic is abysmal much of the time as cars, taxis, buses, and horse-drawn carriages called *calesas* clog traffic circles (*glorietas*). An architectural cacophony of restaurants, bars, and souvenir shops lines the avenue, which looks more like a busy city street than a road by the beach.

kids Part of a national chain of water parks, **CICI,** or the Centro Internacional Convivencial Infantil (Costera Miguel Alemán at Colón; ☎ 744-484-4035) sits beside several condo buildings on the Costera. The park has waterslides, wave machines, a small aquarium, and a dolphin pool. It's not as fancy as parks in the States, and looking worse for wear these days, but it's still fun for kids. The park is open daily, 10 a.m. to 6 p.m.; admission is about $10 per person.

Costera Miguel Alemán becomes much prettier as it climbs into the Las Brisas hills and its name appropriately changes to **Carretera Escénica,** or Scenic Highway. This section of the road passes by expensive hotels, restaurants, and private villas. A tall white cross beside the **Capilla de La Paz** (**Chapel of Peace**), a small chapel at the top of a steep hill, is visible from much of the city. The drive up the hill to the chapel takes you past enormous mansions and the multi-acre compound of a wealthy family who constructed the chapel as a monument to two sons killed in a plane crash.

Though much of this area has been taken up by high-end developments, the beaches at **Puerto Marqués** remain open to the public. Rows of umbrellas and palapas line the beach, which curves around a small bay; cafes and beach vendors supply seafood meals, cold drinks, and water toys. The beach is surrounded by banana, mango, and coconut plantations. Farther down the road is **Playa Revolcadero,** a long expanse of sand subject to rough, open surf. Although there is a public section of this beach (at the eastern end), the beach is primarily the turf of the Fairmont Acapulco Princess and Fairmont Pierre Marqués resorts.

Acapulco is part of an enormous jungle area, though you don't really see that side of the city unless you're around when rainstorms create instant rivers and waterfalls. The natural side of the region is more evident around **Tres Palos** and **Coyuca** lagoons, and the settlement of **Barra Vieja** on the outskirts of the city. Boat tours are available at the lagoons, where herons and egrets nest in peace. Tour companies offer lagoon tours, or you can get to the area on your own in a rental car.

 Pie de la Cuesta, a small beach settlement about eight miles west of the city, is the antithesis of the Costera. Small hotels cater to escapists who prefer this long stretch of sand that faces fierce waves and spectacular sunsets. Consider taking a cab there (it's about $20 each way) just before sunset, and watch nature put on a show while you dine at a beach restaurant.

In 2002, the archaeological site of **Palma Sola** opened to the public, but it hasn't undergone much restoration. The site is believed to have been a center for the Yope people, who lived in the area from around 600 BC to AD 200. A dozen or so petroglyphs have been uncovered, along with a few modest structures. The site is above the Costera on Avenida Palma Sola. The road is narrow and steep, and you must hike about 20 minutes after the road ends. Visit with a tour company—hours are erratic, and there are no guides or written info at the site.

unofficial **TIP**
About an hour from Acapulco, the **Tehuacalco** archaeological site opened in December 2009. Under excavation are the remains of a ball court, temple, and residential area.

TOURS *and* SIDE TRIPS *from* ACAPULCO

INLAND FROM ACAPULCO in the Sierra Madre mountains, **Taxco** is Mexico's most famous silversmithing town. There must be more than 100 silver shops lining the town's steep, narrow streets; shopping here can be utterly mind-boggling. **Santa Prisca** church rises above the plaza in this colonial town that feels like it's stuck in another era (until you hear the constant grinding of gears from cars trying to get up the hills). Travel agencies in Acapulco offer day and overnight tours to Taxco, or you can take an **Estrella de Oro** bus (☎ 744-485-8705) on your own. The company runs six or seven first-class buses between Acapulco and Taxco daily. The trip takes about four hours and costs $16 each way.

BOAT TOURS

YOU REALLY SHOULD GET OUT ON THE WATER at least once during your stay. Most of the boat cruises are a bit hokey, pushing open bars and silly games. Still, it's great fun to get out on the water (and certainly cooler than on land). The narration is rather like that of a Hollywood bus tour—Sly Stone, Luis Miguel, Plácido Domingo, and countless other celebrities apparently have handsome homes above the bay. Go in the late afternoon and watch the lights on the hillsides start to twinkle as the sun sets. A word to the wise: skip the cheap tequila. **Yates Fiesta & Bonanza** (Costera Miguel Alemán, Glorieta Tlacopanocha, Locales 4 y 5; ☎ 744-482-2055) offers three cruises per day. Costs are $22 per person for a sunset cruise, $45 for a dinner cruise, and $22 for a moonlight cruise. All include open bar and dancing. For a more peaceful tour, book a spot on a private yacht with **Fish-R-Us** (Costera Miguel Alemán 100; ☎ 744-482-8282; 877-3-FISH-R-US U.S.; **www.fish-r-us.com**). Most boats stop by La Quebrada so passengers can watch the cliff divers.

TOURS

IF YOU'RE A FIRST-TIME VISITOR and want an overview of Acapulco, you'll save money on cabs by taking a city tour. Routes vary—look for a tour that goes to the Chapel of Peace, the *zócalo*, Playa Caleta, the fort, and the House of Masks. **Servicios Turísticos Constelación** (Costera Miguel Alemán 116–105, Fracc. Club Deportivo; ☎ 744-484-1988; **constellationservices.com.mx**) is a full-service agency that can arrange just about anything you want to do, from city tours to sportfishing, to day trips to Taxco. They also arrange tours for cruise-ship passengers. We've found their guides tend to bend the truth a bit, but they do come out with some interesting tidbits.

EXERCISE *and* RECREATION *in* ACAPULCO

THE MOST POPULAR CALORIE-BURNER in Acapulco is dancing. You can work off quite a few piña coladas if you stay on the dance floor until dawn. There are plenty of daytime activities at most

Acapulco hotels, especially those on the Costera. Bungee jumping, parasailing, swimming, and riding personal watercraft are all popular on **Playa Hornos,** where the water is usually calm. Snorkeling is best around **Playa Caletilla** and **Isla Roqueta.** Sportfishing boats can be chartered at the docks by the *zócalo.* There isn't much surfing action in Acapulco, and there are far better places for scuba diving. More and more hotels are adding gyms and spas; see our accommodation profiles, starting on page 322, for more information.

GOLF

OIL MAGNATE J. PAUL GETTY TOOK A LOOK at the coconut plantations by Pierre Marqués Bay and envisioned a golf course. The original **Club de Golf Pierre Marqués** (Playa Revolcadero s/n, Granjas del Marqués; ☎ 744-469-1000) opened in the 1950s beside Getty's vacation home. Robert Trent Jones Sr. remodeled the 18-hole course for the 1982 World Cup Championship; his son did another renovation later. The 6,855-yard, par-72 championship course has 65 sand bunkers and is adjacent to the **Fairmont Acapulco Princess Golf Course** (same address and phone number). Ted Robinson designed the Princess course, which incorporates plenty of challenges in a small space bordered by tall palms. The 6,335-yard, par-72 championship course has water hazards on more than half the holes and an out-of-bounds area on one side. Each course has a full driving range, rental clubs and shoes, and lessons. Shared carts are included in the greens fees ($130 for hotel guests, $145 for nonguests, $100 after 3 p.m.) at the Princess course; add $10 for the Pierre Márques's.

The **Mayan Palace Golf Club** (Avenida Costera de las Palmas s/n; ☎ 744-469-6000) overlooks the ocean. The 18-hole, 6,507-yard, par-72 course is open daily from 7 a.m. to 6 p.m.; greens fees are $140 for nonguests, price for guests depends on the type of booking they've made. If you don't have time for 18 holes, try the **Club de Golf Acapulco** (Costera Miguel Alemán s/n; ☎ 744-484-0781). This 9-hole, par-36 course is open daily from 7 a.m. to 6 p.m. Greens fees are $38.

SHOTOVER JET

IMPORTED FROM NEW ZEALAND, THE **Shotover Jet** is a sleek red boat that carries up to a dozen passengers on a dizzying ride along the Papagayo River. The big thrills come from the boat's ability to spin a 360-degree turn and skim along the water at 40 miles per hour. It takes about 45 minutes to reach the staging point at Puente Viejo, and the actual boat ride lasts about 15 minutes. Reservations are required. The company has vans that depart from the office on the Costera, and the outing includes time for lunch. If you enjoy short spurts of hair-raising excitement and don't mind getting soaking wet, you'll have a great time. The rates are $45 for adults, $20 for kids 3 to 12, including transportation. The office is at Costera Miguel Alemán s/n,

Plaza Marbella Local 116c; ☎ 744-484-1154;. **shotoverjet.com.mx.** The Shotover Jet company's **Pueblo Bravo** complex at Puente Viejo also offers river rafting on the Papagayo River several times a week during the rainy season. Cost is $80 for the two-hour adventure, plus driving time. Transportation and a small lunch are included. They also arrange diving and snorkel tours at $70 and $35, respectively.

SPORTFISHING

THOUGH MARLIN, SAILFISH, DORADO, and tuna visit the waters around Acapulco, sportfishing isn't as big a deal as it is in Los Cabos, Mazatlán, or Cozumel. Still, fishing fanatics have to try all waters. **Fish-R-Us** (see page 342) sets up fishing trips on yachts from 38-footers ($380 is the least expensive) to luxury craft. Most of the year you can also get a place on a party boat for about $75 per person.

SHOPPING *in* ACAPULCO

THERE'S LITTLE TO SHOP FOR IN ACAPULCO if you have a collector's eye. Artisans' markets and shops tend to carry manufactured crafts that leave a lot to be desired. We have, however, found some unusual, high-quality items at the market by the *glorieta* with a statue of Diana, the market at Playa Caleta, and at the downtown **Artisans' Market** at Calle 5 de Mayo and Calle Velázquez. Look for hand-carved ceremonial and dance masks typical to the state of Guerrero. When shopping in these markets, it's best to get into a chatty mood and choose a vendor who's friendly without being obsequious.

Silver jewelry and figurines abound in the street markets and shops, and sellers often claim their goods came from Taxco. This mountain town about four hours from Acapulco is known for its silver workshops and its jewelers (who would be horrified to be associated with most of the cheap items in these markets). You'll find excellent silver shops in some of the hotels. The well-respected jeweler **Tane** has a shops at Las Brisas; **Minette** at the Fairmont Princess hotel also sells fine jewelry.

You can find well-made folk-art items in the various **Sanborn's** coffee shops–department stores around town. Check out the one in the **Oceanic 2000** shopping plaza, near the Grand Hotel (Costera Miguel Alemán 3111, Fracc. Costa Azul; ☎ 744-484-3368). The malls along the Costera are good for browsing in air-conditioned comfort during the midday heat, and some have movie theaters.

NIGHTLIFE *in* ACAPULCO

FOR MANY OF ACAPULCO'S FANS, partying is the whole reason for being here. The discos are legendary, and the pace after midnight is astonishing. The city seems to burst into sound and color after dark as locals and visitors don their best dancing shoes and hit the town.

The discos feature the latest trends in music and special effects; the crowds range from hip youngsters to ultrachic celebrities. Most venues have a strict dress code—no T-shirts, sneakers, sandals (other than high-heeled, dress-up sandals), jeans, or shorts are allowed. People dress up to go out dancing. If you want to fit in, wear your skimpiest dress or finest shirt and slacks. Cover charges can be steep—as much as $30 to $60 in the classiest spots—though that usually includes at least a few drinks. (Women pay at least $10 less than guys as a general rule.) Most discos open at about 10 p.m. and close around 4 or even 6 a.m., when the hangers-on depart for all-night cafes serving tacos and *huevos rancheros.*

An affluent, young, singles crowd frequents **Baby'O** (Costera Miguel Alemán 22; ☎ 744-484-7474), which is so popular it has offspring in Cancún and Tijuana. **Palladium** (Carretera Escénica; ☎ 744-446-5490) is glitzier, with glass walls overlooking the bay, firework shows after midnight, and plenty of high-tech effects. Tunes range from electronic to dance rhythms. Salsa and cumbia set the beat at **Salon Q** (Costera Miguel Alemán 3117; ☎ 744-481-0114), sometimes called the Cathedral of Salsa.

An older, dress-to-impress clientele favors **Mandara** (Carretera Escéncia; ☎ 744-446-5711), where guests sit in comfy banquettes by the bars or in rows of seats facing the dance floor. Beside the disco, waiters deliver champagne to an eclectic late-night audience who listen to salsa music and songs from the piano bar at **Siboney** (in Mandara; ☎ 744-446-5711).

Piano bars cater to a calmer crowd, though patrons tend to sing along as the night goes on. **Pepe's** (Carretera Escénica s/n, Fraccionamiento Guitarrón; ☎ 744-483-4373) is the granddaddy of Acapulco's piano bars, and visiting celebrities often stop by the casual bar for a song or two.

The party scene is far more casual at **Señor Frog's** and **Carlos'n Charlie's** (Costera Miguel Alemán 112; ☎ 744-484-1285), where patrons dance in wild, T-shirted mobs to recorded rock and roll. Similar action takes place at **Paradise/Paraíso** (see profile in "Where to Eat in Acapulco," page 336) and other beach bars on the Costera.

PART TWELVE

PUERTO ESCONDIDO

_A_ BEACHIN' HIDEAWAY

SINCE IT WAS "DISCOVERED" by surfers and sybarites in the 1960s and 1970s, **Puerto Escondido** (simply called Puerto by locals) has grown steadily but has never reached anything near resort status—which is just what its admirers like about it. Beach rats and snowbirds hole up for months during the winter, hanging out in small, moderately priced hotels and eating seafood and fresh pasta at restaurants by the sand. Vacationers, on the other hand, find enough worthwhile beaches, bars, and restaurants to keep them happily exploring for a week or more.

Surfers make pilgrimages to Puerto Escondido and the waves at **Playa Zicatela,** rated one of the best surf spots in the world. Bird-watchers seek out the mangroves, estuaries, and marshes west of Puerto Escondido to spy on a wealth of wildlife. Even nonornithological types enjoy half- and full-day trips to **Manialtepec** and **Chacahua** lagoons. Others hop on horses, riding to a secluded hot spring originally used by local inhabitants in cleansing ceremonies.

In between Puerto Escondido and the small town of **Puerto Ángel,** a string of pretty beaches lure more inquisitive travelers and those looking for bargains and a bohemian lifestyle. The best known of these beaches is **Playa Zipolite,** a longtime hangout for budget-minded and independent travelers content to swing in hammocks at small, cabana-style hotels on the sand or a smattering of more fashionable (and comfortable) digs. More Europeans are found here than at other Pacific Coast resorts, due in part to the fact that this beach has a topless scene, and nude sunbathing is tolerated at one end of the beach.

The city of Puerto Escondido is divided into the upper town, north of the Carretera Costera (the Coast Highway), or simply **La Costera,** where you'll find the market, shops, and people's homes, as well as some hotels and restaurants. The other section of town is on the beach side of the highway; most traveler services are here, along with a four-block pedestrian street called the **Adoquín,** which means "the pavement." One- and two-story shops, restaurants, and hotels line this busy promenade fronting the main beach, **Playa Principal.** At the west end of the beach, stairs lead to a cement walkway that hugs the rocks, ending in a residential neighborhood. On the east side of the main beach, across a small estuary, is **Marinero Beach,** where fiberglass fishing skiffs double as water taxis.

If you're looking for a more private and picturesque beach, you can hire one of these boats by the hour, or just arrange to be dropped off (and retrieved at the hour you desire) at delightful **Manzanillo Beach,** on tiny **Puerto Angelito Bay.** This is a sandy beach scalloped by rocks, and a great, protected cove for swimming and snorkeling. Just beyond, **Carrizalillo Beach,** on the bay of the same name, is another very attractive beach that has small restaurants offering a modicum of shade from the powerful sun. Both are accessible by foot, car, or boat. East of town proper, long and wide **Zicatela Beach** is the reason many folks are here. The megawaves draw surfers, and a string of hotels appeal to those wanting to spend a good deal of everyday surfing, lounging, or walking on the beach. You'll find lots of great restaurants here, and bars, shops, and mini–grocery stores, too. At the other end of town, **Bacocho Beach** is another long beach where, because it's on the open sea, only the strong and aquatically confident should swim. Bacocho is a semi–spread-out neighborhood with a few mainly dispirited-looking hotels. Between downtown Puerto and Bacocho, the neighborhoods of Rinconada and Carrizalillo are beginning to offer more choices in restaurants and accommodations.

QUICK FACTS *about* PUERTO ESCONDIDO

AIRPORT AND AIRLINES The **Aeropuerto de Puerto Escondido** (Carretera Costera Km 3; ☎ 954-582-0491) is about five miles northwest of the town center. At press time, **Aerocaribe** (**aerocaribe.com.mx**) had cancelled its service from Mexico City because of financial problems. Visit the Web site for information.

Several small regional airlines connect the capital city of Oaxaca to Puerto Escondido. **MexicanaClick** (☎ 954-582-2023), a Mexicana subsidiary, flies twice daily between Puerto Escondido and Mexico City. The flight takes about an hour.

unofficial **TIP**
Flights may depart prior to or later than their scheduled time. Get to the airport early and be prepared for delays as well.

Puerto Escondido

ACCOMMODATIONS
1. Best Western Posada Real
2. Casa Rosada
3. La Hacienda
4. Le P'tit Hotel
5. Paraíso Escondido
6. Santa Fé

RESTAURANTS
7. Bouganvilleas
8. Cafecito
9. Flor de María
10. La Galería
11. El Jardín
12. Las Margaritas
13. Restaurant Mandil
14. Santa Fé

NIGHTLIFE
15. Bananas
16. Bar Fly
17. Casa Babylon
18. Cinemar
19. Danny's Terrace
20. El Son y la Rumba
21. Wipe Out

Airport
Beach
Church
Information
Post Office

0.1 mi
100 m

Carretera Costera
Calle del Morro
To Puerto Angel, Huatulco, & Tehuantepec

Playa Zicatela
Playa Marinero
Playa Principal
Playa Manzanillo
Playa Carrizalillo
Playa Bacocho

Laguna Agua Dulce

El Adoquín

Av. 4 Norte
Av. 3 Norte
Av. 2 Norte
Av. 1 Norte
Av. Hidalgo
Av. Revolución
Av. Maris
Av. Libertad
Av. Pérez Gasga
Av. Soledad

Av. 8 Norte
Av. 7 Norte
Av. 6 Norte
Av. 5 Norte
Av. 3 Oriente
Av. 2 Oriente
Av. 1 Oriente
Av. Oaxaca
Av. 1 Poniente
Av. 2 Poniente
Av. 3 Poniente

Av. Benito Juárez
Av. Unión

To Oaxaca

Carretera Costera
Av. 5 Poniente

Camino a Puerto Angelito

Faro (lighthouse)

PACIFIC OCEAN

Bahía de Puerto Angelito
Bahía de Carrizalillo

Av. Juárez
To Acapulco

Gulf of Mexico
VERACRUZ
MEXICO CITY
OAXACA
GUERRERO
MICHOACÁN
PACIFIC OCEAN
Puerto Escondido

200 mi
200 km

DRIVING Puerto Escondido is 190 miles south of Oaxaca city and 70 miles west of Huatulco. Cars can be rented at the airport, major hotels, and from offices along the Adoquín, Zicatela Beach, and Fraccionamiento Bacocho. However, because car-rental prices are steep, you might spend less and avoid the hassle by simply taking taxis around town or renting one by the hour.

GETTING AROUND Taxis are available at the airport and bus stations, and taxis park at both ends of the tourist walkway, the Adoquín. Economical city buses run among the main parts of the city and stop on the Carretera Costera one block inland of the Adoquín.

> *unofficial* **TIP**
> Mexico's small airlines have been having trouble staying in business and tend to start and stop service frequently. Check **Aerotucán (www.aero -tucan.com)** to see if it's operating between Oaxaca City and Huatulco when you are traveling.

SWIMMING SAFETY Puerto Escondido has beautiful beaches, and some are safe for swimming—but don't take that for granted. The waves at Zicatela beach are strictly for the pro surfers. Others should stick to the gentler waters at Carrizalillo and Puerto Angelito bays, both between the downtown tourist zone and the rougher, open sea in the Bacocho, at the west edge of town. Bacocho is only recommended for strong swimmers.

TELEPHONES The area code is ☎ **954;** all phone numbers should be seven digits. The old numbers were only five digits (and locals still refer to them this way), so if you have a five-digit local phone number, try adding 58 at the beginning.

TOURIST INFORMATION Once in Puerto Escondido, visit the main **Tourist Information Office** (Boulevard Benito Juárez near the Aldea del Bazar Hotel, Fraccionamieonto Bacocho; ☎ 954-582-0175). Hours are Monday through Friday, 9 a.m. to 4 p.m. More convenient for most folks (and more informative) is the tourism department's adjunct, Gina Machorro (more about her later under Cultural Walking Tours), who speaks excellent English and is very knowledgeable about what there is to see and do in her town. You'll find Gina at the **Information Kiosk** at the west end of Pérez Gasga (aka *el adoquín*) Monday through Friday, 10 a.m. to 2 p.m. and 4 p.m. to 6 or 6:30 p.m.; and Saturday, 10 a.m. to 1 p.m. The commercial Web site **www.puertoescondidoinfo.com** is filled with helpful info.

WHERE *to* STAY *in* PUERTO ESCONDIDO

PUERTO ESCONDIDO HAS NO FIVE-STAR FACILITIES and, except for the **Best Western,** no international chain hotels. Those who want

How Accommodations Compare in Puerto Escondido

ACCOMMODATION	OVERALL	QUALITY	VALUE	COST
Santa Fé	★★★★	★★½	★★★½	$$
Casa Rosada	★★½	★★½	★★★	$
La Hacienda	★★½	★★★½	★★★	$$
Paraíso Escondido	★★	★	★★★½	$
Le P'tit Hotel	★½	★½	★★★½	$
Best Western Posada Real	★½	★½	★½	$$

that sort of luxury head for other parts of the country. The fact that the properties listed here have few stars reflects mainly a lack of amenities and services; nonetheless, they are not without charm. What Puerto offers are mainly family-owned, low-key, small-to-medium-sized hotels with a restaurant, bar, and swimming pool. You'll find this sort of accommodation at Zicatela Beach, as well as various sizes of bungalows and rooms designed with kitchenettes or hot plates to accommodate surfers and other long-term budget travelers. Hotels by the Adoquín are convenient for proximity to restaurants, taxis, and water taxis from the main beach. At the west end of town, several hotels overlook the water from the cliffs in Fraccionamiento Bacocho, and the more charming Rinconada, the latter a mixed neighborhood of accommodations and houses, with a few mini-groceries and restaurants.

ACCOMMODATION PROFILES

Best Western Posada Real $$

OVERALL ★½	QUALITY ★½	VALUE ★½

Boulevard Benito Juárez s/n; ☎ 954-582-0133 or 800-780-7234 U.S.; fax 954-582-0192; www.bestwestern.com

Perched on the cliffs overlooking Bacocho Beach, this is Puerto Escondido's only chain hotel, and what it lacks in charm it makes up for in amenities such as coffeemakers and alarm clocks in the rooms. The immediate neighborhood is dispiritingly lonely, however, and the hotel has gone exclusively all-inclusive. On past trips, we've always found time to settle into a chaise lounge on the huge green lawn and sip a cocktail while watching the sunset from the cliff overlooking Bacocho Beach. You can walk down the many steps (or take the shuttle van) to the beach club at the beach below, which has a bar, restaurant, and a large, lively pool where guests congregate. For more recreation, there's a game room with Ping-Pong, foosball, and other games, and courts for basketball, tennis, and beach volleyball (one each).

A taxi ride to town takes about five minutes, and the airport is one mile away.

SETTING AND FACILITIES

Location Fraccionamiento Bacocho, above Playa Bococho.

DINING 2 restaurants.

Amenities and services Beach, 2 pools, tour desk, shop, 4 bars, room service, tennis courts, putting green, organized children's activities.

ACCOMMODATIONS

Rooms 100.

All rooms AC, windows that open, hair dryer, coffeemaker, cable/satellite TV, Internet.

Some rooms Nonsmoking.

Comfort and decor Cheerful but standard hotel decor with rather cramped accommodations; request one of the larger, airier rooms at no additional cost.

PAYMENT, RESERVATIONS, AND RESTRICTIONS

Deposit Credit card; 2-week cancellation policy.

Credit cards AE, MC, V.

Check-in/out 3 p.m./1 p.m.

Casa Rosada $

OVERALL ★★½	QUALITY ★★½	VALUE ★★★

Calle 3a Sur 303; ☎ 954-582-0585; www.casa38.com

These apartments are the perfect place to set up housekeeping—for as long as your budget and boss will allow. In true Mexican fashion, the complex is surrounded by a high (bright pink) wall, inside which you'll find delightful gardens vibrant with tropical plants, flowers, and vines. Another wonderful perk is the location in a quiet residential neighborhood a short walk from both downtown and several beautiful beaches. Fully equipped kitchens and comfortable dining areas allow you to cook your own meals, and each unit has a hammock. The large pool, naturally heated by the sun and surrounded by plants, is perfect for floating after a long, hot day at the beach.

SETTING AND FACILITIES

Location North side of town, between the downtown strip and the beaches of Puerto Angelito.

Dining No restaurant.

Amenities and services Pool, massage (by appointment).

ACCOMMODATIONS

Rooms 4 units.

All rooms Fan, windows that open, balcony or terrace, kitchenette, nonsmoking; no phone or TV.

Some rooms Ocean view.

Comfort and decor Comfortable beds with crisp linens; baths with colorful tile sinks and shower; Mexican fabrics and furnishings with Oaxacan handcrafts in a cozy, livable setting.

PAYMENT, RESERVATIONS, AND RESTRICTIONS

Deposit Check or wire transfer; forfeit if you cancel and apartment can't be rented.

Credit cards Cash only.

Check-in/out 3 p.m./11 a.m.

La Hacienda $$

OVERALL ★★½	QUALITY ★★★½	VALUE ★★★

Atunes 15, Rinconada; ☎ 954-582-0279; fax 954-582-0096; www.suiteslahacienda.com

French owner Bernadette Lacour de Servat has put her creativity to good use in designing and furnishing six wonderful apartments in Puerto's Rinconada neighborhood. Ms. Lacour worked as a designer and antiques dealer in Paris and has decorated each unit in her tasteful style. Furnishings and decor vary, but most of the spacious suites have tile floors, exposed beams, and brick ceilings with wrought iron and wood furniture, as well as hand-woven spreads covering comfortable beds. Original art hangs on the walls, and antiques give each unit a homey, lived-in feeling. Roomy kitchenettes are fully stocked with utensils, plates and dishes, and pots and pans; guests can also use the outdoor barbecue. Walkways throughout the property are lined in potted plants, and one of several patios has a delightful fountain. Rooms are $130 to $180 per night including tax, depending on the season. For information about the hotel, it's best to call in the morning (between 9 a.m. and 2 p.m.), when the English-speaking secretary is on-site; otherwise, *Parlez-vous français ou español?*

SETTING AND FACILITIES

Location Fraccionamiento Rinconada on the outskirts of Puerto Escondido.

Amenities and services Pool, Wi-Fi.

ACCOMMODATIONS

Rooms 6 furnished apartments.

All rooms AC, kitchenette, refrigerator, coffeemaker, cable TV, Wi-Fi.

Some rooms Bathtubs, balcony or terrace, disabled access.

Comfort and decor Beds are cozy, bathroom is elegant yet functional. Apartment #2 has a distant ocean view.

PAYMENT, RESERVATIONS, AND RESTRICTIONS

Deposit Credit card; $100 cancellation fee (negotiable).

Credit cards MC, V.

Check-in/out 2 p.m./noon.

Le P'tit Hotel $

OVERALL ★½	QUALITY ★½	VALUE ★★★½

Andador Soledad 379; ☎ phone and fax 954-582-3178; www.oaxaca-mio.com/leptit.htm

Here's a charming little hotel at the west end of the Adoquín, near the action of the main street and the tourism information kiosk. Some of the rooms have hammocks in addition to queen beds; little touches such as Tiffany-style lamps and framed, painted tile mosaics on the walls make up for the lack of actual amenities. Winding metal stairways lead to some of the rooms, making access a bit difficult for the mobility-impared. But the overall effect of this budget beauty is clean and bright, if simple.

SETTING AND FACILITIES

Location West end of the Adoquín.

Dining No restaurant, but close to many dining spots on the Adoquín and the main beach.

Amenities and services Pool, Wi-Fi.

ACCOMMODATIONS

Rooms 18 rooms.

All rooms AC, windows that open, cable TV.

Some rooms Air-conditioning, fan, ocean view, balcony or terrace, coffee-maker, refrigerator.

Comfort and decor Rooms smell nice and have charming details like faux painted walls in an array of sunny colors; queen- or king-size beds have bright, pretty, hand-loomed bedspreads.

PAYMENT, RESERVATIONS, AND RESTRICTIONS

Deposit 50% deposit to confirm reservation.

Credit cards Cash only.

Check-in/out 2 p.m./noon.

Paraíso Escondido $

OVERALL ★★	QUALITY ★	VALUE ★★★½

Calle Union 10; ☎ 954-582-0444; fax 954-582-2767

Close to the action on the Adoquín but far enough away (up an alley of cement stairs) to be quiet and peaceful, this German-owned hotel has few amenities but has been painted inside and out. All rooms have screened windows and firm mattresses; some have lovely views of the garden and town and far in the distance, the ocean from the ample terrace. Aside from the tranquility, one of the nicest things about "Hidden Paradise" hotel is the garden dotted with statues and reproductions of pre-Hispanic artifacts. There's a funky old chapel and several other nooks and crannies around the place.

SETTING AND FACILITIES

Location A 5-minute uphill walk from the main beach and tourist area, El Adoquín.

Dining Outdoor dining room open for 3 meals only at Easter and Christmas.

Amenities and services Pool.

ACCOMMODATIONS

Rooms 22 rooms, 2 suites.

All rooms Air-conditioning, windows that open.

Some rooms Distant ocean view, balcony or terrace, stove, refrigerator.

Comfort and decor Rooms are plain, with whitewashed brick walls and red-tile floors, wrought-iron light fixtures, and homely paintings in carved wooden frames.

PAYMENT, RESERVATIONS, AND RESTRICTIONS

Deposit Bank deposit at Banamex bank or foreign equivalent; cancellation policy 60 days.

Credit cards Cash only.

Check-in/out 2 p.m./noon.

Santa Fé $$

OVERALL ★★★★	QUALITY ★★½	VALUE ★★★½

Calle de Morro s/n; ☎ 954-582-0170 or 888-649-6407; fax 954-582-0260; hotelsantafe.com.mx

This two-story hotel meanders around pools and open patios, all surrounded by coconut palms and potted plants. Bathrooms are done in blue-and-white tiles, with rooms in rustic brick-red tile floors. Most rooms have desks and all have screened windows that let in the fresh air and smell of the sea just beyond. This is the prettiest property in Puerto Escondido, although the rooms themselves are nothing to write home about. It's a cab ride or a longish walk (about 15 minutes on the beach or the road) into town from here. Nonetheless, this is a prime location if your main objective is lounging by the pool (where free wireless service is available) or enjoying the scene: days at the beach and evenings eating and drinking at the main street's many restaurants and bars. Zicatela beach is a big surf spot, but it's not appropriate for most swimmers. Still, the beach is wide and long and perfect for strolling, with your toes being occasionally sucked by the sea. Next door to the main property, nicely furnished bungalows, complete with well-stocked kitchenettes, have a wide, shady veranda and are ideal for couples or small families who want to prepare some of their own meals. The hotel celebrated its 25th anniversary in 2008 and remains the most popular in town. They added a conference center for meetings and weddings in 2008, along with a cafe serving coffee from the owners' coffee farm, called Finca las Nieves. There are three suites at the finca high in the mountains, about 90 minutes from the coast. Rates are $250 per night, including meals and transportation from Puerto Escondido. Staying a night or two is a wonderful way to experience the lifestyle of the people of Oaxaca.

SETTING AND FACILITIES

Location West end of Playa Zicatela.

Dining Open-sided restaurant overlooking the beach features yummy vegetarian dishes and seafood (see review, page 361), cafe.

Amenities and services Beach, 2 pools, hot tub, tour desk, shop, bar, room service, Internet.

ACCOMMODATIONS

Rooms 58 rooms, 4 suites, 8 bungalows.

All rooms AC, fan, windows that open, minibar, cable/satellite TV.

Some rooms Ocean view, balcony or terrace, safe, bathtub, kitchenette, whirlpool tub, refrigerator, coffeemaker, disabled access, Wi-Fi.

Comfort and decor Practical and comfortable rooms and suites decorated with Oaxaca crafts and materials. Some of the air-conditioning units are old and noisy.

PAYMENT, RESERVATIONS, AND RESTRICTIONS

Deposit Credit card; cancellation policy varies by season, but up to 30-days' notice required.

Credit cards AE, MC, V.

Check-in/out Noon/noon.

WHERE *to* EAT *in* PUERTO ESCONDIDO

EATING OUT IS A PLEASURE in this laid-back fishing town. Restaurants are unpretentious, but that doesn't mean they don't provide good service and delicious eats. Of course, menus center on seafood, but Italian, German, and Canadian immigrants (to name just a few) have opened restaurants and diversified the local restaurant scene with their own ideas and talents.

RESTAURANT PROFILES

Bouganvilleas ★★★

INTERNATIONAL FUSION   EXPENSIVE   QUALITY ★★★★   VALUE ★★★

Playa Bacocho at Hotel Villa Sol; Avenida Loma Bonita 2, Fracc. Bacocho; ☎ 954-582-0350

Reservations Required.

Entree range Prix fixe meals only, $37 per person for 4-course meal, including 1 glass of wine.

How Restaurants Compare in Puerto Escondido

RESTAURANT | CUISINE | COST	OVERALL	QUALITY	VALUE
El Jardín | **Italian/vegetarian** | Inexp	★★★★	★★★★	★★★★★
Bouganvilleas | **International fusion** | Exp	★★★	★★★★	★★★
Santa Fé | **Mexican/vegetarian** | Inexp/mod	★★★	★★★★	★★★
Flor de María | **International** | Inexp	★★½	★★★½	★★★½
La Galería | **Italian** | Inexp	★★½	★★★ ½	★★★½
Restaurant Mandil | **International/seafood** | Inexp/Mod	★★½	★★½	★★
Cafecito | **Breakfast/international** | Inexp	★★	★★½	★★★★
Las Margaritas | **Mexican** | Inexp	★★	★★	★★★★★

Payment AE, MC, V.

Service rating ★★★★.

Parking Lot at hotel or on the street at the beach club (you can also take a shuttle to the beach club).

Bar Full service.

Dress Mexicans dress up here, but it *is* at the beach, so anything goes, really, beyond shorts and T-shirts.

Disabled access None.

Customers Locals celebrating special occasions, travelers in the know.

Hours 7 a.m.–11 p.m.

SETTING AND ATMOSPHERE Blue sailcloth umbrellas over white-clothed cafe tables between the beach and the pool.

HOUSE SPECIALTIES A different prix-fixe, four-course meal every day.

SUMMARY AND COMMENTS Although tucked away at Bacocho Beach and available by advance reservation only, this restaurant merits your patronage simply because the food is divine. Chef Jacobo Jimenez, who trained under our favorite Swiss-Franco chef Terry Faivre, of Huatulco's L'Echalote, and later studied in Paris, is a natural talent and the spirit behind the whole operation here. Call ahead to reserve a meal for 2 or 20, giving input about the menu selection or better yet, letting this master pick out the freshest ingredients each day to create something truly special. Your multicourse masterpiece will start with a seasonal appetizer, and then a soup or similarly light dish, moving on to a couple of scallops marinated in mandarin orange juice and mint and served like an edible work of art, before proceeding to the main course and dessert. Chef Jacobo is passionate about his work, and the proof of this, as they say, is in the pudding.

Cafecito ★★

BREAKFAST/INTERNATIONAL   INEXPENSIVE   QUALITY ★★½   VALUE ★★★★

Playa Zicatela; Calle del Morro s/n; ☎ 954-582-0516

Reservations Not accepted.

Entree range $6–$9.

Payment Cash only.

Service rating ★½.

Parking Limited street parking.

Bar Full service.

Dress Ultracasual, as in flip-flops, bathing suits, and sarongs.

Disabled access No problem outside on the first level, but bathrooms are inaccessible.

Customers Surfers and breakfast junkies; it's wildly popular with the locals, for breakfast especially.

Hours Daily, 7:30 a.m.–10 p.m.

SETTING AND ATMOSPHERE Girls in bikini tops and sarongs and sun-streaked guys make this open-fronted beachfront restaurant sandy and scenic.

HOUSE SPECIALTIES Breakfast, coffee, French toast, locally made baked goods.

SUMMARY AND COMMENTS Some folks spend half their morning, every morning, at this happening spot in the action zone on Zicatela beach. Mornings are crowded, and service isn't particularly impressive; nonetheless, this is a fabulous place for great Oaxaca-grown coffee, fresh-ground and brewed. The owners have been baking wonderful things and serving gringos for so long now it's second nature to conjure up cinnamon-sprinkled French toast and large, luscious, fresh-fruit salads with mounds of yogurt and fresh granola for the perfect, healthful breakfast. Pastries are fresh and varied; portions are large. For lunch or dinner, have chicken, fish, beef, Mexican dishes, a BLT on a fresh bread roll, or a healthful salad.

Flor de María ★★½

INTERNATIONAL   INEXPENSIVE   QUALITY ★★★½   VALUE ★★★½

Entrance to Playa Marinero s/n; ☎ 954-582-0536 or 954-582-2617; www.mexonline.com/flordemaria.htm

Reservations Not accepted.

Entree range $5–$8.

Payment MC, V.

Service rating ★★★.

Parking Street.

Bar Full service, specializing in *mojitos,* a refreshing, mint-infused cocktail.

Dress Casual.

Disabled access None.

Customers Locals and travelers who want consistently good food.

Hours Daily, 8 a.m.–11 a.m., 6–10 p.m.; closed May, June, September, and October, and Tuesdays between Easter and December. SETTING AND ATMOSPHERE Simple dining area overlooking the sand road to the beach.

HOUSE SPECIALTIES New takes on international favorites, such as roast pork in a mustard, wild mushroom, and cream sauce.

Summary and comments The decor is simple and the service can be leisurely, but locals come again and again for Joanne's consistently yummy recipes and winning desserts. Dinner is the main meal here. Breakfast draws mainly hotel guests; at dinnertime, the white board lists Joanne's numerous nightly specials such as the oven-baked poblano chiles stuffed with your choice of chicken or cheese. There's always at least one offering for vegetarians. For dessert, the lemon pie is legendary, and the pecan pie also is worth every carb and calorie.

La Galería ★★½

ITALIAN	INEXPENSIVE	QUALITY ★★★½	VALUE ★★★½

El Adoquín; Pérez Gasga s/n (west end); ☎ 954-582-2039 and Calle del Morro s/n, north of Hotel Arco Iris; no phone

Reservations Not generally needed or accepted.

Entree range $6–$13.

Payment Cash only.

Service rating ★★★.

Parking Limited street parking several blocks away.

Bar Full service, with liqueurs like sambuca.

Dress Casual.

Disabled access None.

Customers Locals and travelers.

Hours Daily, 8 a.m.–11 p.m.

SETTING AND ATMOSPHERE Gallery restaurant, open to the street, with rotating ceiling fans to swirl the heat.

HOUSE SPECIALTIES Pizza and homemade pasta.

SUMMARY AND COMMENTS If you're up to your gills in fresh fish or Mexican specialties, head directly to La Galería for wonderful Italian eats. Everything's served à la carte, but at these prices, go ahead and order a cream of spinach soup or a traditional Swiss salad containing lettuce, cheese, apple, and chopped nuts (ask for the dressing on the side, as it tends to drown the salad). The most recommended dishes are the homemade pastas, including ravioli stuffed with smoked salmon. Pizzas are delicious, as are the homemade lemon pie and the chocolatey-but-not-too-sweet chocolate cake. Decorating the original space floor to ceiling are works of art; the newer locale at Zicatela sports admirable tile mosaics along with Ping-Pong and small billiard tables.

El Jardín ★★★★

| ITALIAN/VEGETARIAN | INEXPENSIVE | QUALITY ★★★★ | VALUE ★★★★★ |

Playa Zicatela; Calle del Morro s/n; ☎ 954-582-2315

Reservations Generally not needed, but accepted.

Entree range $5–$11.

Payment Cash only.

Service rating ★★★.

Parking Limited street parking.

Bar Full service.

Dress Casual, dude.

Disabled access None.

Customers Travelers and local businesspeople interested in Italian food and healthful vegetarian fare.

Hours Daily, 8 a.m.–11 p.m.; closed October 16–30.

SETTING AND ATMOSPHERE An unpretentious eatery with a peaked thatch roof; musica "lite" like Arabic instrumentals play unobtrusively. Pretty, square wooden tables are embellished with glossy paintings of flowers and fruit; straw-bottom chairs make a nice change from the usual plastic.

HOUSE SPECIALTIES Wonderful, medium-crust pizzas with generous toppings; homemade ravioli.

SUMMARY AND COMMENTS The menu is huge; even the beverages range far and wide, from smoothies with orange or grapefruit juice or milk or yogurt to mineral water with ginger, lime, and pineapple, to name just a few options. The menu is almost endless, running the gamut from enchiladas and vegetarian gado gado to a few meat dishes (burgers, breaded chicken), eggplant Parmesan, and potato croquettes. The medium-crust pizza, heaped with toppings, is sublime. The wonderful salad we ordered, with spinach, tofu, black olives, avocado, and tomato was large and not overdressed. And the breakfast menu is just as expansive, healthful, and yummy, with such Mexican classics as *entomatadas* (tortillas in a mild tomato sauce) and *chilaquiles* to eggs, crêpes, frittatas, and home-baked pastries. The Italian owner has a lot of restaurant experience in Puerto, having owned La Gota de Vida natural foods restaurant here for many years.

Las Margaritas ★★

MEXICAN	INEXPENSIVE	QUALITY ★★	VALUE ★★★★★

Playa Zicatela; Calle 8a Norte s/n; ☎ 954-582-0212

Reservations Not normally accepted.

Entree range $4–$11.

Payment Cash only.

Service rating ★★.

Parking Street.

Bar Beer, *micheladas,* and mixed drinks.

Dress Casual.

Disabled access None.

Customers Locals and expatriates.

Hours Wednesday–Monday, 8 a.m.–6 p.m.

SETTING AND ATMOSPHERE Large, open-sided dining room painted goldenrod with cobalt blue columns; blue or orange cloths on square tables; white plastic chairs.

HOUSE SPECIALTIES Daily lunch specials, *birria* (goat stew).

SUMMARY AND COMMENTS It's the talk of the town! Near the market in the more business-oriented upper town, "The Daisies" is all about budget meals. Most folks go for the lunch specials: soup, rice or pasta, entree, dessert, and handmade tortillas for less than $4. The dessert is often gelatin, if that clues you in to the sort of Mexican menu we're talking about. But the stews and local specials are tasty, and the little *sope* appetizers—a tiny tortilla smeared with a smidge of lard and a sprinkling of cheese—are delicious. Less successful are the budget cuts of thin beef; it's generally best, near the coast, to stick with seafood. Locals come on Sunday afternoons to dance to salsa, merengue, and cumbia and to eat the special of the day, be it *birria* or perhaps *cochinita pibil,* a Yucatecan pork specialty marinated in sour orange juice of that region.

Restaurant Mandil ★★½

INTERNATIONAL/SEAFOOD	INEXPENSIVE/MODERATE	QUALITY ★★½	VALUE ★★

Fraccionamiento Bacocho, at Hotel Aldea del Bazar; Avenida Benito Juárez Lote 7; ☎ 954-582-0508

Reservations Accepted.

Entree range $7–$15.

Payment AE, MC, V.

Service rating ★★★★.

Parking Hotel lot.

Bar Full service.

Dress Casual.

Disabled access None.

Customers Travelers for meals, locals for drinks and appetizers.

Hours Daily, 7 a.m.–11 p.m.

SETTING AND ATMOSPHERE *Casablanca* attitude with Mexican flavor.

HOUSE SPECIALTIES Seafood.

SUMMARY AND COMMENTS Locals find this sparkling-white hotel restaurant north of town perfect for an after-work drink and appetizer. Waiters are approachable and friendly, the marble floors are cool, and the large fountain tinkles delightfully. With more time on their hands (and more discretionary income), travelers park themselves in white-wicker chairs under the Middle East–style outdoor awning and Moorish arches any time of the day. The open-sided restaurant gets a pleasant breeze off the ocean, just steps away beyond the bluff (but not visible from the tables), and overlooks green lawns and the hotel's large, blue pool. The rather lengthy menu offers a range of recognizable international favorites, such as breaded and grilled chicken breast stuffed with seafood, served with French fries and steamed veggies.

Santa Fé ★★★

MEXICAN/VEGETARIAN   INEXPENSIVE/MODERATE   QUALITY ★★★★   VALUE ★★★

Playa Zicatela; Calle del Morro s/n; ☎ 954-582-0170 or 888-649-6407 U.S.

Reservations Not normally accepted.

Entree range $5–$14.

Payment AE, MC, V.

Service rating ★★½.

Parking Hotel lot.

Bar Full service.

Dress Casual.

Disabled access None.

Customers Travelers and local professionals.

Hours Daily, 7:30 a.m.–10:30 p.m.

SETTING AND ATMOSPHERE Open, second-floor venue with big vases of cut flowers, soft lighting, and an outstanding ocean view.

HOUSE SPECIALTIES Chiles rellenos, seafood tacos, strawberry pie.

SUMMARY AND COMMENTS Vegetarians will think they've stumbled into hog heaven, where the hogs are alive and well and the diners pig out instead on grilled quesadillas and *sopes* (small corn cakes topped with avocado, minced onion, and *crema,* a Mexican dairy product halfway between sweet cream and sour). Fish lovers might try the red snapper (*huachinango*), served whole (head, tail, and all) in the traditional fashion, or filleted and prepared *al mojo de ajo* (sautéed in lots of garlic). For vegans, there are tofu dishes, soyburgers, and mushroom-and-prickly-pear-cactus crêpes (spines removed, of course) served with a chipotle chile sauce. The restaurant is simple and unpretentious, under a tall, circular palapa roof, with the ocean, surfers, and fab sunsets for decoration.

SIGHTSEEING *in* PUERTO ESCONDIDO

MOST OF THE PEOPLE WHO VISIT PUERTO ESCONDIDO are in relaxation mode, meaning they're content with days on the beach and evenings sipping a frosty drink, and diving into a delicious meal at an unpretentious restaurant. Those wanting more cultural activities and entertainment plan to come in November (when the weather is at its most pleasant) for the **Fiesta de Música y Baile,** usually held the second week in November. This music and dance festival precedes the yearly **international surfing contest** and the **sailfish tournament,** which take place later in November. Be sure to make hotel and plane reservations well in advance. There is a lively fiesta in December as well, in honor of the **Virgen de la Soledad** (Virgin of Solitude), which culminates in a candlelit boat procession to honor the Virgin and bless the local fishermen.

At other times of the year, sightseeing involves exploring the coast. In addition to the beaches described in the introduction to this chapter, many visitors head for the beaches around the tiny port of **Puerto Ángel,** including **Zipolite, San Agustanillo,** and **Mazunte** (see Part Thirteen, Huatulco, page 385).

TOURS *and* SIDE TRIPS *from* PUERTO ESCONDIDO

BAHÍAS DE HUATULCO TOUR

TOUR OPERATOR **Viajes Dimar** (Avenida Pérez Gasga 905-B, next to Casablanca Hotel; ☎ 954-582-1551 or 954-582-0734 (phone and fax); and Calle del Morro s/n, Zicatela; ☎ 954-582-2305; **www.viajes dimar.com**) leads full-day trips to the **Bays of Huatulco.** Passengers go by land to Santa Cruz Bay, where along with other day-trippers they explore Huatulco's undeveloped bays and beaches, with an open bar and time for swimming and snorkeling as well as a seafood lunch (the latter not included in the tour price). It's a full day and a fun way to see not only Huatulco's lovely bays but also the countryside en route. The 12-hour tour costs $50 per person, and there's a required minimum of four people. Dimar also leads surfing safaris in a van or Suburban with surf racks to Barra de la Cruz, a beautiful virgin beach about an hour south of Huatulco, for about $185 for up to ten passengers.

BIRDING AND BOAT TOURS

PARADISE FOR BIRD-WATCHERS, **Manialtepec** and **Chacahua lagoons** are home to some 250 types of birds; mainly aquatic species inhabit these two large lagoons and the mangrove swamps that line their shores. Even nonbirders enjoy exploring the lagoon by small boat and spending time on the water. **Viajes Dimar** (see previous page) and other area tour operators arrange the excursions. The $33 half-day tours to Manialtepec Lagoon depart in morning or afternoon and include the boat trip (about three and a half hours), English-speaking guide, and land transportation. During the winter months, Dimar's tours are led by Canadian ornithologist Michael Malone and his wife, Joan Walker, who charge about $10 more per person. Or take a full-day tour to Chacahua Lagoon (approximately $40). When cruising through mangroves, you'll spot roseate spoonbills, boat-billed heron, and tiger heron, as well as a number of elegant wading birds. There's time for a swim and a simple fish lunch on the beach (for an additional cost) before the return trip.

Several interesting eco-trips to Manialtepec are offered through **Lalo Ecotours** (☎ 954-582-2468 or cell 954-588-9164, adding 044 before the number if you're in Puerto Escondido; **www.lalo-eco tours.com**). In addition to the half-day birding tour in the morning, there's a sunset glide through the lagoon and the chance for a swim and wine on the beach, or a walking tour for birders. Each of the above costs about $32 and includes transportation and guide but no food. Marine conditions permitting there is also a "phosphorescence tour" of two hours ($19) where you can enjoy the beautiful spectacle of swimming around phosphorescent plankton in the lagoon.

CULTURAL WALKING TOURS

ON WEDNESDAYS AND SATURDAYS during the winter, take a two-hour walking tour with the personable Gina Machorro, who works at the information booth at the west end of the Adoquín. Participants leave from the booth promptly at 8 a.m. Gina attended high school in the United States, and she speaks English well. She'll be happy to tell you everything you need to know about tamales and tortillas, chocolate, and the church. Cost is about $20 per person. She also leads Sunday-afternoon tours in the winter, lasting from about 4 p.m. to sunset, to the Colotepec River. The $50 fee includes transportation, tacos, and beer. There's no phone there, but you can contact her ahead of time by e-mail at **ginainpuerto@ yahoo.com**.

EXERCISE *and* RECREATION *in* PUERTO ESCONDIDO

IT SEEMS THAT MOST PEOPLE EITHER COME to Puerto to surf or to lie around in a hammock. There's not much middle ground when it comes to expending energy. Active people on the go might be happier in Cancún, Puerto Vallarta, or Acapulco, where there is easy access to parasailing and other adrenalized adventures. Still, the diligent sportsman or woman can come up with a few activities to fill idle days.

BODYBOARDING

SURFING HERE IS BEST LEFT TO THE PROS. Known as the Mexican Pipeline, **Zicatela** beach gets some huge, shapely waves that attract top professional and amateur surfers. One of the world's top surf spots, this beach also has a powerful undertow that makes it dangerous for anyone but expert swimmers. But intrepid souls can rent bodyboards or surfboards at Zicatela beach and head to the less formidable surf at La Punta (point at the east end of Zicatela Beach); beginners can practice at Playa Carrizalillo. **Crickets** (Calle del Morro s/n, Playa Zicatela; ☎ 954-582-1872) rents bodyboards for $2 per hour or $5 per day and surfboards for $3 an hour or $10 a day, along with a hefty deposit of more than $100.

HORSEBACK RIDING

ARRANGE A HORSEBACK-RIDING EXCURSION to the hot springs in **Atotonilco.** It's a more pleasant excursion during the cooler winter season, as the ride goes through some open country, and the last thing you want in the tropical heat is a dip in a really hot spring. Also, area rivers often become too deep during the summer rains, and mosquitoes can be bothersome. It's easiest to make the trek through **Viajes Dimar** (Avenida Pérez Gasga 905-B, next to Casablanca Hotel; ☎ 954-582-1551; **viajesdimar@hotmail.com**). The agency's tour departs at 9 a.m., and after an hour's horse ride, a soak in the spring is just the ticket. Riders can order food at the simple restaurant (extra cost) before returning to the starting point, near Manialtepec, arriving back in Puerto Escondido by about 2 p.m. The tour costs $35 per person, with a required minimum of two people. If you have a spirit of adventure and want to pay about half that price, get yourself to the village of Manialtepec and ask around for the guide.

KAYAKING AND RAFTING

RENT KAYAKS FOR ABOUT $6 OR $7 an hour at **Manialtepec,** about 12 miles from Puerto Escondido. You can paddle around for an hour to get a taste of the mangroves, or dedicate a bit more time (usually about two-and-a-half hours) to reach the end of the lagoon and return. Go as early in the morning as possible, when birds are feeding and the temperatures are cooler. For a bit more money ($10 per hour) but with transportation included, you can make arrangements through **Viajes Dimar** (Avenida Pérez Gasga 905-B, next to Casablanca Hotel; ☎ 954-582-1551; **www.viajesdimar.com**).

SCUBA DIVING

Aventuras Submarinas (Pérez Gasga 601-A; ☎ 954-582-2353; **www.scubaescondido.com**) offers certified divers a variety of opportunities. Although there's little coral in this area, divers explore the **Coconut Trench,** about 200 meters off the coast. You're most likely to see dolphins in November and December, while gray whales appear in March at the end of their southward migration from the Bering Sea. Visibility varies, depending on water temperature, the presence of plankton, and even the weather in the coastal mountains; typical range is only 30 to 45 feet. The shop offers night dives in addition to open-water, deep-water, and PADI certification courses. Jorge Pérez Bravo—owner, divemaster, and guide—charges $60 for two tanks and night dives to reefs from 30 to 120 feet deep, depending on the client's experience.

SPORTFISHING

SPORTFISHING CAN BE ARRANGED AT **Viajes Dimar** (Avenida Pérez Gasga 905-B, next to Casablanca Hotel; ☎ 954-582-1551; **www.viajesdimar.com**), the **Best Western Posada Real Hotel** in Bacocho (Boulevard Benito Juárez s/n; ☎ 954-582-0133), or directly with the anglers on Playa Marinero. Some of the species you might hope to catch (and if you're not planning to eat them, to release) include tuna, red snapper, marlin, and sailfish. Prices are generally around $37 to $40 per hour (one to three anglers) for a minimum of four hours.

SHOPPING *in* PUERTO ESCONDIDO

IT'S A TESTAMENT TO PUERTO ESCONDIDO'S obscurity and lack of sophistication that you'll find not one Los Castillo jewelry store, Gold Duck boutique, or Sergio Bustamante gallery (which are a given in most tourist destinations). In fact, shopping for quality souvenirs in Puerto is pretty bleak. The Adoquín, or pedestrian walkway that is the main tourist drag in Puerto Escondido, is paved with nearly identical boutiques selling T-shirts, batik sarongs, visors, and beach towels. Others favor Oaxacan artifacts, although none stands out as a beacon of fine art or handcrafts.

More shops are found north of Carretera Costera, in and around the municipal market, **Mercado Benito Juárez** (named for Mexico's only fully indigenous president, who was born in Guelatao, Oaxaca, and is the state's most important hero). The market encompasses several city blocks around Calles Novena (9a) Norte and Tercera (3a) Poniente. Although the selection is not terribly impressive, this is one of the best places to search for Oaxacan and Guatemalan crafts, textiles, and other mementos of your trip. Puerto Escondido is an excellent place, on the other hand, to buy a cute Brazilian bikini. Prices are on par with U.S. shops, but **Bikini Brasil** (two locations on Calle del Morro s/n, Zicatela Beach; ☎ 954-582-3331 or 954-582-2555) has an excellent selection of well-made suits and cute flip-flops, too.

NIGHTLIFE *in* PUERTO ESCONDIDO

FOR MANY PEOPLE, NIGHTLIFE here tends to consist of a drink and dinner—period. But for those who want to get out and party, there are some diversions, which tend to multiply in the high season (December through Easter; July, and August) and then disappear or shrink to weekends only for the rest of the year.

For a musical evening, check out **El Son y La Rumba** (far east end of Zicatela Beach; no phone), an unassuming little cabaret that special-izes in *nueva trova* (politically inspired ballads) and Latin jazz, with dance music starting after midnight. Famous names sometimes drop in to join the local boys in an impromptu jam session, but things don't start until about 11 p.m. Nearby, **Bar Fly** features Latin and rock (and Latin rock) until 3 a.m. Locals swear there's more than the usual splash of alcohol in the two-for-one happy-hour drinks at **Bananas,** found about in the middle of Calle del Morro at Zicatela Beach (☎ 954-582-0005); it's a lively sports bar with several TVs. Locals enjoy tiny, Eastern-styled **Casa Babylon,** next to the Arco Iris hotel at Zicatela Beach, for board games, coffee, Red Bull, good tunes, book exchange, and spontaneous dancing. Its attractive terra-cotta–colored walls are covered in dozens of authentic masks. On the Adoquín, **Wipe Out** (no phone) is a lively bar with back-ground music that's easy on the ears. **Danny's Terrace,** right on the beach off the Adoquín (Avenida Perez Gasga 900; ☎ 954-582-0257) has a nightly happy hour from 5 to 7 p.m. It's a good place to watch the sunset and not a bad choice for dinner, either.

Cinemar, aka **P.J.'s Books** (Calle del Morro s/n next to La Galería restaurant; ☎ 954-582-2288), has video functions at 7 and 9 p.m., usually showing the latest DVD releases or those titles requested by popular demand. Cost is about $5 per person but includes popcorn. Two-for-one specials during the early part of the week are meant to draw in customers.

PART THIRTEEN

HUATULCO

The **BAYS** of **OAXACA**

LOCATED ON THE PACIFIC SHORES of the state of Oaxaca, **Huatulco** is a peaceful, picturesque beach resort that has yet to grow into a major destination. It's the perfect hideaway for those who want to feel as though they've escaped civilization while enjoying the creature comforts of a modern resort. Set on the shores of nine gorgeous bays backed by mountains, Huatulco has some excellent luxury and budget hotels, a golf course, and a smattering of interesting shops and restaurants. Options for adventure tourism have increased in recent years, and vacationers now spend their days exploring the bays, and their evenings sipping cocktails under a starry sky.

Huatulco's original interlopers were pirates seeking not gorgeous sunsets and gold-sand beaches, but the booty stolen in the New World and sent by ship to the Old World. Sir Francis Drake and Thomas Cavendish are among the most famous of the pirates who antagonized the Spanish during Huatulco's short tenure as one of the New Spain's important shipping ports. San Blas, Zihuatanejo, and Acapulco later became important ports of call, and Huatulco slipped into a blissful obscurity. But it's hard to hide paradise from hungry developers, and in the 1980s, promoters of Mexican tourism noted the allure of Huatulco's sand beaches scalloping the coast in a series of jade, turquoise, and gray-blue bays.

Like Cancún, the coastal resort of **Huatulco** was planned by FONATUR, the tourism-development arm of the Mexican government. By 1984, a master plan for development had been drawn up, hotel construction begun, and coast-dwelling families relocated or integrated into the new plan. Mindful of the challenge of creating an ecologically friendly

unofficial **TIP**
Unlike those in Ixtapa, hotels and other services are set relatively far apart, so it's best to choose your accommodations according to your interests.

unofficial **TIP**

Grupo Asur, which operates airports throughout Mexico, purchased 321 acres in Huatulco for a major development. The company plans to build at least 1,300 hotel rooms on the property by 2012.

tourist town where no infrastructure currently existed, planners limited hotels to four stories, promised not to dump sewage in the bays, and set aside large tracts of land as ecological preserves.

The resort has never attained the popularity of Cancún or even Ixtapa. The economic downturn of the early 1990s derailed development, bringing investors to their financial knees and growth to a thumping halt. As a result, Huatulco had for its first decade a semiabandoned feeling that made the destination hard to sell. Restaurants still struggle to survive, and of the five-star hotels, the all-inclusives have become the most popular and successful. Despite these problems, Huatulco offers a beautiful tropical climate and a more palatable price tag than more popular destinations like Los Cabos or Cancún. In 2008, FONATUR announced that it is redirecting its focus onto Huatulco and will initiate efforts to get more flights to the destination and more services for tourists. The agency announced that Huatulco will have 5,000 rooms (about twice as many as exist now) by 2012.

Tangolunda Bay has the most glamorous and pricey accommodations in Huatulco, with water-sports equipment rental on the beach, the area's only golf course, and a few restaurants and shops. West of Tangolunda, **Chahué Bay** offers a half dozen moderately priced accommodations a short walk from the beach, along with a slowly blossoming restaurant and bar scene.

The inland town of **La Crucecita,** about five minutes by cab from Tangolunda or Chahué, was created by FONATUR street by street, and it now resembles any tourist-oriented town, with budget and moderately priced hotels, a municipal market, some bars, and plenty of restaurants. Even though it was built "from scratch," it's the only spot in Huatulco that looks and feels like a real town. Next in line, **Santa Cruz Bay** has a marina and cruise ship pier, restaurants and bars, and a nice mix of hotels in various price ranges. Santa Cruz Bay has several nice beaches as well, including La Entrega, which is good for snorkeling.

QUICK FACTS
about HUATULCO

AIRPORT AND AIRLINES The **Aeropuerto Bahías de Huatulco** (☎ 958-581-9004) is 12 miles northwest of town. **Mexicana de Aviación** has flights from Mexico City, with connections from the U.S. and major Mexican cities in high season only. The small airline **Aerocaribe** was running daily fights between the city of Oaxaca and

Bahías de Huatulco

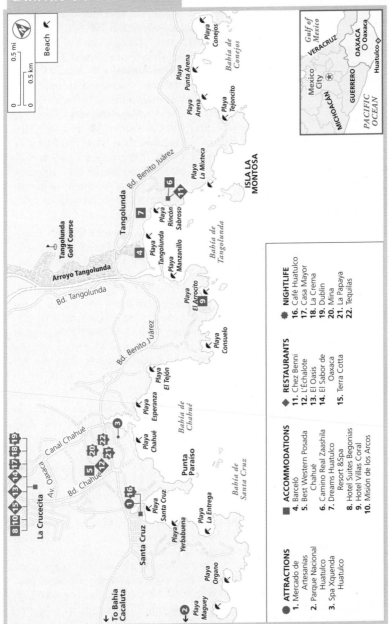

ATTRACTIONS
1. Mercado de Artesanías
2. Parque Nacional Huatulco
3. Spa Xquenda Huatulco

ACCOMMODATIONS
4. Barceló
5. Best Western Posada Chahué
6. Camino Real Zaashila
7. Dreams Huatulco Resort &Spa
8. Hotel Suites Begonias
9. Hotel Villas Coral
10. Misión de los Arcos

RESTAURANTS
11. Chez Benni
12. L'Échalote
13. El Oasis
14. El Sabor de Oaxaca
15. Terra Cotta

NIGHTLIFE
16. Café Huatulco
17. Casa Mayor
18. La Crema
19. Dublin
20. Mina
21. La Papaya
22. Tequilas

unofficial **TIP**

Mexico's small airlines have been having trouble staying in business and tend to start and stop service frequently. Check Aerotucán (www.aero -tucan.com) to see if it's operating between Oaxaca City and Huatulco when you're traveling.

Huatulco at press time but has been having some financial problems. Check **aerocaribe .com.mx** for schedules. **ClickMexicana,** a budget subsidiary of Mexicana (☎ 800-112-5425; **click.com.mx**), sells through the Internet and has three flights daily from Mexico City year-round. **Continental Airlines** (☎ 800-523-3273; **www.continental.com**) flies small aircraft nonstop from Houston on Saturdays from December through April. **Magnicharters** (Calle de Sabali 304, La Crucecita; ☎ 958-587-0413 or 958-587-1232) flies daily from Mexico City (except Tuesday) once or twice a day. Expect to pay $8 to $10 for van shuttle service to hotels on the bays or in La Crucecita, or about $35 for a private van. No private taxi service is authorized from the airport; it's $10 to $15 for a cab to the airport from Huatulco's hotels.

DRIVING The resort is about 162 miles due south of Oaxaca (capital of the eponymous state), 31 miles east of Puerto Angel, and 65 miles east of Puerto Escondido. When exploring outside Huatulco, or doing a lot of traveling between the bays, your hotel, and the town of La Crucecita, you'll want to rent a car for a day or two. Two car-rental agencies have desks at the airport and representatives at the hotels: **Dollar** (Boulevard Chahué, Lote 22, Manzana 1; ☎ 958-587-2221) and **Advantage** (Hotel Dreams; ☎ 958-587-0491). However, since car-rental prices are steep, you might spend less and avoid the hassle by simply taking taxis around town or renting one by the day or the hour.

GETTING AROUND You'll find taxis at major hotels, stationed along Calle Gardenia as you're leaving La Crucecita and at the marina on Santa Cruz Bay. Taxis cruise the streets as well. Huatulco taxi drivers are known for their honesty, and they have rate sheets listing the cost for various area destinations. Cab fare from Santa Cruz Bay to La Crucecita is $1.50, and it's $2.50 from Tangolunda to either La Crucecita or Santa Cruz. A cab from Tangolunda to the beach at La Entrega is $7. *Colectivos* (shared cabs) cost just $0.50 within these zones. If you want the bargain of a shared cab, just wave at any passing taxi with customers aboard; if it stops and you can squeeze in (and we are talking serious squeezing here), you're on your way. If you're unsure whether the woman in the front seat is a fare or the driver's girlfriend, ask, "*¿Es colectivo?*" ("Is this a collective taxi?").

unofficial **TIP**

If you have a five-digit local phone number, just add 58 at the beginning.

TELEPHONES The area code is ☎ **958;** all phone numbers should be seven digits. The old numbers were only five digits (and locals still refer to them this way).

TOURIST INFORMATION The best resource for information before you go to Huatulco is the Web site of the **Convention and Visitor's Bureau** at **baysofhuatulco.com.mx;** toll-free from the United States ☎ 866-416-0555; it has a link to the Hotel and Motel Association page, **hotelshuatulco.com.mx.** Once in Huatulco, contact the bureau at the Hotel Crown Pacific, Tangolunda Bay, ☎ 958-581-0486 or 958-581-0487.

WHERE *to* STAY *in* HUATULCO

HUATULCO'S MOST GLAMOROUS ACCOMMODATIONS are in **Tangolunda Bay,** which is also the hotel cluster nearest the area's only golf course. **Santa Cruz Bay** has some pretty, moderate-to-expensive properties and the best access to Huatulco's marina. **Chahué** offers mostly mid-priced accommodations and is about a 15-minute walk from La Crucecita. Most of the inexpensive accommodations are found in the town of La Crucecita, about five minutes by cab from Chahué and Tangolunda Bays, and ten minutes from Santa Cruz.

ACCOMMODATION PROFILES

Barceló $$$

OVERALL ★★½	QUALITY ★★½	VALUE ★★★

Paseo Benito Juárez s/n; ☎ 958-581-0055 or 800-227-2356 U.S.; fax 958-581-0113; www.barcelohuatulco.com

An attractive hotel located at Tangolunda, the only bay so far to offer accommodations right on the sand, this beachfront property started life as a Sheraton. The strong decorative lines and elegant appointments of public spaces have been sullied since the property was sold to the Barceló chain,

How Accommodations Compare in Huatulco

ACCOMMODATION	OVERALL	QUALITY	VALUE	COST
Camino Real Zaashila	★★★★	★★★½	★★★	$$$–$$$$
Misión de los Arcos	★★★★	★★★	★★★★½	$
Dreams Huatulco Resort & Spa	★★★½	★★★½	★★★	$$$
Hotel Villas Coral	★★½	★★½	★★★★	$
Barceló	★★½	★★½	★★★	$$$
Best Western Posada Chahué	★★½	★★	★★½	$$
Hotel Suites Begonias	★	½	★★	$

which has introduced incongruous color schemes in some areas. In keeping with the times, the Barceló now offers clients an all-inclusive plan exclusively, and its elevators—which many Huatulco hotels lack—makes it popular with older English as well as Canadian and American couples. Rooms are pleasant, with dark wood furnishings and deep green drapes. Adjacent to the gym, the small spa has couples-dedicated (read: tiny) sauna and steam rooms and offers massage. Make a reservation at the luxurious Don Quijote or El Agave for a romantic a la carte dinner (guests are allowed one dinner in these specialty restaurants), or partake of the nightly buffet dinner at La Tortuga, where there's a different theme and cuisine each night. Added hotel perks include three lighted tennis courts, miniature golf, and a beauty salon.

SETTING AND FACILITIES

Location Bahía Tangolunda.

Dining 4 restaurants.

Amenities and services Beach, 2 pools, gym, massage, water-sports center, tour desk, organized children's activities (ages 5–12), shops, 2 bars, 24-hour room service, Internet.

ACCOMMODATIONS

Rooms 351 rooms and suites.

All rooms AC, windows that open, balcony or terrace, bathtub, hair dryer, safe, minibar, coffeemaker, cable/satellite TV.

Some rooms Ocean view, whirlpool tub, refrigerator, kitchenette, CD, non-smoking.

Comfort and decor Rooms are simply but tastefully decorated, with comfortable furniture and tile floors. Refurbishing in 2005 replaced TVs, air-conditioning units, mattresses, and minibars.

PAYMENT, RESERVATIONS, AND RESTRICTIONS

Deposit Credit card; 1-day cancellation policy (with $5 fee).

Credit cards AE, MC, V.

Check-in/out 3 p.m./1 p.m.

Best Western Posada Chahué $$

OVERALL ★★½	QUALITY ★★	VALUE ★★½

Calles Mixie and Mixteco, Bahía Chahué; ☎ 958-587-0945 or toll-free within Mexico 800-780-7234; fax 958-587-1240; www.bestwestern.com

unofficial **TIP**
Year-round, the price includes free transportation to the airport, and free local calls under 30 minutes.

In typical Best Western style, rooms are functional rather than fun or arty, but they are comfortable. Free wireless Internet is available from the restaurant area, but not from guest rooms. The price for a double superior room seems high, but discounts are often available—to government employees and AAA members, for example. Specials like "third night free" are often available too, and these bring the price down to a very reasonable rate. Employees are typically friendly and helpful.

SETTING AND FACILITIES

Location Around the corner from L'Echalote Restaurant, about a mile from the beach at Chahué.

Dining Informal restaurant serving national and international dishes.

Amenities and services Pool, beach club, bar, room service, tour desk.

ACCOMMODATIONS

Rooms 19 rooms, 1 suite.

All rooms AC, fan, cable/satellite TV, coffeemaker, hair dryer, room safe, windows that open.

Some rooms Balcony or terrace, refrigerator, whirlpool tub, kitchenette.

Comfort and decor Comfortable yet unexciting beds and decor: standard-issue orange cloth cushions on sofas or armchairs and heavy drapes to block morning sun. Some rooms have cordless phones.

PAYMENT, RESERVATIONS, AND RESTRICTIONS

Deposit Credit card; 72-hour cancellation policy.

Credit cards MC, V.

Check-in/out 3 p.m./noon.

 ## Camino Real Zaashila $$$–$$$$

OVERALL ★★★★	QUALITY ★★★½	VALUE ★★★

Boulevard Benito Juárez 5; ☎ 958-581-0460 or 800-722-6466; fax 958-581-0468; www.caminoreal.com/zaashila

Graceful and gorgeous, and with an enviable location in the crook of Tangolunda Bay, the Camino Real is the place to relax in elegant comfort. Sit in comfortable rattan furniture at the open bar overlooking the pool and the sea beyond, lulled by the sound of water falling in the nearby fountain. Wander the property's pathways, admiring the thousands of plants that grow in riotous profusion. Slide into a lounge chair surrounding the cool, blue, freeform pool—better suited for floating than for serious swimming—over which tranquil New Age music emanates from unseen sources.

SETTING AND FACILITIES

Location Playa Rincón Sabroso, Bahía Tangolunda.

Dining European plan. Three restaurants, including Chez Benni, with Oaxacan and international specialties, and Azul Profundo, with seafood-fusion-Asian dishes. Some packages include free buffet breakfast.

Amenities and services Beach, 2 pools, hot tub, gym, water-sports center, organized children's activities (seasonal), tour desk, shops, 2 bars, 24-hour room service, Internet, Wi-Fi.

Rooms 120 rooms, 24 suites.

All rooms AC, fan, windows that open, ocean view, balcony or terrace, bathtub, hair dryer, minibar, cable/satellite TV, high-speed Internet.

Some rooms Safe, kitchenette, bathtub, coffeemaker, refrigerator, nonsmoking.

Comfort and decor Chic, with clean, spare lines and quiet elegance; marble appointments in bath, comfortable beds with wrought-iron headboards; no elevators, plenty of steps and walking along meandering paths may be off-putting to some folks.

PAYMENT, RESERVATIONS, AND RESTRICTIONS

Deposit Credit card; 3-day cancellation policy.

Credit cards AE, MC, V.

Check-in/out 3 p.m./1 p.m.

 Dreams Huatulco Resort & Spa $$$

| OVERALL ★★★½ | QUALITY ★★★½ | VALUE ★★★ |

Boulevard Benito Juárez 4; ☎ 958-583-0400 or 866-2DREAMS **U.S.; fax 958-581-0220; www.dreamsresorts.com**

This all-inclusive hotel (formerly the Gala) was taken over by the Dreams Resorts company in 2008. Like any beachfront all-inclusive worth its salt, it provides the opportunity to either play hard and try new things, or just to recharge depleted batteries. There are buffet restaurants and à la carte restaurants, nightly theater and theme shows, and, after 11 p.m., a disco. Rooms have been completely remodeled. During the day, check out windsailing, kayaking, and tennis clinics at no extra cost. In the pool, work off the nachos and extra desserts with aquaerobics or a rousing game of water volleyball. For the kids, separate "clubs" keep toddlers, children, and teens entertained with activities, videos, and sports. Adults may opt to pay an additional surcharge for Preferred Club rooms, which guarantee an ocean view and offer concierge service, extended check out, whirlpool tub on the balcony, and their own pool and beach.

SETTING AND FACILITIES

Location Tangolunda Bay.

Dining 4 restaurants.

Amenities and services Beach, 4 pools, gym, water-sports center, tour desk, organized children's activities, shop, 4 bars, 24-hour room service, business center, Internet, airport transfers.

ACCOMMODATIONS

Rooms 228 rooms, 12 suites.

All rooms AC, windows that open, bathtub, patio or balcony, hair dryer, safe, minibar, satellite TV, DVD/CD, MP3 docking station.

Some rooms Ocean view, whirlpool tub, nonsmoking, disabled access.

Comfort and decor Rooms have been completely remodeled with plush bedding, flat-screen TVs, fresh paint, and updated bathrooms and are far more comfortable than in the past.

PAYMENT, RESERVATIONS, AND RESTRICTIONS

Deposit Credit card; 8-day cancellation policy with stiff penalities.

Credit cards AE, MC, V.

Check-in/out 3 p.m./noon.

Hotel Suites Begonias $

OVERALL	★	QUALITY	½	VALUE	★ ★

Calle Bugambilia 503, La Crucecita; ☎ 958-587-0390; fax 958-587-1390

Budget travelers willing to accept no-frills accommodations will appreciate this hotel's location in the midst of downtown Crucecita, if not its decor. It's not on the beach nor does it have a pool, but it's central to many inexpensive and good restaurants, bars, and shopping (venues where you can spend the cash you're saving on accommodations). Rooms have firm queen beds; those for four people have two bedrooms and cost just about $50. For the same price as a standard, rooms #106 and #206 are larger corner units overlooking the plaza; they have tiny balconies and a round table for snacking or playing board games. Still, for almost the same price, two people can stay at the much more glamorous Misión de los Arcos, also in La Crucecita.

SETTING AND FACILITIES

Location Across from the plaza at La Crucecita.

Dining No restaurants, but close to many.

Amenities and services Beach-club access.

ACCOMMODATIONS

Rooms 13 rooms.

All rooms AC, fan, cable TV, windows that open.

Some rooms Balcony or terrace.

Comfort and decor Talavera-tile sinks cheer the bathrooms of these otherwise institutional rooms; most rooms have two queen beds.

PAYMENT, RESERVATIONS, AND RESTRICTIONS

Deposit Bank deposit; 3-day cancellation policy.

Credit cards MC, V.

Check-in/out 3 p.m./1 p.m.

Hotel Villas Coral $

OVERALL	★ ★ ½	QUALITY	★ ★ ½	VALUE	★ ★ ★ ★

Lotes 7 y 8 Manzana. 2, Paseo El Arrocito; ☎ 958-581-0500; fax 958-581-0477; www.hotelvillascoral.com

unofficial **TIP**
The two-bedroom, two-bath villas with complete kitchen doesn't even make it into the $$$ range and accommodates four adults and two kids, although a bit crowded if all six take the bait.

Perched above lovely little Arrocito Bay, which is between Tangolunda and Chahué Bays, this family-owned-and-operated hotel has great ocean vistas and breezes. Even the white-and-blue-dressed restaurant is blessed by a bird's-eye view of the water. Below the red-roofed, whitewashed, Mediterranean-style hotel is a tiny private beach; or just a few minutes' walk away is public Arrocito beach. The rooms are clean, but although nearly new, are already showing signs of age. Still, the one-bedroom suites are ideal for families.

SETTING AND FACILITIES

Location Between Tangolunda and Chahué Bays.

Dining Restaurant serving breakfast and lunch in low season, dinner also in high season.

Amenities and services Beach (down many stairs), pool, tour desk, bar (high season only), limited Internet access in reception area.

ACCOMMODATIONS

Rooms 16 rooms, 5 suites, 4 villas.

All rooms AC, balcony or terrace, cable/satellite TV; no room phones.

Some rooms Ocean view, minibar, refrigerator, coffeemaker, kitchenette.

Comfort and decor Mexican- and Mediterranean-style buildings; light, charming, pastel-oriented rooms with seaside feeling, conch-shell studded headboards. Ask for a room with a new air conditioner.

PAYMENT, RESERVATIONS, AND RESTRICTIONS

Deposit Credit card; 7-day cancellation policy.

Credit cards MC, V.

Check-in/out 3 p.m./noon.

 Misión de los Arcos $

OVERALL ★★★★	QUALITY ★★★	VALUE ★★★★½

Gardenia 902, La Crucecita; ☎ 958-587-0165; fax 958-587-1904; www.misiondelosarcos.com

Serene and tasteful, this oasis of chic uses the finest Mexican handcrafts, such as hand-woven, cream-colored bedspreads and wrought-iron-and-glass tables, without going for the overblown "super-fiesta" ambience to which some tourist hotels and restaurants fall prey. With the same clean lines and striking architecture as in the rest of the hotel, the on-site cafe serves almost two dozen different ices and ice creams as well as espresso, American coffee, and dessert. The restaurant (see Terra Cotta, page 381), serving Mexican and international meals all day, is as bright, appealing, and well managed as the rest of the hotel. The garden suite, perfect for honeymooners, has a large, private garden and fountain. If you want classy and understated surroundings, and don't mind the lack of amenities and services, this may be the hotel for you. It's certainly one of our all-time favorite budget hotels. In addition to the high-speed Internet in the cafe (free for hotel guests), there's free wireless Internet access in guest rooms and in the public spaces.

SETTING AND FACILITIES

Location La Crucecita.

Dining Restaurant, cafe.

Amenities and services Gym, Internet.

ACCOMMODATIONS

Rooms 13.

All rooms AC, fan, windows that open, safe, Internet.

Some rooms Balcony or terrace, whirlpool tub, cable/satellite TV.

Comfort and decor Tasteful, muted decor in beige and white, with wrought iron and wood furnishings and comfortable beds.

PAYMENT, RESERVATIONS, AND RESTRICTIONS

Deposit Credit card; first night paid to reserve (nonrefundable); 72-hour cancellation policy.

Credit cards AE, MC, V.

Check-in/out 2 p.m./1 p.m.

WHERE *to* EAT *in* HUATULCO

BECAUSE SOME OF THE LARGEST PROPERTIES offer all-inclusive plans, and because accommodations are spread throughout the slowly developing resort, restaurants have a hard time flourishing. Over time a few good restaurants have been established, and those that thrive by gearing themselves toward local business have wonderfully competitive prices. While innovation and competition are not the norm here (serious epicureans are better off in Puerto Vallarta), the destination attracts some excellent chefs who put to good use fresh seafood and locally grown herbs, fruit, and veggies to produce interesting international dishes and Oaxacan specialties. For dining options outside the hotel zones, head for the town of La Crucecita.

RESTAURANT PROFILES

Chez Benni ★★★

INTERNATIONAL	MODERATE/EXPENSIVE	QUALITY ★★★½	VALUE ★★★

Zona Hotelera Tangolunda; Hotel Camino Real Zaashila; Boulevard Benito Juárez 5; ☎ 958-581-0460 or 800-722-6466

How Restaurants Compare in Huatulco

RESTAURANT | CUISINE | COST	OVERALL	QUALITY	VALUE
L'Échalote | International | Mod	★★★★	★★★★	★★★★
Chez Benni | International | Mod	★★★	★★★½	★★★
Terra Cotta| International/Mexican | Inexp	★★★	★★	★★★
El Oasis | Mexican/Japanese/American | Inexp	★★	★★½	★★★½
El Sabor de Oaxaca | Oaxacan | Inexp	★★	★★★	★★★½

Reservations Recommended.

Entree range $13–$21.

Payment AE, MC, V.

Service rating ★★★½.

Parking Valet.

Bar Full service; the Zaashila, the house cocktail, combines coconut and pineapple creams with vodka, gin, and tequila.

Dress Casual chic–dressy.

Disabled access None.

Customers Mexican businesspeople and international travelers.

Hours Daily, 6–11 p.m.

SETTING AND ATMOSPHERE A narrow dining room on several levels, with high ceilings, smooth stucco walls, and large, open windows overlooking the pool and beach below. Some days they serve at the beach club below.

HOUSE SPECIALTIES Continental classics updated using New World ingredients.

SUMMARY AND COMMENTS This elegant, intimate restaurant has reasonable prices, and our party found the chef's daily specials a real treat. If ordering off the menu, you might start with an appetizer from the international menu, such as the lobster quesadillas. The Tangolunda salad, with lettuce, shrimp, and citrus fruits, is dressed in a light balsamic vinaigrette. Coconut shrimp served with guava, rice, and a tangerine sauce is a favorite main dish, as is the traditional *tlayuda,* an oversized corn tortilla with various condiments atop a bed of dried beef, spicy pork loin, or sausage.

L'Échalote ★★★★

INTERNATIONAL   MODERATE   QUALITY ★★★★   VALUE ★★★★

Calle Zapoteco s/n, Plaza Chahué at Hotel Posada Eden Costa; ☎ 958-587-2480

Reservations Recommended.

Entree range $10–$25.

Payment MC, V.

Service rating ★★★½.

Parking Small lot, street.

Bar Full service, with wine cellar.

Dress Resort casual.

Disabled access Yes.

Customers Travelers and a loyal local following.

Hours Tuesday–Sunday (daily during school holidays), 2–11 p.m.

SETTING AND ATMOSPHERE Thatch-roofed main restaurant with art by a well-known local painter on the walls; tables outside in a mini-garden surrounded by plants.

HOUSE SPECIALTIES Traditional Swiss fondue made with Gruyère cheese, white wine, and a touch of nutmeg and garlic; Thai fondue, an innovative (and yummy) combination of vermicelli, spinach, shrimp, and meat simmering in a little fondue pot, with delicious broth served separately.

SUMMARY AND COMMENTS A meticulous chef of French and Swiss parentage, Thierry Faivre brings to Huatulco worldly recipes and an unwavering work ethic, both of which lead to consistent presentation. Very popular with locals and visitors, this warm-and-cozy restaurant fuses successfully several different cuisines. Go wild with a Mexican hybrid, *chimichanga de chapulines* (fried burrito with grasshoppers), or take it down a notch with Quiche Lorraine or Vietnamese *nems* (fried egg rolls). For something light, try the lemongrass soup with shrimp and mushrooms, Thai-style.

> *unofficial* **TIP**
> There's often live music at L'Échalote after 9 p.m., with jazz on Thursday and melodic guitar ballads the rest of the week.

 El Oasis ★★

| MEXICAN/JAPANESE/AMERICAN | INEXPENSIVE | QUALITY ★★½ | VALUE ★★★½ |

La Crucecita; Avenida Flamboyan 211 at Bugambilias;
☎ **958-587-0045**

Reservations Accepted but not usual.

Entree range $6–$13.

Payment AE, MC, V.

Service rating ★★★.

Parking Street.

Bar Full service.

Dress Casual.

Disabled access None.

Customers Locals and travelers of all ages.

Hours Daily, 7 a.m.–midnight.

SETTING AND ATMOSPHERE Casual patio dining.

HOUSE SPECIALTIES Teppanyaki (seafood, steak, or chicken—or a combo—grilled with onion, green pepper, broccoli, and other veggies).

SUMMARY AND COMMENTS Locals join visitors at this plain restaurant in the center of La Crucecita for its quick service and the consistency of its food, always prepared exactly the same, so you know what to expect. Owner Ernesto Tostados, a transplant from Mexico City, was one of the pioneers of Huatulco tourism in the 1980s, and has since established himself as one of La Crucecita's most reliable restaurateurs. Sit on the outside patio, diagonally across from the town plaza, for a hearty breakfast, a snack with coffee, or sushi and teppanyaki. What the wait staff lacks in polish they generally make up for in speed.

El Sabor de Oaxaca ★★

OAXACAN	INEXPENSIVE	QUALITY ★★★	VALUE ★★★½

La Crucecita; Avenida Guamúchil 206; ☎ 958-587-0060

Reservations Recommended in high season.

Entree range $10–$11.

Payment AE, MC, V.

Service rating ★★★.

Parking Street.

Bar Full service; *ponche,* the local specialty drink, combines mezcal with grenadine and orange, pineapple, and grapefruit juices.

Dress Casual.

Disabled access None.

Customers Mexican and foreign travelers.

Hours Daily, 7 a.m.–11 p.m.

SETTING AND ATMOSPHERE Festive and intimate, just across from the town square.

HOUSE SPECIALTIES Oaxaca plate for two; may vary, but the platter usually contains an Oaxacan *tamale,* string cheese, guacamole, black beans, sausage, thin beef and pork steaks, *chile relleno* (stuffed chile), salsas, and tortillas.

SUMMARY AND COMMENTS This is the place to sample Oaxacan fare, period. The sample plate mentioned above gives you a taste of some of the state's most traditional dishes, from mild *quesillo* (a ball of tangy string cheese) to *cecina* and *asajo* (chewy but flavorful cuts of pork and beef, respectively), and tortillas. Children and fussy eaters will appreciate the more recognizable offerings: hot dogs, burgers, French fries, *tortas* (sandwiches on fresh bread rolls), and even spaghetti with butter or garlic butter. Those wanting an authentic regional dish might opt for pigs' feet, fried grasshoppers, or a *tlayuda*—a giant, somewhat tough tortilla (typically smeared with a tad of pork lard)—topped with meats, cheese, and hot salsa. For the less adventurous, there's a variety of soups, including cactus soup and bean soup; and for vegetarians, satisfying fruit or mixed green salads.

Terra Cotta ★★★

INTERNATIONAL/MEXICAN   INEXPENSIVE/MODERATE   QUALITY ★★   VALUE ★★★

Avenida Gardenia 902, at Hotel Misión de los Arcos; La Crucecita; ☎ 958-587-0165

Reservations Accepted but not needed outside high season.

Entree range $8–$13.

Payment AE, MC, V.

Service rating ★★.

Parking Street.

Bar Full service.

Dress Casual.

Disabled access None.

Customers Locals, Mexican business travelers, travelers staying at the hotel Misión de los Arcos.

Hours Daily 7:30 a.m.–11p.m.

SETTING AND ATMOSPHERE Set up like an upscale coffee shop, with comfortable booths.

HOUSE SPECIALTIES French toast stuffed with cream cheese and orange marmalade and orange liquor.

SUMMARY AND COMMENTS Mingle with the local businesspeople consulting over breakfast at this American-owned restaurant. Done in the same soothing palate as the adjoining hotel, Terra Cotta has faux-painted earth-tone walls, fawn-colored booths and creamy, natural stone-tile tables grouted in white. The lighting is recessed and the soundtrack soothing and modern. Dishes are international and Mexican: mango chicken with rice; shrimp and beef tenderloin in creamy, smoky sauce; or baguette sandwiches or a burger. For dessert there's caramelized pineapple with coconut ice cream.

▌SIGHTSEEING *in* HUATULCO

IN HUATULCO, THE BEACH is the place to be. Whether you choose to bay-hop on an organized tour, snorkel around a rocky cove, or hang

unofficial **TIP**
To get oriented, consider hiring a cab and driver-guide for a few hours, or rent a car for a day or two.

out at a favorite beach, the Huatulco experience centers around its gold-sand beaches and the clear waters that fringe them. A bay tour is a great way to spend a day on the water, get to know the area, and plan for subsequent days of lounging or activity.

Because the resort is so spread out, transportation is a key issue. Just a few of Huatulco's string of nine stunning bays have been developed, others (for the moment) have been left pristine or with beachfront fish restaurants or other minimal services. Comprising these bays are 36 beaches—some solitary, some with all the soda, beer, munchies, and water toys you'll need for a long day of strenuous relaxation.

But remember: If you'll spend most of the day at the beach, it's generally cheaper to use taxis than a rental car. (If being dropped at an isolated beach, ask the driver to return for you at a specific hour.) The highlights of each area are described below, along with some further suggestions for exploration. Check out "Tours and Side Trips from Huatulco," lower right, and "Beautiful Beaches and Basic Services," page 385, for advice on adventures farther afield.

ATTRACTIONS

THE FIRST TO BE DEVELOPED, tongue-twisting **Tangolunda Bay** is where you'll find the **Barceló, Dreams,** and **Camino Real Zaashila** hotels (see profiles earlier in this chapter), and other high-pedigree accommodations as well as the golf course. The Dreams and Barcelo are all-inclusive, but the others have nice restaurants open to the public. The beach also is public, but lounge chairs are reserved for hotel guests, especially during high season. Water-sports stands on the beach rent all the usual toys.

Just east of Tangolunda, **Conejos Bay** has a pretty beach called **Tejón** (the local word for the coatimundi, a raccoonlike animal), with calm water. There are no services except for a palapa restaurant on the beach at **Punta Arena. Conejos** (Spanish for "rabbits") is the next beach slated for development by FONATUR (the tourism-development arm of the Mexican government), and some luxury homes, condos, and time-shares have been built on the cliffs overlooking the bay.

West of Tangolunda, **Chahué Bay** has a beach club (open to nonmembers for a small fee) with a pool, children's play area, shaded lounge chairs on the beach, and a small restaurant. The beach at Chahué slopes down at an angle to the water; currents are a bit strong, making it unsuitable for water-sports and even swimming. Chahué now has a half dozen three- and four-star accommodations, but none right on the beach. The **Spa Xquenda Huatulco** (Bahía Chahué s/n; ☎ 958-583-4448) offers a variety of spa services and treatments and has a gym, tennis courts, and a lap pool. Chahué has a growing number of restaurants (such as L'Échalote and the popular sandwich shop–cafe Viena).

Santa Cruz Bay has a few four-star accommodations as well as restaurants, bars, and several banks. Along the main road you'll find the **Mercado de Artesanías,** a strip of shops selling souvenirs and sarongs, and a plaza that *almost* resembles that of a real town. During the day young men with photo albums tout fishing trips and bay cruises; follow them to the nearby marina, where you can book these excursions. Alternatively, you can hire a water taxi (read: an angler in his skiff) through the **Sociedad Cooperative Tangolunda** (☎ 958-587-0081), a co-op of local fisherfolk. Private round-trip service costs range from $25 to $100, depending on distance; day-long bay cruises cost just $20 to $25 per person. The main beach in town has the same name as the bay, and it's fronted by seafood restaurants where you can rent banana boats, personal watercraft, or snorkel equipment, as well as hire a motorboat for water-skiing. The west side of the bay, called **Playa la Entrega,** is a good place to snorkel.

unofficial **TIP**
Boat captains will insist you wear a lifejacket as you pass the port captains office—but they don't mind if you shed them afterwards.

Continuing in a westward direction, **Organos Bay** (accessible only by boat) has a virgin beach. The water here is clean, calm, and great for swimming. Contiguous **Maguey Bay** is accessible by two decent roads, one originating at La Entrega, the other, from the town of Santa Cruz or Crucecita. Visit the seafood restaurants on the beach, and it's a great place to swim or snorkel. Bay tour operators often deposit their guests here for lunch and beach time.

Lovely **Cacaluta Bay** comprises part of **Parque Nacional Huatulco,** a land and water park inaugurated in 1998. You can get here by ATV, but because the route to the bay goes through the protected area, visitors are allowed only as part of a group tour (see "ATV Tours," next page). There's no restriction on visitors arriving by boat, however, and you can hire a water taxi at Santa Cruz Bay. You won't find services at all on Cacaluta, nor on neighboring **Chachacual Bay,** whose long, au naturel beaches are perfect for swimming. It also is only accessible by water. Behind some rocks at the west end of the bay, **Playa la India** is protected and therefore the best place for paddling around uninhibited by the surf.

TOURS *and* SIDE TRIPS *from* HUATULCO

CULTURAL TOURS

SWIM, EAT, DRINK, AND OBSERVE during **Bahías Plus**'s eight-hour Discover Huatulco tour. The day starts with a bay cruise; then participants snorkel and eat lunch at **Maguey Beach** (food and gear cost extra). After about six hours, they continue to the town of

La Crucecita, where they visit the Catholic church; watch the weaving process and shop for handicrafts; and sample Oaxacan specialties such as string cheese, pork sausage, hard tortillas called *tlayudas*, and many different flavors of *mezcal* (tequila's unrefined cousin). The tour ends with a bird's-eye view of the bay from a mirador. The cost is $50 (higher with fewer than 20 guests); contact Bahías Plus at ☎ 958-587-0932, **www.bahiasplus.com,** or visit their office in La Crucecita at Avenida Carrizal, No. 704.

ATV TOURS

THERE'S NO MINIMUM NUMBER of passengers required to rumble into Huatulco National Park on an ATV tour. Three- to four-hour tours offered by different tour operators (including Bahías Plus, above) include time for swimming at the beach and bouncing along dirt roads through the jungle as well. Tours usually depart around 9:30 or 10 a.m. and again in the early afternoon. Wear sunscreen, sunglasses, and a head scarf or close-fitting hat; goggles and helmets provided. Tours cost $45 to $63 per ATV (some companies charge slightly less for solo drivers).

BOAT TOURS

 BOARD A LARGE CATAMARAN (for up to 300 people) or a smaller yacht (30 to 60 passengers) for an all-day adventure on the bays of Huatulco. The tour price includes transportation, with stops for swimming and snorkeling at San Agustín and Maguey (or other beaches depending on crowds, tides, etc.), as well as free soft drinks and beer at the bar. Guests have time for lunch at simple restaurants on the sand, but the lunch isn't included in the tour price ($20 to $25 per person).

COFFEE PLANTATION TOURS

A GREAT WAY TO GET AWAY from the hot weather at the coast and up into the cooler air of the foothills of the Sierra Madre del Sur is to take a tour into coffee country. It's a full-day trip, most often to **La Gloria** coffee plantation. Depending on the time of year, you may see coffee beans ripening on the trees, or you may observe the drying, roasting, or other stages of the coffee-making processes. Enjoy a typical country lunch in the plantation's dining room, and a swim in some attractive waterfall-fed pools in the Copalita River. Tours require a minimum of six people, so to be sure you get hooked up, sign up soon as possible after hitting town. Prices run $40 to $50 per person, including lunch. Contact Explore Huatulco 4 Less (**www .explorehuatulco4less.com**).

TOURS OUTSIDE HUATULCO

THE BEACHES WEST (it seems as if they should be north, but the Oaxaca coastline runs west to east) of Huatulco are gorgeous and great for exploring, either on your own or on a day tour. Most tour operators charge about $20 to $25 per person (not including lunch or entrance fees) and stop at **Puerto Ángel,** a tiny town on a sheltered bay where a few hotels accommodate more-solitary, budget-oriented travelers. Puerto Angel itself has so-so beaches, but just west is **Zipolite,** a beautiful, wide, long, white-sand beach favored by European (which often means topless) sun-worshippers; at one end a rocky cove provides a semi-secluded area where nude bathers are generally ignored (by the authorities, that is). Just beyond is equally pretty **San Agustinillo,** framed by groups of rocks extending out into the water.

BEAUTIFUL BEACHES AND BASIC SERVICES

Less than an hour northwest of Huatulco, **Zipolite, San Agustinillo,** and **Mazunte** are gorgeous beaches offering palm-thatch restaurants on the sand and basic accommodations where you can keep an eye—and an ear—on the surf. In past years, surfers and nature lovers have been content to rent hammocks or a bare-bones palapa (often with a musty-smelling mattress) right on the beach. Today, as entrepreneurs fall in love with and invest in the area, there are a few more appealing alternatives for combining a laid-back, au naturel lifestyle with comfier digs.

Highly recommended **Casa Pan del Miel** (Cerrada del Museo de la Tortuga, Mazunte; ☎ 958-589-5844; **www.casapandemiel.com**) combines the wonderful hospitality of French-Mexican owner Anne Gillet with an unbeatable view of the coast from its lofty perch above the junction of San Agustinillo and Mazunte beaches. The excellent room rate ($–$$) gets you one of four tastefully furnished, "beach-elegant" suites with coffee-maker and microwave, room safe, satellite TV, fan, and air-conditioning. Each has an ample patio with chairs and a big, airy hammock. Views from the property's open kitchen and dining room, infinity pools, and deck are to die for, and the sound of the sea hitting spiky black rocks just offshore is as soothing as can be. Rooms closed for renovation from December 2008 to February 2009.

Exploring the coast en route to Zipolite or Puerto Angel, make a pit stop at **Piña Palmera** (Carretera Puerto Angel Mazunte, Playa Zipolite s/n; ☎ 958-584-3145; **www.pinapalmera.org**), open Monday through Saturday, 9 a.m. to 3 p.m. Purchasing some hand-made artifacts supports the hundreds of physically handicapped adults and children who reside there.

At Zipolite beach, the best bet for accommodations is **El Alquimista** (north end of beach). Here surfers grab the good waves and nudists work on their all-over tans. The cabins ($) are far and away the nicest on the beach, with screened doors and teak furnishings. And the best news is that right outside your door is also the town's best bar/restaurant, offering fine pizza, pasta, and international dishes; it's a popular hangout as well for evening drinks, and so the tables right on the sand fill nightly with locals as well as visitors.

Continue to **Mazunte,** where you can learn about endangered Olive Ridley and *Golfina* turtles at the **Centro Mexicano de la Tortuga** (Domicilio Conocido, Mazunte; ☎ 958-584-3376; **www .centromexicanodelatortuga.org**). It's open Tuesday through Saturday, 10 a.m. to 4:30 p.m., and Sunday, 10 a.m. to 2:30 p.m., closed Mondays; admission is about $2 for the obligatory 45- to 60-minute tour. You'll see tanks of tiny turtles and larger specimens before continuing to a shop selling natural cosmetics and creams, an alternative for the townspeople to the turtle-butchering businesses of previous years.

Tour operators include **Bahías Plus** (Calle Carrizal 704, La Crucecita; ☎ 958-587-0932; **www.bahiasplus.com**), which offers coffee plantation trips, ATV tours, and jaunts to the beaches west of Huatulco. **Paraíso Huatulco** Calle Ceiba 202, La Crucecita; ☎ 958-587-2878; **www.paraisohuatulco.com;** with offices at Barceló, Dreams and Camino Real Hotels on Bahía Tangolunda) has bay cruises with drinks but not food included, at $25 per person; fishing; horseback riding, coffee plantation, and ATV tours; and tours to Puerto Angel; and offers travel agent services and incentive group tours.

EXERCISE *and* RECREATION *in* HUATULCO

OPPORTUNITIES FOR ADVENTURE TOURISM are slowly growing in Huatulco. Arrange dive or snorkel trips, sport fishing, or ocean kayaking along the area's beautiful bays. While Pacific Coast diving is neither as easy (the currents are stronger) nor as rewarding as Caribbean diving, small coral reefs and shipwrecks draw divers into the warm, blue water.

BODYBUILDING

FOR A WORKOUT WITH LIKE-MINDED bodybuilders, go to **Sam's Gym** (Hotel Misión de los Arcos, Calle Gardenia 902, La Crucecita; ☎ 958-587-0165). There's a trainer on-site, free weights, and machines. Cost is $3 for the day, or get a bimonthly or monthly rate.

GOLF

THE 18-HOLE, PAR-72 **Campo de Golf Tangolunda** (Avenida Juárez s/n, next to Hotel Barceló; ☎ 958-581-0059) was designed by Mario Schetjnan. The air-conditioned clubhouse has a restaurant, bar, and pro shop, as well as a swimming pool and four lighted tennis courts. Greens fees are $69 for 18 holes, with an extra $32 for cart rental.

HORSEBACK RIDING

AREA TOUR OPERATORS are happy to arrange horseback riding expeditions, many of which begin at Conejos Bay and traverse the low tropical jungle to the mouth of the Copalita River. After a ride on the beach, equestrians head into the hills before returning to the coast at Conejos Bay. There's a small palapa where refreshments are sold, and there's time for a swim before the ride back to the ranch. Trips normally leave around 10 a.m. and 2 p.m. If possible, wear loose, cool, long pants (jeans are awfully hot), a hat, and everything you need for sun protection. Three-hour rides cost around $50.

KAYAKING AND RAFTING

ALTHOUGH TAME BY WORLD RAFTING standards and available only during or just after the rainy season (usually July through November, for example) one of the most exciting "off-road" adventures from Huatulco is to descend the **Copalito River** in kayak or raft. Beginners usually put in at La Ceiba, where they'll float and paddle past exuberant tropical vegetation and several Class III rapids.

*un*official **TIP**
A slightly longer and more challenging option is to put in at La Hamaca and descend some 25 miles to La Bocana, where the river empties into the Pacific Ocean. Contact **TTBC (Transportes Turisticos Bahía Chahué)** (Calle, Chahué s/n, ☎ 958-587-0509; ttchahue@hotmail.com) for current schedules and prices.

SCUBA DIVING AND SNORKELING

HUATULCO'S REEFS ARE AMONG the best of Pacific North America. Growing not more than 25 feet below the surface, reefs off **Cacaluta** and **Riscalillo** are appropriate for novice divers, while **San Agustín** offers a sunken ship at a more challenging 100 feet below sea level. In this translucent underwater world, you'll see giant parrotfish and delicate-looking angels as well as lobsters, starfish, seahorses, and myriad other underwater types. Highly respected **Hurricane Divers** (Santa Cruz Bay; ☎ 958-587-1107; **www .hurricanedivers.com**) is a full-service PADI dive shop. Owner Robert Kraak is a professional Dutch diver who worked for years in the Dominican Republic before relocating to Huatulco; his wife often prepares a seafood feast postdive. Hurricane offers dive and snorkel tours, PADI and DAN certification, and equipment repair. They also offer just about any land tour you could imagine, from coffee plantations to the city of Oaxaca.

SPORTFISHING

SPORTFISHERS REGULARLY HOOK MARLIN, dorado, tuna, and red snapper on full-day or half-day fishing adventures out of Bahía Santa Cruz. You can book through your hotel or through tour operators, such as **Paraíso Huatulco** and **Hurricane Divers** (info on previous page and above), or contact **Sociedad Cooperative Tangolunda** (☎ 958-587-0081). The latter, located at the Santa Cruz marina, is a co-op of local anglers that we always are happy to support. Prices for either of these range from $15 per hour for a skiff (four-hour minimum) to about $120 a day for a small fishing yacht.

SHOPPING *in* HUATULCO

HUATULCO OFFERS A MAINLY UNASSUMING mix of souvenirs ranging from tacky and tasteful—as well as a small selection of folk art, jewelry, and fine art. In La Crucecita and at the major hotel gift shops, you'll find some good examples of rugs, weavings, pottery, tin work, embroidered blouses and dresses, and other items from the state of Oaxaca. Beware of mass-produced goods of dubious quality. For shopping like the locals do, go to the **Mercado 3 de Mayo** in La Crucecita (corner of Calles Bugambilias and Guanacaste; no phone). Although mostly you'll find butchers, fishmongers, and purveyors of plastic goods, blue jeans, and halter dresses, you'll see some traditional, embroidered blouses and handicrafts as well.

For more artistic souvenirs, **Museo de Artesanías Oaxaqueñas** (Calle Flamboyan 216, La Crucecita; ☎ 958-587-1513) is filled with bright cotton tablecloths with matching napkins, *tapetes* (thick, hand-loomed rugs) from Teotitlán del Valle, and other goodies from throughout the state. The store's open late, so you can stop by after dinner in town.

La Probadita (Calle Bugambilia 501; ☎ 958-587-1641) sells a range of Oaxacan foods—including chocolate (for hot chocolate), concentrated *mole* for making regional dishes, mezcal in many presentations—and a small stock of handicrafts. Next door, **Artesanías Oaxaqueñas** (Calle Bugambilia 501; ☎ 958-587-1750) carries a large inventory of *alebrijes* (brightly painted wood figurines) and some adorable, tiny, painted wooden chairs.

Mantelería Escobar (Calle Cocotillo 217; ☎ 958-587-0532) looms cloth to order in Oaxacan style; order curtains, bedspreads, tablecloths, or even hammocks, or buy from their stock.

Plaza Oaxaca (Flamboyan and Gardenias; no phone) has a half-dozen shops selling arts and crafts, magazines, casual wear, and more. In Bahía Santa Cruz, **Maria Bonita** (Santa Cruz Marina; ☎ 958-587-1400), offers high-quality jewelry from Taxco, Guerrero as well as arts and crafts from all over Mexico. Also at Santa Cruz Bay is the **Mercado de Artesanías** (Boulevard Santa Cruz at Calle Mitla; no phone), a string of shops selling a rather uninspired collection of sarongs, T-shirts, and shell and ceramic knickknacks, along with a few more-interesting pieces.

NIGHTLIFE *in* HUATULCO

WHILE A FAR CRY FROM THE PANACHE of Acapulco or the rowdy, nonstop pulse of Los Cabos, Huatulco's nightlife offers entertainment for most tastes and budgets. Most of the hotels in Tangolunda Bay have at least one dinner-show per week open to the public, and La Crucecita and Chahué have a limited but growing number of bars and dance clubs with live or canned tunes. Most of the clubs charge $5 to $8 cover (sometimes with a drink or two included) in high season and are open throughout the week; in low season most are open weekends only and may lower their cover charges to attract locals and stray tourists.

Canned techno complete with flashing strobe lights can be found at **Mina** (Calle Mixie s/n, next to the Best Western; ☎ 958-587-2731), the town's most popular disco for the young. **La Papaya** (Boulevard Benito Juárez s/n, ☎ 958-583-4911) has a downstairs restaurant and mezcal bar, and another bar upstairs where showgirls swim around in giant fish tanks. Danceable tunes meander among house, trance, electronica, salsa, merengue, and rock. The bar **Tequilas** (Boulevard Chahué s/n, Suite 6, ☎ 958-583-4055), a lively outdoor bar surrounding a fountain, is a popular stop for an after-dinner drink and a listen to folk music (sometimes live) from all over the world.

In the town of La Crucecita, **La Crema** (Calle Gardenia 311; ☎ 958-587-0702)—in addition to serving (after 8 p.m.) huge baked potatoes with various toppings and the destination's best, brick-oven pizza—is a friendly bar where multi-generational families are as comfortable, inside or on the open back patio, as 20-somethings. The friendly owners have a huge discographic collection for your listening pleasure. Across the street, **Dublin** (Calles Carrizalillo and Flamboyan; no phone) recreates a chummy Irish pub—except the Guinness is in a can, not on tap! Overlooking the town square, **Casa Mayor** (Calles Flamboyan and Bugambilia; ☎ 958-587-1881) is an excellent place to mix with the locals for coffee, drinks, snacks, and conversation; live *trova* (ballads) are performed most nights after 9 p.m.

Café Huatulco, within the open-air gazebo in Santa Cruz Plaza ☎ 958-587-1228), is a convivial evening scene with a background of canned classical music. Most evenings between 6 and 8 p.m., musicians entertain the crowd on their magical marimbas.

PART FOURTEEN

LOS CABOS

From **SERENE RETREATS** to **PARTY CENTRAL**

THE RAGGED SIERRAS BISECT THE **Baja California Peninsula,** a skinny, often-barren apostrophe between the Pacific Ocean and **Sea of Cortez.** Baja, as it's commonly called, stretches nearly 1,000 miles south from the international border between Southern California and Mexico to a stone horseshoe called **El Arco**—"the arch."

Los Cabos, which spreads north from the arch along both coastlines, is gorgeous, luxurious, and exciting. It's also outrageously expensive and completely unlike any other Mexican resort. Some call it "Newport Beach South," referring to the Southern California influences that have turned a desert landscape into a lush swath of golf courses and million-dollar villas with awesome views. A generous wad of discretionary cash comes in handy at this extravagant resort area—though there are ways to enjoy the scenery without maxing out your credit cards.

It's hard to believe this barren, desolate landscape has become a high-class resort destination. When the Spaniards arrived in the mid-1500s, the area was populated by small groups of Pericú Indians who lived and dressed sparsely. The conquistadors paid little attention to the tip of Baja, focusing more on the city of **La Paz** to the north, where pearls were abundant in the bay. Dutch, Spanish, and English pirates found refuge in southern Baja for two centuries, from the mid-1500s to

unofficial **TIP**
Los Cabos has the dubious distinction of being a beach resort where the ocean is usually too dangerous for swimming. The safest swimming is at **Playa Médano** in Cabo San Lucas. The **Hilton** has one of the few safe swimming beaches on the Corridor. Nonguests are allowed access; if you pay for snacks or drinks, you should be able to use the hotel's lounge chairs under shade umbrellas.

the 1700s. Jesuit missionaries arrived in the 1600s and attempted to impose "proper" dress and manners upon the local populace. The padres' insistence on monogamy and other foreign concepts was unwelcome. A tiled scene above the door at one church portrays the locals dragging Padre Nicolás Tamaral to a raging fire where he died, becoming Baja's first martyr. The foreigners brought new diseases to Baja as well, and the indigenous population was nearly wiped out.

A different class of immigrants arrived in the 1940s, when the action was focused on **Bahía San Lucas** and its profitable tuna cannery. Sportfishing became an important local industry in the 1950s, after word of the fertile fishing grounds where the Sea of Cortez meets the Pacific Ocean spread through a community of hardy, independent travelers. A few rustic-yet-luxurious lodges with private airstrips catered to adventuresome, wealthy anglers, while hardier, less-affluent adventurers began driving down the long, rugged peninsula to its tip. A paved road connecting **Tijuana** and Los Cabos opened in 1973. FONATUR, the tourism-development arm of the Mexican government, designated the area for development in 1974 and coined the name "Los Cabos," encompassing the towns of **San José del Cabo** and **Cabo San Lucas** with the **Corridor,** an 18-mile strip of highway connecting the two towns. As it has grown, Los Cabos (often simply called Cabo) has developed into three distinct destinations.

unofficial **TIP**
The key to enjoying a Los Cabos vacation lies in your location. It costs about $40 to travel between the two towns in a cab, and about $20 each way to go from either town to the Corridor. Rental cars are expensive, and you don't want to waste time and money just getting around. Choose a hotel in the area that best suits your budget and expectations.

Most travelers arrive at the international airport north of San José, the civic and commercial hub of the area. San José's town center is located a few blocks inland from a wild stretch of the Sea of Cortez, where all-inclusive hotels and time-shares line a broad beach. You can't swim in the sea in San José—the waves are far too treacherous even for pros on surfboards, who head to Playa Azul in the Corridor just south of San José. But you can enjoy a taste of real Mexico.

Lavender blossoms from jacaranda trees decorate Boulevard Mijares, the main street into downtown San José. A simple, double-spired yellow church overlooks the main plaza, where art shows and concerts are held. Locals and enterprising entrepreneurs have rescued early–20th-century homes in this neighborhood and turned them into classy restaurants and shops. Some of the finest meals in Los Cabos are served here, and owners of multimillion-dollar vacation homes shop for furnishings in San José's boutiques.

Those who stay in and around San José appreciate its relative tranquility, especially in the evening when the day-trippers from the

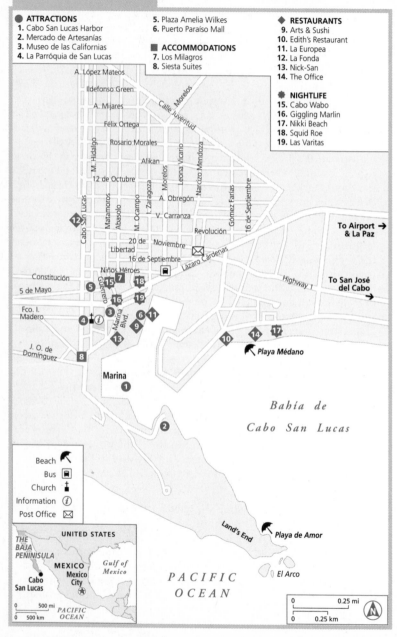

Cabo San Lucas

● ATTRACTIONS
1. Cabo San Lucas Harbor
2. Mercado de Artesanías
3. Museo de las Californias
4. La Parróquia de San Lucas
5. Plaza Amelia Wilkes
6. Puerto Paraíso Mall

■ ACCOMMODATIONS
7. Los Milagros
8. Siesta Suites

◆ RESTAURANTS
9. Arts & Sushi
10. Edith's Restaurant
11. La Europea
12. La Fonda
13. Nick-San
14. The Office

✹ NIGHTLIFE
15. Cabo Wabo
16. Giggling Marlin
17. Nikki Beach
18. Squid Roe
19. Las Varitas

A. López Mateos
Ildefonso Green
A. Mijares
Félix Ortega
Rosario Morales
Alikan
12 de Octubre
Calle Morelos
Calle Juventud
M. Hidalgo
Leona Vicario
Morelos
Narcizo Mendoza
Cabo San Lucas
Matamoros
Abasolo
M. Ocampo
I. Zaragoza
A. Obregón
V. Carranza
Gómez Farías
16 de Septiembre
Revolución
20 de Noviembre
Libertad
16 de Septiembre
Lázaro Cárdenas
Constitución
5 de Mayo
Niños Héroes
Guerrero
Fco. I. Madero
Marina Blvd.
J. O. de Domínguez

To Airport & La Paz →
To San José del Cabo →
Highway 1

Playa Médano

Marina

Bahía de Cabo San Lucas

Beach
Bus
Church
Information
Post Office

Land's End
Playa de Amor
El Arco

PACIFIC OCEAN

THE BAJA PENINSULA
UNITED STATES
MEXICO
Mexico City
Gulf of Mexico
Cabo San Lucas
PACIFIC OCEAN
0   500 mi
0   500 km

0   0.25 mi
0   0.25 km

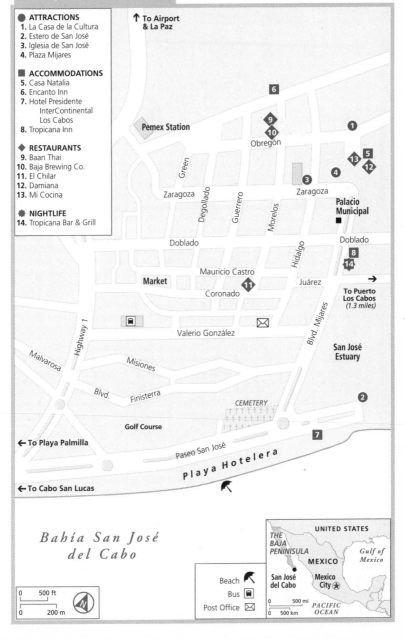

San José del Cabo

ATTRACTIONS
1. La Casa de la Cultura
2. Estero de San José
3. Iglesia de San José
4. Plaza Mijares

ACCOMMODATIONS
5. Casa Natalia
6. Encanto Inn
7. Hotel Presidente
    InterContinental
    Los Cabos
8. Tropicana Inn

RESTAURANTS
9. Baan Thai
10. Baja Brewing Co.
11. El Chilar
12. Damiana
13. Mi Cocina

NIGHTLIFE
14. Tropicana Bar & Grill

To Airport & La Paz

Pemex Station

Obregón

Green

Zaragoza

Degollado

Guerrero

Morelos

Zaragoza

Palacio Municipal

Doblado

Doblado

Hidalgo

To Puerto Los Cabos (1.3 miles)

Mauricio Castro

Market

Coronado

Juárez

Valerio González

Blvd. Mijares

San José Estuary

Highway 1

Malvarosa

Misiones

Blvd. Finisterra

CEMETERY

Golf Course

To Playa Palmilla

Paseo San José

To Cabo San Lucas

Playa Hotelera

Bahía San José del Cabo

0 500 ft
0 200 m

Beach
Bus
Post Office

UNITED STATES

THE BAJA PENINSULA

MEXICO

Gulf of Mexico

San José del Cabo

Mexico City

0 500 mi
0 500 km

PACIFIC OCEAN

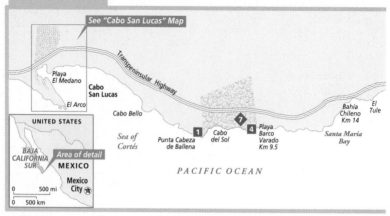

Los Cabos

See "Cabo San Lucas" Map

Transpeninsular Highway

Playa El Medano

Cabo San Lucas

El Arco

Cabo Bello

UNITED STATES

BAJA CALIFORNIA SUR   Area of detail   MEXICO

Mexico City

Sea of Cortés

Punta Cabeza de Ballena

1

7

Cabo del Sol

4

Playa Barco Varado Km 9.5

Bahía Chileno Km 14

El Tule

Santa María Bay

PACIFIC OCEAN

0   500 mi
0   500 km

BEWARE THE HARD SELL

Booths advertising tourist information are located all over the airport, hotels, and streets in the tourist areas of both San José and San Lucas. They're all connected to some commercial entity, usually a time-share property. The sales pitches are intense and ever-present. We've even been approached by time-share salespeople in fancy, expensive restaurants. You'll feel the pressure the moment you arrive at the airport, where sales reps beckon passengers with free rides to their hotels. There's no such thing, as the saying goes. You'll be hit up with a pitch to attend a time-share presentation as soon as your bus is under way. Some visitors swear they'll never go back to Los Cabos because of the time-share assault—it's that intense. For tips in dealing with this situation, see "The Time-share Hustle" in Part Three, Arriving and Getting Oriented, page 70.

---

other parts of Los Cabos have returned to their rooms. There's precious little nightlife in town—if you're looking for discos and dance bars, stay in Cabo San Lucas. If you want peace and reasonably priced relaxation, stay in San José.

The Corridor is reserved for the wealthy or those who've saved a bundle for a vacation splurge. Its canyons and mesas have been transformed by championship golf courses, and extraordinary resorts claim the best views of the Sea of Cortez. Guests in these exclusive digs tend to play a few games of tennis or a few rounds of golf, lounge around serene blue pools, indulge in spa treatments, and dine on nouvelle Baja cuisine. If you like the high life, sample a bit of the Corridor lifestyle even if you can't afford to stay here. Reserve a massage, a tee time, or a table for dinner at one of the Corridor's resorts.

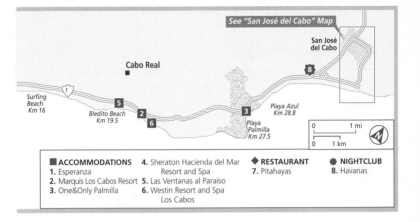

■ **ACCOMMODATIONS**
1. Esperanza
2. Marquis Los Cabos Resort
3. One&Only Palmilla

4. Sheraton Hacienda del Mar
   Resort and Spa
5. Las Ventanas al Paraíso
6. Westin Resort and Spa
   Los Cabos

◆ **RESTAURANT**
7. Pitahayas

● **NIGHTCLUB**
8. Havanas

Cabo San Lucas is action central—the place that gives Cabo its party-hearty reputation. The former cannery town has retained a Wild West sort of ambience. Its graffiti-painted streets are lined with a discordant jumble of bars, shops, and restaurants, most blaring loud music to get your attention. It's an in-your-face kind of place where topless bars abut interior-design galleries. A large percentage of the travelers in Cabo are into drinking, dancing, and carrying on like they never would at home.

San Lucas has the best swimming beaches, several large time-share resorts, and a few of the oldest hotels in the area. It also has a bay and marinas filled with private yachts, and fishing and tour boats.

You'll most likely get a glimpse of all three areas your first visit here. If you're like the thousands of Americans and Canadians who have purchased vacation property here, you'll feel quite at home. But if you're looking for an authentic Mexican experience, you won't find it in Cabo San Lucas.

unofficial **TIP**
Cabo's best nightlife and party beach bars are in Cabo San Lucas. If you're heavily into the nightlife scene, pick a hotel near Playa Médano.

▪ **QUICK FACTS** *about* **LOS CABOS**

AIRPORT AND AIRLINES **San José International Airport** is eight miles north of San José and is served by **Alaska, Aeroméxico, Continental, Delta, American, America West, Mexicana,** and **Northwest.** A 2009 expansion will feature a new terminal, shops, and car-rental booths. There are direct flights from most major U.S. gateways, with increasing service during the winter months.

DRIVING You'll probably want to rent a car for a day or two to visit outlying beaches or tour the towns and Corridor. Most major U.S. car-rental agencies have desks at the airport and representatives at the hotels. Beware of the convertible VW bugs and four-wheel-drive vehicles that look like they'd be so much fun. You may get sunburned, shiver on chilly evenings, and have no secret space to stash your belongings. But they're also the least-expensive rentals, and many adventurers wouldn't think of driving anything else.

unofficial **TIP**
You can usually get a better deal on rental-car prices by reserving your car on the Internet. If you haven't arranged it before your trip, do so at an Internet cafe or hotel business center.

GETTING AROUND Taxis are abundant and expensive. Taxi vans are common, and you can cut costs considerably by sharing a cab whenever possible. There is a public bus that runs along the Corridor between the two towns, and new bus stops are becoming more common. But it's a long walk in the heat to most of the resort accommodations from the main road.

unofficial **TIP**
A few hotels in the Corridor are close to the road and bus stops. Ask about the proximity to the road if you plan to use public transportation.

TELEPHONES The area code is ☎ **624;** calls among the three Los Cabos destinations are local.

TOURIST INFORMATION The best resources for information before you go to Los Cabos can be found on the Web sites **www.visitcabo.com** and **www.loscabosguide.com.** The Baja Sur State Tourism Board operates a Web site, **www.visitloscabos.org,** and provides some recorded information at ☎ 866-567-2226.

WHERE *to* STAY *in* LOS CABOS

LOS CABOS HAS SOME OF THE HIGHEST ROOM RATES in Mexico. Rooms in the many lavish resorts start at $350 a night in high season (January through April), and it's almost impossible to find a decent place for less than $100. Suites in some of the finest establishments run $5,000 a night—and they're actually booked solid during major U.S. and Mexican holidays.

Rates are highest at the self-contained resorts in the Corridor, which typically sit beside a championship golf course and a man-made beach. Both San José and Cabo San Lucas have resort hotels with all the crucial accoutrements—lavish pool areas, several restaurants, and plenty of activities—at lower rates. But you won't be sleeping under Egyptian-cotton sheets or sunbathing in privacy. Nearly all the resorts have some kind of children's program, which may be seasonal.

The major hotel chains have moved into Cabo, and more are on the way. The Spanish chain **Sol Meliá** has two spectacular hotels in the area; the Mexican-owned **Pueblo Bonito** chain has four. **Hilton**

How Accommodations Compare in Los Cabos

ACCOMMODATION | LOCATION	OVERALL	QUALITY	VALUE	COST
Las Ventanas al Paraíso | **Corridor**	★★★★★	★★★★★	★★★★	$$$$$
One&Only Palmilla | **Corridor**	★★★★★	★★★★★	★★★½	$$$$$
Esperanza | **Corridor**	★★★★	★★★★½	★★★	$$$$$
Casa Natalia | **San José**	★★★½	★★★★★	★★★½	$$$$
Marquis Los Cabos | **Corridor**	★★★½	★★★★	★★★	$$$$
Sheraton Hacienda del Mar Resort and Spa | **Corridor**	★★★½	★★★½	★★★	$$$$$
Los Milagros | **San Lucas**	★★★½	★★	★★★★	$
Hotel Presidente InterContinental Los Cabos | **San José**	★★★	★★★	★★★★	$$–$$$
Westin Resort and Spa Los Cabos | **Corridor**	★★★	★★★	★★★½	$$$$
Siesta Suites | **San Lucas**	★★½	★★★	★★★★	$
Encanto Inn | **San José**	★★	★★½	★★★½	$$
Tropicana Inn | **San José**	★½	★★½	★★★	$$

and **Sheraton** each have one, and persistent rumors of a Ritz-Carlton will apparently be realized in 2011. Many of the large resorts have a time-share program, which is often (along with all-inclusives) the least-expensive way to vacation in Cabo. But part of Cabo's charm is its abundance of one-of-a-kind properties, some owned by the region's earliest entrepreneurs. Several boutique hotels in both towns (usually not by a beach) that have reasonable rates and a friendly *mi casa es su casa* ambience.

Advance reservations are absolutely essential at all accommodations, especially during Christmas and spring break. Room rates change several times during the year. They're usually highest at Christmas and drop as much as 30% in the summer. Look for packages including transportation, sports, spas, meals, and other activities.

ACCOMMODATION PROFILES

Casa Natalia $$$$

OVERALL	★★★½	QUALITY	★★★★★	VALUE	★★★½

San José del Cabo; Boulevard Mijares 4; ☎ 624-146-7100 or 888-277-3814 U.S., 866-826-1170 Canada; fax 624-142-5110; www.casanatalia.com, www.mexicoboutiquehotels.com

Husband-and-wife team Loic and Nathalie Tenoux chose a quiet corner by San José's plaza for their chic boutique hotel that blends perfectly with the town's old adobe structures. A pathway to a small pool and gardens passes several three-story buildings housing spacious rooms. Wooden doors lead to private terraces shielded by bamboo and bougainvillea; sliding-glass doors separate terraces from bedrooms. All rooms are filled with carefully chosen folk art and have king-size beds covered with silky-smooth linens. The grounds are particularly lovely at night, when torches flame atop walls and around the edges of Mi Cocina, one of Cabo's finest restaurants. The service is remarkably attentive, and the concierge will set up any activities you desire including a shuttle to a beach club in the Corridor and in-room spa treatments. Note that children under age 13 are not permitted at the hotel.

SETTING AND FACILITIES

Location Just off Plaza Mijares in San José del Cabo.

Dining Restaurant serving dinner nightly; complimentary full breakfast in your room.

Amenities and services Bar, pool, spa, tour desk, room service, Wi-Fi.

ACCOMMODATIONS

Rooms 14 rooms and 2 suites.

All rooms AC, fan, windows that open, balcony or terrace, hair dryer, safe, satellite TV, CD/DVD, high-speed Internet.

Some rooms Hot tub.

Comfort and decor Rooms are large, with cushy couches in front of the TV; all have king beds, no doubles. Decor is a refreshing combo of minimalist and modern, earthy and homey. Bathrooms have door on water closet and large showers (no tubs). Spa suites have enormous terraces with hot tubs, lounge chairs, and hammocks.

PAYMENT, RESERVATIONS, AND RESTRICTIONS

Deposit Credit card; Reservation: 2 nights charged to credit card; 15-day cancellation policy (no refund some holidays).

Credit cards AE, MC, V.

Check-in/out 3 p.m./noon.

 Encanto Inn **$$**

| OVERALL | ★★ | QUALITY | ★★½ | VALUE | ★★★ |

Morelos 133, San José del Cabo ☎ **624-142-0388; fax 624-142-4620; www.elencantoinn.com**

Standard rooms are pretty if simply decorated with oil paintings of traditional Mexican scenes. Most rooms have white-tile bathrooms with shower only. Corner suites are a bit larger and decorated with statuettes from Tonalá, candelabra, and other artistic touches. The main structure, a two-story yellow building facing the pool, is surrounded by tropical plants and cacti, a stone statue, and a tinkling fountain. Across the street, a second building is farther from the pool but has tables outside the first- and second-story rooms, and a rock and cactus garden. The sweet-smelling spa and proximity to good restaurants and art galleries are two real pluses.

SETTING AND FACILITIES

Location Downtown San José.

Dining No restaurant.

Amenities and services Pool, gym, spa, Internet.

ACCOMMODATIONS

Rooms 29.

All rooms AC, fan, windows that open, coffeemaker, cable TV.

Some rooms Kitchenette, refrigerator, minibar, whirlpool tub.

Comfort and decor A classic older building renovated into a snug little budget hotel, with comfortable, individually decorated rooms.

PAYMENT, RESERVATIONS, AND RESTRICTIONS

Deposit Reserve through Web site; cancel 1 month in advance or forfeit cost of 1 night's lodging.

Credit cards AE, MC, V.

Check-in/out 3 p.m./noon.

Esperanza $$$$$

OVERALL	★★★★	QUALITY	★★★★½	VALUE	★★★

Corridor; Highway 1 Km 7; ☎ 624-145-6400 or 866-311-2226 U.S.; fax 624-145-6499; www.esperanzaresort.com

In the lineup of luxury hotels along the Corridor, the Esperanza stands out for its spectacular spa and enormous suites. The independent spa offers luxurious treatments in a soothing setting, along with a fitness center with yoga/pilates classes at no additional charge. Allow time to sample the herb- and fruit-blended juices, the stone steam caves, rain shower, and the peaceful sun terrace. Guest rooms—renovated in 2007—open to large decks and terraces with padded lounge chairs, and you can see the sea from the pillowlike beds topped with Frette linens and fluffy comforters. The buildings sit on a sloping lawn that leads to the horizon pool, open-air restaurant and bar, and two secluded coves. Once or twice a week there are complimentary gallery tours, Spanish lessons, and painting clinics. Between tax and service charge, add 28% to room price. No children under 16.

SETTING AND FACILITIES

Location Corridor.

Dining 3 restaurants.

Amenities and services 3 pools, hot tub, gym, yoga studio, spa, tour desk, shop, 24-hour room service, Internet.

ACCOMMODATIONS

Rooms 57 villas with separate bedrooms and private pools and whirlpools.

All rooms AC, fan, windows that open, ocean view, balcony or terrace, bathtub, hair dryer, safe, minibar, refrigerator, satellite TV, DVD/CD, Internet, Wi-Fi.

Some rooms Rooftop patio, separate bedroom, private pool, coffeemaker, kitchenette, wheelchair access, nonsmoking.

Comfort and decor Down comforters on the beds, oversized bathrooms. The smallest room is 925 square feet of indoor and outdoor space. One-bedroom suites feature infinity-edge hot tubs on the private balcony.

PAYMENT, RESERVATIONS, AND RESTRICTIONS

Deposit Harsh reservation policy: 50% charged on credit card upon booking; remaining amount charged 30 days before arrival; entire amount forfeited if cancelled less than 30 days before arrival.

Credit cards AE, MC, V.

Check-in/out 3 p.m./noon.

 Hotel Presidente InterContinental Los Cabos $$–$$$

OVERALL ★★★	QUALITY ★★★	VALUE ★★★★

San José del Cabo; Boulevard Mijares s/n; ☎ 624-142-0211 or 888-424-6835 U.S.; fax 624-142-0232; www.ichotelsgroup.com

This low-lying cluster of golden-brown structures beside a broad, beige beach has been thoroughly updated (except for its dated stucco exterior) to attract families, couples, and groups who want simplicity and comfort at a set price. The all-inclusive concept works well here because it takes 10 to 15 minutes to walk to San José's best restaurants. The Presidente's eateries include El Napa, featuring California cuisine, and a Mexican restaurant (make reservations for both) as well as a steakhouse and several more casual options. If you want peaceful seclusion, opt for the rooms in the oldest section by the estuary—it has an adults-only pool. Volleyball games and water-aerobics classes are held in the pool in the middle part of the complex. Those who favor swim-up bars and sunbathing can choose the newest section with its large, free-form pool, and sun deck. You can't swim off this beach, but the sound of crashing waves is always present.

SETTING AND FACILITIES

Location Outside San José del Cabo by the estuary.

Dining 5 restaurants, 7 bars; all-inclusive.

Amenities and services Beach, 4 pools, 24-hour gym, tour desk organized children's activities, shops, bars, 24-hour room service, 24-hour business center, Internet (free), Wi-Fi (charge).

ACCOMMODATIONS

Rooms 390.

All rooms AC, satellite TV, coffeemaker, hair dryer.

Some rooms Windows that open, ocean view, balcony or terrace, bathtub, safe, refrigerator, Wi-Fi, nonsmoking, wheelchair access.

Comfort and decor Rooms vary greatly, from ground-floor suites with charming lanai patios with hammocks to larger rooms with windows sealed shut on the second floor, and third-floor rooms whose cement patios obstruct the view. Most have sleeper sofas, but families may feel cramped in the available space.

PAYMENT, RESERVATIONS, AND RESTRICTIONS

Deposit Credit card with 1-night deposit; cancellation policy varies depending on where purchased.

Credit cards AE, MC, V.

Check-in/out 3 p.m./noon.

Marquis Los Cabos Resort $$$$$

OVERALL	★★★½	QUALITY	★★★★	VALUE	★★★

Corridor; Carretera Transpeninsular Km 21.5, Fracc. Cabo Real; ☎ 624-144-2000 or 877-238-9399 U.S.; fax 624-144-2001; www.marquisloscabos.com;

A curving yellow wall shields the guest rooms from highway noise at this art-filled architectural stunner. Most rooms are in the main building overlooking the sinuous pool and broad beach. Casitas are on the sand; some have rooftop decks with hot tubs. Meals are very reasonably priced— a nice surprise at an upscale Corridor hotel. The gourmet Canto del Mar dinner-restaurant feels like an elegant, personal dining room, with the chef attending your every request. Vista Ballenas restaurant is less formal; Dos Mares sits beside a waterfall crashing from the lobby level to the pool and serves excellent ceviche. The gym is enormous, with a climbing wall and all the requisite machines, and the spa's hot tubs overlook the sea (but are also visible from rooms above). There's a $38-per-day service charge.

SETTING AND FACILITIES

Location Corridor in Cabo Real development.

Dining 3 restaurants, 2 bars; complimentary Continental breakfast.

Amenities and services Beach, 3 pools, hot tub, gym, spa, tour desk, organized children's activities, shops, bars, 24-hour room service, business center, Internet.

ACCOMMODATIONS

Rooms 210 suites, 28 casitas.

All rooms AC, fans, windows that open, ocean view, balcony or terrace, whirlpool bathtubs, hair dryer, safe, minibar, satellite TV, high-speed Internet.

Some rooms Refrigerators, kitchenette, DVD player, hair dryer, Wi-Fi, nonsmoking, wheelchair access.

Comfort and decor Oversized rooms have entryways with long tables, the perfect spot for keys, hats, and beach gear. Desks with high-speed Internet cables face the sky and sea view. Shutters by the whirlpool bathtubs can be open to the view or shut for privacy. Continental breakfast is placed in a niche by the doorway.

PAYMENT, RESERVATIONS, AND RESTRICTIONS

Deposit 1 night's charge on credit card; cancel 30 days prior to arrival to avoid cancellation fee.

Credit cards AE, MC, V.

Check-in/out 3 p.m./noon.

Los Milagros $

OVERALL	★★★½	QUALITY	★★	VALUE	★★★★

Cabo San Lucas; Matamoros # 116; ☎ 624-143-4566 or 718-928-6647 U.S.; fax 624-143-6004; losmilagros.com.mx

Guests are tempted to stay extra days once they've settled in at this small, budget hotel. Rooms with kitchenettes are on the first floor near an outdoor seating area. Owner Sandra Scandibar often joins her clients there, discussing best beaches, taco stands, and such. Bougainvillea drapes from railings in front of the upstairs room; Scanibar has even planted a desert garden in the rocks behind the property. Readers can count on finding something interesting on the shelves, and comparing favorites with strangers. This is a great place to stay when you're working or just want a comfortable escape.

SETTING AND FACILITIES

Location Side street 1 block from plaza.

Dining No restaurant.

Amenities and services Pool, free Wi-Fi throughout hotel.

ACCOMMODATIONS

Rooms 11.

All rooms AC, fan, windows that open, cable TV, nonsmoking, , Wi-Fi.

Some rooms Balcony or terrace, bathtub, refrigerator, coffeemaker, kitchenette, disabled access although not really wheelchair-equipped.

Comfort and decor Rooms that feel like home, with lots of drawers and tables for your things. Most have showers only.

PAYMENT, RESERVATIONS, AND RESTRICTIONS

Deposit Credit card, personal check, or PayPal; full refund if canceled before 2 weeks, otherwise forfeit deposit.

Credit cards AE, MC, V.

Check-in/out 2 p.m./11 a.m.

One&Only Palmilla $$$$$

OVERALL ★★★★★	QUALITY ★★★★★	VALUE ★★★½

Corridor; Highway 1 Km 7.5; ☎ 624-146-7000 or 800-637-2226 U.S.; www.oneandonlypalmilla.com

Oprah Winfrey treated her staff to a week's stay at Cabo's trendiest property; John Travolta celebrated his 50th birthday here. A $90-million renovation in 2004 transformed the venerable Palmilla (one of the first hotels in Cabo) into a totally chic hotel while protecting its Mediterranean Moorish style. White arches, domes, and lavish gardens prevail on the exterior, but the interior is decidedly modern. Charlie Trotter (who gained fame in the Chicago area) oversees the sleek C restaurant, one of several excellent eateries. Privileged guests book private villas with outdoor beds and hot tubs at the Mandara Spa; others make do with the serene waterfall in the sun lounge. Jack Nicklaus designed the adjacent course, where million-dollar villas continue to proliferate.

SETTING AND FACILITIES

Location Corridor close to San José del Cabo.

Dining 3 restaurants.

Amenities and services Beach, 2 pools, hot tub, gym, spa, water-sports center, tour desk, organized children's activities, shops, 24-hour room service, business center, Internet.

ACCOMMODATIONS

Rooms 172 rooms and suites.

All rooms AC, fan, windows that open, ocean view, balcony or terrace, bathtub, hair dryer, safe, minibar, cable/satellite TV, DVD/CD, telephone, high-speed and wireless Internet, nonsmoking, disabled access.

Some rooms Kitchenette, private pool, multiple bedrooms.

Comfort and decor The decor is a sometimes-jarring blend of Asian and Mexican, contemporary but comfortable. High beds are loaded with pillows and bolsters; the curved desk at the foot of the bed has an ingenious design. Bathrooms take up half the space, with "wet rooms" containing open rain-showers, and tubs on pedestals. Some patios and terraces have daybeds facing the sea. All rooms have Bose sound systems, flat-screen TVs, and minibars stocked with high-end labels. Butlers are assigned to each building and serve as private concierges 24 hours a day.

PAYMENT, RESERVATIONS, AND RESTRICTIONS

Deposit Seasonal; 21-day cancellation policy (higher at holidays, lower in summer); 2-night deposit.

Credit cards AE, DC, MC, V.

Check-in/out 3 p.m./11 a.m.

Sheraton Hacienda del Mar Resort and Spa **$$$$$**

| OVERALL ★★★½ | QUALITY ★★★½ | VALUE ★★★ |

Corridor Turístico Km 10; ☎ 624-145-8000 or 800-325-3535 U.S.; fax 624-145-8002; www.sheratonloscabos.com

Yellow buildings with arches and domes sit between the golf course and beach at Cabo del Sol, one of the largest Corridor developments. Guests receive discounts at the golf course. A series of palm-fringed pools and sun decks edge a broad beach. The hotel runs a $10 per person shuttle to Cabo San Lucas—a big savings over taxi fares. It takes about 15 minutes to walk the road from the rooms to the highway. The restaurants are excellent—even nonguests should not miss having dinner at Pitahayas. Use the gym first to avoid a charge for use of the sauna, steam, or Jacuzzi (if you go for the steam et al without using the free gym first, there is a charge.)

SETTING AND FACILITIES

Location Corridor in Cabo del Sol.

Dining 4 restaurants and snack bars, 3 bars.

Amenities and services Beach, 4 pools, 3 hot tubs, gym, spa, tour desk, organized children's activities, shops, 24-hour room service, business center, Internet.

ACCOMMODATIONS

Rooms 241 rooms, 39 suites, 14 villas.

All rooms AC, fan, windows that open, balcony or terrace, whirlpool tub, hair dryer, safe, minibar, coffeemaker, satellite TV, high-speed Internet.

Some rooms Ocean view, refrigerator, kitchenette, VCR/DVD/CD, high-speed Internet, nonsmoking, wheelchair access.

Comfort and decor Corner rooms have the largest balconies with lounge chairs. Cushy beds, desks, and whirlpool tubs are all pluses. The hacienda-style hotel's decor is classy, not fussy, with dark-wood furnishings and burgundy and brown accents on creamy walls and beds.

PAYMENT, RESERVATIONS, AND RESTRICTIONS

Deposit Credit card; cancel with no penalty 48 hours before check-in date, some major holidays exceptedancellation with no penalty, except for Christmas.

Credit cards AE, DC, MC, V.

Check-in/out 3 p.m./noon.

Siesta Suites $

| OVERALL ★★½ | QUALITY ★★★ | VALUE ★★★★ |

Cabo San Lucas; Calle Zapata s/n (between Calles Guerrero and Hidalgo); ☎ 624-143-2773 or 866-271-0952 U.S.; www.cabosiestasuites.com

Impressively inexpensive, these suites have kitchen areas with full refrigerators, wide couches that can be used as beds, and two double beds in a sleeping area away from the kitchen. The hotel is a great find in the midst of San Lucas, and the rates can't be beat. The proprietors are founts of knowledge when it comes to the ins and outs of vacationing inexpensively in Los Cabos. They even list economical restaurant selections and public-transportation info on a central bulletin board.

SETTING AND FACILITIES

Location On side street near marina.

Dining Restaurant.

Amenities and services Room service, outdoor barbecue, sun deck, small pool, secure parking, Internet.

ACCOMMODATIONS

Rooms 20.

All rooms AC, cable TV, fan, microwave, refrigerator, nonsmoking rooms.

Some rooms Full kitchen

Comfort and decor Rooms have recently been upgraded, with new mattresses and linens; from the bed you can watch the recently purchased TVs. Also replaced were tile, window treatments, fans, and even water heaters, so you know things are newish, even though their budget price tags are evident. The Italian restaurant on the patio offers dinner daily after 5 p.m.

PAYMENT, RESERVATIONS, AND RESTRICTIONS

Deposit Credit card, 50%; 2-week cancellation policy.

Credit cards MC, V.

Check-in/out 2 p.m./noon.

Tropicana Inn $$

OVERALL	★ ½	QUALITY	★ ★ ½	VALUE	★ ★ ★

San José del Cabo; Boulevard Mijares 30; ☎ 624-142-1580; fax 624-142-1590; tropicanainn.com.mx

A good option for those on tight budgets or those craving nightly entertainment: the lounge bar offers San José's most consistent shows, often Cuban or mariachi bands. The Tropicana sits right in the middle of San José. Tiled murals replicating Diego Rivera paintings, as well as sculptures and fountains, decorate the public areas; rooms face a heated pool with palapa-shaded swim-up bar surrounded by plants. There's no swimming beach nearby.

SETTING AND FACILITIES

Location Center of San José del Cabo's tourist area.

Dining Tropicana Bar & Grill specializes in Mexican dishes and fresh seafood; if the large, attractive dining room with booths along both sides appears abandoned, you can order off the same extensive menu in the charming and more intimate lounge-bar. Brunch is served on weekends.

Amenities and services Bar, pool, gym, self-service Continental breakfast included in price, wireless Internet at pool area.

ACCOMMODATIONS

Rooms 35 rooms, 4 suites.

All rooms AC, fan, cable TV, coffeemaker, hair dryer, refrigerator, Wi-Fi.

Some rooms Bathtub, balcony or terrace, king bed.

Comfort and decor Designed for economy, the rooms are plain but clean-smelling. Fabrics tend toward florals, and windows look out to the pool or to undeveloped land. Honeymooners favor the *troje*. Styled after a typical Michoacán dwelling, it has wide plank walls and floors and a palapa-thatch roof. The bedroom with its mosquito net is at the top of a spiral staircase.

PAYMENT, RESERVATIONS, AND RESTRICTIONS

Deposit Credit card or 1-night deposit; 2-day cancellation.

Credit cards AE, MC, V.

Check-in/out 2 p.m./12:30 p.m.

Las Ventanas al Paraíso $$$$

OVERALL	★★★★★	QUALITY	★★★★★	VALUE	★★★★

Corridor; Carretera Transpeninsular Km 19.5; ☎ 624-144-2800 or 888-767-3966 U.S.; fax 624-144-2801; www.lasventanas.com

It's hard to fault any aspect of this luxurious hotel, part of the Rosewood chain of deluxe properties. The architecture is outstanding, with sleek, white buildings interspersed with cactus gardens, and curving pathways inlaid with stone patterns. Fireplaces, whirlpool tubs, and in-room tele-scopes for viewing whales in the Sea of Cortez make you want to stay in your room forever. You do need to step out eventually, however, if only to survey your options. The pool areas are serene and soothing, with low, padded lounge chairs under white umbrellas, and hammocks swing-ing under palapas on the sand. The spa is divine, and the restaurants are superb. Every vista seems to have come straight from *Architectural Digest;* no detail has been overlooked. There's a special program for pets, including a menu for meals and box lunches for the ride home in their masters' private jets. Celebrities find ultimate privacy here, and nonguests must have reservations at the restaurant or spa in order to enter the property.

SETTING AND FACILITIES

Location Corridor.

Dining 3 restaurants.

Amenities and services Beach, pools, hot tubs, gym, spa, water-sports center, tour desk, shops, 24-hour room service, Internet.

ACCOMMODATIONS

Rooms 61 suites.

All rooms AC, fan, windows that open, ocean view, balcony or terrace, bathtub, hair dryer, safe, minibar, cable/satellite TV, VCR/CD, high-speed Internet, non-smoking, wheelchair access.

Some rooms Rooftop patio, separate bedroom, private pool, whirlpool tub (outdoor Jacuzzi), kitchen, refrigerator, coffeemaker.

Comfort and decor High-standing beds with plenty of pillows; huge bathtub; distinctive decor with nearly everything handcrafted. Some suites come with butler service.

PAYMENT, RESERVATIONS, AND RESTRICTIONS

Deposit 2-night minimum credit card deposit; 28-day cancellation policy (14 days in summer; more than 28 days for holidays); penalties vary.

Credit cards AE, MC, V.

Check-in/out 3 p.m./noon.

 Westin Resort and Spa Los Cabos $$$$

| OVERALL | ★★★ | QUALITY | ★★★ | VALUE | ★★★½ |

Corridor; Highway 1 Km 22.5; ☎ 624-144-9000 or 800-WESTIN-1 U.S.; fax 624-142-9153; www.westin.com/loscabos

A broad, curving road leads up a hillside to the Westin's dramatic yellow and pink walls boldly standing out against a brown, desert landscape. Another winding path runs from the open-air lobby to sandstone-colored buildings facing the sea. The hotel, inspired by the designs of architect Ricardo Legoretta in the 1980s, was renovated in 2003 and is as sophisticated and pleasing as its high-end neighbors. The spa is fabulous, with an airy lounge, excellent therapists, and a spacious gym with machines facing the ocean. An Asian restaurant features a sushi chef preparing sashimi with fish fresh from the sea; other dining venues are consistently very good. A nine-hole seaside putting course keeps golfers in shape.

SETTING AND FACILITIES

Location Corridor near San José.

Dining 4 restaurants.

Amenities and services Beach, 7 pools, hot tub, gym, spa, organized children's activities, 5 bars, tour desk, shops, 24-hour room service, business center, Internet.

ACCOMMODATIONS

Rooms 243.

All rooms AC, fan, windows that open, or terrace, bathtub, hair dryer, safe, minibar, refrigerator, coffeemaker, kitchenette, satellite TV, high-speed Internet.

Some rooms Ocean view, balcony, whirlpool tub, nonsmoking, wheelchair access.

Comfort and decor Westin's trademark Heavenly Bed and Heavenly Bath make it hard to leave the room with a (smallish) balcony looking out to pools and the sea. The beds are like clouds, with pillow-top mattresses, feather-light duvets and a selection of pillows. You can watch TV from the sitting area with coffee table, but why leave heaven? Guests in the Royal Beach Club (Concierge Level) and suites are treated to daily hot breakfast as well as two hours of cocktails and hors d'oeuvres in a private lounge. One drawback—the distance between the rooms and lobby is daunting, and it's a pain to run back for forgotten items.

PAYMENT, RESERVATIONS, AND RESTRICTIONS

Deposit Credit card; 2-day cancellation fee.

Credit cards AE, DC, MC, V.

Check-in/out 3 p.m./noon.

WHERE *to* EAT *in* LOS CABOS

THE DINING SCENE IN LOS CABOS has exploded in the past few years as European, American, and Mexican chefs opened cafes, trattorias, and chic restaurants serving everything from pâté to pizza. Seafood is still the local specialty, and you'll find it prepared in dozens of imaginative ways. Chefs coat dorado (also called mahimahi) with pecan or wasabi crusts, drizzle tamarind or mango sauces on shrimp, and serve snapper with tomatillo or guajillo chile salsas. The meat selection has vastly improved as restaurateurs import New Zealand lamb and Angus beef from the U.S. Many upscale restaurants use organic herbs and vegetables grown in hotel gardens or in the fields around Todos Santos (see "Tours and Side Trips from Los Cabos," page 420).

unofficial **TIP**
If you happen to catch your own fish, take it to a local restaurant and ask the chef to prepare it any of several ways—*mojo de ajo* (grilled with oil and crusty bits of garlic) is particularly tasty.

A nouvelle Baja cuisine emphasizing fresh herbs, vegetables, fruits, and fish is emerging, and chefs compete to create new takes on standard fare. Their efforts are sometimes successful and sometimes overwhelmingly strange. Menus change frequently, and the quality of the food is often inconsistent. Ask your fellow travelers for recommendations—a new chef or management will drastically affect the quality of your dining experience.

The most exciting, innovative restaurants are located in San José and along the Corridor. The Cabo San Lucas dining scene is more mainstream, with an overabundance of theme and chain restaurants. We've included a few truly outstanding hotel restaurants in our profiles, but have skipped over some well-known places because of their inconsistency. Unless you've heard rave reviews from other guests, order sparingly until you've gauged the quality at your hotel's restaurants. Most rooms have a refrigerator and coffeemaker, and many

How Restaurants Compare in Los Cabos

RESTAURANT	LOCATION	CUISINE	COST	OVERALL	QUALITY	VALUE
Mi Cocina	San José	Nouvelle Mexican	Exp	★★★★★	★★★★★	★★★★
Nick-San	San Lucas/Corridor	Japanese	Mod	★★★★★	★★★★★	★★★★
Pitahayas	Corridor	Pan-Asian	Exp	★★★★½	★★★★½	★★★½
El Chilar	San José	Mexican	Mod	★★★★	★★★★	★★★★
Baan Thai	San José	Thai	Inexp/mod	★★★½	★★★½	★★★★
Arte & Sushi	San Lucas	Sushi	Mod	★★★	★★½	★★★
La Fonda	San Lucas	Mexican	Mod	★★★	★★½	★★★
Damiana	San José	Seafood	Mod	★★½	★★½	★★½
Baja Brewing Co.	San José	Brew pub/pub fare	Mod	★★½	★★	★★★
Edith's Restauranté	San Lucas	Seafood	Mod/Exp	★★	★★½	★½
La Europea	San Lucas	Salads and sandwiches	Inexp	★½	★★	★★★★
The Office	San Lucas	Mexican/American	Exp	★	★½	★½

have additional kitchen appliances. You'll save a bundle by stocking up on drinks and snacks for your room.

Dining in Los Cabos is expensive. You can easily spend $100 on dinner for two with a couple of glasses of wine or beer. Try to stay away from imported liquors and wines, which are frightfully expensive. Both towns have simple taco stands where you can eat relatively cheaply. Wander a few blocks away from the main tourist areas, and you'll find the budget places where locals dine on whole fried fish, *carne asada,* enchiladas, and homemade tamales.

Reservations are essential at the more upscale places, especially during high season. Some places automatically add a 10%-to-15% service charge—check the bill before leaving a tip. Dress is casual everywhere, though you'll want to wear slacks and a polo shirt or a sundress at the more expensive places. Disabled access is hard to find. Few restaurants have bathrooms equipped to handle wheelchairs. We've noted the few places that do accommodate disabled visitors.

RESTAURANT PROFILES

Arte & Sushi ★★★

SUSHI	MODERATE	QUALITY	★★½	VALUE	★★★

San Lucas; Behind Olé Olé Restaurant at Marina San Lucas

Reservations Accepted.

Entree range $15–$22.

Payment MC, V.

Service rating ★★★★.

Parking Puerto Paraíso Mall, or on the street near the marina.

Dress Casual.

Bar Full service.

Disabled access Outdoor patio yes; inside tables and restroom, no.

Customers Locals and travelers looking for something different, art lovers.

Hours Daily, 11 a.m.–10:30 p.m.

SETTING AND ATMOSPHERE The inside space is intimate (read: small), with oversized art of many genres on the walls. Sculptures, mainly nudes, stand on pedestals. Inside and out on the patio, jazz, house, and chill music complete the modern ambience.

HOUSE SPECIALTIES No Name Roll: a wrap of shrimp, tuna, and salmon with cilantro sauce.

SUMMARY AND COMMENTS Something new on the dining scene, Arte & Sushi fills up with folks looking for fresh (and mainly raw) fish, good music, and attentive service. Pendant lamps and track lighting shed a cozy light over the sushi bar and the small square tables—those backed up to a central column have bench seats as well as aluminum chairs. Choose from a long list of appetizers, seafood salad, sushi combos (plenty of tuna and sea bas), teriyaki, teppanyaki, yakatori, and tempura. On the wall, fantasies in oils (an iguana riding a bike, its tongue catching a butterfly) and realistic beach scenes compete for diners' attention. It's a very pleasant change of pace.

Baan Thai ★★★½

THAI	INEXPENSIVE/MODERATE	QUALITY	★★★½	VALUE	★★★★

San José del Cabo; Morelos at Obregón s/n; ☎ 624-142-3344

Reservations Recommended.

Entree range $10–$27.

Payment AE, MC, V.

Service rating ★★★.

Parking Lot.

Bar Full bar serving Mexican, Latin American, and California wines.

Dress Casual.

Disabled access No.

Customers Locals and travelers.

Hours Daily, noon–10:30 p.m.; closed Sunday, July–September.

SETTING AND ATMOSPHERE Serene dining room and patio with fountain.

HOUSE SPECIALTIES Vietnamese summer rolls (marinated chicken and spices wrapped in lettuce and rice paper), catch of the day with black bean sauce.

SUMMARY AND COMMENTS The exotic cuisine and the imported Asian furnishings are a welcome change from a steady diet of seafood and tacos, making a delightfully different dining experience in the heart of San José del Cabo. The chef likes to change the menu every few months, but repeat customers demand that certain favorite dishes remain, including green-papaya salad, Vietnamese summer rolls, and lamb shank braised in green curry. The restaurant offers Thai teas and espresso cappuccino, but sadly, no Thai beer.

Baja Brewing Co. ★★½

TRADITIONAL AND INNOVATIVE PUB FARE   MODERATE   QUALITY ★★   VALUE ★★★

**San José del Cabo; Morelos 1227 between Comonfort and Obregón;
☎ 624-146-9995; www.bajabrewingcompany.com**

Reservations Recommended for dinner.

Entree range $10–$25.

Payment MC, V.

Service rating ★★.

Parking 2 small lots.

Bar 8 styles of home brew, from lager to stout; full service.

Dress Casual.

Disabled access No.

Customers Displaced brewmeisters and pub fans; locals looking for a lively atmosphere with international eats.

Hours Monday–Wednesday, noon–midnight.

SETTING AND ATMOSPHERE A noisy, convivial brew pub with outdoor patio dining, a traditional pub feel with long bar.

HOUSE SPECIALTIES Beer! Burgers and fries; pork chop in reduced-honey glaze with cauliflower-purée side.

SUMMARY AND COMMENTS There's a buzz in San José as this original brew pub enlivens the downtown art district. Copper beer vats are visible through a glass windows along one side of the pub; small square tables and a long, shiny bar conjure up images of England and Ireland. (The only thing missing is the rain on the roof.) But aside from Shepherd's pie, the fare is mostly American, with big burgers, crinkly or curly fries, and thin-crust pizza (arguably more American than Italian). There's a big-screen TV behind the bar, but lively music usually prevails. Out on the patio is a wood-fire oven where the pizzas are cooked.

 ## El Chilar ★★★★

MEXICAN	MODERATE	QUALITY ★★★★	VALUE ★★★★

San José del Cabo; Juárez 1490 at Morelos; ☎ 624-142-2544

Reservations Recommended.

Entree range $12–$25.

Payment No credit cards.

Service rating ★★★.

Parking Plenty of street parking.

Bar Full service, large wine selection.

Dress Resort casual.

Disabled access Limited.

Customers Loyal Cabo regulars and locals.

Hours Monday–Saturday, 4–10 p.m.

SETTING AND ATMOSPHERE Purely Mexican with bright orange walls, murals of the Virgin of Guadalupe and angels floating over clouds, open kitchen and festive clientele.

HOUSE SPECIALTIES Salmon napolean with mango, shrimp with roasted garlic and guajillo chile.

SUMMARY AND COMMENTS Chef Armando Montaña uses chiles from all over Mexico to enhance the flavor (without heating up the spice) of traditional and continental dishes, coating rack of lamb with chile ancho and sugar-cane honey, and boosting the flavor of lobster bisque with smoky chile guajillo. The menu changes frequently, inspiring many return visits.

Damiana ★★½

SEAFOOD	MODERATE	QUALITY ★★½	VALUE ★★½

San José del Cabo; Boulevard Mijares 8; ☎ 624-142-0499; damiana.com.mx

Reservations Recommended.

Entree range $11–$22.

Payment AE, MC, V.

Service rating ★★.

Parking Limited street parking.

Bar Full service.

Dress Dress-up casual.

Disabled access Limited.

Customers Frequent Los Cabos visitors (repeat customers).

Hours Wednesday–Monday 10:30 a.m.–10:30 p.m. Closed September.

SETTING AND ATMOSPHERE Romantic, especially the tables under the bougainvillea in the patio.

HOUSE SPECIALTIES Imperial shrimp, steak, Damiana margaritas.

SUMMARY AND COMMENTS Owners Luis and Leticia Klein are long-time Los Cabos boosters (he was once the head of the state tourism board). Their restaurant was a San José landmark long before the neighborhood became trendy, and it continues to attract a loyal following. The back patio, with its overgrown trees and flickering candlelight, is one of the most romantic spots in town. Favorite dishes include lobster and the "shrimp steak," a grilled patty of chopped shrimp. Preparations are simple and satisfying rather than trendy, and the service is courteous (though a bit slow at times). The restaurant is named after a local liqueur said to be an aphrodisiac.

 Edith's Restaurante ★★

SEAFOOD	MODERATE/EXPENSIVE	QUALITY ★★½	VALUE ★½

Cabo San Lucas; Camino a Playa Médano s/n; ☎ 624-143-0801; www.edithscabo.com

Reservations Recommended between 7 and 9 p.m.

Entree range $17–$35.

Payment MC, V.

Service rating ★★★.

Parking Very limited street parking.

Bar Full service; extensive wine list, lots of specialty drinks.

Dress Casual.

Disabled access No.

Customers Travelers, families in early evening, couples later at night.

Hours Daily, 5–10:30 p.m.

SETTING AND ATMOSPHERE Romantic dining with a view of Land's End.

HOUSE SPECIALTIES Mesquite-grilled fish and beef; homemade tortillas and salsas.

SUMMARY AND COMMENTS Edith's has long been considered one of Cabo's more adult-oriented, romantic restaurants. But the patio, with tables at the edge overlooking Playa Médano, is often filled with children and large groups in early evening. Things do calm down later at night, and Edith's is removed from the rowdy action in downtown Cabo. At its best, the cafe is filled with quiet chatter and a trio playing melodic music (most nights after 6 p.m.). Waiters courteously serve excellent salads, grilled fish, and flambéed crêpes.

La Europea   ★½

| SALADS AND SANDWICHES | INEXPENSIVE | QUALITY ★★ | VALUE ★★★★ |

San Lucas; Plaza Puerto Paraíso, Avenida Lázaro Cárdenas at Calle Cabo Bello ☎ 624-105-1818

Reservations No.

Entree range $5–$9, plus wine.

Payment AE, MC, V.

Service rating ★★.

Parking Lot at Puerto Paraiso.

Bar This wine and spirits shop boasts about a thousand different labels.

Dress Casual.

Disabled access No.

Customers Hip-looking locals and yachties.

Hours Monday–Saturday, 9 a.m.–9 p.m.

SETTING AND ATMOSPHERE A simple, open patio in front of the wine shop at the entrance to Puerto Paraíso mall, with partial view of the San Lucas Marina.

HOUSE SPECIALTIES European-style squid sandwiches.

SUMMARY AND COMMENTS Locals and travelers on the inside track congregate here in the late afternoon for salads, ceviches, and sandwiches. It's a great place to have a simple, healthful and inexpensive meal and a glass or two of vino, which you can purchase inside this extensive liquor store and open without corkage fee. Stop here on your way to the excellent mall or the marina, or just on a walk around town. Note that the La Europea in San José does not sell food.

La Fonda   ★★★

| MEXICAN | MODERATE | QUALITY ★★½ | VALUE ★★★ |

San Lucas, Avenida Hidalgo and 12 de Octubre (across from Telmex); ☎ 624-143-6926.

Entree range $12–$25.

Payment MC, V.

Service rating ★★★.

Parking Small lot, street.

Bar Full service; house margaritas with choice of fine tequilas.

Dress Neat and casual or a bit more dressy.

Disabled access No.

Customers Local businesspeople, gangs of mavens doing lunch, and travelers who want an authentic Mexican dining experience.

Hours Wednesday–Monday, 1:30–10:30 p.m.

SETTING AND ATMOSPHERE Elegant hacienda-style dining room with fountains and arches; nicely dressed tables have blue-glass water goblets from Guanajuato and comfortable chairs.

HOUSE SPECIALTIES Executive meal, weekdays 1:30–4 p.m. Choose from a special menu of soup, salad, main dish, dessert, and fruit drink.

SUMMARY AND COMMENTS Stone arches frame doorways, and Talavera tiles beautify several four-tiered fountains. This repurposed house has two dining rooms and a small garden patio. Inside, the air-conditioning is just right, and the mariachi music or romantic ballads in the background set the mood. The extensive menu has typical Mexican snack foods like quesadillas, tacos, and "grandma's turnovers." Full dinners include traditional food from around Mexico, including hot-and-spicy shrimp, meatballs in sauce, and grilled chicken; exotic pre-Hispanic dishes include ant eggs, grasshoppers, and maguey worms. Most of the typical dishes come with rice, refried beans, and made-in-the-moment tortillas. Around comes the dessert cart just when you think you can't take another bite.

Mi Cocina ★★★★★

NOUVELLE MEXICAN	EXPENSIVE	QUALITY ★★★★★	VALUE ★★★★

San José del Cabo; Boulevard Mijares 4; ☎ 624-146-7100 or 888-277-3814 from the U.S.

Reservations Recommended.

Entree range $14–$30.

Payment AE, MC, V.

Service rating ★★★★.

Parking Street parking, small lot.

Bar Full service; good wine and martini list.

Dress Dressy or resort casual.

Disabled access Dining room accessible, but there are stairs to the restroom.

Customers Affluent locals and travelers.

Hours Daily, 6–10 p.m. (closed Tuesday, end of May–early September).

SETTING AND ATMOSPHERE Modern Mexican with candlelight, torches, and custom-made tableware; subdued and romantic.

HOUSE SPECIALTIES Mediterranean octopus salad, grilled filet mignon, risotto with seafood.

SUMMARY AND COMMENTS Owner-chef Loic Tenoux creates a pleasing selection of European-influenced dishes, changing the menu frequently. Most of the tables are in the courtyard and spaced far enough apart for private conversation. Plan to linger over a tequila martini, excellent breads, and an appetizer of fried Camembert or tequila-cured salmon. Select any special Tenoux prepares, especially the lobster chunks in puff pastry. Chefs visiting the area tend to eat here at least once during their visits, and some diners ask for the same table and waiter for several nights. Tenoux and his charming wife, Nathalie, wander about the room, making sure guests are comfortable and satisfied, and they're eager to suggest a meal to suit your mood. Keep an eye out for celebrities—the exclusive hotels often send their guests here for a meal.

Nick-San ★★★★★

JAPANESE	MODERATE	QUALITY ★★★★★	VALUE ★★★★

Cabo San Lucas; Boulevard MarinaPlaza de la Danza, next to Hotel Costa Real; ☎ 624-143-4484; Las Tiendas de Palmilla, Corridor; ☎ 624-144-6262; www.nicksan.com

Reservations Recommended for dinner.

Entree range $9–$15.

Payment MC, V.

Service rating ★★★.

Parking Small parking lot behind businesses.

Bar Full service; sake, Japanese beer.

Disabled access Possible.

Customers Office workers on lunch break, Cabo regulars, loyal locals.

Hours Daily, 11:30 a.m.–10:30 p.m.

SETTING AND ATMOSPHERE Three or four chefs are kept busy at the long sushi bar that takes up one full side of the restaurant, separating the open kitchen from the dining area. Paintings by local artists hang on the white walls.

HOUSE SPECIALTIES Cilantro sashimi, soft-shell crab sushi, lobster (most lobster dishes cost around $35).

SUMMARY AND COMMENTS Nick-San's sushi bar stations are full most nights. Regulars (many are visitors who return to Cabo frequently) sit in front of their favorite sushi chefs and order consecutive dishes. The salmon-skin hand rolls make a tasty starter, followed by sashimi (the fish is impeccably fresh), the spicy tuna roll topped with chopped cubes of translucent pink tuna, and maybe the signature Lobster Angel with mustard sauce, named for the owner, Angel Carbajal. Save room for the almond-chocolate cake. The Tiendas de Palmilla location, at the One&Only Palmilla resort, is slightly more expensive, and in high season offers concerts, fashion shows, and art expos.

 The Office ★

MEXICAN/AMERICAN	EXPENSIVE	QUALITY ★½	VALUE ★½

Cabo San Lucas; Playa Médano; ☎ 624-143-3464; www.theofficeonthebeach.com

Reservations Recommended for dinner.

Entree range $20–$45.

Payment MC, V.

Service rating ★★★.

Parking Valet parking, very limited street parking.

Bar Full service; happy hour daily, 7 a.m.–5 p.m. (beer only).

Disabled access No.

Customers Middle-class locals, cruise-ship passengers, and kicked-back travelers.

Hours Daily, 7 a.m.–10 p.m.

SETTING AND ATMOSPHERE A super-casual place right on the sand.

HOUSE SPECIALTIES Seafood combo, fish taco, burgers and fries.

SUMMARY AND COMMENTS It started as a simple shack on the sand, where travelers posed for photos in front of a THE OFFICE sign while lounging in beach chairs; it has since become a Playa Médano landmark. Some cruise-ship passengers take a taxi here and hang out the entire day at waterfront tables sipping margaritas and *cerveza,* snacking on nachos, and playing in the surf. The food is surprisingly good, although way overpriced, the portions generous, and the scene an ever-changing panorama of fun in the sun. You might get a bit annoyed by the endless stream of vendors selling everything from jewelry to gum; simply indicate indifference, and they'll move on. The scene gets calmer at dinner, except on Thursday after 7:30 p.m., when the mariachis hold forth at the Mexican Fiesta.

Pitahayas ★★★★½

PAN-ASIAN	EXPENSIVE	QUALITY ★★★★½	VALUE ★★★½

**Corridor; Highway 1 Km 10, Sheraton Hacienda del Mar;
☎ 624-145-8010**

Reservations Recommended.

Entree range $28–$38.

Payment AE, DC, MC, V.

Service rating ★★★★.

Parking Self-parking at Sheraton hotel.

Bar Full service; 300+ wines from around the world.

Dress Dressy casual.

Disabled access Yes.

Customers Affluent locals and travelers.

Hours Daily, 5–10:30 p.m.

SETTING AND ATMOSPHERE Elegant alfresco dining on five terraces overlooking the beach; especially romantic on dark, starry nights.

HOUSE SPECIALTIES Flank steak, lobster chile relleno, shrimp enchiladas.

SUMMARY AND COMMENTS You won't find anything made of the restaurant's namesake *pitahaya* (the sweet cactus fruit long favored by Baja's desert dwellers) at this elegant restaurant. But you will find courteous service and delicious Pacific Rim cuisine. The large, interesting menu features Chinese and Thai dishes, each uniquely interpreted by Chef Volker Romeike. Recommended entrees include the duck with lemon risotto, as well as the salmon medallions, served with a side of mashed potatoes with chunks of lobster. For starters, order the yummy shrimp coated in coconut and served with a chipotle chile and radish sauce, or the restaurant's famous shredded-pork Kahlúa pot stickers. End your meal with crème brûlée—the chocolate, passion fruit, and ginger versions of this classic French dessert are served as a trio, so you can try all three. Surprisingly, this is one of precious few restaurants right on the water's edge in the Corridor. Break out the sport jacket or collared shirt and your fanciest dress for a special dinner.

SIGHTSEEING *in* LOS CABOS

EACH OF THE THREE LOS CABOS destinations has attractions worth exploring and plenty of opportunities for adventure. To get oriented, consider taking a city tour or hiring a cab and driver or guide for a few hours ($30 and up per hour, depending on language and guiding abilities). Better yet, rent a car for a day or two (but be sure to read our caveats in Part Three, Arriving and Getting Oriented, page 70).

unofficial **TIP**
Be extra cautious about stashing your belongings in the car's trunk before parking at isolated beaches. It's worth paying a tip to park in a guarded lot.

Plan to spend a half-day in each area sightseeing and shopping. Adventure seekers and naturalists may need a bit more time. Your choice of activities could determine your surroundings. Golfers head for the Corridor; anglers for Cabo San Lucas.

ATTRACTIONS

San José del Cabo

The main sightseeing street in San José is Boulevard Mijares, which runs from the hotel zone past the golf course, firehouse, and artisan's market to **Plaza Mijares.** Traffic becomes amazingly congested on this narrow, shady street during business hours and high tourist seasons, and the police are sometimes quite vigorous in their enforcement of traffic rules—watch out for one-way street signs. It's best to park soon after the turnoff to La Playa and walk around the town, which is not large.

Boulevard Mijares is lined with interesting restaurants and shops, especially along the two blocks before the road dead-ends at the plaza recently redone with seemingly more cement than is necessary and busts of locally famous persons.

Locals gravitate toward the plaza in the evening, when church services are held at the plain, 1940s-era **Iglesia de San José,** and during fiestas and holidays. The Catholic church and the centuries-old homes surrounding it are among the few things in modern, tourist-oriented Los Cabos with the ambience of Old Mexico. Kids munch on ears of roasted corn lathered with mayonnaise and run up and down the stairs of the bandstand. Ladies chat on park benches beside travelers fanning themselves and reapplying sunscreen. Be sure to check out the tiled mural over the church's front door.

Many of San José's best restaurants, bohemian bars, and shops are located around the intersections of Boulevard Mijares and Obregón and Zaragoza. Here you'll find **La Casa de la Cultura,** a simple terra-cotta–colored building used for art, theater, and music classes and performances, as well as community gatherings.

In this land of little water, the Río San José etches its way through the eastern mountains to the Sea of Cortez, ending at the ever-changing **Estero de San José** (San José Estuary). A 2,000-acre marina development called Puerto Los Cabos is under construction just north of the estuary; when completed in early 2009, it will feature golf courses, hotels, private homes, and a cactus garden with 1,500 different species of cacti. Promoters say it will be the largest private marina in Mexico. Once it's proven to be a safe harbor it will drastically change the boating scene in this stretch of the Sea of Cortez. A paved road leads east from Boulevard Mijares to Puerto Los Cabos, crossing the Río San José. The small communities that existed on the beaches beside the development have disappeared, but small fishing companies have been granted a section of the marina for docking their skiffs.

The Corridor

Much of the Corridor's land is taken up by hotels and golf courses, and sightseeing here consists of visiting lavish hotels or partaking in a sport or spa treatment. The snorkeling is excellent at **Bahía Santa María** by the now-defunct Twin Dolphin hotel; the beach is also perfect for relaxing, sunbathing, and picnicking. There are large parking lots; don't leave valuables in sight when leaving your car. Vendors usually rent snorkel gear and sell everything from drinking water to sarongs, but bring plenty of water and snacks along.

Some of the more exclusive hotels discourage visitors. Make lunch reservations in advance and you'll be able to wander around the grounds. Schedule a meal or spa treatment at the **One&Only Palmilla, Marquis Los Cabos Resort,** or the inexpensive **Encanto Inn.**

unofficial **TIP**
Avoid driving the highway in the Corridor at night, when the lack of lights and the crazy antics of other drivers create dangerous conditions. Figure in the cost of a cab when deciding where to dine.

Cabo San Lucas

First impressions of Cabo San Lucas (aka Cabo) are usually not favorable. The town consists of an unsightly jumble of streets crowded with businesses all competing for your attention. Boulevard Marina curves along San Lucas Bay. Unfortunately, shopping arcades and hotels block most of the ocean breezes and views.

The Cabo most travelers see begins at the intersection of Highways 1 and 9. The former becomes Boulevard Lázaro Cárdenas, which runs straight to the main plaza. **Playa Médano,** the most popular beach in Los Cabos, sits a few blocks east of the boulevard at the foot of Calle del Pescadero. Large hotels and condo complexes line the north end of this beach, which is packed with bars, restaurants, water-sports concessions offering everything from parasailing to kayaking, and vendors selling baskets, toys, beach blankets, and jewelry.

The stoplight at the intersection of Cárdenas and Boulevard Marina is practically a historic landmark—drivers were shocked when it appeared in the late 1980s. The infamous restaurant and dance club **Squid Roe** long dominated this corner. Now **Puerto Paraíso,** an enormous glass-and-steel shopping mall, is the biggest show in town (see "Shopping in Los Cabos," page 430).

Puerto Paraíso's sweeping stairways and gardens front the *malecón,* a pedestrian walkway that runs from Playa Médano to the cruise-ship pier and fishing docks at the south end of the Boulevard Marina. Stroll along this path to the **Cabo San Lucas Harbor,** and check out the wood carvings, jewelry, and standard souvenirs at the large **Mercado de Artesanías** by the water.

El Arco, the most famous sight in Los Cabos, is visible from businesses along the malecón. The famed rock arch between the Pacific Ocean and the Sea of Cortez is indeed dramatic, as are the many rock formations at the tip of the peninsula. Party boats cruise the arch and **Playa de Amor** (Lover's Beach), a small beach stretching between the inland sea and the ocean. The best snorkeling and swimming is on the Sea of Cortez side around rocks jutting above the mild surf.

kids Cabo's tourist-oriented business district runs inland from Boulevard Marina to the **Plaza Amelia Wilkes,** a small park with a white gazebo in the center. (The plaza is named after a local schoolteacher and community leader.) The building at the northwest side of the plaza holds the **Museo de las Californias** (Boulevard Cárdenas at Avenida Cabo San Lucas; ☎ 624-143-0187). A local volunteer group supports the museum's small collection of archaeological, nautical, and agricultural artifacts; the museum is open Tuesday through Saturday, 10 a.m. to 7 p.m. and Sunday, noon to 6 p.m. **La Parróquia de San Lucas** (Calle Cabo San Lucas near Madero) is a simple church that serves as the parish headquarters.

TOURS *and* SIDE TRIPS *from* LOS CABOS

ATV AND RACE-CAR TOURS

PEOPLE LOVE TO ROAR AROUND the desert in small vehicles with big tires, and there are plenty of reputable companies to accommodate them. Goggles and helmets are provided, as are kerchiefs to keep the sand out of your nose and mouth. Wear a baseball cap or snug headgear, sneakers or other comfortable closed shoes, and your grubbiest duds.

ATVs streak across the desert in groups small (safer) and large, speeding up and down sand dunes and careening along cactus-lined desert trails. **Amigo's Cabo Moto Rent** (Camino al Camino Real, Col. Médano, Cabo San Lucas ☎ 624-143-0808) offers desert-and-dune ATV tours to La Candelaria (5–6 hours, $90 single or $120 double) and Migrino (about 3 hours, $65 single, $85 double). The company also rents scooters and ATVs by the hour or the day and leads horse rides on the beach and then into the hills ($35 for an hour or $55 for two hours).

Race car drivers are fond of Baja's long, sandy roads—the Baja 1000 is one of the premier off-road races in the world. Now regular folks can don helmets and zoom around a 1,500-acre ranch on the coast north of Cabo with **Wide Open Adventures** (Boulevard Marina at Plaza Nautica, Cabo San Lucas; ☎ 624-143-4170; ☎ 866-734-9651 U.S.; **www.wideopencabo.com**). The heart-thumping, dusty off-road ride doesn't come cheap at $250 per person (including transportation from Cabo), but does provide a pure adrenaline rush for thrill-seekers.

BOAT TOURS

YOU REALLY CAN'T GRASP THE BEAUTY of Los Cabos unless you view it from the water. The opportunities to do so are abundant. Water taxis and glass-bottom boats ferry passengers between Playa Médano, El Arco, and the fishing docks, and vendors on the beach lead kayak tours to El Arco and other rock formations. Check out the following options.

CaboRey (Cabo San Lucas Marina; ☎ 624-143-8060) takes clients on a catamaran for snorkeling tours at Chileno Bay ($46.50, with buffet and open bar, although the latter seems anathema to snorkeling); sunset/margarita tours at Land's End (hors d'ouerves, open bar and live music); and deluxe dinner cruises for $96.50 per person.

During the winter, **Cabo Expeditions** (Tesoro Los Cabos, Cabo San Lucas; ☎ 624-143-2700; caboexpeditions.com.mx) uses Zodiac rafts to bring their clients up close and personal with migrating gray and humpback whales. Boats depart every two hours, 8 a.m. to 4 p.m.;

the tour costs about $50. At other times of year they offer two-hour kayaking tours toward Los Arcos, with snorkeling on the return trip. ($50 per person; 9 and 11 a.m. and 1 p.m.). The three-hour Snorkel Two Bays tour gets you to Santa María y Chileno Bays ($45; 10 a.m. and 1 p.m.). In addition to reasonably priced sunset and snorkel cruises aboard 33- to 48-foot catamarans, **Princesa Sailing Charters** (San Lucas Marina; ☎ 624-143-7676) offers whale-watching trips in the mornings. Whale-watching and sunset cruises cost about $30 per person, or add $10 if you choose a cruise with alcoholic drinks and appetizers. **Tío Sports** (ME Cabo by Meliá, Playa Médano, ☎ 624-143-3399; **www.tiosports.com**) is a respected operator offering kayak, snorkel, scuba, sailing, whale-watching, and fishing tours.

Pez Gato I and **Pez Gato II** (☎ 624-143-3797; **www.pezgatocabo .com**) are two 42-foot catamarans that sail daily on snorkeling ($45 per person) and evening bay cruises ($35 per person). The upscale sunset cruise ($59) offers Mexican buffet and international open bar while the Jazz and Wine Tour (**www.tropicatcabo.com**) offers five different international wines by the glass as well as canapes like smoked crab and salmon, fresh veggies and fruit, and French cheeses. Freelancers and formal concessions on Médano Beach (including **Andromeda Divers** (☎ 624-147-7136; **www.scubadivecabo.com**) offer glass-bottomed boat tours to Los Arcos and Playa del Amor. Boats depart from Playa Médano, the Tesoro Los Cabos dock, and the sportfishing dock. Prices start at $5 per person.

kids Children appreciate a cruise aboard the 19th-century **Buccaneer Queen** (Marina Tesoro Los Cabos, Cabo San Lucas; ☎ 624-144-4217). Deckhands dress as pirates and tell spooky tales of luckless landlubbers and ruthless buccaneers. During winter whale-watching jaunts, passengers listen to the whales sing with special headphones. The two-and-a-half-hour cruise costs $55 for adults, $30 for kids ages 4 to 12, and $10 for kids under 4.

CULTURAL TOURS

Capeland Tours and Expeditions (5 de Febrero and Zaragoza; ☎ 624-143-0775) specializes in city tours: Los Cabos, Todos Santos, and La Paz. Their sister company **EcoTours de Mexico** takes clients to the ranching community of Caduaño, located outside Cabo San Lucas in the Sierra de la Laguna. Eat lunch at a typical area rancho and bump down a dirt road to see fossilized shells of clams and oysters and a giant graveyard of whale bones. The tour costs $85 for adults and kids alike and lasts four hours. Capeland Tours also offers nature excursions to the mountains and tours of leather and woodworking factories in the small town of **Miraflores.**

EAST CAPE

THE TENTACLES OF LOS CABOS development reach up the Sea of Cortez coast to the communities of Buena Vista and Los Barriles, where investors are chortling with glee. Those who bought land in this area 10 or 20 years ago have seen the value of their parcels double and triple, and the established hotels (once considered remote fishing lodges and windsurfing camps) are flourishing. The East Cape is gringolandia, populated primarily by North Americans who have established permanent and vacation homes in instant neighborhoods. An unnamed dirt road runs north about 40 miles from San José to the main East Cape towns. It's a great adventure if you rent a car or take a tour.

Cabo Pulmo, a small village with about 100 residents, sits beside Baja Sur's largest coral reef. Scuba companies in Los Cabos run trips to Cabo Pulmo, and the village has a dive shop and rental cottages. There's no electricity or water system; drinking water is trucked in. If you're on a day-long driving trip, stop here to snorkel and chow down on fish tacos. For more information, contact **Cabo Pulmo Beach Resort** (☎ 624-141-0885; **www.cabopulmo.com**). Windsurfers gravitate to **Los Barriles** from November to March, when the winds are at their best. Anglers hang out at casual lodges in **Buena Vista.** Both communities have shops and restaurants you can explore. Drive back from the East Cape to Los Cabos on Highway 1, which is paved.

LA PAZ

CAPITAL OF THE STATE OF BAJA CALIFORNIA SUR, La Paz is the commercial and bureaucratic headquarters of the region. Eventually, everyone living in Los Cabos has to make the trek through the mountains to the city. The 130-mile drive takes about two hours on Highway 1, which rambles down arroyos and up steep hills and passes by the old mining town of El Triunfo. Highway 19 is more direct and less scenic; it intersects with Highway 1 at Cabo San Lucas.

Easy access from the U.S., lower prices than those in Los Cabos, and a vibe that is more traditionally Mexican are luring retirees and vacationers to La Paz these days. New hotels and residential communities are springing up within the city, on the outskirts, on previously undeveloped beaches, and even inland on desert mesas. The city has an important university as well as a busy port, and a new and improved ferry, now privately owned, connects it to Mazatlan, on mainland Mexico.

Once you've reached La Paz, park near the waterfront *malecón* (Paseo Alvaro Obregón), a classic seaside promenade with playgrounds, small restaurants, and several piers jutting into the Sea of Cortez. Wander a few blocks inland on Avenida 16 de Septiembre or Avenida Independencia to the main plaza, alternately called **Plaza Constitución, Jardín Velazco,** or just *el zócalo.* The plaza has all the right touches—shoeshine stands, an ornate kiosk, lots of benches and shade trees, and vendors selling balloons and roasted corn in the evenings. The **Museo de Antropología** (Altamirano at Cinco de

Mayo; ☎ 612-122-0162) has interesting displays on Baja's history and natural attributes. The museum's hours are 9:30 a.m. to 6 p.m. daily; admission is $3.

Both boaters and artists are fond of La Paz because it has several marinas and a burgeoning arts and culture scene. Several European entrepreneurs have transformed some of the city's best early–20th-century buildings into hotels and restaurants. You can easily spend a couple of hours wandering around the bustling downtown. La Paz has several great seafood restaurants and one-of-a-kind hotels if you care to linger. For more information, visit the **La Paz Tourist Information Office** on the waterfront (Alvaro Obregón between Nicolás Bravo and Rosales; ☎ 612-122-5939) It's open weekdays 8 a.m. to 3 p.m.

ROCK CLIMBING AND HIKING

FEEL LIKE JUMPING OFF A BIG BOULDER . . . backward? Then contact **Baja Wild** (Highway 1 Km 28, Plaza Costa Azul, San José del Cabo; ☎ 624-172-6300; **www.bajawild.com**). ATV tours are combined with rappelling on trips lasting approximately three hours ($98). The company offers a variety of routes, some with great ocean views, others farther into the desert interior. Excursions can be booked with a minimum of just two clients, from novices to expert climbers. They also offer an eye-opening hiking tour into the mountains. After reaching the starting point by van, clients will negotiate the harsh and starkly beautiful canyon zone to be rewarded with pines at the higher elevations. The full-day trips ($98) lead you past cold springs and natural pools—don't forget your swimsuit. Your best source of information on nature tours, Baja Wild—recommended by AMTAVE (the Mexican Association of Adventure Travel and Ecotourism)—also offers surfing, kayaking, and other sports-related tours; see "Exercise and Recreation in Los Cabos," page 430. (They also offer a six-day, multisport "inn-to-inn" package including various water sports as well as hiking and mountain biking.) Tell them what you're interested in, and they'll come up with something to please.

TODOS SANTOS

SOME CLAIM THIS SMALL TOWN on the Pacific Coast, 45 miles north of Cabo San Lucas, is the Baja equivalent of Santa Fe, New Mexico. But that cultural character is hard to capture in a short day trip, leaving many visitors to wonder what all the fuss is about. You have to spend some time in town or know somebody who lives in the area to catch the real vibes of Todos Santos. Several artists, writers, and entrepreneurs have chosen to follow their dreams to this small farming town, which has grown steadily since the early 1990s. The Mexican government weighed in on the town's importance by declaring it a Pueblo Mágico in 2006. The designation provides the town with money for infrastructure and tourism promotion and puts it on the map as a unique and special part of Mexico.

The streets around the main plaza contain some of southern Baja's best examples of traditional adobe architecture. Several of the buildings have been restored to house small inns, galleries, and cafes. Take time to browse around Calle Juárez, Calle Topete, and side streets with no visible names. Some businesses close in September and October when tourism is low.

It's fashionable to spend long afternoons in the courtyard of the **Cafe Santa Fe** (Calle Centenario 4; ☎ 612-145-0340; closed Tuesday), dining on homemade pastas and organic vegetables for lunch or dinner. The adjacent **Galería Santa Fe** (☎ 612-145-0301, closed Tuesday) maintains bankers' hours but contains an ever-changing array of Mexico's finest folk art.

Cindy Murray, owner of **Fénix de Todos Santos** (Calle Juárez between Topete and Hidalgo; ☎ 612-145-0808), has an eye for Mexico's more unusual ceramics, including lead-free pottery from Michoacán and colorful majolica from Guanajuato. Her store has a small selection of jewelry as well as fine furnishings, candle holders, hand-carved saints, and other gifts and housewares. We wouldn't dream of going to Todos Santos without stopping by **El Tecolote Bookstore** (Calle Juárez and Hidalgo; ☎ 612-145-0295; closed Mondays and in September). The shelves are always stacked with current books on Baja and interesting used paperbacks.

The **Charles Stewart Gallery & Studio** (Centenario at Obregón; ☎ 612-145-0265; **www.charlescstewart.com**) contains the paintings of one of Todos Santos's earliest artists-in-residence. Stewart moved from Taos, New Mexico, to Todos Santos in 1986 and restored one of the town's 19th-century homes. His gallery and home reflect the trends in architecture so popular in the area. The representational and abstract works of other local and visiting artists are displayed at **Galería de Todos Santos** (Legaspi 33 at Topete; ☎ 612-145-0500).

Most visitors wander around during midday, linger over a long lunch at one of several excellent restaurants, and then drive back to their hotels in Los Cabos before dark. Locals chat over coffee and pancakes at **Caffé Todos Santos** (Calle Centenario 33; ☎ 612-145-0300). The bright yellow, blue, and green chairs and tables are tucked beneath bougainvillea vines and shade trees, and the menu includes plenty of tempting and healthful salads, sandwiches, and full meals. Open after 7 a.m.; no dinner on Mondays. The fried and steamed shrimp are to die for at **Mi Costa** (Militar at Ocampo; no phone), a humble palapa-covered restaurant where local Mexican families assemble for Sunday lunch. For more information on the area, check out **www.todossantos-baja.com** and **www.todossantosguide.com**.

unofficial **TIP**
Check out the surf scene at El Pescadero, Km 59 on the drive to Todos Santos. Diehard surfers camp out for weeks on beaches that still have a wild Baja vibe.

EXERCISE *and* RECREATION
in LOS CABOS

SPORTS AND LOS CABOS ARE SYNONYMOUS. Fishing put the region on the map Los Cabos has now secured its position as an internationally known golf destination. Surfers have long staked out favorite breaks along both coasts of the peninsula's tip; kayakers and windsurfers are fond of the Sea of Cortez. Professional equestrian centers offer some excellent horseback-riding tours, and companies are beginning to offer nature tours into the surrounding desert and mountains.

unofficial **TIP**
Some courses lower their rates substantially for twilight play (usually about $50 after 2 p.m.) year-round which also gives you a chance for some spectacular sunset views, especially from the oceanfront Cabo del Sol course and the hilltops at the Palmilla course.

GOLF

GOLF IS A SIGNIFICANT SOURCE OF entertainment for Baja-philes, despite the withering heat common during much of the year. Most people prefer to hit the links in early morning or late afternoon. Great courses abound (there are currently ten courses, and eight more on the way)., High season is October through June. Prices, which are comparable to those at major U.S. golf resorts, drop by about 30% during the summer months. Fees below are for winter high season.

Cabo del Sol Course

ESTABLISHED 1994	STATUS PUBLIC COURSE

Highway 1 Km 7.5, on the Corridor; ☎ 624-145-8200 or 800-386-2465 U.S.; www.cabodelsol.com

Championship tee 6,698 yards, par 72.

Men's tee 6,252 yards, par 72.

Ladies' tee 6,252 yards, par 72.

Fees $220 for desert course; $350 for ocean course.

Facilities and services Clubhouse, pro shop, putting/chipping green, equipment rental, lessons, restaurant, snack bar, bar.

The Ocean Course at Cabo del Sol, designed by Jack Nicklaus (and called "one of Nicklaus's finest creations" by *Pacific Golf* magazine), has five holes overlooking the ocean. There's a serious water hazard—a 178-yard shot over a rocky inlet—on the 17th hole, while the 18th was modeled after the final hole at Pebble Beach, California. The course appeared on *Golf Digest*'s list of the top 100 courses in the world, and it hosted the Senior Slam in 1995 and 1998. Inaugurated in winter 2002 after suffering damage from Hurricane Juliette in 2001, the Desert Nine was designed by Tom Weiskopf. While less challenging than the Ocean Course, the desert course has magnificent views of the sea from nearly every hole.

Cabo Real Golf Course

ESTABLISHED 1989   STATUS PUBLIC COURSE

Highway 1 Km 19.5, on the Corridor; ☎ 624-144-0243 (pro shop) or 877-795-8727 U.S.; www.caboreal.com

Championship tee 7,037 yards, par 72, rating 73.8.

Men's tee 6,437 yards, par 72, rating 73.8.

Ladies' tee 5,068 yards, par 72, rating 69.4.

Fees Winter rates start at $280 ($100 less for 9 holes at twilight hour).

Facilities and services Practice facilities, putting green, lessons, equipment rental, snack bar, bar, beverage carts on course, box lunches.

A difficult course designed by Robert Trent Jones Jr., it offers a variety of terrains and lots of bunkers. The front nine offer elevated vistas, while the 15th sits right on the sand. In between, the terrain is varied, with superb views. This was the site of the PGA Senior Slam in 1996, 1997, and 1999. The facilities were upgraded in 2006 with new locker rooms and showers and an expanded clubhouse. Guests staying at Cabo Real hotels receive priority tee times.

Mayan Palace Golf Los Cabos

ESTABLISHED 1988   STATUS PUBLIC COURSE

Highway 1 Km 31.5, San José del Cabo; ☎ 624-142-0905 or 866-465-7316 U.S.; www.mexicomayanresorts.com

Championship tee 3,141 yards, par 35.

Men's tee 2,909 yards, par 35.

Ladies' tee 2,444 yards, par 35.

Fees $100 for 9 holes; optional cart rental, $38.

Facilities and services Restaurant, snack bar, 2 outdoor tennis courts ($22 an hour; reservations accepted 1 day in advance); a $16 day pass for use of the swimming pool (except when classes are going on) and the gym; club rentals available.

No reservations are accepted at Cabo's first golf course, making it perfect for families and duffers. This is a great warm-up before playing the more challenging—and expensive—Cabo courses. Designed by FONATUR, the economic-development arm of the Mexican government, the public course's fairways are accommodating, and there are few impediments to reaching the greens. (Of the course's 32 sand traps, only 5 are on the fairways.)

Palmilla Golf Resort

ESTABLISHED 1992   STATUS PUBLIC COURSE

Highway 1 Km 7, on the Corridor; ☎ 624-144-5250 or 800-637-2226 U.S; www.oneandonlypalmilla.com

Championship tee 6,939 yards, par 72.

Men's tee 6,130 yards, par 72.

Ladies' tee 4,858 yards, par 72.

Fees $240.

Facilities and services Pro shop, driving range, putting green, snack bar; lessons available, clubs for rent.

Cabo's largest course opened in 1992 as a private course with two nine-hole sections: Mountain Nine and Arroyo Nine. The now-public club was augmented in 1999 with the new Ocean Nine course. Located on the 900-acre grounds of the prestigious One&Only Palmilla, the course hosted the 1997 PGA Senior Slam. The lovely and challenging 14th hole requires a force carry onto an island fairway. It's recommended that you reserve your tee time at least a week in advance.

GYMS

ALTHOUGH MOST OF THE UPSCALE RESORTS have gyms, these vary widely in terms of machines and classes available. Listed here are a few nonhotel gyms that accept walk-ins or short-term memberships. Locals frequent **Gimnasio Rudos** (Lázaro Cárdenas and Avenida Guerrero, Plaza Candido, behind Tavernos bar; ☎ 624-143-0534, Closed Sunday), a basic gym in the heart of downtown Cabo San Lucas. Walk-in rates for both gyms run about $8 per day and $55 per month.

HORSEBACK RIDING

IF YOU AVOID THE HOTTEST HOURS of the day, riding in Los Cabos is a picturesque and rewarding experience. Stick with the reputable operators whose horses are well cared for. Most offer riding on the beach as well as more diverse sojourns in the foothills, desert or area canyons. Prices hover around $35 to $40 per person per hour, with a slight break for longer rides. **Cuadra San Francisco Equestrian Center** (Highway 1 Km 19.5, Corridor; ☎ 624-144-0160; **www.loscaboshorses.com**) offers classes on several dozen well-fed, well-trained show horses. If you don't need lessons, opt instead to ride along the beach or choose a canyon trail—the latter with a more diverse landscape and an occasional shady spot. One or more guides accompany a maximum of 20 clients per trip; most speak English, but request an English speaker one or more days in advance if that's important to you. Closed Sundays. **Red Rose Riding Stables** (Highway 1 Km 4, Cabo San Lucas; ☎ 624-143-4826) offers group beach and desert rides.

SCUBA DIVING AND SNORKELING

SCUBA DIVERS ARE TREATED TO THE UNUSUAL sight of the "sand falls," located just 150 feet off Playa de Amor at Land's End. This underwater river of sand flows quickly along the bottom of the bay before plunging into a deep pit. Other wonderful sites, including coral reefs, can be found off the shore of the tourist corridor and north of San José. Arrange dive trips with English-speaking guides or rent equipment from full-service **Amigos del Mar** (Boulevard Marina, Plaza Galicota, near harbor fishing docks, Cabo San Lucas; ☎ 624-143-0505; **www.amigosdelmar.com**). Two-tank dives cost $75; add $25 more if you need gear. Snorkel tours start at $30. Snorkelers can take a three-hour trip aboard the 48-foot catamaran *La Princesa* (Cabo San Lucas Harbor; ☎ 624-143-7676). Trips depart daily at noon; $49 cost includes drinks, a light lunch, and equipment. *Pez Gato I* (Tesoro Los Cabos marina; ☎ 624-143-3797) offers similar snorkeling trips and prices.

SPORTFISHING

It's almost a crime to not go fishing at least once while you're in Los Cabos. The marlin, sailfish, wahoo, and dorado that congregate around the tip of Baja attract anglers of all levels, and several championship billfish tournaments are held here each year. Most of the fishing fleets are based at the marina in Cabo San Lucas and offer a wide range of boats and fishing trips. The most comfortable option is a half-day trip in a good-sized boat (28 feet or more) with a bathroom and plenty of shade. If you don't have friends to fish with, most companies have sign-up lists for those who want to share a boat.

If you're serious about fishing, wander down to the marina around 1 p.m., when boats start returning with the daily catch. Flags flying from the outriggers broadcast the type of fish that have been caught. Talk with the anglers who've been out on the water and you'll get a feel of which boats, captains, and crews are best. Though there are usually plenty of fish brought into the docks daily, catch-and-release is alive and healthy in Los Cabos. Anglers are strongly urged to return any captured marlin and sailfish to the sea. The fish are brought up close enough to the boat to be tagged and safely released. Conscientious anglers release any fish they aren't going to eat so that populations of tuna, dorado, and wahoo continue to thrive.

The following companies offer fishing trips with topnotch boats, gear, and crew.

Minerva's (Madero between Boulevard Marina and Guerrero; ☎ 624-143-1282; fax 624-143-0440; **www.minervas.com**) offers reputable charter fishing on its small fleet of Bertrams. Cost is $650 for 1 to 4 people; $760 for up to 6 anglers; and $975 for 1 to 8. Minerva's is also the place for anglers in need of tackle. **Pisces Sportfishing Fleet** (Cabo Maritime Center, Marina 8-6, Suite D-1; ☎ 624-143-1288; ☎ 619-819-7983 U.S.; **www.piscessportfishing.com**) is a large, professional fleet offering 28- to 110-foot Bertrams, yachts, and Hatteras in addition to the luxurious yacht *Mick,* available for custom charters and dinner cruises. Top-of-the-line equipment and service can be had from **Solmar Fleet** (Boulevard Marina across from sportfishing dock; ☎ 624-143-0646; 800-344-3349 US; fax 624-143-0410; **www .solmar.com**).

If you can't afford to go fishing on a big boat, don't despair. Some of the most enjoyable fishing trips we've taken have been in *pangas,* the 12- to 18-foot skiffs used quite successfully by local anglers. Panga fleets are also available at the marina, and they are less expensive to book.

SURFING

SURFERS ARE DRAWN TO POWERFUL WAVES on both coasts. On the Corridor, **Costa Azul Surf Shop** (Highway 1 Km 27.5; ☎ 624-142-2771) is located at the eponymous surf break, one of Cabo's most popular; it's just south of San José. They rent surfboards for $20 per day and offer surfing lessons at $85 an hour, including equipment and transportation. **Baja Wild** (Highway 1 Km 31, San José del Cabo; ☎ 624-142-5300; **www.bajawild.com**) offers surfing safaris to spots around Los Cabos appropriate for beginners. A fee of about $105, depending on the destination, includes transportation, equipment (including wetsuit or rash guard), snacks, beverages, lunch, and instruction.

WATER SPORTS

MANY CABO VISITORS SPEND MORE TIME in the water than on land, and consequently water-sports companies also offer a wide array of beach toys. You can rent personal watercraft or sign up for a parasailing ride with vendors on Playa Médano. Kayaking is a popular sport and an excellent means of exploring the myriad coves and inlets along Cabo's rocky shore. Most kayaks rent for around $15 per hour for a single and $20 for a double. Some operators offer package tours of $65 to $130, combining kayaking with snorkel or dive expeditions. **Andromeda Divers** (☎ 624-147-7136) has a stand at Playa Médano, and they rent kayaks at the prices above as well as boogie boards and snorkel equipment ($10 an hour and per day, respectively) and lead snorkeling and diving trips and PADI certification. **Baja Wild** (Highway 1 Km 28), San José del Cabo; ☎ 624-142-5300; **www.bajawild.com**) offers surf lessons and full- and half-day guided kayak tours to Lover's Beach and El Arco and a few other sites, with time for snorkeling.

SHOPPING *in* LOS CABOS

SHOPPING IN LOS CABOS is becoming more time-consuming and enjoyable. It used to be the only souvenirs were cotton blankets (useful for picnics and sunbathing on the sand) and tacky trinkets. Now it's possible to spend several hours browsing through excellent folk art, jewelry, and sportswear boutiques. The presence of an ever-increasing number of cruise ships in Cabo San Lucas has brought the inevitable onslaught of duty-free shops selling perfumes, watches, and jewelry. Everything starts looking the same very quickly. Fortunately, some excellent Mexican designers have opened galleries in Los Cabos, displaying classy Mexican silver jewelry.

The best shops are in San José, where interior designers, jewelers, and artists have set up shop in restored adobe homes. Prices are high, but so is the quality. San José has developed an exciting arts scene with galleries lining Calle Obregón and the surrounding streets. The galleries hold a Thursday night Art Walk from November through May, offering wine to inspire buyers. It's a good time to explore the town's restaurants and mingle with locals. Most of the elegant hotels in the Corridor have shops, though the selection is limited. Those intent on wildly splurging on T-shirts, sombreros, shell and silver jewelry, and inexpensive mass-produced souvenirs are better off in Cabo San Lucas. The arts and crafts market at the marina is jammed with stalls displaying silver charms, seashell picture frames, abalone earrings, and ruffled blouses and dresses. Vendors carry piles of straw hats and baskets, Balinese sarongs, and serapes along Playa Médano and other beaches—bargaining is definitely expected here. Think twice about purchasing an ironwood carving of marlin and sailfish, once a staple souvenir. The slow-growing tree is becoming over-harvested and scarce.

If you're looking for souvenirs made in Baja, stop by the **Glass Factory** (Avenida Lázaro Cárdenas s/n, two blocks west of Highway 1; ☎ 624-143-0255) in Cabo San Lucas. Their blue-rimmed shot glasses with green cactus designs are fairly lightweight. Damiana, a liqueur made from a local herb, is sold in amusing bottles shaped like voluptuous naked women. A few shops sell primitive baskets and wooden boxes made by the indigenous people living in mountain villages.

Puerto Paraíso Mall (Avenida Lázaro Cárdenas at entrance to Cabo San Lucas, ☎ 624-143-0000; **www.puertoparaiso.com**) is by far the largest mall in the area. The flashy marble-and-glass structure takes up several blocks and a large chunk of the waterfront, and it includes several high-end name-brand shops such as (**Kenneth Cole** and **Nautica**). **Häagen-Dazs** ice cream, a **Johnny Rockets** diner, **Harley Davidson** bar and shop, and a **Ruth's Chris Steakhouse** help cure any cravings for familiar food and drink. The movie theaters show current films in both English and Spanish.

At the marina, **Plaza Bonita** (Avenida Lázaro Cárdenas at Boulevard Marina) has several worthwhile shops as well as cafes, bars, and restaurants. At the south end of Boulevard Marina, the **Mercado de Artesanías** is a warren of stands selling competitively priced abalone frames and hair clips, colorful ceramics, blankets, and other low-end but pretty items. Also in Cabo San Lucas, **H2O de Los Cabos** (Madero at Guerrero; ☎ 624-143-1219, closed Sunday) has a great selection of sportswear, swimsuits, and accessories for men and women. The clothing for sale at **Magic of the Moon** (Calle Hidalgo off Boulevard Marina; ☎ 624-143-3161; **www.magicofthemoon.com**) is designed by owner Pepita in a tropical-vacation style. Choose among the inventory of women's dresses and intimate apparel or have your own outfit designed and stitched in short order. The accessories are handcrafted as well. **Tropica Calipso** (Puerto Paraíso; ☎ 624-143-9792) has an extensive inventory of bikinis and tank suits, as well as pretty resortwear in natural fibers.

San José is the place to shop for jewelry, clothing, and accessories. Visit **Amethyst** (Boulevard Mijares and Doblado; ☎ 624-142-4160) for semiprecious and precious stones as well as finished jewelry. You can place a custom order or choose from the shop's inventory of bracelets and baubles. For unique silver jewelry, check out **Sax** (Boulevard Mijares 2; ☎ 624-142-6053; closed September–October 15) and **Opalos de México** (facing the main plaza; ☎ 624-142-6599). Choose silver or gold (14 or 18K) and one of many types of opals or semiprecious stones, then select a design and have it made in a few days.

Those who want to fill their homes with Mexico's fabulous home furnishings (and who don't mind paying the added cost of shipping) can shop for both rustic and more modern treasures to their hearts' content. Fabulous interior-design pieces can be found at **El Callejón** (Hidalgo between Cárdenas and Madero; ☎ 624-143-1139; closed Sunday). **Galería Gatemelatta** (Camino al Hotel Marina frente Marina Fiesta; ☎ 624-143-1166) has a fine inventory of colonial-style furniture, antiques, paintings, and light fixtures as well as smaller items for tasteful souvenirs or gifts. **Necri** (Boulevard Marina between Ocampo and Madero; ☎ 624-143-0283 and at Boulevard Mijares 16; ☎ 624-130-7500 in San José) sells lovely items for the home, mainly pewter items and majolica and Talavera place settings and housewares. In San José, purchase gifts and larger pieces such as lamps and furniture at **Arte, Diseño y Decoración ADD** (Avenida Zaragoza at Hidalgo; ☎ 624-143-2055). Wonderful folk art from creators throughout Mexico is artfully displayed at **Galería Veryka** (Boulevard Mijares 6-B; ☎ 624-142-0575). You'll find unusual jewelry, fine ceramics, rustic pottery, wooden statuary, and much more. Search for unique small gifts and indigenously made handcrafts at **Copal** (Plaza Mijares at end Boulevard Mijares; ☎ 624-142-3070). **Pez Gordo Arte Contemporáneo** (Calle Obregón 19; ☎ 624-142-5788) is one of the leaders in the San José arts scene, displaying the works of more than 40 artists.

In San Lucas, the venerable **Galería Zen-Mar** (Cárdenas between Matamoros and Ocampo; ☎ 624-143-0661) is an owner-run business with an excellent selection of indigenous folk art, including wooden masks from Oaxaca and Guerrero and wool rugs from the Oaxaca Valley.

If you're interested in the work of local artists, **Kaki Bassi** (Calle Morelos at Alikan; ☎ 624-143-3510) shows the work of Baja artists in watercolor, pastels, and other media, and offers workshops for artists and would-be artists. Also in San Lucas, **Golden Cactus Gallery** (Calle Guerrero and Madero; ☎ 624-143-6399) offers art classes in addition to monthly shows. Owners Chris MacClure and Marilyn Hurst, both fine artists themselves, usually hold an open house the first Thursday of the month. It's a great time to meet local artists and purchase original art.

NIGHTLIFE *in* LOS CABOS

CONSIDERED BY MANY TO BE THE NIGHTLIFE capital of Mexico, **Cabo San Lucas** is jammed with bars packed with party-animal crowds. Spring break, when young people from all over the U.S. and Mexico arrive en masse, is especially raucous. The drinking age in Mexico is 18 (and often not strictly enforced), so it's an attractive destination for those who are not yet old enough to be served in the States. There are, however, a few places where adults can carry on a conversation while listening to background music. The nightlife scene in **San José del Cabo** is not nearly as frenetic as in Cabo San Lucas, with most of the action taking place at hotel bars and smaller cantinas. Nightlife in the **Corridor** is confined to the hotels, which have lounges and bars and live music some nights.

So if you want to party, head for Cabo San Lucas. The young and the restless gravitate to **Cabo Wabo** (Calle Guerrero between Madero and Lázaro Cárdenas, Cabo San Lucas; ☎ 624-143-1198; **www.cabo wabo.com**), owned in part by Sammy Hagar, rock musician and former member of Van Halen. This place rocks when Sammy's in town, making music on the huge stage until the wee hours. There's live music every night, with the bands usually starting up at 9 p.m. As vast as this venue is, most nights it's packed by 10 p.m. Try the "Waborita," a specialty of the cantina made with their own signature line of tequila, while you shoot a game of pool at one of the four tables. You can't miss Cabo Wabo if you're wandering the streets at night—just look for the giant lighthouse jutting up amid the sea of shops and restaurants.

Opened in 1984, the **Giggling Marlin** (Boulevard Marina at Matamoros; ☎ 624-143-1182; **www.gigglingmarlin.com**) continues as one of the hot spots on the Cabo scene. The dirty-dancing–salsa floor show starts at 9 p.m., and patrons are encouraged to join in. If your stomach isn't full, you might not mind being strung upside down at the fish scale and fed a tequila shot while having your picture taken. The music varies from night to night, as does the age of the crowd, but it's always packed. The restaurant serves decent Mexican food as well as burgers, sandwiches, and breakfast.

It doesn't get much wilder than **Squid Roe** (Avenida Cárdenas; ☎ 624-143-0655; **www.elsquidroe.com**), considered by many to be the ultimate party bar. It's the club where the party-hearty set winds up at the end of the night. Waiters walk around with a spray tank of tequila, and waitresses sashay by with trays of Jell-O shooters. The main floor of the three-level club is the open-air dance floor, with plenty of room for moving to the pulsating beat. Just about anything and everything goes here, so if you have a prudish bone in your body, pick another bar.

unofficial **TIP**
You're never too old to rock and roll at Squid Roe. If you feel uncomfortable amid the young crowd head upstairs to the back balcony overlooking the craziness below.

A smaller version of the Puerto Vallarta venue, **The Zoo** (Boulevard Marina s/n across from Puerto Paraíso mall; ☎ 624-143-5500; **www.zoobardance.com**) plays almost exclusively hip-hop. Look for cheetah-print bar stools, zebra-striped booths that invite tête-à-têtes, and an elephant statue that invades the room in front of a savannah mural. The bar opens at 7:30 p.m., gets going just before midnight, and closes at 4 a.m., with a mainly 20- and 30-something crowd.

If you're looking for a more sophisticated place to start off the night, head for **B Lounge** (Hotel Casa Dorada, Avenida Pelícano s/n at Médano Beach, ☎ 624-143-9168), with chill out and lounge music and a good selection of international beer. The bar overlooks the hotel pool and the beach beyond it.

On the sand, the hippest gathering spot is **Nikki Beach** (Playa El Médano, Me by Meliá San Lucas hotel; ☎ 624-145-7800; **www .nikkibeach.com**). Guests lounge about on padded beds under white umbrellas and nibble on chicken satay as DJs spin house and dance music. **Las Varitas** (Calle Gómez Farias s/n at Camino a San José; ☎ 624-143-9999; **www.lasvaritas.com**) features DJs or live rock music, including appearances by Mexican rock bands.

Insiders tend to hang out at **Havanas** (Highway 1, San José del Cabo; no phone; **www.havanasjazzclub.com**). This jazz club and restaurant presents high-caliber live music by local bands and singers. Visiting musicians are encouraged to take the stage. The club is closed Sunday and Monday.

In San José, the bar at the **Tropicana Bar & Grill** (Boulevard Mijares 30; ☎ 624-105-2703) is a popular hangout for guests of the hotel, as well as for locals seeking a a cold drink. Sit outside at the sidewalk cafe and sip a margarita, or watch a sporting event on TV and have a beer inside the air-conditioned bar. This is also about the only place in San José where you can count on shows and dancing to live music almost nightly; usually they involve Latin music, including Cuban, salsa, and merengue.

ELEMENTARY SPANISH

SPANISH PRONUNCIATION IS CONSISTENT, so if you learn the sounds of the vowels, you'll be on your way to speaking like a local. Remember, even taking a first step means you're on your way.

---

a is pronounced as the first "a" in "always"

e sounds like the "a" in "way"

i as the "e" in "see"

o as in "sold"

u as in "too"

ñ is pronounced like "n" combined with a "y" (Think of the Irish singer, Enya.)

j sounds like the English "h"

g sounds like the English "wa," as in wallet, when it comes before "e" and "i";
   before other vowels it sounds like the "g" in "guest"

qu is pronounced as a "k"

In the glossary below, English words and phrases are followed by their Spanish translations. Pronunciation is then given in parentheses, with accented syllables shown in capital letters.

GENERAL CONVERSATION

Yes *Sí.* (SEE)

No *No* (NOH)

Please *Por favor* (POR fah-VOHR)

Excuse me (pardon me). *Con permiso.* (CON pair-MEE-so.)

Excuse me (I'm sorry). *Discúlpeme.* (dees-COOL-pay-may.)

Hello. *Hola.* (O-lah.)

Good morning. *Buenos días.* (BWE-nos DI-as.)

GENERAL CONVERSATION (CONTINUED)

Good afternoon. *Buenas tardes.* (BWE-nas TAR-days.)

Good evening. *Buenas noches.* (BWE-nas NOH-chays.)

Good-bye. *Adiós.* (AH-dee-os.)

Thank you [very much]. *[Muchas] gracias.* (MOO-chas GRAH-see-as.)

You're welcome. *De nada.* (DAY NAH-dah).

Where are you from? *¿De dónde es usted?* (DAY DOHN-de ES u-STED?)

I'm from _____. *Soy de* _____.
  (SOY DAY _____.)

What time is it? *¿Qué horas son?* (KAY ORE-ahs SON?)

Do you speak English? *¿Habla usted inglés?* (AH-blah u-STED in-GLASE?)

I don't understand. *No entiendo.* (NOH en-TIEN-doh.)

Could you help me please? *¿Me puede ayudar, por favor?* (MAY PWAY-day a-yoo-DAR, POR fah-VOR?)

Help! *¡Socorro!* (soh-COR-ro!)

Let's go! *¡Vamos!* (VAH-mos!)

That's fabulous! *¡Qué padre!* (KAY POD-ray!)

NUMBERS

1	*Uno* (OO-noh)		8	*Ocho* (OCHO)
2	*Dos* (DOS)		9	*Nueve* (NEW-ayv-ay)
3	*Tres* (TRACE)		10	*Diez* (DEE-es)
4	*Cuatro* (KWATRO)		20	*Veinte* (BEN-tay)
5	*Cinco* (SINKO)		50	*Cincuenta* (sin-KWEN-ta)
6	*Seis* (SAES)		100	*Cien* (SEE-en)
7	*Siete* (ci-ET-ay)			

FOOD AND DINING

Breakfast *Desayuno* (day-sigh-OO-noh)

Check *Cuenta* (QUEN-ta)

Lunch *Comida* (coh-MEE-dah)

Dinner *Cena* (SAY-nah)

Ice *Hielo* (YELLOW)

Menu *Carta* (CAR-ta)

Purified water *Agua purificada* (AH-wah poo-ree-fee-CA-dah)

With *Con* (CONE)

Without *Sin* (SEEN)

Beef *Carne de res* (CAR-nay DAY RES)

FOOD AND DINING (CONTINUED)

Pork *Puerco* (PWER-coh)

Chicken *Pollo* (POY-yo)

Meat *Carne.* (CAR-nay)

Vegetables *Verduras, vegetales* (ver-DUR-ahs, ve-hay-TAL-es)

Fish *Pescado* (pes-CAH-doh)

Seafood *Mariscos* (mah-REES-cohs)

Salad *Ensalada* (en-sa-LA-dah)

Soup *Sopa* (SOH-pah)

Vegetarian *Vegetariano* (ve-hay-tarry-AH-no)

Appetizer *Antojito* (an-toe-HEE-toh)

Dessert *Postre* (POH-stre)

Beer *Cerveza* (ser-VAY-sa)

Wine *Vino* (VEE-noh)

Without alcohol *Sin alcohol* (SEEN al-COHL)

Coffee *Café* (cah-FAY)

Cream *Crema* (CRAY-mah)

Milk *Leche* (LAY-chay)

Sugar *Azúcar* (ah-SUE-car)

This is not good. *No está bien.* (NOH es-TAH BEE-en.)

This is delicious. *Es delicioso.* (ES day-lee-see-OH-so.)

BEACH AND OUTDOORS

Beach *Playa* (PLY-ah)

Cap *Gorro* (GORE-o)

Hat *Sombrero* (some-BRAY-ro)

Mosquito repellent *Repelente* (ray-pe-LEN-tay)

Pool *Alberca.* (al-BARE-cah)

Sunscreen *Bloqueador del sol* (blo-key-ah-DOR DEL SOL)

Towel *Toalla* (tow-AH-ya)

SHOPPING

Boutique *Boutique, tienda de ropa* (bow-TEAK, tee-EN-dah DAY RO-pa)

Can you give me a discount? *¿Me da un descuento?* (MAY DAH UN des-QWEN-to?)

Handcraft *Artesanía* (ar-tay-sah-NEE-ah)

Handmade *Hecho a mano* (EH-cho A MA-no)

I'm just looking. *Sólo estoy mirando.* (SO-lo es-TOY mi-RAN-do.)

In another color *En otro color* (EN OTRO coh-LOR)

SHOPPING (CONTINUED)

In my size *En mi talla* (EN MEE TAY-a)

It's very expensive. *Es muy caro.* (ES MUY CA-ro.)

Larger *Más grande* (MAS GRAN-de)

Smaller *Más pequeño* (MAS pay-CANE-yo)

Market *Mercado* (mare-CAH-doh)

Pharmacy *Farmacia* (far-MAH-see-ah)

Supermarket *Supermercado* (soo-pare-mare-CAH-doh)

What is the price? *¿Cuánto cuesta?* (QUAN-to QWES-ta?)

PLACE-NAMES

Acapulco (a-cah-POOL-coh)

Baja California (BA-ha cah-lee-FOR-nha)

Cabo San Lucas (CA-bow san LOO-cahs)

Cancún (cahn-COON)

Cozumel (coh-soo-MEL)

Huatulco (wha-TOOL-coh)

Isla Mujeres (EES-lah moo-HAIR-es)

Ixtapa (Eesh-TAH-pah)

Los Cabos (lohs CAH-bows)

Mazatlán (mah-saht-LAN)

Oaxaca (woe-HA-cah)

Puerto Escondido (pwer-TO es-con-DEE-doh)

Puerto Vallarta (pwer-TO vie-ART-tah)

San José del Cabo (sahn hoe-SAY del CA-bow)

Zihuatanejo (zee-wha-tan-EH-ho)

OTHER COMMON WORDS

You'll see these words in our regional chapters and hear them around town. For that reason we've listed the Spanish term first, then the English translation.

Calesa (cah-LES-sa) Horse-drawn carriage

Colectivo (coh-lec-TEE-voh) Shared taxi or bus, usually meaning a van or minivan

Embarcadero (em-bar-ca-DAY-roh) Pier, dock

Glorieta (glow-ree-YET-a) Traffic circle.

Malécon (mah-LEH-cone) A waterfront walkway.

Palapa (pah-LAH-pah) A structure made of palm fronds, or an open structure with a roof of palm fronds.

Panga (PAN-gah) Skiff

ACCOMMODATIONS INDEX

RESTAURANT INDEX

SUBJECT INDEX

Unofficial Guide Reader Survey

If you'd like to express your opinion about traveling in Mexico or this guidebook, complete the following survey and mail it to:

Unofficial Guide Reader Survey
P.O. Box 43673
Birmingham, AL 35243

Inclusive dates of your visit: _____

Members of your party:

	Person 1	Person 2	Person 3	Person 4	Person 5
Gender:	M F	M F	M F	M F	M F
Age:					

How many times have you been to Mexico? _____
On your most recent trip, where did you stay? _____

Concerning your accommodations, on a scale of 100 as best and 0 as worst, how would you rate:

The quality of your room? _____ The value of your room? _____
The quietness of your room? _____ Check-in/checkout efficiency? _____
Shuttle service to the airport?_____ Swimming pool facilities? _____

Did you rent a car?_____ From whom?_____

Concerning your rental car, on a scale of 100 as best and 0 as worst, how would you rate:
Pickup-processing efficiency?_____ Return-processing efficiency?___
Condition of the car?____ Cleanliness of the car?____
Airport-shuttle efficiency?____

Concerning your dining experiences:
Estimate your meals in restaurants per day? _____
Approximately how much did your party spend on meals per day? ____

_____

Favorite restaurants in Mexico: _____

_____

Did you buy this guide before leaving? _____ While on your trip?_____

How did you hear about this guide? (check all that apply)

Loaned or recommended by a friend ☐   Radio or TV ☐
Newspaper or magazine ☐   Bookstore salesperson ☐
Just picked it out on my own ☐   Library ☐
Internet ☐

What other guidebooks did you use on this trip? _____

_____

_____

_____

On a scale of 100 as best and 0 as worst, how would you rate them?

_____

_____

_____

_____

Using the same scale, how would you rate the *Unofficial Guide*(s)?

_____

Are *Unofficial Guides* readily available at bookstores in your area? _____

Have you used other *Unofficial Guides*? _____

Which one(s)? _____

_____

_____

Comments about your Mexico trip or the *Unofficial Guide*(s):

_____

_____

_____

_____

_____

_____

_____

_____

_____

_____

_____

_____

_____

_____

_____

_____

_____

_____

_____